15/3

booksonline

## this book online today:

With SAP PRESS BooksOnline we offer you online access to knowledge from the leading SAP experts. Whether you use it as a beneficial supplement or as an alternative to the printed book, with SAP PRESS BooksOnline you can:

- Access your book anywhere, at any time. All you need is an Internet connection.
- Perform full text searches on your book and on the entire SAP PRESS library.
- Build your own personalized SAP library.

## The SAP PRESS customer advantage:

Register this book today at *www.sap-press.com* and obtain exclusive free trial access to its online version. If you like it (and we think you will), you can choose to purchase permanent, unrestricted access to the online edition at a very special price!

## Here's how to get started:

1. Visit *www.sap-press.com*.
2. Click on the link for SAP PRESS BooksOnline and login (or create an account).
3. Enter your free trial license key, shown below in the corner of the page.
4. Try out your online book with full, unrestricted access for a limited time!

s8ky-zmrq-ex56

# SAP® Security and Risk Management

SAP PRESS is a joint initiative of SAP and Galileo Press. The know-how offered by SAP specialists combined with the expertise of the Galileo Press publishing house offers the reader expert books in the field. SAP PRESS features first-hand information and expert advice, and provides useful skills for professional decision-making.

SAP PRESS offers a variety of books on technical and business related topics for the SAP user. For further information, please visit our website: *www.sap-press.com*.

Loren Heilig et al.
Understanding SAP NetWeaver Identity Management
2010, app. 300 pp.
978-1-59229-338-4

Marc O. Schäfer, Matthias Melich
SAP Solution Manager Enterprise Edition
2009, app. 550 pp.
978-1-59229-271-4

Markus Helfen et al.
Testing SAP Solutions
2007, 350 pp.
978-1-59229-127-4

Volker Lehnert et al.
Authorizations in SAP Software
2010, 700 pp.
978-1-59229-342-1

Mario Linkies and Horst Karin

# SAP® Security and Risk Management

Bonn • Boston

Galileo Press is named after the Italian physicist, mathematician and philosopher Galileo Galilei (1564–1642). He is known as one of the founders of modern science and an advocate of our contemporary, heliocentric worldview. His words *Eppur se muove* (And yet it moves) have become legendary. The Galileo Press logo depicts Jupiter orbited by the four Galilean moons, which were discovered by Galileo in 1610.

**Editor** Stefan Proksch
**English Edition Editor** Kelly Grace Harris
**Translation** Lemoine International, Inc., Salt Lake City,
**Copyeditor** Mike Beady
**Cover Design** Graham Geary
**Photo Credit** Getty Images/RR/Thomas Northcut
**Layout Design** Vera Brauner
**Production Manager** Kelly O'Callaghan
**Assistant Production Editor** Graham Geary
**Typesetting** Publishers' Design and Production Service
**Printed and bound in** Canada



**ISBN 978-1-59229-355-1**

2nd edition, updated and revised, 2011
2nd German edition published 2010 by Galileo Press, Bonn, Germany

**Library of Congress Cataloging-in-Publication Data**
Linkies, Mario.
SAP security and risk management / Mario Linkies, Horst Karin. — 2nd ed.
p. cm.
Includes bibliographical references.
ISBN-13: 978-1-59229-355-1
ISBN-10: 1-59229-355-7
1. Computer networks — Security measures. 2. SAP ERP. 3. Business enterprises — Computer networks — Security measures. I. Karin, Horst. II. Title.
TK5105.59.L567 2010
005.8—dc22
2010031622

# Contents at a Glance

# Dear Reader,

You know the problem: Your IT processes must be as safe as possible, and must also meet your country's legal requirements. The ability to integrate your needs and your country's legal requirements in a way that achieves a holistic security and risk management solution is truly an art — and this is precisely what you'll learn to do with this updated and expanded edition of our standard work on SAP security.

Using numerous examples of established methods, Mario Linkies and Horst Karin will show you, step-by-step, how to implement security in SAP NetWeaver. For ail SAP applications, the authors explain where and how to secure processes and improve the security of existing systems. You will also learn the best practices of SAP security strategy, information about international standards, and how to integrate new technologies into your risk analysis. With the information contained in this book, I'm confident that you will find the task of maintaining secure SAP systems much simpler and easier to understand.

We always look forward to praise, but are also interested in critical comments that will help us improve our books. We encourage you to visit our website at *www.sap-press.com* and share your feedback about this work.

Thank you for purchasing a book from SAP PRESS!

**Kelly Grace Harris**
Editor, SAP PRESS

Galileo Press
Braintree, MA

*kelly.harris@galileo-press.com*
*www.sap-press.com*

# Contents

# Preface by Wolfgang Lassmann

For many years, companies in the information technology (IT) industry (e.g., SAP, Microsoft, Software AG), scientific institutions, and consulting firms have supported initiatives to improve IT security. Some examples include Deutschland sicher im Netz in Germany and the SAP Global Security Alliance of the International Association for SAP Partners (IA4SP). These initiatives help customers and solution providers collaborate on designs and implementations of procedures and control solutions for IT security.

The increasing global networking of computers, the reach of national and international business processes over the Internet, and complex information systems magnify the risk potential of negligent actions or intentional attacks on information systems. Unauthorized, anonymous attackers with an Internet connection can enter remote systems from any location and cause significant damage.

It is the task of IT-related academic and research institutions to highlight the complex relationships and risks and to suggest effective defensive solutions against real and potential attacks on system security.

Mario Linkies and Horst Karin have dedicated themselves to such a task in this book. As experienced specialists in IT security — particularly with SAP— they not only possess experience and practical knowledge, but also the theoretical background required to understand security and risk management.

This book provides a clear introduction to SAP security and risk control. The authors have succeeded in joining externally oriented technological security management (security control) with internally oriented business risk management (risk control). Integrated solutions, attention to risks, and a holistic approach are all important aspects of IT security.

This book encourages a critical review of security solutions that companies have used and a reevaluation of them in light of new requirements. Step by step, readers move from risk analysis to effective methods of control and, ultimately, to IT security that meets legal requirements.

With the enterprise risk management (ERM) Navigation Control Map, this book illustrates the relationships between SAP solutions and other IT components with the required communications and security solutions. The ERM Navigation Control

Map is used to detect and observe risks and to simulate control and security solutions of an IT landscape using SAP and other solutions.

I am sure that this book marks a significant contribution to important work in security and risk management in the IT industry. The authors are to be thanked for their efforts.

**Prof. Wolfgang Lassmann**
Professor of Business IT and Operations Research
at Martin Luther University, Halle-Wittenberg, Germany

# Preface by Monika Egle

Data protection wasn't given much thought for a long time; but now it has everyone's attention due to a multitude of incidents in recent years. From internationally oriented telecommunications providers to large logistics companies to supermarkets: Data protection breakdowns make headlines. Customers and employees of a company are sensitized and claim their right to information more and more frequently. Due to the higher awareness for data protection and due to the complexity of information technology (IT) structures, the requirements of data protection have increased.

The linking of IT systems enables the creation of complete personality profiles. For example, data protection discussions on SAP were mostly focused on employee data protection. Staff and works councils primarily discussed to what extent employee data could be used for performance and behavioral controls.

With SAP Customer Relationship Management (CRM) and SAP NetWeaver Business Information Warehouse (BW), however, there are new challenges to data protection. The goal is to understand these complex structures beyond their actual responsibilities and to check them for lawfulness and risks with regard to data protection. Check within the meaning of data protection to consider the information security of IT systems, and the technical and organizational measures.

In this book, the authors managed to clearly present the complex relationships between information security and SAP systems, and they identified effective solutions for risk management. This creates a practically oriented basis that blends data protection with information security in SAP systems.

One thing is for sure: Data protection must meet the challenge and get involved with the structures of complex IT systems. This book provides a valuable basis for data protection, including complex SAP systems.

**Monika Egle, Graduate Engineer**
Area Manager Information Security and Data Protection of ditis Systeme, NL der JMV GmbH & Co. KG — a company of the Voith Group

Member of the German working group "External Data Protection Officers" and of the Regional Group South of the Professional Association of Data Protection Officers (Berufsverband der Datenschutzbeauftragten (BvD) e. V.), Germany

# Preface by Jose Estrada

Risk management and risk control are very important to companies and administration organizations. In recent years, the number of individual and organized computer crimes has increased rapidly. The risk of attacks on information, its owners, and users has become a major threat to organizations and can cause considerable damage that can threaten entire national economies. The development and effects of global financial and economical crises can be traced back to causes in missing or insufficient risk management.

Therefore, a large part of this book is dedicated to risk and compliance management. The book accounts for the significance of this topic. The majority of technical solutions must go along with a solid understanding of the risk factors involved at various levels to successfully protect companies and organizations and ensure long-term success.

In this book, Mario Linkies and Horst Karin have covered the complex subject of SAP security and risk management. They discuss difficult process and technical relationships and bridge the gap between theoretical/scientific procedure and pragmatic implementation. The authors describe many essential concepts and give practical recommendations for identifying and handling risks, and establishing appropriate protection and control measures for SAP customers. They invoke all of the important components for securing SAP systems and business processes to comprehensively establish security within a company.

The book includes many years of experience and leads readers from a pictured presentation of requirements and control objectives to pragmatic, yet technically challenging IT security measures that can be achieved using standard SAP solutions and additional tools. Even if the concepts are described with a high level of detail, the readers never lose sight of the basic idea and the requirements of security solutions.

**Prof. Jose Miguel Estrada**
Professor for Risk Management and Corporate Governance
at the University of Montevideo, Uruguay

# Introduction

We live in an insecure world. Our ideals have changed, and the values that are created in ever-faster value-added cycles seem to be jeopardized more than ever before. Investments and companies, people and markets, work and health, education and environment — all parts of our existence alter and show to what degree human achievements are vulnerable and worth protecting.

Therefore, security is not only a basic need of people, but an essential condition for building an economy and life. Risks are omnipresent, but must be calculable. Ethics and transparency are required. Independent actions are no longer sufficient to overcome the problems in our world. Comprehensive, logical, coordinated, and internationally designed steps are required to build an innovative, ecology-minded, quality-based, and performance-oriented global economy.

Since the beginning of the new millennium, the financial collapse of large companies in the last decade, the massive market crashes, and the momentous loss of economic moral have profoundly shaken shareholders', employees', and consumers' trust in publicly traded companies, in particular. This reinforces the introduction of new laws and the extension of governmental control and security standards. The Sarbanes-Oxley Act (SOX) in the United States applies to publicly traded companies, and due to tightened restrictions on senior managers it has indirectly expanded its global influence on companies that are not publicly traded.

This similarly applies to the Basel laws for the financial industry, and REACh for the chemicals industry. Japan has even developed its own version of SOX, the J-SOX. The objective of all of these laws is to establish stronger controls and improved security measures within companies and organizations, and processes to better protect investors, companies, traders, employees, and consumers. One way to implement the laws for national control, which partly include fines for the managers responsible, is to ensure the security of information technology (IT)-supported processes and business and financial transactions through consistent security measures.

This requires a risk management that promotes risk identification on one hand and integrates effective controls and integrated security measures on the other. Setting up comprehensive security and control systems with a justifiable effort is a main topic of business transactions and an essential goal for securing investments and values. International agreements, laws, industry-specific guidelines, and corporate specifications already set the framework conditions today.

The control of risks and the reduction of possible threats are two of the main elements that will shape IT in the coming years. Growing functionality; changing technology; the external opening of internal processes; and stricter national, industry-specific, and international regulations will result in new requirements for secure processes, IT-supported systems, applications, and users. The globalized intertwining of companies, partners, and customers increases the requirements for flexible IT-supported communication components.

Employees, consumers, producers, suppliers, and service providers use mobile and multifunctional communication devices to exchange all forms of business information. Distributed systems, service-oriented architectures (SOAs), the increasing focus of applications, and changing conditions for economic and social satisfaction are parts of change for economic processes and technologies.

These economic and technological changes are reflected in business and market processes. These changes not only entail risks, but are also accompanied by new threats. These developments and the interaction of business partners, employees, and customers can only be protected via new approaches and an actual quantum leap in security strategies and their implementation. This book presents essential elements of security measures in IT-related applications and controls.

### Our Motivation

Due to changing requirements, SAP has expanded its function offerings along with its implementation of new technologies; these can be found, for example, in SOAs and their implementations using services. An essential step was the transition from the previously separate ABAP environment toward a new basic architecture: SAP NetWeaver with components like SAP NetWeaver Process Integration (PI), SAP NetWeaver Portal, and SAP NetWeaver Mobile. On the one hand, the new technologies and enhanced applications improve integration between business partners. On the other hand, the risks that the new developments pose require serious consideration.

In addition, a lot of companies that use SAP software have "relics" that still exist due to negligence in the past. Therefore, such companies need to catch up with regard to authorizations, both for developing and establishing secure and optimal management processes. The authorization systems that have grown over the years still pose major challenges for most companies. The diversity of different solutions, the lack of IT security processes integration, and insufficient risk considerations usually don't prevail over effective and transparent access systems.

Based on many years of experience in international consulting and examination work, and close collaboration with SAP, partners, and customers, this book presents the essential options for implementing enterprise risk management (ERM) in a targeted manner. The focus is on the connection to legal specifications, SAP applications, and IT security for the protection and development of the company and the local environment.

### Objectives of this Book

This book provides an overview of SAP NetWeaver security. In addition to the standard applications and the Governance, Risk, and Compliance (GRC) solutions in SAP BusinessObjects, you'll learn about a secured SAP implementation. A description of problems, needs, and general conditions leads to a presentation of strategies, regulatory measures, and conceptual and technical solutions based on numerous examples. Moreover, you'll learn about the latest methods, legal requirements, and industry-specific requirements.

Another goal of the book is to provide help for implementing legal requirements for risk and control management. The descriptions are mainly governed by the theory of an integral, possibly postponed, holistic consideration of IT security components and risk control measures. You must consider security as a holistic and, in particular, strategically positioned task to effectively establish it for the company's benefit and for business partners and shareholders.

This book is supposed to motivate you and offer help. Good practical solutions provide insight into the complex, yet necessary world of IT-related risk management, which must meet current and future requirements by means of efficient methods, new solutions, and improved strategies.

### Content and Structure of this Book

This approach divides this book into a theoretical and conceptual Part 1 and an SAP-specific, practical-pragmatic Part 2. The following provides an overview of the content of the individual chapters:

- **Part I: Basic Principles of Risk Management and IT Security**
  - **Chapter 1**, Risk and Control Management, gives an initial introduction to the topic. It presents the most critical components; explains terms such as company assets, risks, controls, and threats; and covers methods like risk analysis and control consulting.
  - **Chapter 2**, ERM Strategy, outlines the requirements and basic principles of a comprehensive strategy; procedures for implementation, methods, and principles; and security solutions and examples.

- **Chapter 3**, Requirements, introduces important legal, industry-specific, and country-specific guidelines and regulations that have immediate or indirect influence on IT-related security and its parameters.
- **Chapter 4**, Security Standards, describes the country-specific and international security standards that should serve as guidelines for security projects.
- **Chapter 5**, IT Security, describes the conceptual basics of technical security solutions for active inclusion in company-wide control measures.

- **Part II: Security in SAP NetWeaver and Application Security**
  - **Chapter 6**, ERM Navigation Control Map, provides a basic introduction to SAP NetWeaver security. This book is supplemented by a map that acts as a navigation, orientation, and motivation aid that provides an overview of the SAP NetWeaver technology and the ERM solution components in the SAP environment.
  - **Chapter 7**, Web Services, Enterprise Services, and Service-Oriented Architectures, covers these new technologies that are supported by the SAP platform, presents the security concept for this topic, and describes measures for risk management.
  - **Chapter 8**, GRC Solutions in SAP BusinessObjects, discusses the basic contents and procedures for GRC in the SAP solution environment.
  - **Chapters 9 through 28** cover the essential components of SAP NetWeaver along with potential risks and control measures. These chapters explain threats based on examples and the concepts of application and system security tailored for individual examples.

This book discusses the essential concepts and solutions in SAP applications independent of their release.

#### Target Groups and How to Read this Book

This book is aimed at IT managers and authorization administrators, economists and management consultants, shareholders, executives, data protection officers and project leads, security officers, and persons responsible for compliance and financial control in the company and in governmental organizations.

This book features a modular structure to serve not only as a text, but also as a reference book. It offers an introduction to the requirements of ERM and aims to provide a comprehensive overview of the complex world of securing SAP-supported processes and connected systems.

The chapters are partly based on one another — the appropriate passages are indicated respectively — they are coherent, and they usually structured according to the same principle. But as individual text components they also offer direct support for the search and definition requirements. Chapters and content on the basics, examples, and best-practice methods supplement the explanatory material. Best-practice methods are solutions that were used very successfully by numerous customers in the past or that show new developments in security consulting.

**Acknowledgments**

The authors wrote this book in their free time, that is, in addition to their many responsibilities in national and international consulting and teaching. Above all, this book came about with the support from many customers at home and abroad, from close cooperation with partners in Germany, North America, South Africa, and Japan; collaboration with economic-research institutes and the universities of Leipzig (Germany), Halle-Wittenberg (Germany), and Montevideo (Uruguay); from families; friends; and professional supporters from all over the world.

In appreciation of all who provided support, we would like to thank the following: Monika Egle (ditis Systeme), Stefan Proksch (Galileo Press/SAP PRESS), Kelly Harris (Galileo Press/SAP PRESS), Volker Lehnert and Dr. Frank Off (SAP AG), and Prof. Jose Estrada (Universidad de Montevideo). The ERM Navigation Control Map was created in close collaboration with LINKIES. Management Consulting, ditis Systeme, and DELTA Information Security Consulting. We would like to thank everyone involved for their support.

**Mario Linkies**
President LINKIES. Management Consulting Canada Inc.
CEO LINKIES. Unternehmensberatung GmbH

**Dr. Horst Karin**
President DELTA Information Security Consulting Inc.

# PART I
# Basic Principles of Risk Management and IT Security

*Risk and control management provides the central means of structuring and controlling protective measures for the company and other assets. This chapter introduces security objectives and covers the components of comprehensive risk and control management.*

# 1 Risk and Control Management

Risk and control management is a comprehensive set of procedures used to determine company assets, potential risks, and the required control and security solutions. It protects assets and processes in the short term and for the future and ensures effective and optimal use of funds and resources. Risk and control management is the central means of identifying and assessing risks that jeopardize the assets of an organization and its individual parts. It classifies risks and defines appropriate countermeasures in the form of control and security solutions.

Over the past three decades, companies and organizations have standardized their business operations with enterprise software, namely, with Enterprise Resource Planning (ERP) systems such as SAP R/2, SAP R/3, mySAP ERP, and SAP Business Suite. The development from mainframe systems to client/server architecture, mobile infrastructures, and Internet services led to the increased networking of business processes and systems. Providing and acquiring information electronically enabled business partners to execute their transactions with new forms of communication, such as Electronic Data Interchange (EDI).

The invention of the Internet opened new possibilities for merging information technologies and economic processes. The resulting increase in productivity, however, also led to new requirements for system security and communication methods. New potential threats emerged daily. Companies suddenly no longer had the option of executing their business transactions based on traditional forms of commerce and communications. The Internet and the increasingly networked business worlds were evermore rapidly becoming the most important channels for information, sales, procurement, distribution, management, and marketing.

And the next new architectures are already being developed: network-centered multitier and service-oriented system architectures. The opening of company activities and information to transactions and communications over the Internet; the transition from one-dimensional connections to networked systems; and the increased collaboration among organizations, companies, and people lead to faster data exchange and work cycles, increased efficiency, just-in-time production, expanded sales opportunities, and capital expansion because of information technology (IT)–supported systems. This also increased the requirements for employee flexibility, organizational units, and entire companies, which respond to changing market conditions rather than act proactively.

Nevertheless, the advantages of networking and collaboration are obvious: aggregated purchasing; lowered labor costs; higher revenues; transparent prices; increased visibility of suppliers, more rapid market evaluation, penetration, and global expansion; strategic competitive advantages; and increased shareholder value. But these and other strategic and operating advantages cannot be attained without protecting the systems and persons involved. However, the new IT technologies and high level of networking that exists today also bring risks.

Immature, unproven, and, in particular, insecure technologies and areas of use lead to new challenges. Risks are newly defined and arise around the globe. Potential attackers who exploit existing vulnerabilities within companies and external attackers who are imminent threats for business processes and technical systems use the weaknesses of new technologies and gaps in security systems to attack companies in many ways. The potential risks for the companies targeted by such attackers are primarily financial.

## 1.1 Security Objectives

The requirements for trouble-free business processes entail general security objectives. These objectives serve as a guideline when determining concrete needs for security, assessing criteria for risk analyses, and the measurability of risks and security measures.

*Security* means a condition of relative rest, not only in terms relevant to IT, but to other topics as well. The adjective "secure" is derived from the Latin *securus* and means "without worry." Security thus describes an apparently constant state that must be reached and endlessly ensured.

Mathematically, maximum rest and complete security cannot exist except as a subset of an achievable, imaginary quantity that approaches the maximum value. All of the components that contribute to security are therefore incomplete subsets of an unachievable condition of security. That means that although security can be defined as a concrete objective, it can never be completely reached in actual practice.

But how can the existing needs for protection and security among participating business partners be converted into a high level of security in an IT environment? The answer to this question leads to the definition of the term IT security. *IT security* describes the need for data, processes, systems, networks, business partners, and employees to be in a condition of relative rest without any kind of interfering influences to implement continuous value and market chains. It means that no significant break-ins, interruptions, or losses in IT-supported processes are occurring or are foreseen. The primary concern here is the protection of company assets and the systematic control of risks with adherence to all legal and regulatory guidelines. The development of objectives relevant to security helps to determine the required influencing variables required to reach IT security.

Important IT security objectives include the following:

- The establishment of an awareness of threats and risks and their classification
- The description, integration, and protection of all company assets
- The guarantee of the availability of business information, data, and communication processes
- The confidentiality of commercial activities, transactions, and personal data
- The integrity of business processes, internal processes, information, and persons involved
- The reliability of systems, networks, and responsible information owners
- The ability to reproduce, control, and check business activities
- The data retention and data protection of master, transaction, and personal data
- The adherence to legal and internal company requirements and influencing factors (their legally binding nature and compliance)
- The accountability of business transactions
- The ability to control and manage systems, applications, users, and actions influencing the company assets
- The guarantee of the authenticity of application data and user activities
- The flexibility of applications, communications channels, and users

Additional security needs can enhance these core objectives of IT security (see Figure 1.1). Depending on the type of company, industry, geographical area, and local environment, IT security objectives can be variously defined and evaluated to enable the company to respond to specific risks and to invest in appropriate measures.

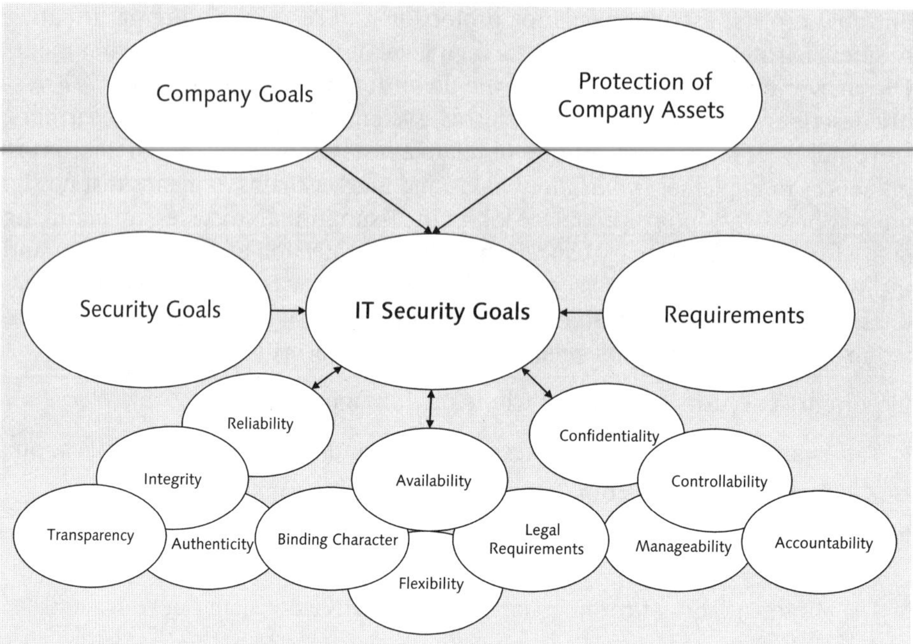


**Figure 1.1** Security Objectives and Influencing Components

**Best-Practice Method: Analysis of Objectives**

An analysis of objectives examines company objectives, company assets, and the information and processes most important to a company's success. The analysis determines general IT security objectives as control objectives and then documents them in a strategy document.

The IT security objectives are generally binding guidelines or directives to establish and support a company-specific IT strategy.

## 1.2 Company Assets

IT security must be established throughout a company to create the necessary trust for all those who participate in processes supported by IT. The protection of company assets and of processes used dynamically within an organization helps ensure continuity within a company. The measures taken to develop IT security thus lead to providing the supporting IT systems, applications, and employees involved with total protection from active and passive threats.

Table 1.1 lists the components that should be protected in a company environment.

| No. | Level | Description |
|---|---|---|
| 1 | Physical level | Buildings and facilities, material |
| 2 | Technical level | IT infrastructure with systems, networks, and applications, and their architecture in the company |
| 3 | Transaction level | Business and administrative processes |
| 4 | Humanoid level | Organization, employees, partners |
| 5 | Data level | Data and information |

**Table 1.1** Components to Be Protected

Recognizing and evaluating the threats and risks to the components of a company's business process chains is one of the most critical prerequisites for establishing successful defensive and control methods as security solutions. These actions limit the existing threats and the related risks for the company as a whole can be reduced and made controllable. Potential risks exist because the previously mentioned components to be protected have vulnerabilities and because of threats from internal and external attackers (see Figure 1.2).

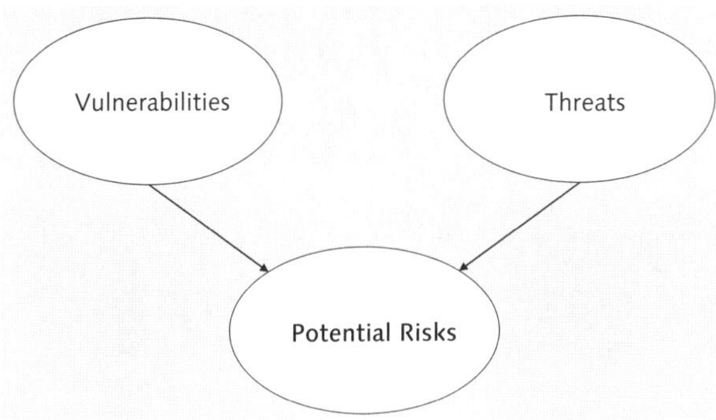


**Figure 1.2** Vulnerabilities and Threats

Various types of dangers exist and are a variable risk to the company depending on the individual case. The establishment of countermeasures requires a targeted analysis of a company's legal, organizational, process-related, or technical vulnerabilities and an evaluation of scenarios that simulate an attack by potential attackers. Company assets are the focus of the examination.

### 1.2.1 Types of Company Assets

Direct company assets that are affected by IT and are thus threatened and need to be protected can be grouped into physical and informational assets.

- **Physical assets**
  Physical assets like technical servers, networks, lines of communication, mobile end-devices, and computers are concrete assets in a company; they are procured and are investments, and they represent a company's inventory. Influencing factors like procurement price, depreciation, and so on define the loss of these assets.
- **Informational assets**
  The characteristics of informational assets, on the other hand, often make it more difficult to set an actual value when evaluating the need to protect such assets. In the worst case, the total value of the company is threatened. Informational assets include personal data, development and product information, price calculations, a company's reputation, brands, experience, and the knowledge of employees.

Company assets are determined, categorized, and evaluated based on the definition of value categories and their assignment to factors like costs, sales volume, and profit margins. Subdividing company assets into types and determining the values of those types are important tasks for establishing the required security solutions in an IT environment. Relevant company assets and parameters must be known to determine the potential for risks related to the components that should be protected. Figure 1.3 illustrates this relationship.

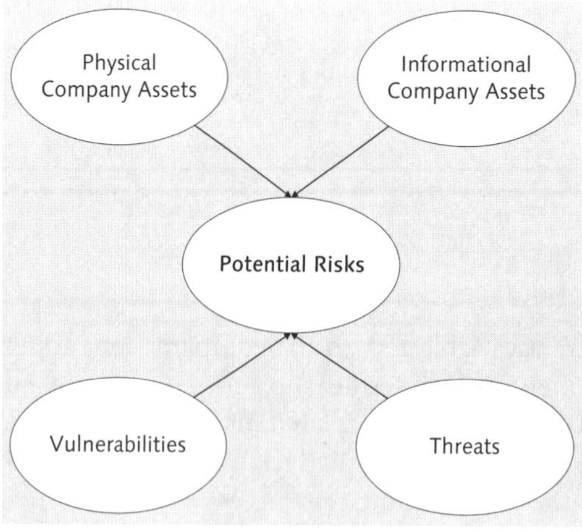


**Figure 1.3** Company Assets and Potential Risks

Indirect company assets, such as the local level of education, reputation, social security in the business environment, transport routes, and so on, that may be a potential risk for the company must also be considered when analyzing the risks, but they are hard to control by means of IT security measures.

### 1.2.2 Classification of Company Assets

The medium-term and long-term protection of company assets is the objective of every IT security solution. An organization's need to protect itself from potential threats is called its *protection need*. A protection analysis determines the protection need. The following classification values for company assets can be used as examples to be applied during the analysis:

- The availability of business information, personal data, and systems
- The confidentiality of commercial actions and data
- The integrity of business processes, flows, information, and persons
- The measurability and transparency of financial and other data
- The relevance of decisions
- The innovation and investment level for products and services
- The time-to-market, delivery continuity and quality, customer base
- The legally binding nature of business processes and adherence to legal requirements (compliance)
- The ability to control and manage equipment, systems, investments, applications, and users

The company assets to be protected are determined based on these and other classification parameters. In IT, the analysis of the protection needs primarily includes the information and data to be protected; the technical infrastructure and other company assets can also be included. This also refers to contracts and terms of delivery, and receivables, interest charges, and payables.

Information is classified according to various levels of confidentiality, such as generally available, available to a limited extent, secret, top secret, or private. In individual cases, the value results from where the information originates from in the company, how the information adds or creates value to the company, how the information is examined in the event of damage (loss, criminal falsification, and so on), and how the information will be used going forward in the company.

The classification parameters mentioned previously help classify and define the company assets that define the protection need. Accordingly, company assets can be classified as worth protecting and not worth protecting. The company assets worth protecting can be further subdivided into the following levels of protection need: low, normal (medium), high, and extremely high. A low protection need is given if the damage or loss of these assets does not affect the company's overall results significantly. If an extremely high protection need is required, the existence of the entire company is usually threatened.

**Best-Practice Method: Protection Requirements Analysis**

The analysis of the protection need sets, evaluates, and classifies the various types of company assets. The evaluation primarily depends on a consideration of information worth protecting and its systematic storage, processing, and communication in IT systems, networks, and processes. The analysis defines and documents a special value for the company or the related organization in a strategy document. The evaluation of company assets and the resulting protection need is the precondition for a targeted risk analysis that determines the potential dangers and the resulting risk for the company assets.

## 1.3 Risks

Once the assets in the various areas have been determined, an analysis of the threats and risks can begin. The determination of risks requires concentrating on the necessary company assets that were identified by the protection requirements analysis to optimize investments in IT security. The risk depends on the potential dangers to the applications involved, the IT systems, the data, the communications channels, the processes and their users, and parameters such as the probability of occurrence and the effects of damage.

Because appropriate measures can minimize and monitor risk, the security solutions for reducing risk are themselves a relevant influencing parameter (see Figure 1.4).

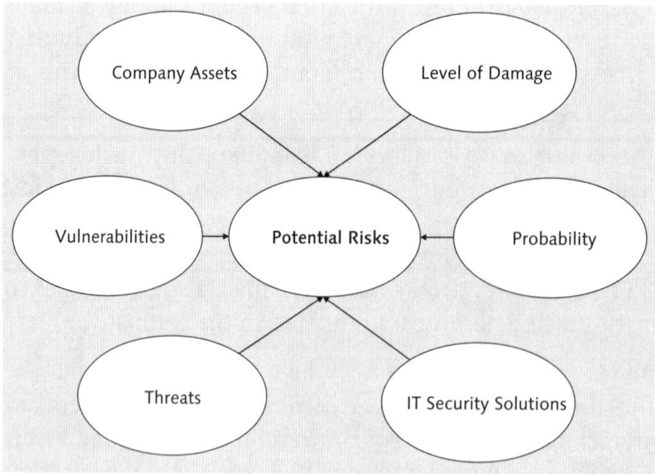


**Figure 1.4** Influencing Parameters for Potential Risks

The IT security solutions, the potential risks, and the size of the potential risks all influence each other. Threats are not only posed by individual and financially motivated attackers but also by white-collar criminals, spies, and terrorists. It is therefore critical to analyze risks comprehensively, early, and carefully, and identify vulnerabilities.

**Best-Practice Method: Risk Analysis**

Risk analysis summarizes the results of threat and effects analyses. The result is a detailed list of company components and their relevant protection need and a list of threats, possibilities, and single risks and overall risks. Risk analysis includes the classification of the risks and serves as the necessary preparation for determining countermeasures and controls, which are defined in this control analysis.

The analysis assigns the risks to areas like data, systems, processes, organizational units, and legal units. The risk analysis examines the data, the information to be processed, process flows, individual process steps, applications, IT systems, functions and transactions, authorizations, and users for possible risks. This also includes regulatory and legal requirements, which are also threats and need to be considered in the risk analysis.

### 1.3.1 Types of Risks

Risks with IT relevance result from the consideration of company assets that are worth protecting. Because analyses primarily consider data, IT systems, processes, and employees, risks are basically subdivided into the following types:

- **Risk of loss**

  The risk of loss involves a consideration of the potential risks and threats arising from the loss of important information (caused by an operating or application error, for example), personal data or company data ending up with an unauthorized third party (caused by unauthorized user rights in a master data transaction in SAP NetWeaver Business Information Warehouse (BW) or SAP ERP HCM, for example), or being changed, or simply theft of technical devices. Depending on the influencing parameter, risks from loss can involve significant effects such as the loss of reputation, the loss of investments, or unfavorable judicial decisions.

  Risks of losses can arise in any segment of the company assets. These risks usually entail the irrecoverableness of the original asset or an unreasonably high recovery effort that involves high costs. The worst loss is the insolvency of the entire company. Therefore, the main objective of risk and control management is to avoid partial and total losses.

- **Process risk**

  Process risks result from a threat that interrupts internal business processes, external business transactions, and communication. This can interrupt the process flow, which can result in massive financial losses depending on the content. A further process risk is the unauthorized and often criminal modification of data by third parties during communication, for example. Release processes are also affected if control functions do not work and damage is done due to insufficient process steps, limits, or authorizations. Risks affect administrative processes and business procurement, distribution, communication, financial, investment, control, and other processes.

  Missing process documentation is usually the initial cause for process interruptions or insufficient process designs. Frequently, however, custom structures and inappropriate technologies also do not meet the requirements in the internal administration process, for example, if too many user rights are granted without this process being controlled. In the worst case, these risks lead to a loss of business partners, interrupted production, and multifaceted reductions of company assets.

- **Technical risk**

  Technical risks are usually symptoms of vulnerabilities in the IT architecture, in the systems, in the communication and data networks, and in the applications in the broader sense. In many cases, individual components of the system landscape are secure or categorized as secure, while the analysis of vulnerabilities reveals significant defects for other components. The complete risk control can therefore no longer be guaranteed. The whole affected structure is not secure.

  Technical risks can occur in individual system components and in transport equipment, storage media, communications channels, and output devices. These risks affect data storage, the loss of information, and the continuity of process flows. Risks for applications can result from defective functions and nontransparent, complex, and not user-friendly interfaces. This risk type also includes risks that arise from open authorization systems that grant technical users overly broad access rights, for example. Furthermore, technical risks need to be controlled in the network area, for databases, during load balancing, for backup methods, or when deleting data.

- **Legal and industry-specific risk**

  In the years to come, legal and industry-specific regulations will be tightened due to economic and financial crisis but also due to permanent incidents in data protection and financial reporting, and due to national and international insolvencies. The greed of investors, managers, and employees, irregular accounting practices, or the mere failure of the persons responsible in the control processes strengthened the demand for stricter requirements for capitalist companies worldwide.

The existing and future legal requirements will be an enormous risk for the companies affected, because this usually entails drastic consequences for companies and managers. Legal obligations and requirements have existed for some time and won't only involve financial but also personal consequences, such as imprisonment and liability in serious cases. These legal risks primarily affect the management level of companies, and they are real and therefore pose a great potential risk to the shareholder value of a company and its employees. You must therefore appropriately include these risks in the overall concept of risk and control management.

- **Organizational risk**
  Because of their direct effect on employees, partners, and the users of IT applications, organizational risks are extremely important when determining overall risk. The erroneous use of SAP applications due to human error belongs to this type of risk category, as does incorrect maintenance of authorization components like roles or user-specific values. Structural risks that do not allow for a segregation of duties must therefore be compensated by enhanced technological solutions. The negative influence exerted on a company's culture, rapid expansion of the company, organizational processes, and problems like an uncontrolled expansion of access rights in various SAP systems and the use of such rights by unauthorized users entail risks that need to be addressed.

All types of risk almost always result in financial losses. The repeated identification of security issues, vulnerabilities, and risks in internal checks and by auditors and consultants clearly indicates the need for an urgent evaluation of necessary IT security and control measures. Because the interaction of technical IT components, processes, organizational units, users, and legal requirements as a whole leads to significant overall risks, only a comprehensive examination of these risks enables the fulfillment of security objectives (see Figure 1.5).

Too many companies trust their experience and accept numerous risks, because they don't identify or document them, or misjudge or simply ignore them due to nontransparent processes and integrated systems. Operating in the dark, however, is no protection from loss, aggressive attackers, and stabilization policies. In many cases, proper execution of a risk examination saves a company from unnecessary failures and allows it to focus its investments on the necessary measures required to effectively control and continuously reduce risks.

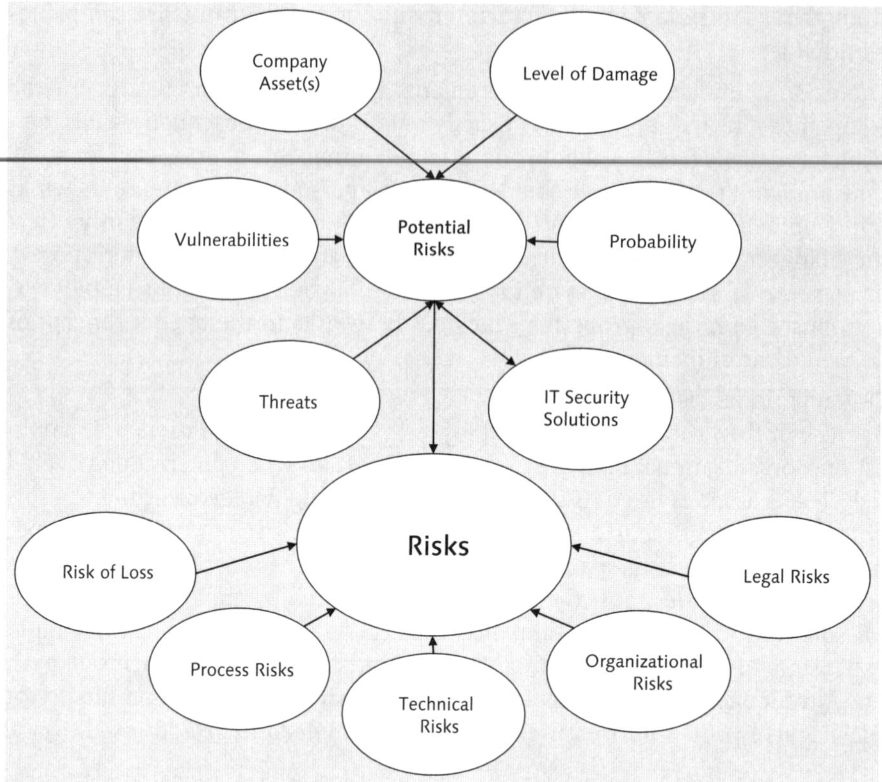


**Figure 1.5** Influencing Factors for Risks

**Best-Practice Method: Danger Analysis**

A danger analysis examines and analyzes the vulnerabilities of and threats to IT systems and architectures, the information worth protecting, and the processes and applications important to the success of the company. An examination of the threats posed by internal and freelance employees, partner companies, competitors, and international attackers completes the analysis of potential dangers. The analysis also estimates the likelihood of occurrence for individual risks to determine the threat potential.

### 1.3.2 Classification of Risks

As a general rule, the evaluation and classification of a risk results from an examination of the potential level of damage (effect) and the expected likelihood of the occurrence of an attack (threat) that causes damage (effect). Risks can be grouped as follows: low risk, normal risk, high risk, and extremely high risk.

The evaluation of risks is critical to determining the protective measures a company must take. The insights gained during the danger analysis are classified according to the influencing factors of probability and effect in the next step. As the amount to be invested in IT control and security measures typically depends on the expected amount of damage, information on the effects of vulnerabilities of and threats to IT is an important source for estimating and making decisions about relevant security measures.

**Best-Practice Method: Impact Analysis**

The impact analysis details the consequences of attacks, failures of IT systems, and human errors. An examination of the potential risks and the company assets worth protecting leads to a determination of the effects in various areas such as technical systems, processes, or applications.

The effects that can result from vulnerabilities, threats, or mutual influences are the foundation for the control measures to be defined in the subsequent step. The documentation of the impact analysis becomes part of a risk control matrix.

## 1.4 Controls

The term *controls* is defined as all measures that protect company assets. This includes the consideration of protection needs, the associated risks, and the possible means and methods of minimizing risk.

In IT, control measures are just as important as all of the necessary items that result from threats to company assets as a whole. The task of controls is to recognize vulnerabilities early, to inspect the identified vulnerabilities, and to prevent passive and active attacks. Controls also help monitor existing company assets and company assets being developed. In the event of damage, controls can be used to investigate and explain the matter. The objective of control measures is to generally lower the probability of damage occurring, minimize the effects, control the risks that remain, and identify new risks and eliminate them at an early stage.

Because the various analyses described previously have defined the necessity for IT security measures, the following sections identify and describe general and concrete controls.

### 1.4.1 Types of Controls

The determination of controls can be quite comprehensive. Depending on the area of IT security and its relevance to the objective, measures can have a controlling character — the required critical activities, for example — or can have an active influence on existing IT systems and their components, processes, applications, and users. Controls are therefore subdivided into two types:

- **Upstream controls**
  Upstream controls help a company avoid and reduce risks using measures such as strong authentication, the separation of user rights in applications, the installation of release steps in business flows, and the encryption of communication channels for transferring business data. The objective of this type of control is to capture a potential threat and eliminate weaknesses in the long term, to reduce risks drastically, and, ultimately, to protect the company assets.
- **Downstream controls**
  Downstream and investigative controls help uncover damage to avoid having the situation become even worse and to avoid further harm to the company. As a rule, this type of control is used to improve existing processes and protective measures considering the changing company assets.

Depending on the objectives for specific company assets, controls can be established as technical measures, authorization solutions, or administrative process solutions. In the SAP environment, technical measures are subdivided into internal IT security solutions by SAP and solutions from SAP partner or security companies. The solutions of other security companies can complete the security solutions from SAP in various applications and systems, which also include the tools that are summarized under Governance, Risk, and Compliance (GRC).

**Best-Practice Method: Control Analysis**

A control analysis helps identify possible solutions to define upstream, downstream, and investigative control measures. This procedure lists the possible control options as technical, process-related, organizational, and automated solutions as part of a risk control matrix, without, however, evaluating specific solutions. The control analysis contains concrete measures to reduce risks, such as the separation of authorizations and the implementation of release steps in the order process. Various solutions can be included as options with advantages and disadvantages. They are evaluated at a later stage.

### 1.4.2 Classification of Controls

An evaluation of the various solutions is performed based on the results of the risk control analysis. Above all, companies should note the evaluation criteria given in Table 1.2.

| No. | Evaluation Criterion | Description |
|---|---|---|
| 1 | Fields of use and functionality | SAP applications, transactions, functionality |
| 2 | Reduction of existing risks | Evaluation in percentages |
| 3 | Strategic principles | Standardization, central storage, data protection, information ownership principle, multiple eyes principle |
| 4 | Best-practice solution for existing risks and handling | Conceptual and technical solutions |
| 5 | Adaptability and integration | Integratability of the control solutions with existing processes, organizational structures, and technical infrastructures |
| 6 | Support from solution suppliers | Scalability of the control solutions, support structure of the solution supplier (also with regard to geography) |
| 7 | Market experience and customer satisfaction | Empirical values from using control solutions from other markets or market segments, feedback provided by existing customers |
| 8 | Effort needed to implement and operate | Specifications made with regard to nonmonetary effort considering the use of control solutions |
| 9 | Initial and ongoing costs | Specifications made with regard to initial implementation costs and ongoing costs for use in production |
| 10 | General benefits for the company | Overall evaluation of all individual parts |

**Table 1.2** Evaluation Criteria for Controls

Based on the results of the risk analysis and the prioritization of the existing need for protection, the control list then ranks the recommended measures and solutions. These results are entered to the risk control matrix, which is the recommendation for the use of IT security solutions and other control measures. The following classification can be used to prioritize the recommended control measures: low priority, normal (medium) priority, high priority, and extremely high priority.

All individual analyses are part of the overall risk control analysis (see Figure 1.6) and are summarized in the risk control matrix.

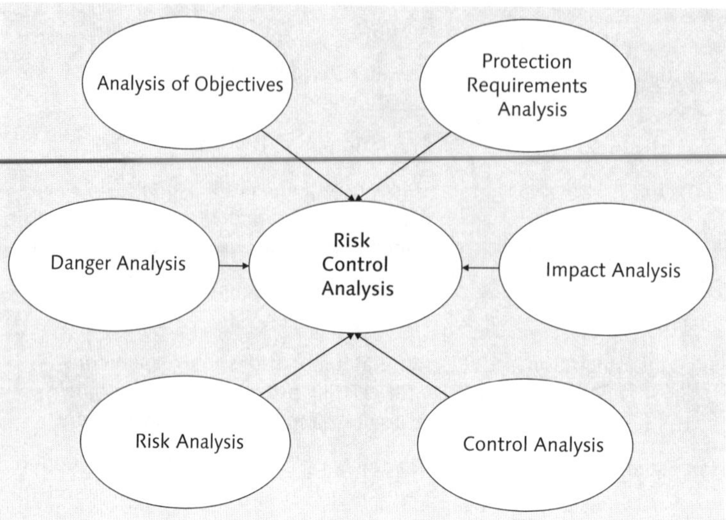


**Figure 1.6** Components of the Risk Control Analysis

**Best-Practice Method: Risk Control Analysis**

The risk control analysis is the superordinate concept for the required individual analyses that are summarized in a risk control matrix as part of the evaluation of company assets, the determination of the protection need, and the determination of the appropriate controls.

A risk control analysis is performed for various areas and aspects. As a result, it is a substantial process mapping the necessary protection and control measures. The measures are then transferred to a catalog of countermeasures that helps prepare an action plan and a work plan. Once created, the risk control matrix should be updated on a regular basis to protect the investments made in analyses and the established security measures

*Enterprise risk management comprises all of the components required for a comprehensive risk control of an enterprise. A corresponding enterprise risk management strategy is the framework for evaluating a company's need for protection and for determining the controls required to guarantee the required level of security. This chapter describes the components needed to successfully establish such a security strategy.*

# 2 Enterprise Risk Management Strategy

The increasing globalization and international orientation of business and financial processes — along with the continuous expansion of linked technical information technology (IT) infrastructures, networks, and program applications — lead to new challenges and requirements in strategic decisions, management, and control of these processes and technologies.

The amount of work performed with computers is escalating quickly: In industrialized nations, more than 60 percent of the labor force already works with computers in some form or another. Economy, science, administration, trade, finances, and culture can no longer manage without digital support. Mankind could not control space probes through millions of miles of space if IT was not available. Foreign trade, grocery shopping, and online banking via your home computer are all based on digital networks. The digital world has established itself everywhere and increasingly defines our working world and our everyday life.

Innovations in IT have reached a fast pace. Mobile devices like calculators, cell phones, and portable computers become smaller and smaller and are brought on the market with an unexpected variety of functions with an ever-improving quality and in ever shorter production cycles. Today, cell phones are no longer limited to their original use as a telephone, but in addition to saving contact data, music, and pictures, the portfolio offered by mobile devices can also include the retrieval of weather data, location determination, financial services, purchasing activities, and numerous other functions. These devices also contain word processing and spreadsheet programs — and, ultimately, SAP systems as well. Due to their mobile properties, these devices are exposed to a considerably higher risk of loss than permanently installed computers. This necessitates coordinated measures in risk management.

The increased rate of criminal activities in IT is growing globally at an alarming rate. The lack of risk controls in the financial industry and economy on a national and an international level are among the basic causes for the catastrophic extent of the economic — and social — disaster at the end of the first decade of the new millennium. The international economy crisis and various data protection scandals are examples of this: The failure and the partly arrogant ignorance that is displayed with regard to comprehensive risk management are considerably intensified by an evermore complex economy, ownership, and IT structures. Greater competition among companies, organizations, and countries also puts added stress on employees and therefore pressure on users of IT applications. As a result, users are making more errors, and various opportunities are provided for criminal behavior.

Moreover, criteria like profitability, effectiveness and productivity, transit times, alliance cycles, the creation of new markets, customer management and retention, return on investment, security, continuity, and transparency become more and more significant in business life. There are no breaks on the Internet; online orders can be made 24/7. The following trends emerged that express the rapid changes in electronic business:

- Besides the Enterprise Resource Planning (ERP) and production systems, the Internet is integrated with various economic processes as an essential technological communication and information element, and it therefore revolutionizes all microeconomic and macroeconomic processes.
- Economic models change constantly; firms experience a transformation into enterprises with a global reach (multinational groups). Other trends exist at the same time that force companies to focus on their core businesses. Companies therefore reevaluate their role in the value chain.
- The speed of economic developments and cycles increases continuously. The result is that saturation times and competition are further intensified and that critical conditions are reached faster.
- The fight for customers increasingly becomes the focus of business activities and information flows, which extend to all areas of economic, social, and political life.
- Knowledge and experience become evermore important as strategic components. Education, science, and multiculturalism therefore become increasingly significant parts of a healthy economic life and social freedom.
- Threats to company and social assets grow, which can no longer be considered separately. These also include environmental, moral, and ethical values.

Enterprise Risk Management (ERM) is a central component in the fight against such risks that have direct or indirect influence on the conservation of or decline in values of a company. It is an essential component for preventing and correctly handling crises. Besides the original elements of enterprise risk management such as market risk, investment risk, and capitalization risk, it also increasingly includes components like environmental risk, identity and access management (authorizations management), data protection and security, information politics and distribution, technical security, process security, organizational control, and regulatory and legal compliance, and corporate governance.

## 2.1 Status Quo

Based on these insights, enterprise risk management as a strategic core measure for long-term protection of company assets becomes a central component and increasingly important. One of the components of enterprise risk management, IT security, has become more high profile in recent years. The topic was often considered a necessary evil; but the situation has gradually changed since the mid-1990s. Companies and organizations are increasingly anxious to protect their investments with appropriate security measures. This development established important elements of IT security, even if a holistic concept was omitted in most cases. In the course of this development, SAP equipped the components of SAP systems and applications with versatile control options and the required IT security structure, and has provided corresponding interfaces for external solutions.

But many of these solutions are individual measures that are slowly integrated with the overall landscape of systems, applications, communication and data networks, user rights, and legal requirements. Although companies pay attention to technical security measures by using antivirus programs, firewalls, encryption mechanisms, and authentication solutions, they are guilty of ignoring things like authorization systems.

Furthermore, some companies have made significant investments to develop an orderly authorization concept for their SAP systems, but they lack or insufficiently follow the administrative and supporting processes needed to remain at that level. Because many companies try to establish individual security measures without examining their own risks, they play a great deal of catch-up to achieve the current level of risk management and security investments— despite the progress that has been made.

The interaction of individual areas in a company, its employees, controlling bodies, and consulting and auditing firms is another critical area. Company-wide risk management requires the involvement of most, if not all, business areas, and a large number of decision-makers, managers, information providers, and others who must contribute to a successful implementation of enterprise risk management and therefore a comprehensive security strategy. The coordination of these areas and this information is truly a difficult task. Accordingly, it must be planned, executed flexibly yet promptly, and appropriately further developed and controlled as much as possible with clear and standardized procedures.

In addition, ignorance and bad advice only make the road to a comprehensive ERM and security strategy with objective-oriented solutions more difficult. Nevertheless, SAP, suppliers of security solutions, and consulting firms have increased their efforts to develop solutions for a comprehensive enterprise risk management. These solutions are used to solve individual problems and to establish the holistic structure of an integrated catalog of security and control measures; technical support, however, must also consider innovative security solutions.

In the meantime, enterprise risk management in the sense of company security has reached a status that forces more and more enterprises and organizations to actively search for solutions to obtain protection and financial added value for the company and the environment through targeted and holistic investments. Individual solutions are replaced by a centrally defined, transparent, coordinated, and holistic risk management or they are further developed. The security trend is clearly toward mandatory overall solutions.

## 2.2 Components

The word risk presumably originates from the Latin, *rixicare* or *rixari*, which means argue or dispute. It is likely that this referred to the incalculable resistance in combat operations. *Risco* is the Spanish word for a rock that is a danger to a vessel. Management can mean the following: control, lead, achieve, handle — the Latin *manus* stands for hand. According to this, risks must be identified, calculated, and handled. Risk management is an important protection function of human life because you are surrounded by risks of all kinds, you must concern yourself accordingly and develop preventive and protective measures.

This also applies to companies and organizations that need to set up a comprehensive protection and defense system against threats and wrong decisions within the scope of enterprise risk management. The strategy includes all of the activities and solutions that lead to an improved security situation in the company and therefore to protecting the company assets and establishing trustworthy business connections and activities. Particularly in the SAP environment, the number of highly integrated systems, functions, and roles and the related emphasis require you to regard these tasks as an important criterion for a company's long-term success. Security is not only a means to reduce risks, but also a way to build a foundation of trust for business partners.

A professional enterprise risk management, combined with common sense and active actions, increases the success factors for implementing strategic control measures without which a long-term business success cannot be guaranteed. Because security without a strategic concept only leads to insufficient results, a methodical procedure with a high-quality implementation is needed. A transparent ERM strategy captures all areas worth protecting, including SAP systems and networks, data and applications, organizational structures and users, external business partners, and processes. Only a comprehensive examination of risks and control options in all areas touched by IT helps companies establish an IT security strategy that truly offers them the required standard of security.

According to this, enterprise risk management comprises several components, which need to be merged and handled successively in an overall strategy. The following lists some examples:

- **First component: Enterprise Risk Management Strategy (ERMS)**
  By means of ERMS, you determine and conceptually process the components of a security strategy that are relevant to the company or the company area. It is specified at which level and for which information and areas you implement risk analyses and which methodology and procedure is followed. ERMS is closely linked to risk, control, and security management and entails topics such as project planning, documentation, security standards, requirements management, change management, and security intelligence and continuity.
- **Second component: Risk, Control, and Security Management (RCSM)**
  RCSM is used to establish a risk culture within the company. It lays the foundations so that strategic risks and risks that are partly relevant are identified, classified, and provided with corresponding security and controlling measures. These, in turn, are the preconditions for using and implementing appropriate solutions that can only be created through acceptance at the highest management level and the entire organization.

  In addition to technical risks and solutions, RCSM also includes procedural, organizational, legally binding, manual, and many other risks and solutions that are mutually dependent and should be balanced. Strategic topics like market and sales risks, product and development risks, geographic and regional risks, legal and compliance risks, industry and competition risks, and investment and financial risks are considered just like political developments and changes in location, environmental and environmental-load risks, and structural and future risks. In addition, there are internal risks such as sufficient insurance coverage, process and organizational risks, technical and system risks, infrastructure and personnel risks, data protection and data security risks, defect and quality risks, and application and authorization risks. The control and security measures for the previously mentioned areas are handled as separate ERM components respectively.

On the solution side, it is a stated goal to establish a lot of automated and preventive controls. These controls must be able to access the risk databases, for example, to make faster and more efficient decisions and to ensure a high quality for these decisions. Moreover, there are protective mechanisms that minimize the probabilities of threats and thus reduce the risks. These measures are accompanied by manual controls, system and auditing checks, and analyses and periodic inspections by consultants and ERM experts to ensure the continuity of the security level.

- **Third component: Legal and Compliance Risks and Corporate Governance (LCCG)**
  The enterprise must regard national legislations and international specifications that, for example, concern the economic, trade, social, financial, and data protection law as an integral part of risk considerations. The more far-reaching the consequences for the company, the more urgent the interest in a consistent integration with the ERM strategies. In addition, there are trade-specific and industry-specific guidelines and instructions that regulate company-internal and business areas like occupational safety, dangerous goods transports, production safety, food safety, pharmaceuticals specifications, and so on.

  Corporate governance includes legal specifications for internal company organizations and control structures and is an integral part of company management. The central specification and integration of internal requirements into a transparent risk control structure lead to the distribution of responsibilities to information owners. The goals of corporate governance comprise the protection of company assets (e.g., real estate, living beings, information, investments, market values, product and industry knowledge, unique attributes); protection of processes, business decisions, and transactional responsibilities; integration of internal and legal requirements; establishment of an independent executive monitoring entity (corporate legislative supervisory); and a risk and governance culture that defines control and self-control as a critical part of corporate governance.

- **Fourth component: Identity, Access, and Application Management (IAAM)**
  The main control elements of a company comprise the governing of internal and external (virtual) identities (see Section 2.3.3, Identity Management) and the build-up of a well-functioning authorization system to secure functional and technical accesses. IAAM concerns itself with the identification, creation, administration, authorization control, management, and scheduling of identities that have access to physical premises, information systems, data, applica-

tions, and functions. These identities include company employees, technical system users, and other users.

The objectives are to build up and manage personal identity data, to assign identities to organizational and asset units, to secure company assets with regard to identities and their functional and activity scope, automated controls for managing identities, and to establish a complete lifecycle management for all identities. This way, you not only control process flows, data accesses, and activities, but you also control and reduce risks.

However, the control of individual users and processes through user departments and internal controlling bodies only forms the basis for another level of security measures. The internal and external employees that are restricted to their actual working fields through single authorizations must also be controlled from time to time with regard to the development of criminal activities. The process risks are always related to modules and topics. Common control methods include release controls, functional authorizations, and expenditure restrictions.

The topic of data protection and security also comes within the limits of this area. The specifications from the data protection law defined in the third component must be translated into a corresponding system and authorization solution in systems and applications.

- **Fifth component: Technical Infrastructure and Architecture Landscape (TIAL)**
  The technical security of an ERM strategy comprises all risks and solutions related to the system and application. These include areas such as network security, backup and alarm management, operation system management, interface management, and the hardening of systems. The consideration and symbiosis of technical, process, administrative, authorization, and other solutions results in secured, transparent, and effective enterprise risk management.

Topics such as investment risks, market risks, and environmental protection that are also a part of enterprise risk management are not discussed here. However, these topics are an integral part of a comprehensive ERM strategy. The area of enterprise risk management described here, that is, IT or SAP security strategy, is part of the company's superordinate risk management strategy, which is discussed in the following text.

Figure 2.1 shows the general components that lead to building an SAP security strategy: general framework, strategy, methods, and Best Practices. The following sections describe these.

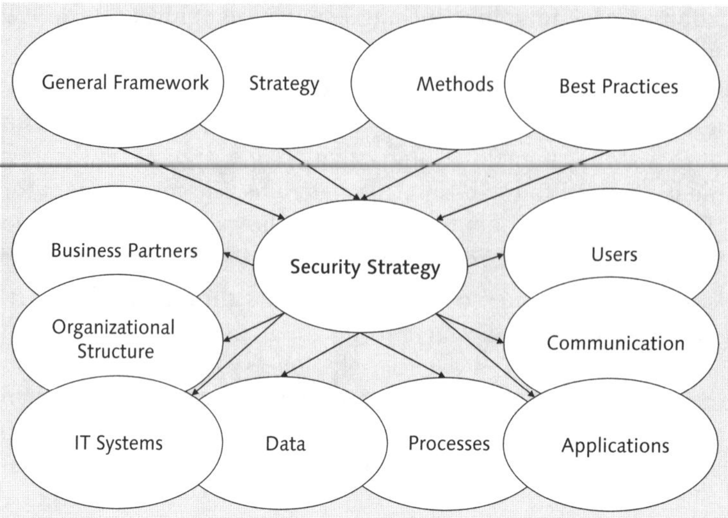


**Figure 2.1** Security Strategy — Components and Objectives

### 2.2.1 General Framework

The general framework must be known before an ERM strategy can be developed. The general framework includes requirements that affect the security strategy. Such requirements include internal, legal, and industry-specific requirements, previous and future goals of the company, main risk areas, growth strategy, the types and number of IT systems and applications, the functional scope for applications and authorizations, the number of users and technical system users in individual systems and applications, the technical architecture with communication channels, the type of information to be processed, and other indicators.

The identification of the general framework is important for targeted planning of individual security components. Such identification primarily uses strategic corporate definitions, technical architecture, documentation of business processes, legal determinations, general instructions from internal security guidelines, inspection reports, existing risk analyses, and incidents from the past. The general framework also determines the priorities and the sequence the specific parts of the ERM strategy are supposed to be implemented. Because the overall strategy for enterprise risk management is comprehensive, the implementation can only be performed gradually and in individual projects. Any critical problems must therefore be processed first with high priority to successively implement the holistic strategy.

Some possible examples for the general framework include the following:

- Legal determinations: Sarbanes-Oxley Act (SOX), Japan's SOX (J-SOX), the Principles for IT-Supported Accounting Systems (GoBS), REACh, and data protection laws
- Internal requirements: reporting and segregation of duties
- Guidelines: internal security guidelines and data protection specifications
- Processes: requirement documentation for purchasing processes, transport processes, identity, access, and application management

**Best-Practice Method: Requirements Analysis**

All requirements are mapped out in a requirements analysis and summarized in a requirements catalog. The requirements catalog is part of a strategy document for enterprise risk management. Besides legal requirements, it also comprises a strategic, conceptual, geographic, environmental, industry-specific, personnel, and technical general framework and goals.

The strategy document is a component of the ERM strategy for SAP risk management and IT security, which should be the written foundation for the company's security strategy for SAP applications. This includes, for example, requirements that result from the SOX regulations (see Chapter 3, Section 3.1.1, Sarbanes-Oxley Act), human resources (HR) department, data protection, the IT department, the employee representatives, and the user departments.

### 2.2.2 Strategy

Strategy is a central component of the overall strategy for enterprise risk management. It comprises all of the characteristics required to form a strategy document. The strategy helps describe the scope and reach of the studies in risk management, the planned ERM components and goals, the activities required, the general concepts to be considered, the critical documentation, and processes. The strategy is part of the overall document that describes the ERM strategy and serves as a template for detailed planning and documentation. It serves as a decision-making aid and definition when planning the use of security and control measures in a risk management environment in general and in an SAP environment in particular.

Some examples for the strategy include the following:

- Scope and reach: concretion of the company assets and risk goals, functional scope, technical scope, geographical scope, and timing
- Concepts: market analyses, financial analysis, environment protection concepts, development programs, data classification concepts, risk analysis concepts, identity management concepts, authorization concepts, standard SAP solutions in the technical security area

- Documentation: strategy document for risk management and IT security; risk control matrix
- Processes: documentation on authorization and user management

**Best-Practice Method: Strategy Concept**

The strategy concept is a central core aspect of the ERM strategy. All relevant requirements, general framework, target areas, and solutions are determined and described with a rough outline. Because the SAP security and authorizations area affects various components of enterprise risk management, you must also describe components that directly or indirectly refer to SAP topics when you define suitable structures. Examples in this context include legal aspects, company goals, planned risk analyses, data classification, organizational and personnel requirements, and so on.

### 2.2.3 Methods

Methods describe the procedures, required activities and targeted steps, suggestions for possible solutions, and examples for working out and implementing an ERM strategy in an enterprise environment. The required components and ranks result from the general requirements described in the requirements catalog. A methodological procedure should be a basic condition for using security measures, to plan and make optimal investments, and to attain the highest possible levels of use and benefits.

Some examples for methods include the following:

- Procedure: risk-controlled project phases such as analysis phase, security strategy, design, implementation, continuity phase, methods of audits for IT security, IT security as part of enterprise risk management
- Staffing: identification of project team members
- Options for solutions: strategic financial management, data security concepts, authorization concepts with functional and organizational roles
- Planning: work plan with activities, results, and milestones split into short-term, medium-term, and long-term work phases

**Best-Practice Method: Method Concept**

The method concept is an important component of the ERM strategy and is also described in the strategy document. It introduces the procedure models, the advantages and disadvantages of strategic solution options, and plans as a decision-making aid and basis.

### 2.2.4 Best Practices

Best Practices (or good practices) involve a company's requirement to establish the best risk and control management solutions in all company-critical areas. Best Practices are proven solutions that have been tested and used successfully in other locations, large industrial companies, and in small- and medium-sized companies — nationally and internationally. They include processes and procedures, and new technologies, innovative principles, and improvements for individual solutions.

The introduction of these solutions as part of an overall strategy and their evaluation by those responsible and decision-makers is important for ensuring short-term successes when handling threats and for making the correct long-term decisions when selecting security solutions. Appropriate advice from experienced consultants covers the introduction of Best Practices.

Some examples of Best Practices include the following:

- Principles: topic selection, prioritization, step-by-step procedure in phases, the principle of information ownership, and establishing a change management
- Integrated risk and authorization management: SAP Best Practices for Governance, Risk, and Compliance (GRC)
- Communications security: Secure Sockets Layer (SSL), Supply Network Collaboration (SNC)
- Authentication: digital certificates
- Methods: BSI Baseline Protection manual, risk-based authorization management, risk-based organizational and decision management

**Best-Practice Method: Best-Practice Analysis**

As a necessary part of the ERM strategy and its components, the best-practice analysis helps evaluate solutions in IT security. The analysis addresses concepts and solutions, describes functionalities and benefits, and shows advantages and disadvantages — it helps those responsible to evaluate the items and make a decision.

### 2.2.5 Documentation

There are two basic rules for a simple documentation of the ERM strategy and its components:

- The number of documents should be minimized.
- The documents must contain all of the necessary information.

The necessary information includes the requirements and an explanation of the requirements, the protection required for company assets, determination of ERM components and topic areas, a consideration of the risks and the control objectives and control measures, the design of the security components, and a description of the administrative security and monitoring processes.

The documentation should include the security policy of the entire company, general and specific guidelines, laws and internal rules to be followed, forms, and technical descriptions that are important for decision-makers, information owners, user departments, security and data protection officers, and employees and system users.

## 2.3 Best Practices of an SAP Security Strategy

The necessity of security measures and continuous monitoring and improvement of the processes and measures arises from the requirements that exist in every company and organization. Individual measures, as a rule, only lead to temporary or limited security. Therefore, the topic of IT security should always be looked at as a critical part of the overall ERM strategy. All dimensions of security — technology, applications, operational processes, organizational structure, users, and company and communication partners — must be considered, examined with regard to risks, and protected accordingly.

The following sections describe examples of Best Practices that are important for an SAP security strategy.

### 2.3.1 Procedure

The procedure or methodology used in establishing a security strategy in an SAP environment is one of the first strategic decisions that a company must make when determining its security risks. The company must see what previous documentation is available, when security solutions must be established, and if and how it needs to perform a risk control analysis. The estimated degree of overall protection needed and a focus on a security area affect the components of the security strategy. The correct procedure is of vital importance for the success of security measures and for the protection of such investments.

Targeted and comprehensive development of a security strategy requires the components illustrated in Figure 2.2, which are described in more detail in the following sections.

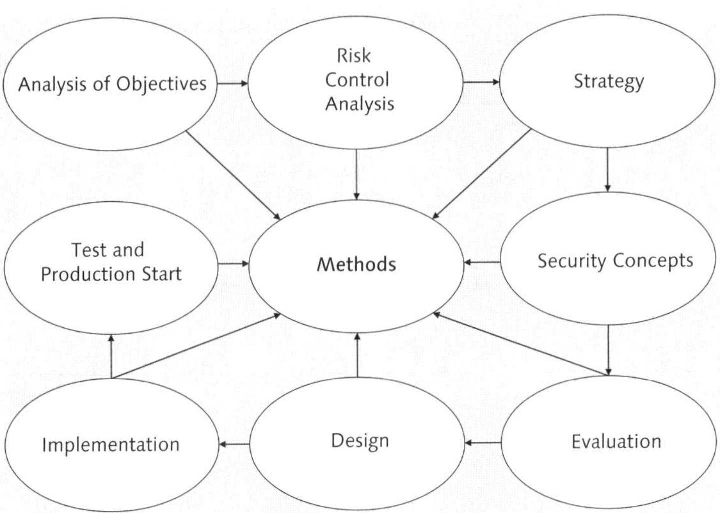


**Figure 2.2** Methodology to Implement a Security Strategy

### Analysis of Objectives

An objective analysis defines important control objectives and general rules. In an SAP environment, the risks play a special role in technical architecture and SAP-supported operational processes, identity management, transaction determination, authorization assignment, separations of functions in individual applications, and adherence to legal requirements. Control objectives — such as reliable SAP systems and related networks, the guaranteed availability of information and systems, and improved confidentiality of transactions and data — are important indicators and must be taken into account when you define security objectives and the procedures necessary for attaining these objectives. The sources of information include the requirements catalog, which contains important information on legal requirements like SOX, FDA, REACh, Basel II, and their relevance to the company, and the protection requirements analysis (see Figure 2.3).

### Risk Control Analysis

The risk control analysis helps identify risks in SAP technology, applications, organization, and legal requirements. For example, it classifies data, processes, and transactions according to their risk evaluation. Risky transactions and combinations of transactions with a high or very high risk factor are labeled as such and given control measures.

| Analysis of Objectives | | | | Protection Requirements Analysis | | | | | |
|---|---|---|---|---|---|---|---|---|---|
| No. | Description | Type | SAP System/ Application | Confidentiality | Integrity* | Availability* | Evaluation* | Estimated Percentage Share in Overall Revenues | Approximate Qualitative Financial Equivalent |
| 1 | Confidential Product Information Containing Formula Details | Corporate Knowledge | SAP NetWeaver BW | H | H | H | H | 20% | $238,000 |
| 2 | Compliance with SOX Requirement | Legal Regulation | All | H | H | H | H | 90% | $1,100,000 |
| * (L = Low, N = Normal, H = High, E = Extremely High) | | | | | | | | | |

**Figure 2.3** Protection Requirements Analysis

The risk control analysis is one of the basic components of a successful security strategy. Risks are examined in terms of data and information, business processes, applications and functionalities in SAP applications, SAP systems, organizational structures, and authorizations (see Figure 2.4).

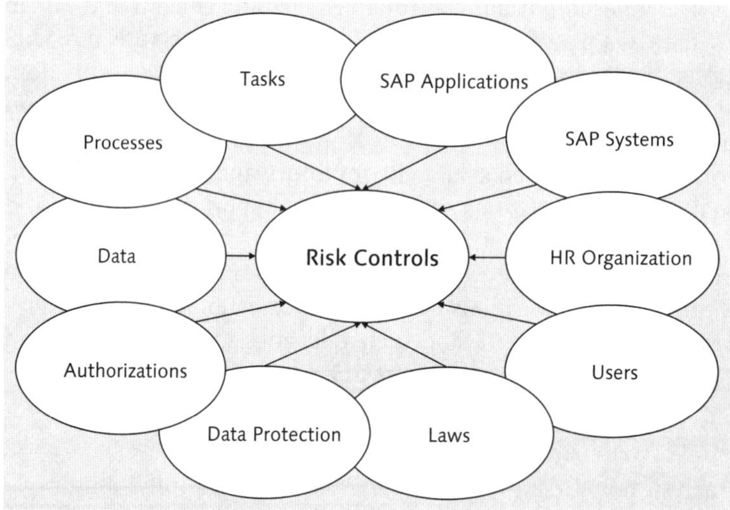


**Figure 2.4** Scope of a Risk Control Analysis

A risk control analysis is performed in four steps: danger analysis, impact analysis, risk analysis, and control analysis. The evaluation of the risks leads to control and security measures. Figure 2.5 shows the risk control analysis as the main analysis procedure for risk evaluation and solution determination in an organization.

| Goal analysis area | No. | 1 | 2 |
|---|---|---|---|
| | Area | Technology | Processes |
| | Subarea | Web server | SAP ERP HCM |
| Danger analysis | Vulnerability | No encrypted-SSL connection is established. | Each user has authorizations to display tables using Transaction SE16.<br><br>Tables are not restricted in any way. |
| | Threat | Information can be viewed and modified without authorization. | Person-related data can be viewed |
| Impact analysis | Effect | The production process can be viewed and adopted by a competitor.<br>A decisive competitive advantage would be lost. | Violation of the data protection law. Loss of reputation. Damage for the person affected. Legal consequences for the company due to action by injured party. |
| Risk analysis | Damage potential * | H | H |
| | Probability ** | H | H |
| | Overall risk factor | H | H |
| | Approximate qualitative financial equivalent according to probability | X | X |
| Control analysis | Control measure | SSL encryption of communication channels | Revision of authorizations for tables in the role concept |
| Rec. evaluations | Implementation costs | L | N |
| | Financial equivalent implementation costs | X | X |
| | Implementation speed | H | N |
| | Simplicity of administration | L | H |
| | Efficiency of solution | H | N |
| | User-friendliness | H | H |
| | Degree of compliance with business priorities | H | H |
| Rec. priority | Priority of security recommendation | H | H |
| | Priority calculation | H | H |
| Activity planning | Planning steps | Development of solution, evaluation, pilot test | Development of the authorization solution, evaluation, decision and role design |
| * (L = low, N = normal, H = high, E = extremely high) ** (L = 2%, N = 15%, H = 25%, E = 40%, Basis: 24h) | | | |

**Figure 2.5** Risk Control Analysis

**Strategy**

The strategy component determines the individual parts of the SAP security strategy. It's best to avoid using a lot of different documents in your security strategy. One document can contain all of the strategic descriptions, important remarks on protection needs and options for solutions, and so on. This strategy document can then be consulted as needed. It serves as the basis for all conceptual statements, such as security and control objectives, requirements, and naming of security components to guarantee a uniform procedure in the entire company. Various departments that handle different tasks within the holistic security process can use the strategy document as a template for developments, processes, and activities.

**Example: Contents of a Strategy Document**

- Background and Objectives
- Scope and Reach
  - Functional scope for application security
  - Functional scope for IT security
  - Technical scope for IT security
  - Geographical scope
  - Organizational scope
  - Scope of risk examination
  - Timing
- Requirements and Protection Needs
  - Legal requirements
  - Data protection regulations
  - Industry-specific requirements
  - Internal requirements
- Risk Control Matrix
- General SAP Concepts
  - Identity management
  - IT security for SAP systems
  - Authorizations in SAP applications
  - Risk controls for SAP modules
- Best Practices
  - Technology solutions with functional description, advantages and disadvantages, and recommendations
  - Principles

- Evaluation Criteria and Evaluations
- Decision Sheet
- Design
  - Technical design
  - Authorization design
- Targets for Conversion and Implementation
- Administrative Processes
  - Identity management
  - Authorization management
  - Security management
  - Monitoring and reporting
  - Internal auditing
- Appendix
  - Work planning with short-, medium-, and long-term tasks
  - Example for evaluations
  - Role and authorization documentation
  - Technical representation of SAP systems (architecture)

### Security Concepts

Security concepts can be derived from the security solutions taken from the risk control matrix, as described in the following steps. The description helps companies prepare for and make decisions.

Examples of security concepts in an SAP environment include authorization concepts for SAP ERP Financials (FI), Controlling (CO), SAP NetWeaver Business Warehouse (BW), Materials Management (MM), and SAP Customer Relationship Management (CRM). Remarks on various solution options with regard to Single Sign-On (SSO), and the presentation of best-practice methods and principles to follow legal regulations are also part of the concept presentation. Security concepts are later enhanced with technical guidelines and instructions to guarantee comprehensive and correct administration measures.

In all security phases (see Figure 2.6), security concepts must be known to all responsible parties, that is, information owners, those responsible for IT, security managers, and administrators. The security phases described here (or similar phases) can also be seen as best-practice methods.

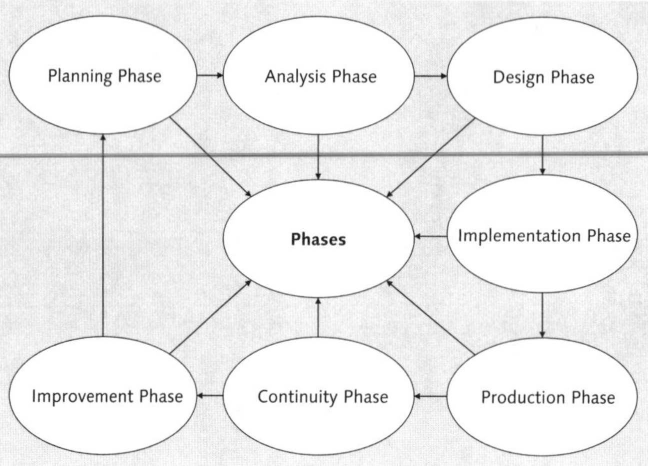


**Figure 2.6** Security Phases

**Best-Practice Method: Security Phases**

The following security phases exist:

- **Analysis phase**
  Recording the requirements and evaluating the security needs in a company
- **Planning phase**
  Planning activities to establish comprehensive security measures in a company
- **Design phase**
  Designing security and control measures
- **Implementation phase**
  Implementing security and control measures
- **Production phase**
  Using the security and control measures in the company in a productive environment
- **Continuity phase**
  Ensuring a smooth flow of control measures and monitoring the measures
- **Improvement phase**
  Continuously checking the relevance of control measures, improving the measures, and adjusting the measures as needed

## Evaluation

Security measures must be evaluated to guarantee long-term protection and correct decisions regarding company assets. Decisions are made easier when the security concept clearly works out the advantages and disadvantages of individual solutions. Evaluation is important work. It's not reserved for technical consultants and experts from the IT department. It must be performed by the information owners in the individual departments, data protection officers, internal auditors, a compliance team, SAP project managers, and consultants.

The topic of security, with all of its influencing factors, pertains to every area of a company. That's why an evaluation requires including these areas in decision-making. The advantage here is that many departments can participate in the decision-making process. However, it can often make the decision-making process itself tedious and it can exhibit losses in efficiency. So it is important to have experienced project leads and coaches, who can compromise solutions.

That's why, from the very beginning, an SAP risk control or security team should be formed — a team that unites people from all important areas and defines the strategic discussions and solution evaluations with qualified diversity under the direction of subject-matter experts and corporate consultants. Ultimately, the company's employees responsible for their particular area must make a decision by paying attention to the efficiency, the functionality, the required implementation and administration effort, the sustainability, and the benefits and potential improvements of the security solution along with the long-term support guarantee offered by its manufacturer.

#### Design

The design phase can then begin to set up the control and security measures. Starting with the risk control matrix, data security and master data concepts, identity management, authorization solutions, technical security measures, and administrative and control processes are worked out and included in the SAP security strategy. Apart from the risk control analysis, the design demands one of the most involved efforts in the whole process and it must therefore be accounted for accordingly in the planning document with regard to time and effort. Some design examples include:

- The design of an authorization system for SAP ERP, SAP NetWeaver BW, or SAP CRM with the GRC product solutions in SAP BusinessObjects
- Design of a solution to meet SOX requirements when using GRC solutions in SAP BusinessObjects
- Design of a technical security solution for secure authentication of employees
- Design of an administrative and technical authorization process solution to control orders

The design must also be accepted and released by the information owners involved. Implementation of the security design can begin afterward.

### Implementation

During implementation, it is very important that the individual departments are actively involved to ensure that the principle of information ownership is carried out consistently throughout the company. A thorough test phase of the implementation of authorizations is required. Authorization components like roles, user groups, functionality, and operational processes should be examined in the context of positive and negative authorization tests, and integration tests examined in terms of their ability to function and for errors. Positive authorization tests involve comprehensive tests of all of the transactions and functional assignments in an authorization role. Negative authorization tests help spot-check the implemented functional assignments and their positive mapping in authorization components.

The objective of authorization tests is to make sure the authorization components work. They are the basis for the further use of authorization components in integration tests and user rights. Integration tests, however, test functions and business flows within and among SAP applications. The byproduct of integration tests is a check of the authorization component's ability to function. However, the disadvantage of these tests is that they don't test all authorizations. Individual tests are needed when special functions are tested or after normal administrative authorization changes for individual authorizations. External solutions can be used to authorize tests that support both extensive mass tests and the daily handling of authorization problems in the production phase.

For technical security solutions such as SSO, encryption mechanisms, the use of digital certificates, development of identity management solutions, and biometric authentication, pilot tests are usually performed prior to a tedious company-wide implementation. Pilot tests also involve positive, negative, and integration tests (see Figure 2.7).

Note that test scenarios are worked out for each security test so that the success of the tests is repeatable and measurable.

## 2.3.2 Principle of Information Ownership

Over the years, with regard to authorizations, SAP has created a number of solutions that implement authorization components and general requirements flexibly. Consider the *SAP Profile Generator*. It helps users work with roles according to groups of transactions and the related menu structures in any form. The new GRC solutions in SAP BusinessObjects follow an integrative concept and they have technically connected the risk management with the design of authorization components and the user management:

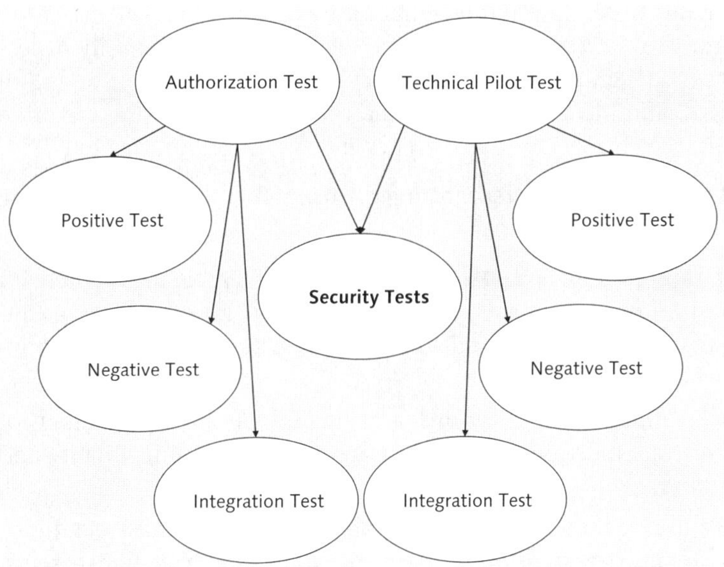


**Figure 2.7** Security Tests

- In SAP ERP HCM, for example, structural authorization profiles are used.
- In SAP NetWeaver BW, separate authorization objects are defined that specify access to business information and reports.
- The use of only a few transactions in SAP industry solutions must be limited.

Because of the high level of flexibility of these tools, their design is rather technical and complex. Therefore, after an initial and often complex design and implementation phase, only the IT department can manage these authorizations. The department has the technical knowledge to do so, but is often overwhelmed when it comes to evaluating the risks and the authorizations being requested. Authorization checks on transactions are simply taken as is, without asking those responsible if it is really necessary to accept them because of the risks involved, the organizational structure, or internal or legal requirements. A consideration of risk for business processes and technical components is often avoided or the quality does not deal with the reality.

Many companies haven't adapted their authorization design to this situation for years. This has caused a lot of problems. The content and number of authorization components grow over time. This leads to nontransparent, complex, non-user-friendly and therefore insecure authorization structures. The number of authorization concepts and solutions is almost infinite. Therefore, a variety of strategies and concepts — even within an industry or within the company itself — can be produced. Either too many or too few authorizations are granted. The level of security and the administrative processes linked to it are designed unsatisfactorily or less than optimally in many companies. Transparency into the assignment of authorizations, the design, and the administration and the ability for control are often lacking. Why is there such a lack of transparency in assigning authorizations?

One reason is not understanding or recognizing the real risks inherent in designing and granting authorizations.

- Many authorization systems are just too complex: the types and number of roles and authorization components, the inner structure, and the naming conventions often make sense to technical administrators, but not to those responsible for the specific areas.
- Comprehensive standard authorizations are created because a number of optional requirements must be handled that are reflected in functionality and the scope of activity.
- The number of authorization checks often creates very comprehensive authorization systems; administration of the systems provides only little transparency and serves only limited security needs.
- Authorization administrators must rely on expert input only from those responsible for roles or processes in user departments – and these people do not speak the technical language of IT administrators.
- Important decisions are only rarely handled as such, because it's impossible to go into the details of comprehensive checks.
- Integrated solutions that handle authorizations along with risk and control options are lacking.
- No reproducible and meticulous rules process exists; vulnerabilities are often only discovered later on. The cost of ineffective management is very high in the long run.

All of these circumstances lead to reduced control and less security, significant risks, continuously increasing expenses for ineffective management, frustration and errors among participants, and the failure to comply with legal requirements and auditors' specifications. Figure 2.8 illustrates this vicious circle of vulnerabilities.

The protection of intellectual and material property is becoming more and more important. The continuous provision of business processes and efficient administration are basic elements of secure economic life. These elements affect the profitability of companies and organizations at a fundamental level. That's why a proactive limitation of damage is becoming increasingly important. With legal frameworks (see Chapter 3, Sections 3.1.1 through 3.1.4), legislatures have forced companies to take topics like application security, reporting, change management, and internal controls seriously and dedicate themselves to these tasks to ensure self-protection.

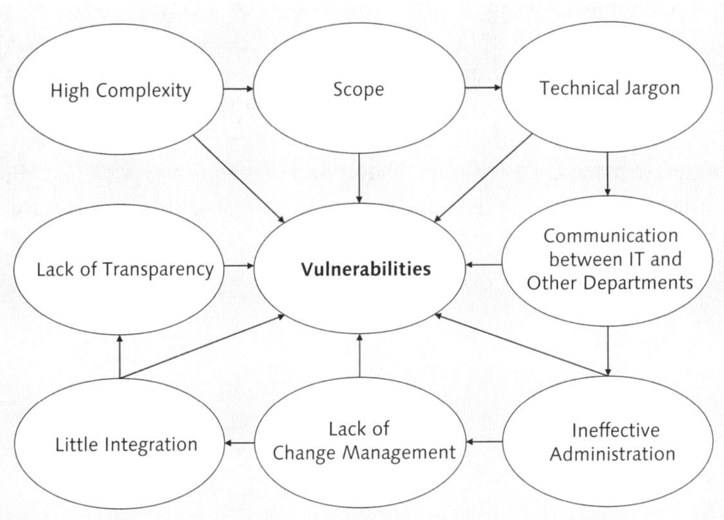


**Figure 2.8** Vulnerabilities of Authorization Solutions

That's why there's an urgent need for standardized simplifications, for the establishment of transparency in authorization processes, and for a consideration of the potential risks as an integrated component of the authorization and control structure. Authorization components must be created simply and transparently based on the required functionality, the existing risks, and the control objectives. Administrative processes need a general overhaul.

Security is related to responsibility. Authorization administrators usually know two to three specialized applications, if they have sufficient experience, it could be one to two solutions or products. But it often happens that specific requirements simply cannot be implemented. A check is not usually performed, but if it is, it is performed later on by auditors. This situation leads to permanent procrastination with regard to problems and risks. In a serious case, it can lead to significant losses.

Figure 2.9 shows the required, but often disordered, communication channels between individual owners of information and the areas responsible. The components of application security must be considered as a whole. And this approach requires a new qualitative and conceptual leap that supports these requirements.

The assignment of authorizations in SAP systems directs access to functionalities, transactions, and information for the users of SAP applications. Expert business and organizational decisions are needed to materialize user rights to SAP systems, applications, information, transactions, activities, and reports. IT can support this process, but it cannot initiate it or assume full responsibility for it. That responsibility must remain with the owners of information in the individual departments: those responsible for processes and areas, owners of roles, and those responsible for functions. Only they are in a position to make expert judgments in their areas, to estimate and evaluate risks, to identify the required control options, to define the controls, and to exhibit responsibility for these decisions. That responsibility must flow into the departments: where it is needed and where the experience and knowledge lie. Fundamental and efficient decisions are crucial to the ongoing success of a company.

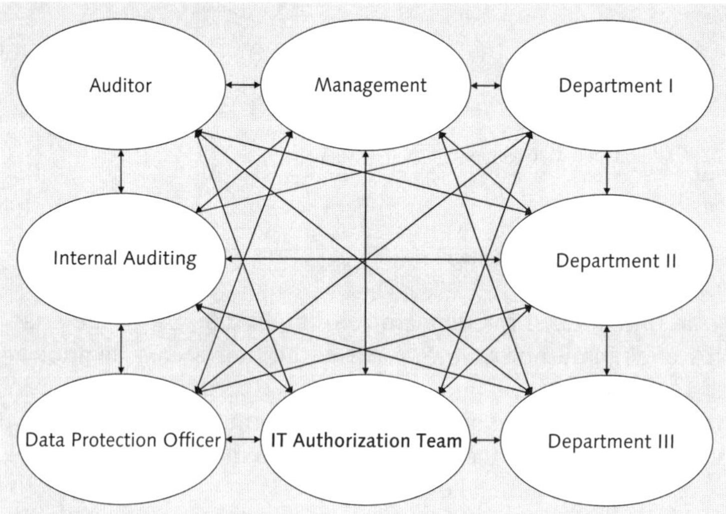


**Figure 2.9** Traditional Structure without Clear Information Ownership

The responsibility — with or without legal consequences — can and must be taken. An increased number of complex structures, the growing functionality of SAP applications, increased legal requirements to minimization risks, for a greater transparency, and for the control of business decisions produce the need to involve the individual departments in the control of information, authorization, and users relevant to security. SAP authorization administrators set the conditional framework and establish the basics of process control in the entire company. Each responsible person creates the content.

With the right information, processes, and authorizations, users can now manage and control access to their own business applications themselves. The design of the processes becomes more secure and data protection is significantly improved.

Comprehensive transparency, integrated control, and efficiency can be implemented with this method. But the corporate culture should not be underestimated. Security and best-practice methods can only be achieved if the corporate culture is oriented in that direction and if the company is willing to accept and provide active support for new solutions.

The novelty in this approach is that tasks relevant to security and consistent involvement of risk evaluation and controls move from IT-led administration to the company's departments that can execute the activities much, much better because of their expert knowledge. A transparent and plausible authorization system supports the tasks of internal and external auditing, which lowers the effort involved for all participants. Management must understand this fundamental change to authorization management, accept it, and support its implementation and daily use. Only then can profound success and a stable level of security be achieved.

Figure 2.10 shows the distribution of responsibility to information owners in a uniform and communicative control system. The principle of information ownership is a best-practice method and can only be initiated and implemented successfully in a company as an integrated strategy with the support of management and technology. The ownership of information and authorizations can only be established with a combination of technical solutions, appropriate authorization design, and process measures.

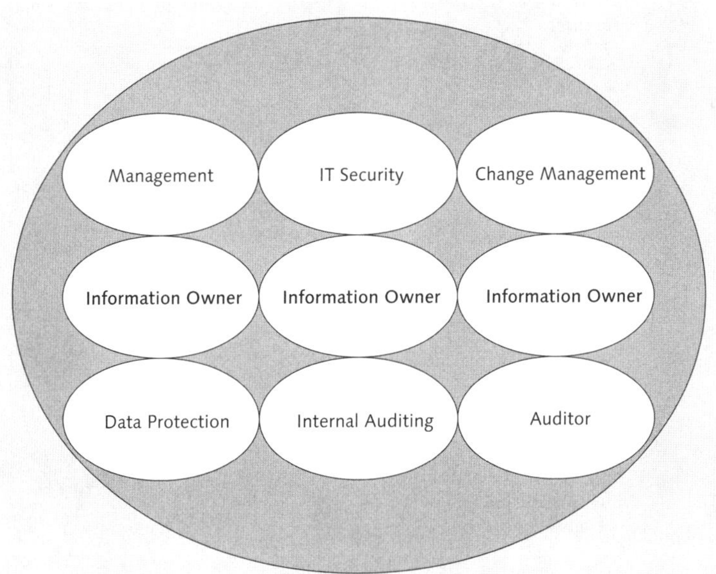


**Figure 2.10** Distribution of Responsibilities and Integrative Management Based on Information Ownership

### 2.3.3 Identity Management

As users of applications, data consumers, and employees, users of SAP systems play a central role in internal company processes. They hold responsibilities, maintain operations, and control the security of the established procedures. Employees secure the protection of company assets. Accordingly, employees themselves become an object worth protecting within the process of IT security. In this context, this is referred to as identities.

#### Starting Point

These days, the design of administrative processes for identity and authorization management is still too complex, involves too much effort, and is inefficient. The processes are thus a considerable cost factor that do not really guarantee security and cannot reduce the existing risks as required. The results include inconsistencies, a small amount of transparency, and users with inappropriate, incorrect, or too much authorization (see Figure 2.11).

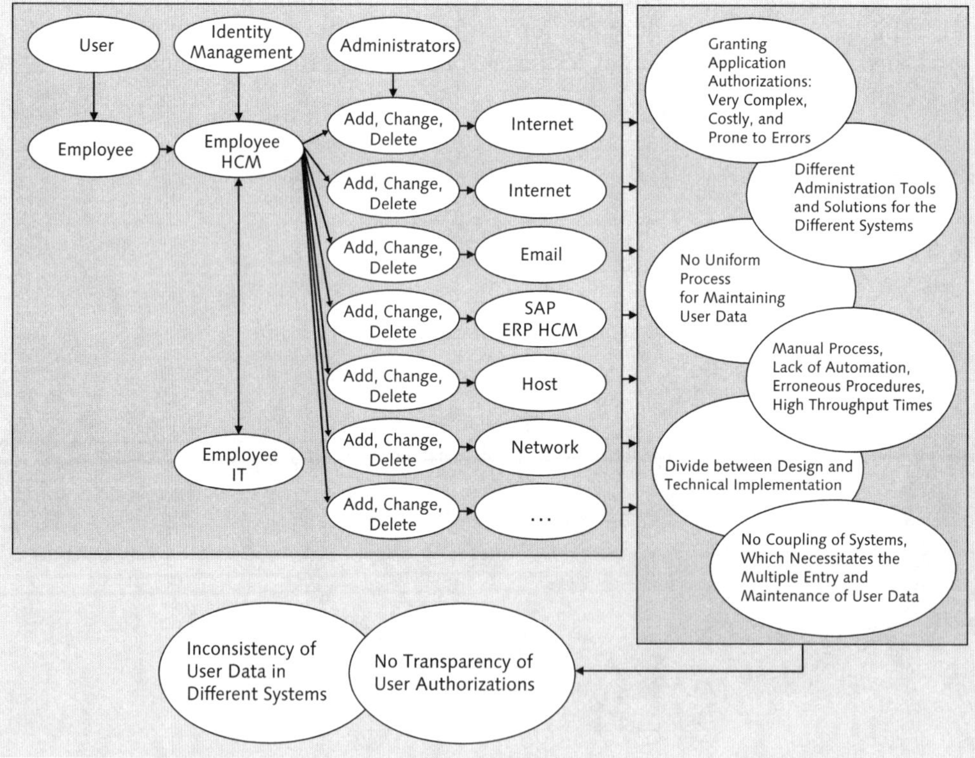


**Figure 2.11** Starting Point for Identity Management

In many cases, increased complexity and costs result from the drastic increase in the number of identities and authorizations. Users have too many authorizations because identity management does not permit real-time processing. Employees who have long since left the company still have access to various systems within the organization. The security requirements lead to the need to establish a uniform solution to manage identities. Control helps improve internal administrative processes related to employees and users of systems, and protect against external attacks by inimical identities that can destabilize internal company processes. If identities and system access are unprotected, even the best authorization systems can't provide help; all company assets are in danger.

### Objectives and Influencing Factors

The main problem is the decentralized management of identities and their related rights for all types of systems and applications. A central identity management system used throughout the entire organization only exists in the most unusual cases. The objective can therefore only be a holistic consideration of the weaknesses, the individuals coming into question as identities, and the systems being managed along with the related processes (see Figure 2.12).

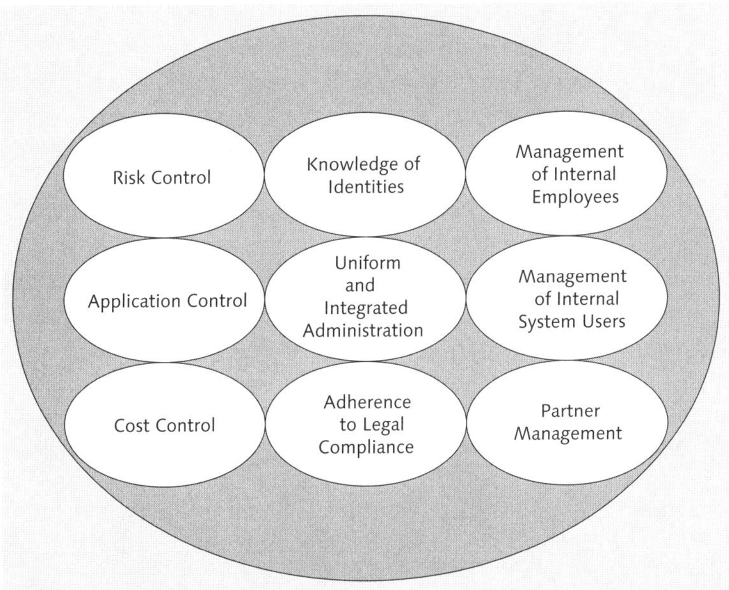


**Figure 2.12** Requirements and Objectives of an Integrated, Central Identity Management

That comprehensive objective includes the following preliminary objectives:

- A reduction of risks and increase in security in the company
- Uniform knowledge, transparency, and management of identities throughout the entire company (avoiding multiple identities for an employee, for example)
- A reduction of effort and administrative costs
- Effective management of external partners with and without access to systems and applications
- Adherence to legal requirements like SOX, Basel II, and data protection laws by controlled management of all identities, assigned rights to data, and functional access. Examples include personal data such as an employee's medical information, which might be stored centrally or in a distributed manner.

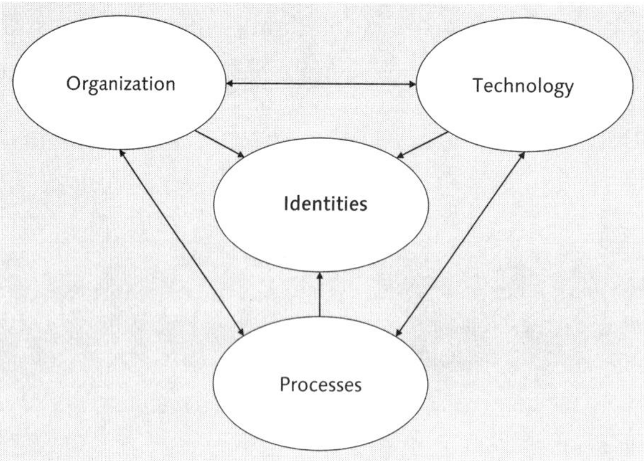


**Figure 2.13** Determining Factors for Identity Management

The most important factors that affect identity management (see Figure 2.13) include:

- The technology that tackles authentication. It creates control options for authorization and must therefore take over the management of identities.
- The accompanying processes that regulate administration, operation, monitoring, and exceptions.
- The organization. Its structure must map identities as positions, jobs, and external partners. It must also manage the required assignments and authorizations and distribute responsibilities.

### Solution

Companies must decide on a leading identity management system (User Persistence Store (UPS)) for a more centralized design of management, building upon standards and rules, clearing out the sources of errors, and using best-practice solutions. Several alternatives exist and, like the processes to be managed, they seek to distribute tasks in the future according to organizational, functional, legal, and internal company requirements. Technology supports the various solutions at different levels and therefore directly affects the selection of an identity management solution.

User and employee data must be stored, managed, distributed, controlled, called, and archived. Users need authorizations for applications, email, Internet access, or their own desktop computers. These activities must be coordinated uniformly to meet the growing requirements.

The roles of the administrative units like HR, the IT help desk, the heads of departments, the IT department, and other responsible persons must be unambiguously defined and assigned. They must also be mapped consistently by the system and technologically. Who should be responsible for creating new users? How are passwords changed and by whom? Who releases user rights? What supporting technology and which security solution have been selected? These questions must be answered ahead of time to secure the required investments in the correct identity management methods and the sustainability of the investments in these control measures. A well-functioning identity management can be established using solutions like SAP NetWeaver Identity Management, for example.

The risks in this area will continuously grow without the targeted use of technically supporting identity management solutions. Identity management by itself won't help much, but as part of a general IT security strategy, it can contribute to the overall success of establishing efficient and comprehensive control measures for IT security. Chapter 6, ERM Navigation Control Map, discusses SAP NetWeaver Identity Management.

**Best-Practice Method: Involving the Organizational Structure and Identifying a Leading Identity Management System**

Three scenarios provide solution alternatives:

- The first solution is decentralized management and involves various Central User Administration (CUA) systems, a Lightweight Directory Access Protocol (LDAP) directory service, and the organizational structure mapped in SAP ERP HCM. It manages various types of identities like internal employees, internal and external users, users with an internal status, and additional types of users. The participating identity management systems manage various groups of identities. Synchronization and process control make the solution up to date, even if it is not the optimum alternative for many companies.

- The second alternative provides a simpler and more manageable solution. Identities are completely managed in a directory service (metadirectory) and distributed to the various systems. However, this efficient and objective-oriented solution assumes cleansed datasets, uniform rules on procedures or naming conventions, clarity with regard to the technical implementation, and distribution of the tasks involved in identity management. To use this solution, a company must overcome existing sovereign rights for functional claims and historical areas of responsibility — without affecting harmonious operations and creating new potentials for risks.
- A third option is to integrate SAP NetWeaver Identity Management as a central security and control component to determine authenticities and to manage application users. An administration of all user types (internal, external, technical, and dialog users) is enabled at a high level within the SAP system and beyond system boundaries. This administration also provides for integration into the GRC solutions in SAP BusinessObjects.

*An efficient internal control system can only be established based on the requirements and needs of a company. This chapter explains the various types of requirements with examples.*

# 3 Requirements

Legal and internal requirements serve as signposts for choosing the correct information technology (IT) security measures in an SAP environment. Each company must identify individual procedures and solutions with regard to laws and industry-specific regulations to ensure compliance; make future-oriented, profitable, and value-conserving investments; and guarantee its endurance and effectiveness. Internal requirements for security systems and measures should always be defined upon the basis of necessity, especially all risks, including legal requirements.

**Best-Practice Method: Avoidance**

To meet all requirements, companies should not only implement methods and solutions to monitor and report on critical activities, but also reduce risk in general with active avoidance measures. Compliance is attained with knowledge and control of requirements and risks. A comprehensive risk management system tuned to the entire company and defined on the basis of legal and internal requirements is the foundation for compliance. Ensuring adherence to these measures and their timeliness are part of the administrative activities of a risk control system that meets the requirements of a company's departments, including IT, and also fosters responsibilities.

## 3.1 Legal Requirements

Secure and efficient investments in company controls and security solutions result from all of the required elements of the values conservation in an organization and from the protection needs of creditors, shareholders and investors, partner companies, and other private or public individuals and statutory corporations. Persons, information, decision-making processes, and responsibilities are the objects of protective activities. The needs are recognized by regulatory institutions and associations and emerge from legal instruments such as regulations, directives, guidelines, and laws.

However, legal requirements demand that companies respond and take action to improve the security of business activities, transactions, and investments, and to make this action worthwhile. The rules established by directives or laws involve regulations at the national and industry-specific level and regulations with international impact.

**Best-Practice Method: Requirements Analysis**

The requirements analysis outlines all of the important requirements for choosing the correct methods and solutions to protect company assets and selecting investments for IT security. It summarizes the requirements in a requirements catalog. The requirements catalog is also a component of a strategy document for enterprise risk management; it is supplemented by a necessary compliance analysis (for legal requirements) that focuses on individual SAP components.

Many of these laws and general conditions aim at improving financial reporting and establishing uniform rules for financial statements. This chapter cannot cover all national and international laws. The following sections describe some of the more important laws to give you an introduction to the current legal situation with examples.

### 3.1.1 Sarbanes-Oxley Act (SOX)

One of the most important laws affecting SAP security is SOX. SOX is a legal set of rules primarily directed toward companies traded on the New York Stock Exchange or the NASDAQ in the United States and their subsidiaries outside the United States. The law affects both American and foreign companies. So although it is a national law, SOX has direct and indirect international effects. The regulations affect both publicly traded organizations and auditing firms. Most auditing and IT consulting firms have already developed a great deal of expert knowledge surrounding SOX and work actively with SAP clients on individual solutions.

SOX came about in the United States as a result of stock-market financial scandals in 2002. The law was written by Paul S. Sarbanes (a senator from the Democratic Party) and Michael Oxley (a representative from the Republican Party). The objective of the law is to improve corporate reporting and to reestablish shareholder trust in the correctness of financial data published by companies. The central topic of the law is the successful establishment of organizational structures within companies to guarantee the reliability of annual reports and to contribute to greater transparency and correctness in financial processes.

A positive effect of SOX is that organizations must deal with it and establish an effective internal control structure for appropriate control measures in their companies according to the relevant requirements. This creates areas of responsibilities and persons responsible that increasingly draw the focus of attention to corporate governance. This situation finally gives IT security some long-overdue attention. Overall, SOX helps companies develop a uniform consideration of processes, IT solutions, and control measures to create fundamental and continuous improvement of accounting methods, organizational management, and internal control systems. IT security plays a central role in this task.

However, the implementation of improved standards in financial processes alone is insufficient to achieve the required process security, even though this is the defined primary goal of SOX. In the past, and to this day, missing internal controls and poor leadership qualities on the part of management have led to a series of spectacular scandals (Enron, for example) ultimately caused by insufficient risk management processes in the company involved. The consequences were dire: company bankruptcies, and cheated investors and employees. For many companies and organizations, SOX is one of the most important legal directives, because it has created a sound basis for serious ratification: consequences.

There is a legal foundation for managers to be made directly responsible for the negative consequences of missing control and security, including several years in prison. The effects on business and capital markets are much more important: Today more than ever, these incidents in an industry or country quickly become economic crises with global impact. The intertwining of companies and corporate entities with international investment structures and the increasing globalization of production, trading, and financial activities force investors, companies, and employees to make a quantum leap with regard to internal and legal controls so that the economy can flourish in the future — freely but secured.

Although more strict regulations and controls for internal operating and financial security also involve higher costs, today, intelligent risk management solutions provide a high degree of security and lead to substantial success in reducing your costs and achieving a good return on security investments if they are used consistently. SOX helps protect a company's needs and those of participating partners.

The American Security and Exchange Commission (SEC) and the Public Company Accounting Oversight Board (PCAOB) handle the enforcement of SOX. The SEC can investigate and issue sanctions. The role of auditors becomes more important, because as control instances they are monitored by the PCAOB. Audits of publicly traded companies are the responsibility of the PCAOB.

#### Contents of SOX

SOX regulations require the members of a company's board of directors and financial board to explicitly confirm the correctness of annual reports and the ability of publicity control systems to function. That means that processes relevant to finances, and all other processes that affect finances and operations, along with their utilities (like IT), are to be controlled and designed transparently and more securely. Evaluating accounting activities and their controlled involvement in business flows are important parts of the compliance process. Another equally important aspect of SOX is the total protection of data, processes, IT, and applications, because they have a direct or indirect influence on the financial success or failure of a company.

SOX includes the following:

- Corporate governance to manage a transparent and proper cooperate governance and liability for insider trading
- Expanded requirements for the disclosure of closing statements, such as annual reports, and the related upper management confirmation requirement (with the use of Form 20F)
- Regulations regarding the creation of a supervisory agency for auditors (PCAOB)
- Introduction of a notification requirement for when companies become aware of internal damage like embezzlement or comparable crimes
- A notification requirement for when the financial or operative situation of a company changes
- New regulations on the responsibilities of managers of publicly traded companies and the introduction of auditing committees at the board of directors level
- The threat (and implementation) of significant penalties for not fulfilling the notification requirements for the persons responsible for and attempted deception and obstruction, such as the destruction of electronic data as evidence (Section 802/1102 of SOX)
- The duty to set up an internal control system and monitor the system continuously to guarantee compliance by company management to eliminate recognized risks and vulnerabilities in the long term (Section 404 of SOX)
- Rules for independent auditors and increased penalties for them
- A requirement regarding a company's regular disclosure of risks and vulnerabilities
- Real-time implications (Section 409 of SOX)

Section 404 of SOX requires the definition, documentation, and creation of appropriate control procedures for company transactions to minimize the risk of erroneous information, misinterpretations, incorrect balances, and so on. Most of the companies and auditors only interpret these specifications for financial processes. Processes that directly or indirectly affect the financial results and reports are often not considered. However, because these processes have comprehensive effects on corporate governance, the effectiveness of SOX needs to be enhanced. This results in concrete requirements for ensuring data and process security, especially in IT security.

### Effects of SOX on IT Security

Sections 302, 404, and 409 of SOX are particularly important with regard to IT security:

- The requirements of Section 302 regulate a company's responsibilities. This section makes the chair of the board of directors and the director of the finance department responsible for the correctness of quarterly and annual reports. Their signatures confirm that the reports don't contain false statements and that they faithfully represent the financial situation and net operating profit. The signatories declare that they are responsible for the setup and maintenance of internal control systems, and that conclusions about the effectiveness of control measures have been derived from the most recent evaluation. The chair of the board of directors and the director of the finance department further confirm that they have informed the auditors and auditing committee about any important deficits and irregularities ahead of time. If the report nonetheless contains something other than the truth, fines can be assigned and the CEO and CFO can be made personally liable.
- Section 404 requires management to create an appropriate, internal control structure and to set up transparent processes for creating financial reports. The effectiveness of the internal controls and measures must be assessed at the end of every fiscal year. The auditors confirm the correctness of the report.
- Section 409 regulates the necessity of continuous control measures that the company must monitor without limits and in real time using an internal risk control system.

Violations of the requirements of SOX are met with severe consequences that can include the delisting of a publicly listed company and serious prison sentences. The expanded responsibilities of company management consistently lead to required measures in IT security:

- Acceptance of the requirements of SOX
- Translating the requirements into a catalog of countermeasures that's based on national conditions and conditions in the company

- Identification of risks in the company that can lead to violations of SOX requirements
- Establishment of control measures including monitoring processes, evaluation criteria, information rules, and protection of the ongoing performance of all measures as a whole

Because responsibility lies at the company management level, it can only be exercised by a distribution of the control processes throughout the entire company. It's not simply a matter of identifying and presenting risks, but of establishing efficient protective measures and controls that will significantly contribute to the elimination and monitoring of those identified risks. To secure the protection of information, transactions, and financial data, a strategy that covers all operations must be established. This generally involves the setup of specialist teams that include employees from the financial department, the auditing department, and persons with responsibilities in data protection, IT security, authorization administration, and process operations. Because the requirements of SOX demand significant investments in the company, experienced consultants should have a role in the development of the solution.

Most problems occur because of the everyday use of systems by company employees. Accordingly, IT security measures become a necessity. Some common problems are:

- The relevance of critical data or the risk group to which the data belongs is often unknown — therefore the data is often not protected. And this applies to business transaction data, financial data, and personal data.
- Functional separations of tasks have been insufficiently implemented in the SAP systems. This situation results in users with authorizations that reach far beyond their normal activities. Even today, it often happens that authorizations without restrictions, including SAP_ALL, are given to administrators, technical users, consultants, or even experts in the user departments. In many cases, even the activities of the administrators are not subject to further monitoring.
- The documentation of processes, risks, and controls is either missing or only partially available, has omissions and errors, or is no longer up to date. As a result, the documentation does not correspond to the SAP system configuration and procedures. Therefore, verifiability does not exist or only to a limited extent. This, in turn, has an effect on the verification costs.
- Risks are not identified or are inadequately identified. Internal controls are hardly ever reconciled and are often the task of the IT department.
- Authorization systems do not meet the necessary requirements. Changes to user authorizations are frequently carried out by simply adding more informa-

tion to the profiles. Employees with development tasks often have authorizations that are too extensive for their actual requirements.

- The management of users and identities is insufficient. Experience shows that at least 20% of user master records are no longer up to date (problems arise with temporary, external, and former employees and consultants, for example).
- There is no integrated system with risk, control, and change management dedicated to the management of users and authorizations.

The preceding problems only represent a sample and demonstrate how comprehensive the tasks in most companies must be to reach full compliance with SOX requirements. The measures developed for SOX in IT include the following activities:

- Recognition and analysis of vulnerabilities and threats and their relevance to SOX
- Internal company analysis of internal controls and security measures
- Evaluation of data, processes, and systems relevant to SOX and their need for protection
- Evaluation of risks relevant to SOX within SAP applications
- Assignment of internal control objectives to SOX requirements
- Addressing the relevant differences between the actual state and the target objectives for SOX compliance
- Definition of a process to implement SOX requirements on schedule
- Definition of user authorizations for data, transactions, and systems with segregation of responsibilities
- Selection of methods and tools for IT security that provide conceptual, methodological, and technological support
- Introduction of principles for the integration of decision-makers to distribute responsibilities better — according to the principle of information ownership, for example
- Reallocation of administrative processes like identity management, authorization administration, function and process risk control, and user management
- The use of SOX as a driver for additional critical IT security measures that directly or indirectly affect the ability to comply with SOX
- Setup of an effective change management system — to provide controlled management of users and authorizations, for example

- Definition of monitoring and quality assurance processes to ensure the continuity and integrity of internal and business flows

**Best-Practice Method: Monitoring and Reporting**

The use of standardized monitoring and analysis tools like the Audit Information System, Security Audit Logs, reporting in SAP NetWeaver Business Warehouse (BW), or SAP BusinessObjects with Governance, Risk, and Compliance (GRC) solutions as along with other solutions round out the required complete solutions. Note that the effectiveness of the control measures must be continually monitored and real events identified to ensure that conclusions for the continuous enhancement of enterprise risk management solutions are reached.

This procedure can be used for the practical and technical implementation of other legal requirements. Therefore, SOX supports the general demand for more transparency and security of financial and commercial transactions and business processes.

Responsibilities are now direct and indirect tasks for the company's upper management and employees. Internal control structures and procedures that maintain these responsibilities must be continuously analyzed in terms of their efficiency and usability to recognize vulnerabilities up front and remove them before damage results.

SOX also directly affects user authorizations and identity management. Unilateral measures can no longer be accepted for implementing compliance requirements. For example, the assignment of authorizations gives users of SAP applications access rights to critical data, business transactions, confidential data, and personal information. Because wrongdoing can come from a lack of knowledge or a deliberate act, correct authorization assignments protect users and the company and helps a company comply with SOX requirements.

SAP systems and applications are needed to perform all types of activities related to business processes. Every day, SAP users execute thousands of transactions and combinations of transactions. As a logical consequence, risks that result from executing functions and function calls in SAP applications should be determined and avoided ahead of time.

The introduction of comprehensive control measures must involve the use of professional change management to ensure user acceptance. Effective change management improves the ability to control and the security of processes and systems, because users assume responsibility according to their work area.

The control measures must also lead to more transparency in all business areas. Accordingly, consistent implementation of the principle of information ownership is an important element. In most cases, the IT department still handles the concerns of and controls users. Central security administrators traditionally handle the administration of authorizations and users. This approach records the requirements of the various business units and processes them according to the administrators' best knowledge and intentions.

But central management of security and control systems is not usually transparent for those responsible for processes. In the past, oftentimes risks were not considered or were considered inadequately. The result is decisions based on estimates, and this type of situation leaves too much leeway. Thus, the administrating processes develop in such a way that the administrators simply record and execute requirements of the individual departments. In serious cases, responsibilities are difficult to prove, alert or crisis management solutions are usually not implemented in these cases.

**Best-Practice Method: Information Ownership**

The principle of information ownership resolves the conflict described previously: Owners of information are data owners, process owners, role owners, and system owners. They assume responsibility if the principle is used consistently. Decision-makers are selected by organizational and content-related aspects. Areas of responsibility are assigned and responsibility for data, processes, systems, and users is distributed. For example, each department creates authorizations, assigns them to users, and controls everything transparently. The IT department provides supporting and controlling tasks.

The traditional "black box of IT" no longer exists in these companies. Administrative processes are designed more efficiently and with more transparency, erroneous estimates that arise from a lack of knowledge are avoided, and overall risk and operating costs are lowered. Responsibility is distributed across the persons responsible for the processes, data, or departments, because — owing to their daily tasks — they are best able to evaluate and manage the information to be processed and the relevant risks. Management now enjoys the advantage of increased transparency for processes and information being processed, because it would otherwise be unable to confirm the correctness of the information with a signature. The concept of information ownership also corresponds to the requirement to establish an appropriate internal control system.

IT security is increased because those responsible in each user department assign access rights themselves. They can assess the processes and risks that arise from overly broad user rights better than a global administrator. As a result, they will only grant users the access rights that they truly need.

Without IT-based solutions, you cannot meet the SOX requirements sufficiently. Various compliance software providers have made a place for themselves on the market. These offerings, combined with SAP's GRC solutions, form good comprehensive packages. Here, it's a matter of looking closely at the functionalities of the individual solutions and matching them with the requirements and needs of an individual company. Recognition and monitoring of risks are not the key to long-term success. Rather, the key involves consistent redesign of incorrect processes, risk-related access rights, and creating a comprehensive catalog of measures to meet the requirements of SOX and to guarantee the security of a company's activities. You should always consider operational risks in the risk examination and manage them appropriately.

**Best-Practice Method: Integrated, Holistic Solutions**

SOX demands the setup of new processes, control methods, and technologies. The more integrated and coherent the strategy and the sought-after solution are, the more successful the implementation of the measures in the company. SOX and other legal requirements should be considered a chance to significantly enhance internal risk control systems.

The significance of SOX for IT security is highlighted in a study of the Computer Security Institute (CSI) and the Federal Bureau of Investigation (FBI). According to the study, 8 of the 14 companies surveyed think that SOX has increased the importance of IT security (see Figure 3.1).

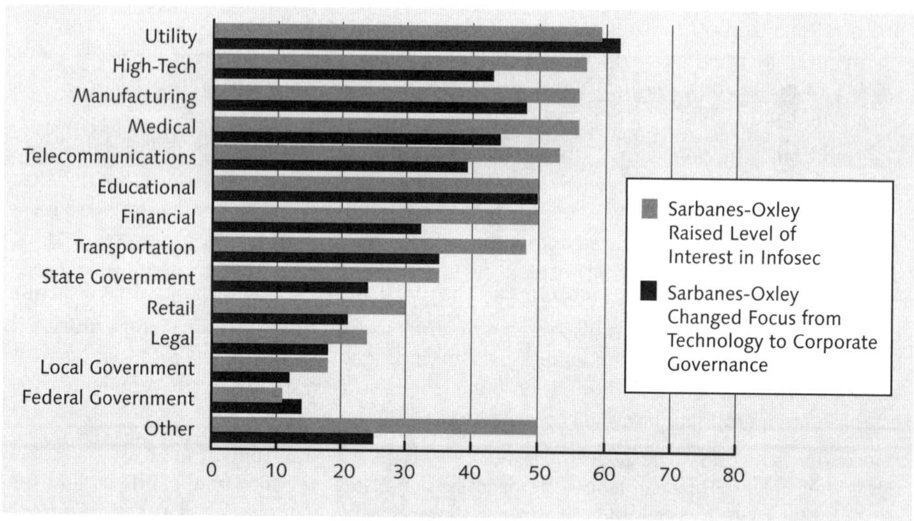


**Figure 3.1** Influence of SOX on IT Security (Source: SOX)

The SOX demand for adequate control structures for operative risk management within publicly traded companies will force improvement of international legal standards and rules, and thus improve IT security in general. The benefits of a company's investments depend upon the procedures, the solutions in place, and the stability of those solutions.

### 3.1.2 SOX Implementation in Japan

As one of the most important and powerful economies, Japan's industry has become extremely technical. Compared with all other Western industrial nations, Japan is a pioneer in IT.

#### Content of J-SOX

With the typical Japanese attitude toward precision and calm, Japan has put risk and control management on their agenda for the last few years. As this is also common practice in other areas in this Asian country, the state considers itself responsible and used the SOX specifications of the United States to establish a new set of rules for Japanese publicly traded companies and their subsidiaries: The Financial Instruments and Exchange Law (Kin'y shhin torihiki-h) has been binding since 2008. The Japanese SOX version defines the requirements for the conditions of the Japanese market. The rules of Sections 302 and 404 of the U.S. original are also used in Japan. On the one hand, specifications for financial reporting are defined, on the other hand recommendations for operational risk controls and the setup of an Internal Control System (ICS) are given, which is unofficially called J-SOX. The objectives of the ICS are defined as follows:

- Integrating internal controls into a superordinate control process
- Encouraging all employees to participate in the internal control process
- Ensuring the effectiveness and efficiency of operation
- Ensuring the reliability of financial data and reports
- Adhering to legal and regulatory requirements
- Protecting the company assets

The J-SOX is highly standardized and more detailed in some parts, which assumes a central role for the implementation by the companies affected because there is less room for individual interpretation. The number of qualified auditors in Japan is significantly lower than in the U.S., for example. This leads to increased requirements for automated controls and standardized audits and requires a great deal of discipline regarding the implementation of security requirements and solutions, particularly in IT.

#### Effects of SOX on IT Security

J-SOX mainly focuses on the creation of a comprehensive internal risk control system based on standardized requirements and IT-supported risk analyses and security solutions. Using a reference model for internal control systems, management must evaluate the company's internal controls. Auditors not only evaluate the control system but also make statements regarding content-related results for the management and provide recommendations.

Therefore, Japan is one of the countries that have adapted the U.S. act rather quickly. The national initiatives lead to establishing internally binding standards to make economic processes and activities controllable, more transparent, and more secure.

### 3.1.3 Principles for IT-Supported Accounting Systems

The Principles of Computer-Based Bookkeeping (GoBS in its German abbreviation) is another set of legal rules in Germany and is part of the general fiscal law of the (German) Federal Ministry of Finance. The GoBS provides regulations for electronic accounting. Regulations include requirements of IT-based accounting systems and rules for their implementation, use, and documentation. The GoBS is a continuation of the Principles for Accounting (GoB). Storage media for data and requirements for proper, IT-supported accounting in companies are regulated. The GoBS provides the regulations for electronic accounting. The GoBS is binding and, despite its scope, it is a minimum requirement for companies and organizations with SAP systems.

#### Content of the GoBS

The GoBS consists of the following content:

- **Responsibility**
  The person responsible for compliance with the GoBS is the person responsible for accounting.
- **Documentation**
  The IT systems in use must be able to reproduce all business transactions that are subject to accounting. Such reproduction requires document, journal, and account functions. The document function helps create proof of the business transactions and their financial mapping in the related IT systems. Quantity and time references are just as important as entering the name of the authorized accountant. The journal function serves as a log. Entries must be complete and factually and chronologically correct; legal periods of retention must be taken into account. IT-supported systems must fulfill the document and journal functions with their internal document and archiving processes; verifiability must be guaranteed at all times. The documentation of IT-supported systems must reflect reality and be able to prove that it does.

- **Data security**
  All data — especially confidential and risk-related data — must be protected with the appropriate authorization systems for applications and systems. Authorization for the relevant systems and applications help protect data and transactions. Data and transactions are to be protected from loss, unauthorized disclosure, and change; they must be stored according to legal requirements. Data must be stored according to a schema and controlled at regular intervals. For example, tables and master data are to be secured.
- **Creation and storage of postings**
  Access to individual business events and transactions must be possible at all times, and the applications and data for processing must be stored. Plausibility checks and controls are just as important as logging. Follow-up changes to transactions must be documented and traceable.
- **ICS**
  Implementation of an ICS with established IT-supported and manual controls is mandatory. Best-practice solutions such as segregation of duties help create a clear separation of functions and responsibilities — even in terms of data and transactions in applications and systems. Control measures must be documented and technically implemented in systems. Specifications for programming, the system landscape, and the use of text systems must exist.

Please see the original text of the GoBS for regulations on the reproduction of documents on storage media, the verifiability of IT-supported accounting, and other instructions.

#### Effects of the GoBS on IT Security

The GoBS regulates accounting requirements and processes in IT-supported systems in terms of the legality of the accounting transactions, documentation and verifiability, data security, and process control. Accordingly, only an integrated and comprehensive solution can realize the requirements that result from the GoBS for the relevant companies.

SAP applications have numerous solutions to fulfill the requirements of the GoBS, including table logging, archiving, process control, and authorization systems. These solutions must be coupled with related internal flow and control measures to guarantee the integrity and security of accounting processes and data. The separation of functions and their assignment with technical authorizations to transactions and data, the establishment of release processes, and the setup of archiving and external control cycles are all measures covered by standard products from SAP.

**Best-Practice Method: Integrated, Holistic Solutions**

The GoBS also demands integrative flow and control structures. Risks must be evaluated and requirements must be recorded and implemented in measures. Supplementing standard SAP products with additional security components like archiving systems leads to competent solutions in this area.

### 3.1.4 International Financial Reporting Standards

The International Accounting Standards Committee Foundation (IASCF) in the United States was the driving force for establishing international accounting principles and their interpretation, for example, for accounting rules that are summarized as International Financial Reporting Standards (IFRS). These rather comprehensive recommendations basically apply to globally active companies.

#### Content of IFRS

IFRS is supposed to facilitate the comparison of capital market-oriented companies worldwide and promote an integrated capital market that is efficient, transparent, and secure. This also strengthens the trust in financial markets and is supposed to stabilize free capital flows on the single market and improve the protection of (small) investors in the long term. Consequently, doing international business and getting listed on foreign stock exchanges is easier for companies.

The standards therefore define qualitative requirements for annual reports, such as clarity, transparency, materiality, decision relevance, reliability, and comparability. Reports that comply with IFRS are supposed to provide information on net assets, financial positions, and results of operations of the company. Common German accounting according to Book 3 of the German Commercial Law, for example, mainly focuses on the protection of the debtor for annual reports. Information on net assets, financial positions, and results of operations of the company is treated secondarily. The IFRS principles are supposed to change this: IFRS lays the foundation for an internal standardization of requirements and becomes national law due to the ratification of the individual countries or European Union.

#### Effects of IFRS

In Germany, due to the Accounting Reform Act, adhering to IFRS became mandatory for companies whose securities are not publicly traded yet but have begun the registration process for being listed on the stock exchange. Many binding recommendations of IFRS are more comprehensive than the German Commercial Law. According to IFRS, for example, all types of provisions for operating expenses are not allowed.

The introduction of IFRS and its step-by-step enhancements have already shown a positive development for capital market–oriented companies, in particular regarding payables, intangible and fixed assets, and return on assets. The measures therefore result in noticeable improvements of critical key performance indicators and thus directly and indirectly promote transparent and successful enterprise risk management in companies.

## 3.2 Industry-Specific Requirements

Industry-specific requirements for enterprise risk management and IT security result from influencing factors like the type of company, industry and branch, production requirements, and transport needs. In addition to general requirements like financial reporting and data protection, industry-specific considerations cover various requirements. Banks or investment companies usually have other requirements than energy suppliers or the country's Department of Defense. National law or international rules and regulations stipulate and define these requirements.

### 3.2.1 Food and Pharmaceutical Industry and Biomedical Engineering

The U.S. Food and Drug Administration (FDA) monitors the security of drugs and food for products and substances that are manufactured in the U.S. or imported for the single U.S. market. This leads to requirements and controls for food safety, drugs for humans and animals, research, veterinary medicine, toxicology and radiation safety, and for medical devices and food industry equipment. Therefore, the FDA not only assumes a critical role in the U.S. but increasingly gains in international importance for the companies and research facilities affected. Approval documents and declarations of no objection are just as important as quality, risk assessment, or inspection.

#### Content of the FDA Specifications

Each country has its own approval and control boards that use the FDA specifications for orientation. Numerous EU directives control drug and food regulations in the European countries, for example. In the case of drugs, health risks and pharmaceutical risks influence an approval; here, the risk-benefit ratio plays a major role. Despite standardized FDA processes and requirements, the respective country decides the approval of drugs and import licenses or bans for food. This sometimes leads to different evaluations of the same product and a different market treatment through the respective authorities. Consequently, the time-to-market and distribution of specific drugs vary and depend on national law or evaluations.

Both nationally and internationally, approvals are time-consuming processes for determining product safety. This means that holistic internal security systems need to be implemented in advance. They must consider administrative control solutions just like measures for research, product, and production safety. Examples include pharmaceutical companies, beverage companies, or manufactures of biomedical engineering equipment.

#### Effects of the FDA Specifications

The Federal Ministry of Health in Germany, for example, consists of several institutes that monitor the registration of drugs and epidemiology — the production of chemicals that are used as pesticides that can enter the food chain. The complexity of research, production, and approval processes requires controls at early decision stages, data security, secure communication methods, and many other security and control measures. This affects risk management areas such as FDA compliance, document and data management (retention periods, modification and loss risk), process monitoring, and system security. These FDA components lay the foundation for trust in generated and managed data.

System security means to maintain the validated operation of quality-relevant IT systems. FDA regulations in the pharmaceutical area require that the operator proves compliance with this security, and inspectors increasingly pay more attention to this during inspections. That means that system and application authorizations and access protection are critical parts of a catalog of measures for achieving compliance and secure processes in the food and pharmaceutical industry.

### 3.2.2 Finance and Banking Industry — Basel (I, II, III)

The evaluation of risks in the financial sector is one of the most important economic activities of financial institutions — at least until now. Worldwide liberalization of financial markets has also rapidly increased the risk involved in every type of financial transaction. That's why special supervisory rules for banks and financial institutions were created to promote and control the granting of loans and careful handling of all types of financial transactions. The Basel Committee on Bank Supervision works to ensure that financial markets remain as stable as possible. To do this, various stages of financial regulation have been established (Basel I, II, and III). They define binding regulations for banking control areas such as minimum capital requirements, reviews by bank supervisory authorities, and expanded disclosure and are supposed to be used as international guidelines. This leads to transparency specifications for using equity regulations, equity structure, and mapping of risks related to the banking business.

Reality requires strict regulation specifications: The industry had protested successfully against the introduction of solid control measures for cost reasons for several years and then invested a lot in IT systems but only halfheartedly in appropriate enterprise risk management. For some time now, it won't be able to get rid of its reputation of being primarily responsible for the worldwide economic crisis due to speculative financial transactions. However, this is not the fault of individuals; the entire industry assumes a general responsibility for this as well.

The Basel Committee has existed since the mid-1970s and is supported by the regulatory financial agencies and central banks of the most important industrialized countries. The decisions of the Basel Committee have no international legal force in and of themselves, however, legal guidelines of individual states and the European Union can make them law. In Germany, for example, the legal basis for Basel II is the Banking Act (KWG is its German abbreviation).

Unfortunately, the proposed law, Basel II, opened all doors for shifting the risk from banks to investor groups (hedge and bond funds, for example). Nevertheless, if all companies applied to Basel II, this disastrous financial situation would never have occurred because certain developments and risks would have been identified better and preventive measures could have been taken. Basel II could have helped avoid the banks' liquidity concerns and significant impacts of the financial crisis at the end of the decade.

#### Content of Basel II

Basel II consists of three pillars: minimum capital requirements, supervisory review, and market discipline. Basel II requires that a creditor has its own capital reserves for each loan. According to this requirement, risks are to be valued higher than they were before, and individual errors or incorrect estimates by participating companies are to be avoided. The objectives of Basel II are to reduce the risk of bank insolvencies with appropriate regulations, to foster the stability of and ability to schedule investments, and thus to provide more secure incentives for economic development. The security of investments must be guaranteed for borrowers and creditors. If a borrower goes bankrupt, the financial institution that granted the loan loses all or part of the money. If such cases accumulate, the creditor will soon develop its own liquidity problem.

To limit this risk, even today the credit-granting banks must reserve a specific amount of their own capital as security against the credit risk. Basel I set the rule in 1992. Basel I defined fixed rates of capital for an institution's own capital reserves. Basel II was intended to make the fixed rules set by Basel I more flexible (see Figure 3.2). Basel II includes two important innovations: the capital requirement according to a risk analysis, along with scoring and rating. Capital requirements are not fixed, but based on the ability of the borrower to pay and the risk that the bank customer cannot repay the loan. Scoring and rating is used to evaluate the risk of individual customers. Financially weak clients must pay a higher rate of interest in the future for their loans. A creditor has to reserve less financial means for a borrower with good creditworthiness. Credit is less expensive for these clients.

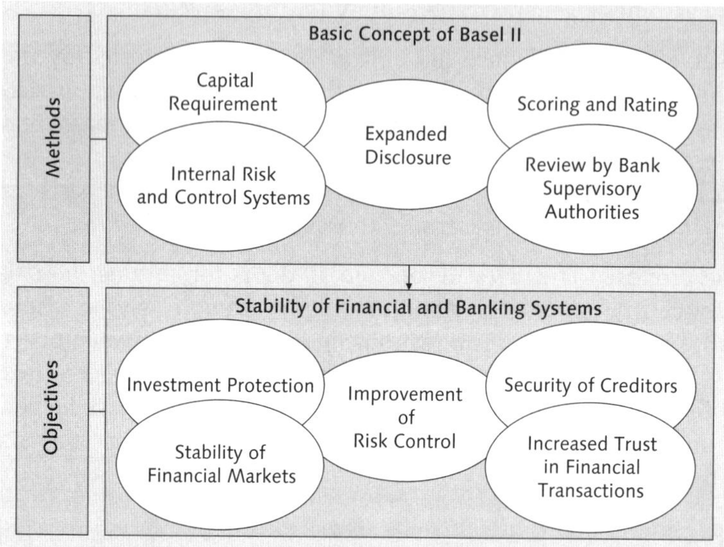


**Figure 3.2** Objectives and Methods of Basel II

Supervisory agencies see to the continuous improvement of internal risk and control procedures at financial institutions. Now more than ever, internal bank procedures and processes that evaluate internal and economic risks are the standard of evaluation.

Furthermore, expanded disclosure promotes more transparency in the financial processes of business and supervisory partners. The objective is for banks and financial institutions to increase the amount of information available to partners, the responsibility of upper management, and the effectiveness of risk and control systems.

In Germany, for example, the legal requirements of KWG (§ 25a) and of Basel II are realized with the help of minimum requirements for risk management (MaRisk in its German abbreviation). MaRisk is an initiative of the German Bundesbank and the German Financial Supervisory Authority. It contains requirements for the setup of a proper business organization and the introduction of internal control procedures to establish uniform standards along with appropriate and comprehensive risk and control structures in financial institutions.

#### Effects of Basel II on IT Security

To ensure the security and solidity of national and global financial institutions, the internal (and therefore IT-supported) control systems and management of banks, financial supervision, and transparency are held in high regard. But capital reserves alone cannot guarantee the security and solidity of a bank. Qualitatively improved risk management and reviews by bank supervisory authorities are also decisive criteria for meeting security objectives.

The implementation of Basel II, therefore, has a significant influence on the IT security of participating organizations. Adequate risk and control management is achieved with the support of IT systems and the implementation of processes. Protection of important information, such as data on borrowers, is to be secured. Appropriate controls avoid manipulations that affect scoring and credit ratings. Authorizations for relevant applications, along with the correct evaluation of the risk factor and the related controls, can thus be appropriate parts of measures to set up a proper internal control structure. Electronic payment methods must stay secure to ensure the security and functionality of cashless payments.

Basel II and its successor (Basel III, which is supposed to allow for more flexible adaptations of the strict Basel II specifications) are not responsible for the overregulation and bureaucratization of control systems. They demand consistent penetration of risk and control procedures throughout financial institutions, promote an internal awareness of risk in all critical areas, and conduct a market-oriented examination and handling of investment-related banking activities.

**Best-Practice Method: Highly Integrated and Holistic Solutions**

Only the combination of a sound ERM strategy, efficient IT systems, internal and external control measures, and the awareness of governmental controlling bodies can guarantee a reduction in the number of incorrect processes, risk-related access rights, organizational shortcomings, opportunities for manipulation, and incorrect estimates and process behavior across the control units.

Therefore, holistic and integrated approaches and solutions are of primary importance. In an SAP environment, solutions like SAP for Banking help establish internal control and monitoring methods. Other GRC solutions can be integrated to enhance and complete these solutions.

### 3.2.3 Chemical Substances and Environmental Protection

In 2007, the REACh regulation on chemical substances was established as an equivalent to the FDA. Like other motivating regulations, REACh promotes the industry's overall responsibility. Within its area of application, solely registered chemical substances can be brought to market. This is relevant to manufactures, importers, and carriers.

#### Content of REACh

The European Chemicals Agency (ECHA), headquartered in Finland, regulates the administrative, technical, and scientific aspects of the registration, evaluation, and approval of chemical substances. REACh deals with the registration, evaluation, authorization, and restriction of chemical substances. Chemical substances entail risks, for example, if they are toxic, carcinogenic, or harmful to the environment. In these cases, chemical safety reports and exposure scenarios need to be created. Because they must also consider the lifecycle of a specific substance — from production, to use, to disposal — this may lead to consequences resulting from international agreements, such as the Kyoto Protocol for the reduction of harmful environmental emission.

#### Effects of REACh

The steps for approval result in either an approval with or without restrictions or in a prohibition of the chemical substance. The affected economic areas are production, use, and transport. Registration requires critical information and a high level of security-technical controls because the confidential information, the manufacturer's identity, and the identity of the substance to be registered need to be guaranteed.

Another critical security aspect is the information chain between manufacturers, sales and trading partners, and persons who use the substance. This leads to various legal obligations regarding the acquisition and distribution of information. The safety data sheet is also a critical instrument for communication during transport. Planned tests on vertebrates to determine toxicological and ecotoxic data can only be conducted when it has been clarified that useful comparative studies exist. For animal welfare purposes, the manufacturers and all partners involved are obliged to share all pieces of data without restriction. Companies that want to export to the EU economic area are a further potential risk. Here, the controls aim at avoiding misuse. Only companies that are headquarted in the EU economic area can apply for registration.

The requirements for the activities initiated by REACh place a high security demand on individual process steps and general aspects. Consequently, the implementation of REACh regulations is particularly protected by means of enterprise risk management measures, such as identity management; data security and protected access control; secure transfer of confidential information; and monitoring of registration, production, and use chains.

## 3.3 Internal Requirements

Internal requirements for enterprise risk management and IT security result from influencing factors such as the type of company, industry and branch, organizational structure, legal environment, geographical distribution, strategic orientation, and the related needs for protection. The required IT-supported division of labor in a modern company must be accompanied by the appropriate segregation of duties, realized as authorizations granted to individual employees.

**Best-Practice Method: Segregation of Duties**

The segregation of duties and transactions should allow users of SAP systems to assign authorizations as minimally as possible without withholding from employees the authorizations they need to accomplish their daily work. The segregation of duties is also a critical control element for implementing of process controls, for example, for releases or the reduction of the loss risk in purchasing processes.

In principle, decision-making must focus on risks and legal requirements. Organizational and subjective, historical consideration often plays too great a role, which leads to very complex authorization systems. For example, different authorization components might be developed for user groups with the same functional requirements of SAP software, but without logical or legal reasons for doing so. The administrative costs for such authorization structures can be enormous. Legal requirements and conditions within a company must be adjusted to each other to avoid risk and administrative effort, and thus optimize costs.

A company's experience with SAP systems, the level of training among employees, and the depth of the use of the systems play an important role during the definition of internal requirements for IT security. Evaluation of the separation of duties should involve those responsible for authorizations in individual user departments, IT security personnel, data protection officers, and internal auditors to define company-specific requirements and use the technology available to translate them into SAP terminology. For example, transactional separations, organizational distribution, and temporary authorizations are important tools in the context of protecting data, establishing process controls, and producing secure reports.

However, companies must also ensure that the users of SAP applications have the user rights they need to guarantee the continuity of business flows:

- In many countries, the protection of personal data is a legal requirement. In any case, it is the responsibility of all companies to handle personal data carefully and to secure it according to its use in IT-supported SAP systems.
- Monitoring and reporting are also important internal requirements. Each department has different requirements because of differing functional content and legal conditions. The differences must be identified and documented in the requirements catalog.
- It's just as important to document business and administrative processes, responsibilities, change-management documents, reporting cycles, and measures for security control and administration reasons as it is for legal and auditing reasons.
- The authorization system should mirror authorizations based on the identified risks and the related control measures. Persons who leave the employ of a company or external employees may not have access authorization. All SAP systems enable temporal limits for user master data.

**Best-Practice Method: Four-Eyes Principle**

The four-eyes principle is used when critical activities are divided by content and executed by various persons so that the business processes and related transactions function correctly. The release of purchase orders is a good example

*Legal regulations, like the Sarbanes-Oxley Act (SOX) and the International Financial Reporting Standards (IFRS), don't define direct security requirements for SAP systems in the texts of the respective laws. However, their data and system security is part of the general framework for adhering to legal regulations. For this reason, there are national and international security standards in place. This chapter describes the most important one briefly.*

# 4 Security Standards

Legal regulations, as they were presented in Chapter 3, Section 3.1, Legal Requirements, define goals for controls in company and accounting processes. To achieve these goals, you need a basic information system security. However, this system security is not sufficient to comply with the goals of legal regulations. The goals must be implemented technically with special controls in information and SAP systems where financial and accounting transactions occur. In general, these controls are set up in intensive company-internal projects, frequently with the support of consulting firms.

Companies usually develop their own standards for the security of their systems, which consider their specific business processes and systems. It has proven very successful to compare the specific standards with the generally acknowledged and accepted security standards for implementing legal regulations and to align the specific guidelines accordingly. Relevant international standards and concepts include the following:

- ISO/IEC 27002:2005
- Control Objectives for Information and related Technology (CobiT) 4.1
- Committee of Sponsoring Organizations of the Treadway Commission (COSO)
- Infrastructure Library (ITIL) v3

Selected country-specific standards may be, for example:

- IT-Grundschutz catalogs of the Federal Office for Information Security (BSI; Germany)
- NIST (USA)
- PIPEDA (Canada)

These security standards and concepts offer valuable guidelines and approaches that can be implemented in your company to establish legal regulations or Best Practices in the information technology (IT) and information security area. The implementation of generally acknowledged standards also offers companies an opportunity to make even more future-proof investments in enterprise risk management and IT security. Long-term cost savings can be achieved by integrating controls during the implementation of standards in company processes, where these controls strive for a continuous adherence to legal requirements. This can be achieved, for example, if new systems, projects, and changes are planned and aligned according to the standards from the outset.

This chapter introduces the most important security standards, because they should be used in SAP environments. It does so not in terms of special, technical implementations, but rather in terms of security fundamentals defined for management, organization, and processes.

## 4.1 International Security Standards

The following section describes the most important international security standards. In addition to ISO/IEC 27002:2005, CobiT 4.1, ITIL v3, and COSO, which are covered here, ISO/IEC 15408 (Common Criteria for Information Technology Security Evaluation) also exists. However, it focuses on the inspection of detailed technical security procedures and is therefore inappropriate for establishing an organizational and management-oriented framework. The common goals and the basic statements of these standards are similar, however. They often only differ in methodological approach, definition, and focus.

### 4.1.1 ISO/IEC 27002:2005

International security standard ISO 17799 was originally developed by the British Standards Institution (BSI, which is the same abbreviation as the German Federal Office for Information Security) and published as a British standard as *BS 7799 Part 1* and *BS 7799 Part 2*[1]. The British standard was published as an international standard in 2000. This standard was revised again and in 2007 published as ISO/IEC 27002:2005 as part of the ISO/IEC 27000 series by the International Organization for Standardization (ISO, *http://www.iso.org*). Today, it is considered as the code of practice for information security management.

1 Replaced by the ISO 27001 standard.

Since 2008, this standard is also available as a DIN standard (DIN ISO/IEC 27002). A certification according to ISO/IEC 27002:2005 is not possible because the standard is only a recommendation. Certifications are being performed according to ISO/IEC 27001. The ISO/IEC 27002:2005 standard considers the entirety of the business processes and framework of internal guidelines for information security, controls, and risk management as an Information Security Management System (ISMS). A certification check evaluates this system according to the requirements of ISO/IEC 27001. A successful result confirms that the system is effective and appropriate.

The information security management system is the core of ISO/IEC 27002:2005. Its goal is to ensure that the company manages information appropriately and securely considering an effective risk management. In particular, the requirements of SOX explicitly directed toward the integrity of financial data can be supported effectively. After it has been implemented, the ISMS must enjoy ongoing development and continuous improvement. Such development occurs by checking new potential risks and the controls required for them, along with ongoing communication of the controls in the company.

Ideas and suggestions for improvement from the organization must be recorded and integrated as appropriate into the ISMS. Moreover, there must be regular checks or audits of the ISMS. It involves an external or internal audit of the controls that have been established and a review of the processes and documentation defined in the ISMS. Records must be kept that document the security management process. For example, auditors must be able to determine how many access authorizations were granted and why and by whom they were approved.

ISO/IEC 27002:2005 is subdivided into eleven control areas with 39 control objectives and 133 security measures. These security measures are valuable recommendations that should be integrated with the information-processing areas taking into account the special conditions of the respective company. An effective mode of operation of the security measures in systems and applications supports you in meeting the control objectives. A risk analysis should always be performed before you create and implement specific security controls. The ISO/IEC 27005:2008 standard contains advanced notes.

The following sections briefly discuss the eleven control areas of ISO/IEC 27002:2005, including notes on risk management:

- **Security policy**
  Guidelines for management to protect data, systems, networks, applications, and risk management.
  Management must define a clear direction in the information security policy and show support and involvement by publishing and adhering to these guide-

lines throughout the company. If these management tasks are not performed in the scope necessary, the result is a lack of strategy, weak guidelines on information security, and, ultimately, security gaps. Therefore, this control area holds a key position in the business framework for information security and thus for the information security management system. Information security starts here. For this reason, this control area supports all measures for risk management and consequently lays the foundation to design business guidelines appropriately and effectively and to ultimately develop the readiness and responsibility for their adherence.

- **Organization of information security**
  Management of information security and responsibility.
  For the administration of risk management and IT security, a framework must be defined to enable the company to reach the security objectives that have been defined. Under the leadership of management, appropriate management forums must be set up to approve the information security policy, distribute roles in security, and coordinate the implementation of security throughout the organization. If needed, an expert help desk for information security should be set up and made available within the organization.

  Contact with external security experts must be established to keep up with industry trends, monitor standards and methods of evaluation, and create appropriate contact points to handle security issues. An approach across the organization for information security should be promoted for example by the cooperation and collaboration of managers, users, system administrators, application designers, auditors, and security personnel, for example. The procedure should also involve experts from areas like insurance and risk management.
- **Responsibility and classification of information assets**
  Management of information assets.
  Accountability must exist for all information assets. Therefore, persons must be assigned responsibility for them. This ensures that appropriate protection for the company assets is maintained. The same persons who are assigned responsibility for all important company assets should also be responsible for maintaining the appropriate security measures. Responsibility for implementing measures can be delegated, however, accountability should remain with the persons responsible for the company assets. This is the *information ownership* principle, which plays a significant role in SAP, because very important company assets are processed there.
- **Human resources security**
  Management of information security if the number of staff changes.
  Personal backgrounds must be checked during the hiring process. Applicants

should undergo an appropriate background check, especially for confidential tasks.

All users of IT devices — in other words, all employees, including external companies — should sign a confidentiality agreement.

- **Physical and environmental security**
  Protection of the information technology and its institutions.
  The data processing devices for important or confidential business data must be located in secure zones protected by a defined security perimeter that must have appropriate security barriers and access controls. They should be physically protected from unauthorized access, damage, and interruption. The protection should be appropriate to the level of risk that has been determined. It's a good idea to implement guidelines for cleaning desks and locking screens to reduce the risk of unauthorized access or damage to paper documents, data storage media, and IT devices.
- **Communications and operations management**
  Management of technical security controls in network and operations to protect data, networks, and telephone systems.
  Responsibilities and procedures for administration and operation of all IT systems and applications should be implemented. This includes the creation of adequate operating instructions and specifications for notifying incidents that are relevant for information security. A division of duties with regard to functions and system access must be implemented to reduce the risk of inadvertent or intended misuse of the system.
- **Access control**
  Control of access to networks, systems, applications, functions, and data. Access to information and business processes with a business application (for instance, in the SAP system) should be controlled on the basis of business and security requirements. Existing guidelines for IT and access control must be considered here. The guidelines must be documented appropriately in an authorization concept. The assignment of access rights must follow the guidelines exactly.
- **Information systems development and maintenance**
  Integration of information security with acquisition, development, and maintenance of systems and applications.
  These areas include infrastructure, business applications, and in-house developments. The design and implementation of the application that supports this business process determine the level of security that the process can achieve. Security requirements should be identified and agreed upon before developing business applications. All security requirements, including the need for backup

plans, must be determined, agreed upon, and documented in the requirements phase of a project.

- **Information security incident management**
  Detection, handling, and countermeasures in the case of security incidents. Operating regulations must be created and implemented to ensure that correct and required notification processes are initiated by management in the case of security incidents and that appropriate, required, and approved measures are taken to reduce any negative effects.
- **Business continuity management**
  Protection, maintenance, and reconnection of company-critical systems and processes.
  A process for managing continuing business operations must be implemented to reduce downtime to an acceptable minimum in the event of a catastrophe or security failure. The need can arise from natural disasters, accidents, device failure, or intentional damage. The process includes a combination of preventive and restoring controls. The results of catastrophes, security failures, and the loss of business applications must be analyzed. Emergency plans must be developed and implemented to ensure that business processes can be reestablished in the required time.

  The plans must be secured and practiced so that they become an integral part of all other management and operating processes. The management of continuing business operations also includes measures to identify and reduce risks, to limit the effects of incidents that can produce damage, and to guarantee that basic processes can be quickly resumed. Measures must also be taken to maintain the information security appropriately in the event of a catastrophe or failure.
- **Compliance**
  Compliance with security guidelines, legal regulations, and a check of compliance using audits.
  The goal of the compliance control area is to avoid breaking any criminal or civil laws; legal, regulatory, or contractual obligations; or security requirements. The development, operation, use, and management of information and information systems can be subject to legal, regulatory, and contractual security requirements. Such requirements must be recognized and met to avoid fines or damages to the company. The business processes, guidelines, and control objectives should be designed in such a way that a continuous adherence to internal and legal regulations is possible, even if changes occur in the information technology, or in the internal or external requirements (sustainable compliance).

In general, the ISO/IEC 27002:2005 standard clearly focuses on establishing a required security management process. The specification of detailed technical security measures is a necessary component of a complete security framework. These specifications must be created at the system, network, and application levels to ensure that the superordinate control objectives are met. With regard to the goals of SOX, the recommendations of the standard form an excellent starting point at the technical system level to support the fulfillment of requirements.

### 4.1.2 CobiT

The IT Governance Institute (ITGI, *http://www.itgi.org*) created and published another important security standard, CobiT (*Control Objectives for Information and related Technology*). CobiT is a generally acknowledged framework for internal controls in IT processes. CobiT 4.1 is the current version.

Business and accounting processes are handled in SAP systems, and the data quantities with regard to content are processed in other IT systems. Often, these are forwarded to or received by external business partners. To create and monitor a structured and clear framework of effective security measures in these complex linked systems, CobiT provides a valuable concept with corresponding measures. If the concept of CobiT is implemented effectively, first, you can design the IT and SAP processes with sufficient assurance (IT assurance) so that enterprise goals are reached and undesired IT incidents are identified, corrected, and prevented in time.

Second, CobiT offers a model for a more objective quantification of the status of control activities and control objectives in IT processes. Therefore, it becomes possible to determine where improvements need to be made and to what extent IT processes are matured. By means of this approach, you can evaluate the improvement process quantitatively and monitor developing trends.

Compared to the ISO/IEC 27002:2005 standard, CobiT features a stronger IT process orientation, but it is compatible with the rather technically focused standard. Details of the two concepts are often compared and parallelized. In contrast to ISO/IEC 27002:2005, CobiT provides models that enable a quantification of the achieved maturity level of an organization's IT processes with regard to the adherence of control objectives (CobiT Maturity Model of Internal Controls). Due to the complexity of IT processes and systems, it is not easy to develop a criterion for quantification. However, the status measurement is important, and it provides an enormous benefit if this is performed on a regular basis to assess a developing trend. The CobiT Maturity Model of Internal Controls is an acknowledged approach to perform this analysis.

Another essential difference is that CobiT focuses on the management, organizational structures, and processes to ensure that the IT-relevant company processes are aligned with the company's strategy and goals to support and expand them.

Furthermore, CobiT details and emphasizes the responsibility of managers and the members of the supervisory board (IT governance). Companies are provided with a valuable instrument for creating information security and risk management in SAP system landscapes and their integration with IT processes.

CobiT focuses on four domains with a total of 34 IT processes and numerous security control objectives and measures. The four domains are:

- **Plan and Organize (PO)**
  IT strategy and tactic for implementing the strategic vision.
  Information technology supports company processes; or the enterprise activity completely depends on IT, in the extreme case. This shows that IT is a decisive factor to achieve company goals. Therefore, the company vision must clearly identify the requirements, goals, and risks for information technology, formulate them as an IT strategy, and specify a corresponding direction and responsibility. This CobiT domain provides control objectives to identify and meet these important tasks so that the IT systems and the management of the information risk fulfill the company's conditions.
- **Acquire and Implement (AI)**
  Development and integration of IT processes with business processes.
  The implementation of the company and IT strategy comprises the acquisition, development, and implementation of new applications and systems. This involves a risk for acknowledged strategies of the company with regard to financial, scheduling, production-specific, and IT-security planning. This risk must be mastered with the goal that new solutions align with existing strategies and then meet the intended business purpose. The IT control objectives of this domain are specifically aligned with this problem. They help create control points that let you evaluate and control the IT development to continuously orient them toward enterprise goals.
- **Deliver and Support (DS)**
  Performance provision, management of security, and continuity.
  After new IT systems and applications have been introduced in the company, they must continuously meet expectations. Among other things, this refers to their usability, user-friendliness, service, costs, and information security. The inclusion of the control objectives of this CobiT domain into the running operation of IT systems and applications reduces the risk that they are beyond the expectations within the period of use. This is analogous to the goals of the ITIL framework for IT services.
- **Monitor and Evaluate (ME)**
  Monitoring and evaluation of compliance with control objectives, regulations, and ensuring management leadership and responsibility.

ystems and applications not only need to meet
rformance and costs, but – despite changes –
ılfill the internal obligations for compliance with
ılations and laws, for example, within the scope
o information security, for instance, data protec-
include control and monitoring points that let
early stage and thus initiate corrective measures in
sents corresponding processes and control objec-
ustainable compliance.

losely interlinked, supplement one another, and
he entire lifecycle of IT processes, systems, and
rmation security and risk management. Figure 4.1
ced.

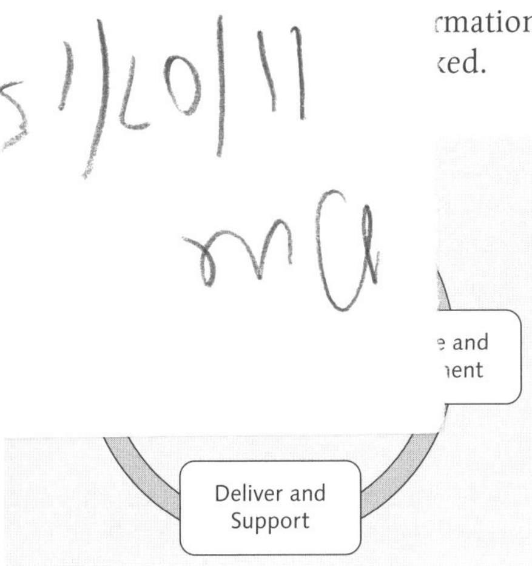


**Figure 4.1** CobiT Domains for the IT System and Application Cycle

Furthermore, the *CobiT Security Baseline* (2nd edition 2007, *http://www.isaca.org*) is derived from CobiT 4.1 and focuses on the most essential security control objectives and detailed security control steps that can be used for all companies and acts as a guideline for establishing security. The special value of this baseline is that, based on the general CobiT 4.1 concept information security risks and control objectives were selected that are typical for the six categories of IT system users. These six categories differ in their usage type of IT systems and the resulting information security risk. They refer to the user with information technology in domestic use, the professional user, and four different usage type levels in company management. However, you must interpret this baseline according to the conditions of your own security environment. However, it supports your risk analysis and development of control objectives because valuable information is provided as the starting point.

Overall, the CobiT standard offers a generic framework that can help companies attain and maintain good basic security and a risk management for IT, particularly for SAP systems and their users. Together with the CobiT Security Baseline and other CobiT products not mentioned here, you are provided with a useful catalog for best-practice behavior rules that effectively support the respective IT system user, SAP practitioner, or manager in terms of security. Companies that must meet the requirements of the SOX should use the valuable suggestions and concepts of CobiT.

### 4.1.3 ITIL

The IT Infrastructure Library (ITIL) has been available since 1989 (version 1) and is a collection of publications whose goal is to provide a best-practice standard for the management and lifecycle of IT services in a company. For SAP practitioners and managers, the benefit of ITIL is that they are provided with a guideline that describes a structured approach to complex IT and SAP system processes in the company.

The basic idea is that most business processes are supported by IT systems and therefore IT represents a service (for company processes). This is obvious if, for example, the entire IT service or individual parts of it are outsourced to an external IT service provider. Such IT service has its own lifecycle that must be led in a targeted manner to attain and maintain the company goals and to continually improve. If the concepts of ITIL are employed within the company, you can detect weaknesses, design IT processes more effectively, and reduce risks. In this context, ITIL has parallels to the ISO/IEC 20000 standard (service management).

The current version, ITIL v3 (*http://www.itil-officialsite.com*), has been available since 2007 and is being further developed further by the British Office of Government Commerce (OGC). ITIL v3 includes the following publications (see Figure 4.2):

- **Service strategy**
  Service strategy includes the integration of IT and the company with the goal that IT is aligned with today's and future company requirements. If, for example, you consider IT as a service that attends to internal needs, it becomes obvious that this service must be adapted to the business requirements so as not to reduce the company's performance or let IT security gaps challenge the result of internal processes. Here, you can also see a task of the internal risk management where discrepancies between IT performance and the requirements for IT must be determined and corrected. A balance between the two factors can be aimed for and achieved in the long term by aligning the IT service strategy with the company strategy or by integrating it.

- **Service design**
  The objective of a service design is the creation of an effective IT service. The IT service must be designed in such a way that the company requirements are met with a balance of design, function, and effort (expense) of the IT service. This way, you can take into account the business demands for information security, risk management, and compliance in a cost-saving and time-saving manner during the design phase of the IT service.
- **Service transition**
  The service transition focuses on the implementation of internal requirements to the actual IT services. Important parts of this process include change management and risk analysis, for example.
- **Service operation**
  The service operation describes the daily IT processes, the adherence to service agreements, and measures for processes with as little interruptions as possible.
- **Continual service improvement**
  Continual service improvement aims at implementing service parameters and their adherence, when weaknesses are detected, and the implementation of improvements. The cycles ensure that the present and future requirements are met and increasingly better. The actual value added of the IT service becomes apparent here.

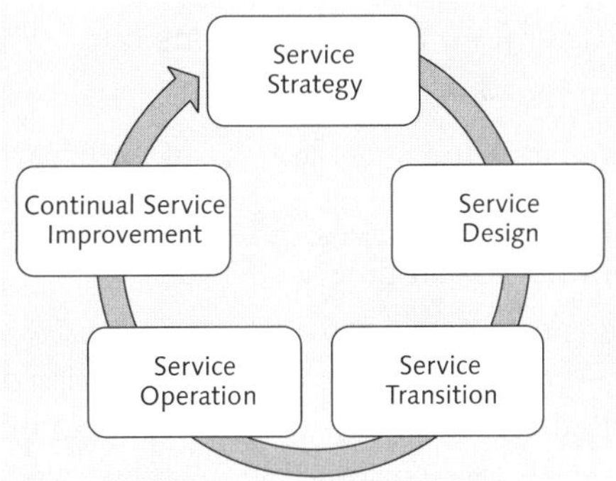


**Figure 4.2** ITIL Topics for IT Services

The value of these ITIL publications is, among others, that critical success factors and risk for IT service are indicated universally. This knowledge and the concepts offered should be applied creatively to your own IT service processes. More effective IT services with service agreements that can be adhered to better or that are shorter will have an immediate positive influence on operating results. Another interesting aspect is the idea, which is offered in the ITIL concept, that IT service users and their expectations set the benchmark for the actual value of the IT service. ITIL v3 is simply a very useful tool for IT management to better understand the internal processes, reduce process risks, and support entrepreneurial risk management.

### 4.1.4 COSO

The *Committee of Sponsoring Organizations of the Treadway Commission* (COSO; *http://www.coso.org*) published an internal and integrated framework for managing internal controls in the 1990s. It was further developed into an integrated framework for company risk management in 2001.

Particularly due to the financial scandals and the resulting SOX of 2002, the COSO framework enjoys broad use in numerous companies because the COSO framework is especially dedicated to the primary demand of SOX: effective management of all risks to the company related to finance and the related controls. Whereas CobiT and ISO are oriented toward risk management in IT, the focus of COSO is on the broader level of risk management in financial reporting. However, the basic idea of the COSO framework for the control concept can clearly be found in CobiT and ISO.

Company risk management is defined in the COSO framework as follows:

- It is an ongoing process anchored in all parts of the company, and it is initiated and controlled by upper management.
- It must be shared by all persons, regardless of their level in the company.
- It must be used in the definition of the company strategy.
- It must be applied in all parts of the company, and specific risks of each part must be considered.
- It must inform management about current risks at all times.

In 2004, the original COSO control concept was expanded to form the COSO enterprise risk management framework and contains the essential activities listed in Table 4.1. The activities are described with an example from financials (posting entries).

| Activity | Example from Financials |
|---|---|
| Description of the internal control environment | These entail the posting entries for financial transactions. |
| Description of the control objective | Posting entries must be correct and approved. |

**Table 4.1** Examples of COSO Activities from Financials

| Activity | Example from Financials |
| --- | --- |
| Identification of events that cause risks | SAP users of financial accounting can perform uncontrolled and incorrect postings. |
| Analysis of risks and their consequences | Incorrect postings that were made by mistake or intentionally can have serious consequences on the results of financial reporting and posting checks. |
| Definition of control activities | Postings must be approved by a second person before the data is posted. To do this, the FI authorization system is configured in such a way that a user can only enter the posting data (for instance, SAP Transaction FB50, Enter G/L Account Document, Park Document option) and a second person can then only post the data (for instance, SAP Transaction FBV0, Post Parked Document). The separation of document entry from document posting is also referred to as a segregation of duties. |
| Information and communication for financial reporting to support appropriate management measures | The control activities must be documented and provided to management and for audits. Persons who check the posting test the effectiveness of control activities during the checks to better assess the validness of financial reporting. |
| Constant monitoring and evaluation of control compliance and control effectiveness | It's the company management's task to specify measures for implementing the necessary controls and periodic checks of their effectiveness and compliance. Standard SAP reports are available to monitor the segregation of duties in the company's SAP system. In the simplest case, you can implement this control by using Transaction SUIM (Information System of the Authorization Concept). |

**Table 4.1** Examples of COSO Activities from Financials (Cont.)

Company risk management forms the foundation of the COSO framework, which can define and control the following primary objectives of a company:

- **Balance between the company's possible risk acceptance and business strategy**
  The equivalence is reached by balancing possible business strategies and their associated risks.
- **Improved decision-making on risks**
  Improved risk reporting can help a company decide more quickly if a risk should be accepted, avoided, lessened with a control, or shared by taking out insurance.

- **Reduction of operating losses and losses as a result of unforeseen events**
  Effective risk management helps minimize operating losses by identifying and evaluating possible risks ahead of time.
- **Improved use of capital**
  The use of capital can be improved by considering the possible financial risks before investment planning.
- **Adherence to legal requirements**
  If you include legal requirements in risk management, you can effectively ensure the adherence to these requirements.

COSO defines the framework for company risk management in three dimensions: first, with the definition of a company's security objectives; second, with the specification of eight components (tasks); and third, with the definition of the geographical-organizational scope (company entity, division, department, and so on). Together, these three dimensions create the framework for risk management and define the dependencies among the dimensions. A company's security objectives are also divided into four categories:

- **Strategic**
  The strategic objectives are seen at a high level and can in an example be formulated as follows: A company's success depends on an effective supply chain. Financial losses from purchasing must therefore be kept at a minimum.
- **Operative**
  The strategic objectives must be translated into detailed operative objectives in this step. For example, all purchase orders must be uniquely authorized. For example, order quantities above a certain amount (determined by the company's acceptance of risk), must be released by the financial department or highest management.
- **Reporting**
  The operative business transactions, such as the entire order quantity and the offsetting supply, must be supported by manageable and, above all, correct reporting. For example, reporting must recognize discrepancies immediately and implement appropriate corrections.
- **Adherence to legal regulations**
  An obvious security objective is adherence to legal regulations. For companies listed on the *New York Stock Exchange*, the legal regulations involve SOX as administered by the *Securities and Exchange Commission* (SEC). From the COSO framework's viewpoint, these regulations are the primary, but not the sole, means of mandating that companies create an effective internal control system for business processes that influence financial data. Similar laws exist in Ger-

many, such as the *Law on Control and Transparency in Enterprises* (KonTraG in its German abbreviation) and the Principles for IT-Supported Accounting Systems (GoBS), which was mentioned in Chapter 3, Requirements. Data protection laws (BDSG in Germany) also define legal regulations for personal data. Industry-specific regulations are often also in effect, especially in the pharmaceutical industry and the financial industry. Chapter 3 provides a detailed overview of legal requirements.

A company must address the following eight tasks to maintain and fulfill the risk acceptance defined in the strategy:

- **Preparation of the internal organization**
  The company's security objectives and, in particular, the level of possible acceptance of risk, must be communicated to the organization. The organization must be prepared for enterprise risk management; it must accept and use these objectives.
- **Setting objectives**
  The security objectives must be harmonized with other company objectives. The level of risk acceptance must be defined so that it does not impede new business models and sources of revenue. It should support the models and sources instead.
- **Early warning system**
  Negative incidents that endanger the security level of the company must be recognized at an early stage. A clear distinction must be drawn between positive (for example, a new source of revenue) and negative events.
- **Risk analysis**
  Risks must be analyzed according to their effects on the company and in terms of their likelihood of occurrence.
- **Risk evaluation**
  The risks must be evaluated after the analysis. The evaluation determines if a risk must be avoided, accepted, lessened, or shared. It defines the necessary steps to bring the risk in line with the risk acceptance of the company.
- **Control steps**
  The steps described in risk evaluation to lessen, distribute, and avoid risk must be checked accordingly. The check is performed with controls monitored by a management system.
- **Information and communication**
  The information necessary for enterprise risk management must be obtained and communicated to the persons responsible. Only when these persons are informed as best as possible and in a timely manner, the security objectives

themselves can be maintained, because then the required decisions can be made.

- **Monitoring**
  The entire risk management system of a company is continuously monitored with an appropriate reporting structure. Internal and external audits can provide such monitoring.

Many companies often operate globally and in different industries — consider automobile companies that also operate in the financial services industry. Accordingly, security objectives and the respective risk acceptance can be defined differently for individual local entities. The COSO framework allows such differentiation with the implementation of a geographic or business-specific dimension. Such a dimension must determine the company objectives, types of objectives, and how the objectives are included in overall enterprise risk management. Particularly in mixed corporate groups, local characteristics can color the objectives significantly.

But the company must clearly recognize that various objectives and tasks depend upon each other to a great extent. The effectiveness of enterprise risk management should always be evaluated on the basis of the eight components (tasks). Particularly in the case of different local security objectives, the objectives must be managed at the local level and ultimately consolidated into the overall enterprise risk management. If the objectives are implemented correctly, the overall efficiency of the COSO framework is high. It's also important that senior management, above all, considers establishing such a system positively and wants to implement it throughout the company.

The COSO framework to establish effective enterprise risk management thus aims at the important regulations in Sections 302 and 404 of SOX that demand an effective, internal management system of risks and the necessary controls. The procedure is supported, for example, by the Governance, Risk, and Compliance (GRC) solutions in SAP BusinessObjects (see Chapter 8, GRC Solutions in SAP BusinessObjects).

## 4.2 Country-Specific Security Standards

The following sections briefly describe three national security standards. They were selected to give you suggestions and to show how different national conditions result in different approaches to specify guidelines for data protection and risk management.

Even if the objective, interpretations, and documentation forms may vary, the request and the core idea of the three following standards is still very similar: On the one hand, companies have a legal obligation to protect financial, personnel, and business data, and, on the other hand, data and information systems must be protected in the company's interest to enable business processes permanently. The objective of this standard is to provide organizations and companies with guidelines and recommendations in the various areas of managing information risks.

### 4.2.1 NIST Special Publication 800-12

The NIST Special Publication 800-12 (National Institute of Standards and Technology) is structured like a computer security manual (*http://csrc.nist.gov/publications/nistpubs/800-12*). It describes specific control objectives for management, operations, and the technology necessary for secure IT systems.

It describes a methodology for risk analysis as a foundation that helps select and implement the required and correct security controls. It describes concrete evaluation methodologies for basic information values and lists the most common threats. To respond effectively to these threats, it lists important control measures, as shown in Table 4.2.

| Control Objective | Description |
|---|---|
| **Management Controls** | |
| Computer security guidelines | The computer security guidelines describe the objectives of IT security and, above all, their importance to the organization — at a high level. It also outlines and defines responsibilities. |
| Computer security program management | This control must ensure that the objectives defined for IT security are met. This panel is therefore responsible for establishing additional controls. It must use audits to guarantee that the controls have been implemented. |
| Computer security risk management | This control provides ongoing analysis of the risks and lowers them with appropriate security measures. |
| Security and planning within computer lifecycle management | This aspect of security must be considered with every implementation of a new IT system. |
| Security management | Audits must be used to monitor if the intended security measures have been implemented correctly and according to requirements. |

**Table 4.2** Control Measures of NIST Special Publication 800-12

| Control Objective | Description |
|---|---|
| **Operating Controls** | |
| Personnel controls | During planning and staffing for security, special checks must be carried out to see if the skills necessary to maintain the level of security are present. The background and integrity of employees must also be checked when they are first hired. |
| Planning measures for emergencies and system outages | Appropriate redundancies must be planned for systems whose availability is critical to the company. Such planning especially applies to a situation in which the entire data center is affected by a fire or other catastrophes. |
| Management of security incidents | All security incidents must be captured by an appropriate system. In this context, it's important that appropriate operative countermeasures are available and that they have already been executed in test runs. The responsibilities must be clearly defined: shutting down the system, for example. |
| Improved awareness of security with training and continuing education | The organization's employees must undergo training to be aware of and educated on the topic of security. The personnel responsible for operations must also receive training on the correct operation of security technologies. |
| Security consideration during operation of IT systems | Correct configuration and change management is evident during operation of the IT systems. Also, documentation must be kept at the most current level. It must indicate the operative security settings that must be implemented in detail. |
| Physical security | The correct choice of location for the data center and the correct physical security measures (access control and monitoring systems) are fundamental requirements of IT security. |
| **Technical Controls** | |
| Identification and authentication | Before they are allowed to access the IT system, business partners, customers, and so on must be clearly identified. These persons are assigned an ID or authentication characteristic that uniquely identifies them whenever they use the IT system. The most important authentication characteristics are the user name and password. But stronger options are available, such as digital certificates created according to the X.509 standard. |
| Logical access control | After successful authentication, users are only allowed to execute the functions for which they have authorization. In this context, functional separation must be observed: a failure to do so can result in significant business risks. |

**Table 4.2** Control Measures of NIST Special Publication 800-12 (Cont.)

| Control Objective | Description |
|---|---|
| Technical logging | Required technical logging can record access to IT systems and changes to data. The log can monitor any unauthorized changes that might have occurred. |
| Cryptography | Cryptography is the foundation of technical security controls. |

**Table 4.2** Control Measures of NIST Special Publication 800-12 (Cont.)

Briefly summarized, NIST Special Publication 800-12 is a manual that describes measures for a secure implementation and operation of IT systems. The descriptions of the measures are not detailed; they simply outline the basic underlying concepts. This manual offers a general and internationally valid approach for computer and IT security questions. It was acknowledged as a standard when it was published in 1995 and promoted the publishing of further NIST publications in the subsequent years.

These NIST Special Publications are published periodically on current security questions about new IT and computer technologies. Some selected publications — on "historical," but also current questions about IT security and enterprise risk management — include the following:

- SP 800-14: Generally Accepted Principles and Practices for Securing Information Technology Systems (1996)
- SP 800-15: Minimum Interoperability Specification for PKI Components (1997)
- SP 800-25: Federal Agency Use of Public Key Technology for Digital Signatures and Authentication (2000)
- SP 800-27: Engineering Principles for Information Technology Security (A Baseline for Achieving Security) (2004)
- SP 800-30: Risk Management Guide for Information Technology Systems (2002)
- SP 800-34: Contingency Planning Guide for Information Technology Systems (2002)
- SP 800-50: Building an Information Technology Security Awareness and Training Program (2003)
- SP 800-62: Computer Security Incident Handling Guide (2008)
- SP 800-64: Security Considerations in the System Development Life Cycle (2008)
- SP 800-100: Information Security Handbook: A Guide for Managers (2006)

- SP 800-122: Guide to Protecting the Confidentiality of Personally Identifiable Information (PII) (Draft, 2009)

### 4.2.2 IT Baseline Protection Manual

The German standard, IT-Grundschutz (IT baseline protection manual), was developed by the Federal Office for Information Security (BSI). The new edition of the manual was enhanced as IT-Grundschutz catalogs and published in 2005 (10th supplement set). The catalogs describe the components of the IT environment, threats, and appropriate countermeasures. Moreover, the catalogs are updated frequently.

BSI's IT-Grundschutz catalogs provide a structured security concept for a company's IT systems. They assume that a large portion of existing IT systems and applications is operated by users in similar ways and in comparable environments. For example, servers run UNIX, client PCs run Windows, and systems include database applications or SAP systems. If no special security requirements are present, the potential dangers to IT systems exist independently of the usage scenario.

From this situation, two ideas result for a way to approach the creation of a companywide security concept.

- A comprehensive risk analysis is not always necessary. The dangers to IT operations and the likelihood of the resulting damage can be limited in certain situations, particularly when the IT systems do not need increased security.
- It is not always necessary to develop new security measures for every situation. Catalogs of standard security measures can be derived that offer appropriate and sufficient protection from such dangers in the context of normal security requirements.

Based on these assumptions, the IT-Grundschutz catalogs suggest a procedure for creating and checking IT security concepts. They describe standard proven security measures for typical IT systems that are to be implemented with the current technology to provide an appropriate level of security, or *baseline protection*. The procedure pays special attention to infrastructure, organization, personnel, technology, and emergencies and thus supports a comprehensive approach. It places special value on procuring the required technical knowledge. Accordingly, the IT-Grundschutz catalogs are also a reference book. The basic components of the IT-Grundschutz catalogs include the following:

- Basis for IT security
- Layer model and modeling
- IT modules

- Threat catalogs
- Safeguard catalogs
- Utilities

The IT-Grundschutz catalogs use the IT baseline protection model for a structured security package (see Figure 4.3). The IT security aspects of an information network are assigned to the individual layers as follows:

- **Layer 1**
  Layer 1 considers the questions of IT security management and the associated processes. The subject matter of this area is particularly suited for company and IT management.
- **Layer 2**
  The basic IT infrastructure is the subject of Layer 2. The IT infrastructure decisively determines the constructional physical circumstances and environment conditions for IT, for instance, the company's SAP data center with critical and confidential databases. Employees and management from data network technology to safety operations to building protection will find information on standard security questions for the physical protection of IT.
- **Layer 3**
  Questions on information security and data protection within the scope of IT systems, the information network, individual components of the network infrastructure, servers, and computer units are answered in Layer 3. So the subject matter is significant to IT management, the network technology, and system administration and its employees.
- **Layer 4**
  Layer 4 deals with the security aspects of linking computer systems and network connections. Network and communication risks are discussed here. They must be given special attention because, for example, incorrect configurations and security weaknesses are often not detected until a security incident occurs. IT management, network technicians, and system administrators are responsible for information security in this area.
- **Layer 5**
  Layer 5 handles the security aspects of server-based and computer-based IT applications. This enables system and application developers, IT management, and, just as in the other four layers, the persons responsible for information security to use the appropriate catalogs of Layer 5.

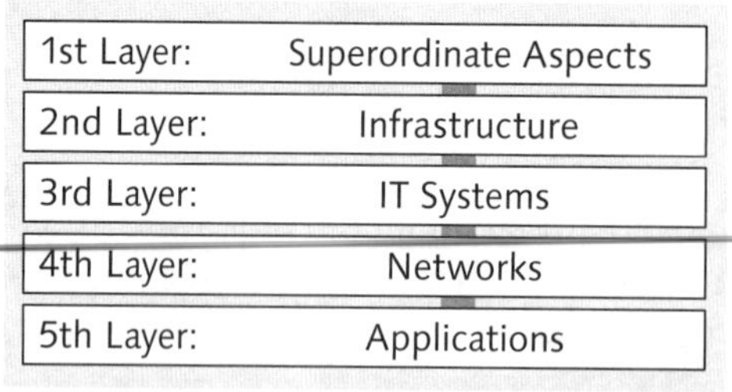

| 1st Layer: | Superordinate Aspects |
|---|---|
| 2nd Layer: | Infrastructure |
| 3rd Layer: | IT Systems |
| 4th Layer: | Networks |
| 5th Layer: | Applications |

**Figure 4.3** Layers of the IT-Grundschutz Model
(Source: IT-Grundschutz Catalogs, 10th Supplement Set)

The benefit of this concept is that the components of every layer can be assessed and secured with regard to risk and information security before you consider the entire information network with its interrelations.

The IT-Grundschutz catalogs of the BSI thus offers a proven methodology for developing a comprehensive security concept based upon standard modules. It comprises the technology and the organization. The measures are described in detail and do not remain at a purely generic level. The IT-Grundschutz catalogs are less helpful when analyzing and evaluating the risks of fraud relevant to business processes, for example. It focuses on IT security.

The catalogs were not particularly helpful in the past when dealing with SAP system landscapes because they did not include a module for SAP security. The IT-Grundschutz catalogs now describe the security aspects of SAP systems with an adequate level of detail; for example, the section, "B 5.13 SAP System" (*https://www.bsi.bund.de/cln_183/ContentBSI/grundschutz/kataloge/baust/b05/b05013.html*) comprises comprehensive recommendations and a structured procedure for a security concept and risk management in the usage phase and for the entire lifecycle of an SAP application. Therefore, the IT-Grundschutz catalogs are a valuable aid and an instruction for developing company-internal concepts for IT and SAP risk management.

### 4.2.3 PIPEDA

The Personal Information Protection and Electronic Documents Act (PIPEDA, *http://www.priv.gc.ca*) was developed in Canada in the late 1990s; in 2000, it became law and was implemented gradually. Since 2004, all Canadian companies and organizations that process personal data must develop and permanently implement corresponding data protection measures. This necessity resulted from the close international trade, tourism, and arising exchange and storage of personal data between Canada and the countries of the European Union.

The law defines what data needs to be protected and what measures and processes are required for data protection. The act's core defines the following personal data:

- **Personal data**
  Personal data include information which can be used to identify an individual.
- **Data about the state of health**
  This includes any data of an individual relating to the:
  - physical or mental state of an individual
  - health services provided to an individual
  - donation of any body part or bodily substance and the associated test results
  - information on health care and treatments
- **Data carriers and electronic documents**
  This includes all data that belongs to following categories:
  - manual correspondence, notes, documents, graphics
  - photographs, film material, microfiche
  - electronic data carriers, sound and video recordings, machine-readable recordings
  - any copies of these data carriers

In addition, ten principles for data protection are defined according to PIPEDA. These include the following (in simplified presentation):

- **Responsibility**
  Companies and organizations are responsible for protecting personal data. This includes the creation and enforcement of business-internal regulations, processes, and the training of employees. The identity of the persons responsible for data protection must be disclosed upon request.
- **Disclosure of the intended use**
  The intended use for personal data collected must be defined and documented. Furthermore, data may only be collected and processed for the use stated. If the data is supposed to be used for another purpose, the persons concerned must give their consent (except for legal uses).
- **Knowledge and consent**
  Persons must be informed about the type of collected and processed data, including its intended use and its possible public access, and they must give their consent.

- **Restricted data entry**
  Data may only be entered to the scope as required by the intended use and if the individual's consent is granted.
- **Restricted use, publication, and retention time of data**
  Data may not be processed, forwarded, published, or stored beyond the intended use permitted. Enterprises must create and comply with guidelines on the retention period of data. Sometimes legal regulations must be considered as well.
- **Correctness of data**
  Personal data must be correct and current as it is required by the intended use stated. However, data must not be updated as a matter of routine if this is not expressly required by the intended use.
- **Technical data protection measures**
  Technical measures must protect data against misuse, theft, unauthorized access, copying, and loss. These measures, for example, must also include physical-constructional security measures. Further technical measures include, for example, password-protected data access, data encryption, and access authorizations.
- **Public**
  Companies and organizations must make their data usage guidelines publicly available in a generally understandable form. This means that individuals must be able to, without much effort, view the company's data protection guidelines. Many companies usually fulfill this requirement by making their guidelines available at the point where personal data is collected. In general, the individual's legally required consent is obtained and documented at this point as well. This process can be in print format or on the company's website.
- **Individual access**
  Companies and organizations must make data available for inspection upon request of the individuals. The individuals may challenge the correctness of data and request corrections.
- **Criticism on the compliance with data protection regulations**
  Individuals are supposed to be able to pass criticism on the persons responsible for data protection with regard to compliance with data protection guidelines. For instance, companies must establish a procedure for accepting, processing, and responding to complaints. Individuals who want to pass criticism or complaints to a company must be informed about the existence of this procedure in an easily understandable form.

Based on a definition on the terms, personally identifiable data, health data, and electronic documents, PIPEDA specifies which technical measures (for instance, data encryption or access controls) are required for protection. This means that companies that must obey PIPEDA are not only obligated to include data protection in the acquisition, processing, and storage of information, but they must also apply the legally required technical measures in a verifiable form. Consequently, companies run the risk that they come into conflict with the regulation, for example, if the protective measures are no longer effective as required in the case of changes within an application. This example reveals that companies must design their change processes so that the internal and external regulations are continuously met (sustainable compliance).

In summary, it can be said that, on the one hand, the control objective of PIPEDA is to protect personal data against misuse, illicit publication, or unauthorized circulation. On the other hand, persons gain some control of the personal data processed by companies. These PIPEDA regulations have decisive influence under which circumstances personal health data may be collected and processed and how it is managed, for example, in SAP ERP HCM or in IT systems on health and work safety.

However, the example of PIPEDA clearly reveals that the protection of personal data depends not only on how effectively the authorization system is technically configured in the SAP system, but also on the company's ability to maintain corresponding data protection processes. For this reason, companies periodically use internal or external audits (privacy impact assessment) to test their compliance with PIPEDA data protection regulations at the technical and process levels. Such self-initiated checks are an advisable component of internal risk management because it enables companies to determine and remedy security weaknesses at an early stage.

As a result, the risk to violate data protection provisions can be kept to a minimum. This approach is not only useful from an information security perspective, but it is also economic and vital for a company. The reason for this is that possible court proceedings, fines, and costs arising from damage claims as a result of data protection violations can sometimes be considerable, not to mention the negative publicity and loss of reputation.

*A lot of conditions influence the security of information systems. To better control risks under specific conditions, security models have been developed that encrypt data using mathematical methods to protect information against unauthorized access and loss. This chapter briefly introduces the basic concepts.*

# 5 IT Security

It is generally known that electronic data can be easily falsified, misused, or copied using computer technology. This applies to stored data and, in particular, to data in transit between systems. Mathematical methods for data encryption are commonly used as a solution to specific security issues. Often, these encryption processes run in the background and cannot be accessed by the user.

The security concepts and methodologies used in SAP products are based on the basic procedures of cryptography. Without them, it would be impossible to use SAP NetWeaver securely. A secure authentication of users, for example, would be impossible without asymmetric encryption. Enabling asymmetric encryption for a large number of users, as is the case on the World Wide Web, requires the use of a trustworthy Certificate Authority (CA) and a Public Key Infrastructure (PKI).

The following sections describe encryption technology (cryptography), Public Key Infrastructure, and some aspects of network security (the Open Systems Interconnection (OSI) model) as parts of IT security. The main focus is not on the data-technical principles of these protocols but on the selection of the products used, their security potential and risk-relevant configuration, and their use in data protection.

## 5.1 Cryptography

Cryptography describes the methodology for making the transmission of a sender's message to the recipient so incomprehensible that unauthorized third parties cannot view the message and use it for their own purposes. It has its roots in prehistory. In nineteenth century BC, Egyptians used methods to encrypt texts by exchanging blocks of text according to a specific schema. This method was quite simple and could easily be decrypted with today's utilities.

Julius Caesar used a somewhat more complex algorithm in 60 BC. This Caesar Code encrypts a message by juxtaposing it with a secret alphabet. The secret alphabet, however, was simply an exchange of the regular alphabet by k number of places. In general, the value of k could be guessed quite easily. Table 5.1 shows a simple example of a Caesar Code. In this case, k = 1.

| Status | Character String | | | | | | | | | | | | |
|---|---|---|---|---|---|---|---|---|---|---|---|---|---|
| Regular text | S | A | P | | N | E | T | W | E | A | V | E | R |
| Encrypted text | T | B | Q | | O | F | U | X | F | B | W | F | S |

**Table 5.1** Caesar Code for Message Encryption

Those procedures underwent constant refinement and, basically, remain the foundation of symmetric encryption. In this age of electronic data processing, however, encryption is implemented using binary methods instead of exchanging letters.

### 5.1.1 Symmetric Encryption Procedure

In a symmetric encryption procedure, the same key is used to code and decode a plain-text message. A simple way of using symmetric encryption is to use the XOR function (exclusive "or"). Table 5.2 provides an example of a symmetric encryption for an 8-bit key.

The first row of the table displays the data to be encoded as bits. The encryption key given in the second row is then applied to the first row with the XOR function. A bit can only be set for the encoded data record if the record to be encrypted and the encryption key have different bits set. Decryption occurs in the same manner; the last row of the table contains the original data record to be encrypted. That proves the possibility of symmetric encryption with the XOR function.

| Status | 8-Bit Key | | | | | | | |
|---|---|---|---|---|---|---|---|---|
| Data record in plain text | 1 | 0 | 1 | 1 | 0 | 0 | 0 | 1 |
| + XOR (symmetric key) | 0 | 0 | 1 | 0 | 1 | 1 | 0 | 1 |
| Encrypted data record | 1 | 0 | 0 | 1 | 1 | 1 | 0 | 0 |
| + XOR (symmetric key) | 0 | 0 | 1 | 0 | 1 | 1 | 0 | 1 |
| Data record in plain text after XOR | 1 | 0 | 1 | 1 | 0 | 0 | 0 | 1 |

**Table 5.2** Using XOR for Symmetric Encryption

The following conditions apply to use symmetric encryption:

- The key cannot simply be determined from the encrypted data record. To prevent such a determination, the key must be long enough and the encryption cannot use a simple function.
- The key must be kept completely confidential. If encoded data is transferred from a sender to a recipient, both parties must know the key.

Some, important examples of symmetric encryption include the Data Encryption Standard (DES) and Triple DES (3DES). The Advanced Encryption Standard (AES) is the successor to the DES. The International Data Encryption Algorithm (IDEA) also plays a critical role. Like the DES, the AES algorithm is a block algorithm with a bit length of up to 256 bits, and a contest held by the National Institute for Standards and Technology (NIST) in the United States found AES to be the most secure procedure. Since then, it has been considered a standard (FIPS 197).

### 5.1.2 Asymmetric Encryption Procedure

As the name indicates, asymmetric encryption differs from symmetric encryption because it uses two different keys: one for encryption and one for decryption. The procedure is similar to the normal lock on a door; the key is the counterpart to the lock.

Everyday use of asymmetric encryption means that the following requirements must be met:

- A secret private key, s, and the appropriate public key, p, are implemented for an identity. Messages encoded with the public key, p, can only be decrypted with the related private key, s. Decryption with the public key, p, is impossible.
- Messages encrypted with an identity's public key, p, can only be decrypted with the identity's secret private key, s. Decryption with the public key, p, is impossible.
- The correlation between the private key, s, and the public key, p, is unambiguous. No other pair of keys results in the same encryption.
- It is impossible to derive the private key, s, from the public key, p.
- The pair of keys (s and p) can be determined by a relatively simple and efficient algorithm.

The Rivest, Shamir, and Adleman (RSA) algorithm is an asymmetric encryption procedure that meets these requirements and was introduced by three American mathematicians — Rivest, Shamir, and Adleman — in 1978. The keys of the procedure are determined as follows:

- Public key p: A pair of integers (n, p)
- Secrete private key s: A pair of integers (n, s)

The number n can consist of 1,024 binary digits, or 2,048 in a higher quality procedure. The numbers s and p can also consist of up to 1,024 binary digits, but that is not absolutely necessary. The following rules apply to RSA encryption:

- RSA encryption with public key p:
  - Split the plain-text message t into a series of blocks ($m_1$ ... $m_k$) with a minimal k so that every block $m_i$ (in binary form) corresponds to a number smaller than n.
  - Calculate $c_i = P(m_i) = m_i^p$ `mod` n.

  `mod` is the modulo function that returns the integral remainder of a division of integers.
- RSA decryption with the secret private key, s:
  - Split the coded text c into a series of blocks ($c_1$ ... $c_k$) with a minimal k so that every block $c_i$ (in binary form) corresponds to a number smaller than n.
  - Calculate $m_i = S(c_i) = c_i^s$ `mod` n.

  The entire plain-text message, t, can then be determined from the sum of all mi.

Multiplication and determination of the coset (modulo function) of 1,024-bit-long numbers requires a great deal of computing. That's why the procedure should not be used for very large quantities of data. The greatest advantage of the asymmetric procedure is that it does not require the exchange of a private key.

Using these mathematical processes in software applications or database systems requires some time. Even though recent systems have extraordinary computing capacity, there may be delays, which cannot be neglected for large data volumes.

### 5.1.3 Elliptic Curve Cryptography

To avoid the RSA encryption and decryption procedure, which requires a lot of system resources, Neal Koblitz and Victor S. Miller developed an encryption method in 1985 that is based on the determination of cryptographic keys using elliptic curves (ECC). ECC is a combination of asymmetric and symmetric procedures — a hybrid encryption procedure with a private, public, and symmetric session key, as described in Sections 5.1.2, Asymmetric Encryption Procedure, and 5.1.4, Hybrid Encryption Procedure. PKIs (see Section 5.2, Public Key Infrastructure) can use this technology in general. In contrast to RSA, ECC is a very effective alternative procedure because it uses a considerably shorter key and still achieves an encryption security that RSA only achieves with long keys.

The general formula for an elliptic curve is y2 = x3 ax – b. It forms the basis for determining the secret session key for the encryption and decryption of plain text. The following steps describe how the sender and receiver of an encryption specify the private key, exchange the public key, and determine the secret session key:

1. Both sender and receiver know the elliptic curve and a high prime number P on this curve (range: 160 decimal places).
2. The sender selects a secret integer, a, as the private key on the curve and multiplies it by the known prime number, P. The product (a × P) is the public key of the sender.
3. The receiver selects a secret integer, b, as the private key on the curve and multiplies it by the known prime number, P. The product (b × P) is the public key of the receiver.
4. Sender and receiver exchange their public keys.
5. Sender and receiver determine the secret session key for the encryption and decryption by multiplying the public key received by their private key (a × (b × P)) or (b × (a × P)). The session key is not transferred.

It is important to note that the entire mathematical process is significantly shorter and requires less system resources. In addition, you can use the session key for a fast symmetric encryption procedure (see also the following section on hybrid encryption procedures). These advantages allow for a wide range of options for using elliptic curve cryptography in technical security solutions that provide for data backups through encryption without extensive computing or large data volumes. It is used, for example, in Secure Socket Layer (SSL) for Windows, Secure Shell (SSH) for UNIX and Linux, mobile and wireless devices, or web servers that need to encrypt and decrypt large data volumes in a very short time.

### 5.1.4 Hybrid Encryption Procedure

Hybrid encryption procedures combine the advantages of both methods: the lack of a need to exchange keys with the asymmetric procedure and the obvious performance advantages of the symmetric procedure. The first message between a sender and recipient exchanges the private, symmetric key by using asymmetric encryption between the two parties. For each communication, the symmetric key can be selected at will. After the symmetric key has been exchanged, the actual encrypted transfer of the plain-text information occurs with the fast symmetric procedure.

The following steps are required at the first level (the exchange of keys with the asymmetric procedure, see Figure 5.1):

1. The sender selects a random session key for the symmetric encryption that follows (marked as *secret*).

2. The sender encrypts the session key with the public key (marked as *public*) of the recipient, which produces the encrypted session key.
3. The sender then transfers the encrypted session key.
4. The recipient decrypts the encrypted session key with the private key (marked as *private*), which produces the session key for the recipient.

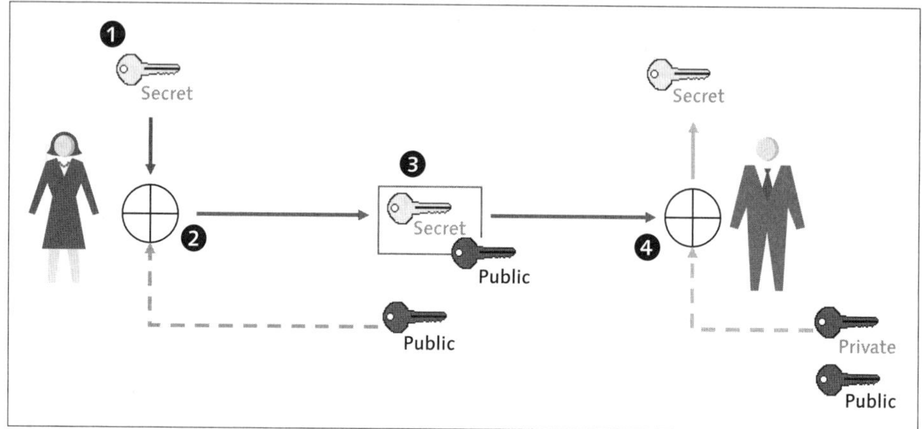


**Figure 5.1** Hybrid Encryption (First Level: Exchange of Keys)

The following steps are required at the second level (symmetric encryption of information, see Figure 5.2):

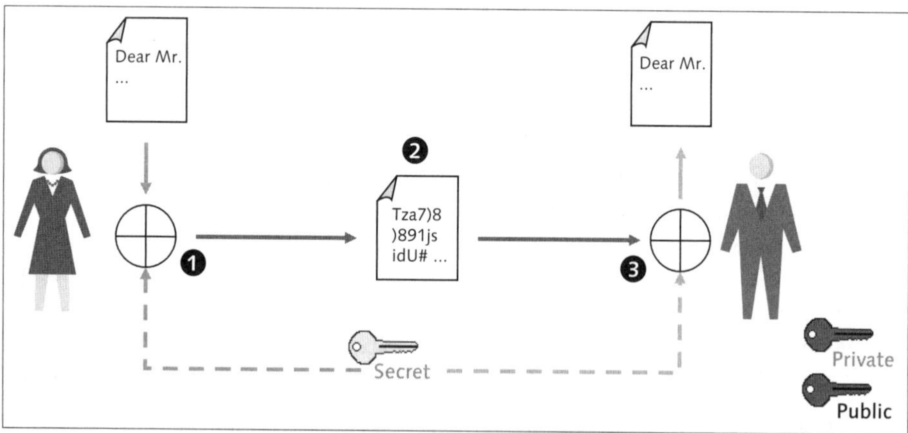


**Figure 5.2** Hybrid Encryption (Second Level: Secure Message Exchange with Symmetric Encryption)

1. The sender encrypts the plain text with a symmetric session key (marked as *secret*), which produces the encrypted text.
2. The sender transmits the encrypted text to the recipient.
3. The recipient decrypts the encrypted text with the symmetric session key, which produces the plain text.

The hybrid procedure is the de facto standard in encrypted communications and is used by the SSL protocol.

### 5.1.5 SSL Encryption

The SSL network protocol is used to protect data during data transfer. Encryption of the data occurs as it does with the hybrid procedure, with a symmetric key selected at random for the session. The key is exchanged ahead of time with an asymmetric procedure. SSL can also be used for the unidirectional or mutual authentication between sender (client, for example) and receiver (web server, for example) for SSL-encrypted data. This way, the sender can ensure that the data is transferred to the correct web server or that the correct web server receives the data.

In this context, the authentication procedure for a web server is described as an example. Authentication of the server and the exchange of the symmetric key with the server is called the handshaking phase. The phase functions as follows:

1. A client wants to set up a secure communication connection to a specific server with SSL. The client requests the server's certificate with the server's public key.
2. If properly configured, the client can contact the CA (see Section 5.2) that generated the server certificate, and check the validity of the certificate against the Certificate Revocation List (CRL) issued by the CA. If the certificate is valid, the client can continue.
3. In this case, the client selects a random number that it uses to encrypt the public key of the server. It then sends the number to the server.
4. The server receives the encrypted random number and decrypts it with its own private key. The decrypted random number is sent back to the client.
5. The client compares the random number sent by the server with the original. If the two numbers are identical, the client can be sure that it's connected to the correct server.
6. If mutual authentication is called for, the same procedure must occur between the server and client in the opposite direction. This step does not usually occur.

7. Next, a randomly generated symmetric key (usually 128 or 256 bits) is exchanged between client and server.
8. Communication can continue with the symmetric key and the appropriate encryption. The key can also be renegotiated after a short time, which is often the case in Virtual Private Networks (VPN).

The SAP NetWeaver Application Server (AS) is an application server that is specially designed for SSL data encryption. It lets you establish an SSL communication with other SAP and non-SAP applications (see Chapter 9, SAP NetWeaver Application Server).

### 5.1.6 Hash Procedures

Hash procedures are used to generate an unambiguous numerical value from a message text or any quantity of data. The unambiguous numerical value is referred to as the hash value. The hash function is often used in applications to encrypt passwords. If a password is checked for validity, the system compares the hash values of the password that is stored and the password that is supposed to be tested.

The following three conditions apply to the hash function:

- No conclusions about the original message or data record can be drawn from the hash value created by the hash function.
- The generated hash values do not collide; an unambiguous and unique hash value is generated from each data record. Every hash value must therefore be unique and unambiguous.
- The hash value must be calculated efficiently.

Figure 5.3 provides an overview of the hash procedure. It shows that when using the hash procedure on large data records, the records must first be split into n blocks (*a*) — of 32 bits, for example. The hash function is then applied to the individual blocks, and the total hash value is calculated by addition. As a variant, a start value for the hash total can also be selected.

Well-known hash functions include the Secure Hash Algorithm (SHA) and the Message Digest Algorithm 5 (MD5). SHA was standardized by the NIST in the United States and is the foundation for the Digital Signature Standard (DSS). The MD5 was developed at the Massachusetts Institute of Technology (MIT), see RFC 1321 for its exact specifications.

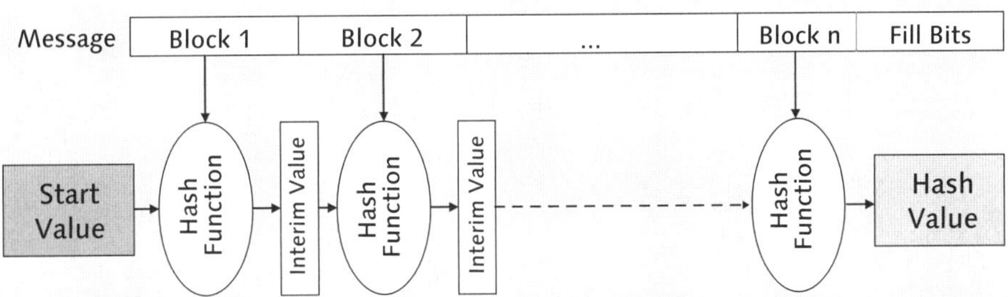


**Figure 5.3** Processing Principle of a Hash Procedure with Larger Data Records by Separation into Blocks

### 5.1.7 Digital Signature

A digital signature can be generated by the interaction between asymmetric encryption and the unambiguous calculation of a hash value. A signature is generated as follows:

- A hash function (SHA, for example) generates an unambiguous and collision-free hash value from a text — for instance, from an accounting document.
- The hash value is then encrypted with the secret private key of the signatory and stored together with the document. This procedure is known as signing.
- Let's say that the recipient of the document wants to check to see if anything in the document was changed during transmission, which means that the document is no longer authentic and by the signatory. The recipient would use the public key to decrypt the attached hash value and compare it with the hash value of the document, which is calculated with the same SHA function.
  - If both hash values are the same, the document comes from the person who signed it, and it has not been changed.
  - If the hash values differ, the document has been changed or the public key does not fit the signatory. When the values differ, the document does not come from the person who signed it. The digital signature is therefore counterfeit.

Generating a digital signature involves the following steps (see Figure 5.4):

1. Generating a collision-free hash value for the message
2. Encrypting the hash value with the private key
3. Combining the message with the signed hash value

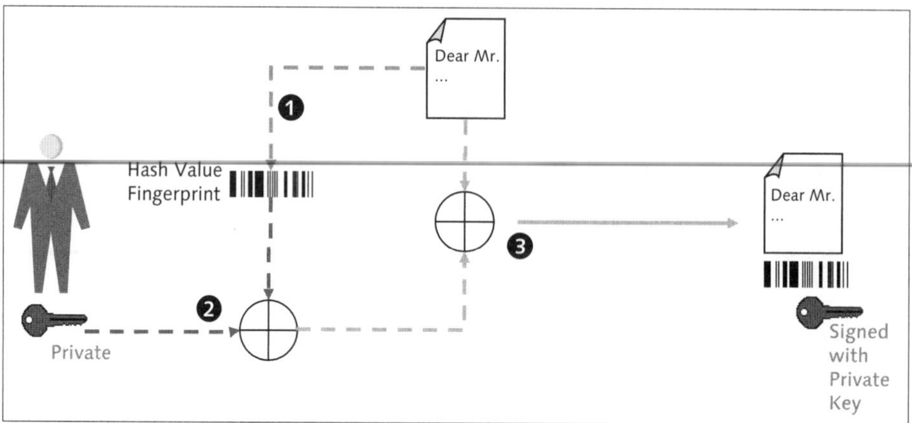


**Figure 5.4** Generating a Digital Signature

Verification involves the following steps (see Figure 5.5):

1. Extracting the digital signature from the message
2. Generating a collision-free hash value for the message
3. Decrypting the digital signature with the sender's public key
4. The signature is valid if the generated hash value matches the decrypted hash value of the digital signature. If the values differ, the document was not digitally signed by the sender or it was changed afterward.

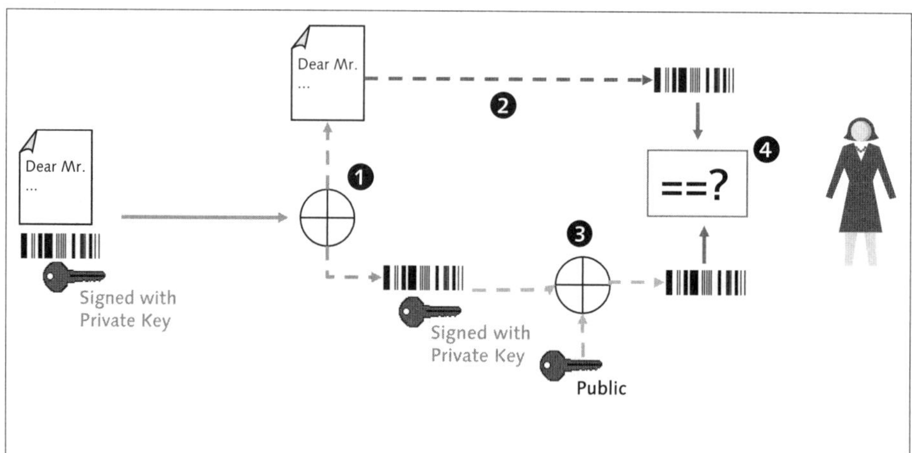


**Figure 5.5** Verifying the Digital Signature

The quality level of a digital signature depends on the quality rating of the asymmetric pair of keys being used, because asymmetric key pairs are handled by a public key infrastructure (see Section 5.2) using digital certificates according to the X.509-v3 standard. There are some advanced signatures that are generated with certificates that have a rather low level of security. That means that no high-quality registration process occurred to capture the identity. The certificate, particularly the secret private key, is stored at the operating system level rather than on dedicated media, such as a smart card. Qualified personal certificates must be used to generate signatures for example those that meet the requirements of German law. Only an accredited CA can issue such certificates, which must be stored on smart cards.

Other legal issues may determine which signature can be used. For example, in some countries, when citizens deal with governmental agencies and the transactions have legal merit, the citizen can only use signatures that meet the requirements of that country's signature law. Furthermore, using digital signatures is not only a data security issue within the company but can also be required by law (for example, medical data, or in the pharmaceutical industry).

SAP applications can protect data with digital signatures using Secure Store and Forward (SSF). SSF is a function provided by SAP that lets you encrypt and protect data via digital signatures at the file system level. To use this function, however, the SAP system and the SAP user must be configured and have corresponding certificates. So there are already certain out-of-the-box transactions that support digital signatures. A good example that is frequently used in the industry can be found in the inspection lot creation transactions in SAP Quality Management (QM). For other transactions that do not directly support digital signatures, you can use ABAP interfaces to enables this function. This digital signature function also meets audit requirements.

Another example for using digital signatures is the SAP-specific Secure Network Communication (SNC) protocol. SNC is based on the GSS-API standard and uses digital signatures to authenticate systems and secure data communication via networks. This is a good measure to provide security for the data transfer with SAP NetWeaver. Because the SNC protocol can transfer authentication information securely, it is also used to configure Single Sign-On (SSO) for users of SAP applications in combination with public key infrastructures (see Chapter 9).

## 5.2 Public Key Infrastructure

As noted for creating and verifying digital signatures, asymmetric encryption methods only function if the public keys of the identities are managed securely and efficiently. For example, the recipient of a message can only check the validity of the sender's signature if it is completely certain that the sender's public key truly belongs to that sender.

This can occur when senders transmit their public key to the recipients ahead of time over a secure and trustworthy channel. In an Internet scenario with numerous participants and an enormous number of identities, it becomes obvious that this way of managing public keys soon reaches its limits and simply becomes impossible.

To avoid this difficulty, the PKI was implemented. It helps manage the public keys of individual identities. A public key infrastructure consists of two parts: the certificate authority and the registration authority.

Think of the certificate authority as a passport office that issues passports so that travelers can identify themselves when they cross into another country. The officials at the border trust the passport office that confirms the identity of the travelers with its seal and signature. The registration authority confirms the true identity of the traveler before the passport is issued. The certification authority only issues a passport when unique characteristics exist to indicate that the traveler truly is who they claim to be.

Now transfer this process to the digital world, and you'll see how the principle is the same. Instead of a passport, a digital certificate is issued for the institution making the request. A certificate is a digital attestation of an institution's public key by a trustworthy certificate authority. Certificates are generated according to the international standard, X.509 v3, which essentially contains the following attributes:

- **Version number**
  Specification of the X.509 version being used.
- **Serial number**
  Unique serial number of the certificate. It may exist only once.
- **Signature**
  Signature of the certificate and the algorithms and parameters needed to validate the public key of the certificate authority.
- **Certificate issuer**
  Name of the issuing certificate authority.
- **Validity period**
  Validity period for the certificate.

- **User name**
  Name or pseudonym of the certificate owner. This is the Distinguished Name (DN) of the identity. It can also be a server.
- **Key information**
  Public key of the owner and the algorithms to be used.
- **Unique identification characteristic**
  An additional identification characteristic is required if the name is used multiple times.
- **Enhancements**
  Additional specifications on the use of the key, such as several validity periods, and on the conditions of the issue.

The certificate authority must sign the certificate with its secret private key so that the validity of the certificate can be verified at any time. The application must store all of the validating certificates of all trustworthy certificate authorities. Certificate authorities can also be cascaded in a hierarchy. That means that only a few root certificate authorities exist that confirm the trustworthiness of another certificate authority by issuing a certificate. The trust relationships between the individual participants (or institutions) are created like a cascade.

In addition to issuing certificates, a certificate authority is also responsible for managing certificates. If, for any reason, a certificate becomes invalid before its validity period expires, the participating institutions must be informed. Certificate authorities use a certificate revocation list to handle this task. With this list, an application can determine if the certificate presented by a user is still valid.

The certificates can be issued in various quality classes. The certificate practice statement defines the quality classes that a public key infrastructure may issue. This statement determines the purpose of the certificate and the type of registration process for issuing the certificate to the user.

Another task of the public key infrastructure is to maintain the certificates, for example. This involves the following:

- Actually creating certificates
- Monitoring the validity period
- Automatically renewing certificates after the validity period has been expired
- Recovering processes if the certificates have been damaged or lost; to enable recovery, the certificate authority securely stores the private keys

Simplified, a public key infrastructure has a Lightweight Directory Access Protocol (LDAP) server that stores certificates according to a defined structure and provides them for use. A public key infrastructure must also have the corresponding interfaces for applications, such as those that check the validity of certificates. Redundancy and the absolutely secure setup of the required server systems are extremely important. In many cases, the servers not only manage the public key of the certificate, but also the private key.

If required, Hardware Security Modules (HSM) are used to store private keys with a particularly high level of security. From a design-technical, electronic, and software-related perspective, these modules are very secure. However, complete security can't be achieved, because the modules permanently exchange information via a network and operators can access the hardware security module during maintenance work. This constantly involves risks even though password-protected smart cards are used for access control.

## 5.3 Authentication Procedures

Authentication procedures help recognize previously registered identities before granting permission to execute a specific action, such as starting an application or executing application functionality.

### 5.3.1 User Name and Password

The simplest and most common procedure is based on a user ID and password. Upon registration, users are assigned a unique user ID and the required password. The application, such as a database, then stores the values. Users are identified and allowed to access an application only when they enter the correct combination of user ID and password during authentication.

This method is called a one-factor procedure, because users are authenticated based only upon "what they know." Authentication does not require a second factor, such as possession of a smart card. The security risk for a user ID and password combination mainly depends on the confidentiality and length/complexity of the password.

### 5.3.2 Challenge Response

The challenge-response procedure is a noncryptographic procedure primarily used as a schema for authentication in Windows NT networks (Windows-NT-LAN-Manager, (NTLM)). The target system (a server application, for example) issues a randomly generated challenge. The user, which can be a Windows client, for example, who wants to be authenticated on the target system, answers with an appropriate response. The response to the challenge is calculated by software or a token card.

This procedure is much better than using traditional passwords, because only one correct response to a challenge exists to allow access. Even eavesdropping on the two partners does not help a potential attacker gain access. The security risk for this methodology is significantly lower because each challenge is only used once, and no passwords are transmitted over the network.

### 5.3.3 Kerberos

Kerberos takes its name from a figure in Greek mythology. Kerberos (or Cerberus) is a hound of hell, standing guard at the gates of the underworld. He has three heads and keeps the dead from reentering the world of the living.

In the world of computers, Kerberos is a network authentication procedure developed at MIT at end of the 1980s; see RFC 1510 for its exact specifications. The procedure was first developed for UNIX networks. Microsoft adopted the procedure and has used it as their standard network authentication protocol (SPNEGO, Simple and Protected GSS-API Negotiation) since Windows 2000. It has since replaced NTLM as the standard in the Windows environment. Just as the original hound of hell had three heads, Kerberos has three components: the client; the application server the client wants to connect to; and the trustworthy authentication server, also referred to as a Key Distribution Center (KDC).

The Kerberos procedure is relatively complex. The procedure is essentially based on a symmetric encryption process that does not transmit an encrypted password but uses it as a secret shared between two parties. For example, assume that "Alice" transmits her name and the current time in encrypted form with her password (called an authenticator) to a trustworthy institution, "Bob." Bob can then use Alice's password (stored at Bob's location as a shared secret) to decrypt the message and compare the current time in the message with his own current time. If the time systems are sufficiently synchronized, Bob can then authenticate Alice as long as the time specifications lie within the allowed period (five minutes, for example). So that Alice can know that she is linked to Bob, Bob uses the same password to encrypt the time stamp that Alice transmitted and returns it to her as a message. Alice can now use her key to decrypt the message and compare it with the time stamp that she originally sent. If the two are the same, she can securely assume that she is connected with Bob.

Bob can now send Alice a Ticket Granting Ticket (TGT) for the day. Alice can use the ticket to access the actual application servers because Bob also manages the application keys of the application servers. Alice receives the keys with the TGT (in encrypted form) when she wants to access the application servers. Alice can then authenticate herself on the application server, using the same principle she did when authenticating herself to Bob. The institution, Bob, is a key distribution service and is necessary for effective administration of the symmetric keys, which have a limited period of validity, and to function as a trustworthy instance (much like a certificate authority).

The SPNEGO authentication schema can thus be used by systems for mutual authentication or for authentication of a user in the system. If several applications or systems are configured for SPNEGO and integrated with the Microsoft Active Directory, for example, SSO can be effective for users. SSO means to give users access to all of the applications they are authorized to have by signing on just once. The authentication data from the first logon is used to let the user log on to other applications without interaction from the user again. The advantages are obvious.

**Note: SSO Only Increases Security to a Limited Extent**

However, it should be noted that SSO does not increase security. The security risk is basically on the first entry of the user password and therefore depends on password security. All other authentications trust in the first authentication being correct and secure. SSO is only a method to avoid additional authentication processes.

The usability of SPNEGO has been enhanced in the past so that user authorizations can now also be transferred to applications to a limited extent (Privilege Attribute Certificate (PAC)). The respective authorization information is read from the Microsoft Active Directory (group assignment of the user).

SAP NetWeaver can use the SPNEGO authentication and accept user authentications from non-SAP systems and allow for SSO. The SAP NetWeaver AS supports the process using the SPNegoLoginModule. You can also use SPNEGO to create SSO structures for SAP users if they have been authenticated with the Microsoft Active Directory first and then obtained SAP system access via an SAP GUI. This access does not require any additional SAP password entry by the user.

### 5.3.4 Secure Token

Secure token procedures are typical two-factor authentication procedures. In this case, users have a secret password or PIN and a secure token card. Users need the card to authentication a network or with an application.

The SecurID method from RSA Security is one of the most common secure token procedures. With this method, a one-time password, the passphrase, is produced, which is valid for about one minute. The SecurID card uses a specific algorithm and a PIN (entered by the user) to generate the passphrase. The passphrase is then transmitted to the required authentication server, which works with the same algorithm to identify the passphrase. If the passphrase is correct, the user is authenticated. The authentication server can then act as a trustworthy instance and transfer the successful authentication to an application server. The transfer can be implemented using Security Assertion Markup Language (SAML) Assertions.

Because the passphrase is only valid for about one minute during authentication and is only used once, an unauthorized attacker cannot take advantage of the procedure. Two-factor authentication achieves a very high level of security.

### 5.3.5 Digital Certificate

In certificate-based methods, authentication occurs with a certificate issued by a trustworthy certificate authority. Authentication on an application server checks the validity of the certificate with the asymmetric encryption procedure and the certificate revocation list. The user's unique name and the unique serial number of the certificate must already be stored in the application, or a directory service must exist with access to the certificate. These certificates basically follow the X.509v3 standard. You can also use certificates for system servers and users to establish an SSL connection (see Section 5.1.5, SSL Encryption).

Compared to other authentication procedures, the security risk of digital certificates is relatively low. Nevertheless, there is a high risk when the user is provided with the certificate. For example, a user could feign an identity to obtain a certificate. You must therefore pay particular attention to a secure and risk-free identification of the user.

### 5.3.6 Biometric Procedures

Biometric methods are increasingly used as authentication procedures where a unique identification of persons is required and the process speed is not that critical. If the biometric method is combined with a password or PIN query, it is a secure two-factor authentication.

Authentication is based on unique biometric characteristics of a user. For example, a fingerprint can be used as a unique characteristic because a given fingerprint only exists once in the world. The eye's iris is also absolutely unique. But problems exist when trying to determine the exact differences between the characteristics. In most cases, only a high-resolution scanner can recognize the differences. A biometric procedure requires users register ahead of time so that they can later be authenticated with the stored biometric characteristics.

This relatively time-consuming registration process also limits the use of this procedure. Nevertheless, it has been gradually introduced to physical access security, facility access security, and mobile computer devices. Typical areas of use are person access control systems for data centers, security facilities, and selected border crossings, for example. Today, this authentication procedure is also used as an access control for operating systems or applications in mobile or stationary computer systems. When using SAP NetWeaver Mobile in mobile devices, for example, biometric authentication procedures can efficiently protect end devices against unauthorized access. This requires specially equipped end devices and external security products. For specific areas of use with high security demands, SAP provides direct support for biometric authentication procedures, such as fingerprint scanners.

The benefit of the biometric authentication procedure is the low security risk. However, it has the disadvantage of an inefficient registration process, especially if a high number of users are involved. When analyzing this procedure, you must also consider the additional costs. As already mentioned, you must always find a balance between actual threat, moderate remaining risk, and acceptable costs.

## 5.4 Basic Principles of Networks and Security Aspects

To make the security mechanisms related to networks outlined in the previous sections clearer, this section offers a short excursus into network technology, especially because network considerations continue to play a role when using SAP NetWeaver on the Internet. This section uses the OSI model to discuss this subject. It makes sense to refer to the OSI model here because it describes complex network processes in a simplified way.

### 5.4.1 OSI Reference Model

The OSI model is an open layer model for organizing communications technology. It was developed in 1979 and is currently the standard for network communications. The OSI model serves as the foundation for a variety of proprietary network protocols that are used almost exclusively in public communications technology in transport networks.

It subdivides the various application areas of network communication into seven layers (see Figure 5.6). Each of the layers is designed to perform the tasks assigned to it independent of the other layers.

In a computer network, other participants in the network provide various hosts with the most varied types of services. The communication required to do so is not as trivial as it might seem at first glance. The communication must handle several tasks and fulfill requirements related to reliability, security, efficiency, and so on. The problems that must be solved in the process cover questions about electronic transmission of the signals, a regulated sequence in communications, and abstract tasks that arise between the communicating applications.

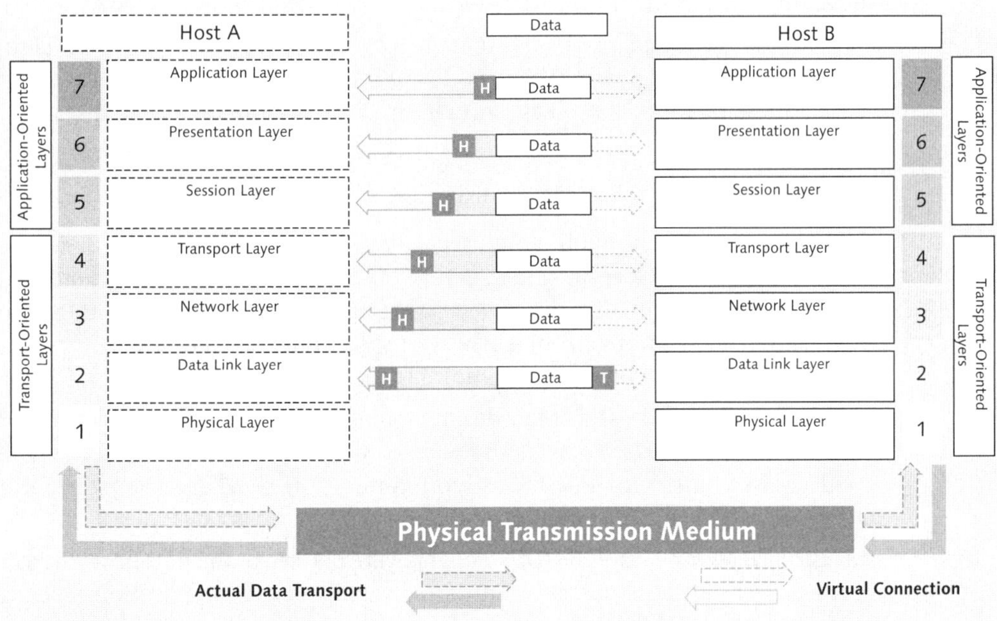


**Figure 5.6** OSI Network Reference Model

The number of these problems and tasks makes it reasonable to assign a network's services to specific categories rather than viewing the network as a single service provider. The benefit of this approach is that the security aspects of each category or layer can be analyzed separately. In fact, each technological layer involves specific risks and the corresponding security technologies. If the interactions between the layers are then linked to the corresponding security measures, a holistic security concept can be created for the information flow through the network. This security concept is also known as defense in depth.

A subdivision of the network into seven layers has proven particularly helpful. In the OSI model, the degree of abstraction of the functions increases significantly from layer 1 to layer 7. Data is redirected from one layer to the next. In other words, communication occurs in a vertical direction. On the sender's side, the communication flows from the top to the bottom; on the recipient's side, the communication flows from the bottom to the top. Seen logically, communication between the sender and the recipient occurs horizontally in every layer. The following sections describe the seven layers, including their restrictions, security risks, and possible risk management measures.

### Layer 7: Application Layer

The application layer (also referred to as the processing layer or user level) is the highest of the seven hierarchical layers. It provides applications with a variety of functionalities: data transfer, email, virtual terminal, remote login, HTML, and so on.

This layer involves the following security risks or possible countermeasures:

- This application layer entails a high security risk because application data from desktop computers or application servers can be directly accessed, stored, and processed. The risk management level that can be achieved depends on the existing security options of the software applications installed in this application layer and their effective utilization for security measures.
- Host-based firewalls in servers or desktop computers can be efficiently used for risk management because — if they are configured correctly — they enable good access control for open local communication ports (see Section 5.4.2, Overview of Firewall Technologies).
- Intrusion Detection Systems (IDS) recognize the pattern of the data flow directed to the server and can thus be used to analyze data at the application level, to avoid unauthorized data requests or suspicious programming commands, and to reduce the risk of hacker attacks.
- The security concepts that are provided with SAP NetWeaver or with the authorization procedures in the SAP system are already effective in this application layer and can be used to establish information security.

### Layer 6: Presentation Layer

The presentation layer (also referred to as the data presentation layer or data provision level) converts the system-dependent presentation of data (ASCII, EBCDIC, and so on) into an independent form and thus enables a syntactically correct exchange of data between various systems. Layer 6 also includes tasks like data compression and encryption.

This layer involves the following security risks or possible countermeasures:

- The presentation layer has the critical task of transferring data from applications to the network and vice versa. This already determines the security risks because application data in common formats is easy to access, the data can be falsified, or incorrect data can be provided.
- Risk management here basically uses data encryption technologies such as SSL, SSH, or SNC. Another way to reduce the security risk is to control and filter the data flow from the network to the applications by analyzing all incoming data-

base commands and not transmitting untypical commands that have the character of hacker attacks, for example (see Chapter 28, User Interfaces). A similar security concept is used to protect applications against Internet risks.

#### Layer 5: Session Layer

To correct interrupted sessions and similar problems, the session layer (also referred to as the communications control layer, control of logical connections, and the session level) provides services for organized and synchronized data exchange. It sets up check points that can be used to synchronize a session after a transport connection fails without having to restart the transmission from the beginning.

This layer involves the following security risks or possible countermeasures:

- This layer supports technologies such as FTP, Telnet, or Voice over IP (VoIP). It entails the corresponding risks if passwords or data to be protected is transmitted in plain text, communication partners are not authenticated securely, or insufficient security measures are configured for avoiding IP falsification and spoofing.
- Risk management measures include, for example, data encryption, no transfer of passwords in plain text, session management, and secure authentication methods for communication partners (see Chapter 9).

#### Layer 4: Transport Layer

The tasks of the transport layer (also referred to as end-to-end control or transport control) include the segmentation of data packages and congestion control. The transport layer is the lowest layer that provides complete end-to-end communication between a sender and a recipient. It provides the application-oriented layers 5 - 7 with uniform access, so that they do not need to consider the characteristics of the communications network.

Five different service classes of various qualities are defined in layer 4 for use by the higher layers. They range from the simplest to the most user-friendly services with multiplex mechanisms, error-protection procedures, and error-correction procedures.

This layer involves the following security risks or possible countermeasures:

- Because the transport layer provides the main support for the TCP/IP communication via UDP, TCP, and ICMP network protocols, this leads to the corresponding risks, such as transport problems or IP falsification and spoofing.

- Effective risk management measures include, for example, well-configured (stateful) firewalls that monitor and control the transport of information packages (see Section 5.4.2).

#### Layer 3: Network Layer

The network layer (also referred to as the package level) switches connections for connection-oriented services and redirects data packages for package-oriented services. Data transmission in both directions flows over the entire communications network and includes routing between the network nodes. Because direct communications between the sender and the target IP address are not always possible, the nodes on the path must redirect the packages. The redirected packages do not go to the higher layers, but are given a new, intermediate destination, and are sent to the next node.

The tasks of the network layer include setting up and updating routing tables, flow control, and network addresses. Because a communications network can consist of several subnetworks with various technologies, the conversion functions needed for redirection between the subnetworks can also reside in this layer.

This layer involves the following security risks or possible countermeasures:

- Because this layer basically supports IP communication, it entails all related security risks, for example, IP falsification and spoofing or intended redirecting of data communication to wrong network directions.
- Risk management in this area includes, for example, well-configured firewalls and network elements that allow you to control source and target IP addresses for communication (see Section 5.4.2).

#### Layer 2: Data Link Layer

The task of the data link layer (also referred to as the connection level or procedure level) is to ensure almost error-free transmission and to regulate access to the transmission medium. This layer is responsible for logically linking network partners.

This layer involves the following security risks or possible countermeasures:

- Risks and security gaps can emerge if network segments (VLAN) or network support devices, such as routers, switches, gateways, or firewalls, have not been configured properly or WLANs have been operated without the necessary security level.
- Options for risk management include splitting the bit stream of data into blocks and inserting sequence numbers and checksums. Recipients can use receipt and repeat mechanisms to newly request blocks corrupted by errors or lost blocks

(frames). Flow control gives a recipient dynamic control of the speed at which the other side may transmit blocks.

- In this layer, critical risk management elements are a secure network architecture, the use of firewalls, data encryption measures, and a secure authentication of communication partners.

### Layer 1: Physical Layer

The physical layer (also referred to as the bit transmission layer) is the lowest layer. This layer describes the physical characteristics of telecommunications. The characteristics can include electrical signals (cables), optical signals (optical fibers or lasers), electromagnetic waves (wireless networks), or sound. The type of procedure used is referred to as the transmission procedure.

Devices and network components assigned to the physical layer include the network card, transceiver, antenna, amplifier, plugs and sockets for the network cable, the cable itself, the repeater, the hub, the tee, and the terminator.

Digital transmission of bits with or without wires occurs on the physical layer. The topology of the network also plays a role in a wired procedure. Static or dynamic multiplexing can handle common use of a transmission medium at this layer. It requires the specification of specific transmission media (for example, copper wires, fiber optic cables, electrical grid, or air) the definition of plug-and-socket connections, and additional elements. The way that a single bit is transmitted must also be determined at this layer.

This layer involves the following security risks or possible countermeasures:

- These markedly physical processes bear a very high security risk because the mere interruption of a network cable connection, eavesdropping of communication data via stationary data or radio networks, unauthorized access to data centers including theft, or the deactivation of computer systems, data storages, or network devices, for example, could lead to enormous data security or data availability violations.
- Measures for reducing the risk include sophisticated physical and biometric control and data protection systems in data centers that comply with the general security standards (see Chapter 4, Security Standards). The encryption of stored and transferred data also reduces the risk.

SAP applications use a standalone communication protocol (network interface protocol), which is based on the TCP and UDP protocols and optimized for SAP data communication. The NI protocol can be assigned to layer 4 (transport layer) of the OSI model, which enables you to identify potential risks.

### 5.4.2 Overview of Firewall Technologies

While various firewall types are used in several layers of the OSI model, traditional firewalls only work at the network and transport layers. Accordingly, the traditional firewall is a package filter at the network layer. Such simple package filters can also be designed to be stateful by involving the transport layer. Firewalls that only work at the application level are generally referred to as application level gateways (host-based). The following sections briefly introduce the three types of firewalls.

- **Package filters**
  Package filters represent the simplest form of firewall. They work exclusively at the IP level and are basically network routers with a filtering option. A package filter analyzes the IP header information.

  A package filter can define which of the superior protocols (FTP, HTTP, and so on) may pass between two network segments. Communication can also be limited to specific ports, like port 80 for HTTP. Users can also define which IP address of a network segment is allowed to set up communication with another network segment. Communication can be controlled and limited in this manner.

  The advantages of such a solution include cost-efficient and high-performance technology. Some disadvantages are also involved. Complex infrastructures can require a great deal of effort to define rules and susceptibility to IP spoofing, in which an unauthorized client uses another IP address to gain access to another network segment.

- **Stateful package filters**
  Stateful package filters work much like stateless package filters and generally provide the same types of rules. But a TCP session can be used to determine which clients have a communications connection with each other. The advantage of this method is that these kinds of firewalls can defend against network scanning based on half-open syn queries.

  Half-open syn queries are generated, for example, when numerous queries are sent to a server due to an attack from an inaccessible IP address (IP address spoofing, syn spoofing). Because the source IP address cannot be accessed, the server cannot establish a complete communication (half open), and the queries are queued and repeated later on. The server can no longer process the amount of the incoming queries and thus cannot process any queries (syn flooding).

  In addition, this type of firewall can use both the IP header and the message body to analyze the superior protocol a message is using. This way, dynamic filter rules can be created. In other words, the firewall itself can flexibly respond to changing conditions.

- **Application level gateway**
  Because package-filter firewalls cannot defend against attacks at the application level, application level gateways — also referred to as application level firewalls (host-based) or Web Application Firewalls (WAF) — are gaining popularity. But only a combination of package filters and application level gateways can provide the required level of security.

  Application level gateways offer additional protection against Internet attacks, such as:

  - Cross-site scripting
  - SQL script injection
  - Parameter tampering
  - Buffer overflow
  - Stealth commanding
  - Hidden field manipulation
  - Directory traversal
  - URL blocking

  The application level gateway can offer such protection because the data flow is actually analyzed at the level of the application. Predefined rules can determine if a query has been formulated correctly.

  Many users work with a white list, that is, a positive security model. In other words, rules must be defined for acceptable queries. Queries outside the rules are then blocked automatically. But the definition of such rules can create problems. It is especially difficult with very dynamic Internet applications. That's why many manufacturers try to use a learning algorithm that can learn the defining rules.

  Use of application level gateways can often be problematic in terms of performance, which means that another dedicated computer must be set up for it.

Firewalls assume an important role in network security. They can map its strengths or weaknesses. Experience has shown that firewalls are not always optimally configured regarding security technology or that the configuration hasn't been adapted to changing conditions.

Enterprise risk management requires a good balance between the opening and closing of communication options via firewalls with the goal to only allow and secure data traffic the company or organization needs. A prerequisite for finding this balance is a clear definition of data communication that is permitted and communication that the firewall is supposed to prevent. On this basis, the technical service can implement the correct configuration with the respective requirements.

The relevance of this process should be emphasized here because SAP applications always process company-critical data and SAP NetWeaver provides numerous options for connecting SAP applications with the Internet or external networks. The security of SAP applications always depends on the network security.

# PART II
# Security in SAP NetWeaver and Application Security

*This chapter describes critical applications, components, and technologies within the SAP NetWeaver product portfolio, and some possible security technologies to protect them. From this point of view, the SAP components are presented in an example of a security architecture considering enterprise risk management. This architecture is also visualized in a map which has been included in this book.*

# 6 Enterprise Risk Management (ERM) Navigation Control Map

The numerous components and technologies in SAP systems and related functions present a complex system of interactions with regard to enterprise risk management. The applications and solutions used determine the security requirements and security strategies. To help you understand these interdependencies, this book comes with an ERM Navigation Control Map (see Figure 6.1), which is also referenced in the following chapters. It provides a comprehensive overview of SAP applications and SAP NetWeaver components and visualizes security aspects, possible solutions, and vendors in a comprehensive security architecture. You can also access the ERM Navigation Control Map online at *http://www.linkies.eu* and *http://www.deltaisc.com*.

The arrangement of the individual components in the various security zones is not static and just an example. The ERM Navigation Control Map is more like a "visual checklist" for necessary security measures and solutions with regard to system, application, and communication security and risk and control management. The increasing complexity of system landscapes makes it indispensable to have a uniform security strategy that considers all SAP components in terms of technology, processes, organization, and other issues. This is the only way to achieve comprehensive and stable security for risk and control systems between the various heterogeneous systems.

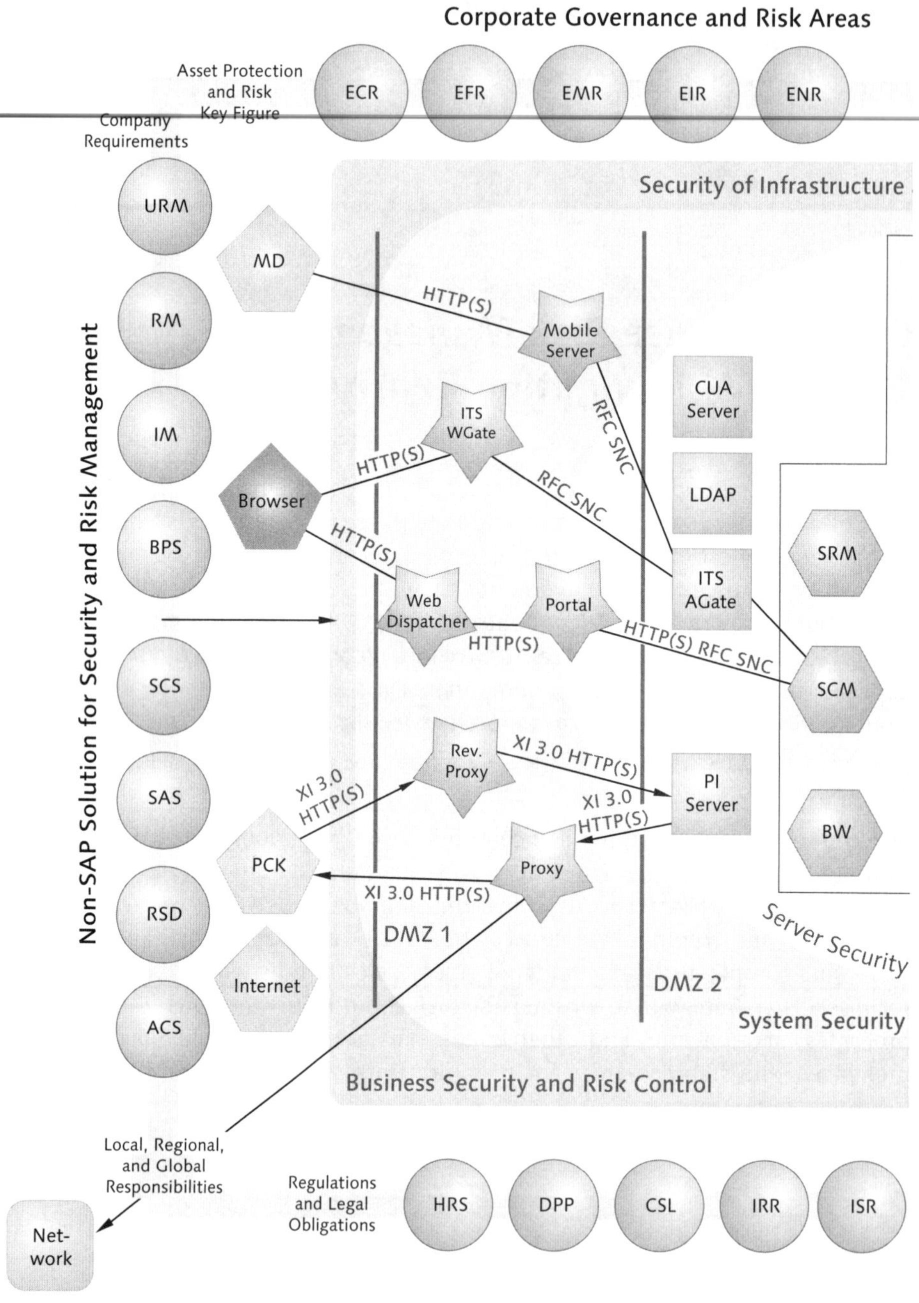


**Figure 6.1** ERM Navigation Control Map (Source: LINKIES. Unternehmensberatung GmbH)

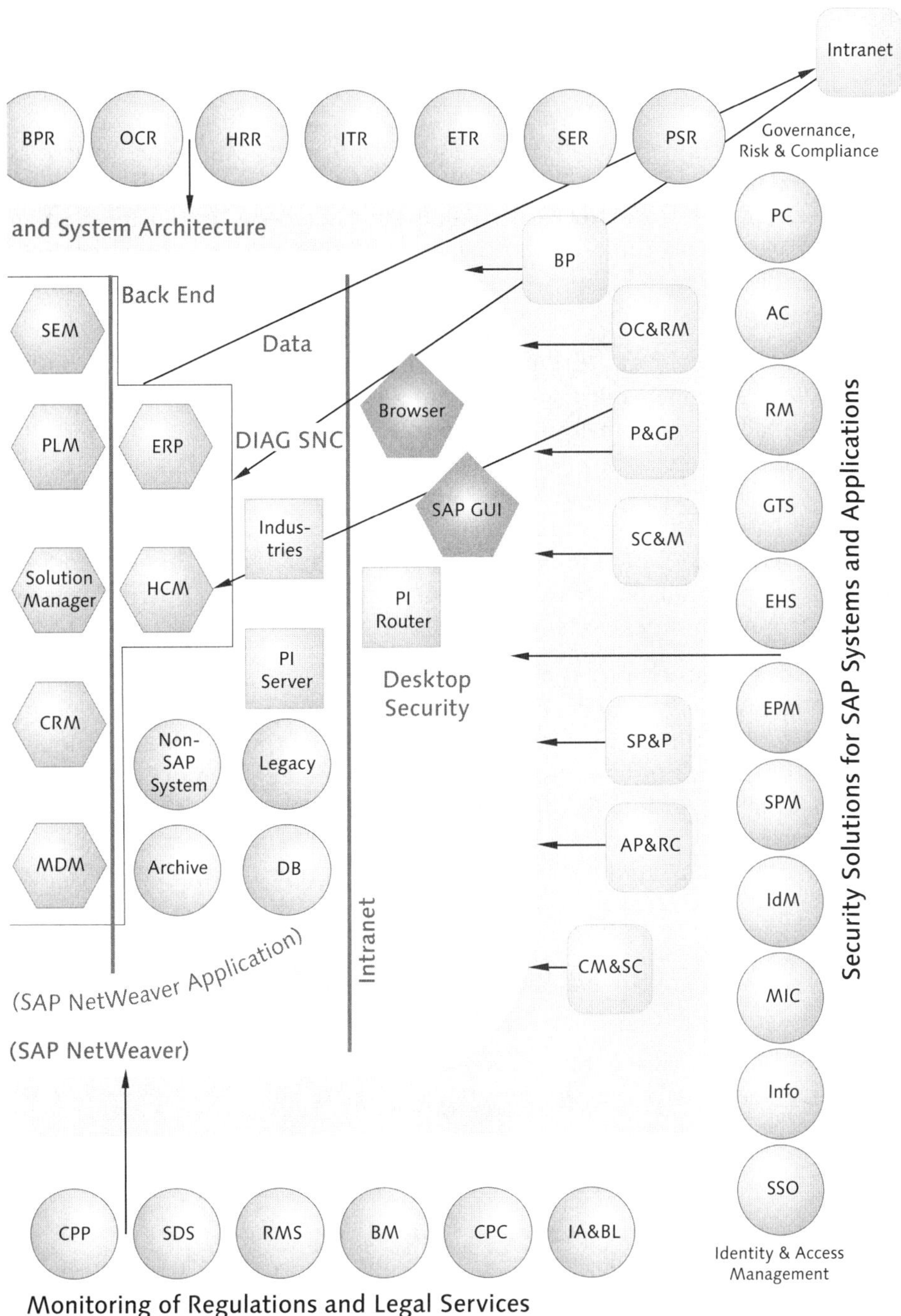

Intranet
BPR
OCR
HRR
ITR
ETR
SER
PSR
Governance, Risk & Compliance
and System Architecture
BP
PC
Back End
SEM
OC&RM
AC
Data
Browser
RM
PLM
ERP
DIAG SNC
P&GP
SAP GUI
GTS
Indus-tries
SC&M
Solution Manager
HCM
PI Router
EHS
PI Server
Desktop Security
EPM
CRM
Non-SAP System
Legacy
SP&P
SPM
MDM
Archive
DB
AP&RC
IdM
Intranet
CM&SC
Security Solutions for SAP Systems and Applications
(SAP NetWeaver Application)
MIC
(SAP NetWeaver)
Info
SSO
CPP
SDS
RMS
BM
CPC
IA&BL
Identity & Access Management
Monitoring of Regulations and Legal Services

The ERM Navigation Control Map, which is contained in this book as a supplement, can be used for orientation and navigation purposes. To maintain the overview character of the ERM Navigation Control Map, only the most important SAP applications are mapped and arranged in the center of the security zones. These applications run on the SAP NetWeaver Application Server (AS), which is used as the technical platform here and determines the essential parts of the security architecture (see Chapter 9, SAP NetWeaver Application Server). Internal authorization concepts of SAP applications are generally not affected by this and are therefore not further discussed here; they will be described in more detail in other chapters of this book.

The System Security (SAP NetWeaver) security zone that surrounds the center includes SAP components that support communication functions in the network group, internally, and externally (to the Internet, for example). The related security aspects are defined in the SAP NetWeaver security concept (see Chapter 5, Information Technology (IT) Security). The zones at the periphery of the ERM Navigation Control Map map aspects of risk management that address risks affecting the system infrastructure from the outside. This also includes components and SAP solutions that are available for risk management of external and internal security risks concerning the access to functions and data.

The basic idea of this chapter is to provide you with an overview of selected SAP applications, SAP NetWeaver components, external security solutions, and security technologies. The selection is limited to some essential components to maintain the general focus of this book. To explain the terminology used in Figure 6.1 or in the map, Tables 6.1 and 6.2 briefly introduce the concepts and abbreviations used in the ERM Navigation Control Map. Table 6.1 explains the elements mapped in Security of Infrastructure and System Architecture in the center of Figure 6.1.

| Abbreviation | Description |
|---|---|
| **Security of Infrastructure and System Architecture** | |
| SEM | SAP Strategic Enterprise Management |
| PLM | SAP Product Lifecycle Management |
| ERP | SAP ERP, the SAP Enterprise Resource Planning System |
| SRM | SAP Supplier Relationship Management |
| Solution Manager | SAP Solution Manager |

**Table 6.1** Explanations of Abbreviations Regarding the Security of Infrastructure and System Architecture

| Abbreviation | Description |
|---|---|
| HCM | SAP ERP Human Capital Management |
| SCM | SAP Supply Chain Management |
| CRM | SAP Customer Relationship Management |
| BW | SAP NetWeaver Business Warehouse |
| MDM | SAP NetWeaver Master Data Management |
| CUA server | Server of the Central User Administration |
| LDAP | Lightweight Directory Access Protocol |
| ITS AGate | AGate of the SAP Internet Transaction Server |
| PI Server | Server of SAP NetWeaver Process Integration; external business-to-business (B2B) communication |
| Mobile server | Server of SAP NetWeaver Mobile |
| ITS WGate | WGate (web server) of the SAP Internet Transaction Server |
| Web Dispatcher | SAP Web Dispatcher |
| Portal | SAP NetWeaver Portal |
| Rev. Proxy | Reverse proxy |
| Proxy | Proxy in the demilitarized zone |
| MD | Mobile devices, that is, all mobile end devices |
| Browser | Web browser (see also browser entry) |
| PCK | SAP Partner Connectivity Kit |
| Internet | Any type of Internet application |
| Network | Any type of network access |
| Browser | User interface for internal access to the SAP system, usually supported by web browsers |
| Industries | SAP Industry Solutions, industry-specific SAP solution portfolio |
| SAP GUI | SAP Graphical User Interface, user interface for traditional SAP access |
| PI Router | Router of SAP NetWeaver Process Integration |
| PI Server | Server of SAP NetWeaver Process Integration; internal application-to-application (A2A) communication |

**Table 6.1** Explanations of Abbreviations Regarding the Security of Infrastructure and System Architecture (Cont.)

| Abbreviation | Description |
|---|---|
| Non-SAP System | All ERP applications that have not been developed by SAP |
| Legacy | Legacy systems that existed before implementing an SAP system and still used for certain processes |
| Archive | Systems for archiving data and documents |
| DB | Database and database server |
| BP | Business Process Controls, the business processes and their controls |
| OC&RM | Organizational Change and Risk Management, risk management addressing changes in the business organization |
| P&GP | Principles and Good Practices, generally accepted principles and practices |
| SC&M | Security Controls and Monitoring, control measures for information security and monitoring for identifying security-relevant incidents |
| SP&P | Security Policies and Procedures, internal guidelines and processes to support information security |
| AP&RC | Audit Procedures and Routine Controls, audits and regular controls of the efficiency of the control measures |
| CM&SC | Continuity Measures and Sustainable Compliance, continuous maintenance/recovery of compliance in case of business or technological changes |

**Table 6.1** Explanations of Abbreviations Regarding the Security of Infrastructure and System Architecture (Cont.)

Table 6.2 describes the functions that are mapped in the periphery of the ERM Navigation Control Map. These functions are external risk management components and external SAP security solutions.

| Abbreviation | Description |
|---|---|
| **Corporate Governance and Risk Areas** | |
| ECR | Enterprise Compliance Risks; risks for existing control measures of losing existing compliance with internal or legal regulations due to changes |
| EFR | Enterprise Financial and Commercial Risks; business and financial risks |
| EMR | Enterprise Market Risks; risks resulting from market fluctuations and production and product features |

**Table 6.2** Explanation of External Risk Management Components and External SAP Security Solutions

| Abbreviation | Description |
|---|---|
| EIR | Enterprise Investment Risks; risks related to investments and currencies |
| ENR | Environmental Noncompliance Risks; risks resulting from the fact that production processes or products could generally have negative environmental effects and that production processes no longer comply with existing regulations and guidelines |
| BPR | Business Process Risks; risk resulting from business processes related to the administration and management of information security |
| OCR | Organizational and Change Management Risks; risks resulting from the methods of how organizational and technological changes (such as virtualizations or the modeling of processes within service-oriented architectures (SOAs)) are implemented by management |
| HRR | Human Resources Risks; risks related to employees or labor markets, for example, subject matter experts or employees in key positions that are no longer available |
| ITR | Information Technology Risks; risks resulting from the use of IT infrastructures |
| ETR | Enterprise Technology Risks; risks caused by production technologies |
| SER | Social and Educational Risks; risks resulting from social environments and education, for example, insufficiently qualified employees and lack of education |
| PSR | Political and Stability Risks; risks resulting from the environment of external (political) conditions, including terrorism |
| **Security Solutions for SAP Systems and Applications** | |
| PC | SAP BusinessObjects Process Control |
| AC | SAP BusinessObjects Access Control |
| RM | SAP BusinessObjects Risk Management |
| GTS | SAP BusinessObjects Global Trade Services |
| EHS | SAP Environment, Health & Safety |
| EPM | SAP BusinessObjects Enterprise Performance Management |
| SPM | SAP BusinessObjects Sustainability Performance Management |
| IdM | SAP NetWeaver Identity Management |
| MIC | Management of Internal Controls |
| Info | SAP BusinessObjects solutions for information management |

**Table 6.2** Explanation of External Risk Management Components and External SAP Security Solutions (Cont.)

| Abbreviation | Description |
|---|---|
| SSO | Single-Sign-On solutions |
| **Monitoring of Regulations and Legal Services** | |
| HSR | Health and Safety Regulations |
| DPP | Data Protection and Privacy; legal regulations for data protection and privacy |
| CSL | National Laws and Country-Specific Regulations; country-specific law to which the company must adhere |
| IRR | International Rules and Regulations; international regulations to which the company must adhere (for example, the Sarbanes-Oxley Act (SOX)) |
| ISR | Industry-Specific Regulations (for example, for the financial or chemical industries) |
| CPP | Company Policies and Procedures; internal regulations and defined procedures |
| SDS | IT Security and Documentation Standards; standards regarding the use of IT security and its documentation |
| RMS | Risk Management Standards; generally accepted risk management standards |
| BM | Bilateral and Multilateral Agreements; bilateral or multilateral agreements must be known and considered respectively |
| CPC | Crisis Prevention and Control; measures, especially the development of measures, to avoid and handle potential crises, such as hacker attacks on the corporate website, which can lead to significant data protection and PR crises |
| IA&BL | Insolvency Acts, Bankruptcy Laws; compliance with the respective acts and regulations for extraordinary business cases, such as insolvency |
| **Non-SAP Solutions for Security and Risk Management** | |
| URM | User and Role Management; various non-SAP applications for managing SAP users and their authorization assignments |
| RM | Risk Management; risk management applications within SAP processes; the assignment of users, roles, and transactions is evaluated and risky assignments are identified using risk libraries |
| IM | Identity Management and User Provisioning; non-SAP solutions for the central management of user identities, role assignments, and system accesses |

**Table 6.2** Explanation of External Risk Management Components and External SAP Security Solutions (Cont.)

| Abbreviation | Description |
|---|---|
| BPS | Business Process Security; security support within business processes using non-SAP applications |
| SCS | Secure Communications Solutions; security solutions for encryption and secure authentication of the communication to and from SAP systems |
| SAS | Secure Authentication Solutions; solutions for user and system authentication |
| RSD | Risk, Security, and Audit Documentation; documentation of risk management processes |
| ACS | Advisory & Consulting Services; external consulting and security solutions supplementing risk management |

**Table 6.2** Explanation of External Risk Management Components and External SAP Security Solutions (Cont.)

## 6.1 SAP Applications

The following list provides an overview of the most important SAP Business Suite applications, which are also included in the ERM Navigation Control Map.

- **SAP ERP**
  SAP ERP is the SAP application for comprehensive enterprise resource planning. It comprises classic ERP applications, which were previously called R/3 modules. The functional areas in SAP ERP include analytics (reporting), financials (financial accounting and corporate governance), procurement and logistics execution, product development and manufacturing, sales and services, and corporate services.

  Chapter 20, Authorizations in SAP ERP, describes the risks, controls, and aspects of governance for SAP ERP —particularly the technical core, SAP ERP Enterprise Central Component (ECC). Due to the special nature of security topics, the risks and controls for the SAP ERP HCM solution are discussed in Chapter 21, SAP ERP HCM and Data Protection. Chapter 22, SAP Strategic Enterprise Management, deals with the risk and control options for SAP Strategic Enterprise Management (SEM).

- **SAP CRM**
  SAP CRM is SAP's central customer and sales management application. Its functional areas include marketing, sales, service (customer-oriented services), and analysis (market and customer analysis). Chapter 23, SAP CRM, describes the important risks and controls.

- **SAP SCM**
  SAP SCM is SAP's central planning and control application. It covers the following functional areas: supply and demand planning (capacity planning), service parts planning (component logistics), procurement, manufacturing (production planning), warehousing, order fulfillment, transportation (transport management), and supply chain design and analytics. Chapter 24, SAP SCM, describes the risk and control options.
- **SAP SRM**
  SAP SRM is the central SAP solution for procurements and for managing suppliers and business partners. Its functional areas include sourcing, procurement, and supplier enablement. Chapter 25, SAP SRM, describes the risk and control options.
- **SAP PLM**
  SAP PLM is part of the SAP Business Suite and supports the management of the entire product cycle: from product idea, to production, to customer service. SAP PLM runs on the SAP NetWeaver AS ABAP, which also determines the security environment and risk management for SAP PLM. Chapter 9 describes the risk and control options.
- **SAP BusinessObjects**
  SAP Business Suite provides comprehensive options for mapping business and product data. To better manage the increasing data volume, applications for data management and data reporting can be used, for example, SAP NetWeaver BW or SAP NetWeaver MDM. To determine and map the increased volume of complex information in a company more easily and flexibly, the company can use the SAP BusinessObjects solution portfolio. Chapter 11, BI Solutions in SAP BusinessObjects, discusses the related information security and risk management aspects.
- **Industry solutions**
  SAP's industry-specific solution portfolios provide specific applications that meet the requirements of individual industries and branches. There are industry solutions for financial service providers and the public sector (banks, healthcare, higher education and research, internal and external security, insurance companies, and so on), for service providers (trade/wholesale trade, logistics, media, telecommunications, utilities, residential rental, and so on), for manufacturers (automotive industry, engineering, plant engineering and construction, and shipbuilding industry, high tech and electronics, consumer products, aerospace, mechanical engineering, metal industry, mill products, and so on), and for the processing industry (mining, chemicals, pharmaceutical industry, oil and gas, and so on).

Because not all industry solutions can be discussed here, Chapter 26, Industry-Specific SAP Solution Portfolios, describes the complexity of the supplemental control solutions for industry solutions based on an important example from the SAP Defense and Security solution portfolio.

## 6.2 SAP NetWeaver Components

All of the SAP solutions listed previously are based on SAP NetWeaver, the technology and integration platform from SAP. The ERM Navigation Control Map covers its main components:

- **SAP NetWeaver AS**
  SAP NetWeaver AS is the central unit of SAP NetWeaver. All SAP and non-SAP applications run on this platform. In addition to the traditional ABAP stack (ABAP programs and applications, AS ABAP), it also offers Java middleware for Java applications (AS Java). Chapter 9 describes the risks and controls for the SAP NetWeaver AS.
- **SAP NetWeaver Portal**
  SAP NetWeaver Portal provides a complete portal infrastructure in which SAP and non-SAP systems and applications are combined in a central user interface. The portal facilitates navigation for users because the user interface runs in a web browser and is thus easy and intuitive to understand. The portal itself is an application with a wealth of powerful functions for collaboration within and across company boundaries (Knowledge Management & Collaboration, SAP NetWeaver Enterprise Search, business packages, and so on). Chapter 16, SAP NetWeaver Portal, describes the risks and controls for the SAP NetWeaver Portal.
- **SAP NetWeaver PI**
  SAP NetWeaver PI is the integration solution for data and applications, which enables process-oriented collaboration between SAP and non-SAP components. To do this, SAP NetWeaver PI provides a central, versatile, and open interface solution and thus contributes to simplifying complex landscapes made up of SAP NetWeaver and non-SAP components (enterprise application integration). SAP NetWeaver PI constitutes the basis for connecting heterogeneous systems and applications and also provides the technical basis for setting up SAP transactions and complete business processes between heterogeneous systems. The technical solution also supports process modeling. Chapter 12, SAP NetWeaver PI, describes the risks and controls for SAP NetWeaver PI.
- **SAP NetWeaver BW**
  SAP NetWeaver BW is the central application for analysis, evaluation, and over-

all reporting for the SAP Business Suite and its applications. Chapter 10, SAP NetWeaver BW, describes the essential risk management and control measures for SAP NetWeaver BW.

- **SAP NetWeaver MDM**
  SAP NetWeaver MDM is an upper-level system for the central consolidation, creation, and distribution of master data for all SAP applications in a company's heterogeneous SAP NetWeaver landscape. Chapter 15, SAP NetWeaver MDM, describes the special considerations for risk and control management with SAP MDM.
- **SAP NetWeaver Mobile**
  SAP NetWeaver Mobile is a component of SAP NetWeaver and offers solutions for operating and managing mobile applications. The ERM Navigation Control Map maps the SAP NetWeaver Mobile server — including a connection to an MD. Chapter 17, SAP NetWeaver Mobile, describes the risks and controls for SAP NetWeaver Mobile.
- **SAP Auto-ID Infrastructure**
  SAP Auto-ID Infrastructure is the platform for integration and system programming of automatic communication modules, such as contactless sensors (RFID), Bluetooth technology, and so on. Depending on the specific case, the SAP Auto-ID Infrastructure solutions and components can be used in versatile network environments internally and externally; therefore, they are not mapped in the ERM Navigation Control Map. Chapter 18, SAP Auto-ID Infrastructure, describes the risks and controls for SAP Auto-ID Infrastructure.
- **SAP Solution Manager**
  SAP Solution Manager is the central operations management component for SAP system landscapes. SAP Solution Manager can be used to manage SAP systems. In addition to implementation and monitoring assistance, SAP Solution Manager provides solutions for technical and functional measures for effective operations management and supports the IT Infrastructure Library (ITIL) core processes. Chapter 19, SAP Solution Manager, describes the risks and controls for SAP Solution Manager.
- **SAP PCK**
  The SAP PCK enables the connection of partner solutions if various technologies are in use. Chapter 13, SAP PCK, describes the risks and controls for the SAP PCK.
- **Database server**
  The database server is the storage area for all SAP system data. Chapter 27, Database Server, describes the risks and controls for the database server.

- **Middleware**
  Middleware ensures effective communication between various applications. Chapter 14, Classic SAP Middleware, describes the risks and controls for the following SAP middleware tools:
  - **SAP Web Dispatcher**
    The SAP Web Dispatcher is the load balancer for all SAP system clusters. In addition to load distribution, the Web Dispatcher offers limited security functions like reverse proxy and encryption.
  - **SAProuter**
    SAProuter is a small but critical application for establishing and protecting data communication and filtering access to systems that run on the SAP NetWeaver AS.
  - **SAP Internet Transaction Server**
    SAP Internet Transaction Server is the link between AS ABAP and SAP GUI for HTML (web browser). It is needed to format ABAP-based applications in HTML so that a web browser can control them.
- **User interfaces**
  User interfaces are the interfaces between user and application. This also involves risks and controls, which are described in Chapter 28, User Interfaces, for the following user interfaces:
  - **SAP GUI**
    SAP GUI is the graphical user interface for users of traditional (not web-based) SAP applications on the AS ABAP.
  - **Web browser**
    The web browser provides the technology for graphical user interfaces in web-based SAP applications.
  - **Mobile devices**
    Mobile devices are used for mobile SAP applications. They include notebooks, Personal Digital Assistants (PDAs), cell phones, and scanners.

## 6.3 Security Technologies

The following security solutions and suppliers make substantial contributions to improving security, control, and compliance measures for SAP NetWeaver products and applications. These partner solutions and providers are only examples. This does not mean that other vendors do not meet the same quality requirements.

### 6.3.1 Authorizations, Risk and Change Management, and Auditing

The following solutions serve security when dealing with authorizations, the identification of risks, control management, and change management to guarantee compliance with legal requirements and auditing requirements.

- **Securinfo for SAP**
  Securinfo for SAP offers an integrated solution for risk control, authorization control, user management, and control management that adheres to auditing requirements for a change management process. The focus is on consistent use of the information ownership principle. It is a preventive solution for reducing potential risks and minimizing company risks. A predefined risk library within the overall solution can help identify potential risks.

  Securinfo provides a broad range of functions for risk management and is mapped with several symbols in the NON-SAP SOLUTIONS FOR SECURITY AND RISK MANAGEMENT section of the ERM Navigation Control Map. This includes URM, RM, IM, BPS, and RSD, for example.

- **Approva BizRights for SAP**
  With BizRights, Approva offers a solution for risk analysis and monitoring of SAP ERP, including SAP NetWeaver Portal. The solution is designed around detective control and enhanced with preventive risk analysis. Risk libraries allow for analyses of processes and access authorizations and thus for reductions of potential risks supporting compliance with control objectives.

  The Insight product line is a comprehensive range of tools for user, risk, and compliance management. Approva is mapped with several symbols in the Non-SAP Solutions for Security and Risk Management section of the ERM Navigation Control Map, such as URM, RM, IM, BPS, and RSD.

- **Governance, Risk, and Compliance (GRC) solutions in SAP BusinessObjects**
  With its GRC solutions in SAP BusinessObjects, SAP offers its own product portfolio for this application. Chapter 8, GRC Solutions in SAP BusinessObjects, discusses these GRC solutions.

- **SAP Audit Information System**
  SAP Audit Information System is a tool to support internal and external audits. Because audits reveal vulnerabilities in financial and settlement processes and in technical applications, SAP Audit Information System is an important component of a comprehensive control and compliance solution for companies. SAP Audit Information System comprises transactions for analyses and special reports.

- **Profile Generator/role management**
  The SAP Profile Generator for role management (Transaction PFCG) is the traditional tool used to create ABAP roles and authorization components. It is the standard solution for authorization management in the AS ABAP. The SAP Profile Generator can assign roles to users; it does not consider risks or controls when doing so.
- **User Management Engine (UME)**
  The UME creates UME roles and authorization components. It is the standard solution for authorization management in AS Java. The UME can assign roles to users; it does not consider risks or controls when doing so.

### 6.3.2 Identity Management

Managing identities (users of SAP systems and applications and business partner users) is a central task in an internal risk and control system. Opening applications and systems to the Internet and external partners makes it necessary that information stored on system users is always up to date, audit-proof, and correct. The following sections list some sample solutions for SAP NetWeaver.

- **SAP ERP HCM**
  SAP ERP HCM can manage employees and users of SAP NetWeaver AS applications. It uses the organizational structure in SAP ERP HCM to accomplish this task. Authorizations can also be assigned to users via the organizational structure — for jobs, for example. Linking administrative processes and SAP ERP HCM to external central user management or LDAP directory services leads to a comprehensive identity management solution (see also the descriptions on SAP NetWeaver Identity Management (IdM)).
- **SAP NetWeaver IdM**
  The SAP NetWeaver IdM software component can be used for user administration and authentication in various SAP and non-SAP applications within the business system architecture. Other functions including assigning authorization roles, password management, and reporting to support audits; this also includes approval workflows for authorization assignments, which are relevant due to audit and compliance reasons.

  SAP NetWeaver IdM lets you control user information and system authorizations from a single source. For example, if SAP NetWeaver IdM is synchronized with SAP ERP HCM, the HCM system, as the "authoritarian" system, can couple HR tasks with system authorizations. So the employment of a person can automatically lead to access authorizations for an application — and, if required, include approval processes for authorizations. The central deletion of system authorizations and accesses can also be automated, for example, if a person leaves the company, which is then reflected in the HCM system.

These centralized and automated functions, however, lead to increased requirements for integrity, security, administration, and auditing of user master data because incorrect or misused administration tasks have far-reaching effects on system access and authorizations. To reduce this risk, the comprehensive portfolio of audit data in SAP NetWeaver IdM must be used for monitoring.

- **Microsoft Active Directory Service (ADS)**
  Microsoft ADS is an LDAP directory service that helps companies manage SAP and non-SAP user master data according to the X.509 standard. Its wide market penetration means that Microsoft ADS is often used in SAP environments. The service can be used, for example, to authenticate users before system access authorizations are assigned — regardless of whether SAP GUI or SAP NetWeaver Portal is used as the front end. Microsoft ADS is mapped with the IM symbol in the NON-SAP SOLUTIONS FOR SECURITY AND RISK MANAGEMENT section of the ERM Navigation Control Map.
- **Siemens DirX product line**
  Siemens DirX, in particular, the DirX Identity component, is a metadirectory service for the central maintenance of user master data and is assigned to authorizations in various SAP and non-SAP systems. DirX is mapped with the IM symbol in the Non-SAP Solutions for Security and Risk Management section of the ERM Navigation Control Map.
- **Computer Associates (CA) Identity Manager**
  With its CA Identity Manager and CA Role and Compliance Manager solutions, CA offers applications for the central maintenance of user and authorization assignment data for SAP and non-SAP systems. Compliance with control objectives is also supported on the process side. These solutions are mapped with the URM and IM symbols in the Non-SAP Solutions for Security and Risk Management section of the ERM Navigation Control Map.
- **Oracle/Sun Identity Manager**
  With Sun Identity Manager, Sun or Oracle offers a complete solution for managing user identities and user administration with role assignment in heterogeneous systems and applications. These solutions are mapped with the URM and IM symbols in the NON-SAP SOLUTIONS FOR SECURITY AND RISK MANAGEMENT section of the ERM Navigation Control Map.
- **Entrust PKI**
  Entrust PKI is a certificate-based, complete solution for secure and controlled administration of identities. Entrust PKI can be combined with other metadirectory services and offers increased security using digital certificates and their

audit-proof management. Entrust also provides solutions for data encryption and digital signatures. Entrust PKI is mapped with the URM, IM, SCS, and SAS symbols in the NON-SAP SOLUTIONS FOR SECURITY AND RISK MANAGEMENT section of the ERM Navigation Control Map. Chapter 4, Security Standards, describes the advantages of the public key infrastructure for information security and risk management.

- **IBM Tivoli software**
  IBM Tivoli software solutions are part of a product line for managing user identities and role assignments in heterogeneous system landscapes. This enables companies to centralize user administration and better assess their risks and meet compliance requirements. These solutions are mapped with the URM and IM symbols in the Non-SAP Solutions for Security and Risk Management section of the ERM Navigation Control Map.
- **Novell eDirectory**
  Novell eDirectory is an LDAP directory service used to maintain and manage SAP and non-SAP identities. The X.509 standard is applied here and supports multifactor authentication of user identities. Novell eDirectory is mapped with the URM and IM symbols in the Non-SAP Solutions for Security and Risk Management section of the ERM Navigation Control Map.

### 6.3.3 Secure Authentication and SSO

Secure authentication is one of the most important methods of granting controlled access to internal SAP systems and keeping unauthorized persons at bay. SAP has developed procedures that can be enhanced or replaced by partner solutions.

- **User ID and password**
  In the standard version, SAP uses one-factor authentication. Each user is granted a unique user ID and a password. This authentication method is used as the basic procedure throughout the entire SAP environment. Password rules can also be defined.
- **SAP logon tickets**
  SAP offers SAP logon tickets as an authentication method for SSO. The SAP logon ticket is a cookie created and signed upon successful initial authentication on a primary SAP NetWeaver AS or SAP NetWeaver Portal. All connected SAP systems use the logon ticket for further authentication.
- **Authentication using X.509 certificates**
  X.509 certificates that are created by a certification authority (using the public key infrastructure, for example) can be used for secure authentication and SSO. There are various commercial vendors who create solution variants, including two-factor authentication with tokens or chip cards.

### 6.3.4 Technical Security

Technical security is a basic precondition for linking all components of an SAP system landscape together. SAP itself offers several security solutions, such as SAP WebDispatcher, SAProuter, and the encryption of network communication links based on the SAP Cryptographic Library.

To guarantee secure identity and authorization management, secure and encrypted communication, and other technical components, in addition to offering its own solutions, SAP also collaborates with numerous partners to support the open system architecture of SAP NetWeaver. This includes the following solutions. These solutions are not listed in the ERM Navigation Control Map, but belong to the symbols in the Non-SAP Solutions for Security and Risk Management section.

- **RSA Access Manager, RSA Federated Identity Manager**
  RSA offers solutions for authenticating identities in heterogeneous networks. RSA Federated Identity Manager is also an SSO solution for authenticating access to SAP systems via Security Assertion Markup Language (SAML) between different network domains.
- **Entrust Public Key Infrastructure**
  With its numerous products, Entrust offers a comprehensive technical security portfolio for network and communications security via Secure Network Communication (SNC), encryption, digital signatures, Secure Store and Forward (SSF) mechanisms, and X.509 certificates for authentication.
- **F5 TrafficShield Application Firewall**
  F5 TrafficShield Application Firewall secures web applications at the application layer. It offers security solutions for attack scenarios in web applications. F5 TrafficShield is available as a standalone solution or as a component of BIG-IP Security solutions.
- **Deny All rWeb**
  Firewalls for web applications can be used to support web-based applications and portal installations that can be accessed via the Internet with various security measures at the application level. rWeb, the Web Application Firewall (WAF) by Deny All, is certified for SAP NetWeaver, for example.
- **Computer Associates**
  The Host-Based Intrusion Prevention System by Computer Associates (CA HIPS) is a combination of control solutions for proactive server protection that provides protection against unauthorized access at the operating system level. CA HIPS is a server management tool that recognizes vulnerabilities at the operating system level – and thus provides an investigative control solution using incident analyses.

- **Avira**
  Antivirus scanners lay the foundation for IT system protection. Numerous antivirus scanner products by various software vendors are available for SAP NetWeaver. AntiVir by Avira, for example, is one of the products that can be integrated with the SAP NetWeaver AS using a virus interface (VSI).

## 6.4 Influencing Factors

As described in the previous sections, a number of influencing factors determine the value and need of security solutions. Considerations of risk, legal requirements, adherence to security guidelines, security standards, and physical security must be embedded in comprehensive risk and control management. The ERM Navigation Control Map shows SAP NetWeaver components worth protecting, influencing factors, and security solutions in their totality. Every company must define its own security requirements in consideration of the influencing factors and the evaluation of risk.

All components of the ERM Navigation Control Map are part of a necessary and comprehensive security strategy. The following chapters focus on determining potential risks to help you define the "correct" security strategy and any related controls. The presentation of standard SAP methods, notes, and best-practice solutions are to help readers understand the controls.

*Service-oriented architectures (SOAs) are based on the principle of dividing software into independent components that each provides functionality as services — usually as web services. Particularly in a constantly changing environment, this provides several advantages compared to classic static information technology (IT) architectures. This chapter discusses the related security risks and how to handle them.*

# 7 Web Services, Enterprise Services, and Service-Oriented Architectures

Companies use both old and new SAP and non-SAP applications that were integrated with the system landscape and have since grown with it. The integration of SAP and non-SAP applications has always been of particular importance for executing IT processes to transfer data and transactions between internal systems and external applications of business partners, customers, and organizations. Communication formats, such as Intermediate Documents (IDocs), Business Application Programming Interfaces (BAPIs), and various web protocols —including SAP-specific formats — have always been and still are vital for this. This results in the following solution concepts:

- Applications communicate via various interfaces to allow for interactions between nonuniform and heterogeneous system groups.
- Within a software application, transactions and business processes follow a defined program flow.
- Controls and conditions within applications are clearly defined. If a business process changes, this can have enormous consequences for the software. Changes can only be implemented by modifying the program code.

Therefore, new application versions are continuously developed and need to be adapted to (and in interaction with) other applications. So system development has become very complex, and minor changes often lead to long-term development projects. Program modifications, testing, and managing program versions became focal points in the development cycle but were insufficiently considered. If you then also keep in mind that you have to ensure a uniform and consistent security concept and manage security risks, linking business applications quickly becomes a complex topic.

In the meantime, however, due to globalization, the concept of establishing IT architectures and data exchanges was supplemented with a conceptual idea in which business processes in heterogeneous applications and IT architectures are implemented using flexible services (web services). This is referred to as an SOA. The basic principle of service-oriented architectures is that functions of applications and data exchange processes between applications are provided and used as services. An example of such a service is a request referring to a specific purchase order within SAP Enterprise Resource Planning (ERP). In this case, the purchase order is the business document (business object), and a query service searches for the respective purchase order upon request.

In addition, interfaces and communication methods are standardized. As concatenations of services, business processes can be modeled, standardized, and executed across applications. Some advantages are the flexibility provided and the fact that a service, once developed and registered, can be repeatedly used by various applications.

So, using service-oriented architectures has the following benefits:

- Global standards reduce or eliminate even complicated adaptations in heterogeneous system landscapes.
- Communication levels and methods are independent of applications.
- Various applications use the same modular, reusable program code.
- Control logic, business process controls, decisions, or conditions can be programmed regardless of the application used.
- It leads to general benefits for application-supported business processes and content.
- The process flow in the system architecture becomes less complex.
- Program-technical process implementation is easier and more effective.

To implement the SOA concept, open international standards have been developed in cooperation with several organizations and companies. Since Release 6.20, the SAP NetWeaver Application Server (AS) supports these standards and — along with SAP NetWeaver Process Integration (PI) — makes SAP's entire technology platform compatible with the SOA concept, particularly for using and processing web services. Due to their flexibility, service-oriented architectures can also be used to collaborate with the existing traditional applications so that a gradual migration to this new architecture can be achieved without a "big bang." This chapter briefly introduces the idea behind service-oriented architectures and discusses related security risks for web services and enterprise services.

## 7.1 Introduction and Technical Principles

The Organization for the Advancement of Structured Information Standards (OASIS) consortium (*http://www.oasis-open.org*) that drives the development of web services standards defines them as follows:

> *Web services allow applications to communicate across platforms and programming languages using standard protocols based on XML.*

Let's take a look at a simplified example using online shopping: You order an article in an online shop. This triggers a process in the vendor's system that checks to see if the article is in stock or from an external business partner. At the same time, a payment process runs with a bank or credit card company; the financial purchase order data is transferred to the company-specific posting system, and the purchase order is forwarded to the warehouse system which automatically generates the invoice and shipping label; finally, you receive an email with the purchase order data confirming the order.

As the example demonstrates, the different applications must be adapted to the various communication formats to connect to each other. This has frequently been done through complex application-specific programs and interfaces. The goal of the SOA concept is to solve this in a simple and elegant way. So the sample purchase order would use a web service for purchase order management. This web service generates a message (XML message) that contains the purchase order data and is understood and processed by all SOA applications involved. If the article had to be ordered from another supplier, the XML message would simply be redirected to the other vendor instead of the complete application architecture being questioned.

Enabling the required data communication using reusable web service messages that are flexible, independent of applications, programming languages, and operating systems generally requires usable standardization rules, also for information security. Basically, web services are based on three standards:

- **Simple Object Access Protocol (SOAP)**
  The SOAP concept provides a standardized XML structure in which all pieces of information in a message are arranged in defined segments. So SOAP forms a kind of "envelope," similar to a letter for the message, whose header (SOAP header) contains information on the sender and recipient and whose body (SOAP body) contains the actual data.
- **Web Services Description Language (WSDL)**
  The WSDL is a standardized programming language that can be used to describe which web service functions a server provides and how data is exchanged. So an application that is connected to this server can determine which SOAP XML

message is used for a specific function. The WSDL standard describes web services with the following seven elements:

- **Type**
  Describes the communication data type for web services.
- **Message**
  Describes the data type of the data transferred.
- **Operation**
  Describes the functions of the web service.
- **Service**
  Describes the network access point for communication.
- **Port**
  Describes the network endpoint including network protocol, data format, and network address.
- **Port type**
  Describes the operations with support from a port.
- **Binding**
  Describes the actual data format and protocol of a specific network access point.

- **Universal Description, Discovery, Integration (UDDI)**
  UDDI is a standardized directory service that is used to register web services on the Internet so that they are publicly available. An application that wants to provide or use web services must be able to localize them on the intranet or Internet. For this task, the UDDI register is the generally accepted OASIS standard. UDDI has a structure that is adapted to the WSDL standard to support the description and registration of the web services provided. The UDDI data structure contains the following elements:
  - **tModel data structure**
    In the WSDL context, this data structure describes the type and technical specifications of the web service. Various tModels are possible.
  - **Business service data structure**
    This data structure describes the web service and how it is used.
  - **Binding template data structure**
    This data structure describes the access point for the web service and contains a reference to the tModel.

For a better overview, Figure 7.1 illustrates the WSDL and UDDI structures. Today, various companies, so-called UDDI operators, maintain decentralized UDDI registers. SAP is one of these UDDI operators and has integrated the UDDI register with the Enterprise Services Repository in SAP NetWeaver PI. If web services are supposed to be described with WSDL and registered in UDDI, these two structures must be reconciled. Therefore, an assignment exists between the following structure elements:

- WSDL port type and UDDI tModel
- WSDL binding and UDDI tModel
- WSDL service and UDDI business service
- WSDL port and UDDI binding template

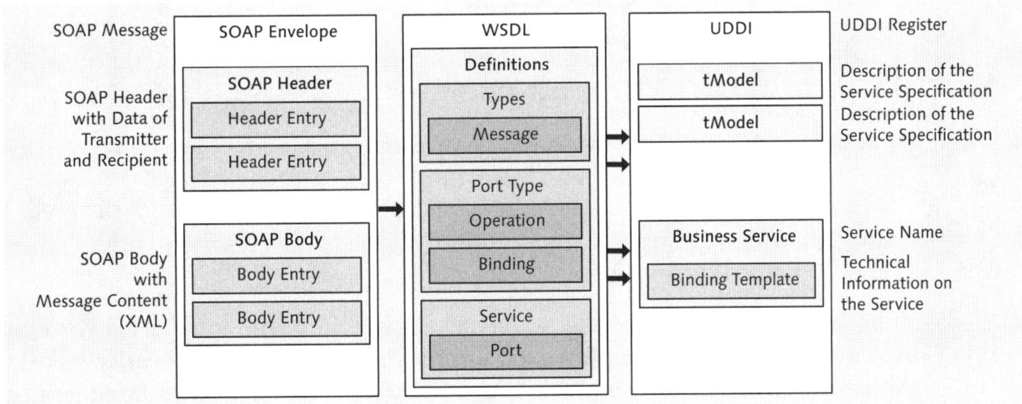


**Figure 7.1** Standardized Structure — SOAP Message, WSDL Structure for Description, and UDDI Data Structure for Registering Web Services

SAP NetWeaver PI provides seamless support for web services and thus contributes to data communication between SAP systems and non-SAP systems as long as all communication partners follow the OASIS standards for web services. The data of a traditional SAP transaction from an ERP system, for example, of a purchase order, is processed by the web services and transferred between the systems in SOAP messages. You can implement entire business processes using this principle, regardless of which IT systems the partners involved in the process use. There are two generally implemented system architectures, which are also illustrated in Figure 7.2.

- In system architecture variant 1, SAP NetWeaver PI is used as an agent and can transfer information for structured data (data entries of the SAP system, for example) but it can also actively modify transferred data. This enables you, for example, to convert nonstructured information, such as documents in DOC, PDF, or HTML format, to XML messages and forward them using SAP NetWeaver PI.

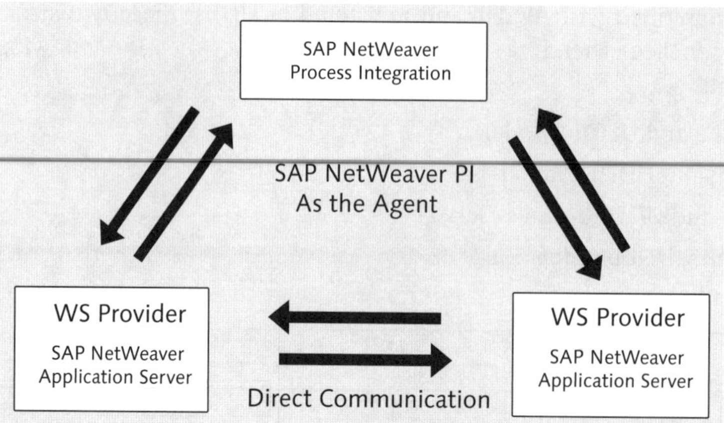


**Figure 7.2** Principle Web Service System Architecture (Direct and Indirect Communication)

- In variant 2, the WS provider (the application that provides the web service) and the WS consumer (the application that uses the web service) are in direct contact without using SAP NetWeaver PI as an agent.

In both variants, SOAP messages are exchanged within the internal network or externally via the Internet. However, both variants include data security risks in the data exchange and data processing processes. These risks must be identified and reduced with the appropriate security measures.

The data transfer in the Open Systems Interconnection (OSI) application layer and in the transport layer involves general risks (see Chapter 5, Information Technology Security). Because a complete business process can run while web services are used, data security and access control may not be sufficient in the application and transport layer.

To reduce security risks for business processes, security mechanisms for processes and process controls and appropriate audit measures must exist. In addition, it must be possible from a security technology perspective to reliably identify business partners, establish trust relationships, and irrevocably complete processes or transactions. Concepts that always need to be mentioned in this context are policies and governance; these topics must always be addressed in the SOA environment.

The success of a web service–based service-oriented architecture depends on how the concept meets the requirements of data security, risk management, and Governance, Risk, and Compliance (GRC) guidelines. The program-technical prerequisites are considered in the SOA concept; how it is followed and used efficiently, however, depends on clear requirement definitions and close cooperation of business process owners, system architects and developers, and of persons responsible for data security, business logic, controls, and audits.

## 7.2 Security Criteria for Web Services

Due to the related flexibility, openness, and universal communication options, the SOA concept or the use of web services involves numerous security risks. Good data security, customized access authorizations, and compliance with business guidelines are some of the basic prerequisites that SOA applications must meet to be successful.

The following security criteria (further specified in Table 7.1) are generally accepted and should be met appropriately in each application or process:

- **Authentication**
  The web service agent (for example, SAP NetWeaver PI) or web service consumer must be able to clearly identify the web service.
- **Authorization**
  To make sure that the web service can only be used by certain consumers, an efficient authorization system must exist.
- **Data integrity**
  The web service concept must support controls that ensure that message content cannot be manipulated during transfer.
- **Data confidentiality**
  Data should be efficiently protected against unauthorized access. This is not only an internal and legal prerequisite that must be met; it also depends on the content of the data.
- **Irrevocability (non-repudiation)**
  It mustn't be possible to revoke completed transactions. This requirement can be met by assigning the transaction (a purchase order, for example) a digital signature of the person who issues the purchase order.

These security criteria for using web services cannot be implemented using randomly and internally developed security technologies. This would jeopardize the universal use and reusability of web services. Instead, web service security must correspond to a generally accepted standard. The World Wide Web Consortium (W3C) developed and published these generally accepted standards. Table 7.1 shows which standardized security options are available for meeting the security criteria mentioned in service-oriented architectures with regard to web services.

| Security Criterion | Security Option for Web Services |
|---|---|
| Authentication | The web service must prove its identity directly to the SOA agent or WS consumer to avoid nonauthorized processing. To do this, the web service generates identifiable information in the header of the SOAP message, for example:<br>▶ User name (not signed)<br>▶ Kerberos token (digital signature)<br>▶ X.509 certificate token (digital signature)<br>▶ Security Assertion Markup Language (SAML)<br>These digital signatures follow the XML security standard. |
| Authorization | The Extensible Access Control Markup Language (xACML) enables the programming of authorization controls. Only authorized WS providers or WS consumers can use web services and process messages. |
| Data integrity | The following options are available for protecting data integrity:<br>▶ Web Services Time Stamp is used to make sure that message data is not modified.<br>▶ SAML<br>▶ XML Digital Signature Standard |
| Data confidentiality | Data confidentiality is supported by encrypting data that is transferred between web service provider and user. The corresponding standard is the SSL/TSL-compatible XML encryption standard. |
| Non-repudiation | The irrevocability of a transaction (a purchase order document in XML format, for example) can be achieved by digitally signing the document when completing the transaction. This signature proves that the transaction is completed. SOAP messages from a web service can also be protected against being revoked using digital signatures. The corresponding standard is XML Digital Signature. |

**Table 7.1** Security Risks and Options for Web Services

With the WS-Security Framework (*http://www.w3.org/TR/ws-policy/ws-policy-framework.pdf*), the W3C laid the foundation for implementing business process controls, such as guidelines and their governance. This framework contains standards that provide a uniform programming syntax for application developers. This lets you program an adequate WS-Policy that implements business requirements for SOA applications, that is, a specific behavior or security-relevant conditions of a web service or process.

This WS-Policy can define what conditions have to be met by a SOAP message before it can be processed. Such a condition can define, for example, that the SOAP message needs to be signed digitally or encrypted. In the web service application, the condition is defined within the WS-Policy as a policy alternative (subgroup within WS-Policy). These policy alternatives contain policy assertions (technical instructions), which are programmed in XML or in a policy file. The XML syntax for policy programming is defined in the OASIS standard for WS-Security (*http://docs.oasis-open.org/ws-sx/ws-securitypolicy/v1.3/ws-securitypolicy.html*).

Listing 7.1 shows a sample XML program code for a WS-Policy, including policy assertions that require encryption, a specific encryption algorithm, a digital signature, and an X.509 certificate for authentication in the SOAP messages (see also *http://docs.oasis-open.org/ ws-sx/ws-securitypolicy/200702/ws-securitypolicy-1.2-spec-os.html*). Furthermore, policy assertions can be assigned a value assignment type, that is, whether a specific option is necessary or only optional, or whether a specific option or all options have to be met.

```
<wsp:Policy xmlns:wsp="..." xmlns:sp="...">
  <sp:AsymmetricBinding>
    <wsp:Policy>
      <sp:RecipientToken>
        <wsp:Policy>
          <sp:X509Token
           sp:IncludeToken=".../IncludeToken/Always" />
        </wsp:Policy>
     </sp:RecipientToken>
     <sp:InitiatorToken>
       <wsp:Policy>
         <sp:X509Token
          sp:IncludeToken=".../IncludeToken/Always" />
       </wsp:Policy>
     </sp:InitiatorToken>
     <sp:AlgorithmSuite>
       <wsp:Policy>
         <sp:Basic256 />
       </wsp:Policy>
     </sp:AlgorithmSuite>
     <sp:Layout>
        <wsp:Policy>
          <sp:Strict />
        </wsp:Policy>
     </sp:Layout>
```

```
      <sp:IncludeTimestamp />
      <sp:EncryptBeforeSigning />
      <sp:EncryptSignature />
      <sp:ProtectTokens />
    </wsp:Policy>
  </sp:AsymmetricBinding>
  <sp:SignedEncryptedSupportingTokens>
    <wsp:Policy>
      <sp:UsernameToken
       sp:IncludeToken=".../IncludeToken/Once" />
    </wsp:Policy>
  </sp:SignedEncryptedSupportingTokens>
  <sp:SignedEndorsingSupportingTokens>
    <wsp:Policy>
      <sp:X509Token sp:IncludeToken=".../IncludeToken/Once">
        <wsp:Policy>
          <sp:WssX509v3Token10 />
        </wsp:Policy>
      </sp:X509Token>
    </wsp:Policy>
  </sp:SignedEndorsingSupportingTokens>
  <sp:Wss11>
    <wsp:Policy>
      <sp:RequireSignatureConfirmation />
    </wsp:Policy>
  </sp:Wss11>
</wsp:Policy>
```

**Listing 7.1** Example of a WS-Policy with Security-Relevant Policy Assertions

The following code segments in Listing 7.1 are security-relevant:

- Policy statement: all criteria of the policy must be met (`<wsp:Policy xmlns:wsp="..." xmlns:sp="...">`)
- Assertion: asymmetric encryption (see Chapter 5), use of a public key for encryption, and a private key for digital signatures (`<sp:AsymmetricBinding>`)
- Assertion: use of an X.509 certificate (`<sp:X509Token sp:IncludeToken= ".../IncludeToken/Always" />`)
- Assertion: encryption using AES algorithms and a key length of 256 bits, digital signature algorithm Sha1 (`<sp:Basic256 />`)

- Assertion: adding a time stamp to the document (<sp:IncludeTimestamp />)
- Assertion: data encryption before digital signature (<sp:EncryptBeforeSigning />)
- Assertion: encryption of the digital signature (<sp:EncryptSignature />)
- Assertion: adding the user name that is supposed to be included in the security header of the SOAP message (<sp:UsernameToken sp:IncludeToken= ".../IncludeToken/Once" />)
- Assertion: digital signature of the user name in the SOAP security header and adding an X.509 certificate (Version 3) in the SOAP header of the document (<sp:SignedEndorsingSupportingTokens>, <sp:X509Token sp: IncludeToken=".../IncludeToken/Once"> and <sp:WssX509v3Token10 />)
- Assertion: verification and confirmation encryption of the digital signature (<sp:RequireSignatureConfirmation />)

The WS-Policy is part of a service or a SOAP message. For demonstration purposes, Figure 7.3 shows the structure of a SOAP message with a security header that contains the WS-Policy.

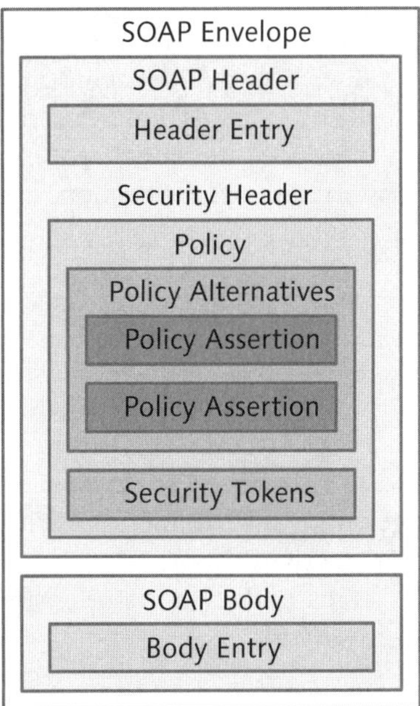


**Figure 7.3** SOAP Message (Illustration) with Security Header for the Security Policy

As you can see from the information provided, the web service security concept clearly differs from the traditional SAP authorization concept — and for establishing information security for transactions and processes that are modeled using web services, a detailed technical implementation concept is necessary. This requires close cooperation of the respective business process owners, the persons responsible for data and authorizations, and the XML developers. This is the only way to effectively implement processes, guidelines, decisions, uniform security strategies, and, ultimately, governance in program code.

The actual challenge is to implement and comply with governance guidelines in service-oriented architectures: It is "simply" about defining basic conditions and rules for the flexible use of web services. They must reflect specific internal business processes and control conditions and have an open structure so that new web services can be developed and integrated with those of existing business processes and partners.

### 7.2.1 Security and Risk Management for Service-Oriented Architectures

Once you have adapted SAP ERP operations or your system landscape based on SAP NetWeaver — together with your business partners — you can benefit from future-oriented advantages, as already described for service-oriented architectures. A focus on service-oriented architectures, however, does not exclude traditional methods of rather inflexible connections between SAP and non-SAP applications. You can still use them in parallel, but must bear in mind the functional requirements and the acceptable method-specific security risk. Traditional connections are possible using the following interfaces, for example:

- Remote Function Call (RFC)
- Business Application Programming Interface (BAPI)
- Exchange Infrastructure (XI) protocol

Figure 7.4 illustrates how two communication partners exchange a SOAP message. In this case, data is supposed to be transferred to a database. To do this, an application server uses a web service provider to generate a SOAP message with data, and the database (as the web service consumer) receives the SOAP message for processing the data. The same method is used to transfer data in the opposite direction, that is, from the database to the application server.

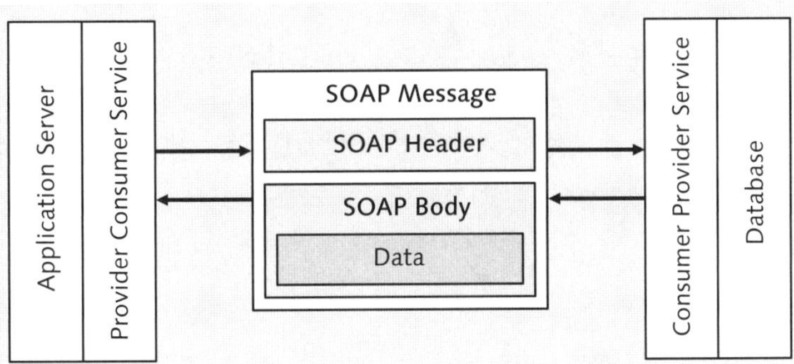


**Figure 7.4** Data Transfer via a Web Service from the Database Using SOAP Message

### 7.2.2 SAP Enterprise Services

If a web service is supposed to be used to implement a purchase order, additional criteria must be defined and met. In particular, it must be possible to apply a business logic to the web service. To do this, SAP publishes industry-specific web services as SAP Enterprise Services. These enterprise services focus on business processes and represent specific business objects. A purchase order is such a business object, for example.

Since Release 6.0, the SAP ERP system installation provides predefined enterprise services. Transaction WSADMIN lets you map and manage the services. In addition, SAP provides enterprise services in the Enterprise Services Workplace and publishes them in the SAP Developer Network (SDN, *http://sdn.sap.com*). Numerous enterprise services are also available in enhancement packages for various business process scenarios. Figure 7.5 shows SAP applications in the Enterprise Services Workplace for which additional enterprise services are available.

Even if the focus is on the flexible use of enterprise services — as is the general case for web services — the following criteria must be met according to OASIS standards:

- Compliance with a global data standard (ISO 15000-5 and UN/CEFACT CCTS)
- Interface design (WSDL) to which you strictly adhere
- Limited configuration options for compatibility between current and future enterprise service versions

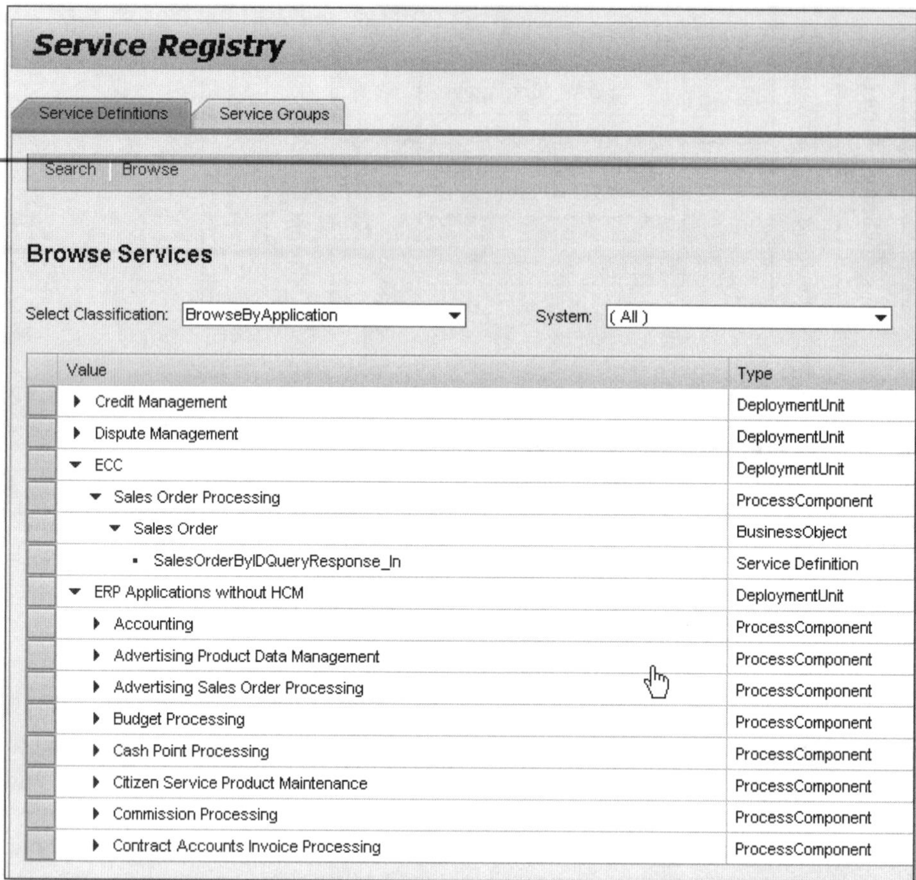


**Figure 7.5** Definitions for SAP Enterprise Services in the Enterprise Services Repository

Even though SAP Enterprise Services are already provided with the system's installation or can be obtained retroactively from the Enterprise Services Workplace, you must consult a security consultant when selecting and implementing the necessary security configuration for the enterprise services. You should always run a risk analysis in advance to optimize the system configuration and keep the risk at an acceptable level.

Table 7.2 compares some critical risks and the countermeasures available for increasing security. This is done using the OASIS security standard for SAML 2.0. Table 7.2 illustrates that the data transfer between service provider and service consumer involves most of the threats and the highest risk to enterprise services.

| Threat/Risk | Security Measure |
|---|---|
| Service messages could be read by unauthorized users (eavesdropping). | ▶ An initial measure is to encrypt network communication in the transport layer using Secure Socket Layer (SSL) or Internet Protocol Security (IPsec).<br>▶ In addition, SOAP messages can be protected according to the XML encryption standard. |
| Service messages could be received and forwarded by unauthorized users (replay, denial-of-service attack). | ▶ An initial measure is to encrypt network connections using SSL or IPsec.<br>▶ The time stamp of the SAML token (assertion) can be evaluated upon Single Sign-On (SSO) authentication and SOAP messages that are invalid with regard to time can be filtered using the `NotBefore` and `NotOnOrAfter` attribute of the SSO assertion.<br>▶ The data integrity of SOAP messages can be protected using digital signatures according to the XML Digital Signature Standard. |
| Wrong service messages could be added and transferred (impersonation). | ▶ An initial measure is to encrypt network connections using SSL or IPsec.<br>▶ Non-authorized SOAP messages can be filtered by creating a SAML correlation to a previous message using the `InResponseTo` SAML attribute.<br>▶ The data integrity of SOAP messages can be protected using digital signatures according to the XML Digital Signature Standard. |
| Service messages could be received and deleted without authorization. | ▶ SOAP messages can be filtered by being put into context with other messages and creating a SAML correlation to previous messages using the `InResponseTo` SAML attribute. |
| Service messages can be received, modified, and forwarded without authorization (high risk of falsification of the message's authentication and authorizations). | ▶ An initial measure is to encrypt network connections using SSL or IPsec.<br>▶ The data integrity of the SOAP messages can be protected using digital signatures according to the XML Digital Signature Standard. |

**Table 7.2** Selected Risks and Possible Countermeasures for SOAP Messages during Transfer in the Network

| Threat/Risk | Security Measure |
| --- | --- |
| Service messages could be caught (man-in-the-middle attack). | ▸ An initial measure is to encrypt network connections using SSL or IPsec.<br>▸ A time stamp (SAML token, assertion) added to the message can be evaluated when the SSO SAML assertion is evaluated using the `NotBefore` and `NotOnOrAfter` attributes. Messages that are invalid with regard to time can be filtered.<br>▸ Mutual authentication of the communication partners supports the measures mentioned. |

**Table 7.2** Selected Risks and Possible Countermeasures for SOAP Messages during Transfer in the Network (Cont.)

Because business processes at the enterprise service level always store data or process transaction results in a database, another data security aspect must be considered — data integrity. Databases, for example, those of the producer and customer, must include the correct data entries related to the process when a specific transaction is completed. Data irregularities have to be eliminated.

To do this, SAP has designed three concepts that provide an important prerequisite for ensuring reliable data transfer and avoiding data irregularities:

- **Synchronous processes**
  Enterprise services run as synchronous processes. Therefore, a service is executed directly and not stored temporarily. A service consumer sends a request to a service provider and waits for confirmation. During this phase, the service consumer cannot send requests to other service providers or a new request to the same service provider. This is a critical feature supported by SAP NetWeaver PI.
- **Full completion**
  Executing an enterprise service always results in the data transaction being fully completed and in a data entry in the database (atomic transaction).
- **Statelessness**
  Data is only stored in the database, and data or transaction information is not stored at the service or application level. Accordingly, enterprise services are characterized by statelessness.

### 7.2.3 Security Guidelines for SAP Enterprise Services

If a service provider sends a SOAP message to a service consumer, the service provider does not know how the service consumer receives, evaluates, and processes this message. Queries would be ineffective. However, in the context of service-oriented architectures this should not be necessary, because they promise " open" communication.

The service provider adds additional information to the SOAP message; in other words, the service provider provides information on the service that explains to the service consumer how it can interact with the service provider or SOAP message and under what conditions the service or message can be used. This necessity of avoiding queries and providing proactive instructions also applies to security. For example, a web service or SAP Enterprise Service must be able to inform the service consumer that authentication or data encryption is necessary to use the service.

This concept is implemented using the WS-Policy. This policy contains behavior rules and instructions that define under what conditions a web service or enterprise service can be used. This concept is relevant to security and risk management of enterprise services and should be implemented. The policy is directly implemented when a service and the SOAP messages are programmed in XML: For example, security-relevant conditions for SOAP messages are formulated and programmed using security standards, such as WSS10, WSS11, WS-Trust, and WS-SecureConversation.

A security example is the requirement that a specific encryption or authentication method has to be used. An enterprise service consumer would therefore not be able to use this kind of service if they cannot use the required method for authentication or meet the encryption requirement. So a WS-Policy defines that data must be encrypted if a web service is used, for example. Two policy alternatives for the encryption algorithm are provided:

- RSA as an asymmetric cryptographic algorithm
- DES as an symmetric cryptographic algorithm

From a program perspective, using these algorithms is defined as an assertion in the WS-Policy. In this case, this would be an asymmetric or symmetric cryptographic algorithm. Listing 7.2 shows an example of such a policy in which these specific conditions for encryption algorithm must be met:

```
<wsp:Policy
 xmlns:sp="http://schemas.xmlsoap.org/ws/2005/07/securitypolicy"
 xmlns:wsp="http://schemas.xmlsoap.org/ws/2004/09/policy">
  <wsp:ExactlyOne>
    <sp:Basic256Rsa15/>
    <sp:TripleDesRsa15/>
```

```
  </wsp:ExactlyOne>
</wsp:Policy>
```

**Listing 7.2** Syntax of a Simple WS-Policy with Two Alternative Encryption Algorithms

The following lines in Listing 7.2 are particularly interesting:

- Policy statement: all criteria of the policy must be met (`<wsp:Policy xmlns:wsp="..." xmlns:sp="...">`).
- Assertion: asymmetric encryption, using a public key to encrypt the document according to the AES algorithm (`<sp:Basic256Rsa15/>`)
- Assertion: symmetric encryption, using a symmetric key to encrypt the document three times according to the TripleDes algorithm (`<sp:TripleDesRsa15/>`)

A security gap of WS-Policies is that a policy could be changed if a SOAP message was caught during transfer and its security guidelines were modified or softened. For example, the requirement for consumer authentication or data encryption could cease. To close this security gap, you must use WS-Security functions. The WS-Policy itself, tokens, and policy assertions can be protected against unauthorized modifications using digital signatures. The OASIS security standard for web services provides the means required for programming (OASIS Standard 1.3, *http://docs.oasis-open.org/ws-sx/ws-securitypolicy/v1.3/ws-securitypolicy.html*).

Using these program-technical options effectively to implement process control objectives, requires cooperation between the business process owner, the person responsible for application security, and the XML programmer. The goal of this cooperation is to identify and define necessary security criteria and implement them in program code. Table 7.3 provides an overview of the resulting responsibilities.

| Function | Responsibility |
|---|---|
| Business process owner | Identification and determination of the necessary process controls and criteria for compliance with auditing guidelines |
| Person responsible for application security and authorizations | Assessment of the risk, integration of the control objectives, criteria, and guidelines with the available models of WS-Policy, security, and data security, and including the enterprise services security in the overall application security concept |
| Developers and programmers for XML, WSDL, or web services | Development of XML or SOAP content considering the specifications of the overall business security concept |

**Table 7.3** Responsibilities for the Development of Enterprise Services

The WS-Policy allows for specifying critical security functions and for appropriately adapting the data and processing security-to-business requirements. As for all security functions usage and configuration issues, the positive support of business processes strongly depends on a clear definition of risks and security requirements. The additional effort involved will definitely lead to subsequent cost reductions and increased efficiency with regard to processes, process security, and troublefree audits.

## 7.3 Service-Oriented Architectures and Governance

You can only create and introduce an effective security concept if the risk has been assessed accordingly and clear guidelines and requirements have been formulated on the business process side and reconciled with the feasible security-technical options. The result must be a balanced security concept that raises the remaining risk to an acceptable level. This process can be complicated, time-consuming, and expensive. However, there are management methods available to make this process more effective.

This includes good coordination of the various processes, intensive risk management, and effective management of the development objects and their documentation with instructions and rules on standardization and its compliance. With these methods, independent and different development objects can interact effectively with each other. And this exact scenario is given when enterprise services are developed or used. If you think of enterprise services as independent, free modules that can be selected at certain times, interact temporarily, and provide targeted results, the result depends on if these modules are compatible, how their functions supplement each other, and how they are reconciled with each other. This requires a uniform concept for managing the modules and functions. This concept must ensure that existing and newly developed enterprise services can cooperate with the various applications and systems now and in future.

To ensure that guidelines that have been agreed upon are adhered to and implemented in a future-oriented, productive, and effective way, you need a comprehensive, managing activity. The "governance" concept describes this process and is part of risk management for business processes that are executed using enterprise services. However, governance is not solely restricted to this, it also applies across the company and across IT and business processes, including integrated security concepts. Some of the general governance characteristics of enterprise services include:

- Business processes are optimally designed according to a uniform concept and well documented.

- Design rules for services are adapted to the business process requirements, standardized, and well documented.
- Design rules contain criteria and guidelines for information security, controls and audits, process components, business objects, interfaces, global data types, transaction behavior, structure of the SOAP message, and service implementation.
- Design rules are used consistently and permanently for the development, design, and implementation of new services.
- A uniform benchmark is developed and used to assess the efficiency of service implementations and service interdependencies with other applications.
- A holistic perspective exists during the development of an enterprise service considering the requirements of service reusability and potential future functions and requirements to optimize the number of services that are supposed to be newly developed.
- Business process owners directly cooperate with service developers and those responsible for information security to define process requirements and the concept of a uniform technical implementation considering future requirements, if possible.

This kind of uniform governance for developing and using enterprise services is a basic prerequisite for a successful implementation of service-oriented architectures. Successful governance provides the following benefits:

- Services that are designed according to accepted, standardized rules make it easier to meet the requirements of business process, audit, and controls and to achieve business process management objectives.
- Services can be reused in various applications.
- During the development phase of enterprise services, developers are more efficient if they adhere to uniform guidelines.
- Developed enterprise services are coherent within defined interfaces, information security environments, and general versatility in usage (global data types, uniform authentication or encryption method, for example).
- A uniform concept for information security is supported in heterogeneous systems, for example, using end-to-end encryption.
- Integration with system landscapes of global business partners or customers is easier.

In summary, and referring to enterprise services, you can say that governance affects the following aspects of the enterprise services concept (see Table 7.4).

| Aspect | Effect |
|---|---|
| Service structure | Governance affects the development, integration, and usage guidelines for the service structure:<br>The number of elements that determine the service within the process model should be kept to a minimum. |
| SOA infrastructure | Governance affects usage guidelines:<br>The connection and interface concept that enables the usage and use in operation of web services should be developed considering an overall business perspective and the system landscape. This supports a coherent implementation of business process and IT guidelines. |
| Service registration | Governance affects service management guidelines:<br>Web services must be managed according to uniform guidelines. This requires that the service within the infrastructure is registered in the Enterprise Services Repository according to an internal standard (specified via UDDI). The goal is effective access (automatic and manual) to the web service from generally accessible interfaces. |
| Interaction with communication partners | Governance affects access and process guidelines:<br>Guidelines for access to web services and execution processes that are based on web services must be consistently designed and implemented for all communication partners of the SOA infrastructure. All users of the service adhere to the required guidelines for the interaction with and usage of the service. |

**Table 7.4** Governance Aspects for Services

The goal of business governance for the IT and processes is a coherent concept with uniform guidelines for implementing information security and managing risks. This is especially critical for the transition to service-oriented architectures when business processes are modeled using enterprise services, and their design eventually affects business performance, remaining risks, and compliance.

*This chapter provides an overview of the most essential Governance, Risk, and Compliance (GRC) solutions within SAP BusinessObjects and their application areas. You learn how to approach Enterprise Risk Management (ERM) topics, corporate governance, risk management, and legal compliance, with the support of SAP.*

# 8 GRC Solutions in SAP BusinessObjects

Not only is the functional information technology (IT) support of business processes an essential characteristic for differentiating companies, but so is the security within company-internal processes and the strategic goals using IT. SAP has recognized this and invested in both external tools and software products and a considerable share in custom developments to protect business processes and applications.

As a result, solutions for GRC have emerged that bear the name SAP BusinessObjects. They provide a solution portfolio for company-wide SAP risk management in corporate governance, risk control, and legal compliance.

The following sections describe the basic concepts of the GRC solutions in SAP BusinessObjects in theory and document them using examples.

## 8.1 Introduction and Functions

The tools that are provided with the GRC solutions of SAP BusinessObjects can be used individually or as parts of a holistic GRC solution. They support you in evaluating SAP-internal and company-wide risks, and in controlling them. By using the appropriate measures, you can see a substantial improvement of your previous situation.

In this context, SAP relies on the three main areas of enterprise risk management:

- The correct and controlled management of the company and its areas
- knowledge of the company risks and how to reduce or remove them via security measures

- The acknowledgement of regulatory or legal specifications and their implementation within the organization

By integrating the individual parts, the GRC solutions in SAP BusinessObjects provide the option to include SAP applications and other systems and areas in the risk consideration to implement an effective, comprehensive, and sustainable company-wide risk control system.

The influence of information and information technologies on day-to-day business processes, which no longer need to be evaluated only in-house, requires solutions that are integrative; can be implemented relatively quickly; whose functions are basically transparent, but comprehensive; feature a robust technology; and are user-friendly for administrators, users, and managers.

### 8.1.1 Goals of the GRC Solutions in SAP BusinessObjects

Protecting company and organizational values is the main goal for using GRC solutions in SAP BusinessObjects. The security for information and processes, which are processed with SAP support, is the focus of activities whereas non-SAP systems can be integrated. The main focus is on information, person-related data, transactions, process chains, applications, and systems.

Industry-specific and legal compliance requirements are also taken into account and evaluated when considering risk aspects such as country-specific legal regulations or internal guidelines. To do this, in addition to industry solutions, SAP offers special GRC components for individual areas.

Other goals involve protecting the organization and employees, and using measures to protect the environment and health of people, and safeguarding the constant development of the company in a socially acceptable and secure environment. By automating control measures and processes, you improve both the work results and drastically relieve the employees responsible for controls in the security area. The improved results of the work processes, in turn, have a positive effect on downtime and reduce interruptions, which becomes noticeable as Return on Security Investments (RoSI).

The basic goals of governance, risk, and compliance go beyond the normal protection requirements of SAP systems both in theory and in practical use. Therefore, they lead to a holistic, standardized, and future-oriented enterprise risk management considering all needs and a transparent company management that complies with legal standards and industry-specific guidelines and with the necessary regional and global framework conditions. These framework conditions are increasingly derived from legislative decisions whose goal is an ideal company.

Ideal companies are not driven by making short-term profits, they aim or medium-term success and the long-term existence of the company. Even though this situation is never reached completely, the strategic orientation and achievement of milestones can be supported using GRC solutions in SAP BusinessObjects. At the same time, general security goals apply, for example, safeguarding the continuity of business processes, creating a transparent and secure work environment, protecting the environment, and other factors that become increasingly important for achieving strategic company goals.

In the future, companies and organizations will be measured on considerably more criteria than just financial goals. These criteria, in turn, have influence on achieving and securing financial goals and must therefore be integrated with the overall solution together with the GRC measures.

### 8.1.2 Methods of the GRC Solutions in SAP BusinessObjects

You achieve the goals of the GRC solutions by establishing a regional or company-wide risk control system. You must therefore establish some basic information on risks that concern the company directly and indirectly. You should also include an evaluation and classification of the information. The basic information is determined by SAP's preliminary content-related contribution in the SAP and legal environment and must then be considered in a company-specific risk control database.

The content of this SAP BusinessObjects repository, also referred to as a GRC foundation or technology foundation, is processed with regard to organizational requirements and serves as the basis for control and security measures that must be defined depending on the strategic orientation and risk acceptance level of the respective level. This repository is the central data and structure repository used by all GRC solution components. Besides tools and documentation options for the embedded GRC workflows, you can also use the SAP BusinessObjects repository to integrate and develop custom and third-party solutions. So the repository retains all GRC data centrally.

Besides the application-technical support provided by the GRC solutions in SAP BusinessObjects, the solution portfolio already offers content specifications, for instance, in the SAP authorization area. The provision of standardized specifications for risks in an SAP environment aims at faster implementation of risk analyses, rapid definition of appropriate control measures, and setting up organizational and administrative control processes. These include design and change processes, and workflows for release, maintenance processes, and check specifications.

By integrating internal and external specifications and the application-technical support, the GRC solutions in SAP BusinessObjects directly influence the control design and their implementation and application via security measures. The selection of the methods and specific procedures offers a lot of freedom. As a result, this supports different measures and the design of these measures or the application-specific implementation and usage.

SAP BusinessObjects also offers the option to focus on specific areas or company parameters and process business data with the appropriate risk sorted by priorities. A successive implementation in internal control structures using GRC solutions is a practicable option to succeed gradually. This applies to both the partial use of GRC solutions in SAP BusinessObjects and to the comprehensive application in certain business areas. The project plan for the implementation is accompanied by measures for determining maturity levels. This means that the classification and the definition of priorities can be used to create a roadmap where the individual measures are defined and implemented geographically on the one hand and company-internal and departmental on the other hand.

### 8.1.3 Planning the Deployment of GRC Solutions in SAP BusinessObjects

Due to the number and versatility of security and compliance topics, problems usually arise with regard to coordination, financing, prioritization, responsibility, and other project and decision topics that necessitate an effective deployment of the GRC solutions. You achieve the best results in a holistic approach, but this entails the highest initial effort. In targeted security and control topics, only individual areas are considered without focusing on a holistic risk control system.

It is therefore advisable to develop a strategic concept that, on the one hand, describes all of the company goals and their risks and specifies the strategy for establishing an internal security system, and, on the other hand, ensures a practicable implementation. In many cases, practicable means that you need to concentrate on the essential aspects of the company parameters, important information, really critical processes, and objects and systems that are worth protecting to organize a plan that is sorted by priorities. Due to the complex information requirements, however, you must involve various departments in subprojects during the preliminary stages.

When you develop a proper SAP authorization concept, you not only include the SAP team or the authorization administrator, but also all concerned user departments, internal auditors, SAP specialists, risk managers, consultants, persons responsible for compliance, and so on to cover the information requirement in advance and obtain optimal results. Because some companies lack the required amount of discipline with regard to documenting work processes, design concepts, detail specifications, and the like, this lack must be compensated by an effective deployment of SAP BusinessObjects. This also influences proper reporting for both internal control and for the legally required external reporting of financial and business data of a company within a specific period of time.

If no conceptual clarity exists, deploying GRC solutions like those in SAP BusinessObjects is not recommended. To achieve a valuable benefit for the company and profitability, you first need to analyze the needs, areas of use, available personnel resources, cooperation of the departments, financial investment means, the Return on Security Investment Planning (RoSIP), and a description of the expected results; this is supplemented by internal sponsoring questions.

These preparatory measures support both the decision process and a better preparation and effective project implementation considering quality aspects and cost control. Because the GRC solutions in SAP BusinessObjects deliver a considerable value added for most company areas, you should also find options for financing such solutions and the related project costs in terms of cost-effectiveness, profitability, and security to allocate accruing initial costs to different cost objects.

It is absolutely essential to include all decision-makers, sponsors, and experienced consultants in the decision-making process and to be prepared at an early stage. Without management's consent, GRC projects will not succeed because the acquisition costs and the implementation effort are relatively high. However, not only the costs are decisive, but also the consistent implementation of the defined target objectives so that the qualities of the solutions can be worked out properly and applied in the company. Changing the ratio of manual controls in favor of automated processes and automatic controls alone considerably improves the financial consideration of such projects.

However, this only works if you have clear consent from the executive floor. Therefore, in addition to a careful cost/benefit list you should also define an appropriate goal for specific areas. This means that the value mustn't only be measured on the project's overall success, but must actually present a success for every participant, which can be demonstrated in advance. This increases the chances of a successful implementation of the GRC project with SAP BusinessObjects and leads to the correct and desired results.

### 8.1.4 Overview of the GRC Solutions in SAP BusinessObjects

SAP's solutions in governance, risk, and compliance comprise applications for risk management; process controls; authorization controls; handling foreign trade; and the work areas, environment, health, and work protection. Although SAP pursues an integrative approach, you can also deploy the GRC components separately and use them to solve specific problems. The following presents the five solution components; the subsequent sections of this chapter provide detailed descriptions for the individual solutions.

- **SAP BusinessObjects Risk Management (RM)**
  RM is the central framework for risk management methods that can be used globally in all business and other internal processes. The management and departments can specify control rules and keep them up to date when handling business information, and then integrate them with day-to-day decision processes. Risk management and governance are central topics of this solution.
- **SAP BusinessObjects Access Control (AC)**
  AC offers solutions for successfully creating authorization components for all SAP applications and ensures the definition, management, distribution, and control of all components that exist in an authorization structure, including roles, users, risk evaluations, and release processes. It takes into account functional requirements, critical transactions and transaction combinations, organizational assignments, and the integration of the design, implementation, and operation phases. Risk management, authorization and user administration, documentation, and segregation of duties are central topics of this solution.
- **SAP BusinessObjects Process Control (PC)**
  PC enables the evaluation and use of control steps at the process level. Moreover, it checks the effectiveness of using security measures and controls and forwards a summary to the RM component. Using PC, you can implement both automated and manual controls. Monitoring, evaluation, test scenarios, compliance controls, and documentation are the central topics of this solution.
- **SAP BusinessObjects Global Trade Services (GTS)**
  GTS supports all business processes that are directly or indirectly connected with the foreign trade activities of a company. The primary focus is on transactions relevant to imports and exports, trade guidelines, and company-internal requirements. Compliance with legal specifications and the control of financial risks are the central topics of this solution.
- **SAP Environment, Health, and Safety (EH&S)**
  Within the GRC portfolio, EH&S covers environmental protection/compliance, health protection, legal specifications, and governmental guidelines and internal security measures concerning occupational safety. It provides controls that are integrated with business activities and company processes. National and international guidelines, constant updating of the information level, and internal implementation of specifications and requirements are the core topics of this solution.

- **SAP BusinessObjects Sustainability Performance Management (SPM)**
  SPM is a solution of SAP for supporting companies in attaining sustainability goals like the improving the sustainability balance. For the first time, you can holistically enter and measure all action-relevant information on sustainability performance.

For the target components of the GRC solutions, that is, proper corporate governance and reporting (governance), risk management (risk), and legal compliance (compliance), a separation is not advisable because only the combination of these three parts is target-aimed (see Figure 8.1). The risk management includes the protection of company goals and values and the legal compliance requirements for proper corporate and business action and reporting. Because the noncompliance of statutory requirements itself presents a broad scope of different risks, the risk management — usually as the leading component — specifies the strategic and practical direction that the basis risks are defined and protected and with which priorities the risks are counteracted.

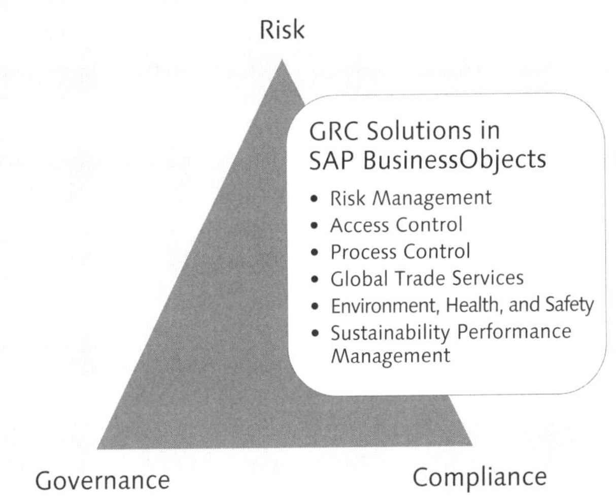


**Figure 8.1** Solution and Target Components of the GRC Solutions of SAP BusinessObjects

SAP BusinessObjects RM is the central collection of methods for process-related risk management, where all ERM activities concerning the company are entered, including compliance management. Besides the central storage of the risk repository, the active risk management is supported by integrated workflows that obtain the approval or denial of new risks from the persons responsible. This way, the information owners can be integrated with all risk control processes.

Nevertheless, the target components exist as equivalent task areas because every component can be both motivating and mandatory. The implementation and optimal use of the GRC solutions of SAP BusinessObjects therefore doesn't necessarily involve strategic decisions in real life, but can definitely show a solution path as an individual measure for specific, and local, control areas. This solution path then successively organizes the GRC integration throughout the company.

You can also use and configure internal controls in the standard version. These controls are deployed within SAP applications, for example, tolerance limits in the order process and in contract processing or price determination in sales processes. These configuration controls within the applications of SAP NetWeaver can be added to the GRC components and their use and benefits are controlled accordingly.

On the one hand, this increases the transparency of the existing internal controls, which are often used without any documentation, and, on the other hand, enhances the effectiveness if you know how to use these controls. If internal controls that have errors in the configuration are used or there are errors in the security application itself, you can take short-term measures or effect long-term changes promptly. Evaluations, checks, and reporting can be defined and used in the individual GRC solutions, but also via interfaces in SAP NetWeaver Business Intelligence (BI).

The use and close link of the individual GRC solutions in SAP BusinessObjects show the significance of how SAP as a manufacturer of company applications, ascribes to risk management in general and the proper company controls, legal compliance security, and the requirements with ecological and social relevance, in particular. The proportionality of using resources of any kind and their effective utilization within a globally, regionally, and nationally controlled rule system not only advances the general security interests, but also promotes the useful handling of internal and external resources within the organizations — and they are an essential component of protecting the value of a company. SAP will further advance the integration of individual GRC components and provide open interfaces for the simpler integration of third-party systems and applications — also with regard to service-oriented architectures (SOAs) that find their way into more and more system landscapes.

SAP has laid the foundation for the integrated and centrally organized risk management that is established throughout the company and is now one of the promoters of proper corporate governance and control at the international level. It can be assumed that the solutions will be gradually enhanced with further components and functions, particularly with regard to the integration of all SAP applications, third-party systems, and technologies that enable you to map company structures practically and provide solutions that can be accepted by the market.

## 8.2 SAP BusinessObjects RM

SAP BusinessObjects RM deals with the company-wide presentation of risks. SAP provides you with a platform for a standardized evaluation of risk potentials and implications for company entities so that you can obtain an overview of your present situation and initiate countermeasures, if required. ERM is one of the most essential systems in an organization to protect company assets by fending off short-term attacks and long-term erroneous developments and to ensure the continuous development of the company success.

Enterprise risk management becomes the essential instrument for securing the company's success. Corporate actions must include the consistent consideration of all risks that can sustainably negatively influence company performance. A critical cause for this situation involves the different risk types and the different areas of responsibility that are confronted with the respective risk. It is therefore not surprising that most organizations don't establish an appropriate global risk management. Also, the heterogeneous system landscapes in most companies make it more and more difficult to identify and evaluate risks in a holistic and organized manner and design all information transparently in this regard.

Risk considerations are not only relevant to the c-level management of a company, but they must also be integrated every day with the work processes at the individual levels and in the organizational departments. Only by using supporting solutions and tools is a company's management able to implement risk evaluations effectively, anticipatorily, and appropriately to achieve a comprehensive reduction of existing risks, and to react appropriately in case of an emergency.

### 8.2.1 Main Components

The initial screen of SAP BusinessObjects RM shows the following components (see Figure 8.2):

- **My Home**
  Custom activities, for example, assigned activities for processing risk management tasks, are available on the My Home tab.
- **Risk Assessment**
  All essential activities for entering, classifying, and defining appropriate control measures can be found in Risk Assessment.

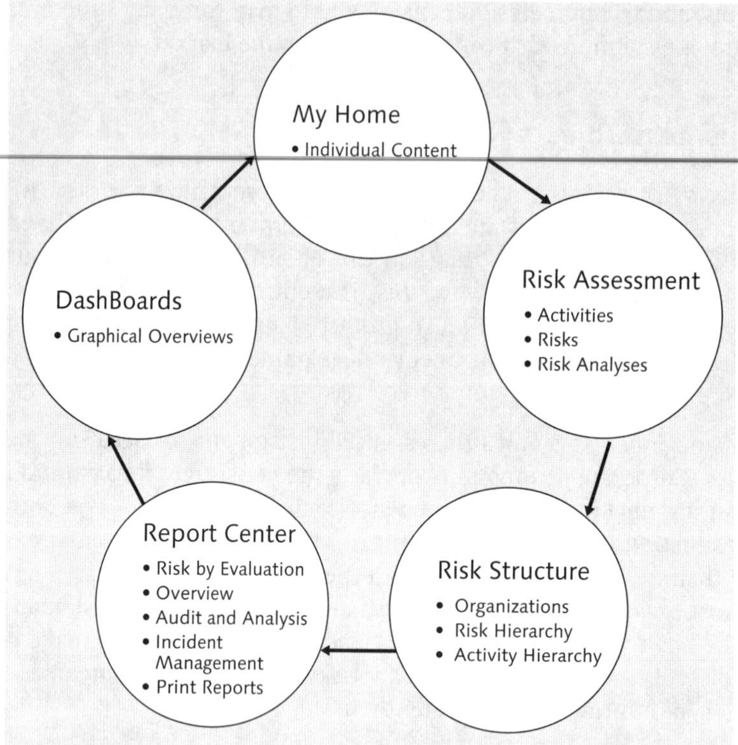


**Figure 8.2** Main Components of SAP BusinessObjects Risk Management

- **Risk Structure**
  The organizational, risk, and activity structure is created and maintained in RISK STRUCTURE.
- **Report Center**
  In REPORT CENTER, you can find the standard reports and restrict access to them using authorizations.
- **Dash Boards**
  In the DASH BOARDS, you can compile views and authorize evaluation functions.

### 8.2.2 Phases

Understandably enough, you can't always monitor all of the risks of a company all of the time, particularly if it involves a comprehensive and company-wide consideration that also includes external influencing factors like market and political risks. For this reason, a practicable approach can ensure the transparency and capacity to act on the basis of predefined Key Risk Indicators (KRI). The necessary risk management process comprises the following steps (see Figure 8.3):

- Planning
- Identification and Analysis
- Measures
- Monitoring

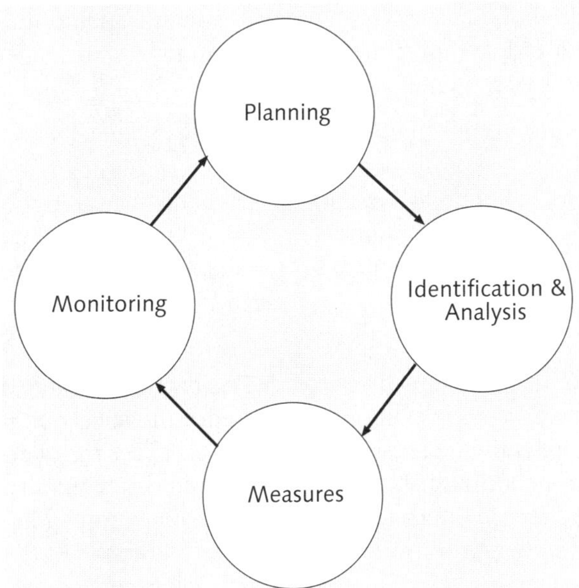


**Figure 8.3** Risk Management Components in SAP BusinessObjects Risk Management

Because in most cases the identification and assessment of risks are very close in terms of time, the following sections describes the identification and analysis of risks as one combined phase, even if the risk determination, the risk evaluation, and subsequent classification can be managed as different responsibilities. The initial methodology and enthusiasm with which risk management is established determine the character, and therefore the success, of the initiated controlling measures.

### Planning

Planning is the goal definition phase. During risk planning, you make the necessary basic statements and set them in the risk management organization. This involves you specifying the risk acceptance level using threshold values.

The planning phase aims at specifying the control areas and determining the sequence of the processing steps. This usually starts without SAP BusinessObjects RM, though the planning process is supported. Here, you should define clear goals for protecting company assets and specify these goals within the scope of the strategy for a company-wide risk management sorted by priorities.

The motivation for starting a structured risk management project is either the insight into the changing conditions of the market and of the strong influence of unforeseen events or far-reaching and substantial external auditing reports. Therefore, you mustn't only deal with individual topics. Moreover, you must determine the user departments and organizational units that contribute to the risk management strategy or delegate project team members.

The planning phase aims at determining the goals and a company's protection requirement. The objective analysis and protection requirements analysis described in Section 8.1, Introduction and Functions, are essential instruments for determining the company goals and the protection requirement. The risks of a company orient not only toward IT-relevant financial problems, but also toward a multitude of objectively existing risk groups, which must be subjected to an evaluation in another phase.

In planning, you should realize that you already made a decision with regard to priorities and process scenarios here. According to this, besides the subsequent identification, the planning phase is the most important prerequisite for the overall success in setting up a well-functioning risk management. To do this, you must define clear protection goals and classify them according to qualitative or quantitative evaluation criteria that not only orient toward the immediate situation of the company, but primarily include medium-term and long-term development criteria in the evaluation. Here, different approaches are possible to achieve the goal.

Because this phase has an initial and basic character, the active and central support of management is a critical prerequisite for success. It is recommended to consult external consultants to determine the company assets and strategic necessities required for the procedure and solution determination to support the risk planning process. Strategies like Management of Risk (M_o_R) help companies define their strategic goals in risk management and derive or develop the necessary control solutions.

For example, based on the ERM Navigation Control Map (see Chapter 6, Enterprise Risk Management Navigation Control Map), you can create a checklist to include risk areas and their evaluation. Information on risk areas like enterprise financial and commercial risks, market risks, environmental compliance risks, organizational and change management risks, information technology risks, and so on are first collected and then evaluated in an impact scorecard. The goal of this evaluation not only includes the risk areas immediately concerned, but you also identify and classify political, social, and geographical risk groups.

The purpose of determining risk goals and categories is the subsequent automation and holistic company-wide implementation of the risk management processes by the participating departments and the identification of the presentation options and the interval for management reports.

### Identification and Analysis

After you've stored the results of the planning phase in SAP BusinessObjects RM, the risk identification phase is used to identify and analyze the threats, influencing factors, probabilities of occurrence, and other factors to determine the relevance of the threats to the company's success. In threat and risk analysis, you identify, evaluate, and assess the risks. A company-wide catalog for identifying, rating, and classifying the risks for all previously determined risk areas is defined and stored in SAP BusinessObjects RM. The amount of damage that a threat can trigger is an essential aspect for determining the risk classification.

With regard to the high-quality assessment of a specific threat, you should also consider development factors. For example, political, environment-relevant, or compliance risks can have a stronger or weaker impact on the threat potential depending on the development of the threat factors.

In the evaluation process, you can also find factors that have a stronger influence on the threat and thus exert a positive or negative influence on the direct company risk. Market risks, for example, are influenced by a variety of factors. These factors in turn, either individually or collectively, then define the market risk. Both are possible in SAP BusinessObjects RM.

Beyond that, it is of vital importance to define each risk with a numeric value. The specification of a quantifiable value is important for the significance of the evaluation quality itself and thus determines the chances of success for the evaluation. Besides the financial evaluation, a qualified qualitative evaluation is also important in the security environment. The noticeable improvement of the security level via appropriate control measures can only be achieved if the risks are known and assessed as objectively as possible.

Today, company risks not only arise from internal processes and actions. Risks can also be found in the environment of a company, in political reactions to products and commercial activities, changes in legal and other specifications, production behavior, and moral considerations.

In risk determination, you differentiate risks that result from the work and the information in the systems affected, for example, SAP applications, and the risks that must be evaluated outside the applications and systems. SAP BusinessObjects RM provides the option for intuitively managed and collaboratively supported areas to include and handle risks in a standardized form.

**Note**

Chapters 1, Risk and Control Management, and 2, ERM Strategy, discuss risk management strategy and the various analyses in detail.

### Measures

In the measures phase, you specify the control and security measures for a specific risk. In doing so, you determine control categories and controls, which also include an evaluation of different solutions in this area.

For an effective and financially profitable investment in security measures you always need to know the risks and the level of acceptance in your company. The risk management culture in general must definitely improve in the international business world. The decision on certain solutions will nevertheless be determined by economic factors to justify investments in this area.

SAP BusinessObjects RM provides the option to support decisions in favor of or against specific control measures with individual or overall responsibility. Furthermore, many risks, or even entire risk areas, can be covered with a specific control instrument. The SAP authorization system is one of the essential central control instruments. With this system, you can implement and centrally manage a variety of individual controls for individual risks in the case of an employees' access to information (which is necessary due to the job) and activities in the work processes.

Conversely, in SAP BusinessObjects RM you have the option of assigning multiple control measures to one specific risk. This might be the case if the risk entails a rather high degree of damage potential and therefore can be controlled through additional security measures.

The risk measures when control and security mechanisms for reducing risk, fending threats, and continuous monitoring can no longer be mastered manually due to the high number of threats. Without an automation of all security processes within the company, you cannot effectively protect company assets and ensure that the company goals are met.

The holistic consideration of all control and security measures leads to a selection of suitable control instruments and solutions to avoid or reduce a high number of risks with an optimal amount of costs. The ratio of benefit and costs of a specific security solution can therefore only be usefully assessed after a proper consideration of the risks and control options. For this reason, an approach involving project stages that build on one another is of high significance. Here, the success really depends on the course and the completeness of the processing objects.

Measures, besides the definition of upstream and downstream individual controls, also require the establishment of all security-relevant control processes ranging from acknowledgement of risks and their evaluation and dealing through control measures to the setup of warning systems and alert messages in the company. SAP BusinessObjects RM actively and automatically supports these processes in the monitoring component.

### Monitoring

Monitoring uses the information collected from the initial phases and includes it in a system of security measures. To do this, SAP provides automated workflow functions to provide employees and managers the option of monitoring the risk level, the effectiveness of control measures, the integration of new risks, and a prompt response. If the information, which consists of single values and consolidations, is used consistently and updated proactively, it leads to a noticeable improvement of the security level within the company, to a culture of adequate self-control, necessary monitoring, and effective use of resources to sustainably protect the values.

Another aspect of the continuous improvement of control measures and processes entails the integration of damages or attacks with the evaluation of the measures' effectiveness, thus the change of these measures with regard to the deployment, usage, and methodological evaluation. The effectiveness of control measures is an important method for the financial evaluation of security solutions and their degree of influence on the reduction of risks. To do this, you must use the SAP BusinessObjects RM analysis functions like scorecards and dashboards with graphical information processing.

Monitoring also includes the individual evaluationfor the individual persons responsible. You can create watch lists that monitor specific areas of the risk control system from the risk catalogs. This lets you transfer the risk responsibilities to organizational areas and control them automatically.

Due to the possibility of disproportionality, in this context you must also consider social, labor law–related, and ethic-moral problems, which are only indicated briefly at this point. Thanks to the new transparency of company performance, protective factors, potential risks, and communication you create a foundation of trust that enables a comprehensive monitoring on a reasonable basis without violating the rights of individuals. This results in a new quality of the enterprise risk management not only within SAP systems but also beyond.

### 8.2.3 Responsibilities

SAP BusinessObjects RM offers a risk management organization that manages the responsibilities in the risk management processes. The risk management organization is part of the risk control system. In the standard version, this organization defines the following risk management user roles, which can be restricted to organizational areas (see Figure 8.4):

- **Organization owner**
  The employee with the ORGANIZATION OWNER role can implement organizational assignments of authorizations within SAP BusinessObjects RM.
- **Risk manager**
  The RISK MANAGER usually determines the risks for their area in the SAP solution and can create security-relevant projects. In doing so, in addition to the risks they also implement activities in the system, which can represent a project, a process, or a risk object. In this context, the objects involve all elements to collect or illustrate a specific situation.

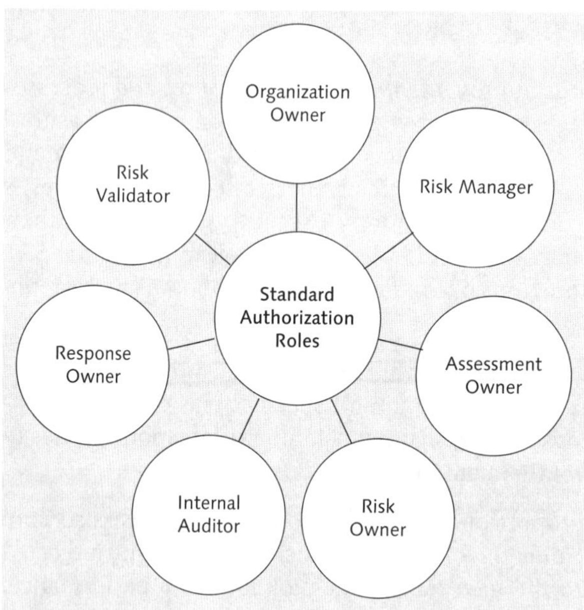


**Figure 8.4** SAP BusinessObjects Risk Management — Standard Authorization Roles

- **Assessment owner**
  The ASSESSMENT OWNERS assess the risks. They plan measures that were defined in cooperation with the risk owners.

Organization owners, risk managers, and assessment owners are responsible for the holistic risk management process, at least within their area of responsibility. The restriction is made via the authorization restrictions to specific activities.

- **Risk owners**
  A RISK OWNER is responsible for specific risks in their area and they define controlling measures or countermeasures for value protection. An authorization restriction to concrete risks is possible in this context.
- **Internal auditor**
  The INTERNAL AUDITOR authorization role is assigned to an employee that assumes controlling tasks with regard to the compliance of security processes, identified risks, and established controls.
- **Response owner**
  Control measures for a specific work or organizational area are coordinated, initiated, and monitored by a RESPONSE OWNER. Therefore, the response owner is of special significance. Just as with the authorization concept, there must be a concept available to distribute responsibilities concerning control measures that extend over the entire company. These responsibilities must be coordinated centrally and executed decentrally.
- **Risk validator**
  These central monitoring and coordination tasks are most likely assigned to the RISK VALIDATOR, who must check, approve, and possibly reject the risks received so that postprocessing or other actions can be implemented.

The roles for risk management can be supplemented or extended with any other functions. You also have the option to create new risk management roles to reflect the security and control processes in the company and the structure of the organization.

The roles can be assigned to existing users as part of their job. This particularly applies if employees are responsible not only for their own task areas in their business departments, but also for the risks and controls in this area. An example would be the human resources (HR) department, which must know, assess, and handle risks on data protection and personnel responsibility.

However, the risk management authorization roles can also be used by persons whose main task involves activities in the risk management process. These users include, for example, chief security officers, risk management officers, internal auditors, and external employees that support the creation of the risk management process, such as, consultants, external auditors, service providers, software providers, and technical experts. They can all obtain access to SAP BusinessObjects RM through a specific authorization role, although this should only be a limited time. The authorization roles are assigned to users of the solution who can then access the web applications via a URL link.

### 8.2.4 Reporting

Besides the SAP BusinessObjects repository and another alternative for mapping an organizational and hierarchical structure, SAP BusinessObjects RM also provides numerous control and evaluation functions in the form of reports, which are already preset in the standard version. Other reports can be adjusted or created as required. The reports always indicate the respective status of the risks. The integration of workflows enables the collaboration of the risk management users in the risk management process.

SAP BusinessObjects RM is SAP's central solution tool to consistently determine and handle company risks via a central repository. This lets you deploy risk management functions for a consistent enterprise risk management with a central control, decentral distribution, and across the system.

## 8.3 SAP BusinessObjects Access Control

The authorization system is the central and most essential security instrument for controlling employee accesses to transaction and master data, activities, and processes in an SAP environment. Due to the high number of transactions and functions in SAP systems, the control of authorizations occupies a special protection position because in most companies a major part of the company-relevant information is processed using SAP applications. Therefore, the control of user authorizations is of vital importance.

SAP BusinessObjects Access Control solves the problem of missing functional and content support for central control and role and user authorizations (also known as access control), including its design, creation, and administration processes. Moreover, the reporting that is required for proper company management and compliance is managed with regard to authorization checks (audits) both inside and outside the SAP system and put on a standardized basis.

### 8.3.1 General Requirements on the SAP Authorization System

The SAP authorization system controls SAP users' access to objects and events worth protecting. These objects worth protecting include, for example, master data, table data, and reports. Security-relevant events can involve transactions, transaction data, and actions. Users need these access rights to implement business processes like purchasing processes, order processes, contract creations, price determinations, and personnel activities using SAP applications.

### Authorization Goals

According to this, the authorizations specify the rights defined for a job to access data, activities, and organizational units. Authorizations can be assigned to individual users or to groups of users. The assignment of work-related user rights requires you to map the organizational structures defined in the company and the segregation of duties using the authorization system.

You must define the segregation of duties in advance based on the current and future situation of the department or company. The reasons for segregation of duties or authorization restrictions can usually be found in the risks, which can result from overly broad rights, or from organizational necessity.

Figure 8.5 shows an overview of the influencing factors for SAP authorizations.

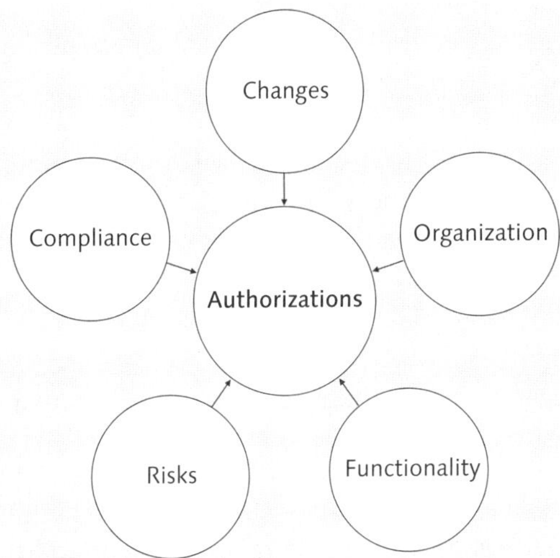


**Figure 8.5** Requirement Objects That Influence SAP Authorizations

### Access Control Components

Chapter 20, Authorizations in SAP ERP, provides a detailed description of the authorization system with all of the main components and risks. At this point, we'll only look at the most essential components for SAP BusinessObjects Access Control:

- **Authorization objects with authorization fields**
  Authorization objects define the check elements in the ABAP code of a program and are part of the authorization checks and authorization assignment. These involve templates for the authorization check and authorization creation.
- **Authorizations with authorization fields and values**
  Authorizations with authorization fields and values are part of the controls and authorization roles. They are defined by the authorization values. Here, you define the check on one hand and the access rights on the other.
- **Authorization profiles with authorizations**
  Authorization profiles are the link between authorizations and authorization roles and include defined authorization objects.
- **Authorization roles with authorization profiles**
  Authorization roles are used for creating and assigning authorizations. They comprise the authorizations that are supposed to be assigned to users in collected form.
- **Authorization composite roles with authorization roles**
  Authorization composite roles represent a collection of roles to obtain a specific type of user management. They are assigned directly to users.
- **Authorization role types**
  Authorization role types, such as functional main and auxiliary roles or value roles present a design form of the authorization structure. The authorization system leaves a lot of freedom for the procedure and type of structuring and coupling authorization components. Authorization roles depend considerably on the design and the strategic orientation toward the authorization concept.
- **Special authorization components**
  Besides the assignment of authorization roles, there are various subordinate and parallel authorization components that you can configure either separately or in conjunction with roles for special authorization checks. These can be authorization groups, user groups, field groups, reports, or tables. Special authorization components are an essential part of the authorization concept and of the SAP system's control options.
- **Control elements**
  You can use control elements like organizational authorization objects to check different elements in the SAP system. For transparency and effectiveness reasons, it is recommended to handle the control elements on the basis of risk analysis with care.

- **Risks**
  Risks can be critical transactions and combinations of transactions. In this context, this is also referred to as the segregation of duties risk. Critical transactions should therefore be known and assigned to users via roles in a controlled manner. Transaction combinations must be considered during creation and the continuous maintenance that is necessary for practical operation.
- **Users with user master records**
  User master records comprise authorization roles and special presets that are relevant to a specific user.
- **User types**
  User types such as dialog users, technical system users, or communications users characterize the type of users assigned a user ID. Different tasks require different user types, for instance, batch users for background processing.
- **User groups**
  User groups, such as basic users, business department users, or transactional users, are used for the organizational or authorization assignment of users to user groups. The authorization usage leads to an assignment of users to user authorization groups.
- **Profile Generator**
  The SAP Profile Generator is the main tool for mapping roles in the SAP system. The combination of SAP BusinessObjects Access Control and SAP NetWeaver Identity Management (IdM) also offers tools for role creation.

### Specifications and Standards

An important category of requirements determines legal regulations, industry specifications, security standards, and company guidelines that influence the initial design of the authorization components and their use in practical operation. Organizational changes, personnel fluctuations, business developments, seasonal fluctuations: Many of these influences require using authorizations in large SAP ERP systems. In most cases, authorizations are historically grown structures that have increased intransparently over the years and only come into the limelight in the case of focused external checks.

A majority of the medium and high risks that can be found somewhere in these systems are usually ignored, even less that the potential of an effective authorization design and management is recognized. The problems manifest in many different ways. In the authorization design, you often only consider the functional and organizational requirements without determining the risks, for example, transactional risks. This way, you can simplify the authorization project, but this leads to unsatisfactory results.

In user management, you usually enhance the authorizations without carefully checking the consequences and considering the solutions for optimizing or effectively using the user rights. As a result, authorization components, such as authorization roles, authorization profiles, and user master records, unnecessarily increase with regard to content and occurrence, and the users receive considerably more user rights than they normally need for their work.

Therefore, roles expand without restrictions, and these authorizations are assigned to users without sufficient checks. Auditors usually only check general risk points without taking into account the design structure and authorization management. This also applies to the check of custom developments. Over the years, SAP customers have developed their own programs and transactions that weren't always provided with the necessary authorization checks. Often, the persons involved, user departments, or authorization administrators don't even know which users have access to specific functions because the documentation isn't updated.

These and other problems result in insufficient authorization systems. Also, documentation on authorization changes, which are complex and completely contradictory to the insufficient authorization concepts, usually miss their target because the release processes are not established on a solid basis. Many organizations lack a basis to evaluate risks in roles and user master records. Users rely on the individual assessment of risks in the evaluation of whether authorizations may be granted to specific users or not without having a repository of critical transactions, risk-relevant transaction combinations, and corresponding rules at hand, which could be accessed manually — at least in the first step.

Accordingly, some of the decisions are not adequately founded. Moreover, there's a lack of knowledge about the requirements in other departments. Risks must be defined at different levels depending on the information content and the classification. The departments must feel responsible for the risk from/in their work area, for example, for data and processes. In addition, there must be a superordinate data basis to determine and evaluate risks in process chains and several applications and systems.

### Implementation Requirements

In terms of implementing authorizations, for some years there has been a strong development with regard to using new methods and options that have been provided by SAP for handling authorizations better. But there is a relatively large customer base that still hasn't found its way out of the long-established paths for the technical design and practical maintenance of roles and other authorization components.

For example, these customers ignore the check indicators required for the authorization check using the Profile Generator and don't maintain the USOBT/USOBX authorization tables accordingly in case of necessary changes. Missing authorization objects for roles are integrated manually into the authorizations without using the procedure that SAP has provided for the automated application.

### Work Processes

Another requirement from the working world: The extent of flexibility has increased from previous years. Due to temporary changes, work peaks, fluctuation, market fluctuations, project work, and other factors, the work process repeatedly demands temporary shifting or time-limited deployment of authorization extensions for a specific user group or usually for a specific individual user.

The SAP Basis department usually has the privilege to have unrestricted, very far-reaching authorizations because the users are supposed to be prepared for all eventualities with an anticipatory and responsible planning approach. Moreover, there are users, such as external employees, that are only supposed to receive authorizations for a specific period of time. There are authorizations that are required for troubleshooting in case of emergency. Vacation replacements are also affected by these requests. What these cases have in common is that they usually become necessary on short notice, are limited in time, and involve an authorization scope that is not precisely defined.

At best, authorizations specify who may view and change what and in which systems. There are various user types like dialog users or technical system users. For everyone involved the basic principle applies that the only authorizations that should be assigned are the ones actually required. In this context, you should still pursue a practicable approach. The aspect of risk consideration prior to the authorization creation or assignment is useful here because decisions on a complex authorization control or reduction can be avoided if the authorizations have little or no risks.

According to this, a correctly evaluated and established authorization system entails a high degree of optimization and cost reduction potential. Particularly for a difficult economic environment, it is essential to control expenses, reduce risks, and optimally utilize resources. Decisions and business processes must be optimized and use every potential for financial improvement of the company's performance.

### Solution Requirements

SAP offers alternatives in response to these problem areas. With SAP BusinessObjects Access Control you can integrate all of the requirement areas of a proper authorization design, although the solution is not only designed for SAP systems but also for non-SAP systems and applications. Therefore, the solution shifts SAP security to the superordinate area of enterprise risk management. Risk can be considered not only in an application, but holistically in the entire company, including non-SAP systems and applications. Moreover, the authorizations are no longer defined as isolated modules only for functional access to transactions and activities, but they also include the consideration of risks in the design and usage process and make this process useful for the first time.

The authorization system as the core component of the SAP control options goes beyond the pure function assignment and serves as an active control instrument for proper company management under automated consideration of risks and controls. Release changes for roles and user authorizations are now no longer brought to a new level by the individual knowledge of a single person, but by the automatic ability to check critical authorizations.

This makes the design and procedural application more secure, and it considerably improves the traceability, transparency, and ability to check. You can more easily check existing and historically grown authorization systems with regard to requirements. Some examples include:

- **Critical authorizations**
  These are available in the form of transactions, authorization objects, authorization object values, authorizations, or authorization profiles, for example, in the maintenance of master data transactions like user master data, supplier master data, or personnel master data.
- **Critical authorization combinations**
  These are available in the form of combinations of transactions, authorizations, or roles within a user master record, for example, in the maintenance of master and transaction data without internal controls or segregations of duties.

You can now also include the requirements of temporarily required authorizations with far-reaching user rights in classified design components and control processes without having to assign authorization profiles like `SAP_ALL` or `SAP_NEW` to the users in an uncontrolled way.

Put simply, the use of SAP BusinessObjects Access Control is based on a conformed structure of the organization with entities and other structure elements and rules for risks and control elements. The main benefit of SAP BusinessObjects Access Control can be found in the provision of information on risks in the SAP system in a solution suite, which helps to achieve a targeted control of authorization systems that already exist or need to be defined anew. SAP has predefined more than 200 control rules for this purpose; you can extend these rules when you use the solution and adapt them to your custom developments.

The predefined rule sets can also be supplemented with non-SAP information and then be configured to become a company-wide security and check tool for access control. The rules are then assigned to different commercial risks and therefore become transparent. This establishes the connection between technical application presentation and company-relevant and area-relevant presentation.

This presentation not only provides support for internal, external, and technical auditors, but it also guarantees a clear language for both the managers responsible and the specialists from the user departments and IT. In a manner of speaking, the experts from IT learn to translate their technical work into company-internal needs. The representatives of the departments quickly understand the technical implications of a functional or control-relevant specification.

One result of the developments in recent years includes the increasing influence of information technology and the associated merging with commercial and other activities of economic life. On the one hand, this deepens the knowledge in this area and, on the other hand, results in the further decrease of transparency, which is necessary but is more and more difficult to achieve without suitable measures and solutions. Solutions like SAP BusinessObjects Access Control help you to improve this situation.

### 8.3.2 Main Components

So what happens now? Via the launch pad you can navigate to the initial screen of the SAP BusinessObjects Access Control application. There are four main components displayed to the user (see Figure 8.6).

Before you get to know these four components in more detail in the following sections, it can already be said that you use SAP BusinessObjects Access Control to create, manage, change, document, and assign authorization structures considering the consistent view of the risks. You are provided with an important component to improve existing authorization systems and for active control. Both GRC-specific applications and standard functions are used in the SAP systems, for example, the Profile Generator (Transaction PFCG). This combination of new and proven technologies and functions gradually improves authorization problems in SAP applications and other non-SAP systems.

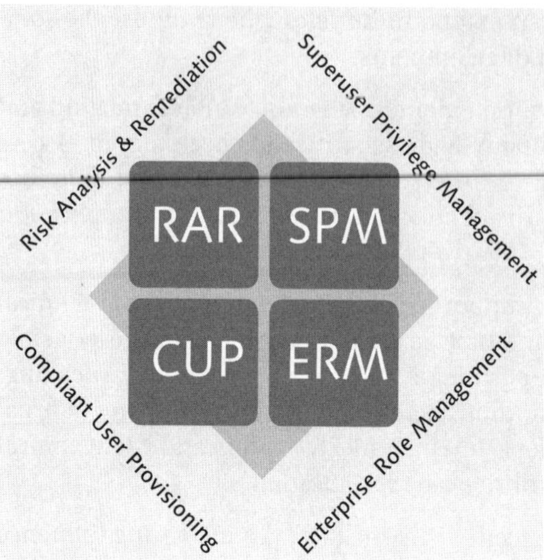


**Figure 8.6** SAP BusinessObjects Access Control — Main Components

### Risk Analysis and Remediation (RAR)

The RAR component in SAP BusinessObjects Access Control is primarily used to determine and analyze risks and to control SAP authorizations. By providing a comprehensive rule set, which defines functional authorization separations, information on the risks in the applications of SAP NetWeaver are made available that you can extend as required — even to non-SAP systems. In this context, tasks are mainly determined by segregations of duties. It is recommended to use a simple risk definition to ensure transparency even if the integration of many critical combinations with the RAR component is possible technically. Every change in the risk definitions in the system also entails an update of the associated check rules that were generated from the risks.

Based on the rules and a comprehensive report structure, you can audit the existing authorization systems for check-relevant events and analyze them for critical authorization combinations in the various authorization components, such as roles and user master records. So the analysis functions are critical elements of the solution component. The deployment in the check and analysis area is an essential target area for the RAR component. Moreover, there is the daily operational and administrative work with the application to support the decisions in the user provisioning process and other administrative processes that comprise a control function for authorizations. Without this help, you couldn't implement simulations within a reasonable period of time, for example. In addition, decisions such as release access rights and allocations to users would be less important, as is the case with the RAR component.

Based on a solid authorization basis (which must first be developed using a proper concept and holistic design), you can transparently present the authorization systems and keep them in a state of relative security with the support of the RAR solution. Existing authorization systems can be successively transferred to a well-functioning state-of-the-art target design and take recommendations into account. However, this is rather difficult without knowing the design options, but it can be supported by RAR on the risk side and implemented successively on the application side. The RAR solution not only attends to the controllers and auditors, but also to the employees of the authorization administration, the departments, and other participants that have direct or indirect influence on authorization creation, authorization distribution, and authorization usage.

#### Checks

For risk analyses and checks, you load the user, role, and authorization data from the systems to be checked into the RAR component. The reports can be summarized in different report types, for instance, reports at the user, role, and organizational level and for HCM objects. You can also implement evaluations, including the SAP Management of Internal Controls (MIC) function . For the implementation, and depending on the evaluation type and size of the report to be expected, you must decide whether the reports should be started in background processing. Here, it is important to include the background jobs in an authorization concept that is provided for this purpose and regulates naming conventions and the like.

#### Analyses

The analysis reports at the user level result in evaluations of the authorization situation in user master records because all individual components of Access Control are summarized for a specific user and constitute the total of authorizations. You can evaluate users individually or in groups. In general, the evaluations should always be implemented based on a specific risk to ensure the transparency and effectiveness of the respective evaluation. In principle, the evaluation always occurs for a specific system.

Evaluations at the organizational level are important to consider for specific organizational segregations that are controlled via authorization components. For authorizations including the HCM organizational structure, you can perform evaluations at the level of positions, work centers, and other defined HCM objects. Among other things, these evaluations are also interesting if further applications are used that require complex functional and technical authorization scenarios, for instance, the connection of SAP Customer Relationship Management (CRM), the SAP IS-U industry solution, and SAP ERP HCM.

Reports can be abstracted as executive summaries and prepared for management. The risk results are classified into risk levels, such as high, medium, or low risk. High risks entail a critical situation in a specific company area that can negatively influence the organization. This must be attended to immediately. Medium risks pose no immediate danger for the respective organizational unit or the company as a whole, but in the medium term increase the probability of damage and must therefore be reduced using countermeasures or at least sufficiently controlled.

There are four essential steps within the scope of processing the results of authorization analyses and checks:

1. You change the authorization components and differentiated assignments of access rights in user master records.
2. You specify compensating measures by including the risk(s), the associated documentation, and the controls in the RAR component. Here, you must differentiate the persons responsible as administrators, approvers, controllers, and risk owners.
3. After reevaluating, you accept the risks while taking into account the business data and organizational necessities or you decrease the level of risk.
4. You create automated alert messages.

Such defined control measures can always have a time limit.

**Benefits of RAR**

The following benefits are obvious if you use RAR:

- Jump start for setting up risk controls in the SAP authorization system
- Check support
- Preparation for risk-based authorization management
- Risk definition of violations of functional authorization segregations in compliance with principles such as the four-eyes principle
- Distribution of responsibilities within the organization
- Compliance with specifications of any kind relevant to user rights
- Analysis of authorizations assigned at the detail level
- Tracking of authorization violations within SAP applications and across the company in other non-SAP systems
- Reduction of the risk potential by recognizing the causes
- Control functions for managing, graphically formatted overviews and consolidated information

### Compliant User Provisioning (CUP)

The CUP component is a workflow component used to integrate a controlled workflow structure with the authorization assignments to users of SAP or non-SAP systems. In this context, you use information from both email systems and SAP applications and integrate it with an application and release process. Integrating personnel data, which can be used for activating authorization changes or creation processes, is a reasonable use of CUP to ensure a better process control of the application system.

The authorization assignment seems to be a simple work step. But it entails the definite assignment and allocation of authorizations to users of system applications. Information protection and other protection objects are at their peak here because users can now use their assigned authorizations to work, while others may be kept from work due to missing authorizations, or exploit overly broad authorizations to the company's disadvantage.

Therefore, special importance is placed on creating authorization components that are functionally sound and consider the risk, as they can be created using the RAR and ERM components in SAP BusinessObjects Access Control. In addition, it is also critical to control the assignment of these authorization components in a holistic management and control process that monitors the assignment of user rights in a standardized way and analyzes the release of these authorizations on the basis of the risk evaluation. In this process, the functional-organizational assessment and the risk relevance plays a role.

Figure 8.7 shows the relevant influencing factors for proper authorization assignments to users of SAP applications.

Besides the influencing factors already mentioned, there are several other important aspects that are necessary when considering the assignment of far-reaching user rights. This also includes the respective employee's level of training. For example, an authorization concept can comprise a stepwise assignment of rights that is based on the completion of specific training courses. Particularly in large, strongly networked companies, it is important to establish clear rules with regard to the employee's qualification level.

The different cases for user management show the need for controlled user management. The following lists some examples:

- There must be a general creation process for employees that join the company.
- A new user orientation must take place after the user changes from one department to another.

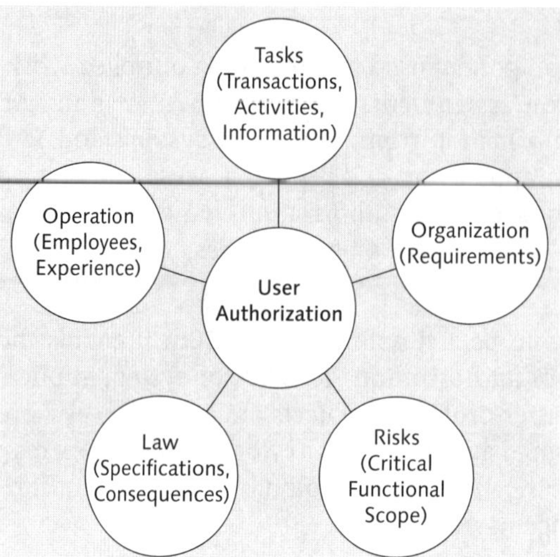


**Figure 8.7** Influencing Factors for User Authorizations

- Changes to authorizations are made from a functional perspective.
- Required function access is not granted in the existing roles.
- The required function access is granted, but erroneous.
- The required function access is only needed temporarily.
- The required function access is granted, but not to its full extent.
- The user temporarily leaves the company.
- The user leaves the company.
- The user accepts addition work in another work area.
- The user has too many authorizations that are no longer required (this is often the case in companies that have used SAP systems for years).
- The working environment is not stable, the authorizations cannot be qualified uniquely.

These examples of user management indicate how important the CUP component is for the overall success of using SAP BusinessObjects Access Control.

The application process is supported by workflows so employees can file the application for authorizations or authorization changes themselves. Moreover, you have the option of detecting employee-related changes to the infotypes of the personnel master data via interfaces and to forward those changes to SAP BusinessObjects Access Control.

**Benefits of CUP**

The following shows the benefits of CUP:

- Simple authorization request for users
- Controlled release considering the risks involved through simulation options
- Prevention of excessive growth of authorizations in user master records

### Enterprise Role Management (ERM)

An instruction on the role creation method exists in the ERM component of SAP BusinessObjects Access Control — in this context, don't confuse the abbreviation ERM with Enterprise Risk Management! In the ERM component, you can define authorization roles via a log-capable mechanism and generate them in the back-end system. To do this, the standard process comprises steps like the definition of authorizations, analysis of risks, setup of authorization criteria for workflows, generation of authorization roles, tests of authorization roles, and so on. Here, you must also determine in which systems the roles are supposed to be generated. This is done by specifying the connectors.

The setup of the role attributes lets you specify roles for the business processes, subprocesses, functional areas, and other attributes. Business processes are usually cross-department attributes, whereas functional areas allow for an authorization role cataloging on the basis of organizational units. The ERM component can be used in SAP ERP, SAP ERP HCM, SAP Advanced Planning and Optimization (APO), SAP CRM, and SAP Supplier Relationship Management (SRM) by default.

Enterprise Role Management therefore provides support for designing authorization roles that observe and closely integrate possible controls and the authorization risks that you previously defined in the RAR component. Decisions improve objectively and usually advance the goal of defining risk-free authorization components in the form of authorization roles and keep them as such in their lowest level modules.

By merging the role modules in composite roles and assigning a large number of authorization roles of different types to user master records, in almost every case you assign authorization combinations that are not risk-free. SAP BusinessObjects Access Control, however, enables the continuous control of these risks using the CUP component by involving process controls in the release of specific authorization components for the user or by using the RAR component for the definition and the deployment of mitigating controls. The individual departments and experts responsible can implement the authorization role definitions and changes themselves because they are done in a controlled manner and in functional dimensions.

**Benefits of ERM**

In combination with the other components of Access Control, ERM has the following benefits:

- Controlled creation of authorizations
- Integration of risk definitions
- Controlled authorization checks
- Assignment of authorization roles to business processes and functional areas
- Responsibility for role definition and control delegated to the managers that are actively involved in the role management process
- Decisions are made based on information from the SAP BusinessObjects repository and are therefore well-founded

### Superuser Privilege Management (SPM)

Flexible handling is one of the requirements that arise from the complexity of today's ERP applications, systems, and company-internal division of labor and economic requirements. This flexibility is required, for example, in emergencies where serious technical problems call for the immediate support of specialists that are equipped with advanced access rights (emergency authorizations) to detect and remedy errors.

Besides the technical emergency assignments, department-related activities also result in needs that require temporary and short-term assignments. In the past, these requirements could only by met via the short-term assignment of comprehensive authorization profiles like `SAP_ALL` and `SAP_NEW` that SAP provides by default. The usage of these authorization profiles was usually subjected to a time limit.

Most basic, authorization, and application administrators therefore used to have some kind of superuser privilege that entitled them to not only use all authorizations in the SAP system temporarily, but to keep them for possible problems in the user master at free disposal. Many SAP consultants are also included here who generally ask for full access, meaning `SAP_ALL`, without actually considering the effect their request can have on the company's risk culture. Over the years, it has been possible to ease this situation slightly although no real alternative has actually been available.

With the SPM component, SAP provides the option to assign selected users an advanced authorization role for short-term usage and linked to a superuser. This role is used separately and in a targeted way and is only assigned if justified and required. The user that is supposed to obtain access to the system logs on using the superuser ID and can utilize it until the problem or emergency is solved. However, every action and activity is logged automatically and can subsequently be evaluated within the scope of the risk management concept and allocated to specific users. The corresponding risk management concept is created separately.

**Benefits of Superuser Privilege Management**

The organized handling of access rights for emergency management results in the following benefits when using SPM:

- Exceptional rules for the temporary use of far-reaching authorizations
- Control of assigning emergency authorizations
- Traceability of actions that are implemented using the emergency authorization ID

## 8.4 SAP BusinessObjects Process Control

Processes essentially determine the actions within an organization. A process is a sequence of individual activities that are performed step by step. Every individual activity is an element of a process chain whose goal is to conclude the previous activity and prepare a new activity. In this context, you can specify starting and end points.

Business processes in the company are subject to the same regulations, are often complex, and must therefore be mapped with many cross connections. Because the processing cycles and therefore the process runs become faster and faster, the control of the proper processing of the individual activities is an essential characteristic of a well-functioning risk management system and is used to protect the company assets.

Processes process transaction data, that is, data that moves from process point A to process point B from a mathematical point of view. Risks objectively exist at starting point A, at the individual activity points, and end at point Z, or somewhere in between. These risks arise from the error-proneness of today's process runs and from a multitude of criminal activities inside and outside of an organization. Therefore, you must define the commercial process scenarios and check them for their risk content. The process scenarios comprise control steps and activities to exploit a responsible monitoring and the active usage of the control options. This involves the use of manual controls and the definition and usage of automated security solutions.

Business applications must also be checked for risks with regard to non-compliance of legal regulations. For this reason, the control steps embedded in the processes are integrative elements of the internal control system that can be enforced not only by a central control department, but by as many employees as possible at decisive points. This means that noncompliance of legal, industry-specific, or company-internal specifications must be defined as a risk and be controllable in the process. This ability to control includes the definition of business processes, risks, controls, and security processes, and the determination of the centrally or organizationally assigned persons responsible. Effective controls must therefore be integrated with the processes and the underlying subprocesses to be efficient.

The integration of manual measures is definitely an alternative from a documentary perspective, but even with all good intentions this has the disadvantage that these measures can be forgotten. Therefore, it is recommended to specify a very large part of the process controls and security-relevant measures as automatic controls and support them technically. Many companies have process owners, but actual process documentation is rather the exception than the general rule. The problems are occasionally caused by structural or historical aspects, but they still don't represent an obstacle for the effective and proper management and control of a company and its areas in conformity with the law.

With the SAP BusinessObjects Process Control component, SAP offers an effective control management solution that establishes internal process controls and monitors their use. Here, not only the functions of the solution itself are used, but also the standard functions of the SAP applications, such as the workflow mechanisms and reporting. SAP BusinessObjects Process Control is an important supplement to the process control management in the SAP BusinessObjects solution portfolio thanks to the graphical dashboard functions, a structured reporting, task definitions, assignment options to employees, and a broad range of additional functions.

The deployment of SAP BusinessObjects Process Control requires comprehensive Customizing settings to be able effectively use the component in the company as a whole at the various process and organizational levels. The following presents the functions and use of the solution to evaluate essential aspects that speak in favor of or against the use in the organization. The following functional areas exist in SAP BusinessObjects Process Control:

- My Home
- Compliance Structure
- Evaluation Setup
- Evaluation Results
- Certification
- Report Center
- User Access

Figure 8.8 shows an overview of these functional areas for SAP BusinessObjects Process Control. SAP BusinessObjects Process Control offers a wide range of standardized reports and options for individual or level control to protect business, administration, and control processes sustainably, consistently, and continuously and further develop and improve the control measures proactively.

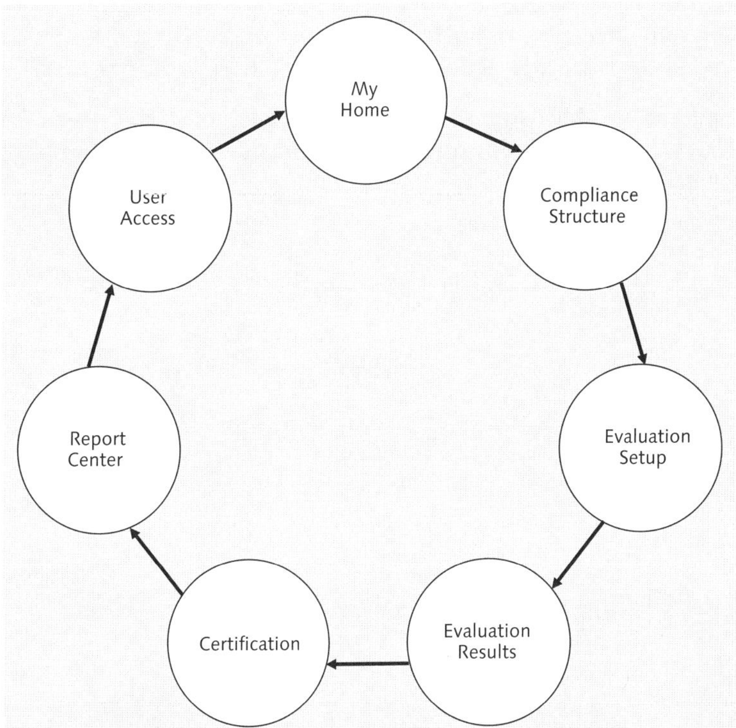


**Figure 8.8** SAP BusinessObjects Process Control — Functional Areas

### 8.4.1 My Home

The My Home menu has four selection functions:

- **Work Inbox**
  The Work Inbox includes the user's tasks, which were forwarded as a subtask for processing via a workflow as part of the process controls. The processing tasks are displayed in a list.
- **Reports and Analytics**
  Reports and Analytics takes the user to their reports and analysis evaluations. Here, the system also displays test results from analytics, revision results, or evaluations and control reports.
- **My Processes**
  My Processes shows the corresponding risk controls for administrating for the user-specific processes and subprocesses or subactivities.
- **My Entity-Level Controls**
  You must define and manage management controls under My entity-Level Controls. These controls were assigned to the user via user authorizations.

Access to the menu and to objects on the home page is assigned and restricted using authorizations. Figure 8.9 shows the selection functions of the home page in SAP BusinessObjects Process Control.

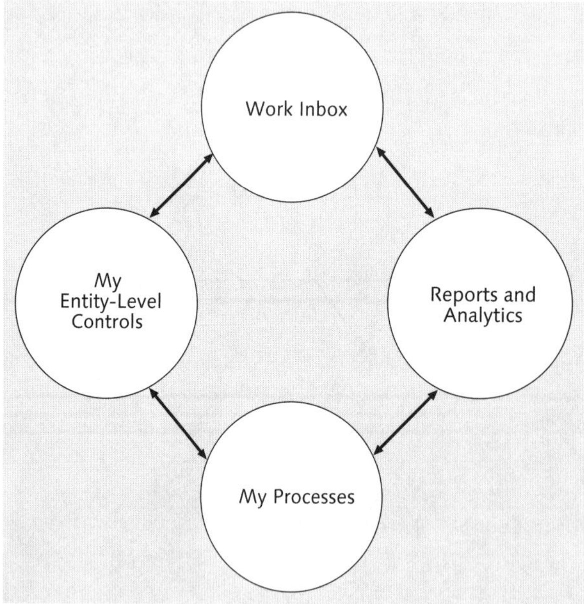


**Figure 8.9** Selection Functions for the My Home Functional Area

### 8.4.2 Compliance Structure

The Compliance Structure menu has five selection functions:

- **Organizations**
  These include the organizational structure of the company, which is important for assigning subactivities and management controls to be able to assign management-relevant and security-relevant objects. This occurs under Organizations.
- **Accounts**
  Under Accounts you manage accounts and account groups. The reason and financial reporting–relevant assignments are also stored in the system.
- **Control Objectives and Risks**
  In the compliance structure you specify the Control Objectives and Risks in a risk control catalog that is valid throughout the company.
- **Central Process Hierarchy**
  In Central Process Hierarchy you determine assignments like account groups/ assertions. Moreover, you maintain test plans for manual control tests here.
- **Entity-Level Controls**
  In this area, you specify the basic settings and definitions and map them in the system.

Figure 8.10 shows the selection functions of the compliance structure in SAP BusinessObjects Process Control.

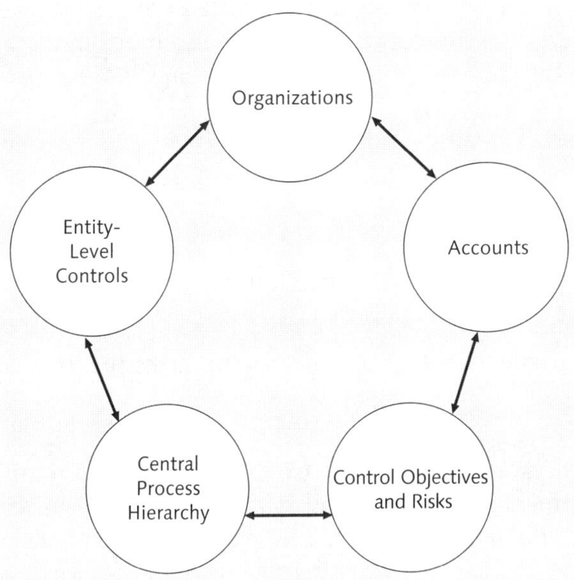


**Figure 8.10** Selection Functions for the Compliance Structure Functional Area

### 8.4.3 Evaluation Setup

The EVALUATION SETUP menu has six selection functions:

- **Assessment Surveys**
  The ASSESSMENT SURVEYS menu item with the Question Library and Survey Library subitems defines questions and surveys for assessing the control design, the self-tests of controls, subprocess design, entity-level controls, and their releases.
- **Manual Test Plans**
  MANUAL TEST PLANS are specified in the menu item bearing the same name. The tests relate to the effectiveness of the controls in their use.
- **Planner**
  Under PLANNER, you create assessment surveys and compliance tests to trigger workflow tasks in the subsequent step.
- **Automated Test Rules**
  Here, you set up automated tests of organization controls, including rule configurations, criteria definitions for application systems, and the assignment of defined controls for rules in the AUTOMATED TEST RULES menu item.
- **Automated Test Customizing**
  In AUTOMATED TEST CUSTOMIZING, you transform queries and SAP standard list reports into process control scripts for rule definitions and control tests.
- **Scheduling**
  In SCHEDULING, you trigger and manage background jobs and process controls for continuous control monitoring. Moreover, this option also provides corresponding monitoring functions under Monitoring Scheduler and Job Monitor.

Figure 8.11 shows the selection functions of the evaluation setup in SAP BusinessObjects Process Control.

### 8.4.4 Evaluation Results

The EVALUATION RESULTS menu has three selection functions:

- **My Tasks**
  MY TASKS is available for troubleshooting and displaying assessments, test results, and issues.
- **Monitoring**
  In Monitoring, you can process issues, perform troubleshooting for control monitoring measures, and process tasks that were assigned to the user via the workflow. The controls for compliance are not monitored in this menu item.

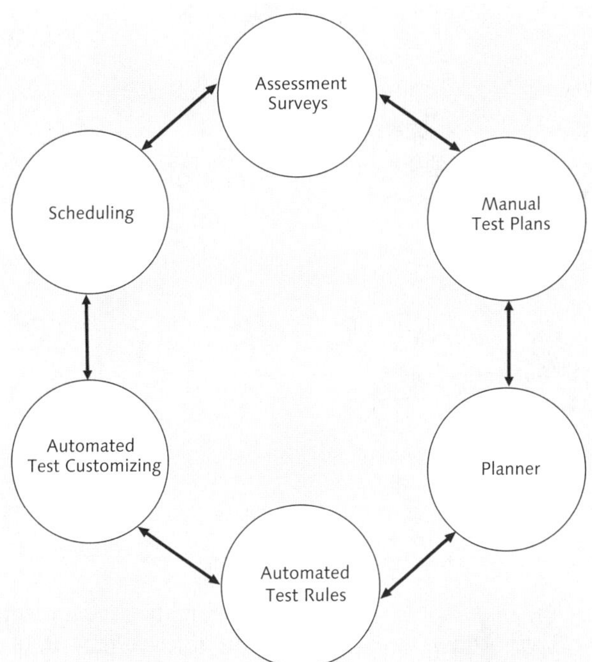


**Figure 8.11** Selection Functions for the Evaluation Setup Functional Area

- **Compliance**
  In COMPLIANCE, you monitor the control measures to comply with the compliance specifications. Here as well, you can process issues and display and manage your own measures for troubleshooting.

Figure 8.12 shows the selection functions of the EVALUATION RESULTS in SAP BusinessObjects Process Control.

### 8.4.5 Certification

The CERTIFICATION area is where you release planning. Here, you plan and distribute tasks for releases. The CERTIFICATION menu has two selection functions:

- **Sign-Off Monitor**
  The sign-off status for the responsibility areas that are assigned to respective users is displayed in the SIGN-OFF MONITOR. This way, the release process can be performed securely and promptly.

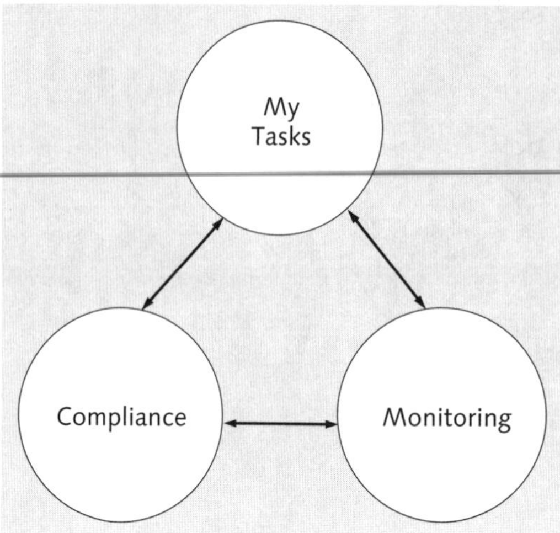


**Figure 8.12** Selection Functions for the Evaluation Results Functional Area

- **Planner**
  The scheduling and triggering of tasks for release to the respective person responsible is done via SAP workflows and executed in the Planner menu item.

Figure 8.13 shows the selection functions of CERTIFICATION in SAP BusinessObjects Process Control.

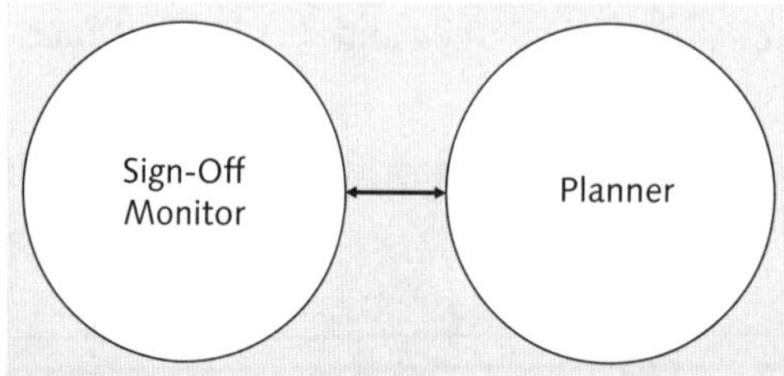


**Figure 8.13** Selection Functions for the Certification Functional Area

### 8.4.6 Report Center

The REPORT CENTER menu comprises six selection functions:

- **Structure and Setup**
  The STRUCTURE AND SETUP menu item is used for the reports of all master data objects that are relevant to this area.

- **Roles and Authorizations**
  The ROLES AND AUTHORIZATIONS menu item aims at report analyses from the process view. This menu item accompanies the report and analytics functions of SAP BusinessObjects Access Control that were described in Section 8.3, SAP BusinessObjects Access Control.
- **Evaluations**
  The Evaluations item is used for all design assessments and tests that are linked to the effectiveness assessments of process controls.
- **Monitoring**
  The MONITORING menu item displays reports for automatic control monitoring.
- **Audit and Analysis**
  AUDIT AND ANALYSIS involves the control reports for revision examinations and change management.
- **Certification**
  The CERTIFICATION item concludes the selection with reports via sign-offs and confirmations.

Figure 8.14 shows the selection functions of the REPORT CENTER in SAP BusinessObjects Process Control.

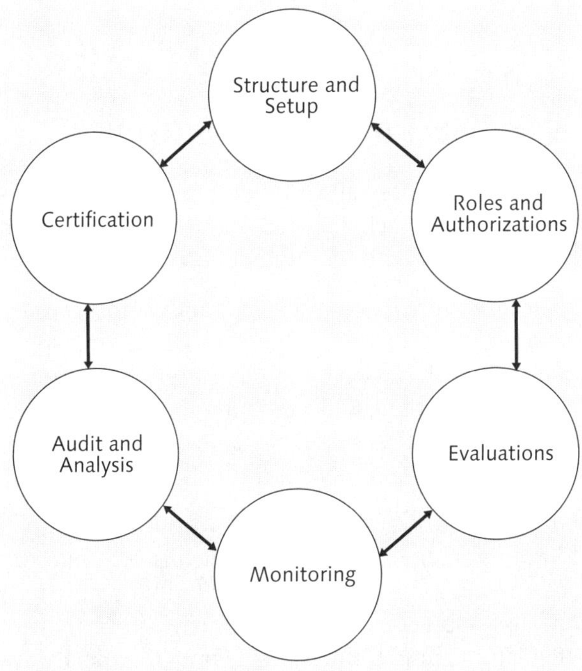


**Figure 8.14** Selection Functions for the Report Center Functional Area

### 8.4.7 User Access

The User Access menu has two selection functions:

- **Roles**
  In the Roles menu item, you maintain the role assignments for the users. Moreover, in this menu item you can manage successors if a user leaves the company.
- **Delegation**
  The substitution policy or the delegation of tasks or application access of a user is stored in the Delegation category.

Figure 8.15 shows the selection functions of User Access in SAP BusinessObjects Process Control.

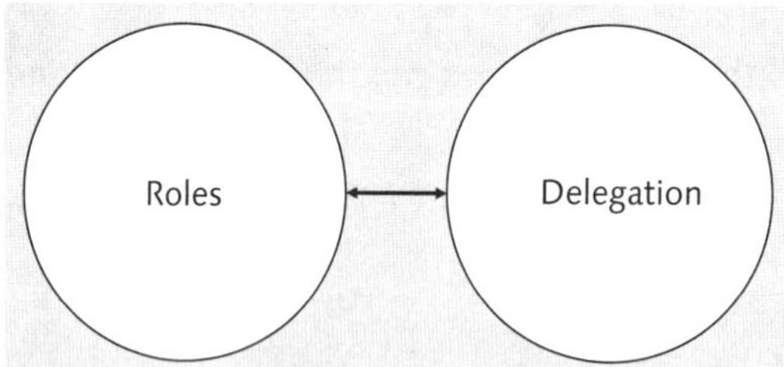


**Figure 8.15** Selection Functions for the User Access Functional Area

## 8.5 SAP BusinessObjects Global Trade Services (GTS)

Today, legal and regulatory compliance is an integral part of enterprise risk management. This involves the legal and industry-specific requirements that are defined by law and must be observed and complied with by individual companies.

Most countries have an active international exchange of goods and services. Because every country has its own legislation in place, the instructions and specifications may vary greatly and must be observed despite international agreements. There are also guidelines and laws for importing and exporting that business processes must follow. Transnational goods and service flows always integrate multiple business partners when handling these commercial traffic flows.

Customs barriers have successively fallen in many parts in the world, for example, with the North American Free Trade Agreement (NAFTA), which is continuously extended with regard to content and geography, or with the binding regulations of the European Union, which is also subject to fast development. Nevertheless, international agreements and regulations mustn't mask that foreign trade always concerns different countries whose laws must be observed.

Furthermore, there are several risks that hardly exist or may not exist at all in your country due to regional proximity or clear political and legal relationships. Partners that manufacture knock-offs of another supplier, financial risk in the handling, or noncompliance of legal regulations can result in considerable losses. Also, a lack of payment or business ethics can lead to losses and represent a high risk for the business partners involved. Foreign trade always means a complete, transparent, and reproducible documentation of processes and deliveries.

Documents such as import and export licenses, sanctions and boycott lists, customs clearance forms, international delivery notes, and intra-European Union and extra-European Union trade statistics are mentioned in this context. In the import and export business, you also need to use nationally and internationally recognized goods numbers and labels for customs and other authorities to comply with the provisions of import and export regulations. An example would be the statistical goods number. It is required for statistical purposes and must be declared to the authorities for foreign trade transactions.

Due to the complexity of the international production, cooperation, service, and commercial relationships that legislatures respond to with continuous adaptations and further developments, application solutions for the functional and technical support of the foreign trade processes are indispensable. GTS, the customs and foreign trade solution within SAP BusinessObjects, provides support for handling foreign trade transactions and the standardized formatting of the necessary information and documents for all company areas and partners involved.

The goal of using this solution is to ensure a fast flow of all processes and activities in conformity with the laws that are involved in transnational goods movements. This includes communication with public authorities and controlling bodies and the interaction with business partners such as suppliers, carriers, customs, agencies, goods recipients, and end customers. Insurances and tax offices can also access a holistic GTS data repository.

SAP BusinessObjects GTS provides a myriad of interfaces to keep information on commercial aspects that concern a company's import or export activities up to date and to update national, bilateral, and multilateral customs and economic regulations and rules in the system. The calculation of the tariff regulation is therefore always based on real-time data, which must be transferred to the system in advance.

From an enterprise risk management perspective, you must periodically check the update processes, interfaces, data quality, and usage successes. To do this, you are provided with the SAP BusinessObjects Risk Management solution (see Section 8.2, SAP BusinessObjects RM), among others. Particularly for countries that have a very export-intensive economy — including Germany, Japan, Great Britain, and China — the comprehensive and highly integrated solutions of SAP BusinessObjects GTS form an important basis to ensure the long-term success of foreign trade transactions.

Depending on the business model, the level of commercial foreign commitment, and the company requirements, the solution can be connected to SAP application systems and to non-SAP systems, if required. The solution focuses on legal control and compliance, customs management, the optimization of financial benefits, and the reduction of risk, particularly financial risk.

The initial menu of SAP BusinessObjects GTS (see Figure 8.16) comprises five processing groups or components, which are discussed in detail in the following:

- Compliance Management
- Customs Management
- Risk Management
- Electronic Compliance Reporting
- System Administration

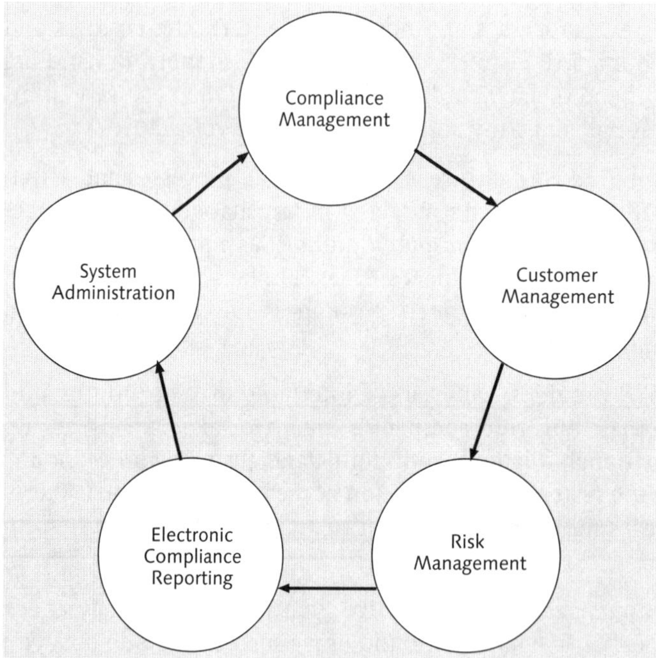


**Figure 8.16** Components of SAP BusinessObjects Global Trade Services

### 8.5.1 Compliance Management

Compliance Management includes all information and handling criteria that are required for the transnational movement of goods in conformity with the law. Compliance with legal regulations is the ultimate goal. Compliance Management involves the following topics:

- Sanction List Check
- Legal Import Control
- Legal Export Control
- Classification/Master Data

Because the individual countries publish different boycott and embargo lists that prohibit trade for specific material groups with specific countries, this information must always be up to date in the system. In this context, not only countries but also individual business partners are included in an embargo list. The current information must be loaded into the repository automatically via EDI (Electronic Data Interchange) or other communication methods.

Most embargo lists originate from the European Union and the United States. National and international boycott lists are equally significant, even if embargos of other countries possibly don't entail direct legal consequences. But as soon as a company maintains business relations with the countries that issue the embargos, the local authorities can proceed against the respective company that bypassed the national embargo list from another country.

Particularly companies with international production locations or sales activities must strictly comply with these requirements. Therefore, the commercial activities must always consider both national and important international boycott lists in the foreign trade process. For every corresponding transaction, SAP BusinessObjects GTS checks the content connection of these lists so that blockings, embargos, boycotts, and the like can be taken into account.

Furthermore, Compliance Management also considers all laws that govern the import and export of specific goods or material groups. The licensing for the production and sales of these goods and services, also beyond country boundaries, is defined by various laws. Some of these laws are increasingly harmonized within regional trade associations such as the European Union or North America. In general, however, the various national legislations apply.

To control and handle trade with specific products, such as weapons or product components and parts to be used for military purposes, or with substances — including chemicals and pharmaceuticals — in conformity with the law, laws such as pharmaceutical laws, weapons laws, narcotics laws, and so on must be mapped in SAP BusinessObjects GTS and observed in business activities.

To do this, there are product classification systems, such as the Harmonized Tariff Schedule (HTS), which is accepted by more than 200 countries worldwide and is applicable to imports and exports. The United States has its own classification system, Export Classification Control Number (ECCN). In SAP BusinessObjects GTS, the necessary product classification is supported by a wide range of functions within the scope of import and export control, for example, by a central goods classification which then has the character of master data. This goods classification ID is then visible and usable in all connected systems and comprises a unique ID of the goods.

Comprehensive tools for processing and checking these goods IDs are used to ensure their proper handling and execution. The product classification is also used to automatically determine whether this involves foreign trade processes that are relevant to importing or exporting. The system automatically checks and assigns licenses for materials and goods that are subject to approval. Usually, these licenses are not only linked with the material group or the specific material, but also with factors such as quantity, value, and so on. The system supports this and controls it automatically.

Figure 8.17 shows the subcomponents for Compliance Management in SAP BusinessObjects GTS.

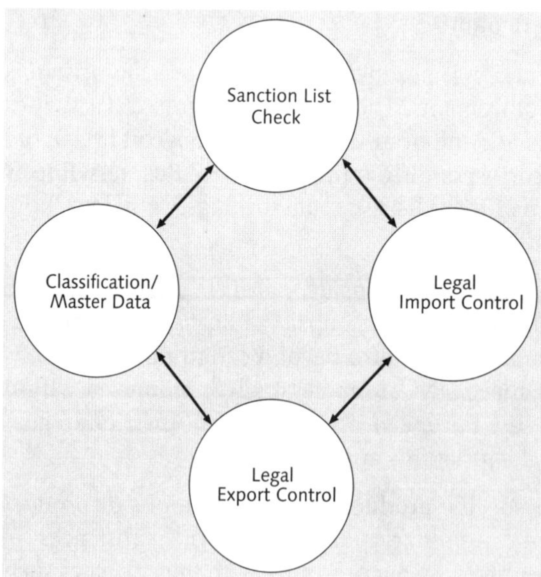


**Figure 8.17** Subcomponents of Compliance Management

### 8.5.2 Customs Management

In SAP BusinessObjects GTS, the customs management attributable to foreign trade is attended to with the Customs Management component where all customs-relevant commercial processes are processed. Here again, the focus is on compliance. One goal is compliance with customs regulations to ensure a smooth processing of the transnational processes. This includes the complete documentation of goods movements and information on business partners, for example, goods recipients. Risk of delays due to missing or insufficient documents are drastically reduced by supporting the solutions of SAP BusinessObjects GTS, which leads to considerable cost savings in the import and export business.

By means of a standardized dataset on goods, material groups, export regulations, import bans, and customs regulations, SAP BusinessObjects GTS can provide the system's communication with IT-supported customs procedures. These national customs handling systems transfer all customs-relevant information from the connected IT systems, such as SAP BusinessObjects GTS, to an electronic customs document — which helps eliminate manual errors from customs documents. Another benefit is the prompt entry and faster processing of customs information, which considerably accelerates the speed of the international movement of goods.

SAP BusinessObjects GTS offers comprehensive interfaces to international customs procedures, for example:

- AES (Automated Export System, U.S.)
- ATLAS (automated tariff and local customs processing system, Germany)
- NCTS (New Computerized Transit System, European Union)
- ZM90 (customs management system, Switzerland)
- ICS (Integrated Cargo System, Australia)

The goods or customs tariff is determined by the customs classification, which in turn depends on the unique ID and the product classification. The more precise and comprehensive the product classification, the more unique the determination of custom tariffs and the sales rate of the foreign trade businesses in the customs processing. International customs authorities provide national custom tariffs in electronic form. These country-specific tariffs can be loaded into the GRC application via interfaces. The tariff and product classification is therefore an important instrument to effectively control the process of transnational movement of goods.

For goods that originate from third countries that are intended for import, SAP BusinessObjects GTS provides functions to automatically calculate the customs duties. Thanks to the electronic determination of information, importers or recipients can include important costs in the accrued costs planning before the goods are sent.

The customs processing also requires correct documents, such as shipping documents, certificates of origin, import customs declaration forms, carrier's delivery notes, export licenses, declaration documents, and so on. All documents required for moving goods to and from a foreign country can be created, printed, or provided in electronic format with SAP BusinessObjects GTS.

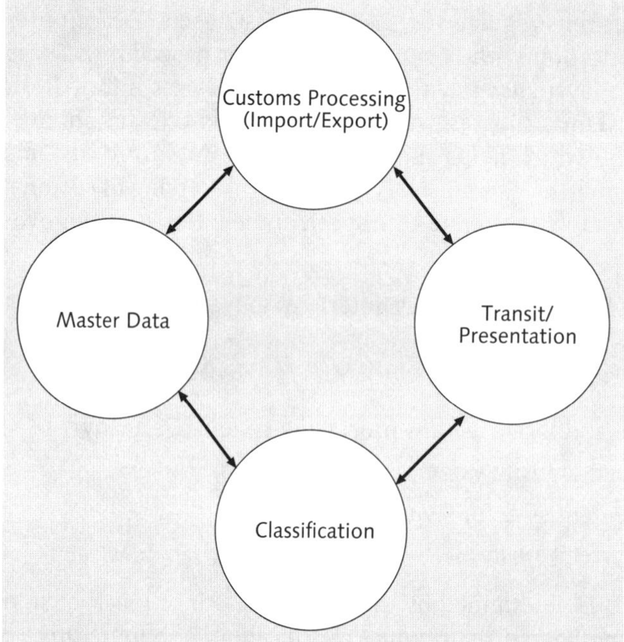


**Figure 8.18** Subcomponents of Customs Management

In the Customs Management area, the following menu items are available (see Figure 8.18):

- Customs Processing (Import/Export)
- Transit/Presentation

- Classification
- Master Data

### 8.5.3 Risk Management

Risk management with regard to foreign trade activities is very versatile. Compliance with legal regulations and the creation of the necessary documents for smooth processing were already described as control and process optimization measures. Risk management in SAP BusinessObjects GTS comprises five subcomponents (see Figure 8.19):

- Preference Processing
- Preference Processing (Master Data)
- Restitution
- Restitution (Master Data)
- Letter of Credit Processing

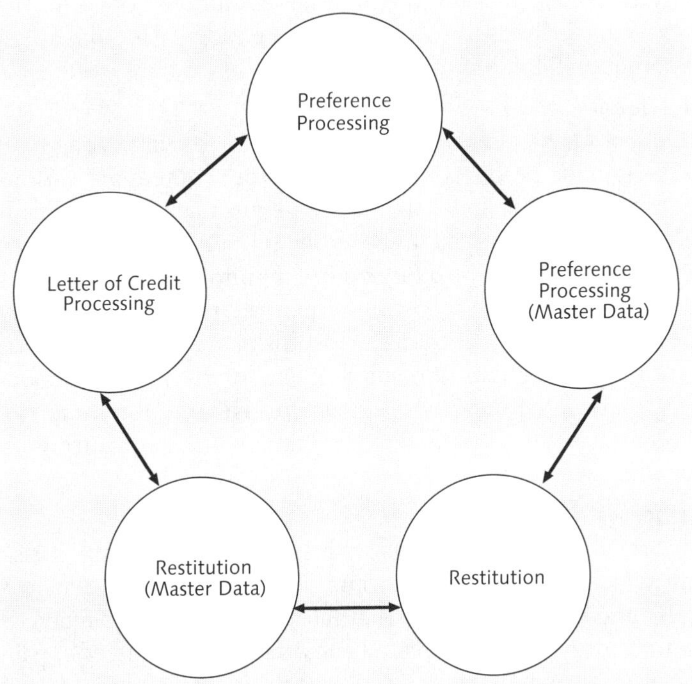


**Figure 8.19** Subcomponents of Risk Management

Another aspect is the utilization of monetary benefits that result from transnational commercial activities. Compared to the rule sets for customs and tariffs, specific material groups in some countries are exempted from customs or at least have reduced customs, which is the case, for example, for product samples. Preferential rates of duty apply to intra-European trade for goods that originate from an EU country. Some of them vary considerably from the standard rates.

Knowing the goods' country of origin is therefore not only mandatory for declaration, but is also used to optimize procurement costs for specific articles and materials. Another effective means of cost control and reduction entails the restitution that exists for some goods thanks to price fixing within the European Union. Here, the price difference between the world market prices and intra-European prices is compensated to stimulate trade between EU countries.

Customs preference calculations and other risk controls are competently supported by SAP BusinessObjects GTS in the following functions (see Figure 8.20):

- **Trade Preference Management**
  TRADE PREFERENCE MANAGEMENT deals with preference calculation. This includes customs and tariff reductions and customs and tariff exemptions. The information on the supplier forms the basis for decisions. Both national decisions about preferences and international trade preferential agreements are observed.
- **Restitution Management**
  RESTITUTION MANAGEMENT handles restitution options for importing and exporting goods. For specific products and material groups, there are various rules that apply in the EU, for example, trading and export companies benefit from subsidies, restitutions, and the like in the foreign trade business, particularly, in exports. Because national controlling bodies monitor the correctness of trading transactions, export licenses are required that the respective company must acquire as the exporter to benefit from the restitutions. Control indicators, such as export quantity, type of goods, time limit of export activities, and so on, are specified here. An integrated security management with risk threshold values and control functions is used to process transactions in compliance with regulatory and customs laws.
- **Trade Finance Services**
  The processing of foreign trade transactions with securities is a common risk control instrument, which can be achieved using the TRADE FINANCE SERVICES function. Using this function, transactions that fall through or other financial risks are supposed to be protected by proven means, such as guarantees of payments, collection collaterals, letters of credit, partial payments, and so on, and limit the amount and impact of the possible damage. The associated effort and

the requirements on foreign trade documents are solved with comprehensive system functions in SAP BusinessObjects GTS.

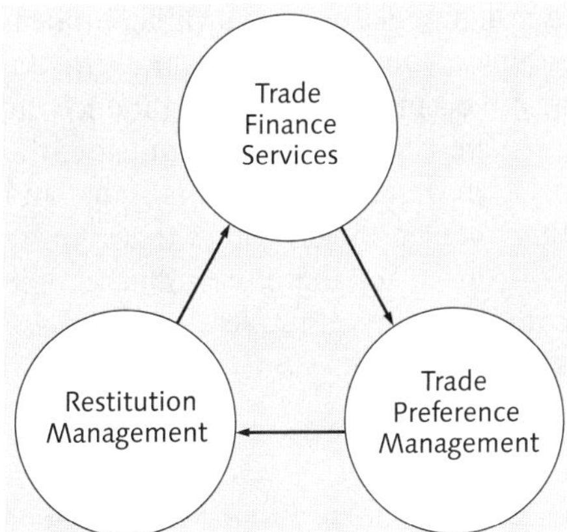


**Figure 8.20** Risk Control Areas of Risk Management

### 8.5.4 Electronic Compliance Reporting

The single market controlled by the European Union reduces the commodity flows that are officially recorded to imports and exports with countries outside the EU. The recording of country-specific commodity flows is significant to record statistics on foreign trade activities, economic potential, and a country's commodity flows. This is essential, for example, for creating a country's foreign trade balance.

Every company is obligated to record the required statistical data. Electronic Compliance Reporting (ECR) supports you with statistics declarations that you have to submit to the authorities for transactions involving trade between two member states of the EU and defined data formats of the national statistical authorities. You can collect the Intrastat-relevant data from the logistics processes and provide it to the national statistics authorities in periodic Intrastat declarations.

### 8.5.5 System Administration

System Administration controls the system maintenance of the system components that are required for the GTS components, for instance, the communication between SAP BusinessObjects GTS, EDI Converter, and customs authorities.

## 8.6 SAP Environment, Health, and Safety (EHS) Management

Profitability, expert economic knowledge, compliance action, and product innovation are no longer the only areas that determine a company's economic success. Environmental protection, health protection, and occupational safety influence the internal behavior of employees, the company's perception from the outside, the company culture, and thus the development of an organization that is stable and established on moral-ethical principles — these are no longer topics that require active actions due to regulatory or legal provisions. They therefore influence the costs, work results, sustainability, and the company's branding. As a result, these factors partly determine the company's success and thus its value.

Besides the specifications that result from legal obligations, several companies have already recognized that they can considerably improve the success changes in the market by means of environmental protection and morally sound treatment of employees. Investments in environmental protection and socially acceptable jobs are a need that the legislation in various countries interprets differently. Standards can only be attained via international frameworks and bilateral obligations.

### 8.6.1 Overview

Environmentally compatible and socially acceptable actions include most areas of entrepreneurial activities and, in particular, the production of goods and services; with regard to EHS, a solution must be integrated with existing work processes of the ERP system and with the production environment that is mapped with SAP Product Lifecycle Management (PLM). Both environmental and international specifications and the necessary code of conduct for employees and other persons to protect the health in the work process are integrated comprehensively with the work areas.

Environment, Health, and Safety (see Figure 8.21) refers to the following situations in particular:

- Environment maps all efforts of a company in the, environmental protection and compliance control areas.
- Health stands for all measures that control the handling of harmful substances, materials, working materials, and finished products.
- Safety refers to the labor law–related provisions and their compliance in the company, particularly with regard to labor protection.

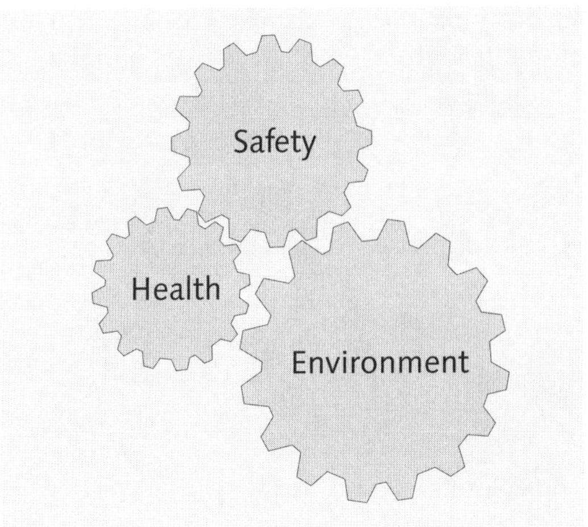


**Figure 8.21** Compliance Areas Environment, Health, and Safety

The EHS goals comprise the following:

- Securing the legal regulations in environmental and labor law
- Transparency of using measures on environmental compliance and laws
- Implementation of a high degree of integration for smooth process control in this area
- Continuous proactive improvement of the EHS development status for utilizing personnel and financial potentials, which result from the consistent application of governmental and company-internal specifications

Legal specifications on handling hazardous goods not only involve environmental protection, but usually also include health risks for the business partners involved, but also persons not involved at all. An example would be the transport of hazardous goods, which have special labeling obligations. Chemical substances or biological material must also be handled with special care. The employees must be informed about the acute dangers and know the protections and risk control processes for the proper handling of these materials.

Today, environmentally compatible action belongs to active risk management as part of ensuring the company's success. Inspired by international agreements and regional and legal specifications, more and more companies take the initiative and promote environment-conscious actions in all value chains. Because these initiatives are regulated by law, and are motivated by perceiving the necessary action, the established specifications and process guidelines must be monitored and checked using suitable security and control measures.

For processing the most essential specifications in this area, the SAP EHS application includes the following four components in three work areas (see Figure 8.22), which are discussed in detail in the following:

- CHEMICALS SAFETY
- ENVIRONMENT, HEALTH, AND SAFETY
- COMPLIANCE WITH PRODUCT-RELATED ENVIRONMENTAL SPECIFICATIONS
- COMPLIANCE AND EMISSION MANAGEMENT

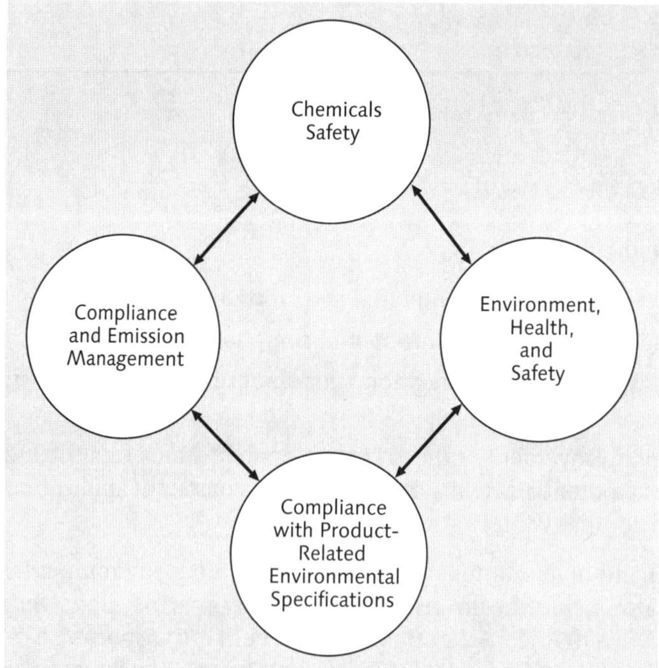


**Figure 8.22** Main Components of SAP EHS Management

The GRC solutions of SAP EHS Management provide for a considerable added value, particularly in foreign trade support, company-wide environmental protection management, risk management, and compliance through a close integration of the SAP system and connection to external applications and business partners.

### 8.6.2 Chemical Safety

The Chemical Safety component controls the information requirement for handling hazardous substances and chemicals that mainly concern the production and transport processes. The core of the solution component comprises the specification database, which includes all data on the content determination of chemicals and can calculate the content data of a specific product in the production flow.

In this context, you can create, manage, assign, and control batches, mixing rations, chemical details and manufacturer information, formulations, mixtures, and other dependencies. The classification characteristics of substances and product compositions result in the risk level and the associated measures for security and control. Information and rule specifications are not only used for the fundamental determination on handling specific hazardous materials, chemicals, and products. The system also allows for comprehensive management control at different levels using reports and collaboration scenarios with suppliers and other business partners.

The entire lifecycle of a chemical from production to disposal must be taken into account and considered in the guidelines on handling chemicals. Therefore, the initial creation and the tracking of the amount of substances are of equal importance. Using a central labeling management, you label materials and substances with regard to content. The chemicals management is a central task of companies that operate with hazardous goods and chemical substances to comply with security and compliance.

The classification and risk evaluation are important control elements for the system's processing of work processes in dealing with chemical substances and for the control and security of the associated work processes and participants in the work processes. A comprehensive reporting equally supports the parties involved and persons responsible in handling hazardous goods and materials. In combination with SAP applications, this reporting monitors the production and all follow-up processes including warehousing, transport, material movements, batch documentations, and other work areas.

Due to the use and control areas in chemicals management, this results in the following subareas of Chemical Safety:

- Basic data and tools
- Product safety
- Hazardous goods management
- Hazardous goods handling
- Waste management

Consistent documentation is important to ensure reproducibility. Therefore, safety data sheets are automatically created and managed in SAP EHS Management. The specification database provides all of the required detailed information that is also used for handling hazardous goods transports. These not only need to be filed once, but are also subject to continuous monitoring.

To do this, there is a close integration with SAP BusinessObjects GTS for dealing with transnational transports, but also with other applications and SAP solutions in the logistics and production areas. The system therefore supports the creation of hazardous goods documents in multiple languages. Cost optimizations through company-internal distribution and assignments can be achieved in waste management via integration with SAP ERP Financials. With this control component, hazardous goods risks and financial risks can be reduced and optimally handled.

### 8.6.3 Environment, Health, and Safety

Environment and labor law–related provisions are mapped in the environment, health, and safety area of SAP EHS Management and are used as the basis for company-internal instructions and precise working environment and area of responsibility.

Regular maintenance and servicing tasks are scheduled for the security of production plants. This ensures integration with SAP Service and Asset Management. Industrial safety is another control area. To do this, data is stored for further evaluation. Regular controls and upstream security measures for preventive protection against accidents and work-related injuries also result in the necessity to provide information related to occupational medicine to take preventive measures on this data. This way, you can schedule influenza vaccinations for departments and preventive measures for individual employees. The provision of medical data for preventive purposes is relevant to data protection.

SAP EHS Management ensures that the necessary prerequisites are met to protect access to this confidential data via a corresponding authorization management and other controls. The requirements to avoid environmental and work center–related impacts are stored in the labor protection documents for each work area, work center, or organizational entity to map security measures, immediate measures, security measures, and other relevant protection measures in the system.

### 8.6.4 Compliance with Product-Related Environmental Specifications

Compliance with product-related environmental specifications is primarily required by legal specifications in the environment area. The goal is to banish substances and parts that are pollutive and imperil the objects of the biosphere from new products and limit the use of such materials. The product-related directive, Restriction of Hazardous Substances (RoHS), is an example of reducing and controlling the use of hazardous substances.

An essential control instrument is the deployment of methods to monitor and control entire product development cycles. All individual activities and operation phases are observed for influences that damage the environment ranging from the initial design, to the prototype phase, to market-ready production and disposal. Because the entire value chain is traced up to the consumption and utilization, you can achieve ecopolitical goals, improve business results, and strengthen the overall national economy; an example would be the Integrated Product Policy (IPP) to improve all, including ecological impacts of a product during its lifecycle.

Compliance with environmental specifications for products determines the system's management of environmental specifications. These can be achieved with solutions such as Compliance for Products (CfP), which control, for example, how to design, produce, market, and dispose of products when considering environmental specifications.

### 8.6.5 Compliance and Emission Management

Companies are confronted with an increasing number of ecopolitical requirements and legal specifications that must be managed effectively and comprehensively. However, environmental protection is not only a duty, but also an obligation for responsible people and companies. The types of environmental protection are as manifold as nature itself. Some essential factors that reflect a company's environmental protection policy include the following:

- Type and scope of environmental risks
- Result of the environmental protection measures already taken
- Setup of a company-wide environment management system (Enterprise Environmental Risk Management (EERM)), including environmental protection officers
- Compliance with environmental protection measures
- Removal of pollution legacy
- Measures for recultivation or renaturation
- Waste management, utilization or disposal of waste
- Disassembly of production plants
- Water protection measures
- Product-related environmental protection, including additional expenses due to changed requirements on environmental safety
- Compliance risks with liability risks and damage claims for damages cause to the environment
- Energy efficiency and energy-saving measures

- Expenses for environmental protection activities and investments, including increasing costs due to production-related or product-related environmental specifications such as shutdowns and company relocations
- Return on Environmental Investment (RoEI)
- Issuing an environmental statement according to the environment audit law
- International specifications
- Regional activities, separately or in the company network

To accommodate the ecopolitical and legal requirements, it is indispensable to have an application support in the system for the numerous national and international specifications. For example, many countries stipulate that they need to implement sustainable measures to reduce greenhouse gases.

SAP EHS Management primarily provides support to gather all of the relevant information and transfer it via interfaces in the SAP Environmental Compliance application to an emission management system where it is processed. This emission management system monitors air, water, and soil emissions. As a result, you can describe operational and production plants and evaluate them with regard to environmental relevance through environmental indicators such as total emission, energy consumption, and other criteria.

You can present regulatory specifications and approval processes and actual savings through environmental measures: new technologies, filter systems, exhaust emission reductions, improvement of environmental data from external environment information systems, and so on. The information on consumption data, such as material consumption, water consumption, chemicals limit values, and so on, can be obtained through integration with SAP solutions, for example, SAP Supply Chain Management (SCM) for data on material consumption, SAP PLM for data on emission-relevant substances and technical plant assets, and SAP ERP Financials for data on operational and environmental costs.

An integrated environment reporting on the basis of target key figures and actual data for emission values of the various company locations is an important control instrument for monitoring limit and threshold values. Environmental loads that result from this measurement data are automatically determined and integrated with comprehensive reporting. Alarm management controls are forwarded in real time via a workflow and communicated to the persons responsible.

The following report types are significant for reporting:

- Global Environmental Data Reporting initiative
- Guidelines for sustainability reporting

- Environmental protection agency reports (Title V reports)
- European Pollutant Emission Register reports (EPER EU)

SAP EHS Management provides further support for the highly complex topic of emission certificate trading. Critical parameters include emission shortfalls or excesses within a specific period of time, where the automatic environment reporting plays a critical role. The trading of certificates and data exchanges with authorities and the business and environment partners involved are always multilateral and are enabled by connecting SAP EHS Management to trading platforms and marketplaces for emission trading.

## 8.7 SAP BusinessObjects Sustainability Performance Management

Sustainability is one of the most critical production and process goals of companies and organizations. Topics like $CO_2$ emissions, energy efficiency, product compliance, ecological production, and financial optimization provide Key Performance Indicators (KPIs) to establish a comprehensive sustainability management. From a multitude of different sources you can record company-wide and external data that is relevant for sustainability. This presents a system for management and reporting.

SAP BusinessObjects Sustainability Performance Management comprises tools and workflows for reporting, benchmarking and analysis, sustainability strategy and risks, and financial reporting. The sustainability management is integrated with the GRC solutions of SAP BusinessObjects and contains further tools and solutions like energy and carbon, product safety and stewardship, sustainable workforce, sustainable supply chain, green IT, and so on. A close integration of the solutions in the environment, health, and safety areas and with the standard SAP applications leads to a systematic entry and use of all data for sustained handling of company assets and resources of any kind.

*This chapter describes information technology (IT) security concepts and risk management aspects for the SAP NetWeaver Application Server (AS). It refers to both the ABAP stack and JAVA stack of the SAP NetWeaver AS.*

# 9 SAP NetWeaver Application Server

The SAP NetWeaver AS is the main technical component of the SAP client-server system and, simplified, the link between SAP users, non-SAP applications, and SAP databases. It serves as the application platform for all ABAP-based and Java-based applications of SAP NetWeaver — hence all SAP NetWeaver components and the service-oriented architecture (SOA) integration options of the SAP system are based on the SAP NetWeaver AS.

Due to this central functionality, SAP NetWeaver AS also assumes critical tasks in security, authorization, and risk management.

## 9.1 Introduction and Functions

In the past, the role of the SAP NetWeaver AS was to function as the technical "basis" for SAP R/3, and all SAP programs only used ABAP. Then, with SAP NetWeaver (and the application server, which was then called SAP Web Application Server), the purely ABAP-based runtime environment was expanded to include Java, based on the Java 2 Enterprise Edition (J2EE) Engine. This move provided better options for supporting Internet-based technologies. The SAP NetWeaver AS is thus not just a "classic" server for R/3 client-server applications; rather, it is more accurately described as a middleware technology platform for web-based applications.

Besides ABAP applications, the SAP NetWeaver AS also supports Business Server Pages (BSP), JavaServer Pages (JSP), and Web Dynpro as user interface technologies for ABAP and Java. Besides the usual application server tasks for various program environments, the SAP NetWeaver AS also provides integration services on the basis of Remote Function Calls (RFC) for Business Application Programming Interfaces (BAPIs). Thus, SAP NetWeaver AS middleware technology makes it possible to gradually switch over what could be described as somewhat monolithic business programs — such as Financial Accounting (FI), Controlling (CO), and Materials Management (MM) — to a service-oriented application architecture (see Chapter 7, Web Services, Enterprise Services, and Service-Oriented Architectures).

The central component of the SAP NetWeaver AS is the ABAP stack (AS ABAP), which contains the runtime environment for ABAP-based applications. These are applications that are developed directly in ABAP or ABAP Objects. The ABAP Workbench (Transaction SE38) can be used to develop these applications and to analyze them to detect any errors. The applications use the database abstraction, a neutral access layer for a range of database manufacturers, to access the database. The SAP NetWeaver AS also has its own logical database, which is separate from SAP NetWeaver AS Java. All ABAP-based applications use the same authorization principles, which are described in Chapter 20, Authorizations in SAP ERP.

A Java part, the Java stack (AS Java), has been added to the classic ABAP architecture of the SAP NetWeaver AS. This opened up the SAP-specific architecture to integrate it into other technologies more successfully, such as Java application servers (IBM WebSphere, BEA WebLogic) or Microsoft .NET, and use the options of service-oriented architectures. The AS Java is a J2EE server that provides the runtime environment for Java-based programs such as JSP and Enterprise JavaBeans (EJBs). The AS Java also accesses its own database by means of database abstraction.

Communication between the AS ABAP and the AS Java is enabled by the Java Connection Architecture. This architecture allows the AS Java to call ABAP function groups in the AS ABAP and vice versa by means of SAP Java Connectors (JCo).

Just as the ABAP Workbench is the development environment for traditional ABAP applications, there is a specific development environment for Java programming in SAP NetWeaver: the Java Integrated Development Environment (Java IDE). The related developer tools for this environment are provided by the SAP NetWeaver Developer Studio (NWDS). The SAP NetWeaver Composition Environment (SAP NetWeaver CE) is the development environment for composite applications in heterogeneous application environments based on services and processes (see Chapter 7). It also contains the SAP NWDS and is based on AS Java as the development platform.

Figure 9.1 illustrates the architecture of the SAP NetWeaver AS. You can see the two independent platforms, AS ABAP (ABAP stack, engine) and AS Java (Java stack, engine), which can be installed together or independently, that is, without the other part. The ABAP Engine supports traditional user access via SAP Graphical User Interface (GUI). It can also process web browser queries, which are then processed by the Internet Communication Manager (ICM) for the ABAP format. During further processing, the dispatcher controls work processes that execute special transactions using program-driven methods. If required, the J2EE Engine can assume further processing that is then directed from the ABAP stack to the Java stack by means of the SAP JCo.

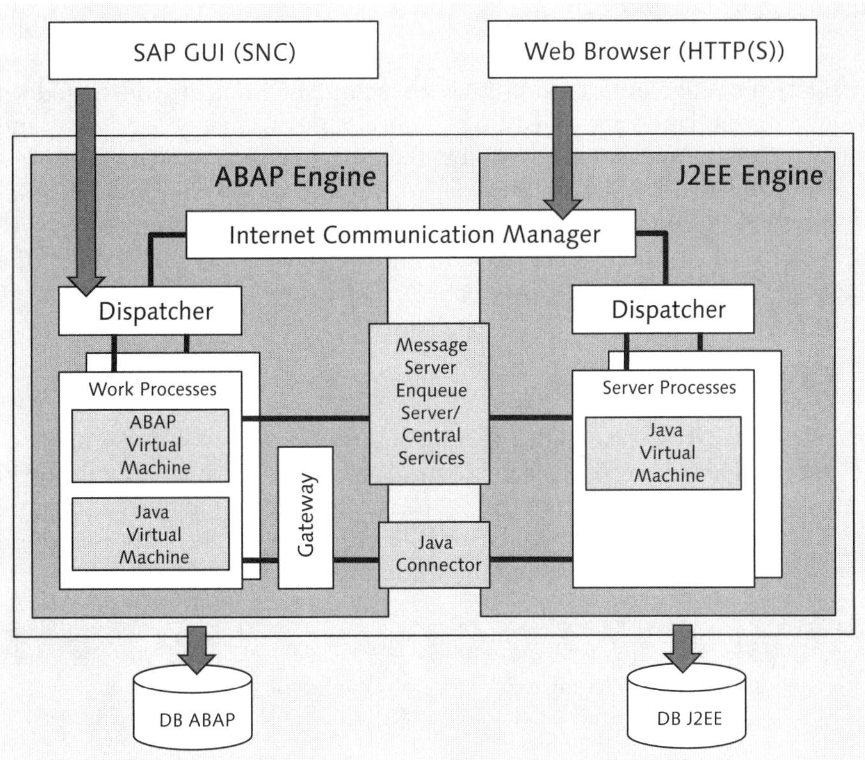


**Figure 9.1** Technical Architecture of the SAP NetWeaver AS with ABAP Stack and Java Stack

The central services component transfers messages, controls the processing process and the logical access of competitive database queries, and supports the load distribution process in the SAP system if multiple SAP instances are coupled (cluster). ABAP or Java Virtual Machines are responsible for isolating user actions during processing. The gateway shown in Figure 9.1 is the interface to transfer RFC queries. If user queries need to be made via the web browser and must then be processed by the J2EE Engine, the same processing scenario as described earlier takes place, that is, the J2EE dispatcher controls Java server processes which then process the Java code of the transaction or user query isolated in Java Virtual Machines.

The ICM, using HTTP(S), is used to handle all web-based programs — that is, programs for both the Internet and intranet. The ICM also controls web services. The

ICM is thus the communication and integration interface to both the user and to other services that use it to call specific functions. In addition to other interfaces, this interface can also be used via SAP NetWeaver Process Integration (PI). All of the usual standard protocols, including HTTP(S), SMTP, Simple Object Access Protocol (SOAP) (XML), are available.

To integrate the SAP NetWeaver AS with a system environment, you should set up a three-system landscape consisting of development, quality assurance, and production system. You should also follow this principle if AS ABAP or AS Java is used as a standalone solution. In this context, you can use also the System Landscape Directory (SLD) together with SAP Solution Manager (see Chapter 19, SAP Solution Manager) to support the planning, maintenance, and monitoring of the maintenance state of the SAP NetWeaver AS.

## 9.2 Risks and Controls

In this section, we'll use a simplified version of the proposed risk analysis methodology described in Chapter 1, Risk and Control Management, to identify the main security risks and the necessary controls. The controls are then discussed in more detail in the following sections and illustrated using examples. References to these sections are provided in Table 9.1, in the section rows.

| No. | Classification | Description |
|---|---|---|
| 1. | Risk potential | Missing or incomplete authorization concept for technical administration of the SAP NetWeaver AS due to insufficient requirements:<br>Administrators and regular users are assigned write access to critical administrative transactions and functions. The four-eyes principle (a predecessor of pair programming) is being disregarded or incorrectly implemented. |
| | Impact | Administrators and regular users can view strictly confidential business information and make unauthorized modifications to this information. This makes it possible for confidential business information to leak to the outside world and poses a serious threat to the integrity of the system. The negative economic effects for the enterprise could be enormous. |
| | Risk without control(s) | Extremely high |

**Table 9.1** Risks and Controls for SAP NetWeaver AS

| No. | Classification | Description |
|---|---|---|
| | Control | Define and implement an administration authorization concept that makes full use of the "four-eyes principle." This applies both to AS ABAP and to AS Java. |
| | Risk with control(s) | Normal |
| | Section | 9.3.1 |
| 2. | Risk potential | No authorization concept for Java applications:<br>There is no authorization concept for Java, which could allow users to access business data that they are not authorized to access. |
| | Impact | The lack of an authorization concept for Java could lead to unauthorized technical system changes being made. However, because current SAP Java applications are not used in critical business areas such as Financial Accounting or Controlling, this situation cannot cause extreme financial losses for the enterprise. Nonetheless, your system may still be compromised, which can include far reaching consequences. |
| | Risk without control(s) | High |
| | Control | Introduce an authorization concept for Java-based applications on the basis of Java Authentication and Authorization Service (JAAS) or User Management Engine (UME) roles. |
| | Risk with control(s) | Normal |
| | Section | 9.3.2 |
| 3. | Risk potential | No authorization restrictions for RFC calls:<br>With RFCs from the SAP NetWeaver AS to another client, to another application, or to another instance that uses an RFC user, the RFC authorizations both in the calling and the called systems have unrestricted authorizations (SAP_ALL profile, for example). |
| | Impact | Even if the RFC user is only of the type COMMUNICATION or SYSTEM, the full authorization status can still be taken advantage of to create a new dialog user with full authorizations in the target system. This entails the risk of unauthorized financial transactions with extremely negative consequences for your enterprise. |

**Table 9.1** Risks and Controls for SAP NetWeaver AS (Cont.)

| No. | Classification | Description |
|---|---|---|
| | Risk without control(s) | Extremely high |
| | Control | Restrict the authorizations for RFC users to the necessary minimum using the authorization objects designed for this purpose. |
| | Risk with control(s) | Normal |
| | Section | 9.3.3 |
| 4. | Risk potential | Passwords that are too numerous and too simple:<br>To authenticate themselves to all of the different applications or clients running on one or more SAP NetWeaver AS installations, users have to log themselves on using a different password in each case. To make it easier to remember their passwords, users either write them down or make them as simple and easy to remember as possible. |
| | Impact | Application passwords that have been written down or that are very simple represent a weak link in the user authentication chain. This situation can enable unauthorized users to abuse applications and to carry out unauthorized transactions. The financial damage from such abuses can be enormous. |
| | Risk without control(s) | Extremely high |
| | Control | Introduce a Single Sign-On (SSO) procedure to reduce the number of user passwords. However, this control is only efficient if the user password for initiating the SSO procedure follows correspondingly secure password rules or if this initial SSO user authentication is secured using a two-factor authentication, for example. |
| | Risk with control(s) | Normal |
| | Section | 9.4.1 |
| 5. | Risk potential | No central user persistence store:<br>Master data is stored in several different user persistence storage locations. In addition to this, there is no unified enterprise-wide employee identifier. The master data storage concept thus contains redundancy and the data is inconsistent. |

**Table 9.1** Risks and Controls for SAP NetWeaver AS (Cont.)

| No. | Classification | Description |
|---|---|---|
| | Impact | Inconsistent user master data causes a large amount of redundancy in user management, not to mention a lack of transparency. Thus, when changes need to be made (for example, if an employee leaves the enterprise or changes the department), user accounts are not managed in an appropriate manner. The result may be the existence of user accounts with excessive authorizations, which could be exploited by other unauthorized users. There are also the additional administrative costs of maintaining redundant user accounts. |
| | Risk without control(s) | Extremely high |
| | Control | Connect the SAP NetWeaver AS to a central Lightweight Directory Access Protocol (LDAP) directory that contains the master data of all users in one central location. This LDAP user management function can be supported by an external LDAP or directory product and by SAP NetWeaver Identity Management (IdM). |
| | Risk with control(s) | Low |
| | Section | 9.4.2 |
| 6. | Risk potential | Default user passwords that have not been changed:<br>The initial default passwords have not been changed for the default users `SAP*`, `DDIC`, and so on. |
| | Impact | Usually, the default passwords for default users are generally known. Therefore, these passwords should be changed as quickly as possible to prevent unauthorized users from using the full authorizations of these default user accounts to make illicit transactions. |
| | Risk without control(s) | Extremely high |
| | Control | Change the default passwords for default users. |
| | Risk with control(s) | Normal |
| | Section | 9.4.3 |

**Table 9.1** Risks and Controls for SAP NetWeaver AS (Cont.)

| No. | Classification | Description |
|---|---|---|
| 7. | Risk potential | The SAP Gateway is not configured:<br>The SAP Gateway controls RFC communication between one SAP NetWeaver AS and another, or between an SAP NetWeaver AS and a CPI-C application. In many cases, this gateway has not been secured. |
| | Impact | The lack of security in the SAP Gateway could allow unauthorized commands to be executed on the target system; for example, a new administrator account could be created. The user of this unauthorized administrator account would then have total control over the target system. |
| | Risk without control(s) | Extremely high |
| | Control | Make RFC communication on the SAP Gateway secure using the *secinfo* file. |
| | Risk with control(s) | Normal |
| | Section | 9.4.4 |
| 8. | Risk potential | No restriction on operating system access:<br>Even regular users can access the operating system from within the SAP NetWeaver AS. |
| | Impact | Operating system commands that are executed using SAP transactions (such as Transaction SM49) could compromise the entire operating system. The integrity of the system is thus not adequately protected, which poses a serious risk to the system. |
| | Risk without control(s) | Extremely high |
| | Control | Take measures to prevent operating system commands from being executed from within the SAP NetWeaver AS. This can be achieved by not assigning transactions with access to the operating system or only to few authorized users, if necessary. |
| | Risk with control(s) | Normal |
| | Section | 9.4.5 |
| 9. | Risk potential | SAP security parameters are not configured:<br>Important security parameters — such as those setting down password rules — are not defined. |

**Table 9.1** Risks and Controls for SAP NetWeaver AS (Cont.)

| No. | Classification | Description |
|---|---|---|
| | Impact | Parameters that have not been configured, or parameters that have been incorrectly configured, cause new weak points in the system. This includes the risk that unauthorized users can carry out transactions or manipulate data for unauthorized purposes. |
| | Risk without control(s) | Extremely high |
| | Control | Correct configuration of system security parameters. |
| | Risk with control(s) | Normal |
| | Section | 9.4.6 |
| 10. | Risk potential | Unencrypted communication channels:<br>The communication channels either between the SAP GUI or web browser and the SAP NetWeaver AS, or between different SAP NetWeaver AS instances, are unencrypted. |
| | Impact | Unencrypted communication channels can allow unauthorized users to view or manipulate confidential business information. This is likely to have negative effects or cause financial losses for the enterprise. |
| | Risk without control(s) | Extremely high |
| | Control | Introduce Secure Socket Layer (SSL) encoding on all HTTP communication channels, or Secure Network Communication (SNC) encoding for Dynamic Information and Action Gateway (DIAG) or RFC connections. |
| | Risk with control(s) | Normal |
| | Section | 9.4.7 |
| 11. | Risk potential | Unnecessary and unsecured Internet services are active:<br>The ICM enables access to and communication with services on the Internet Connection Framework (ICF) of the SAP NetWeaver AS. These services should not be accessible via the Internet. |

**Table 9.1** Risks and Controls for SAP NetWeaver AS (Cont.)

| No. | Classification | Description |
|---|---|---|
| | Impact | If services exist that should not be generally accessible this can indicate security gaps in these service — such as a lack of proper authentication — are used and further unauthorized actions are initiated. In the worst-case scenario, the whole SAP system may be compromised. |
| | Risk without control(s) | High |
| | Control | Deactivate services that are not required and that do not need to be accessible from the Internet. |
| | Risk with control(s) | Normal |
| | Section | 9.4.8 |
| 12. | Risk potential | No network strategy:<br>The SAP NetWeaver AS is not sufficiently secured at the network level for Internet use. |
| | Impact | Inadequate security for the SAP NetWeaver AS in the case of Internet use, with appropriate firewall configuration on the network side, leaves any vulnerabilities at the operating system level open to possible attacks. This can allow system attackers to obtain administrator authorizations, which in turn may compromise the SAP NetWeaver AS. The end result may be unauthorized manipulation of data or unauthorized execution of transactions. |
| | Risk without control(s) | Extremely high |
| | Control | Protect and secure the SAP NetWeaver AS network by dividing up the network segments into trustworthy, less trustworthy, and access-restricted areas. Do this by appropriately setting up and configuring firewalls and other network components. |
| | Risk with control(s) | Low |
| | Section | 9.4.9 |

**Table 9.1** Risks and Controls for SAP NetWeaver AS (Cont.)

| No. | Classification | Description |
|---|---|---|
| 13. | Risk potential | External attacks on Internet applications:<br>Web-based applications (Web Dynpro, BSPs, and JSPs) do not perform adequate checks on the input transferred by the client on the application level, such as URL parameters, form field input, and so on. This involves the risks that hackers carry out the following application-level attacks (these are the main methods of attack):<br>Stealth commanding: changing transfer parameters to obtain a different application status or to modify price information<br>Cookie poisoning and token analysis: enable the hacker to carry out session hijacking |
| | | Buffer overflow: enables a denial-of-service attack<br>Cross-site scripting: enables the hacker to divert the user to a compromised site<br>SQL injection: attacks databases |
| | Impact | Because of inadequately checking input parameters, there is the risk that an application or a database is compromised, and therefore unauthorized users can obtain advanced permissions at the application level. This also means that back-end applications can be accessed, and unauthorized users can retrieve and modify application data. |
| | Risk without control(s) | Extremely high |
| | Control | Transfer parameters and input fields have to be checked for plausibility and correctness on the server side. It is also recommended that you introduce an application-level gateway. This kind of gateway is especially important for in-house applications that will be provided with the SAP NetWeaver AS for Internet use. |
| | Risk with control(s) | Low |
| | Section | 9.4.10 |
| 14. | Risk potential | No security measures at the operating system level of the SAP NetWeaver AS:<br>The SAP NetWeaver AS operating system has not been secured (hardened), resulting in the existence of superfluous operating system services that have not been deactivated. |

**Table 9.1** Risks and Controls for SAP NetWeaver AS (Cont.)

| No. | Classification | Description |
|---|---|---|
| | Impact | This security gap bears the risk that an attacker has gained access to the SAP NetWeaver AS, which means that the SAP NetWeaver AS can now be used in other attacks on the enterprise's back-end applications. |
| | Risk without control(s) | High |
| | Control | The SAP NetWeaver AS has to be hardened adequately on the operating system side. For example, services that are not required by the applications running on the server have to be deactivated.<br>Also, an Intrusion Detection System (IDS) can be established at the server host level. This system can be used to detect possible attacks and to initiate the required countermeasures. |
| | Risk with control(s) | Low |
| | Section | 9.4.11 |
| 15. | Risk potential | No software transport and release system:<br>There is no quality assurance process for newly developed or modified software (such as ABAP or Java applications). |
| | Impact | The lack of a quality assurance process for developing software and transporting it to the production system can cause faulty software to be imported to production servers. This would damage the integrity of the production system. It is thus very likely that the system will be compromised. |
| | Risk without control(s) | Extremely high |
| | Control | Introduce a quality assurance process for developing, assessing, and releasing software, and for transporting it to the production SAP NetWeaver AS. |
| | Risk with control(s) | Normal |
| | Section | 9.4.12 |
| 16. | Risk potential | No quality assurance process:<br>There are no or only insufficient specifications of security requirements for internal or external developers of ABAP or Java programs. |

**Table 9.1** Risks and Controls for SAP NetWeaver AS (Cont.)

| No. | Classification | Description |
|---|---|---|
| | Impact | Business process requirements for quality, authorization controls, and data security are not integrated with customer-specific, newly created ABAP or Java code. This results in security gaps and noncompliance with internal requirements. |
| | Risk without control(s) | High |
| | Control | Establish a quality assurance process for customer-specific program code<br>Define security, authorization, and data security requirements as a part of the program creation requirements<br>Assess and test the new program code with regard to compliance with security specifications |
| | Risk with control(s) | Low |
| | Section | 9.4.13 |

**Table 9.1** Risks and Controls for SAP NetWeaver AS (Cont.)

## 9.3 Application Security

This section describes in more detail the risks and controls that are outlined in Table 9.1 and occur in application security.

### 9.3.1 Technical Authorization Concept for Administrators

Based on the relevance, risks, and complexity of the technical SAP systems, an appropriate authorization concept for authorizations in the technical ABAP environment should reflect the specific conditions and requirements of the relevant server administration and business processes. The authorization concept for administrators of the ABAP stack in the SAP NetWeaver AS is based on the ABAP standard authorization concept, as described in Chapter 20.

This concept defines the procedures, rules, and roles that apply to administrators, and specifies the administrative functions of the SAP NetWeaver AS. As is the case with business-department-specific authorizations, you should also perform a risk analysis of the critical functions of the SAP NetWeaver AS, so that you can make the appropriate functional and logical separations when setting the authorizations (see Figure 9.2).

Unfortunately, it is often the case that very generous authorizations are assigned to the administrators of SAP NetWeaver AS systems. The reason here is often the lack of governance, task-based and requirements roles that are not clearly defined, or missing risk analyses for the task area of the server administrators. It is the responsibility of every enterprise to assess the potential risks of its own situation and define the respective risk management requirements. However, a technology authorization concept is a mandatory component of the overlying authorization and IT security concept, and it should always form part of the enterprise's approach to ensuring that the processes of the SAP ERP system, and all other systems that are based on SAP NetWeaver AS, run smoothly.

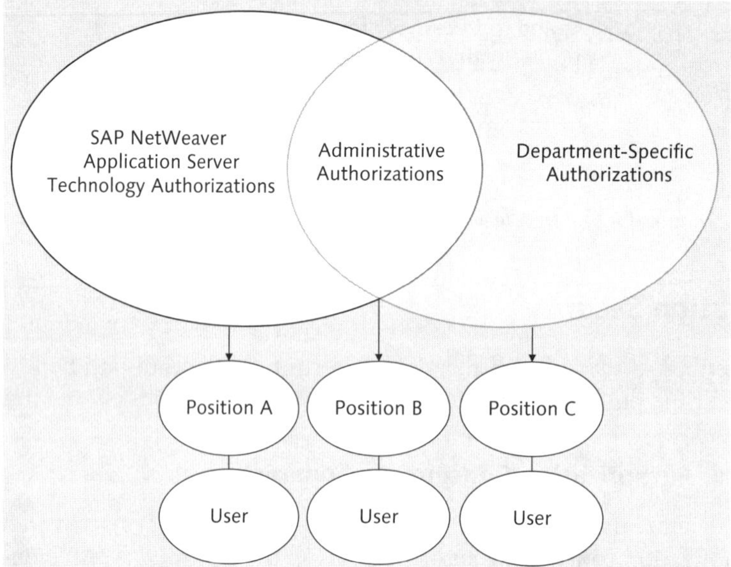


**Figure 9.2** Technology Authorizations Are a Part of a Holistic Authorization Concept

How do you develop such an authorization concept? The basis of a solid authorization concept for the SAP NetWeaver AS is formed by clearly defined task-based roles. They can be grouped into position roles for organizational reasons. Because the size and quality of technology and development teams can vary, we assume here that a work center consists of multiple administrative task roles. A task role in this context is defined in terms of the quantity of transactions that have a logical relationship with each other and bear no functional risks when being combined. Task roles contain the authorizations that are required to execute all transactions of the role. Because an individual task role usually only covers some of the activities of the basic user, multiple task roles are usually assigned to the basic user; or all required transactions are assigned in aggregated form to a basic user as a basic single role.

If at all possible, an administrative user should only be assigned to one work center — that is, to only one position. If multiple positions are involved, transactions are grouped into either a single role or a composite role and then assigned to the employee.

**Example**

An employee may be working as a developer and a customizer at the same time. These roles are often implemented as generic roles in the technology area. This means that they do not contain any restrictions in terms of organizational boundaries.

However, there can also be roles that are specially developed for the development system, the quality assurance system, or the production system. Thus, the authorizations that a developer has in the development system may be more extensive than those that he has in the quality assurance system. Developers shouldn't be able to access the production system. This creates a situation where the developer has different positions in the development system, the quality assurance or test system, and the production system.

However, like with other authorizations, the scope of technology authorizations can be restricted; in this case, the main elements are user group, role name, development class, and program or table authorization group.

The risk analysis process for technology authorizations has the advantage that roles can also be analyzed in terms of their incompatibility with each other. Two technology roles are considered incompatible if, for system security and risk-related reasons, they cannot both be assigned to the same user.

**Example**

The maintenance of roles and authorizations, and the administration of users (such as the assignment of roles to users shouldn't both belong to the access rights or function assignments of the same person. If the roles of these two task areas, which are actually incompatible, are assigned to one administrator, control via the four-eyes principle is not given. These criteria for role incompatibility should be defined in a risk analysis document.

Incompatibility between two roles may also result in incompatibility between two positions, as multiple positions may be assigned to an SAP user due to internal requirements. You will then have to ensure that appropriate measures are put in place to monitor the activities of the employees in question, to minimize the risk involved.

Application areas usually describe the functions and objectives of specific task areas, and are used to delimit the functions that are assigned to employees. The following are some of the application areas in the technology area:

- Integration of data communication between systems (Application Link Enabling (ALE))
- Authorization management and user management
- Authorization management
- Customizing and development
- Operations
- System administration
- Workflow management

Once the risk analysis has been used to divide up the tasks, the organizational factors can be incorporated into the design of the authorization concept. The process of assigning work areas to specific positions in the technology area is also useful in developing and assigning roles and authorizations on the position level. For example, the project coordinator, developer, customizer, and quality specialist positions may be assigned to the Customizing and Development work area. The positions assigned to the Operations work area could be as follows: archiver, batch user in the business department, batch job administrator, help desk worker, and operator.

The following describes some positions from the technology area as examples; the transactions of the individual positions can be grouped together in a single role or a composite role and assigned to technology users:

- **ALE developer**
  ALE is used for closely integrated data communication between SAP and non-SAP systems. The benefit of this concept is the high data communication performance. This position requires authorizations for the following tasks, among others: developing ALE applications, maintaining ALE Customizing settings; using Intermediate Documents (IDoc) test tools; displaying IDoc types; IDoc record types and segments; configuring ALE partner agreements, ports, and change pointers; adapting ALE controls (process code, status); and implementing ALE monitoring. There are also other positions for ALE, such as ALE customizer, ALE administrator, and ALE monitor.
- **Auditor/reviser**
  This position requires authorizations for the following tasks, among others: using reports in the audit information system, the security audit log, and the authorization information system, and displaying tables that are relevant to users and authorizations.
- **Batch user in business departments**
  This position requires authorizations for the following tasks, among others:

scheduling, modifying, and monitoring batch jobs that are relevant to the business department, and analyzing their results.

- **Batch job operator**
  This position requires all authorizations for job management – for example, for scheduling, modifying, monitoring, and analyzing internal and external background jobs.
- **Authorization administrator (central control)**
  This position requires authorizations for the following tasks, among others: maintaining all authorization components, displaying users and tables with authorization data, creating transport requests, and all transactions that restrict or manage authorizations, authorization groups, and authorization views, among others. Authorization administration is not purely a technology task; it is a general position that also includes business department authorizations. Because of the higher relevance of this position, it is important that you put control and monitoring measures in place.
- **Customizer**
  This position requires authorizations for the following tasks, among others: making client-specific and cross-client Customizing settings, using maintenance functions in the development system and display functions in the quality assurance and production system, and maintaining transaction variants, global field values, tables, hypertexts, SAPscript texts, fonts, number range buffers and intervals, transport requests, and so on.
- **Developer**
  This position requires authorizations for the following tasks, among others: performing development activities in the development system, performing display activities in the quality assurance and production system, carrying out web developments, developing CATT and eCATT processes, creating and administrating queries, maintaining hypertexts, SAPscript texts, and fonts and how they are displayed, displaying Customizing projects and settings, maintaining transaction variants and global field values, maintaining table content, using the authorization information system, performing internal basic system administration functions for all trace functions, and generating transport requests. Remember to watch out for users with different authorizations in different systems.
- **Help desk**
  This position requires authorizations for the following tasks, among others: administrating printers, displaying spool requests and user data, locking and unlocking users, modifying user passwords, and other help functions within SAP ERP that are adapted to each real-world situation.

- **Operator**
  This position requires authorizations for the following tasks, among others: displaying the Computing Center Management System (CCMS) system configuration, CCMS database administration functions, system and client changeability, work processes and user sessions, carrying out performance analyses, and displaying transport requests.
- **Project coordinator**
  This position requires authorizations for the following tasks, among others: displaying Repository development work, authorization objects and fields, CATT and eCATT processes, Customizing settings, and Customizing objects, using the Cross System Viewer, and displaying table content. In quality assurance and production systems, it is very important that these authorizations be restricted to table authorization groups to prevent access to sensitive data relating to transactions for table maintenance (Transactions SM30, SM31) and table display (Transactions SE16, SE17).
- **Quality specialist**
  This position requires authorizations for the following tasks, among others: departmental acceptance of transports containing development and Customizing work, displaying and releasing transport requests, and releasing tasks.
- **Administrator for security and user authorizations**
  This position requires authorizations for the following tasks, among others: all transactions to do with authorizations, user management, and IT security, including maintenance and display transactions, monitoring functions, trace activities, master data maintenance, creating new authorization objects and fields, the Profile Generator, the check indicator, administrating profile parameters, creating transport requests, administrating the audit information system, locking and unlocking transactions, and so on. The position of the administrator for security and user authorizations has very wide-ranging authorizations and therefore has to be subject to appropriate monitoring controls.
- **System administrator for SAP data center**
  This position requires authorizations for creating, deleting, and copying clients; modifying the CCMS system configuration; carrying out CCMS database administration tasks; defining and executing logical commands in a controlled manner; displaying the changeability of systems and clients; administrating work processes and user sessions; maintaining RFC and CPI-C connections; configuring National Language Support; authorizations for various display functions, including for number range buffers and intervals, carrying out performance analyses, configuring and analyzing the security audit log, sending system messages, locking and unlocking transactions, activating and analyzing system traces, creating, modifying, and deleting background jobs for spool manage-

ment, displaying user and authorization data, and configuring the Central Transport System (CTS+) by setting up transport routes and administrating transport requests. These tasks can be divided up into smaller units, depending on the organizational structure of the task assignments.

- **Workflow developer**
  This position requires authorizations for development work in SAP Business Workflow workflow management, making Customizing settings in administrating workflows, maintaining organizational structures, using runtime tools, and using utilities and the workflow information system. Workflow development includes workflow administration and workflow monitoring. These positions can be defined either together or separately and can be mapped in roles.
- **Central user administrator**
  This position requires authorizations for creating and administrating user data, either with Transaction SU01 or with the Central User Administration functions. These tasks include locking and unlocking users, making password changes for users, assigning roles and authorizations to users (this task can also be handed over to the business departments as an independent task, at which point the departments take over information ownership), displaying roles, authorizations, authorization objects, authorization object fields, and displaying the Workbench and the tables of the Profile Generator (`USOBT_C`, `USOBX_C`). Security audit log usage can also be included as a task of this position. If a company used SAP NetWeaver IdM, a central user administrator would have comprehensive authorizations for role assignment and user administration.

There are currently no selective administrator authorizations for administrating the AS Java using the Visual Administrator or the config tool. Therefore, the config tool can be started on the operating system level without any authorizations. Thus, you must ensure that access to the operating system is subject to tight restrictions. You can do this using access control lists for Windows or the correct configuration of Unique Identifications (UIDs) for UNIX, for example. You can define an initial administrator account during the installation process for the Visual Administrator, which is connected to the J2EE Engine by the P4 protocol. However, in this case, as before, you should place extra restrictions on operating system access.

You should also implement measures on the network side to ensure that access to the Visual Administrator is restricted:

- Access to the P4 interface (by default, port 50004 for instance 00) must be protected from unauthorized access via a firewall. However, because the P4 protocol can be tunneled via HTTP (by default, port 50001 for instance 00), this port also needs to be protected.

- The Telnet administration service of the AS Java (by default, port 50008 for instance 00), which enables target-oriented administration, should be deactivated if it is not in use.

Table 9.2 contains a list of actions for administrating Java roles on the basis of the SAP UME, the principle of which is explained in more detail in the next section. These actions can be grouped together to form UME roles. UME administration is called using the URL *http:// <SAP_NetWeaver_Application_Server>:<J2EE_Engine_Port>/ useradmin*.

| UME Action | Description |
|---|---|
| `UME.Manage_All` | This action assigns full maintenance authorization — including for ABAP users, if the persistence store has been configured accordingly — for the J2EE Engine, including permissions to perform the following tasks:<br>▶ Administrate users in all departments and subsidiaries, including creating, modifying, deleting, locking, and unlocking users, and confirming new user creation requests<br>▶ Create, modify, and delete user groups<br>▶ Assign UME roles to users<br>▶ Import and export user data<br>▶ Manually replicate user data with external persistence storage |
| `UME.Manage_Users` | This action authorizes the recipient to manage users in their own departments or users in the company. These users can include the administrator to whom this action is assigned. Chapter 16, SAP NetWeaver Portal, explains how to configure assignments to a department or a company in more detail.<br>This action also authorizes the recipient to perform the following tasks: search, create, modify, delete, lock, unlock, reset passwords, and confirm new user creation requests. |
| `UME.Manage_All_User_Passwords` | This action authorizes the recipient to administrate passwords, regardless of the subsidiary. |
| `UME.Manage_User_Passwords` | This action authorizes the recipient to administrate passwords within the subsidiary. |

**Table 9.2** Java Actions for J2EE Administration

| UME Action | Description |
|---|---|
| UME.Manage_Groups | This action authorizes the recipient to view, add, modify, and delete user groups. It also authorizes them to assign users to groups. Administrators to whom this action is assigned can only perform these tasks for users in their own department or subsidiary. |
| UME.Manage_Roles | This action authorizes the recipient to administrate UME roles. This involves the risk that users use this UME action, for example, to assign administrator roles to themselves that allow for full access to the AS Java. |
| UME.Manage_All_ Companies | This action authorizes administrators to maintain users in all department and subsidiaries. This action can be assigned in conjunction with the UME.Manage_Groups action, for example. |
| UME.Sync_Admin | This action authorizes the recipient to synchronize user data with external persistent storage. |
| UME.Batch_Admin | This action authorizes the recipient to import and export users and user groups. However, it is restricted to users and user groups in the authorization holder's own department or subsidiary. |
| UME.Manage_My_Profile | This action authorizes the recipient to display and modify their own user profile. It does not grant any authorizations for assigning new roles. (If the UME property ume.admin. allow_selfmanagement is set to True, this action is not checked, with the result that this authorization stays in place indefinitely.) |

**Table 9.2** Java Actions for J2EE Administration (Cont.)

### 9.3.2 Authorization Concept for Java Applications

The SAP NetWeaver AS supports two authorization concepts for Java applications (that is, JSP and Web Dynpro Java (WDJ) applications):

- Java Authentication and Authorization Standard (JAAS) for J2EE
- UME

These two concepts are described briefly in the following sections, without much detail, as an understanding of the Java security architecture requires in-depth knowledge of how to program Java applications using EJBs. Although the Web Dynpro programming environment is an SAP standard and only the UME role concept is available for this environment — the UME concept adds an improved role concept to the JAAS — the principles of the JAAS are briefly explained as an aid to understanding the UME concept.

### JAAS Concept

The most effective way of creating JSP applications is to use EJBs. EJBs are independent standard components that first and foremost provide the developer with business logic operations. They are managed inside the AS Java with the help of an EJB container and can only be run within this container. The EJB container handles the following standard tasks: lifecycle management, security management in accordance with the JAAS, transaction management, persistence services, and naming convention management.

There are three different types of EJBs:

- **Session Beans**
  They are responsible for communication with the client.
- **Entity Beans**
  They take care of data retention and its persistence in the database.
- **Message-Driven Beans**
  They are required for communication with other beans or objects, including those on back-end systems.

Because EJBs run inside the EJB container, the container has to be aware of their existence, their available methods (in object-oriented programming, methods define program-based access to an object), and their use. This is done using the Deployment Descriptor (an XML file called *web.xml*). The Deployment Descriptor enables declarative programming and describes the properties of EJBs and their security attributes or authorization concepts.

The JAAS authorization concept uses the concepts of principals and roles:

- **Principal**
  A principal is a user of the application who has already been authenticated by the application and is thus known to the application.
- **Role**
  A role in the JAAS context represents a group of principals that, through the role, is assigned certain application permissions. Thus, application permissions are assigned to a role, which in turn assigns these permissions to a group of principals (ultimately, to the user).

An application permission defines the right, or the absence of the right, to run a specific EJB and the methods it contains. The definitions of application permissions are either declarative or program based.

- In the case of a declarative authorization concept, the roles are defined in the Deployment Descriptor of the EJBs. The granularity of the security concept is based on the EJB level and the methods it contains. Thus, a role describes which EJB and which of its methods the role may run and execute. It is possible to authorize a role to run all methods or some of the methods in an EJB; this is the maximum level of granularity.

- If necessary, the programming authorization concept has to cover these requirements. Two methods are available to the developer for this purpose: `getCallerPrincipal` and `isCallerInRole`.
  - `getCallerPrincipal` returns the identity of the user.
  - `isCallerInRole` checks whether a principal has been assigned to a role.

  This way, the developer can program additional authorization checks, such as a rule-based query.

  However, you shouldn't use program-based authorization concepts too much, as "hard-coded" security checks are always time-consuming and troublesome to manage afterward, and are therefore very inflexible. The ABAP authorization concept, with its individuality and flexibility, cannot be used with the JAAS, or at best, can only be used with the JAAS if an enormous amount of time and effort is invested.

The following is an example of a declarative authorization concept, described using the Deployment Descriptor. The Deployment Descriptor is located in a JAR file (Java program code file, developed with the SAP NetWeaver Developer Studio for Java applications), which contains all of the EJBs that have been developed. All of the possible roles are defined in the assembly section of the Deployment Descriptor (see Listing 9.1).

```
...
<assembly-descriptor>
  <security-role>
    <description>
      Decription: general user
    </description>
  <role-name>all</role-name>
  </security-role>
  <security-role>
    <description>
      Decription: administrator
    </description>
    <role-name>admin-user</role-name>
  </security-role>
...
</assembly-descriptor>
```

**Listing 9.1** Assembly Section of the Deployment Descriptor

Listing 9.1 defines the names of the roles `all` and `admin-user`. This is always done inside the <security-role> tag. You can also use the optional <description> tag to provide a description. Now these roles have to be assigned to the EJBs and the available methods inside the JAR file (or Java component). This is done using the <method-permission> tag inside the assembly section (see Listing 9.2).

```
...
<method-permission>
  <role-name>admin-user</role-name>
  <method>
    <ejb-name>SystemLogin</ejb-name>
    <method-name>*</method-name>
  </method>
</method-permission>
<method-permission>
  <role-name>all</role-name>
  <method>
    <ejb-name>LoginMaintenance</ejb-name>
    <method-name>modifyPersInfo</method-name>
  </method>
</method-permission>
...
```

**Listing 9.2** Assigning Allowed Roles to Java Methods Inside the Assembly Section of the Deployment Descriptor

In Listing 9.2, execute access to all methods of the `SystemLogin` EJB is granted to the administrator role `admin-user`. The general `all` user, on the other hand, is only granted execute permissions to the `modifyPersInfo` method of the `LoginMaintenance` EJB. This is the approach that should be used to granting execute access to the different EJBs and component methods for the various roles. It uses positive declaration; that is, only roles that are explicitly named are assigned permissions, and all other roles get no permissions.

In the next step, J2EE roles are assigned to users or to user groups. This is done in the SAP NetWeaver AS using the Visual Administrator, as shown in Figure 9.3. The available J2EE roles are displayed under the SECURITY PROVIDER service for a specific Java component and can then be assigned to the defined AS Java users.

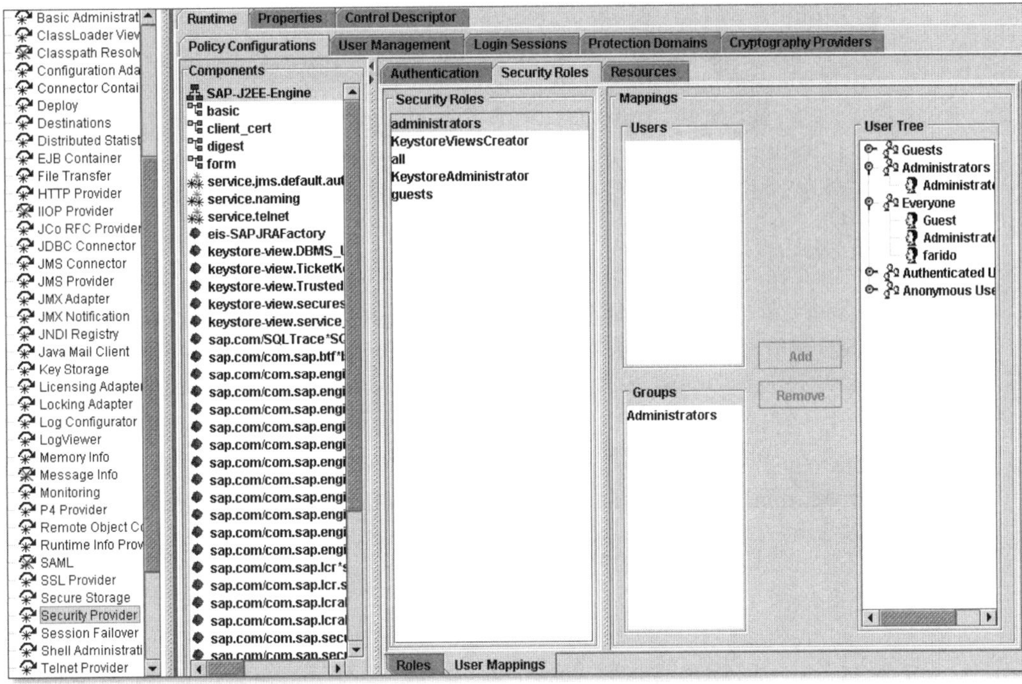


**Figure 9.3** Assigning J2EE Roles to User Groups with the Visual Administrator

As you can see, the J2EE authorization concept very much depends on how the developer configures it, and is thus more flexible than, for example, the ABAP authorization concept. For this reason, SAP extended the basic JAAS concept and further developed it within the UME.

### UME Authorization Concept for Java Applications

The UME is the core of user and role management for Java-based applications in AS Java. It also fulfils an indispensable function as the basis of the SAP NetWeaver Portal, as the SAP NetWeaver Portal uses the AS Java as a runtime environment. Portal roles are based completely on the UME. The technical architecture and functions are therefore described in more detail in Chapter 16.

The UME can be configured in such a way that its own J2EE database, an LDAP directory, or the AS ABAP can be used as the user persistence storage medium (master data and logon data). This is also the case for the SAP NetWeaver Portal and is therefore not described until Chapter 16, which also describes the exact configuration.

This section mainly focuses on the details of the UME role concept for Java applications, which is different from the portal role concept. Portal roles define content that is mapped in the portal (iViews, worksets, and so on), while UME roles are used to specify the authorizations for the Java applications in the portal. In contrast to the JAAS, this is a program-based authorization concept. The developer defines application permissions in the application, which he then bundles together to form actions using the declarative file *actions.xml*. Because the individual application permissions can become very complex, bundling the actions has the advantage of imposing a logical structure on the permissions. The action `UME.Manage_Roles` contains all application permissions required to manage UME roles, without the authorization administrator having to know all of the methods necessary for creating roles.

Ultimately, actions can themselves be bundled to form UME roles, using the UME Console (a web-based front end that can be called via a URL, such as *http://myserver.mycompany.com:50000/useradmin*), and then assigned to users. Figure 9.4 illustrates the UME role concept for Java applications. Actions can also be bundled into roles and administrated in the UME Console.

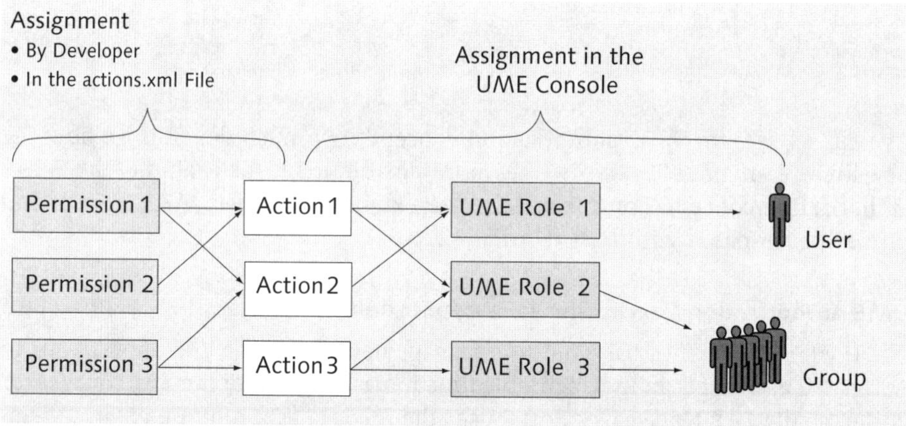


**Figure 9.4** UME Role Concept for Java Applications

One detail should be explained here: If the AS ABAP is used as the persistence storage for the users, a problem arises: there is no group definition for users in ABAP. This problem is solved by the fact that the users who are assigned to a specific ABAP role in the AS ABAP are shown as a user group in the UME Console; in other words, the ABAP role name appears as a group name in the UME. All users who are assigned to this ABAP role are also assigned to this UME group.

A similar situation occurs, for example, if the SAP NetWeaver Portal has been configured in such a way that its persistence storage is the AS ABAP of the SAP back-end system for user authentication. In this scenario, the ABAP roles (simple roles) that have been generated with the SAP Profile Generator in the SAP back-end system correspond to the UME groups in the portal.

### 9.3.3 Restricting Authorizations for RFC Calls

In a server group, or in a situation where different clients are used for production on one SAP NetWeaver AS, one program part (for example, within a specific transaction) often has to call data on another client or another SAP NetWeaver AS instance. This is usually done using an RFC. In an RFC, an SAP NetWeaver AS can be either server or client.

The process of calling ABAP function groups, which then read the required data, takes place in the server system by means of an RFC destination. An RFC destination describes a data record that is stored in the RFC client and contains two types of information: data that describes the network connection, and authentication data for the RFC user. Authentication data is only required if the server system is an SAP NetWeaver AS. The RFC user is used for logons in the server system. This user is active in the server system and has specific authorizations, which we shall now look at in detail.

RFC calls can be one of two basic types: untrusted and trusted. The difference between these two types is that if an untrusted RFC call is made, the client has to authenticate itself to the server using the proper RFC user credentials. If a trusted RFC call is made, no authentication is necessary, as the server system trusts the client.

Figure 9.5 shows the basic procedure of an untrusted RFC call and the authorization objects that are checked in this procedure. With this type of call, a user in system A starts a particular transaction in which an RFC call is made to system B. Here, the authorization object `S_ICF` is checked, which contains the `ICF_FIELD` and `ICF_VALUE` authorization fields. The `ICF_FIELD` field can have either the Service or Dest values.

- Service has to be defined if an ICF service is called.
- Dest can be selected if the call is an RFC call, defined using Transaction SM59.

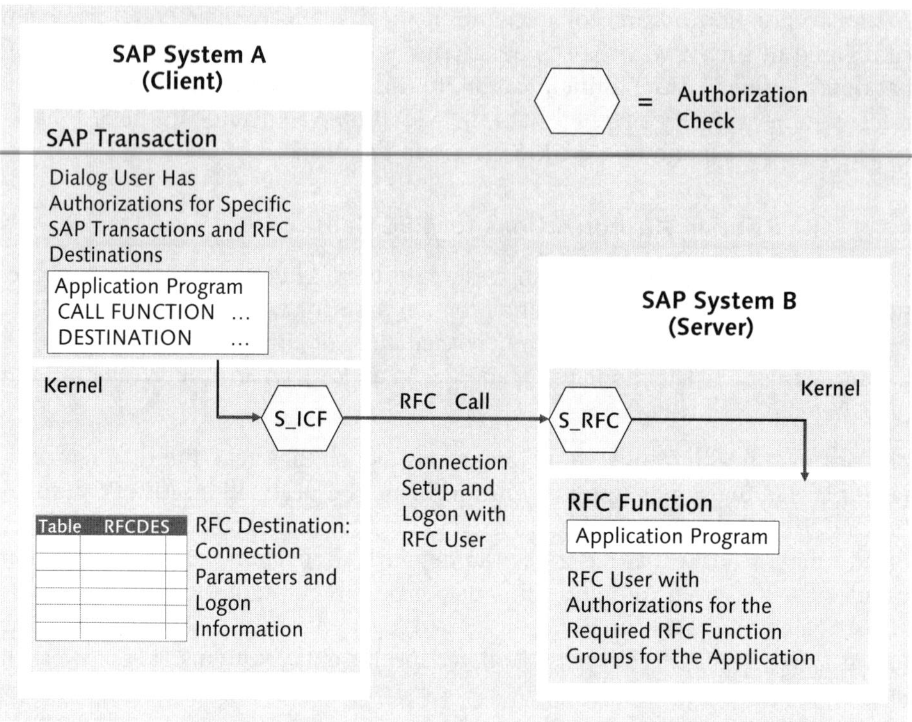


**Figure 9.5** Untrusted RFC Call and Checked Authorization Object (S_RFC)

The ICF_VALUE field can contain the ICF services or RFC destinations for the user, or better still, for the role. Table RFCDES contains a list of the possible RFC destinations.

To make the RFC call to system B, the client has to log on using the RFC user that has been defined in system B for this call. Then, in system B, the RFC call is granted the authorizations that have been defined for the RFC user in authorization object S_RFC. Authorization object S_RFC has the following authorization fields:

- RFC_TYPE
  Type of the RFC object that is to be protected. Currently, this field can only take the value FUGR (function group).
- RFC_NAME
  Name of the RFC object that is to be protected. This field contains the name of the function groups that can be called by the RFC user. It is important that full authorization — that is, an asterisk (*) — is not entered here, or else the user would be able to call critical function groups for creating users. Unfortunately, this rule is often not adhered to. For this reason, we shall now show you how

to use a security audit log to find the function groups that are necessary for the application in question and to restrict these function groups.

- ACTVT
  Activity. Currently, this field can take only the value "16" (execute).

If an RFC call is made between trusted systems, the call proceeds as follows (see Figure 9.6): There is no need for the client to log on using an RFC user. Instead, the user ID of the dialog user that is active in system A is transferred. In this case, this dialog user becomes an RFC service user. For this reason, it is important that there is an additional authorization check in system B, using authorization object S_RFCACL. This check establishes whether the user who is logged on in the client system is allowed to log himself onto the server system under the user ID in question.

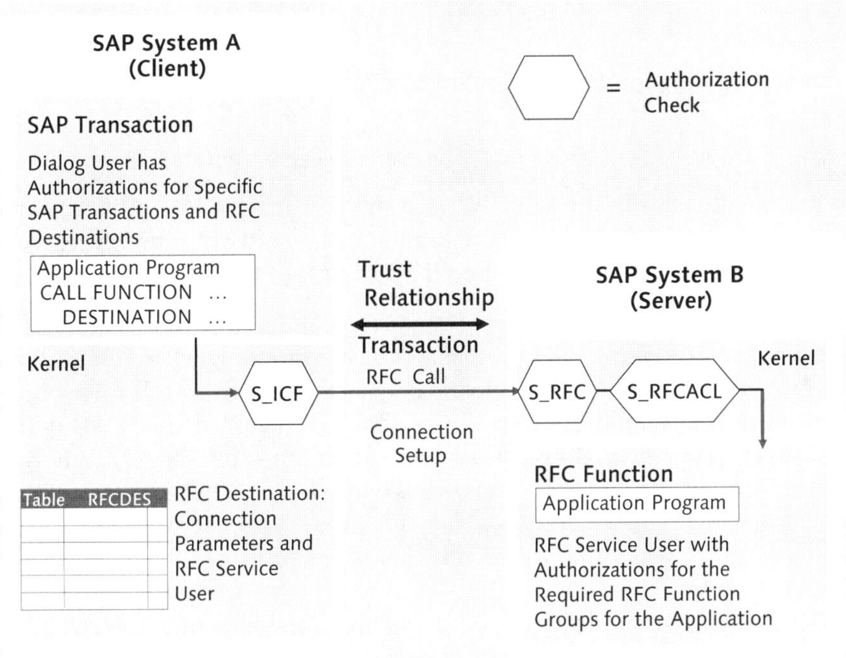


**Figure 9.6** Trusted RFC Call and Checked Authorization Objects (S_RFC and S_RFCACL)

The authorization object S_RFCACL has the following authorization fields:

- RFC_SYSID
  System ID of the calling system A (client system)

- RFC_CLIENT
  Client of the calling system A
- RFC_USER
  User ID of the calling user in system A. It is important that full authorization (*) is not entered here, or else every user in system B would be able to call the function groups in the S_RFC object. This could be a critical problem if, for example, full authorization was defined, as is often the case. It is precisely because of this problem that in many cases trusted RFC calls are not used. We likewise recommend that you use this type of call only in exceptional cases.
- RFC_EQUSER
  Indicator that shows whether the RFC service user can only be called by a user with the same ID (Y=Yes, N=No).
- RFC_TCODE
  Calling transaction; the calling transaction code is entered or checked.
- RFC_INFO
  Additional information from the calling system that is currently inactive.
- ACTVT
  Activity. Currently, only the value "16" (execute) can be entered.

As already mentioned, from a security point of view, trusted RFC calls are more problematic because an incorrect configuration of the authorization object leads to significant security gaps. So you should avoid using this RFC variant as much as possible.

For the risk management of the RFC call, the correct configuration of authorizations for the RFC_NAME authorization field of the S_RFC authorization object assumes a critical role. Full authorization (*) should be avoided at all costs in this case. However, implementation instructions often only allow for full authorization. The concept described in the following text is a way of circumventing this problem, as it allows you to specify the function groups that you want to call. This is done using the Security Audit Log, which is activated using Transaction SM19 and can be analyzed using Transaction SM20. Unlike the system trace (Transaction ST01), the Security Audit Log is not particularly resource-intensive, so it can remain active over quite a long period of time.

To determine which function groups are actually called using RFC, you can implement a special configuration for the Security Audit Log. To do this, the Security Audit Log has to be activated for all clients, users, and events in the audit class for RFC calls. This is done in Transaction SM19. After approximately two months — we can assume that in this time period, the function groups that are necessary for the application will have been called at least once — the audit log can be analyzed using Transaction SM20 (SM20N). The log can then be downloaded to an Excel table and the called function groups filtered out. These can then be entered as authorization values into the RFC_NAME authorization field.

The scope of the authorization is thus set to exactly these function groups. You should follow this procedure for all documented RFC call destinations, so that full authorization can be gradually eliminated.

## 9.4 Technical Security

This section describes in more detail the risks and controls that are outlined in Table 9.1 and occur in the area of technical security.

### 9.4.1 Introducing an SSO Authentication Mechanism

There are a number of different procedures for introducing an SSO authentication mechanism, which allows users to log themselves onto various SAP systems at once. Which procedure you choose depends on the particular scenario in each case.

#### Scenario 1: SAP NetWeaver Portal Used

If an SAP NetWeaver Portal is in use, and to provide the user with a consistent user interface, you should choose one of the SSO mechanisms outlined in Chapter 16. In this case, the leading logon system is always SAP NetWeaver Portal. From the SSO mechanisms possible, the most secure procedure in this context is an SSO mechanism that is based on digital certificates (in accordance with the X.509 standard), as this mechanism is based on a dual-factor approach.

#### Scenario 2: SAP NetWeaver Portal Not Used

If an SAP NetWeaver Portal is not in use but you still want to implement an SSO mechanism for multiple SAP systems, there are, again, a number of ways of doing this, which likewise depend on the type of SAP NetWeaver AS front-end connection that you are using.

- If only the SAP GUI for Windows is in use, choose one of the options described in Chapter 28, User Interfaces, in the SAP GUI section. In this case, as before, because of security concerns, you should seriously consider a certificate-based solution.
- If only the SAP GUI for HTML (web browser) is in use, choose one of the options described in Chapter 28. Again, we recommend that you use X.509 certificates.

- On the other hand, if you want to use the SAP GUI for Windows and the SAP GUI for HTML together, and if you also want to include BSPs, Web Dynpro ABAP, WDJ, and JSPs, you should configure the SAP NetWeaver AS to be the main system and the one that issues SAP logon tickets. SAP logon tickets are web browser cookies that confirm that a user has successfully authenticated himself to a main SAP NetWeaver AS, using that user's digital signature. When this user sends his next request, the browser sends the cookie along with it, enabling other SAP NetWeaver ASs that trust the main SAP NetWeaver AS to use the cookie. The cookie, or the SAP logon ticket as it is more accurately called, can also be transferred to an SAP GUI for Windows, although only with the special shortcut version of the SAP GUI.

  However, there can only be one main system, or else the trust relationships would cross over each other, incurring a high level of administrative work and reducing the level of security due to the increasing risk of an incorrect configuration. All trust relationships have to be defined in accordance with portal scenario 1. There is only one system — that is, either the SAP NetWeaver Portal or an SAP NetWeaver AS — that issues SAP logon tickets, and all other systems must accept this system as trustworthy.

  How this is technically achieved depends on whether the user first logs himself on to the main system using WDJ applications or, as is the usual case, logs on to the AS ABAP. In the former case, the AS Java has to be configured as the system that issues SAP logon tickets; in the latter case, it is the AS ABAP that has to be configured. If the AS Java is the main system, the integrated Windows-Kerberos authentication method can be used instead of the simple user ID and password authentication method. The Windows-Kerberos method is described in greater detail in Chapter 16, but also works with the AS Java.

  In all cases, a trust relationship has to be set up between the systems that are supposed to accept SAP logon tickets, that is, the AS ABAP and AS Java, and the issuing system. This applies in particular to AS Java if Java applications — such as WDJ — are supposed to be incorporated into the SSO mechanism.

The following briefly describes the configuration steps that you need to take if an AS ABAP system is supposed to create SAP logon tickets and these tickets are supposed to be accepted by an ABAP application on another SAP NetWeaver AS. This is a very common scenario.

- **Step 1**

  Configure the AS ABAP to issue SAP logon tickets:

  - A public key infrastructure (public trust center, such as a certificate authority) has to issue and sign a digital certificate for the server on the basis of the

X.509 standard. Alternatively, self-signed certificates can also be used. However, this is advisable only in test scenarios.

- Transaction STRUST is used to import the certificate into the Personal Security Environment (PSE) of the SAP NetWeaver AS. In the case of SSO, this is the PSE system.

- **Step 2**
  Configure the following three system parameters to create SAP logon tickets:
  - `login/accept_sso2_ticket`
    Set this to "1" to specify that the SAP NetWeaver AS itself can accept SAP logon tickets.
  - `login/create_sso2_ticket`
    Set this to "1" to specify that the SAP NetWeaver AS itself can create SAP logon tickets and embed its own digital certificate in them. You can also set "2" here, but you should only do this for self-signed server certificates.
  - `login/ticket_expiration_time`
    This value specifies the validity time period of the SAP logon ticket. It should not be greater than "8" (eight hours). This approximates the duration of a normal working day.
- **Step 3**
  Configure the AS ABAP to accept SAP logon tickets:
  - Set the `login/accept_sso2_ticket` parameter to "1" to activate acceptance of SAP logon tickets.
  - Run the SSO Wizard (Transaction SSO2). Here, you have to enter either an RFC destination for the server that issues SAP logon tickets, or alternatively, the server name and the system ID. The activate button activates the trust relationship. If errors occur, Transaction STRUSTSSO2 can be used to track down these errors.

Once you have completed the configuration, the user can then log on to the main SAP NetWeaver AS using an SAP GUI for HTML and, for example, start the BSP application on the other SAP NetWeaver AS. The application is stored as a link in the user's menu. The user doesn't have to log on to this SAP NetWeaver AS again.

### 9.4.2 Connecting the SAP NetWeaver AS to a Central LDAP Directory

You should use a central LDAP directory to store the user master data of the employees in your enterprise, especially if multiple production SAP NetWeaver ASs are in use in conjunction with the SAP NetWeaver Portal. This scenario is discussed in detail in Chapter 16, which also explains the hierarchy definitions for a flat or deep LSAP directory.

In the portal scenario, the LDAP directory should be used as the main user persistence storage location for all connected SAP NetWeaver ASs. However, unlike the SAP NetWeaver Portal, an AS ABAP cannot access the LDAP directory "online" — that is, during the process of authenticating a user; instead, it has to synchronize the user master data with its own user storage (ABAP user storage). As mentioned at the start of this section, changes should only be permitted in the LDAP directory, so that no inconsistencies arise. The AS Java instead can connect to the LDAP directory online using the UME. This is done in the same way as for the SAP NetWeaver Portal, which also accesses the LDAP directory using the UME. However, the AS Java can also be configured in such a way that the main user persistence storage is the ABAP user storage. This is the recommended variant, because in this case no inconsistencies can arise between AS ABAP and AS Java, and it also allows the assignment of users to groups to be managed using ABAP roles.

The following user master data is usually stored in the LDAP directory and can be synchronized in the AS ABAP using the LDAP Connector:

- Human resources (HR) data (name, department, organization)
- User data and security information (user account, authorizations, public key certificates)
- Information about system resources and system services (system ID, application configuration, printer configuration)

As mentioned already, the LDAP protocol and the LDAP Connector are used for the purposes of synchronization with the LDAP directory. The LDAP Connector is called via ABAP functions and communicates with the LDAP directory server. Various logon methods can be used to establish a connection with the LDAP directory server, such as simple connection (user ID and password) or anonymous connection (guest account without password). It is also possible to use a stronger authentication method on the basis of digital certificates using the LDAPS protocol (LDAP secured with SSL). In general, synchronization is possible with directories that correspond to the LDAP format.

However, after the LDAP Connector has been configured (this handles synchronization), the directory schema also has to be adapted. This involves defining which directory attribute is to be mapped to which SAP attribute. SAP already provides adequate mapping rules for numerous manufacturers. These rules can then be adapted to the requirements of the individual enterprise.

### 9.4.3 Changing the Default Passwords for Default Users

The default passwords for the following default users are widely known, and therefore have to be changed immediately once the SAP NetWeaver AS is installed:

- `SAP*`
  The `SAP*` user in clients 000 and 066 is a super user with comprehensive permissions to set up a new SAP NetWeaver AS. This user has the initial password "06071992".. The `SAP*` user is also used to set up a new client and in this case has the initial password "pass."
- `DDIC`
  The DDIC user in client 000 is used for transports and corrections, mainly in the Data Dictionary. It has the initial password "19920706."
- `EarlyWatch`
  The Early Watch user in client 066 is used by SAP specialists for monitoring and performance management in the system. It should never be deleted, and its initial password is "support."

If default passwords are not changed, there is a significant security gap that entails the risk that default users with their cross-system authorizations can be misused for unauthorized transactions. Risk management should also include that the `SAP*` user is protected in all clients according to SAP recommendations. The user information system (Transaction SUIM) or the technical reports provided by the Audit Information System can be used to check whether the default passwords have been changed for these critical default users.

The user ID and password for the AS Java administrator can be set to anything you like during the installation process. In this case, you should choose a password that is as unpredictable as possible, and that adheres to the following complexity rules:

- Password length should be a minimum of eight characters
- At least one special character
- At least one letter
- At least one number

### 9.4.4 Configuring Security on the SAP Gateway

The SAP Gateway is a work process that is activated on the operating system level to manage communication between various systems, such as SAP NetWeaver AS, using the CPI-C protocol. RFC calls are also based on the CPI-C protocol. Besides an SAP NetWeaver AS, RFC communication partners can also be older R/2 or R/3 systems. Other external applications can also communicate via the SAP Gateway and run programs on remote systems. This involves some security risks, but these can be minimized with the correct security configuration.

A lack of security for the SAP Gateway is a significant security gap. This could allow unauthorized commands to be executed on the target system to take unauthorized full control over the target system. The following lists recommended steps for securing the SAP Gateway and thus reducing the risk:

- The SAP Gateway is activated on every SAP NetWeaver AS instance. Transaction SMGW is used to monitor its status. The *sideinfo* file contains data about all of the possible RFC destinations, and thus has to be protected from unauthorized access. This is done using an access control list on the operating system level. This file exists on every SAP NetWeaver AS instance on which an SAP Gateway is active.
- Because all RFC destinations can be maintained using Transaction SM59 and are stored in table `RFCDES`, authorization for Transaction SM59 should only be assigned with great care, including to administrators. For this reason, you should regularly check the entries in the `RFCDES` table for any changes that may have been made.
- It is important to correctly configure the authorization to execute a specific external CPI-C program or an RFC call. It is also necessary to monitor the registration of an external CPI-C program on the SAP Gateway. A registration means that this program is being made known to the Gateway and can be called from that moment on. This is done using the *secinfo file*, which by default is stored in the data directory of the instance. Alternatively, its location can be specified using the `gw/sec_info` parameter. An external program that is allowed to register itself on the SAP Gateway must be specified in this file. The syntax is as follows:

  ```
  USER=*, HOST=<host>, TP=<tp>;
  ```

  If, for example, the values `USER=*`, `HOST=hw1414`, and `TP=TREX` are set, this means that the `TREX` program on host `hw1414` may register itself on the SAP Gateway. The *secinfo* file can also be used to restrict access to a registered program for specific users. The users are the same as the registered users in the SAP NetWeaver AS. In this case, the syntax is as follows:

  ```
  USER=<user>, [PWD=<pwd>,] [USER-HOST=<user-host>,] HOST=<host>,
  TP=<tp>;
  ```

  In the case of `USER=HUGO`, `HOST=twdf0595`, and `TP=remote_serv`, for example, the user `HUGO` is permitted to start program `remote_serv` on host `twdf0595`. The parameter `USER-HOST` specifies the host on which the program may be started. The `PWD` (password) parameter has to be specified if an external CPI-C program that requires a password is started. Figure 9.7 gives an overview of the functions of the *secinfo* file.

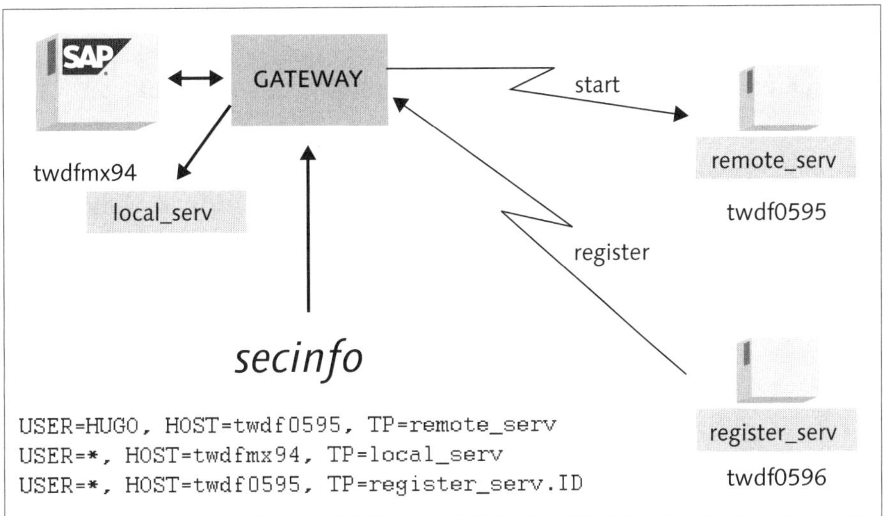


**Figure 9.7** Configuring the SAP Gateway with the secinfo Configuration File

### 9.4.5 Restricting Operating System Access

Transaction SM69 (Administrate External System Calls) and Transaction SM49 (Execute External System Calls) are used for external operating system access and to start operating system commands. The risk of assigning Transactions SM69 and SM49 to users is often underestimated: These transactions enable access to the file system of the operating system, and allow users to execute operating system commands that can be used to compromise the system.

Nevertheless, these transactions have their value, and SAP administrators execute these transactions for technical reasons. However, if these authorizations are made available to users without absolute necessity, this creates a security gap. Authorizations that are assigned for these two transactions must therefore be correspondingly restricted. The following descriptions discuss the corresponding risk management measures.

If these transactions are specified in the authorization, the execution of external operating system commands has to be restricted accordingly, using authorization objects S_RZL_ADM and S_LOG_COM.

- Authorization object S_RZL_ADM assigns authorization to maintain external system calls using Transaction SM69. It only has one authorization field, Activity, in which only 01: Create and 03: Modify are of major significance.
- The authorization object S_LOG_COM has the authorization fields Command, Operating System, and Host, which allow you to specify which operating system command can be executed on which operating system, and on which host.

Because external operating system command calls again use the SAP Gateway — in this particular case, using the *sapxpg* program — access to *sapxpg* using the *secinfo* file should be restricted to specific authorized users. Ideally, authorization should be restricted to users who have access to Transactions SM49 and SM69. The following example restricts permission to execute external operating system commands on host twdf0595 to the user HUGO:

```
USER=HUGO, HOST=twdf0595, TP=sapxpg
```

Thus, the *secinfo* file should contain this kind of entry. If the *secinfo* file is missing altogether, this authorizes every user to execute external commands using the *sapxpg* program. Obviously, this is a situation you should avoid at all costs.

### 9.4.6 Configuring Important Security System Parameters

System parameters are read when the SAP NetWeaver AS is started. They basically determine the operating parameters of the server. In addition to technical parameters, security-relevant settings are also implemented through the system parameters. Security parameters that have been incorrectly configured cause security gaps in the system. This includes the risk that weak password rules are defined. Considering all possible security gaps as a whole, unauthorized users can carry out transactions or manipulate data for unauthorized purposes.

To operate the SAP NetWeaver AS in a secure manner, it is necessary to correctly define some important security-related system parameters using Transaction RZ10. Table 9.3 contains some important system parameters and a recommended Best Practice setting for each one:

| System Parameter | Short Description | Recommended Setting |
|---|---|---|
| login/min_password_lng | Minimum length of logon password (3 to 8 characters) | At least 5 characters |
| login/password_expiration_time | Validity period of the password in months (0 to 999) | 3 to 6 months |

**Table 9.3** System Configurations Relevant to Security

| System Parameter | Short Description | Recommended Setting |
|---|---|---|
| login/fails_to_user_lock | Maximum number of failed logon attempts before user is locked (1 to 99) | 3 failed attempts |
| login/failed_user_auto_unlock | Automatic unlocking of user by batch job at night (0: no, 1: yes) | 0 |
| login/fails_to_session_end | Maximum number of failed logon attempts before logon attempt is terminated (1 to 99) | 3 failed attempts |
| login/disable_multiple_gui_login | Suppression of multiple user sessions (0: multiple logons possible, 1: multiple logons not possible) | 1: multiple logons not possible |
| login/multi_login_users | List of users who are permitted to use multiple logons | List of users, if parameter login/disable_multiple_gui_login equals 0 |
| login/min_password_diff | Minimum number of characters that have to be different from the old password in the new password (1 to 8) | At least 5 characters |
| login/password_max_new_valid | Validity period of passwords of new users (0 to 24,000 days) | 4 days |
| login/password_max_reset_valid | Validity period of reset passwords (0 to 24,000 days) | 4 days |
| Table USR40 | Specifies trivial passwords that are not allowed | There should be at least 100 entries, such as name, month, and so on |
| rfc/reject_expired_passwd | Allows RFC connections to log themselves onto the system with an expired password (0: allowed, 1: not allowed) | 1: not allowed (SAP Note 622464 must be applied first) |

**Table 9.3** System Configurations Relevant to Security (Cont.)

| System Parameter | Short Description | Recommended Setting |
|---|---|---|
| gw/sec_info | Location of *secinfo* file to secure the SAP Gateway | A file should be specified, otherwise there is no security |
| gw/monitor | Allows the SAP Gateway to be monitored from a remote system (0: allowed, 1: not allowed) | 1: not allowed |
| gw/accept_remote_trace_level | Allows trace information about the SAP Gateway to be transferred to an external system (0: not possible, 1: possible) | 0: not possible |
| rdisp/j2ee_start | Start AS Java (0: is not started, 1: is started) | AS Java should only be started if genuinely required |
| icm/HTTP/j2ee_<XX> | Defines whether internal communication between the ICM and the J2EE Engine is encrypted | Parameter should be greater than 0 for every J2EE Engine (serially numbered using <XX>) |
| Root group for the Telnet administration service of the J2EE Engine removed? | Root group includes all users of the AS Java, including guest users | Manually remove root group (see SAP Note 602371) |
| Guest user | J2EE Engine has a guest user by default | Lock guest user |
| Password rules | Password rules can also be set for the J2EE Engine using the Visual Administrator | Define password rules in accordance with the guidelines |

**Table 9.3** System Configurations Relevant to Security (Cont.)

### 9.4.7 Configuring Encrypted Communication Connections (SSL and SNC)

Communication connections are vital for operation and usage, and for the SAP NetWeaver AS. But they are also potential security weaknesses in the SAP system landscape if the corresponding risk analysis, risk management, and security measures are not carried out.

Communication connections should be encrypted to maintain their integrity and confidentiality. To do this, the SAP NetWeaver AS provides the standard encryption methods, SSL and SNC, which are available for important communication connections on both the AS ABAP and AS Java.

### Important Communication Connections for the AS ABAP

Figure 9.8 shows all of the important communication connections for the AS ABAP, while Table 9.4 lists its protocols and encryption mechanisms. This table shows that all of the important communication connections can be encrypted. In the case of the database connection, however, encryption depends on the database manufacturer. In most cases, for performance reasons, no encryption is used for the database connection.

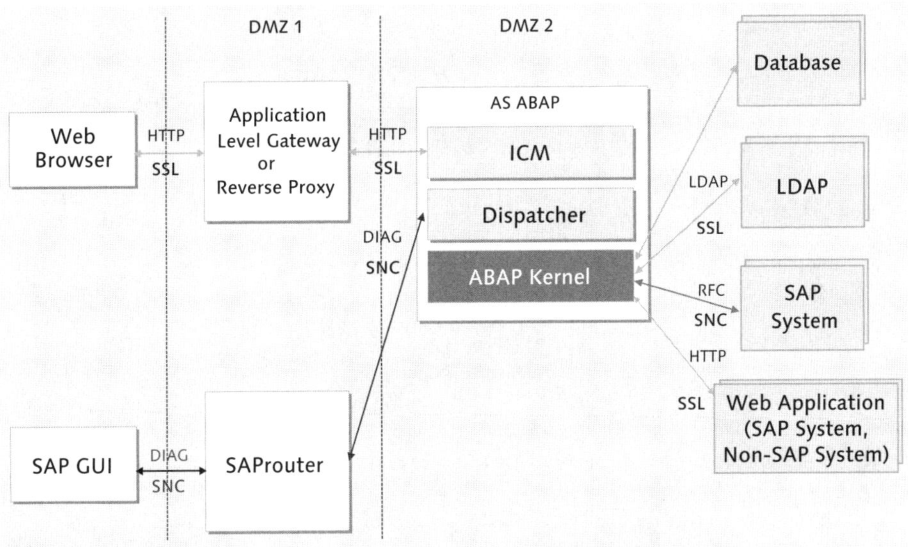


**Figure 9.8** Communication Connections That Can Be Encrypted for AS ABAP

| Protocol | Encryption Method | Communication Connections |
|---|---|---|
| DIAG | SNC | SAP GUI to SAProuter, SAProuter to dispatcher |
| RFC | SNC | ABAP kernel to other ABAP kernel or other external CPI-C program |
| HTTP | SSL | Web browser to application-level firewall (web dispatcher, reverse proxy, and so on), application-level firewall to ICM, ABAP kernel to SAP or non-SAP web applications |
| LDAP | SSL | ABAP kernel (LDAP Connector) to LDAP directory server |

**Table 9.4** Overview of Communication Connections in AS ABAP

### Important Communication Connections for the AS Java

Figure 9.9 shows all of the important communication connections for AS Java, and Table 9.5 lists its protocols and encryption mechanisms.

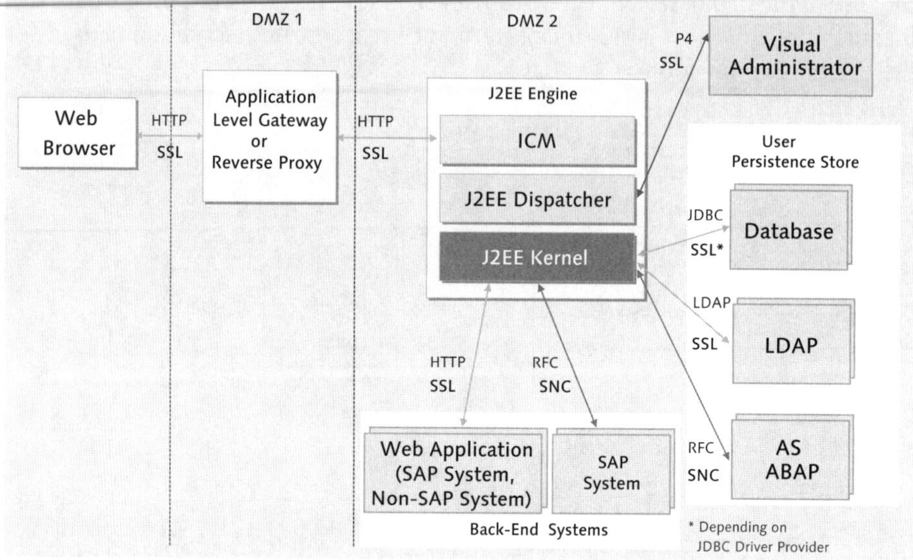


**Figure 9.9** Communication Connections That Can Be Encrypted for AS Java

| Protocol | Encryption Method | Communication Connections |
|---|---|---|
| DIAG | SNC | Not required in the AS Java environment |
| RFC | SNC | J2EE kernel (using Java Connector) to AS ABAP, J2EE kernel (using Java Connection Architecture) to the SAP NetWeaver AS in general |
| HTTP | SSL | Web browser to the application-level firewall (web dispatcher, reverse proxy, and so on), application-level firewall to ICM (or directly to J2EE dispatcher, if it is a pure AS Java installation without ABAP), J2EE kernel to SAP or non-SAP web application |
| LDAP | SSL | J2EE kernel (using Java Connection Architecture) to LDAP directory server |
| JDBC | SSL | J2EE kernel to database server (SSL encryption is only possible if the JDBC or ODBC driver permits it) |

**Table 9.5** Overview of Communication Connections in AS Java

| Protocol | Encryption Method | Communication Connections |
|---|---|---|
| P4 | SSL | Visual Administrator to J2EE dispatcher, J2EE dispatcher to J2EE kernel |
| Telnet | VPN only | Telnet administrator to J2EE dispatcher (not recommended) |

**Table 9.5** Overview of Communication Connections in AS Java (Cont.)

It should also be noted at this point that the configuration shown in Figure 9.9 only applies if the installation in question is a complete SAP NetWeaver AS installation (ABAP and Java) and communication between the available web applications is managed via the ICM. If the installation in question were a pure Java installation, this communication would be directed straight to the J2EE dispatcher.

Also note that the use of an application-level gateway is optional. For security reasons, however, at least one SAP Web Dispatcher should be used. See Chapter 14, Classic SAP Middleware, for more details.

The following section uses an example to explain the installation steps necessary to configure SNC on an AS ABAP and SSL on an AS Java.

### Configuring SNC for the AS ABAP

SAP Cryptographic Library (SAPCRYPTOLIB) can be used to set up SNC communication between two SAP NetWeaver ASs; it is not necessary to purchase any partner software. However, you will need to purchase new software if you want to set up SNC between the SAP GUI and an SAP NetWeaver AS (see Chapter 28).

The following are the steps you need to take to configure SNC on an AS ABAP:

1. Install SAPCRYPTOLIB on all SAP NetWeaver AS where communication via SNC should be possible.
2. Set up the SNC Personal Security Environment (PSE) for each SAP NetWeaver AS involved.

   Alternatively, you can also use an SNC PSE for each system that is involved, but although this option reduces the amount of administration work involved, we do not recommend using it. The better option from a security standpoint is to use individual PSEs, each with a special certificate for each system, as this enables stronger authentication between systems. Transaction STRUST is used to create the PSE. In this transaction, you have to select the SNC PSE and enter a distinguished name with the host name, the organizational unit, the name of the organization, and the country. You can also specify these details in parameter `snc/identity/as`. You also have to set a password to make access to the PSE secure.

3. In this step, the digital certificates of the SAP NetWeaver AS that are stored in the PSE have to be exchanged between the systems so that a trust relationship can be established. As before, this is done in Transaction STRUST. In this transaction, the digital certificate has to be exported to every participating SAP NetWeaver AS. To do this, you again have to select the SNC PSE, and use the Export Certificate function under the certificate list to export the relevant system-specific certificate and save it to the local hard disk. The Import Certificate function is also available here. It can be used to import the certificates of the relevant SAP NetWeaver AS.
4. In this last step, you have to set the relevant SNC system parameters. The most important are the following:
   - **snc/enable** (activate SNC)
     = 1
   - **snc/gssapi_lib** (path for SAPCRYPTOLIB)
     = */usr/sap/<SID>/SYS/exe/run/libsapcrypto.so* (UNIX)
     = *D:\usr\sap\<SID>\SYS\ exe\run\sapcrypto.dll* (Windows)
   - **snc/identity/as** (SNC name of the SAP NetWeaver AS)
     = `Syntax: p:<Distinguished_Name>`, which has to be the same as the SNC PSE
   - **snc/data_protection/max** (maximum security level)
     = '1: authentication only,' '2: integrity protection,' or '3: confidentiality protection'
   - **snc/data_protection/min** (minimum security level)
     = '1: authentication only', '2: integrity protection', or '3: confidentiality protection'
5. Restart the SAP NetWeaver AS, and test the SNC communication.

### Configuring SSL for AS Java

To configure SSL for AS Java, you can use the Visual Administrator, which connects to the relevant J2EE server via the P4 protocol. The installation steps are as follows:

1. Install the SAP Cryptographic Toolkit for Java on the AS Java. The package consists of the following files: *iaik_jsse.jar*, *iaik_jce.jar*, *iaik_ssl.jar*, *iaik_smime.jar*, and *w3c_http.jar*.

2. Configure the start mode for the certificate storage location (keystore), and set the SSL service to Always (this is done with the config tool). Here, select the appropriate server node, and set the start options for both services to Always.
3. You now have to create a certificate (key pair, consisting of a public key in accordance with the X.509 standard and a private key). This is done in the Keystore service of the Visual Administrator. You can also create a Certificate Signing Request (CSR) there, if the certificate has to be signed by a certificate authority. This will be necessary to connect web applications for the Internet via the SAP NetWeaver AS. In the case of test installations, self-signed certificates can also be used.
4. In this last step, assign the certificate to a specific HTTP port that has to be configured for the SSL. This is done in the Visual Administrator using the SSL Service for the corresponding AS Java.

### 9.4.8 Restricting Superfluous Internet Services

If the SAP NetWeaver AS is used in an Internet scenario and provides web-based applications via the ICM, as shown in Figure 9.1, any applications — also known as services — that do not need to be accessible have to be deactivated. Web-based applications of the ICM or a service of the operating system can always be used or provide access for unauthorized purposes and are thus a security gap. To reduce this risk to a minimum, you shouldn't deactivate required services.

There may be dependencies between services, and the deactivation of a service could lead to errors in other services. If the impacts of a deactivated service are not fully known, you should run an analysis. You should always test these analyses and general deactivations in test systems. In addition, this process, including the risk analysis, involves time and effort. As is always the case in risk management, the ratio between effort and achievable risk reduction should be balanced. For the ultimately acceptable remaining risk, you should always consider compensating countermeasures or monitoring, if possible and if useful.

Deactivations can be initiated using Transaction SICF (Administrating the Internet Communication Framework) in Web Dynpro ABAP-based, BSP-based, or ITS-based services on the AS ABAP. Figure 9.10 shows an example of this. By right-clicking on the relevant service (such as IT13: Test Service for IACs), you can deactivate the service. However, you should not use the option to deactivate the whole ICF tree hierarchy under an ICF object at once. Instead, always deactivate services one at a time, or else you may overlook dependencies, which in turn could cause problems with functionality.

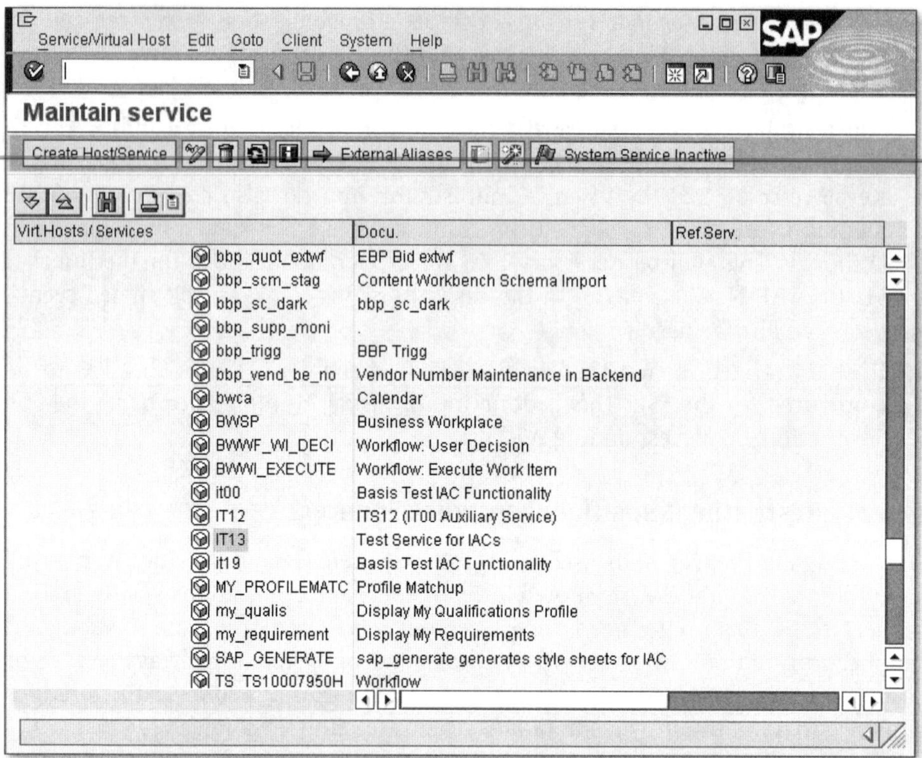


**Figure 9.10** Transaction SICF, Used for Administrating the ICF

AS Java provides external services, even though not all of these are required in every scenario. The problem in this case is that there may be dependencies between services, with the result that if one service is required, other services may also have to be activated at the same time. You also have to differentiate between system services and nonsystem services.

We recommend that you use the following procedure with the Visual Administrator to identify and deactivate superfluous services:

- Identify the system service that is required to execute the application (such as the `servlet_jsp` service for servlet-based applications).
- Next, filter out mutual dependencies between the services. You can view these dependencies on the Dependencies tab. Usually, only the services with a high degree of dependency are required.
- You should deactivate those services that do not have any dependencies. When doing so, be aware that some services will still be required to operate the AS Java, regardless of their degree of dependency.

- Also, you should use the Deployment Tool to remove any applications that are not required.
- HTTP aliases that are not required should likewise be removed.
- After the services are deactivated, you should check to see if the application can still run.
- If the application or AS Java can no longer run, you will have to check the logs. Usually, the logs will contain error messages that relate to services that are required but that have been deactivated. Otherwise, you will have to use trial and error to pinpoint the required combination.
- For system services, you have to change the start setting always so that the AS Java can run again. You do this using the XML configuration file *runtime.xml* in the services directory or the config tool (value: `never` or `manual`).

As already mentioned, because of the level of complexity involved, it is advisable to identify the service combinations that can be deactivated and to carry out the actual deactivations only after you have established that the risks are sufficiently high to warrant this. A system that provides very sensitive Internet applications, for example, counts as a high-risk system, and so the hardening procedure outlined previously should be carried out in this case.

### 9.4.9 Secure Network Architecture for Using the SAP NetWeaver AS with the Internet

If the SAP NetWeaver AS supports applications that can be accessed via the Internet, the server is exposed to additional risks. These risks must be addressed with the appropriate security measures with regard to applications, user access, SAP NetWeaver AS, position of the server in the network architecture, and network design.

Which network architecture you choose for using the SAP NetWeaver AS for the Internet will depend on the individual scenario. Although the SAP Internet Transaction Server has been replaced in the SAP NetWeaver AS, customers still deploy applications that use the SAP Internet Transaction Server. If you will only be providing Internet applications on the basis of the SAP Internet Transaction Server, the network topology proposed in Chapter 14 can be used.

On the other hand, if you are mainly interested in BSP, JSP, and Web Dynpro applications (ABAP and Java), you should choose the kind of network topologies shown in Figures 9.8 and 9.9. For more information, see Chapter 14, in which the SAP Web Dispatcher can be used as a simple reverse proxy in the configurations shown.

### 9.4.10 Introducing an Application-Level Gateway to Make Internet Applications Secure

An application-level gateway will be of most use if you are mainly using BSP, JSP, and Web Dynpro applications (ABAP and Java) that are all accessible via the ICM. To better tackle the threats and security risk from the Internet, you should replace the SAP web dispatcher (see Chapter 14) whose security functionality is somewhat limited with a reverse proxy, which is of higher value from a security point of view, or, even better, with an application-level gateway. The functions of the latter are described in detail in Chapter 16, as the SAP NetWeaver Portal is usually used in Internet scenarios. That chapter also explains the typical methods of attacks on the Internet, against which an application-level gateway may provide protection.

Nonetheless, we must not fail to mention that in these cases, the transferred parameters, such as those in form fields, are always checked. This usually happens on the web application's side. This is especially important in the case of in-house development work.

### 9.4.11 Introducing Hardening Measures on the Operating System Level

If the SAP NetWeaver AS is used for tasks that involve the Internet, it has to be adequately on protected the operating system side. This applies to all areas of application for the SAP NetWeaver AS — for example, if it is used as a runtime environment for SAP NetWeaver Portal, SAP NetWeaver PI, or SAP NetWeaver Mobile.

The security risk at the operating system level is especially high, on the one hand, because numerous applications are available that let you control servers remotely via various networks and the Internet and to carry out administrative work or manipulate the file system (for example, password files stored at the operating system level). On the other hand, the security configurations of the servers are often planned and implemented insufficiently or are too open for access reasons. These security gaps can also be used for unauthorized access from the internal network.

The manufacturers of the individual operating systems now provide good, detailed instructions on how to carry out hardening measures. You should note the following basic principles in relation to hardening:

- Any applications (such as Office applications) on a server that is intended for SAP NetWeaver Portal should be removed. This also applies to additional administrative tools. Such tools sometimes make administrative tasks easier, but they often contain security weak spots that a potential attacker could exploit. Note in relation to this that you should activate services and applications one at a time, so as not to jeopardize the availability of the SAP system.

- Guest accounts have to be deleted or at least deactivated.
- Default passwords for the operating system have to be changed.
- System or server administrators should not share a user account and password; instead individual user names with secret passwords should be common practice.
- Appropriate access permissions have to be assigned to critical operating system directories (such as */etc* in UNIX). This applies, in particular, to the technical service users under which the SAP NetWeaver AS instances run.

In addition to these measures, you can also set up an IDS on the server level. This kind of system mainly monitors any changes made to critical operating system files and triggers an alarm if any change is made to this kind of file without the prior authorization of the administrator. However, this kind of intrusion detection system also triggers false alarms. Therefore, during installation, you should take this into account in your configurations.

### 9.4.12 Introducing a Quality Assurance Process for Software Development

Quality assurance processes or change management processes, or both, are now taken for granted when new SAP systems are rolled out. Because process design always has to be adapted to the individual situation of the organization and the details can be very complex, this section presents only a brief overview of some tips and tools.

There is a general risk that the efficiency, reliability, integrity, and functional interaction with other (non-)SAP applications for SAP systems that are used in production and by the SAP NetWeaver AS are reduced due to insufficient change management and quality assurance processes. This can lead to dramatic failures and data errors.

#### Quality Assurance and Change Management Process for the AS ABAP

Normally, the quality assurance and change management process in a pure ABAP development environment involves a three-tier system landscape:

- Development system (DEV)
- Quality assurance system (QAS)
- Production system (PROD)

New development work, or changes to existing ABAP programs, can only be carried out in the development system. Likewise, customizing work on client-specific and cross-client tables and entries can only be done in the development system. The quality assurance system is used to check the correctness of any newly developed programs. Development work is transported to the production system only once all tests have been carried out in accordance with a predefined test plan and have achieved positive results.

SAP provides tools for the roughly outlined process. Transaction SE06 is used to make the settings for the areas that can be changed. Transaction SE03 allows you to view and check all of the system modifications that have been logged. Transaction SCC4 is used to specify permitted and forbidden settings for maintaining client-specific and cross-client tables and transports. These settings are stored in table `T000`, which means that this table also has to be protected from being accessed via Transactions SM30 and SM31. To ensure that a client — especially the production client — cannot be overwritten, you have to make the corresponding setting in Transaction SCC4 on level 1 (no overwriting).

The following are critical authorizations that you should not assign, at least in the production system:

- Table maintenance `S_TABU_DIS`: activity 02 (change) should only be assigned for noncritical tables where necessary. In particular, the table group that contains table `T000` should not be assigned at all.
- Thus, cross-client Customizing via `S_TABU_CLI` should not be set to `X`, or else it would be possible to assign table `T000`.
- For ABAP software development, authorization object `S_DEVELOP` should be restricted, activity 02 (change) should be `OBJTYPE PROG`, and `DEBUG` should be avoided, as this allows the authorization holder to modify existing programs and to carry out debugging and replace existing code.

The Transport Management System (Transaction STMS) is used to transport software packages. It contains a release process that releases packages for transport only once they have been approved by the responsible development team leader or a quality assurance specialist. You can thus use this tool to set up a standardized change management process with a step-by-step release procedure. You can also choose the number of required release steps.

You should develop a well-documented procedure for the release process and adhere to it. This is not only a best-practice approach, it also reduces the risk that unauthorized or not checked changes are transferred to the production system. In addition, this is necessary to meet audit requirements.

#### Quality Assurance and Change Management Process for AS Java

A quality assurance and change management process can also be set up for AS Java. As before, this process can have a three-tier structure consisting of development, quality assurance, and production environments. However, the tools that are required are different from the AS ABAP tools.

Java applications are developed using the SAP NetWeaver Developer Studio (in the SAP NetWeaver Composition Environment), and software components are stored in the Design Time Repository (DTR). The DTR is also responsible for distribution to the various environments; developer and release roles can be specified for this purpose. The following are the fixed roles in this area: developer, quality manager, and software change manager. These roles can be adapted to suit the individual requirements in each case, so that it is possible to set up a Java development process that is compatible with the ABAP quality assurance process.

### 9.4.13 Security and Authorization Checks in Custom ABAP and Java Program Code

Often, new ABAP or Java program code for applications that the SAP NetWeaver AS supports are further developed by internal or external programmers according to specific customer requirements, or standard SAP programs are modified and transferred to the production system. This is necessary if the standard code does not meet internal or process requirements.

The SAP system is a highly integrated system that consists of numerous applications. Its default code for programs and interfaces provides numerous internal controls and authorization checks that ensure that process and data integrity are maintained at any time. If now internal or external programmers implement new developments or code modifications, it is possible that critical program-internal or cross-process functions, controls, authorization checks, and data access controls are not sufficiently considered—intentionally or unintentionally (see also *Sichere ABAP-Programmierung*, *http://www.sap-press.de/2037*). Examples of insecure program code include:

- Insufficient authorization checks
- Lack of controls for data integrity when data is entered and databases are modified
- Insufficient controls and process controls
- Noncompliance with legal requirements
- Execution of any ABAP and operating system commands

- Manipulation of database queries
- Intentional or unintentional backdoors in the program code

**Example**

A programmer of a financial institute made a seemingly minor change to the program code of an online banking application. The tests of the functions within the application had positive results, and the change was implemented in the production system. Straight after this, incoming payments for private customer accounts could no longer be made in the production system. It took hours to identify the cause and recover the program code of the previous program version.

Effective risk management is characterized by considering causes for security gaps *prior to* the program development and carrying out security and control analyses of the program code after the creation or modification of the program. Examples of causes for errors and security gaps include:

- Insufficient cooperation, awareness of problems, and distribution of the tasks across process owners, decision makers, developers, persons responsible for security and authorizations, and auditors when defining program requirements and evaluating or authorizing completed programs
- Insufficient risk analysis and consideration, including interactions of and effects on other applications and systems
- Insufficient knowledge about security options or their implementation via programs
- Program development and test guidelines with insufficient security and control requirements
- Requirements for the integration of security, authorization, and process controls in programs and their implementation and tests are not specified — or only to a limited extent — in contracts with external developers

After their completion and prior to their acceptance, program developments and program modifications must be analyzed with regard to potential security gaps and evaluated by the persons responsible for security and authorizations. Like the program functions, the efficiency and completeness of the security measures should also be checked against internal requirements and specifications.

Tools that analyze Java or C/C++ program code and automatically identify security gaps have been available for years. However, the results of automatic scanners always require manual evaluation, selection, and interpretation.

*This chapter discusses the security aspects of SAP NetWeaver Business Warehouse (BW). In this context, special security solutions like the new concept for analysis authorizations are detailed.*

# 10 SAP NetWeaver Business Warehouse

SAP NetWeaver BW is the central enterprise information component (Business Intelligence (BI)) within SAP NetWeaver. Here you store, consolidate, and provide transactional and analytical data to various users of the SAP applications for evaluation purposes. This results in a special protection requirement for BW systems and applications.

## 10.1 Introduction and Functions

In transactional systems such as SAP Enterprise Resource planning (ERP), transactional and master data are stored in tables and forwarded to other tables for further processing. SAP NetWeaver BW, however, focuses on individual processes from the respective source systems, whereby it usually extracts historical data from them and formats it into information packages in SAP NetWeaver BW. The goal is to provide BW users with the essential and formatted information for their work area on demand. Historical, nonchangeable data and operational reporting, aggregated views, and multidimensional analyses that were built based on InfoCubes can be called and authorized via SAP NetWeaver BW (see Figure 10.1).

Depending on the type of data objects and data, relevance to the company, and the legally defined requirement of protection, the systems and applications must be protected by appropriate security solutions. Here, for instance, analytical data is very important as it provides information on developments and trends, which makes it susceptible to industrial espionage and other risks. SAP NetWeaver BW provides different applications, tools, and dashboards for an analytical evaluation of the master and transactional data of all processing SAP systems.

Within SAP NetWeaver BW, structured and unstructured data is converted into information; this information supports users, information owners, persons responsible, decision-makers, and external employees in their areas of responsibility in providing any requested information at the right time and in the right form to authorized SAP users. As a central information system, SAP NetWeaver BW provides an option for consolidated information access.

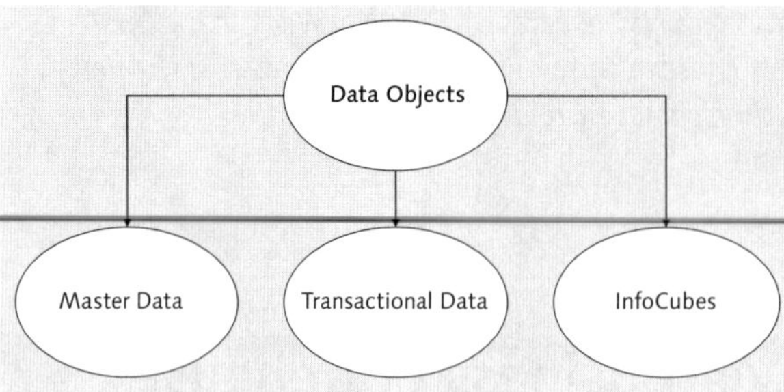


**Figure 10.1** Data Objects

This not only covers the information requirement, but also ensures a higher degree of security for data access. In contrast to a decentralized distribution of data, SAP BW offers a considerably high degree of consistency, a high level of evaluation options, and efficient data access.

Program evaluations, ad hoc reports, and the other tools used for requesting business information in operational BW systems are no longer needed, which eliminates the accompanying additional security risks. The aggregated evaluation of data in a central SAP information system results in an aggregated data retention for the evaluation of risks and the resulting security controls. The central metadata repository facilitates the access and authorization assignment to data and analysis options.

## 10.2 Risks and Controls

Although the central concept of BW objects within SAP NetWeaver BW helps to minimize risks, its open architecture and integrative design leads to a necessary detailed consideration of the possible risks, protection needs, and implementation of security control measures that provide access to the information (see Table 10.1).

| No. | Classification | Description |
|---|---|---|
| 1. | Risk potential | Data presentation:<br>Data can be presented in different forms. Access to information can be permitted, but under certain circumstances (for example, if the information is available in nonaggregated form), individual transactional data can be compromised, which results in loss of integrity. |

**Table 10.1** Risks and Controls for SAP NetWeaver BW

| No. | Classification | Description |
|---|---|---|
| | Impact | For unauthorized persons, evaluations involving real data represent a violation of their scope of authorizations. Even the reading of specific information can lead to potential risks and thus compromise company assets. The effects can be disastrous because the potential risks are often the cause of industrial espionage and the like. |
| | Risk without control(s) | High |
| | Control | Data can be classified according to the potential risks involved. An efficient authorization concept can ensure the protection of this data. For example, SAP NetWeaver BW allows for the presentation of data in aggregated form. This enables users to analyze specific groups of data, but they can't drill down to compromising individual data. |
| | Risk with control(s) | Low |
| | Section | 10.3.1 |
| 2. | Risk potential | Authorization system:<br>The authorization system in SAP NetWeaver BW can be designed in a simple or complex manner. Depending on the requirements, authorization objects can be used to implement access and restriction controls for SAP BW objects, such as InfoAreas, InfoCubes, and queries. The more frequently and more detailed controls are performed, the more complex the monitoring and administrative measures. |
| | Impact | A higher degree of administrative tasks leads to an increase in costs, a potentially higher error rate, and thus a violation of protective measures. |
| | Risk without control(s) | High |
| | Control | The identified need for protection must be the basis for control measures, for example, in reporting. The data for SAP NetWeaver BW must be classified according to its risk relevance and evaluation. The classification of data and evaluation functions in SAP NetWeaver BW result in a targeted authorization concept that reduces the control measures to a necessary minimum and only uses them for an efficient protection of data, processes, and systems. This concept can only be implemented by using appropriate technologies. |

**Table 10.1** Risks and Controls for SAP NetWeaver BW (Cont.)

| No. | Classification | Description |
|---|---|---|
| | Risk with control(s) | Normal |
| | Section | 10.3.1 |
| 3. | Risk potential | Legal requirements:<br>Strategic business information data from the accounting and HR departments is also processed in SAP NetWeaver BW, while the areas of data management, data manipulation, and analysis authorization are subject to legal requirements such as the Sarbanes-Oxley Act (SOX) and Basel II. Inappropriate control measures that don't comply with the existing legal regulations are a violation of the legal conditions and requirements. |
| | Impact | Violations of legal regulations can result in a loss of reputation, penalizations by legal authorities, increased costs, and other business-related and private damages. |
| | Risk without control(s) | High |
| | Control | A consistent authorization concept that's in sync with other security areas reduces the risk of violating legal requirements. The authorization concept must be combined with and be an integral part of administrative and process-related control measures. |
| | Risk with control(s) | Normal |
| | Section | 10.3.1 |
| 4. | Risk potential | Design:<br>An early integration of risk, authorization, and design tasks is particularly important in the business intelligence area so that the necessary authorization requirements can be included in the design of applications right from the beginning. |
| | Impact | An erroneous design in the creation of InfoCubes or queries can lead to incorrect reporting results or to an increase in the costs of the subsequent control design. |
| | Risk without control(s) | High |
| | Control | The design of applications and security measures is a basic requirement for a successful and secure use of SAP NetWeaver BW. |

**Table 10.1** Risks and Controls for SAP NetWeaver BW (Cont.)

| No. | Classification | Description |
|---|---|---|
| | Risk with control(s) | Normal |
| | Section | 10.3.1 |
| 5. | Risk potential | Standard:<br>Tables USOBT_C and USOBX_C don't contain the link between the transaction code and the authorization object, which, for instance, is the case in SAP ERP (OLTP). As a result, the administration effort and error rate increase. |
| | Impact | Therefore, a higher degree of administrative effort, for instance, caused by additional documentation, can be the result. Moreover, an increased number of risks can result when maintaining Transaction SU24 (Check Indicators), which includes the authorization tables. Users could therefore benefit from authorizations that they shouldn't be granted. |
| | Risk without control(s) | High |
| | Control | The maintenance of Transaction SU24 is one of the basic rules for Best Practices in administration. In SAP NetWeaver BW this rule cannot be used nonrestrictively because additional authorization concepts ensure a flexible utilization of BW information structures. Therefore, the concepts of analysis authorizations, external controls, manual authorization maintenance, and sufficient documentation are required, for example. |
| | Risk with control(s) | Normal |
| | Section | 10.3.1 |

**Table 10.1** Risks and Controls for SAP NetWeaver BW (Cont.)

## 10.3 Application Security

SAP NetWeaver BW generally follows the rules of the authorization concept and management based on the SAP role concept as described in Chapters 9, SAP NetWeaver AS, 20, Authorizations in SAP ERP, and 21, SAP ERP HCM and Data Protection; in general, authorizations are assigned to users via the authorization roles. In addition to the concept of authorization roles, there are query and analysis authorizations available, which are described in the following sections.

### 10.3.1 Authorizations

The integrity of business data is also ensured by assigning authorization roles. Corresponding to the activities contained in authorization roles, authorization profiles are generated that limit the access of individual users or user groups to SAP BW data and evaluation information. Authorizations that are generated on the basis of authorization objects and then automatically added to the authorization profiles of a specific user control access to individual cost center hierarchies. This way, you can restrict the drilldown process for cost centers.

BW authorization checks let you protect functions, objects, and data. In an authorization check during the execution of a specific action, the system compares the values for individual authorization fields — of an authorization object assigned to a user via authorization roles — with the values for executing an action that are defined in the relevant program. An authorized user is authorized for a specific activity if the authorization check is successful for each authorization field checked in an authorization object. This way, it is possible to perform complex user authorization checks in SAP NetWeaver BW.

#### Authorization Elements in SAP NetWeaver BW

Figure 10.2 shows the options available for assigning authorizations in SAP NetWeaver BW. Roles are either directly or indirectly assigned to users. They can contain authorization objects for InfoAreas, InfoCubes, queries, and individual InfoObjects. The maintenance effort increases from the tip of the pyramid down to the bottom.

Authorizations must generally be restricted to data, evaluations, transactions, and actions. Depending on their position, users can be authorized for different data and evaluation rules. SAP NetWeaver BW primarily provides authorizations for reporting and data warehouse management. In data warehouse management, for instance, authorizations are required for creating and modifying queries. These authorizations can be granted using the Administrator Workbench in SAP NetWeaver BW, which controls the authorizations for the following activities:

- Data from SAP source systems
  - Structural design
  - Extraction of data
  - Planning and executing the load process
  - Data formatting and analysis

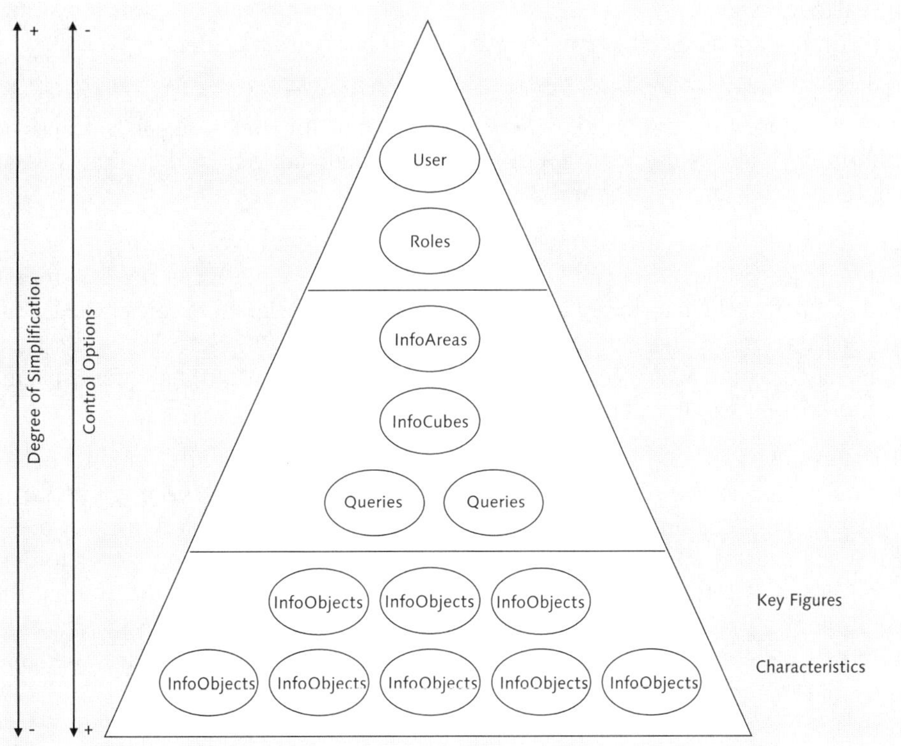


**Figure 10.2** Authorization Pyramid in SAP NetWeaver BW

- Data warehouse management
- Data modeling
- Monitoring and control

The elements relevant to authorization in the data warehouse design are the Data Warehouse Workbench for activating the business content objects and for loading DataStore objects, queries and InfoCube objects, InfoSources and transactional objects, InfoObjects, and source systems. Analyses can be assigned with special analysis authorizations.

In reporting, for example, authorizations can be restricted to specific reporting objects. You can, for instance, specify authorizations for starting queries. It is also possible to restrict authorizations to specific user and query groups. If a user is assigned to a specific group of evaluations, the authorization can be further restricted to specific characteristics. For instance, it is possible to limit the authorization to data of specific cost centers or of only one cost center.

Using the Business Explorer (BEx) in SAP NetWeaver BW, you can restrict the authorizations to activities like query design, reporting, data analysis, and visualization. SAP BEx is used as a reporting tool for data analysis and consists of two components: BEx Analyzer and BEx Browser.

In BEx Analyzer you can define queries based on a group of InfoObjects or predefined query templates of an InfoCube (BEx Query Designer). Queries are embedded in Microsoft Excel–based workbooks that can be assigned to roles in SAP BEx. Thus, data can be analyzed and distributed via MS Excel. The SAP Profile Generator assigns the SAP BW roles to the reporting users. Additional query-specific authorizations can be specified in the SAP Profile Generator.

The Business Explorer Browser (BEx Web) is used to display the contents of the browser, such as the roles, favorites, and tasks of a user, in a specific browser in which you can call reports. You can also address other intranet and Internet pages from the browser. The browser contains drag-and-drop functionality for folders and objects. This functionality can be modified by a user, provided the user has the corresponding authorization. Moreover, you can maintain user-specific favorites in the BEx Web. If BEx Web is used to access data with a mobile device, the communication and the device must be protected appropriately.

#### Authorization Objects in SAP NetWeaver BW

In SAP NetWeaver BW, authorizations are generally granted via authorization objects for administration and reporting. The reporting authorization objects shown in Figure 10.3 are important for granting and restricting authorizations for InfoCubes and other authorization elements. Sensitive data can be controlled using customized authorization objects that can be created via Transaction RSSM and assigned authorizations through the Authorizations menu item. The reporting objects are authorization objects in SAP NetWeaver BW with an additional relationship to InfoCubes. The reporting object authorization fields determine the key figures, authorization-relevant characteristics, and the hierarchy level (see Figure 10.4).

In addition to the authorization objects shown in the figure, there are many other objects available, such as `S_RS_IOBJ` for InfoObjects, `S_RS_ISET` for InfoSets, `S_RS_COMP1` for query component authorizations, and `S_RS_FOLD` for deactivating the overview screen of the InfoArea folder so that roles and favorites are only displayed with queries in the BEx dialog. Other authorization objects, such as `S_RS_MPRO`, can restrict MultiProviders.

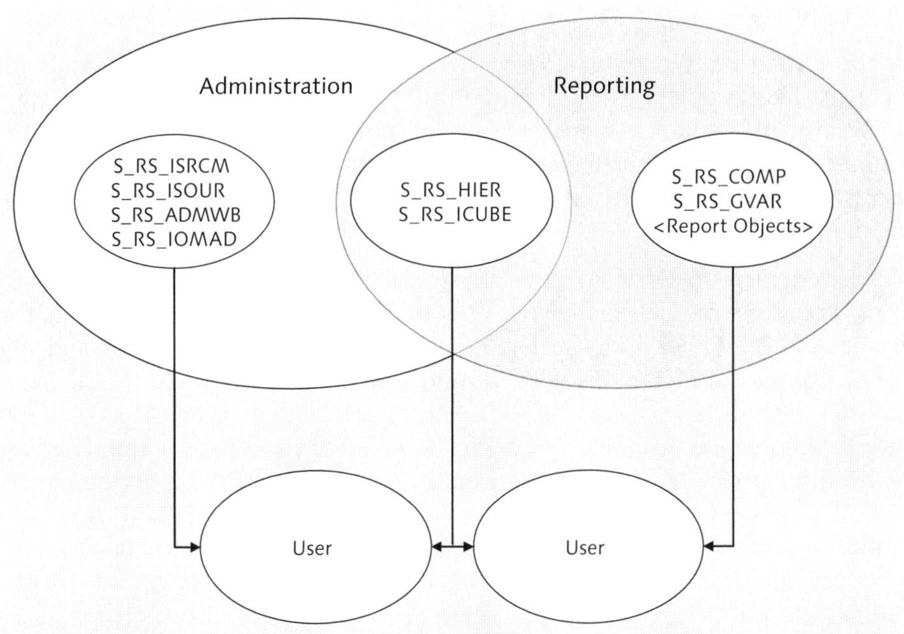


**Figure 10.3** Authorization Objects for Administration and Reporting

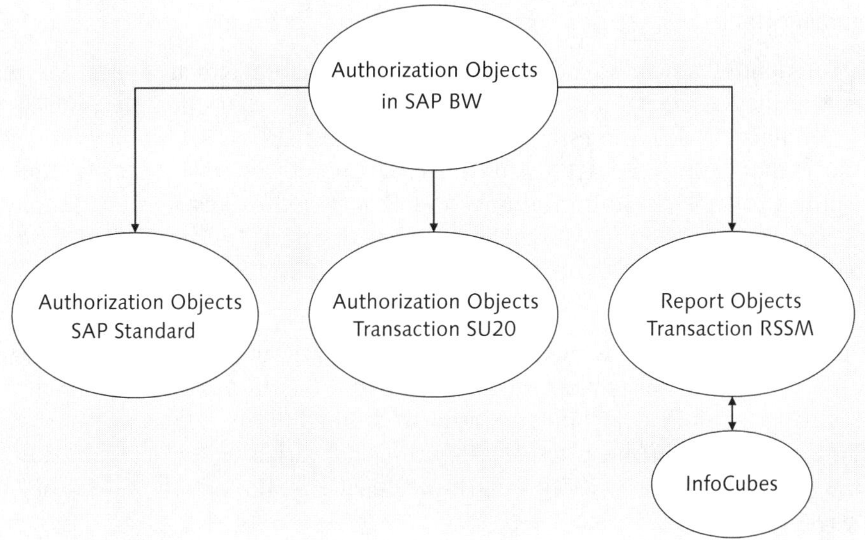


**Figure 10.4** Types of Authorization Objects

### 10.3.2 Analysis Authorizations

In contrast to transaction-based security, where the requirement depends on elements like transaction codes, authorization field values, and activities, SAP NetWeaver BW requires an analysis-focused authorization control. This authorization control is based on elements like InfoProviders, queries, and data mining, that is, on the targeted analysis and evaluation of data for the purpose of extracting information.

This requirement has led to a new authorization concept, the analysis authorizations. The access can be expanded flexibly to different levels of authorization, for example, to InfoCubes, to characteristics like material or product types, and key figures like cost drivers. This goes beyond the scope of the original authorization concepts; the partly rigid authorization objects with a maximum of only ten InfoObjects (mapped as authorization fields) are overcome by the unlimited number of InfoObjects in the analysis authorizations. This way, the original InfoObject authorizations become a new dimension in the control of analytical reports and evaluation structures. The InfoProvider authorizations are no longer separated into individual authorization fields or authorization objects, but directly into analysis authorizations.

The analysis authorization can be defined and controlled via Transactions RSD1 (InfoObject Administration) and RSECADMIN (Central Maintenance of Analysis Authorizations). The procedure for developing analysis authorizations includes the maintenance of InfoObjects via Transaction RSD1 (Data Warehouse Workbench).

Here, you define both authorization-relevant characteristics and authorization-relevant attributes. After the activation of authorization-relevant InfoObjects (`0TCA*`) and InfoCubes (`0TCT*`), the essential InfoObjects like `0TCAACTVT` for activities in analysis authorizations, `0TCAIPROV` for InfoProvider authorizations, `0TCAVALID` for the validity of analysis authorizations, and `0TCAKYFNM` for key figures in analysis authorizations are set to Authorization-relevant status. Individual characteristics and attributes must also be flagged as Authorization-relevant before they are used.

The analysis authorizations themselves are set up and managed in Transaction RSECADMIN. To do this, values for characteristics (for instance, sales organization), attributes, and hierarchies are authorized. In addition, you can define special authorization characteristics, key figures, and variables for authorizations. Besides the real values, you can determine special authorization values for all characteristics:

- The asterisk character (*) defines the authorization to all values or a group of values like LINK*.
- The colon character (:) defines the authorization for viewing aggregated data, for instance, the display of sales figures of all sales organizations in a specific area; here, the display would not be authorized to a single sales organization.
- The plus character (+) defines the name of a single letter value.
- The hash character (#) defines the authorization to an initial value.

Hierarchies can also be authorized on different branches. This way, the hierarchies become authorization structures within the analysis or the InfoObject authorizations.

Special characteristics of the analysis authorizations like InfoProvider, validity, and activity must be defined in at least one analysis authorization and be assigned to a BW user. These characteristics don't need to be included in every analysis authorization, even though this is useful with regard to transparency, completeness, and correctness. The authorizations for the InfoProviders can be defined for individual InfoProviders, a group of InfoProviders, or specific selected InfoProviders. Moreover, you can specify a selection of InfoProviders on the basis of the InfoAreas' hierarchy.

The assignment of analysis authorizations is done either via authorization roles or directly via the assignment of individual analysis authorizations or groups of analysis authorizations using Transaction RSECADMIN. Analysis authorizations can also be grouped in a hierarchy and therefore be assigned to users at different levels. When you use authorization roles, the assignment of analysis authorizations is done via the BIAUTH authorization field in the S_RS_AUTH authorization object. The authorizations are then assigned to the users via special BW authorization roles.

### 10.3.3 Other Concepts

Integrating SAP NetWeaver BW with other systems and applications increases security requirements. Integration options may exist, for example, with SAP ERP, SAP NetWeaver Master Data Management (MDM), and the SAP industry solutions. SAP's open concept requires you to establish special authorization solutions.

- **Check indicator concept**
  Because different customized reporting objects can't be defined up front in Tables USOBT_C and USOBX_C and also because specific authorization objects are directly linked to InfoCubes, the normal maintenance of Transaction SU24 isn't possible in this context. On a case-by-case basis, you must determine whether

or not certain authorization objects for SAP NetWeaver BW can be maintained using Transaction SU24 and, if so, what the possible effects may be.

- **Drag-and-drop authorizations**
  The drag-and-drop authorizations are another example of a security concept. Instead of roles, profiles that can be assigned to users and user groups are used.
- **Hierarchical authorizations**
  For hierarchies, the authorizations can be controlled as shown in Table 10.2 or by using analysis authorizations (see Section 10.3.2).

| Step | Activity | Transaction code |
|---|---|---|
| 1 | Transfer and activate InfoObject `0TCTAUTHH` | RSD1 |
| 2 | Mark InfoObject `0TCTAUTHH` as relevant for authorization | RSD1 |
| 3 | Mark Leaf InfoObject as relevant for authorization | RSD1 |
| 4 | Create authorization objects with `0TCTAUTHH` and Leaf InfoObject | RSSM |
| 5 | Definition of hierarchical authorizations, including technical descriptions | RSSM |
| 6 | Manual integration of authorization object in role (not via Transaction SU24) | PFCG |
| 7 | Maintain authorization values | PFCG |
| 8 | Assign role to user | PFCG (or CUA) |

**Table 10.2** Authorizations with Hierarchies

- **SAP ERP HCM data**
  To extract data, structural authorizations must also be mapped in SAP NetWeaver BW to ensure consistency between the different systems in this area as well. To do this, the following tables are relevant in the context of SAP ERP HCM:
  - `T77PR` for structural authorization profiles
  - `T77UA` for user assignments
  - `T77UU` for users

  In Table `T77UU`, you can select users for the extraction. You can either select all users or specific ones. For structural authorizations in SAP NetWeaver BW, the authorizations can be controlled according to Table 10.3.

| Step | Activity | System |
|---|---|---|
| 1 | Calling program RHBAUS02 for updating Table T77UU — entering users | SAP ERP HCM |
| 2 | Calling program RHBAUS00 for generating an index for structural authorization profiles | SAP ERP HCM |
| 3 | Activating transfer rules for 0HR_PA_2 | SAP ERP HCM |
| 4 | Replicating DataSource 0HR_PA_2 | SAP NetWeaver BW |
| 5 | Activating ODS InfoProvider 0HR_PA_2 | SAP NetWeaver BW |
| 6 | Activating transfer rules for 0HR_PA_2 | SAP NetWeaver BW |
| 7 | Creating an InfoPackage to perform an extraction for 0HR_PA_2 | SAP NetWeaver BW |
| 8 | Loading ODS data from SAP ERP HCM | SAP NetWeaver BW |
| 9 | Mark InfoObjects as relevant for authorization: To use the structural authorizations in SAP BW, all characteristic values (for example, position and employee) relevant to reporting must be defined as authorization-relevant InfoObjects. | SAP NetWeaver BW |
| 10 | Creating the reporting authorization objects | SAP NetWeaver BW |
| 11 | Linking authorization objects to InfoCubes | SAP NetWeaver BW |
| 12 | Calling program RSSB_Generate_Authorizations | SAP NetWeaver BW |

**Table 10.3** Authorizations with Structural Authorizations

### SAP NetWeaver BW Transactions Relevant for Internal Controls

Transactions ST01, RSSM, and RSSU53 carry out different trace functions in SAP NetWeaver BW; Table 10.4 provides an overview of the important transactions.

| Transaction | Transaction Code | Description |
|---|---|---|
| Administrator Workbench | RSA1 | Transaction RSA1 is the main transaction for administrative functions in SAP NetWeaver BW. |
| InfoObject Maintenance | RSD1 | This transaction can be used to mark objects as relevant for authorization. |

**Table 10.4** Transactions in SAP NetWeaver BW

| Transaction | Transaction Code | Description |
|---|---|---|
| Authorizations | RSSM | This transaction can be used to create and modify authorization objects in SAP NetWeaver BW. Authorization objects can be assigned to InfoCubes or removed from them. |
| | | Authorizations can be analyzed using the trace function. The creation and modification of hierarchical authorizations and the corresponding settings occur via this transaction. |
| Variable Maintenance | RSZV | This transaction is used to create or modify the variables for the authorization checks. |
| Business Explorer | RRMX | BEx is the reporting tool in SAP NetWeaver BW and is used for analyzing data. |
| Global Templates | GLOBAL_TEMPLATES | Templates are used for modeling and evaluating data. |

**Table 10.4** Transactions in SAP NetWeaver BW (Cont.)

### Users in SAP NetWeaver BW

It is useful to classify the users in SAP NetWeaver BW. In this context it is possible to group users according to administrative, functional, organizational, or other aspects and assign the appropriate authorizations to them.

A subdivision of the user classes into developers, administrators, power users, expert users, and so on is one classification option. SAP NetWeaver BW uses the concept of user groups. However, with regard to data security and controlled data access, information users who are authorized to use the evaluations and queries must be further classified into subgroups. Information users are only allowed to run queries; they are not authorized to create new queries, or to modify existing ones. This user group is only allowed to display authorizations.

Often, power users and administrators, in particular, have few restrictions placed on their authorizations. Therefore, their actions must be monitored to determine how best to control their activities on the system (that is, how often it is necessary that they use the system and for how long a time are they engaged on the system). This relatively small group of users is allowed to create new queries and to modify existing ones. The authorization can, for instance, be restricted to specific InfoCubes. Administrators should be restricted to their work area and should not have access to critical data outside of their own work area.

Using SAP BEx requires the following three types of user groups:

- Analysts
- Knowledge workers
- Information consumers

Transactional systems (OLTP) like SAP ERP focus on current data, transactions, and process-oriented information. Real-time processing and data consistency are important here. SAP NetWeaver BW, on the other hand, is an online analytical system (OLAP). As was already described, it imports, transforms, and reorganizes historical data based on evaluation criteria, strategic requirements, and statistical aspects, and provides this data for different analytical and informational purposes.

The use of reports and collaborative applications such as the user-specific distribution of information (Information Broadcasting) via BEx and the analysis, and the alert and push functions in SAP NetWeaver BW must be complemented by sufficient protective measures. Other potential risks, such as incorrect information caused by an erroneous query design, for example, can produce negative consequences for decision-makers and executives.

A protection based on risk classifications in the data area, an evaluation of the protection needs of this data for the entire company, and a comprehensive, immediate collaboration between project teams and security experts are all critical factors when structuring appropriate solutions in the internal control system and ensuring its successful implementation. Comprehensive authorization analysis and audit functions are also available to check the use of user authorizations in SAP NetWeaver BW and audit them accordingly.

## 10.4 Technical Security

SAP NetWeaver BW is based on SAP NetWeaver. This means that all technically relevant risks and controls of SAP NetWeaver AS (see Chapter 9) must be taken into account. Moreover, depending on individual use, the technical controls of the following components must also be considered:

- SAP Internet Transaction Server (see Chapter 14, Classic SAP Middleware)
- SAP NetWeaver Portal (see Chapter 16, SAP NetWeaver Portal)
- Database servers (see Chapter 27, Database Server)
- SAP Graphical User Interface (GUI) (see Chapter 28, User Interfaces)
- Web browser (see Chapter 28)

The technical controls described there must be applied without limitation to SAP NetWeaver BW.

*The Business Intelligence (BI) solutions in SAP BusinessObjects provide a new dimension in the evaluation, presentation, and management of business-critical information. This chapter outlines the risks and security aspects that must be discussed in this context.*

# 11 BI Solutions in SAP BusinessObjects

Information processing in traditional SAP applications focuses on the components of SAP Business Suite, which basically support the handling and management of business processes. Business Suite traditionally provides for this in a variety of SAP transactions and retrievable or customer-specific reports.

When these processes run, a large quantity of data may be generated, processed, and stored in the system. This data must exhibit a high quality, that is, the data must be correct and current and correspond to the necessary data format. This data quality is indispensable not only for accounting reasons, but it is also a prerequisite for the effectiveness and the value of the business information system, because, ultimately, the information is retrieved from data that is entered in the information system. An effective information system with good data quality is also indispensable for business management, be it for business and strategic decisions or for the valuation of risks.

On the other hand, the display of data alone is usually not enough because not only data but also more complex information about business processes is required, which is extracted from the analysis of multidimensional and occasionally cross-system, non-SAP databases and presented according to defined rules. This includes, for example, the presentation and assessment of the business performance inside and outside of financial processes and a comprehensive analysis for preparing strategic decisions or valuation of risks and compliance.

To consider this requirement for more complex information and more flexible reporting options, SAP NetWeaver Business Warehouse (BW) already offers a solid basis for profound process analyses and decisions. The resulting higher value of information also increases the security need and requirements on risk management so that independent security and authorization concepts are integrated with SAP NetWeaver BW; Chapter 10, SAP NetWeaver Business Warehouse, provides more information on this topic.

Moreover, SAP's BI solutions in SAP BusinessObjects offer a solution portfolio that is oriented toward complex information management to enable competent decisions in your company. By means of the SAP BusinessObjects solutions for BI you ensure that the users of your company can retrieve, format, analyze, browse, and exchange data and information. To do this, you are provided with dashboards for visualization, analysis tools for retrieval and reporting, reporting tools with search and evaluation functions, and a complex information infrastructure. All of these solutions can also use data from SAP Enterprise Resource Planning (ERP) (see Chapter 20, Authorizations in SAP ERP), SAP NetWeaver BW (see Chapter 10), SAP NetWeaver Master Data Management (MDM) (see Chapter 15, SAP NetWeaver MDM), SAP Customer Relationship Management (CRM) (see Chapter 23, SAP CRM), and non-SAP applications and their databases.

## 11.1 Introduction and Functions

To enable the previously mentioned functions of the BI solutions in SAP BusinessObjects, the following applications and tools are used, among others:

- **SAP BusinessObjects Enterprise**
  SAP BusinessObjects Enterprise is the platform and infrastructure for the BI solutions of SAP BusinessObjects. The Central Management Console (CMC) is the application for administrating SAP BusinessObjects Enterprise, including the user administration, administration of the database's content , and the server platform. But every regular user also has access to this application to make user-specific settings for the user interface. These general access authorizations for regular users, however, exclude the CMC administration functions.
- **Reporting**
  SAP BusinessObjects Crystal Reports is the default tool for creating, presenting, and distributing reports. Crystal Reports enables a structured and formatted design of queries and analyses. The generated reports have a standardized, portable format and are stored as complete files. This way, report files can be easily transferred and presented to other users using Crystal Reports Explorer.
- **Dashboards and visualization**
  The visual, interactive presentation of the analysis reports of what-if scenarios or data forecasts is supported by the applications, SAP BusinessObjects Xcelsius Enterprise and Dashboard Builder. The regular user uses Dashboard Builder, for example, for selecting and monitoring business performance parameters. A developer uses SAP BusinessObjects Xcelsius for designing interactive analysis models and data presentations.
- **Ad hoc query, reporting, and analysis**
  SAP BusinessObjects Web Intelligence and SAP BusinessObjects Desktop Intel-

ligence generate data analyses within relational databases. While regular users access Web Intelligence for displaying information, developers of reports and data analyses mainly use Desktop Intelligence.

- **Advanced analytics**
  Besides other applications, such as SAP BusinessObjects Predictive Workbench, SAP BusinessObjects Voyager is the most important tool in this category to ensure flexible construction and analysis of multi-dimensional data structures within relational databases.

**Note**

Large parts of this chapter refer to Release 3.1 of the BI solutions in SAP BusinessObjects. To ensure that you can benefit from the information provided in this chapter independent of the release, the descriptions are mainly generic because the BI solutions in SAP Business-Objects are increasingly integrated with the overall SAP portfolio and changes in terminology and subject matter occur in this process.

## 11.2 Risks and Controls

A risk analysis according to the methods presented in Chapter 1, Risk and Control Management, is now supposed to present the security risks for the BI solutions in SAP BusinessObjects (see Table 11.1). As usual, you'll also learn about the corresponding controls that reduce the risk, which are then illustrated in detail and with possible examples in the subsequent sections.

| No. | Classification | Description |
|---|---|---|
| 1. | Risk potential | Missing authorization concept:<br>The security concept in SAP BusinessObjects is not implemented or only insufficiently. Administrators, developers, data administrators, or regular users obtain full access to all authorizations for the administration, design, and management of data analyses or the presentation of information, including the user administration and management of access rights. |
| | Impact | Users can view confidential business information and make modifications to this information without any authorization. This makes it possible for confidential business information to leak to the outside world and poses a threat to the integrity of the data. The negative economic impacts could be enormous for the company. |

**Table 11.1** Risks and Controls for the BI Solutions in SAP BusinessObjects

| No. | Classification | Description |
|---|---|---|
| | Risk without control(s) | Extremely high |
| | Control | A clear and well-conceived authorization concept using the predefined security concepts in SAP BusinessObjects for user access is designed and implemented. |
| | Risk with control(s) | Normal |
| | Section | 11.3.1 |
| 2. | Risk potential | Authorization concept faulty or configured without further specification:<br>Administrators, report designers, or regular users obtain authorizations for designing data analyses or reports, or regular users obtain access to critical administration functions for designing data analyses or managing access rights. The principle of separating responsibilities was not implemented. Users have access to all data. |
| | Impact | Administrators or regular users can manipulate access rights without any authorization to obtain confidential business information or falsify data with negative consequences for the company while violating data protection obligations. |
| | Risk without control(s) | Extremely high |
| | Control | A clear authorization concept using the security functions available in SAP BusinessObjects is designed and implemented so that access to administration functions, responsibilities, and access to data administration or data presentation are separated. |
| | Risk with control(s) | Normal |
| | Section | 11.3.2 |
| 3. | Risk potential | Insufficient protection of the superadministrator, the administrator group, and the guest user:<br>The administrator user and the administrator group have unrestricted authorizations for functions, applications, and data. The standard guest user can be misused for anonymous access. |

**Table 11.1** Risks and Controls for the BI Solutions in SAP BusinessObjects (Cont.)

| No. | Classification | Description |
|---|---|---|
| | Impact | The superadministrator or the users of the administrator group could be preyed on for unauthorized or damaging actions. The guest user could be misused for anonymous access to business information with impacts that could jeopardize the business while violating data protection obligations. |
| | Risk without control(s) | Extremely high |
| | Control | A clear authorization concept is defined and implemented. The superadministrator and the guest user are protected particularly against unauthorized access. |
| | Risk with control(s) | Normal |
| | Section | 11.3.3 |
| 4. | Risk potential | Passwords that are too simple:<br>To access SAP BusinessObjects applications, users must authenticate themselves using passwords. To quickly remember the passwords, they select a password with a very simply structure or write it down at a place where it can be found easily. |
| | Impact | Application passwords that have been written down or that are very simple represent a weak link in the access authentication control. Due to this security gap, unauthorized users can access applications and information. The financial damage from such abuses can be enormous. |
| | Risk without control(s) | Extremely high |
| | Control | Password rules are configured in SAP BusinessObjects, which are aligned with the business guidelines and have a sufficiently complex structure. |
| | Risk with control(s) | Normal |
| | Section | 11.3.4 |
| 5. | Risk potential | Users have unrestricted access to all applications in SAP BusinessObjects:<br>The applications are available for all users without any selection according to the task area or the necessary information requirement. |

**Table 11.1** Risks and Controls for the BI Solutions in SAP BusinessObjects (Cont.)

| No. | Classification | Description |
|---|---|---|
| | Impact | If the access to the applications in SAP BusinessObjects is not restricted specifically for tasks or responsibilities, you cannot implement the principle of data protection, information responsibility, or segregation of duties. Moreover, the risk of data falsification or violation of company-wide data integrity exists. |
| | Risk without control(s) | High |
| | Control | Users only obtain authorizations for applications in SAP BusinessObjects, which they require for their work area. |
| | Risk with control(s) | Normal |
| | Section | 11.3.5 |
| 6. | Risk potential | Too many business applications have password authentications with passwords that must be different mandatorily:<br>Usually, many business applications have user authentications that are based on passwords.<br>Consequently, users have a high number of different passwords, which in turn has the result that users select passwords with a simple structure or write them down at a place where they can be found easily. |
| | Impact | Application passwords that have been written down or that are very simple represent a weak link in the authentication control for the access to business applications. Due to this security gap, unauthorized users can access applications and information. The financial damage and the negative impacts for the company's reputation can be enormous. |
| | Risk without control(s) | High |
| | Control | The authentication for the access to applications in SAP BusinessObjects is integrated with a business Single Sign-On (SSO) concept. |
| | Risk with control(s) | Normal |
| | Section | 11.4.1 |

**Table 11.1** Risks and Controls for the BI Solutions in SAP BusinessObjects (Cont.)

| No. | Classification | Description |
|---|---|---|
| 7. | Risk potential | The audit information of the BI solutions of SAP Business-Objects remains unused:<br>Auditing functions are not configured, or audit information of the audit database is not analyzed with regard to incidents or irregularities. |
| | Impact | If no audit information about system or user activities exists or is monitored, no full analysis of the security incidents can be performed, and the principle of user responsibility or the principle of information responsibility cannot be achieved. Moreover, you run the risk that the company doesn't comply with its business audit guidelines or external compliance requirements. |
| | Risk without control(s) | High |
| | Control | Configuration and usage of the extensive audit functions of SAP BusinessObjects |
| | Risk with control(s) | Normal |
| | Section | 11.4.2 |
| 8. | Risk potential | Communication channels between the applications in SAP BusinessObjects are unprotected:<br>The communication within the open SAP BusinessObjects infrastructure that is based on the CORBA technology is not protected, and the data is transferred without encryption in plain text. CORBA security functions and configurations remain unused. |
| | Impact | Unencrypted, unauthenticated communication channels can allow unauthorized users to view or manipulate confidential business information. This is very likely to have negative effects on the company's reputation or cause financial losses for the company. Moreover, you run the risk that the company doesn't comply with its data protection guidelines or external compliance requirements. |
| | Risk without control(s) | High |

**Table 11.1** Risks and Controls for the BI Solutions in SAP BusinessObjects (Cont.)

| No. | Classification | Description |
|---|---|---|
| | Control | Usage of Secure Socket Layer (SSL) communication between internal and external systems. CORBA security functions are used for communication security within the SAP Business-Objects infrastructure. |
| | Risk with control(s) | Normal |
| | Section | 11.4.3 |

**Table 11.1** Risks and Controls for the BI Solutions in SAP BusinessObjects (Cont.)

## 11.3 Application Security

This section describes in more detail the risks and controls that are outlined in Table 11.1 with regard to application security.

### 11.3.1 Authorization Concept for SAP BusinessObjects

When discussing application security for SAP BusinessObjects, you must take into account that SAP BusinessObjects is a (originally) non-SAP technology platform. This results in a different authorization concept than you know from the other SAP systems. All options and restrictions with regard to access to applications, the functionality, and physical and virtual data within SAP BusinessObjects are controlled by a separate authorization concept.

All data accesses and queries from SAP BusinessObjects are directed at the databases of the SAP or non-SAP systems. To do this, SAP BusinessObjects uses a special system user with full database access rights. This direct database access is used to bypass all individual user authorizations for the data access via back-end applications. This means, on the one hand, that the authorization concept of SAP BusinessObjects controls all questions of the user administration, system administration, and data structures, and, on the other hand, authorizations for external data of the back-end databases that are linked with SAP BusinessObjects.

However, the risk analysis and configuration of user access to the information system of SAP BusinessObjects shouldn't occur only from an SAP BusinessObjects perspective, but the authorizations for users should be aligned with the business requirements, control objectives, and the overall risk tolerance permitted. That is, the design of the authorization concept must be aligned with the control objectives of the back-end applications. This means that if a user in the back-end system has no access to specific data, these restrictions should also exist within SAP Business Objects. The general goal is that individual user authorizations in SAP Business-

Objects do not exceed the existing restrictions of data access in the SAP back-end and non-SAP applications or databases.

Chapters 9, SAP NetWeaver AS, and 20 present the SAP authorization concept as it is implemented in the SAP back-end system (AS ABAP). This authorization system is primarily aligned with the authorization check of process transactions. In contrast, SAP BusinessObjects is an information management system with an authorization system (access control) that specializes in objects. Objects include, for example, reports in Crystal Reports, SQL templates for data analyses (referred to as universes in SAP BusinessObjects), directories, applications, a hyperlink, or a connection with the back-end database. Users are also objects in the sense of the authorization system.

The Central Management Console (CMC) is the central tool in SAP BusinessObjects for configuring the user authorizations for objects. This is done using Access Control Lists (ACL). All parameters and authorization configurations are stored in the CMC database.

In SAP BusinessObjects, objects are organized in a hierarchical directory structure, analogous to the Portal Content Directory of SAP NetWeaver Portal. Using the CMC, you can manage this directory and the objects included therein and assign the access authorizations for directories and the objects stored there via the menu path: CMC • ORGANIZE • FOLDERS.

Authorizations (access controls) are distributed based on a ranking: First, in the top-level directory structure in the hierarchy, then for the subdirectories, and then for the object. In this process, the objects accept the authorizations of the directories in which they are contained. This inheritance of authorizations can be canceled intentionally for the directory or manually for the object depending on the requirements. However, this terminates the inheritance of authorizations from the superordinate directory structure.

The following sections present some elements of the authorization concept of SAP BusinessObjects and selected configuration steps.

### User Concept in SAP BusinessObjects

User masters and their data and authorizations are basically configured in the CMC of SAP BusinessObjects. The following information can be added as user master data:

- User ID
- User name
- Email address (for transferring a new password)

- Description of user-specific information
- Password rules
- Configuration of a user-specific password for administrative access to a universe (SQL code template for repeated data queries in the back-end databases)
- Type of the user license
- Deactivation of the user ID
- Alias user IDs, that is, multiple user IDs for the same user

As the administrator, you can configure a user via the following menu path: CMC • USERS AND GROUPS • MANAGE • NEW • NEW USER. After the initial installation of SAP BusinessObjects, there are only two standard users: the administrator user with universal access rights and the guest user that is deactivated by default.

### Group Concept

SAP BusinessObjects offers a user group concept that enables a structured and effective assignment of authorizations for directories, objects, and applications in the same way as for a single user. The basic understanding of the group concept is analogous to the traditional ABAP role concept. Users and user groups are referred to as principals in SAP BusinessObjects. Analogous to the inheritance principle between hierarchical directories, this concept also exists for user groups: A user obtains authorizations for his user group. A subgroup obtains the user rights of the superordinate group (group hierarchy). A user group can be assigned to a profile that determines which information the members of this group can view in a published report.

A user is assigned to a group via the following menu path: CMC • USERS AND GROUPS • ACTIONS • JOIN GROUP. After the initial installation of SAP BusinessObjects, no additional standard user is available except for the one standard user (administrator). User accesses must be configured for all other users. Existing standard user groups with configured access rights provide support to design a roughly structured access for work areas with authorized users (see Section 11.3.2, Application Examples for Authorization Concepts).

### Profile Concept

Within SAP BusinessObjects, users can develop and start their own reports. Data analyses can also be developed and started centrally. As soon as the report data is available, it is published. Users can find these published reports in a special directory within the SAP BusinessObjects system landscape, for example. If specific data is supposed to be filtered when these reports are read (not visible for specific users/user groups), a profile can be assigned to these user groups to support this filter function.

An application case, in which such a profile is effective as a filter, entails the control objective that users of the published report can only view data if they belong to a specific user group or may only view data from a specific country. As the administrator, you can use the following menu path to assign profile values to users or user groups: CMC • PROFILES • ACTIONS • PROFILE VALUES • ADD • CHOOSE. At this point, you can select between users or user groups. You should note that the inheritance principle for users is activated if the profile values are assigned to a user group.

#### Security for the Root Folder and Other Directories

At the highest directory in the directory structure, the root folder, you can specify the accesses (access level) that apply to all subordinate directories and their objects (inheritance). However, this inheritance relationship can be undone at the subdirectories level or directly for the object by setting individual authorizations and manually switching off the inheritance.

As the administrator, you navigate to the root folder via the menu path: CMC • FOLDERS • MANAGE • SECURITY • ALL FOLDER SECURITY • USER SECURITY: ROOT FOLDER. Then, the system displays the access control list for this directory. When you click ADD PRINCIPAL, you can select a user or a user group and then use ADD AND ASSIGN SECURITY to assign the desired authorization.

If required, you can create directories below the root directory. For a selected directory, you can then configure the authorization for a specific principal as follows: MANAGE • SECURITY • USER SECURITY • ADD PRINCIPALS. Users or user groups can now be selected in the list of existing principals. By clicking Add and Assign Security, you select and assign an authorization for the directory for the principal you selected. The authorizations set at the directory level apply to all objects of the directory, including the subdirectories. Here, you should note that at this point you can use a manual configuration step to accept or deactivate the inheritance of authorizations from the superordinate directory directly or indirectly via user groups of this superordinate directory.

#### Object-Typical Authorizations

Authorizations for accessing objects are generally set in the directory of the objects. However, you can also configure an access level directly for a selected object and a specific principal. To do this, follow the menu path: MANAGE • SECURITY • USER SECURITY • ADD PRINCIPALS. You can now select users or user groups in the list of existing principals. By clicking Add and Assign Security, you then select and assign an authorization for the object for the principal you chose. Here as well, you should note that you can accept or deactivate the inheritance of authorizations of the object directory or the user groups of the object directory.

Object-typical access levels exist in addition to the general authorizations for objects. This results from the multitude of different functions that can have objects. For instance, the object of a report has a different task than the object of a user group. For example, for the object of the authorization is it useful to automatically start a report (object type: Crystal Reports) at a specific point in time. This is not useful for the object type of a user group (object type: Users and Groups). There are general authorizations like Add, Delete, or Edit for all object types or special object type–dependent authorizations like exporting reporting data, which exists for the Crystal Reports object type but not for the Word Document object type. Table 11.2 provides four object type groups with their object types.

| Object Type Group (Collection) | Examples of Object Types |
|---|---|
| GENERAL | Authorizations, ADD, DELETE, or EDIT are valid for all object types. |
| CONTENT | ▸ Crystal Reports (.rpt)<br>▸ Adobe Acrobat (.pdf)<br>▸ Desktop Intelligence (.rep)<br>▸ Word (.doc)<br>▸ Excel (.xls) |
| APPLICATION | ▸ SAP BusinessObjects Web Intelligence<br>▸ SAP BusinessObjects Desktop Intelligence |
| SYSTEM | ▸ Users and Groups<br>▸ Calendars<br>▸ Events |

**Table 11.2** Groups of Object Types with Examples

### Standard Authorizations

SAP BusinessObjects comprises standard authorizations (access level) that are already available after the system installation and used to set up the authorization concept. In addition, you can also build customer-specific access levels, either as a modified copy of a standard authorization (CMC • ACCESS LEVELS • ORGANIZE • COPY) or a completely new one (CMC • ACCESS LEVELS • MANAGE • NEW • CREATE ACCESS LEVEL). Table 11.3 summarizes the standard authorizations.

| Standard Authorization | Details | Description |
|---|---|---|
| No Access | No authorization | No access to directories or objects |
| View | Read access for objects and documents | Authorizations for reading directories, objects, documents, and their administration history |
| Schedule | Read authorization, for example, for:<br>▸ Scheduling of reports and their documents<br>▸ Copying objects to another directory<br>▸ Printing reports<br>▸ Exporting reports<br>▸ Managing custom objects | A user with this authorization can, for example, select a data source and request a report for a specific point in time. |
| View On Demand | ▸ All details on the schedule authorizations<br>▸ Repeated starting of a report for updating data | A user with this authorization can, for example, update the data of a report with regard to a data source. |
| Full Control | ▸ All previous authorizations<br>▸ Management of objects<br>▸ Management of authorizations for objects<br>▸ Deletion of objects and reports | A user with this authorization has full control of objects. |

**Table 11.3** Standard Authorizations for Objects

### Advanced Security for Principals

Usually, principals (users, user groups) receive their authorizations from the access level that they have according to the directory or the object. Sometimes, however, it is necessary to further refine these authorizations (advanced rights, included rights), via the following menu path: Manage • Security • User Security. You then select the object and the principal in the CMC. Via the Assign Security • Advanced • Add /Remove Rights menu path, you can then refine the access level and subject it to a special condition.

Advanced rights should be set if a user or a user group is supposed to keep the access level for an object even if the user group or the authorizations for the directory of the object change later on. Table 11.4 summarizes the options for advanced rights.

| Advanced Rights | Description |
|---|---|
| GRANTED | Principal has the access level. |
| DENIED | Principal has no access to the access level. |
| NOT SPECIFIED | The access level is not specified for the principal, which means that the principal has no access to the access level. |
| APPLY TO OBJECT | This option assigns the advanced right to the object (GRANTED or DENIED). |
| APPLY TO SUB-OBJECTS | This option assigns the advanced right to a hierarchical sub-object (GRANTED or DENIED). |

**Table 11.4** List of Advanced Rights

### Solving Authorization Conflicts in an Authorization Check

Considering the different options for how the access level and advanced rights are set or can be inherited indirectly to objects or directories, authorization conflicts may arise. The authorization system of SAP BusinessObjects solves such conflicts with general rules (also see Table 11.4):

- GRANTED + NOT SPECIFIED = GRANTED
- GRANTED + DENIED = DENIED
- GRANTED + DENIED + NOT SPECIFIED = DENIED
- DENIED + NOT SPECIFIED = DENIED

In general, access levels that are directly assigned to an object overwrite those access levels that may apply to the object due to an inheritance. Authorization conflicts can also arise in the authorization check of profiles if a user obtains various profiles due to direct assignment or simultaneously due to inheritance. For this case, SAP BusinessObjects uses two special mechanisms for solving the conflict; the decision of which mechanism is effective is specified manually by the author of the report before a report is published:

- MERGE
  In this case, the conflict is solved by merging the profiles that are not in conflict with one another. The result for the example of the profile concept would be that the user can only view data in a report that corresponds to his user group and the country to which the user belongs.

- Do Not Merge
  In this case, the conflicting profiles are interpreted as different perspectives of the report data. In this example, this would mean for the user that two separate reports are available: one report that is authorized for the data of his country and a second report including data for which only his user group is authorized.

SAP BusinessObjects offers various rules for solving authorization conflicts that are always used depending on the specific conflict type. To ultimately implement the desired control objects in this complexity, you need a sound understanding of the authorization concepts and clear requirements for the control objectives. You should also have a well-conceived test plan that is based on the possible variants and run a sufficient testing of the implemented controls.

### 11.3.2 Application Examples for Authorization Concepts

In SAP BusinessObjects, immediately after the initial installation, no other access for users is created except for a standard administrator. As a result, this standard user must then be used to configure the access rights for all other users. Considering the many authorization concepts available (see Section 11.3.1, Authorization Concept for SAP BusinessObjects), this is a very complex task if not every user is supposed to be granted full access to all solutions in SAP BusinessObjects.

This situation holds the risk that security options are not applied because of a quick granting of system access and thus security weaknesses are integrated with the concept for the user access, or that no well-conceived concept is available in the extreme case. These security weaknesses are not only the cause for a violation of the data protection and compliance, but they will also raise considerable objections in the first audit of the access rights.

Before users are granted access to a production system, it is recommended to sufficiently secure this system, taking into account all of the security concepts in SAP BusinessObjects. This means that you should start with an analysis of the requirements for user access in the context of the control objectives; then you design a balanced authorization strategy that implements the business control objectives and the demands for information access in the sense of risk management. Experience has shown that this requires about 80% of the time of an implementation project; the remaining 20% of the time is used for the system installation and configuration of the SAP BusinessObjects landscape.

The following sections show you how to implement control objectives using the authorization concepts based on some simple application examples.

### Control Objective: User Authorizations Correspond to Task Area

SAP BusinessObjects provides predefined standard user groups. By assigning a user to one of the user groups offered, you can roughly distribute the user rights. Table 11.5 presents these standard user groups.

| User Group (Principal) | Description |
|---|---|
| Administrators | Full access to all functions and data. The standard administrator is a member of this group. Control objectives cannot be achieved with this group due to the universal access. |
| Everyone | Every user is a member of this group. Authorizations can be granted to every user via this group. By default, the Everyone user group has read rights (access level) for the root directory. |
| QaaWS Group Designer | Query as a Web Service (QaaWS) allows for a custom and flexible design of data analyses. Members of this group have the required authorizations to develop data analyses using a predefined universe and then publish it as a web service. This web service can then be used by applications, such as Xcelsius (WS consumer), to have the system run this data analysis of the various applications repeatedly. |
| Report Conversion Tool Users | This group provides access for converting report formats. Users of this group have authorizations to transfer reports from SAP BusinessObjects Desktop Intelligence to the Web Intelligence format. A user would implement this conversion of the report format if a report, individually created using Desktop Intelligence, is supposed to be published for general access via a web browser. |
| Translators | This group provides access to the Translation Manager. The BI solutions in SAP BusinessObjects support multilingual information processing. Users of this group can use the Translation Manager application to convert reports from the local default language into another language or to translate the metadata of a universe accordingly. |
| Universe Designer Users | This user group grants access to the universe development tool and for creating connections to the back-end databases. Users of this group have access to a graphical user interface via which they can establish the physical connection to the back-end databases to create a basis for data analyses. These SQL templates (universes) are user-friendly because they highly simplify the complexity of the underlying SQL structures for the user. |

**Table 11.5** Standard User Groups in SAP BusinessObjects

As you can see in Table 11.5, the standard user groups mainly provide for a separation of functions for the administration and design. This separation of tasks may be sufficient for a development system, but in a production system these standard user groups can only meet the business control objectives insufficiently or not at all. It is indispensable that you develop your own user groups with specifically configured authorizations at the object level, for example, at the reporting level. The following ideas should be considered when developing a simple security concept:

- Analyzing business requirements for information management, the data analysis, report requirements, and control objectives
- Designing an authorization matrix that assigns these analysis results to organizational structures, user groups, and users according to the task area and considering the control objectives identified
- Developing custom directories that are structured by subject groups, organizational forms, and so on (on the basis of the authorization matrix), for example, financials or the personnel department
- Assigning objects to these directories (on the basis of the authorization matrix)
- Configuring the access rights for user groups at the directory level
- Assigning users to user groups (according to the authorization matrix)
- Avoiding the configuration of authorizations at the user level because the user administration work can considerably increase
- Manually switching off the principle of inheriting authorizations because the user administration work can considerably increase due to the complexity and an analysis of the resulting authorization system can also be very complex

#### Control Objective: Protecting Financial or Personal Data in Directories

User access at the directory level can be designed so that the user generally has access to a main directory, but authorizations to subordinate directories, which contain personal or financial data to be protected, are assigned individually to the users. The same concept can be used for controlling the management of objects in directories in a targeted manner.

#### Control Objective: Segregation of Duties

The control objective of segregation of duties or information responsibility can be implemented by assigning authorizations at the directory level so that a user or user group can include objects in a directory but isn't allowed to change these objects. An example of this scenario is the authorization to assign users to a directory, on the one hand, and to deny that the password of these users is changed, on the other hand.

This control objective can be achieved by denying the CHANGE USER PASSWORD right for the USERS AND GROUPS object type using the advanced rights concept. You can use the same methodology — reducing the scope of authorizations in a targeted way — for example, to tailor the user administration to specific functions and user groups (delegated user administration).

### 11.3.3 Securing the Administration Access and the Guest User

The administrator of the CMC and the guest user are standard users of SAP BusinessObjects. They entail a risk that can be reduced using the countermeasures presented in Table 11.6.

| Principal | Risk Management |
|---|---|
| ADMINISTRATOR | Due to his full access to the CMC, including all functions and data, the ADMINISTRATOR should only be used for the initial configuration of SAP BusinessObjects and then only in exceptional cases. The user has no password by default. Accordingly, a password must be structured with complex password rules and protected against unauthorized access (see Section 11.3.4). The audit functions of the CMC should be used for monitoring the activities of the administrator. |
| ADMINISTRATORS | The ADMINISTRATORS user group should only include the administrator as a user due to the full access to the CMC with all functions and data. |
| GUEST | By default, the guest user doesn't have a password to enable SSO. This user should be deactivated to exclude unauthorized access. Applications in SAP BusinessObjects should only be available to regular authenticated users. |

**Table 11.6** Standard Principals and Security

### 11.3.4 Configuring Password Rules

By default, the user authentication for all applications in SAP BusinessObjects is done by means of user ID and password; users can also be created with password only. Password rules that are defined with the appropriate level of complexity should be configured using the CMC to reduce the risk of unauthorized system access. To set the rules, you must navigate to the corresponding CMC area via the menu path: CMC • MANAGE • AUTHENTICATION • ENTERPRISE. Here, you can specify the password properties listed in Table 11.7.

| Rule | Description |
|---|---|
| Enforce mixed case password | This parameter requires that the password contains at least two of the following categories:<br>▶ Uppercase letter<br>▶ Lowercase letter<br>▶ Numbers<br>▶ Punctuation characters |
| Must contain at least N characters | This parameter specifies the minimum password length of N.<br>Recommended parameter value: 6 |
| Must change password every N day(s) | This parameter specifies that the password must be changed after N days.<br>Recommended parameter value: 30 days |
| Cannot use the N most recent password(s) | This parameter defines that when you change the password you cannot select any of the last N passwords as the new password.<br>Recommended parameter value: 3 |
| Must wait N minute(s) to change password | This parameter specifies that a user can try to log on again after N minutes if the user ID was disabled after an incorrect password was entered multiple times (see next parameter).<br>Recommended parameter value: 5 |
| Disable account after N failed attempt(s) to logon | This parameter specifies that the user ID is disabled after an incorrect password was entered N times.<br>Recommended parameter value: 3 |
| Reset failed logon count after N minute(s) | This parameter specifies that after N minutes the count for failed logon attempts is reset.<br>Recommended parameter value: 5 |
| Reenable account after N minute(s) | This parameter specifies that after N minutes a user ID is automatically reenabled. |

**Table 11.7** Standard Password Rules in SAP BusinessObjects

### 11.3.5 Application Authorizations

The BI solutions in SAP BusinessObjects offer a portfolio of applications for information management. Therefore, you are provided with a multitude of applications whose usage depends on the respective case. Due to the different functions, each of these applications has its typical authorizations that you can configure via the

CMC. The Best Practices for handling the authorizations entail that you re-create the application-specific access levels or that you derive them from the application's standard authorizations as a copy and — if necessary — specify them. This is done in three steps:

1. **Create the customer-specific authorization**
   In the CMC, navigate to Access Level Management, and follow the MANAGE • NEW • CREATE ACCESS LEVEL menu path to create a new authorization.
2. **Configure the authorization for the application (advanced rights)**
   You obtain the authorization for accessing an application by first navigating to the Access Level Management in the CMC. Here, you select the new authorization via the ACTIONS • INCLUDED RIGHTS • ADD/REMOVE RIGHTS • APPLICATION menu path, choose the specific application, and then select the application-specific authorization.
3. **Assign authorization to a principal (user/user group)**
   In this last step, you navigate to Applications in the CMC where you select the application. Then follow the MANAGE • SECURITY • USER SECURITY • ADD PRINCIPALS • MODIFY RIGHTS • ADD AND ASSIGN SECURITY menu path, select the authorization and assign it to the principal using Assigned Access Levels. Click OK to confirm your entry.

You can configure a general access authorization for all applications in SAP BusinessObjects individually for users or user groups. The number of the actual applications to which you must grant access depends on the user's respective task. Here, in turn, you should use the principle to not grant the user more access authorizations than is required for his work scope.

## 11.4 Technical Security

This section describes in more detail the risks and controls that are outlined in Table 11.1 with regard to technical security.

### 11.4.1 External Authentication and SSO

The CMC uses a custom standard module or security plug-in for creating, managing, and authenticating users. After a successful identification and authentication of a user, the CMC generates a logon token — a cookie that is saved in the web browser's cache without a password — which is also used for subsequent authentications and the session management within SAP BusinessObjects. The cookie comprises the following parameters to control its usage:

- Validity period (number of minutes)
- Number of permitted accesses to SAP BusinessObjects

The user authentication can have different forms. To do this, you are provided with security plug-ins for external authentications. Table 11.8 provides a selection of the authentication methods currently available. The authentication method can be specified user-specific when you create a user. SAP BusinessObjects supports the use of user aliases for every authentication option. The menu path for selecting an authentication model for a user is: CMC • MANAGE • NEW • NEW USER • AUTHENTICATION TYPE.

| Authentication Method | Name of the Security Plug-in in the CMC | Description |
|---|---|---|
| Enterprise | SAP BusinessObjects Enterprise (standard) | User ID and password (always available) |
| Windows NT (SSO) | Windows NT | User ID and password in Windows NT |
| External Lightweight Directory Access Protocol (LDAP) database (SSO) | LDAP | User ID and password of the external user directory |
| Windows Active Directory | Windows Active Directory | User ID and password of Windows Active Directory; for SSO, the options, NT Lan Manager (NTLM), Kerberos, and SiteMinder, are also possible |

**Table 11.8** Options for User Authentication and SSO

SSO is not a genuine security measure because the authentication is only as good as the initial user authentication. However, the minimization of passwords used indirectly contributes to a reduction of the security risk.

### 11.4.2 Using the Audit Function

SAP BusinessObjects offers comprehensive options for monitoring using audit logs. Functional events (user activity) and system events can be monitored. Log files are saved in the audit database. With the audit function, SAP BusinessObjects can register audit information for a myriad of events. These include, among others, the time when a user accesses the system or when the user leaves the system again, the access to objects, events in connection with Crystal Reports, and system events. In principle, the audit log files include information on time, user, user group, initiator of an event, event/activity, application server, and other selectable customer-specific parameters.

You should configure and use these functions according to your business requirements. This is required not only for reasons of complying with business and legal guidelines, but it also provides important information for possible investigations concerning data security violations or unauthorized accesses.

### 11.4.3 Network Communication via SSL and CORBA Services

Securing the network communication via SSL encryption within the components of SAP BusinessObjects and with the back-end databases is not recommended for data protection reasons because confidential information is transferred, among other things. Another reason is the security of the logon token (see Section 11.4.1, External Authentication and SSO), which is sent to the user with the first successful system access and stored in the web browser. If the network connection between the web browser and the system is not encrypted, the risk exists that the token (cookie) could be intercepted during the transfer and misused for unauthorized access to SAP BusinessObjects. This risk is higher if the network connection is established via insecure channels, for instance, the Internet.

The communication within the server architecture of SAP BusinessObjects is done via Common Object Request Architecture (CORBA) services. CORBA is a known communication technology that is used between distributed systems and equipped with security functions that, if used appropriately, permit risk management of the TCP/IP network connection. Support is provided for security criteria like authentication, authorization checks, audit, encryption in communication, SSL, and SSO within the CORBA infrastructure to external databases.

*Data exchange between internal systems and external applications of business partners, customers, and organizations is an essential process in all system architectures. SAP NetWeaver Process Integration (PI) helps you reduce the number of direct interfaces between SAP and non-SAP applications. Where data is exchanged, however, security aspects assume a critical role; these are explained in this chapter.*

# 12 SAP NetWeaver Process Integration

With SAP NetWeaver PI, SAP provides an enhanced integration platform for processes within distributed business applications. The objective is to integrate both SAP and non-SAP applications via a central platform using flexible web services or via interfaces. Thus, the number of required direct interfaces between individual applications can be reduced considerably. So SAP NetWeaver PI increasingly assumes the role of a powerful SAP middleware that not only enables integration using traditional interfaces but also lays the foundation for service-oriented architectures (SOAs) (see Chapter 7, Web Services, Enterprise Services, and Service-Oriented Architectures) and thus for process integration within and between companies based on an Enterprise Service Bus (ESB).

SAP NetWeaver PI relies on existing standards like web services (Simple Object Access Protocol (SOAP)), Remote Function Call (RFC), File Transfer Protocol (FTP), and other available protocols. It can also use interfaces (called connectors in the PI context) to Enterprise Application Integration (EAI) standards like RosettaNet or the chemical integration standard, Chemistry Industry Data eXchange (CIDX). SAP NetWeaver PI is predestinated for deployment in service-oriented architectures: The current release, Release 7.1, contains the Enterprise Services Repository, which serves as a structured directory for enterprise services.

Because SAP NetWeaver PI can run on both the ABAP stack and the Java stack of SAP NetWeaver Application Server (AS) (AS ABAP usage type, AS Java usage type, JEE5 for SAP NetWeaver PI), the security of "traditional" PI functions from Release 3.0 (SAP Exchange Infrastructure (XI)) and security characteristics and risks of new functions must be considered.

## 12.1 Introduction and Functions

SAP NetWeaver PI supports three communication variants, two of which are controlled directly by the PI architecture and its components:

- **Communication via the PI Integration Server**
  The PI Integration Server controls the forwarding of a message or web service integration between sender and recipient or provider and consumer. The communication partners are determined statically or dynamically using the mapping or routing functions of the integration server.
- **Communication using the PI Advanced Adapter Engine**
  If communication is supposed to be performed via the PI Advanced Adapter Engine, sender, recipient, their connectors, and the communication protocol already need to be defined in the configuration phase. The mapping function of the Advanced Adapter Engine then only statically controls the exchange of messages between the predefined connectors of the communication partners, which increases performance.
- **Direct communication bypassing the PI Integration Server**
  SAP NetWeaver PI also dynamically supports web service communication directly between the WS provider and the consumer without PI Integration Server or the Advanced Adapter Engine. This option is configured in the PI Integration Directory and allows for an increased message throughput.

To describe the preceding PI components, the following sections provide further information on the logical technical PI architecture. If SAP NetWeaver PI is used, three phases are supported: the design phase, the configuration phase, and the runtime phase (see Figure 12.1).

- **Design time**
  During the design phase, the Enterprise Services Builder/Integration Builder is used to define, design, and store the integration components and web services in the Enterprise Services Repository or Services Registry. The Services Registry corresponds to Universal Description, Discovery and Integration (UDDI) Standard 3.0 and plays a central role in provisioning web services. The Integration Directory is used to model the Application-to-Application (A2A) and Business-to-Business (B2B) communication processes.
- **Configuration time**
  The configuration phase involves further configuration of the integration scenario as defined in the Integration Directory. During this phase, communication partners, communication components, and communication channels are configured in communication profiles as defined in the Integration Directory. This includes controls, such as the mapping of senders/recipients, the routing

of messages, or the monitoring of the processes. The Business Process Engine, Integration Engine, and Advanced Adapter Engine, which support process integration for the runtime, are the essential Integration Server components.

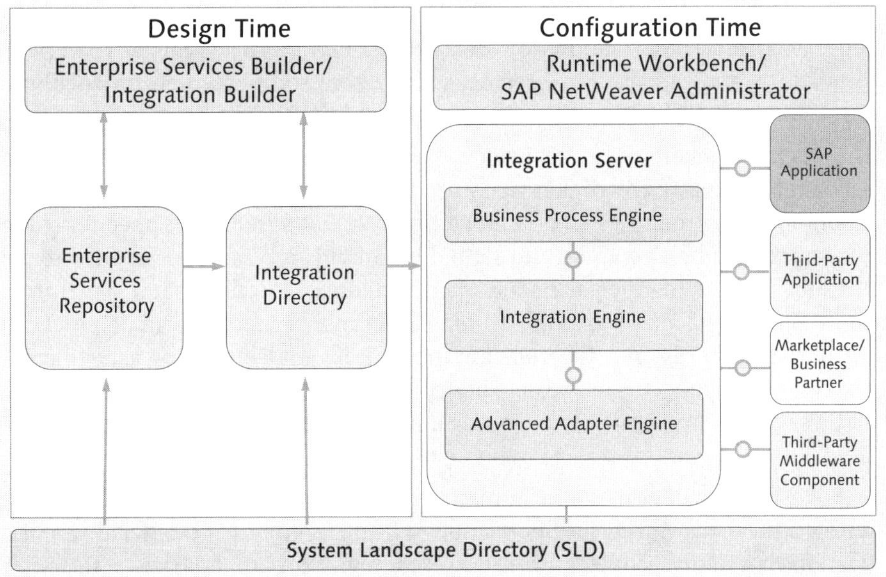


**Figure 12.1** Implementation Phases in SAP NetWeaver PI

- **Runtime**
  At runtime, the communication profiles and integration rules as defined in the Integration Directory are used for process integration by the Integration Server components (Business Process Engine, Integration Engine, and Advanced Adapter Engine). The Integration Engine is responsible for the control, processing, and monitoring of web services, and the Advanced Adapter Engine provides numerous connectors for supporting the direct integration of communication between heterogeneous applications. This often requires a conversion of the communication protocols through the Advanced Adapter Engine. The Business Process Engine implements the process integration at runtime, controls the business process flow, and supports the monitoring processes.

The System Landscape Directory (SLD) stores all metadata that describes the necessary components, adapter versions, and so on. This data is read and updated at runtime, if necessary, by the other PI components, such as the Enterprise Services Repository, Integration Directory, and Integration Server.

From a security validation perspective, the following aspects are therefore particularly essential:

- A direct interaction of a user with SAP NetWeaver PI only takes place during the design and configuration time. Afterward, the processes run automatically in the runtime environment and must be monitored appropriately via monitoring processes. The configuration data stored in the SLD, Enterprise Services Repository, and Integration Directory is only accessed by authenticated administration users during the design and configuration phase.
- The security level to be achieved at runtime, particularly the security of exchanged messages by digital signature and encryption, is specified in the collaboration agreements. This is achieved by receiver agreements specifying that a message is to be encrypted and signed before it can be sent to the final recipient. In the same manner, the sender agreements can define that a signature of an inbound message needs to be validated before the message can be processed further. This holds true whether an application is a sender, or a recipient is always determined by the respective communication partner and not in SAP NetWeaver PI. An application sending a message to the PI system is therefore a sender.
- SAP NetWeaver PI consists of numerous components exchanging information with each other. Mutual authentication is implemented via one-factor authentications based on technical users. Process integration, on the basis of the enterprise service bus using web services, requires that security criteria like authentication, authorization checks, data integrity, and data protection can be used for service-oriented architectures. To meet these criteria and control objectives, the corresponding security concepts are available for web services.

## 12.2 Risks and Controls

SAP NetWeaver PI runs on the SAP NetWeaver AS and uses it at runtime. The two usage types, ABAP and Java, involve similar risks that can also be mastered with the same controls.

In this section, we use a simplified version of the risk analysis methodology described in Chapter 1, Risk and Control Management, to identify the main security risks and the necessary controls for SAP NetWeaver PI (see Table 12.1). The controls are then discussed in more detail in the following sections and illustrated using examples.

| No. | Classification | Description |
|---|---|---|
| 1. | Risk potential | No authorization concept for the design and configuration phase:<br>Via the Enterprise Services Builder, users can access configurations for which they are not authorized. This is enabled by a nonexistent or insufficient authorization concept. |
| | Impact | The configuration of the integration scenario causes it to become unstable, leaving message exchange vulnerable to being impaired and manipulated. The availability of the integration platform can no longer be guaranteed. Message recipients can also be changed so that required postings are not affected in the actual target system, but in a system intended for this purpose by a fraudulent user. |
| | Risk without control(s) | Extremely high |
| | Control | Adequate roles are specified for accessing objects and collaboration agreements stored in the Enterprise Services Repository and Integration Directory. This is set in an authorization concept. |
| | Risk with control(s) | Normal |
| | Section | 12.3.1 |
| 2. | Risk potential | Passwords that are too simple:<br>Passwords and authorizations for technical service users, which are necessary for authentication among the RFC communication partners, are too simple and can be discovered easily. |
| | Impact | If insufficient authentications or incorrect authorizations are selected for technical service users, the component can be accessed directly, and therefore the configuration can be changed by unauthorized persons. This jeopardizes the configuration stability and availability of SAP NetWeaver PI. Unauthorized users can also read and manipulate component information. |
| | Risk without control(s) | High |

**Table 12.1** Risks and Controls for SAP NetWeaver PI

| No. | Classification | Description |
|---|---|---|
| | Control | The passwords for technical service users must be secure, that is, they must have sufficiently complex characteristics. Default passwords must be changed in any case. In addition, the authorizations of technical service users must be determined in accordance with the predefined roles. |
| | Risk with control(s) | Normal |
| | Section | 12.3.2 |
| 3. | Risk potential | Missing authorization concept for the SAP NetWeaver PI components:<br>Via the Services Registry or UDDI server, users can access service definitions and configurations for which they are not authorized. |
| | Impact | The configuration of the central SAP NetWeaver PI components becomes unstable, leaving Services Registry vulnerable to being impaired and manipulated. The availability of the services can no longer be guaranteed.<br>Service definitions can also be changed so that required postings are not affected in the actual target system, but in a system intended for this purpose by a fraudulent user. |
| | Risk without control(s) | Extremely high |
| | Control | Respective roles are specified for administrative access to the services in Services Registry. This is set in an authorization concept. |
| | Risk with control(s) | Normal |
| | Section | 12.3.3 |
| 4. | Risk potential | Passwords that are too simple:<br>The authentication mechanism for administrative access to SAP NetWeaver PI components is based on the user ID and password method. The password is too simple. |
| | Impact | Unauthorized users can gain access by guessing the password in a brute-force attack. This allows them to compromise the service configuration. |
| | Risk without control(s) | Extremely high |

**Table 12.1** Risks and Controls for SAP NetWeaver PI (Cont.)

| No. | Classification | Description |
|---|---|---|
| | Control | Selection of an appropriately complex password for the authentication of administrators |
| | Risk with control(s) | Normal |
| | Section | 12.3.4 |
| 5. | Risk potential | The selected technical service user is the same:<br>The same technical service user (PIAPPLUSER) is used for all communication channels from different SAP systems to the PI server. There is no differentiation of the different SAP systems. |
| | Impact | Because there is no differentiation, other communication channels of SAP NetWeaver PI can be used by other SAP systems as well. Unauthorized transactions can therefore be triggered on other connected SAP systems. |
| | Risk without control(s) | High |
| | Control | For every SAP NetWeaver AS system communication channel via RFC, HTTP, and so on, a different technical system user with another password should be selected. |
| | Risk with control(s) | Normal |
| | Section | 12.4.1 |
| 6. | Risk potential | No encryption of communication channels:<br>Communication channels to the PI server transferring authentication data of technical service users for the communication channel are not encrypted. Furthermore, the communication channels to the connected partner systems that are supposed to be integrated are also not encrypted. |
| | Impact | The authentication data of technical service users can be eavesdropped, and therefore, can be used by unauthorized communication partners connected to the PI system. The unencrypted external communication channels enable third parties to view the exchanged messages and gain insight into confidential data. In addition, unauthorized financing transactions might be effected. |
| | Risk without control(s) | Extremely high |

**Table 12.1** Risks and Controls for SAP NetWeaver PI (Cont.)

| No. | Classification | Description |
|---|---|---|
| | Control | The internal communication channels between the SAP NetWeaver PI components must be encrypted. The communication channels between SAP and non-SAP systems connected to SAP NetWeaver PI should be secured via encryption techniques, such as (SSL) or (SNC). |
| | Risk with control(s) | Normal |
| | Section | 12.4.2 |
| 7. | Risk potential | No signature of XML messages:<br>XML-based messages (per XI or SOAP protocol) are submitted unsigned to SAP NetWeaver PI and forwarded as such to the actual recipient. |
| | Impact | The problem with unsigned messages is that you can't verify the identity of the exact sender, nor can you check whether parts of the message were changed by a third person during the transfer to SAP NetWeaver PI. Moreover, incorrect postings can be triggered. Also, you can't retrace who initiated the financing transaction as completed transactions can later be denied by the sender. |
| | Risk without control(s) | Extremely high |
| | Control | All inbound XML-based messages must be digitally signed by the sender, especially when using SAP NetWeaver PI in Internet scenarios where business partners are supposed to be integrated. |
| | Risk with control(s) | Normal |
| | Section | 12.4.3 |
| 8. | Risk potential | No encryption of external communication channels:<br>XML-based messages (per XI or SOAP protocol) are transferred unencrypted to SAP NetWeaver PI. |
| | Impact | If XML-based messages are transferred unencrypted to SAP NetWeaver PI, the information contained therein can be recorded (sniffed) by unauthorized third persons. If the information is highly confidential, that is, secret business information, the damage potential is accordingly high. |

**Table 12.1** Risks and Controls for SAP NetWeaver PI (Cont.)

| No. | Classification | Description |
|---|---|---|
| | Risk without control(s) | High |
| | Control | The messages should be encrypted, especially when using SAP NetWeaver PI for integration scenarios where business partners have to be integrated via the Internet, and where the business data is highly confidential. |
| | Risk with control(s) | Normal |
| | Section | 12.4.4 |
| 9. | Risk potential | The SAP NetWeaver PI communication channels are not secured:<br>Communication interfaces of SAP NetWeaver PI, particularly in Internet scenarios, are abused by unauthorized third persons. Therefore, unauthorized transactions are triggered on the SAP and non-SAP systems to be integrated via SAP NetWeaver PI. |
| | Impact | If unauthorized transactions are executed, you can't retrace who initiated them. Rollback — restoring the original state — is also not possible, which can result in considerable damage. |
| | Risk without control(s) | Extremely high |
| | Control | A proxy for outbound messages and a reverse proxy for inbound messages should be implemented for SAP NetWeaver PI.<br>Particularly in Internet scenarios, two consecutive PI systems located in different network segments should be used. One in the front-end demilitarized zone for communicating with business partners (B2B) and another one for the back-end for the internal A2A communication. |
| | Risk with control(s) | Normal |
| | Section | 12.4.5 |
| 10. | Risk potential | The message exchange is not audited or monitored:<br>The executed messages and transactions are not checked for potential processing errors by the central monitor. |

**Table 12.1** Risks and Controls for SAP NetWeaver PI (Cont.)

| No. | Classification | Description |
|---|---|---|
| | Impact | Processing errors are not discovered at an early stage and therefore result in instabilities in the integration network. In short, transactions that weren't executed properly cannot be determined in time, which, in turn, can lead to financial losses. |
| | Risk without control(s) | High |
| | Control | Constant monitoring of SAP NetWeaver PI using the central monitor provided for this purpose. |
| | Risk with control(s) | Normal |
| | Section | 12.4.6 |
| 11. | Risk potential | No authentication for the file adapter:<br>SAP NetWeaver PI lets you retrieve files from a sending system and to place them on a receiving system using file adapters. There is no authentication for the file adapter — at a technical or user level. This communication channel, therefore, is easily accessible. |
| | Impact | Files could be introduced to a target system to, for example, overwrite the password file */etc/passwd*. Afterward, the attacked target system could be taken over via a newly created administration account. |
| | Risk without control(s) | High |
| | Control | It is vital that you ensure a correct configuration of authorizations at the operating system level for the relevant file directories, especially when using the file adapter. In particular, this applies to the SYSADM user, under whose tutelage SAP NetWeaver PI is executed. |
| | Risk with control(s) | Normal |
| | Section | 12.4.7 |
| 12. | Risk potential | No encryption of communication channels:<br>The communication channels between the SAP NetWeaver PI components and the connected partner systems are not encrypted. |

**Table 12.1** Risks and Controls for SAP NetWeaver PI (Cont.)

| No. | Classification | Description |
|---|---|---|
| | Impact | The unencrypted HTTP communication channels enable third parties to view the exchanged service messages and gain insight into confidential business data. In addition, unauthorized financing transactions might be effected. |
| | Risk without control(s) | Extremely high |
| | Control | Internal and external communication channels must be secured using SSL or SNC. |
| | Risk with control(s) | Normal |
| | Section | 12.4.8 |
| 13. | Risk potential | Web service security options are not utilized:<br>Web services and enterprise services are not protected against their integrity and confidentiality being compromised. |
| | Impact | Unprotected service message can make confidential business data public. In addition, data might be changed or unauthorized financing transactions triggered. |
| | Risk without control(s) | Extremely high |
| | Control | Web service security needs to be optimally configured considering the technical options. |
| | Risk with control(s) | Normal |
| | Section | 12.4.9 |

**Table 12.1** Risks and Controls for SAP NetWeaver PI (Cont.)

## 12.3 Application Security

This section describes in more detail the risks and controls that are outlined in Table 12.1 with regard to application security.

### 12.3.1 Authorizations for Enterprise Services Builder

SAP NetWeaver PI does not involve direct interaction with the users in the departments at runtime. SAP NetWeaver PI is pure middleware or back-end infrastructure that transports messages from one SAP or non-SAP system to another target system. Using appropriate mapping rules, messages can be converted and translated so that they're understood by the receiving system. SAP NetWeaver PI therefore fulfills the function of a central integration hub for all applications connected via connectors.

The only interaction between SAP NetWeaver PI and users, except for monitoring, takes place during the design and configuration phase. Using the Enterprise Services Builder/Integration Builder, these administrative users access the Enterprise Services Repository, Integration Directory, and SLD. A part of the user authorization is performed on the AS ABAP and can therefore be defined via the ABAP authorization system. The Enterprise Services Builder is a Java application where access to single objects of the Integration Directory can be authorized.

SAP delivers the following standard roles for administration (design and configuration phase) that can be used in this respect:

- `SAP_XI_DISPLAY_USER`
  This role only grants the user read access to the information contained in the Enterprise Services Repository and Integration Directory (integration objects, communication interfaces, and so on).
- `SAP_XI_DEVELOPER`
  This role can create, delete, and change the integration components in the Enterprise Services Repository.
- `SAP_XI_CONFIGURATOR`
  This role can create, delete, and change integration scenarios in the Integration Directory.
- `SAP_XI_CONTENT_ORGANIZER`
  This role can create, delete, and change the contents in the SLD.
- `SAP_XI_MONITOR`
  This role can monitor all SAP NetWeaver PI components and all messages that were processed using SAP NetWeaver PI.
- `SAP_XI_ADMINISTRATOR`
  This role includes all roles mentioned and is thus a master role for SAP NetWeaver PI administration.

Access to the individual object types within the Enterprise Services Repository and Integration Directory can, as mentioned earlier, be designed in a more detailed way. To do this, the following conditions must be met:

- The J2EE parameter in the Exchange profile, `com.sap.aii.ib.server.lockauth.activation`, found at *http://<server>:<HTTP port>/exchangeProfile*, must be set to `true`.

- On the AS ABAP of the PI system, the SAP_XI_ADMINISTRATOR_J2EE role must be assigned to the administrator, because it grants access to the Enterprise Services Builder role configurator, which is available in the Enterprise Services Builder menu. This ABAP role must therefore be granted in a very restrictive way.

Using this role configurator, accesses within the Enterprise Services Builder to the object types can be limited in both the Enterprise Services Repository and in the Integration Directory. In the Enterprise Services Repository, access to individual software component versions, name ranges, and repository object types (software components, integration scenario objects, interface objects, mapping objects, adapter objects, and imported objects) can be limited. The authorizations to Create, Change, and Delete can be granted.

In the Integration Directory, the access to the object types Interface Determination, Recipient Determination, Receiver Agreement, Configuration Scenario, and Special Agreement can be restricted. To do this, the authorizations to Create, Change, and Delete are also available. In general, read access is granted using the SAP_XI_DISPLAY_USER ABAP role.

If new roles are created for the Enterprise Services Builder, the corresponding roles are physically stored in the UME (see Chapter 9, SAP NetWeaver AS). These UME roles for the Integration Repository then start with XIRep_*, or XIDir_* for the Integration Directory. In the UME, they can either be assigned directly to the existing administrator or to a user group.

**Note**

Please remember: The UME group name is identical to the name of the ABAP role. Therefore, if you assigned a specific role in the AS ABAP to a specific person group, this ABAP role can be addressed as a group in the UME. In the same way, the defined Enterprise Services Builder UME roles can be assigned to the same ABAP users.

### 12.3.2 Passwords and Authorizations for Technical Service Users

The various SAP NetWeaver PI components listed previously, like Enterprise Services Repository, Integration Directory, Integration Server, and so on, must access one another during the design, configuration, and runtime phases, for example, to read or write information. During this access, a component; for example, the Integration Directory accessing the Integration Server, reads the relevant technical service user data from the Exchange profile, in this case PIISUSER, and then uses it to authenticate itself to the Integration Server. The service user data is read from PIISUSER via the PILDUSER service user that knows every component.

The following technical service users are used to access the respective component:

- **Exchange profile and System Landscape Directory**
  Access via the technical service user
  PILDUSER using the ABAP role SAP_BC_AI_LANDSCAPE_DB_RFC.
- **Enterprise Services Repository**
  Access via the technical service user
  PIREPUSER using the ABAP role SAP_XI_IR_SERV_USER.
- **Integration Directory**
  Access via the technical service user PIDIRUSER using the ABAP role SAP_XI_ID_SERV_USER.
- **(Advanced) Adapter Engine**
  Access via the technical service user PIAFUSER using the ABAP role SAP_XI_AF_SERV_USER_MAIN.
- **Integration Server**
  Access via the technical service user PIISUSER using the ABAP role SAP_XI_IS_SERV_USER_MAIN.
- **Runtime Workbench (cache at runtime)**
  Access via the technical service user PIRWBUSER using the ABAP role SAP_XI_RWB_SERV_USER_MAIN.

These technical service users are set up during the SAP NetWeaver PI installation and are automatically configured. The passwords need to be chosen during the installation, and it is critical that they are sufficiently complex. The following rules should be applied:

- Password length to be a minimum of eight characters
- At least one special character
- At least one letter
- At least one number

### 12.3.3 Authorizations for Administrative Access to SAP NetWeaver PI

SAP NetWeaver PI can be considered middleware that only administrative employees need to access for configuration or monitoring tasks. Although access is therefore granted to a limited number of people, an authorization concept that assigns appropriate and restrictive authorizations needs to be documented and used.

For the essential SAP NetWeaver PI components, the standard version provides predefined ABAP roles of which — according to Best Practices — copies are adapted to the specific requirements and assigned to the administrative user. The following rules are available for the three components:

- **Enterprise Services Repository**
  - `SAP_XI_ADMINISTRATOR_J2EE` (administrative access to the AS Java)
- **Enterprise Services Registry**
  - `SERVICES_REGISTRY_READ_ONLY` (read-only access to the Services Registry)
  - `SERVICES_REGISTRY_READ_WRITE` (read access to all classifications and write access to classifications that are not predefined or technical)
  - `SERVICES_REGISTRY_BUSINESS_ADMINISTRATOR` (read access to all classifications and write access to classifications that are not technical)
  - `SERVICES_REGISTRY_TECHNICAL_ADMINISTRATOR` (read and write access)
- **Universal Description, Discovery, Integration (UDDI) server**
  - `UDDI_Admin` (object administration, access to user information)
  - `UUDI_TierN` (object administration, no access to user information)
  - `UDDI_Tier1` (service administration, no access to user data)

### 12.3.4 Password Rules for Administrators

It is important that administrators have separate, individual user names and passwords for SAP NetWeaver PI. This is an administrator's individual responsibility. Password rules should be generally applicable and specify that passwords need to be sufficiently complex:

- Password length to be a minimum of eight characters
- At least one special character
- At least one letter
- At least one number

## 12.4 Technical Security

This section describes in more detail the risks and controls that are outlined in Table 12.1 with regard to technical security.

### 12.4.1 Definition of Technical Service Users for Communication Channels at Runtime

At runtime, there are different communication channels that are used to access SAP NetWeaver PI. For these communication channels, an authentication is performed using technical service users.

#### Scenario 1: Communication between Sending System and Integration Server via the XI Protocol

In one important scenario, the sender is an SAP NetWeaver AS (Release 6.20 or higher). In this case, an ABAP application can send a message via the ABAP proxy using the XI protocol. A service user `PIAPPLUSER` then needs to be set up on the Integration Server that enables the SAP NetWeaver AS to log on to the Integration Server. In the ABAP stack, it has the `SAP_XI_APPL_SERV_USER` role.

For every SAP NetWeaver AS that is logged on, a separate technical service user, `PIAPPLUSER`, needs to be configured. The technical service user `PIAPPLUSER` is also used when the sending SAP NetWeaver AS connects to the Integration Server via RFC or IDocs. Communication with the recipient (SAP NetWeaver AS) via the XI protocol requires a technical service user as well.

#### Scenario 2: Communication between Sending System and Integration Server via the Adapter Engine and Various Adapters

For Communication between a sending SAP and non-SAP system via an adapter, the authentication scheme that is necessary for the relevant adapter type is used — usually via technical service users. When using a file, database, or Java Message Service (JMS) adapter, `PIAFUSER` is used. The Adapter Engine (either central or decentralized) communicates with the Integration Server using the technical service user `PIISUSER` via the XI protocol. The technical service user `PIISUSER` must be assigned the ABAP role `SAP_XI_APPL_SERV_USER_Main` as well. For communication between the Integration Server and the Adapter Engine, the initial authentication is performed using `PIAFUSER`, which must be assigned the role `SAP_XI_APPL_SERV_USER_Main` for this purpose. The subsequent communication to the final recipient depends on the respective adapter.

#### Changing the Passwords for Service Users

The passwords used for the technical service users must be changed regularly, at least once a year. This is critical to support password security and to make sure that attempts at decrypting the password are not successful. You make this change in the Exchange profile, which can be called via the following: *http://host:port/exchangeProfile*.

The password must be changed in the corresponding entry `com.sap.aii.<component>.serviceuser.pwd` (for example, `com.sap.aii.integration_directory.serviceuser.pwd` for the Integration Directory). This must also be done in the corresponding entry in the AS ABAP for the technical service user as well using Transaction SU01.

### 12.4.2 Setting Up Encryption for Communication Channels

As mentioned earlier, SAP NetWeaver PI lets you distinguish between the internal communication based on technical service users and the external communication to the connected partner systems. The internal communication among the components takes place via HTTP, which can be secured using SSL (or HTTPS, respectively).

When securing the external communication channels, the encryption type depends on the adapter. For adapters where the protocol used for communication is also based on HTTP, HTTPS can be implemented as well. For communication interfaces based on RFC, SNC can be used.

In general, an encrypted SSL or SNC communication can be configured in the same way as the SAP NetWeaver AS, because SAP NetWeaver PI is built on this technical runtime environment. As a general prerequisite for using SSL, the necessary cryptographic program libraries (for example, SAPCRYPTOLIB for ABAP and the IAIK security package for J2EE) must be installed in both AS ABAP and AS Java. In both cases, the appropriate digital certificates (according to X.509 standard) must be requested by a Certificate Authority (CA). Because SSL is also used for technically authenticating two communication partners, it can be configured so that the server not only authenticates itself to the client but that the client also authenticates itself to the server. In internal PI communication, the components partially function as client and server.

The SSL (HTTPS) communication must therefore be configured for both stacks (AS ABAP and AS Java):

- For AS ABAP, Transaction STRUST must be used to configure the SAP NetWeaver AS for SSL and used for SAP NetWeaver PI; this is where the digital certificate mentioned must be imported. In addition, an appropriate HTTPS service with one port must be set up for the ICM (Transaction SMICM, services).

- For the AS ABAP to function as a client as well, the digital certificate must be imported in the client Personal Security Environment (PSE) using Transaction STRUST. This can be the same client that was used for the server as well. Otherwise, the HTTPS port of the respective server must be used for all destinations (Transaction SM59) where HTTPS with client authentication is to be used.
- In addition, AS Java must be adequately configured as an HTTPS server. This is done using the Visual Administrator. The requested certificate must be imported into the key store `service_ssl` under the Key Storage provider. Also, the certificate must be assigned to the HTTPS service in the SSL provider, and the port for HTTPS must be configured and activated.
- In order for AS Java to act as a client, in addition to importing the server certificate to the `service_ssl` key store, it must also be imported to the `TrustedCAs` key store if self-signed certificates will be used.

#### Configuration of the Internal PI Communication

To change the entire internal communication to SSL (HTTPS), you must set the following parameters in the Exchange profile:

- The `com.sap.aii.connect.secure_connections` parameter must be set to `all`.
- The parameters defining the HTTPS communication ports (for example, `com.sap.aii.connect.integrationserver.httpsport`) must be set to the port that has been defined for the HTTPS service — either AS ABAP or J2EE, depending on the technical runtime environment of the component.

More information about configuring a secure internal PI communication can be found in SAP Note 766215.

#### Configuration of External Communication

For the external communication of messages via the communication channels defined in the Integration Directory, the implementation depends on the relevant carrier protocol. If it is the commonly used HTTP, you can select the corresponding secure equivalent HTTPS in the Integration Directory (provided that the appropriate HTTPS service has been activated on the sender or receiving system, respectively, as already described). Otherwise, it depends on the adapter. For RFC adapters, the secure SNC protocol can be used instead of SSL.

Table 12.2 contains information about the most commonly used adapters and their protection options.

| Adapter | Runs on | Outbound | Inbound | Protocol | Protection |
|---|---|---|---|---|---|
| XI | IS | X | | HTTP | Possible via HTTPS. This is achieved with the selection via the encrypted communication channel in the Integration Directory. |
| | | | X | HTTP | Possible via HTTPS. This is achieved with the selection via the encrypted communication channel in the Integration Directory. |
| IDoc | IS | X | | tRFC | Possible via SNC. The connection must be defined with a technical service user as a communication channel of the IDoc type. The channel must reference an appropriate RFC connection (type 3) between SAP NetWeaver PI and the receiving system (IDoc). The technical service user in the receiving system (IDoc) must have the corresponding IDoc authorizations. |
| | | | X | | Possible via SNC. The connection must be defined as a type-3 RFC destination on the sending IDoc system. The technical service user must have the `SAP_XI_APPL_SERV_USER` role in SAP NetWeaver PI. |

**Table 12.2** External Adapters and Encryption Possibilities for the Relevant Communication Protocols

| Adapter | Runs on | Outbound | Inbound | Protocol | Protection |
|---|---|---|---|---|---|
| Plain HTTP | IS | X | | HTTP | Possible via HTTPS. In the Integration Directory, the communication channel type HTTPS must be selected. Depending on the configuration of the target system, an anonymous login or the authentication using a technical service user is permitted. |
| | | | X | HTTP | Possible via HTTPS. To address this adapter, the sender must address the PI system (Integration Directory) via the *https://<XI host>:<HTTPS port>/sap/xi/adapter_plain* service. An authentication scheme must be stored in the service (to be set via Transaction SICF). The technical service user must have the SAP_XI_APPL_SERV_USER role. |
| RFC | AE | X | | RFC | SNC is not possible. In the Integration Directory, only the RFC type can be selected for the communication channel. For this purpose, an appropriate RFC connection (Transaction SM59) must be set up between the Integration Server and the receiving system. |

**Table 12.2** External Adapters and Encryption Possibilities for the Relevant Communication Protocols (Cont.)

| Adapter | Runs on | Outbound | Inbound | Protocol | Protection |
|---|---|---|---|---|---|
| | | | | | The RFC service user must have the corresponding authorizations in the receiving system. (Note: This adapter should only be implemented in an intranet scenario.) |
| | | | X | RFC | SNC is not possible. You must define an RFC connection from the Integration Server back to the actual target system that can be used to read the RFC metadata. To do this, the adapter should be registered accordingly with the SAP Gateway. There is no authentication via a technical service user. (Note: This adapter should not be implemented in an Internet scenario.) |
| SOAP | AE | X | | HTTP | Possible via HTTPS. In the Integration Directory, SOAP needs to be defined for the receiving channel. The channel can be authenticated to the receiving application using a technical service user. An anonymous login is permitted as well. In addition, the message can be digitally signed. |

**Table 12.2** External Adapters and Encryption Possibilities for the Relevant Communication Protocols (Cont.)

| Adapter | Runs on | Outbound | Inbound | Protocol | Protection |
|---|---|---|---|---|---|
| | | | X | HTTP | Possible via HTTPS. In the sending channel of the Integration Directory, SOAP must be set. The corresponding technical service user can be authenticated via basic authentication or SSL client certificate. This technical service user requires the `xi_adapter_soap_message` role in the Adapter Engine. This must be set via the UME. The signature validation of the message can be enabled as well. |
| Rosetta Net InterFace (RNIF) | AE | X | | HTTP | Possible via HTTPS. In the Integration Directory, the RNIF type needs to be defined for the receiving channel. The channel can be authenticated to the recipient using a technical service user. An anonymous login is permitted as well. In addition, the message can be digitally signed and encrypted. |
| | | | X | HTTP | Possible via HTTPS. In the sending channel of the Integration Directory, SOAP must be set. The respective technical service user can be authenticated via basic authentication or SSL client certificate. |

**Table 12.2** External Adapters and Encryption Possibilities for the Relevant Communication Protocols (Cont.)

| Adapter | Runs on | Outbound | Inbound | Protocol | Protection |
|---|---|---|---|---|---|
| | | | | | The technical service user requires the SAP_XI_APPL_SERV_USER role in AS ABAP. A signature validation of the message can be enabled as well. In addition, the message can be decrypted. |
| Chemical Industry Data Exchange (CIDX) | AE | X | | HTTP | Possible via HTTPS. Use the same options as for the RNIF adapter. |
| | | | X | HTTP | Possible via HTTPS. Use the same options as for the RNIF adapter. |
| File system | AE | X | | NFS | There are security options only at the operating system level. For the SYSADM technical user that runs the PI instance, access to operating system directories must be restricted. There are no encryption options. Using this adapter is not recommended in scenarios with very high security requirements. |
| | | | X | NFS | There are security options only at the operating system level. For the SYSADM technical user that runs the PI instance, the access to operating system directories must be restricted. There are no encryption options. Using this adapter is not recommended in scenarios with very high security requirements. |

**Table 12.2** External Adapters and Encryption Possibilities for the Relevant Communication Protocols (Cont.)

| Adapter | Runs on | Outbound | Inbound | Protocol | Protection |
|---|---|---|---|---|---|
| FTP | AE | X | | FTP | Secure FTP is not possible. Apart from that, you can also use technical service users for FTP authentication. We do not recommend using FTP for integration scenarios with high security demands. |
| | | | X | FTP | Secure FTP is not possible. Apart from that, you can also use technical service users for FTP authentication. We do not recommend using FTP for integration scenarios with high protection needs. |
| JDBC | AE | X | | JDBC | Depending on the manufacturer, database access might be encrypted. The authentication is again implemented using technical service users at the database level. We do not recommend using JDBC for integration scenarios with high protection needs. |
| | | | X | JDBC | Depending on the manufacturer, database access might be encrypted. The authentication is again implemented using service users at the database level We do not recommend using JDBC for integration scenarios with high protection needs. |

**Table 12.2** External Adapters and Encryption Possibilities for the Relevant Communication Protocols (Cont.)

| Adapter | Runs on | Outbound | Inbound | Protocol | Protection |
|---|---|---|---|---|---|
| Mail | AE | X | | IMAP4, POP3, SMTP | Possible via SSL. Except for IMAP4, S/MIME, that is, the signature and encryption option for emails, can be implemented as well. |
| | | | X | IMAP4, POP3, SMTP | Possible via SSL. Except for IMAP4, S/MIME, that is, the signature and encryption option for emails, can be implemented as well. |

**Table 12.2** External Adapters and Encryption Possibilities for the Relevant Communication Protocols (Cont.)

In general, the protection needs for the integration scenario should be determined based on SAP NetWeaver PI when selecting possible adapters. For high protection needs — for example, when connecting systems that are processing highly confidential information and information with high integrity demands — you should only implement those adapters that support digital signatures (high integrity) and encryption (high confidentiality) at the message level.

### 12.4.3 Digital Signature for XML-Based Messages

XML-based messages, like those used for the XI protocol, SOAP, RNIF, and CIDX adapters, can be signed. By digitally signing a message, you can achieve the following security objectives:

- The sender of a message can be unambiguously authenticated at the message level. It is not necessary to rely on the authentication of the communication channel via technical service users, because it may have been compromised by an attacker. In a purely technical authentication, it is impossible to retrace the sender in a legally binding way.
- Using a digital signature, the integrity of the message can be unambiguously determined. An unauthorized change to the message carried out by an attacker at a later stage can be discovered. If the message was changed by an attacker, SAP NetWeaver PI can refuse to process it further.
- A digital signature attests the originality of the message. A sender cannot discard sending the message at a later stage. This is particularly important if business orders are digitally processed. However, you must consider the legal requirements that are to be applied to the business contract. If you want to set

up a legal-proof contract, the signature must comply with the policies of the Electronic Signatures in Global and National Commerce Act. Naturally, this can be circumvented if the business partners have not made any other previous agreements.

Using the XI protocol, you can digitally sign the SAP manifest (part of the XI protocol with information on the processing of the message, and logistic information) and the payloads (that is the actual message), in addition to the SAP main header (similar to the SOAP header in web services). Using SOAP, however, you can only sign the SOAP body (the message only). The RNIF connector uses S/MIME, and CIDX uses the PKCS#7 signature standard.

In SAP NetWeaver PI, messages can be signed using the certificates existing in the certificate store of AS Java (key storage provider) in the PI runtime environment of the underlying SAP NetWeaver AS. The certificate store of AS ABAP is not used in this case. The Integration Server using AS ABAP as the technical runtime environment implements an internal web service for addressing the signature functions of AS Java.

For digital signatures, you must consider the trust model to be applied. There are two variants that can be implemented in this respect:

- There is a direct trust model that does not use a certificate authority: The public keys (certificates) of the sender and the recipient (of the business partners or internal systems) must be exchanged beforehand. In this case, a new key store can be created on the J2EE Engine of SAP NetWeaver PI, where all public certificates of the possible senders are stored. This key store can be freely chosen.
- A public key infrastructure is used: In this case, there is a trust relationship between the business partners that is confirmed by one or more trustworthy certificate authorities. All implemented certificates of the business partners must be digitally signed by these root certificate authorities. The relevant public certificates of the CAs must be stored in the `TrustedCAs` key store of AS Java. However, SAP NetWeaver PI does not support multilevel hierarchical trust relationships. Therefore, the certificates must have been signed directly by the trustworthy certificate authorities. A multilevel certificate hierarchy is not supported.

In order for the access to the key storage provider of AS Java to function correctly, you must assign the appropriate J2EE roles in AS Java (see Chapter 9) to the technical service user (RFC user), which is used by the web service (HTTP carrier protocol) to log on to the Integration Server. This is done using the Security Provider service in the Visual Administrator and affects the following roles:

- On the Policy Configuration tab, the *sap.com/tc~sec~wssec~app*wssprocess.jar* component needs to be selected. It contains the J2EE role WSSecurityProcessing that must be assigned to the RFC service user, so it can be used by the external web service to log on to the Integration Server (HTTP connection type).

- If a new key store has been generated for storing the external business partner system certificates, the aforementioned RFC service user must be assigned to the J2EE role KeystoreAdministrator, which is included in the *keystore-view.<name of the created key store>* component.

To use the J2EE security functions, the IAIK cryptography components first need to be implemented in AS Java. This is done using the software deployment tool. The collaboration agreements for communication partners that have been stored in the Integration Directory define whether it's necessary to use digital signatures and specify the validation of a signature.

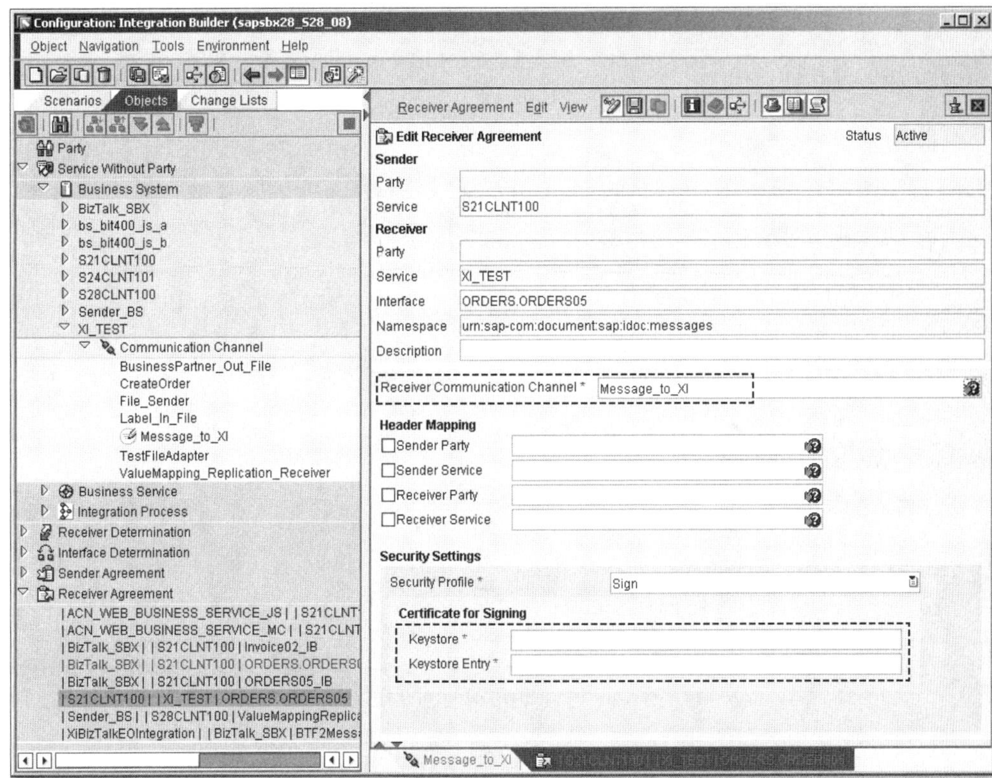


**Figure 12.2** Receiver Agreement — Signature of a Message in the Case of an XI Protocol

The receiver agreement (see Figure 12.2) in the Integration Directory defines whether a message is signed before it is forwarded to the recipient in SAP NetWeaver PI. In this receiver agreement, the key store of AS Java is selected with the corresponding signature certificate (private certificate of the Integration Server). As a prerequisite, either the XI protocol or SOAP (or RNIF or CIDX, respectively) must have been chosen for the communication channel with the recipient.

In the communication channel, Message Security should be set for the XI protocol, for example, Message_to_XI. In the key store, you specify the Key Store Name, and the key store entry contains the actual certificate. In the communication channel, the Message Security checkbox must be selected (see Figure 12.3) to enable a digital signature in the receiver agreement.

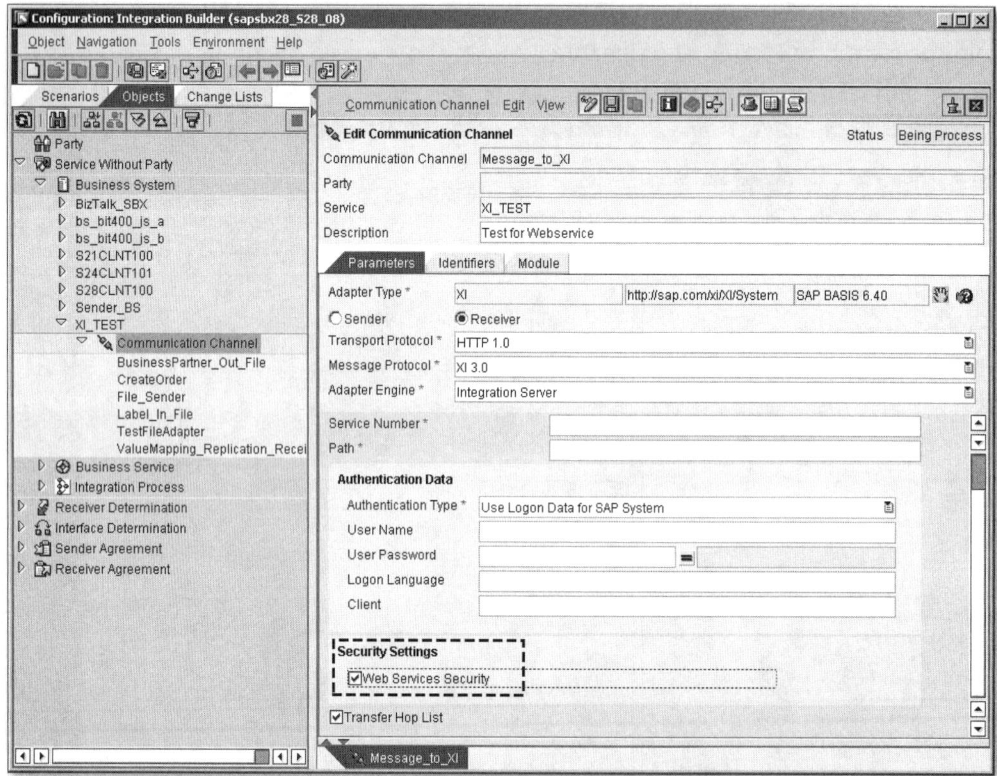


**Figure 12.3** Message Security Option for the Communication Channel of the XI Protocol

The sender agreement (see Figure 12.4) in the Integration Directory specifies the public certificate of the sender to be used for validating the signed message in SAP NetWeaver PI. For self-signed certificates, the public certificates must have been imported into the key storage of AS Java. The self-signed public certificate must also have been imported to the `TrustedCAs` key store. The same applies to the public certificate of the certificate authority that signed the business partner system certificates. In the sender communication channel, the MESSAGE SECURITY option must be set. Therefore, the following must be specified:

- The communication channel with Message Security set for the XI protocol
- The issuer (certificate authority) and the owner of the certificate
- The key store Key Store Name in the J2EE stack

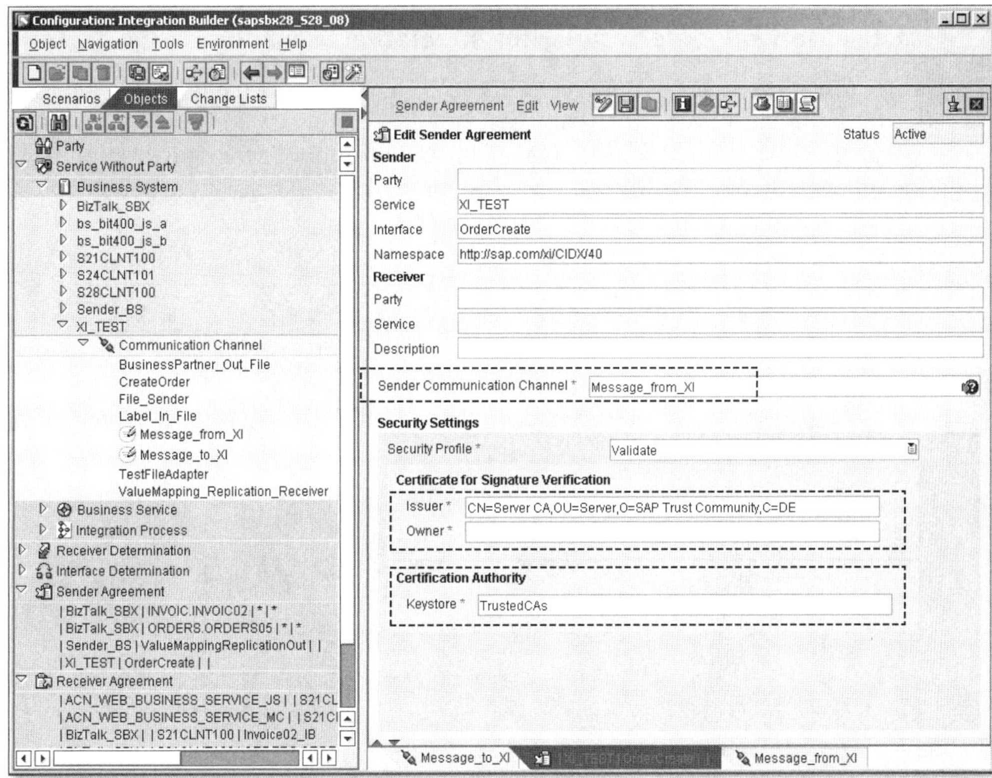

**Figure 12.4** Sender Agreement — Validation of the Sender's Digital Signature in the XI Protocol

Because SAP NetWeaver PI can only sign using server-based certificates, there might be legal problems if more sophisticated signature policies according to the Electronic Signatures in Global and National Commerce Act are observed. To do this, SAP provides direct signature options using SAP GUI (see Chapter 28, User Interfaces).

### 12.4.4 Encryption of XML-Based Messages

To encrypt XML-based message content (SOAP body), you can use the RNIF and CIDX adapters. These protocols enable encryption at the message level. They use the public certificate of the business partner system (receiving system) for encryption. You can also protect messages using the traditional method — via SSL encryption of the communication channel.

### 12.4.5 Network-Side Security for Integration Scenarios

Particularly when SAP NetWeaver PI is used in an Internet scenario, for the integration of a business partner (supplier, reseller, customer), for example, the scenario must be secured via the network. As with portal scenarios, a multilevel demilitarized zone (DMZ) concept must be used for network segmentation, as shown in Figure 12.5.

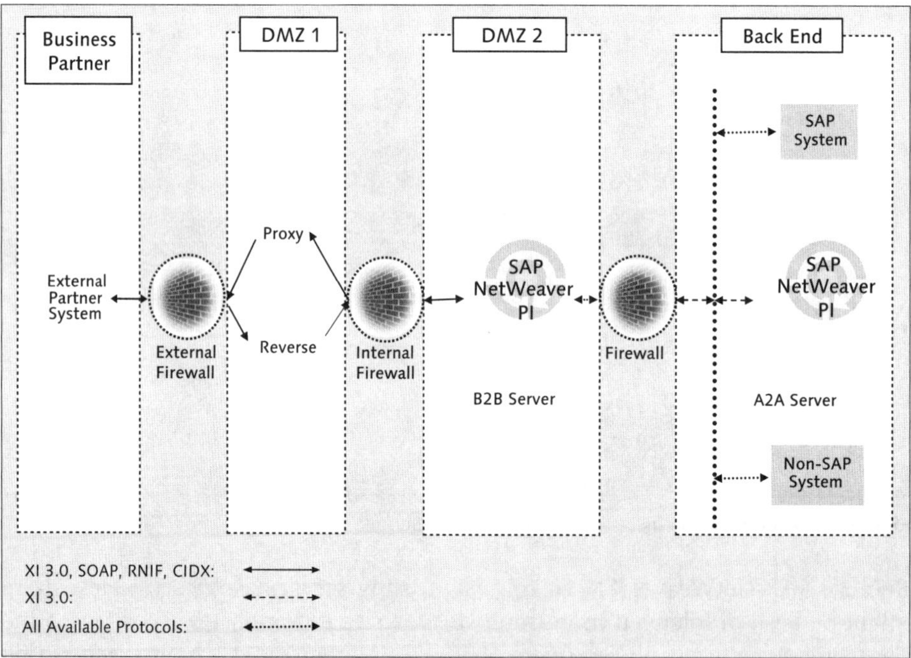


**Figure 12.5** DMZ Concept and Implementation of Two PI Instances in an Internet Integration Scenario

In an integration scenario with business partners where the Internet is used as the network between business partners and your own enterprise, two PI systems should be implemented: one system establishing the integration with the business partners, that is, a B2B system, and a second system for the internal application integration, an A2A integration hub. This ensures that the A2A integration channels cannot be directly accessed from the Internet. Between the B2B PI system and the A2A PI system, you can establish a dedicated communication channel that can be protected and controlled in a more optimal way.

To do this, you can use the XI protocol, which can implement an additional message signature. In addition, this communication channel can be encrypted using HTTPS. This also enables a mutual authentication at a technical level between the B2B and A2A integration systems. The firewall between DMZ 2 and the back-end may only permit communication between B2B and A2A PI systems.

If all systems (for example, SAP Partner Connectivity Kit, see Chapter 13, Partner Connectivity Kit) used by the business partners are known, the outer firewall should also restrict access to these systems. This does not prevent IP spoofing attacks, but it does provide additional protection.

For inbound messages, the communication should be directed via at least one reverse proxy. For outbound messages, from the B2B integration system to the business partner, a proxy should be implemented. We recommend that you only use XI protocol, SOAP, RNIF, and CIDX for communicating with business partners, because this is the only way to achieve good message security with digital signature and encryption. As a reverse proxy, you can use the SAP Web Dispatcher in this integration scenario, which only provides very limited security functions. Only the URL services, which must be called externally, can be restricted.

Preferable solutions would be application-level gateways (or web application firewalls) that are specifically designed for XML-based message communication, that is, web services. They provide the security functionalities necessary for a secure communication based on web services. The web services application level gateways can check the contents of the SOAP header and SOAP body for suspicious, uncommon program fragments. These kinds of program fragments are included in regular messages, for example, to bypass or eliminate the security system (see Chapter 5, Information Technology (IT) Security). In addition, these gateways provide the full range of web services security standards such as Security Assertion Markup Language (SAML) for an additional authentication or web service security.

### 12.4.6 Audit of the Enterprise Services Builder

The investigative security objective — within the security management — can be achieved by using an audit. An audit lets you detect changes made to the configuration or security violations and to take proper countermeasures. By using an audit, you may also find potential security weak spots that require new security controls. SAP NetWeaver PI provides numerous options for an audit.

### Change History in the Enterprise Services Builder

In the Enterprise Services Builder, a change history can be called for every object in the Enterprise Services Repository and Integration Directory that has been changed. Using this change history, you can retrace who made what change to which object at what time. The change history can be called in the object's detail view by selecting History from the main menu of the object.

### Monitoring Outbound Messages

The entire message processing can be monitored in the Integration Server and the Adapter Engine. There you can see if a message transfer failed, or if a recipient is still not reachable. The monitor for the Integration Server is started via Transaction SXMB_MONI (see Figure 12.6).

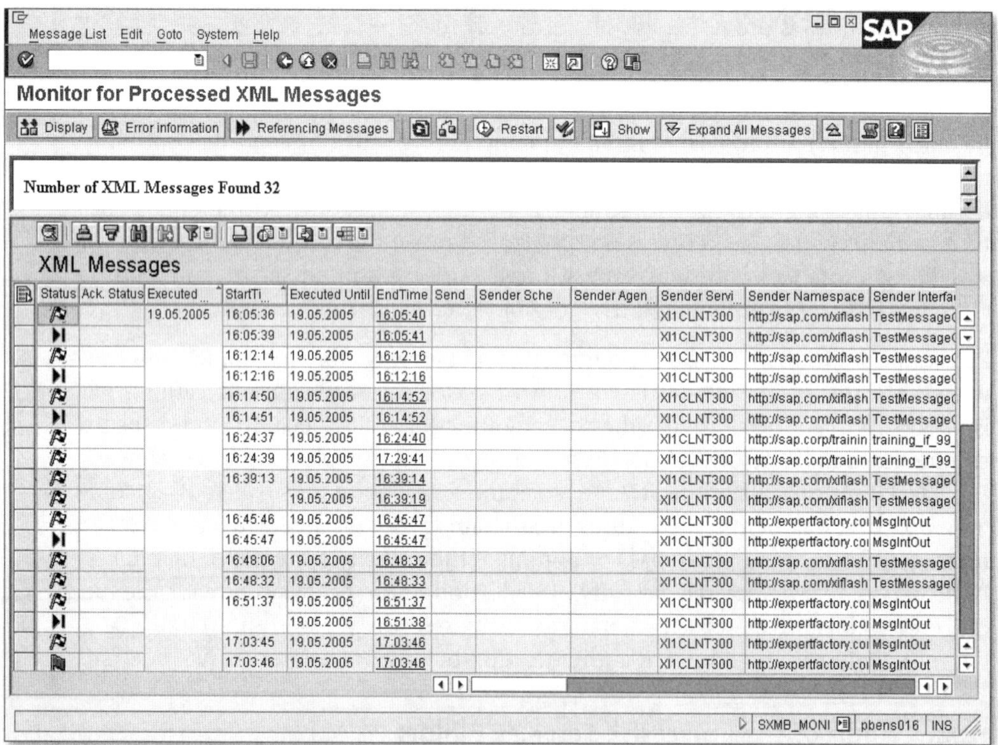


Figure 12.6 SXMB_MONI in the Integration Server

The administration of the Integration Server and of the archive function for processed XML messages is accessible via Transaction SXMB_ADM. The monitor for the Adapter Engine is accessible in AS ABAP via Transaction SXMB_IFR. This transaction starts the web front end, which also activates the Enterprise Services Builder. You can start the monitoring function with a mere click on the Runtime Workbench link.

By default, only XML messages processed in an asynchronous way are made persistent in the Integration Server. XML messages that are processed synchronously are only made persistent if errors occur, or if the logging function has explicitly been switched on. Incorrect message transfers are never deleted automatically. They have to be removed manually by the administrator.

Only messages that were successfully processed in an asynchronous way can be archived or deleted. The archiving of the processed messages can be controlled using Transaction SXMB_ADM. Two archiving jobs need to be set up:

- One archiving job that writes those messages to an archive that was made persistent in the Runtime Workbench.
- One deletion job that deletes those messages that were made persistent in the Runtime Workbench.

Messages that were processed using the Message Security mode (that were digitally signed) are always archived. This applies to both messages that were asynchronously processed and to those that were synchronously processed.

Apart from mere monitoring, an alert function can be defined as well (Transaction SXMB_MONI) that triggers an alarm if messages were not correctly processed. This function can also be linked to the Computing Center Management System (CCMS) so that these alarm messages can also be reported centrally to an SAP system. The important aspect here is that a process has been defined that specifies the measures to be taken if a high-priority alarm is raised. In this case, the required countermeasures need to be initiated.

### 12.4.7 Securing the File Adapter at the Operating System Level

The file adapter provides an immense security leak, because it allows unauthorized access to the Network File System (NFS) file directories of an integration system. We strongly advise against implementing it, particularly in the context of an Internet-based integration scenario.

But, if there is no other option, you should take the appropriate security measures at the operating system level. This includes granting authorizations to the technical `SYSADM` user running SAP NetWeaver PI at the operating system level that enable access to only a specific file directory. On Windows-based systems, this can be done using Access Control Lists (ACLs). On UNIX systems, the correct user ID needs to be set. You should specifically define an exchange directory. All other system-critical directories must be protected using special access restrictions.

### 12.4.8 Encrypting PI Communication Channels and Web Services

Data networks usually have obvious security gaps when confidential data is transferred without encryption. To address the related risks, you can implement standard data encryption methods, such as SSL. This data encryption at the transport level is the simplest and a generally compatible approach for protecting data during transport from communication point to communication point (end-to-end); the AS Java supports SSL by default (see Chapter 9).

This kind of encryption, however, is usually undone when data is received in a system before it is forwarded again. This results in an additional security gap because the data remains in plain text or is stored temporarily before it is encrypted with SSL again and forwarded. You can close this security gap by also encrypting the data. The data should remain encrypted until the recipient receives it. This additional protection is recommended for web services.

To support this concept, the XML encryption standard by the Organization for the Advancement of Structured Information Standards (OASIS) (*http://www.oasis-open.org*) provides standardized guidelines for a direct encryption of web services (XML, SOAP). Before using this method, however, it must be ensured that all communicating systems are able to encrypt and decrypt data according to this standard.

In Release 7.1, SAP NetWeaver PI supports this standard. XML encryption is a part of the WS-Security that defines the guidelines for SOAP message authentication, digital signatures, and encryption of message texts. In Release 7.1, you configure this by performing the following steps in SAP NetWeaver Administrator:

1. You configure the default WS-Security in SAP NetWeaver Administrator via the following menu path: SOA Management • Web Services Administration for WS Configuration • Service End Points • Service Definition Details.
2. Afterward, you configure the PI client in SAP NetWeaver Administrator via the menu path: SOA Management • Web Services Administration for WS Clients Configuration • Logical Ports • Proxy Definitions Details.
3. To define SSL as the standard for clients, navigate to the Security option, and select the HTTPS entry for the Transport Protocol option.
4. Finally, you set the WS encryption and digital signature by selecting the Require Signature and Require Encryption entry for inbound requests and the Add Signature and Add Encryption entry for outbound responses in the Security option under Message Security.

### 12.4.9 Security for Web Services

You can use web services to transfer confidential information. This leads to plain requirements for the security of SOAP messages: data integrity, data confidentiality, and authentication of messages (see Chapter 7). Referring to the information provided in the previous section, Table 12.3 lists the OASIS standards that Release 7.1 of SAP NetWeaver PI currently supports.

| OASIS Standard | Description |
|---|---|
| SOAP (1.1) | SOAP is a transport protocol for data communication between heterogeneous and distributed systems using XML messages. |
| SOAP (1.2) | Version 1.2 of SOAP adds the XML infoset concept to the standard. This concept defines enhancements for the communication format. |
| WSDL (1.1) | The Web Services Description Language WSDL is used to describe document-oriented or procedure-oriented XML information, such as SOAP messages or UDDI as part of the Enterprise Services Repository or Services Registry. |
| UDDI (3.02) | Information on web services needs to be structured, stored, and managed in an inventory directory to make web services available. Universal Description, Discovery and Integration (UDDI) is the standard for this kind of directory. |
| XML (1.0) | Extensible Markup Language (XML) is a programming language to provide information as documents that can also contain instructions for their processing. XML is the basis for all kinds of web service programming. |
| HTTP (1.1) | The Hypertext Transfer Protocol (HTTP) is a transfer protocol for information between heterogeneous and distributed systems. |
| WS-Policy (2004/09) | The WS-Policy standard provides a framework for the description of guidelines on the behavior of web services and their processing. |
| WS-Policy Attachment (2004/09) | The WS-Policy Attachment defines WS-Policy assertions (WSDL 1.1 Attachments only) that describe a condition, characteristic, or behavior of web services. |
| WSIL (1.0) | The Web Service Inspection Language (WSIL) is used to inspect systems that offer web services. This is necessary for user systems of web services to identify appropriate web services. |
| WS-Addressing (1.0) | WS-Addressing is used to identify and exchange web services using XML infosets. |
| WS-Reliable Messaging (1.1) | WS-Reliable Messaging is a concept for reliable message transfer using web services. |
| WS-Security (1.0) | WS-Security is the OASIS framework for web service security. It describes standards for authentication, digital signatures, and encryption of SOAP XML messages. |

**Table 12.3** OASIS Standards for Web Services in SAP NetWeaver PI

| OASIS Standard | Description |
|---|---|
| WS-SecurityPolicy (1.2) | The WS-SecurityPolicy constitutes the framework of guidelines for web services with regard to their security. |
| WS-SecureConversation (1.3) | WS-SecureConversation is a part of the WS-Policy and provides support for avoiding multiple authentication. |
| WS-I Basic Profile (1.1) | The WS-I Basic Profile supports the interoperability of web services in combination with SOAP, WSDL, and UDDI. |
| SAML (2.0) | The Security Assertion Markup Language (SAML) is the current standard for the description of XML documents. SAML communicates, for example, what information is required for authentication and protection of objects and how X.509 certificate are used as a proof of security. SAP NetWeaver Portal 7.0 supports SAML 2.0. |
| WS-Security: SAML Token Profile (1.0) | An SAML Token Profile contains information on the authentication of objects and is used like an X.509 certificates as a proof of security. |

**Table 12.3** OASIS Standards for Web Services in SAP NetWeaver PI (Cont.)

For example, if a web service interacts with an AS ABAP (the SAP system can be both in this scenario, service provider and service consumer), this web service must be authorized in the traditional way according to the known ABAP authorization concept. Table 12.4 lists the standard roles available for this purpose.

| Standard Role (ABAP) | Description |
|---|---|
| SAP_BC_WEBSERVICE_SERVICE_USER | Role for background users of the WS runtime |
| SAP_BC_WEBSERVICE_ADMIN_TEC | Technical administration of web services, for example, for monitoring or managing communication channels |
| SAP_BC_WEBSERVICE_ADMIN_BIZ | Administrator for the administration of the functional use of web services |
| SAP_BC_WEBSERVICE_CONSUMER | System user for the use of web services |
| SAP_BC_WEBSERVICE_OBSERVER | Read authorization for all web services and for information monitoring |
| SAP_BC_WEBSERVICE_DEBUGGER | Authorization for WS debugging (troubleshooting) |

**Table 12.4** Standard Roles (ABAP) for Web Services in SAP NetWeaver PI 7.1

*The SAP Partner Connectivity Kit (PCK) supports internal and external communication of SAP and non-SAP applications with an existing Process Integration (PI) system. This chapter describes which aspects of message and communication security must be taken into account.*

# 13 SAP Partner Connectivity Kit

The SAP PCK is still a beneficial and frequently used solution to connect the in-house SAP or non-SAP system with SAP NetWeaver PI, for example, a PI system of a business partner, and to thus create a full-fledged communication level. The advantage here is that the integration can be simplified and the improved security mechanisms of the Exchange Infrastructure (XI) protocol can be used.

## 13.1 Introduction and Functions

The SAP PCK provides tools for setting up, configuring, and monitoring a data connection of SAP or non-SAP systems to SAP NetWeaver PI, including the required connectors . For example, a non-SAP system can use a PCK connection to SAP NetWeaver PI to access the PI Integration Server to have full access to the SAP infrastructure and process integration. On the other hand, the Integration Server in combination with a connector from the SAP PCK for an SAP system forms the link to non-SAP applications. The SAP PCK therefore creates the technical prerequisite for SAP NetWeaver PI as a middleware.

Standard PCK connectors are available for the following communication types:

- RFCs (SAP protocol; encryption using SNC)
- Small Business Connector (HTTP(S); encryption using SSL)
- File/ File Transfer Protocol (FTP) (FTP, see Section 13.4.6, Securing the File Adapter at the Operating System Level)
- JDBC (HTTP(S), XML messages; encryption using SSL)
- Java Message Service (JMS) (HTTP(S); encryption using SSL)
- Mail (POP3, IMAP4, SMTP; encryption using S/MIME)
- XI (HTTP(S); encryption using SSL)

All of these standard adapters use Application Server (AS) Java and the Java 2 Enterprise Edition (J2EE) Connector Architecture (JCA) and convert structured, semistructured, or unstructured data into the XML protocol for processing in SAP NetWeaver PI and vice versa. The same security environment as in SAP NetWeaver PI is used so that the security environment discussed in Chapter 12, SAP NetWeaver Process Integration, is also relevant for the SAP PCK, which also runs on AS Java.

The SAP PCK provides benefits for integrating smaller supplier companies with a larger regular supplier or manufacturer because the PCK is included in the license price of SAP NetWeaver PI. As in SAP NetWeaver PI, the administration is done via web front ends whose graphical user interfaces (GUIs) are similar to that of the Integration Builder. This enables a simple installation and configuration of the SAP PCK.

## 13.2 Risks and Controls

The risks and controls for the SAP PCK are essentially identical to those of SAP NetWeaver PI. Therefore, this chapter only discusses the risks where the controls differ from SAP NetWeaver PI (see Table 13.1).

| No. | Classification | Description |
|---|---|---|
| 1. | Risk potential | No authorization concept for the design and configuration phase:<br>Via the PCK web front end, users can access configurations for which they are not authorized. This is enabled by a nonexistent or insufficient authorization concept. |
| | Impact | The configuration of the integration scenario technically results in an unstable state so that message exchange can be considerably impaired. The availability of the integration scenario can no longer be guaranteed. Message recipient data can also be viewed and changed without authorization, so that potentially required postings are not affected in the actual target system but rather, in a system intended for this purpose by a fraudulent user. |
| | Risk without control(s) | Extremely high |
| | Control(s) | An authorization concept for administration tasks is developed in the SAP PCK, in which the appropriate roles are specified for accessing the objects and collaboration agreements stored in the SAP PCK. The concept is implemented. |

**Table 13.1** Risks and Controls for the SAP PCK

| No. | Classification | Description |
| --- | --- | --- |
| | Risk with control(s) | Normal |
| | Section | 13.4 |
| 2. | Risk potential | The selected technical service user is always the same:<br>For communication channels in an integration scenario, the technical service user chosen for the partner systems is always the same (PCKRECEIVER). There is no difference between the various systems to be integrated. |
| | Impact | Due to the lack of separation, other communication interfaces of the SAP PCK can be exploited by other partner systems. Therefore, unauthorized transactions can be triggered on other partner systems connected to the SAP PCK, or the service user could be abused for fraudulent programs without any authorization. |
| | Risk without control(s) | High |
| | Control(s) | For every SAP or non-SAP system connected to the SAP PCK, a different technical service user should be set up to enable differentiation. A technical collective service user for all connected partner systems should be avoided. |
| | Risk with control(s) | Normal |
| | Section | 13.4.1 |
| 3. | Risk potential | No encryption of external communication channels:<br>XML-based messages (per XI or Simple Object Access Protocol (SOAP) protocol) are transferred unencrypted to the SAP PCK. |
| | Impact | If XML-based messages are transferred unencrypted to the SAP PCK, then the information contained therein can be viewed by unauthorized third persons. |
| | Risk without control(s) | High |
| | Control(s) | Because the SAP PCK is exclusively used in Internet scenarios, all external communication channels should be encrypted. |
| | Risk with control(s) | Normal |
| | Section | 13.4.2 |

**Table 13.1** Risks and Controls for the SAP PCK (Cont.)

| No. | Classification | Description |
|---|---|---|
| 4. | Risk potential | No signature of XML messages:<br>XML-based messages (per XI or SOAP protocol) are transferred unsigned to the SAP PCK. |
| | Impact | With unsigned messages, the exact sender cannot be verified, and therefore it cannot be determined whether parts of the message were changed by an unauthorized third person during the transfer to the SAP PCK. This can eventually lead to incorrect postings. Furthermore, you cannot retrace who (that is, which legal person) initiated a posting. Requested transactions can later be denied by the sender. |
| | Risk without control(s) | Extremely high |
| | Control(s) | The SAP Partner Connectivity Kit is exclusively used in Internet scenarios. Therefore, digital signatures should always be used when exchanging messages. |
| | Risk with control(s) | Normal |
| | Section | 13.4.3 |
| 5. | Risk potential | The PCK communication channel is not secured:<br>Communication interfaces of the SAP PCK, especially in Internet scenarios, are exploited by an unauthorized third person, and unauthorized transactions are therefore triggered on the SAP and non-SAP systems connected to the SAP PCK. |
| | Impact | When unauthorized transactions are executed, it's often impossible to retrace who requested these transactions. A rollback to the original state is also no longer possible. This can cause considerable damage. |
| | Risk without control(s) | Extremely high |
| | Control(s) | Implement a proxy for outbound messages and a reverse proxy for inbound messages for the SAP PCK. |
| | Risk with control(s) | Normal |
| | Section | 13.4.4 |
| 6. | Risk potential | The message exchange is not audited or monitored:<br>The executed message transfers are not checked for potential processing errors using the central monitor. |

**Table 13.1** Risks and Controls for the SAP PCK (Cont.)

| No. | Classification | Description |
|---|---|---|
| | Impact | Processing errors are not discovered at an early stage and result in instabilities in the integration network. Important transactions might not be carried out, and this can lead to financial loss. |
| | Risk without control(s) | High |
| | Control(s) | Constant monitoring of the SAP PCK using the central monitor provided for this purpose. |
| | Risk with control(s) | Normal |
| | Section | 13.4.5 |
| 7. | Risk potential | No authentication for the file adapter:<br>The SAP Partner Connectivity Kit enables you to retrieve files from a sending system and to place them on a receiving system using file adapters. There is no authentication for the file adapter — at a technical level, or at the user level. This communication channel, therefore, is easily accessible to a certain extent. |
| | Impact | Due to the lack of authentication, files can be introduced to a target system to overwrite the password file, */etc/passwd*, for example. A new user can be created this way. The attacked target system can be controlled by using the new user. |
| | Risk without control(s) | High |
| | Control(s) | It is vital that you ensure a correct configuration of authorizations at the operating system level for accesses from the SAP PCK to the relevant file directories, especially when using the file adapter. This must apply to the SYSADM user, in particular, in whose name the PCK is executed at the operating system level. |
| | Risk with control(s) | Normal |
| | Section | 13.4.6 |

**Table 13.1** Risks and Controls for the SAP PCK (Cont.)

## 13.3 Application Security

For the design and configuration phase (see Chapter 12), just like SAP NetWeaver PI, the SAP PCK is delivered with predefined roles by default. Because the SAP PCK is based on the technical runtime environment of AS Java, it involves Java roles (see Chapter 9, SAP NetWeaver AS) that can be assigned to the administrative users via the Visual Administrator or the User Management Engine (UME) of the J2EE Engine. The Java roles shown in Table 13.2 are available by default.

| PCK role | J2EE Component | Description |
|---|---|---|
| Administrate | sap.com/com.sap.xi.pck*aii_ ib_sbeans | This Java role lets a user fully access the configuration interface of the PCK. This allows for the administration of the integration scenario using the Integration Builder of SAP NetWeaver PI. |
| Display | sap.com/com.sap.xi.mdt*mdt | This Java role gives the user read access to the processed messages in the message monitor. |
| Modify | sap.com/com.sap.xi.mdt*mdt | This Java role enables a user to modify the messages processed in the message monitor. |
| Payload | sap.com/com.sap.xi.mdt*mdt | This Java role gives a user read access to the message payload. This role should therefore be assigned very restrictively. |
| xi_af_adapter_monitor | sap.com/com.sap.aii.af.app*AdapterFramework | Using this Java role, the state of the Integration Adapter for SOAP, HTTP, and so on can be viewed. |
| Support | sap.com/com.sap.xi.pck*pck | This Java role enables access to the administration of system parameters of the PCK. |

**Table 13.2** Java Administration Roles for the SAP PCK

## 13.4 Technical Security

This section describes in more detail the risks and controls that are outlined in Table 13.1 with regard to technical security.

### 13.4.1 Separate Technical Service User for Every Connected Partner System

Just as for SAP NetWeaver PI, in the SAP PCK you should also select a separate technical service user for each connected partner system. In the standard delivery, this is the technical service user `PCKRECEIVER`. This user should be copied and renamed specifically for every connected system. In the SAP PCK, the `xi_af_receiver` role is designed for this purpose. It is included in the Java component `sap.com/com.sap.aii.af.ms.app*MessagingSystem`. For example, this role must be assigned to set up the technical service users using the Visual Administrator.

### 13.4.2 Setting Up Encryption for Communication Channels

The encryption of communication channels for the SAP PCK adapter — HTTP(S) — is set up just like it is in SAP NetWeaver PI. Therefore, the exact details have not been repeated here. Instead, simply refer to Chapter 12, Section 12.4.2, Setting Up Encryption for Communication Channels, for more information.

### 13.4.3 Digital Signature for XML-Based Messages

The mechanisms for establishing message-based security are also identical to those of SAP NetWeaver PI. The XI protocol is used for this purpose (see Chapter 12, Section 12.4.3, Digital Signature for XML-Based Messages). The configuration editor is called via the URL (for example, *http://supplier.pck.de:50000/pck/start*).

### 13.4.4 Network-Side Security for Integration Scenarios

Like SAP NetWeaver PI, the SAP PCK can be secured on the network side using a proxy for outbound messages and a reverse proxy for inbound messages. The application level gateways for XML-based communication, which is recommended for SAP NetWeaver PI, can be implemented here as well.

### 13.4.5 Audit of the Message Exchange

Just as for SAP NetWeaver PI, you should monitor the message exchange in the SAP PCK. To do this, the administration and monitoring tool can be called from the PCK start (*http://<PCK-Host>:<Port>/pck/start*). Using the monitoring tool, you can archive critical messages, that is, those messages that have been digitally signed. Besides monitoring messages, you can also monitor the adapter state. Using graphical symbols, you can easily detect whether problems have occurred during the forwarding and processing of messages.

To perform the audit of the PCK at an early stage and to take quick countermeasures if errors occur, it is recommended that you combine the SAP PCK with the Computing Center Management System (CCMS) monitor if it is already implemented for monitoring other SAP systems.

### 13.4.6 Securing the File Adapter at the Operating System Level

The process of securing the file adapter is analogous to SAP NetWeaver PI. And, as in the PI system, here again, you are strongly advised not to implement this adapter in an Internet scenario. If there are no other options, you must ensure that the operating system access of the technical user, who is running SAP PCK on the server, is greatly restricted. You should assign an authorization to this user for only those directories in which the files for further processing — by the actual target application — are to be stored.

*In the network architecture, middleware is located between SAP and non-SAP applications. It is responsible for connecting incompatible applications with each other effectively. Due to the transfer of information between such heterogeneous systems, information security risks exist not only on the side of the communicating applications but also at the time when the applications or systems start communicating or during data transfer.*

# 14 Classic SAP Middleware

Without middleware, most of the applications would have to be considered islands in the network architecture because no effective technical means for communication between applications with incompatible communication protocols or differing technologies would be available. Depending on the complexity of the problem and on the intelligence of the solution requested, this does not always require dedicated middleware products, such as SAP NetWeaver PI (see Chapter 12, SAP NetWeaver Process Integration). For simple networking tasks that also support communication between SAP systems or between SAP and non-SAP applications, specifically adapted "classic" middleware is available:

- SAP Web Dispatcher (see Section 14.1, SAP Web Dispatcher)
- SAProuter (see Section 14.2, SAProuter)
- SAP Internet Transaction Server (see Section 14.3, SAP ITS).

Regardless of how the systems are connected, all communication scenarios must sufficiently consider security and risk management because connections between inhomogeneous system architectures can lead to risks and security gaps due to the adaptation of heterogeneous technologies, possibly incompatible security functions, or the transformation of data structures.

## 14.1 SAP Web Dispatcher

SAP Web Dispatcher is an application that can perform the following tasks: access point in the demilitarized zone (DMZ) for HTTP(S) requests and their forwarding to downstream applications (SAP NetWeaver Portal, for example), load balancing; as a reverse proxy, it can also assume simple security functions in the demilitarized zone. The resulting risks are discussed in the following sections.

### 14.1.1 Introduction and Functions

In most Internet scenarios, SAP Web Dispatcher is installed as the first access point and to protect a web application (similar to a reverse proxy) — for example, based on Business Server Pages (BSPs), Web Dynpro ABAP, or Web Dynpro Java (WDJ) or JavaServer Pages (JSPs). It serves primarily as a load distributor to distribute incoming requests equally on the SAP systems if the SAP (AS) is a cluster.

However, SAP Web Dispatcher can also handle smaller security functions like URL filtering and SSL for load balancing; it supports SSL termination, SSL reencryption, end-to-end SSL, and X.509 authentication of communication partners. This feature can ensure network-side security for confidential applications, such as business applications that run on the SAP NetWeaver AS. But, you must not confuse SAP Web Dispatcher with an application-level gateway that offers a much higher level of security against Internet attacks, such as cross-site scripting, cookie poisoning, and so on.

### 14.1.2 Risks and Controls

Because SAP Web Dispatcher is not a security solution, the following description of risks and controls refers to the security functions that SAP Web Dispatcher provides. In this section, we use a simplified version of the risk analysis methodology described in Chapter 1, Risk and Control Management, to identify the main security risks and the necessary controls for SAP Web Dispatcher (see Table 14.1). The controls are then discussed in more detail in the following sections and illustrated using examples.

| No. | Classification | Description |
|---|---|---|
| 1. | Potential risk | Direct access to the SAP NetWeaver AS from the Internet:<br>Access from the Internet to applications provided by the SAP NetWeaver AS (a BSP application, for instance) can occur directly. |
| | Impact | Direct access to the SAP NetWeaver AS from the Internet can increase the potential risk of compromising the server. Such a case can result in unauthorized viewing of a file, lead to the loss of data, or trigger unauthorized transactions. |
| | Risk without control(s) | Extremely high |
| | Control | Use of SAP Web Dispatcher as a reverse proxy solution. |

**Table 14.1** Risks and Controls for SAP Web Dispatcher

| No. | Classification | Description |
|---|---|---|
| | Risk with control(s) | Medium |
| | Section | Use of SAP Web Dispatcher as a Reverse Proxy in Section 14.1.4. |
| 2. | Potential risk | Access to unprotected HTTP services (URL):<br>HTTP services only needed for the intranet are active on SAP NetWeaver AS. Only internal employees of the organization should be able to access these services. |
| | Impact | External attackers can exploit the HTTP services and completely compromise the integrity of or take over SAP NetWeaver AS. |
| | Risk without control(s) | Extremely high |
| | Control | Configuration of SAP Web Dispatcher with URL filtering functionality that blocks specific HTTP services from the Internet. |
| | Risk with control(s) | Medium |
| | Section | Configuration of SAP Web Dispatcher as a URL Filter in Section 14.1.4. |
| 3. | Potential risk | Unencrypted Internet connection:<br>Communication between the web browser and SAP Web Dispatcher is unencrypted. |
| | Impact | Unencrypted communication can allow viewing of passwords or other confidential business information. The information can be used for a later attack on the SAP application. |
| | Risk without control(s) | Extremely high |
| | Control | Configuration of the web browser with an SSL-encrypted communications connection from the Internet to SAP Web Dispatcher. |
| | Risk with control(s) | Low |
| | Section | SSL Configuration in Section 14.1.4 |

**Table 14.1** Risks and Controls for SAP Web Dispatcher (Cont.)

| No. | Classification | Description |
|---|---|---|
| 4. | Potential risk | No authentication of the communication partners:<br>SAP Web Dispatcher and SAP NetWeaver AS do not mutually authenticate each other prior to communication. |
| | Impact | If no mutual authentication is implemented, it cannot be ensured that only requests from the authorized SAP Web Dispatcher are forwarded to the SAP NetWeaver AS legitimately. The risk of HTTP or HTTP(S) attacks on SAP NetWeaver AS or SAP applications cannot be reduced efficiently. |
| | Risk without control(s) | High |
| | Control | Requirement for an authenticated SSL communication channel between SAP Web Dispatcher and a downstream SAP NetWeaver AS. The communication partners have to prove their identity using X.509 certificates. |
| | Risk with control(s) | Low |
| | Section | SSL Authentication of the Communication Partners in Section 14.1.4 |
| 5. | Potential risk | Insufficient protection of SAP Web Dispatcher:<br>SAP Web Dispatcher can be accessed from the Internet without any protection, and its security functions are configured insufficiently. |
| | Impact | If the available SAP Web Dispatcher security functions are not used or are configured insufficiently, this results in security gaps that can be utilized for attacks on the back-end SAP application. |
| | Risk without control(s) | Extremely high |
| | Control | Using all SAP Web Dispatcher security functions to reduce the points of attack from the Internet |
| | Risk with control(s) | Normal |
| | Section | Internet Security in Section 14.1.4 |
| 6. | Potential risk | No monitoring of SAP Web Dispatcher:<br>SAP Web Dispatcher and its functions are not being monitored. |

**Table 14.1** Risks and Controls for SAP Web Dispatcher (Cont.)

| No. | Classification | Description |
|---|---|---|
| | Impact | If the main SAP Web Dispatcher functions are not monitored, potential failures or security-relevant changes cannot be determined. Consequently, transactions are not transferred to the SAP back-end system or contain errors. For example, purchase orders that have not been transferred can lead to a loss of revenue. |
| | Risk without control(s) | High |
| | Control | Configuration and monitoring of the SAP Web Dispatcher functionality. |
| | Risk with control(s) | Low |
| | Section | Monitoring in Section 14.1.4 |

**Table 14.1** Risks and Controls for SAP Web Dispatcher (Cont.)

### 14.1.3 Application Security

SAP Web Dispatcher has a relatively limited scope of functions, and usually only administrators must have access to its configuration, maintenance, and monitoring options. SAP Web Dispatcher therefore doesn't provide a highly complex graphical user interface (GUI). It is called via its URL in the web browser.

SAP Web Dispatcher is installed as a service (Windows) or daemon (UNIX) on a separate server. All access controls and configurations are implemented at the operating system level. Therefore, SAP Web Dispatcher doesn't have its own access authorization concept. So the application security of SAP Web Dispatcher doesn't have to be detailed any further. However, it is critical that the corresponding access controls are configured at the operating system level of the server.

### 14.1.4 Technical Security

This section describes in more detail the risks and controls that are outlined in Table 14.1 with regard to technical security.

#### Use of SAP Web Dispatcher as a Reverse Proxy

SAP Web Dispatcher can be used as a reverse proxy (see Chapter 5, Information Technology (IT) Security). It thus functions as a central request point for all incoming HTTP(S) requests from the Internet (see Figure 14.1). It does not offer any filter or security functions on Open Systems Interconnection (OSI) level 7. Its central function is load balancing. It receives load information on the individual instances and Internet processes from the message server of the central instance of the SAP NetWeaver AS, and uses it to distribute the load. It stores the status information in its own memory so that follow-up requests from a given client end up on the same instance of SAP NetWeaver AS. This feature is important for applications that require status information. The HTTP(S) requests are redirected to the Internet Communication Managers (ICM) of the individual SAP system instances.

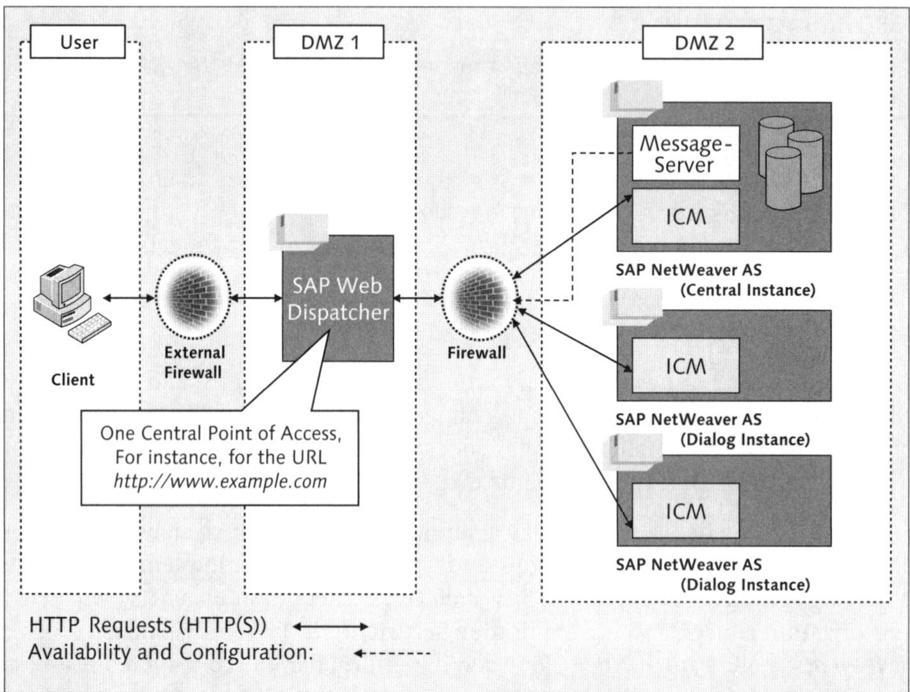


**Figure 14.1** SAP Web Dispatcher as Reverse Proxy for SAP Applications

From a security perspective, SAP Web Dispatcher technically separates the network and implements the DMZ concept. Because SAP systems cannot be accessed directly from the Internet, they can be placed in a trustworthy network segment (DMZ 2).

All communication connections (between the Internet and SAP Web Dispatcher, between SAP Web Dispatcher and the message server, and between SAP Web Dispatcher and the ICM of the SAP NetWeaver AS instances) can completely communicate via SSL encryption. This can also be done using mutual authentication, that is, authentication at the technical level based on X.509 certificates. See the section called "SSL Configuration" later in this chapter for more details.

The configuration file *sapwebdisp.pfl* is used to configure SAP Web Dispatcher. The file is automatically generated after the installation of SAP Web Dispatcher when the application is initially started. The file contains all of the required configuration parameters, which are read when SAP Web Dispatcher is started. At a minimum, a sample configuration file would appear as it does in Listing 14.1.

```
# SAPSYSTEMNAME of SAP Web Dispatcher must be set,
# so that the default profile can be read.
# Otherwise, a warning will be displayed in the console.
SAPSYSTEMNAME = BIN
# SAPSYSTEM (instance number of SAP Web Dispatcher) must
# be set so that the shared memory areas
# can be created. The number must
# differ from other SAP instances on the computer.
SAPSYSTEM = 10
# Description of the message server
# Name of the computer that the message server is running on
rdisp/mshost = binmain
# Port and protocol SAP Web Dispatcher uses
# to get the required load information.
ms/server_port_0 = PROT=HTTP,PORT 8081
# Description of the access points for SAP Web Dispatcher.
# In this case, http requests can be accepted at port 80
# HTTPS requests are accepted at port 443
# and redirected right to the
# SAP systems
icm/server_port_0 = PROT=HTTP,PORT=80
icm/server_port_1 = PROT=ROUTER,PORT=443
```

**Listing 14.1** Sample Configuration File for SAP Web Dispatcher

#### Configuration of SAP Web Dispatcher as a URL Filter

SAP Web Dispatcher can be configured as a URL filter. In this case, specific HTTP services (URLs) provided on the SAP systems can be made inaccessible. Such URLs can include those in the Internet Connection Framework (ICF) of SAP NetWeaver AS that might have to remain accessible only for internal access. These URLs can be deactivated using Transaction SICF (see Chapter 9, SAP NetWeaver Application Server). SAP Web Dispatcher can use the URL filter to block access to these from the Internet.

Here, the file *ptabfile* must be installed on the SAP Web Dispatcher server. The path to the file is defined in the SAP Web Dispatcher configuration file with the following parameter:

```
wdisp\permission_table = <ptabfile>
```

`<ptabfile>` is the absolute or relative path of the appropriate file. The name of the file can be chosen at will without file extension. The example in Listing 14.2 includes a possible definition of an access restriction for a URL using this file:

```
# Sample SAP Web Dispatcher file for
# a Permission_Table
P   /sap/bc/test.cgi
D   *.cgi
P   /sap/bc/cachetest
P   /sap/bc/public/*
P   /sap/bc/ping
D   *
```

**Listing 14.2** Example of a URL Filtering Function of SAP Web Dispatcher

This file is set up so that — from the very start — it searches for an applicable rule. As soon as the rule is found, the search is terminated. You can enter one of three parameters in the first column:

- `P`
  Permitted
- `D`
  Denied
- `S`
  Accessible only with secure HTTP(S) protocol

The sample file in Listing 14.2 only allows a call of the CGI program *test.cgi*, and not any other CGI programs. You can enter a wildcard (*) at the beginning or end of the URL definition. If the position of the first two lines were reversed, no CGI program could be called. The first line would prohibit calling the CGI program — even if the second line would allow it. This situation results because the search is terminated after the first applicable rule. Entry of `D*` at the end of the file means that only the URLs expressly allowed can be called and no others.

The following list contains important security parameters in the context of URL security. They can be set in the SAP Web Dispatcher configuration file:

- **`wdisp\max_permitted_uri_len`**
  Maximum permitted length of a URL in letters (integer, default: 2048)

- `wdisp\max_permission_table_size`
  Maximum number of URL entries in the permission table (integer, default: 300)
- `wdisp\max_permission_table_entry_size`
  maximum length of a URL entry in the permission table (integer, default: 256)

### SSL Configuration

SAP Web Dispatcher supports all possible combinations of SSL communications connections. Figure 14.2 illustrates the combinations. The parameter `icm/server_port_<xx>` with option `Port` determines whether SAP Web Dispatcher accepts HTTP(S) requests. The parameter can accept the following values:

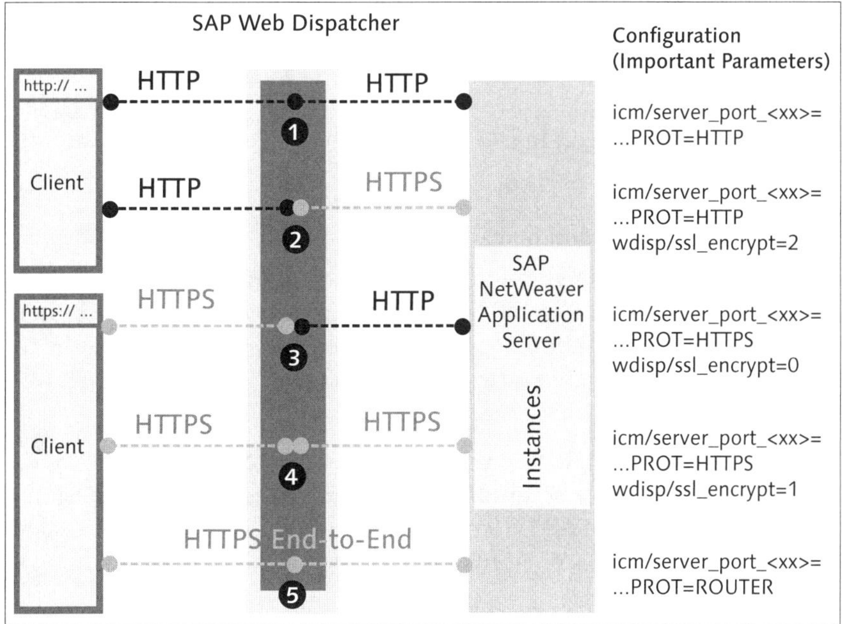


**Figure 14.2** Possible SSL Combinations with SAP Web Dispatcher

- `HTTP`
  SAP Web Dispatcher accepts HTTP requests on the port (see Figure 14.2: cases ❶ and ❷).
- `HTTP(S)`
  SAP Web Dispatcher accepts HTTP(S) requests on the port. It decrypts the

request before redirecting it to an application server (see Figure 14.2: cases ❸ and ❹).

- ROUTER
  SAP Web Dispatcher receives an HTTP(S) request and redirects it without decrypting it; this is the end-to-end SSL example (see Figure 14.2: case ❺).

The parameter wdisp/ssl_encrypt determines if SAP Web Dispatcher (re)encrypts the request using SSL before it redirects it (see Figure 14.2). The parameter can accept the following values:

- 0
  An HTTPS request is decrypted in SAP Web Dispatcher and is redirected without encryption (case ❸, SSL termination).
- 1
  An HTTPS request is decrypted in SAP Web Dispatcher and is redirected with encryption (case ❹, SSL termination).
- 2
  An HTTP request is received in SAP Web Dispatcher and is redirected with encryption (case ❷).

### SSL Authentication of the Communication Partners

The SAP Web Dispatcher configuration file contains another parameter: wdisp/ssl_auth. It determines if SAP Web Dispatcher and the downstream SAP system must undergo mutual authentication. If the parameter is set to 1, mutual authentication is executed. In this case, however, the parameter wdisp/ssl_host = <Common Name of SAP Web Dispatcher> must also be set.

To establish the SSL connection to SAP Web Dispatcher in cases ❷ or ❹, the <Common Name> of the SAP systems must be specified. This <Common Name> must correspond to the <Common Name> of the SAP systems for which the certificates were issued. The names can be viewed on SAP NetWeaver AS using Transaction STRUST.

SAP Web Dispatcher must be equipped with the corresponding cryptographic ability if the HTTPS connection is scheduled in it. This is done with the following steps:

1. Install the SAP Cryptographic Library on the server that runs SAP Web Dispatcher.
2. Define the listed SSL parameters.
3. Create the Personal Security Environment (PSE) and generate a certificate request for SAP Web Dispatcher, for website *http://www.sample.com*, for example.
4. Create a signature of the certificate request via a Certificate Authority (CA).

5. Import the signed certificate into the PSE.
6. Generate access credentials for SAP Web Dispatcher on its PSE so that the certificate can be read at runtime.
7. Restart SAP Web Dispatcher.

After these configuration steps have been performed, SAP Web Dispatcher and SAP NetWeaver AS undergo mutual SSL authentication as communication partners.

#### Internet Security

With its Internet URL or IP address, SAP Web Dispatcher is the first access point for users when they use a downstream SAP NetWeaver Portal or SAP systems in general via the Internet. Therefore, SAP Web Dispatcher should be protected using appropriate firewalls within the DMZ. That is, only the actual SAP Web Dispatcher application file (*sapwebdisp*) and the corresponding configuration file, *sapwebdisp.pfl*, should be located in the demilitarized zone. But this protection is still not sufficient for reducing the risks of attacks from the Internet. The following describes the SAP Web Dispatcher security functions that are available for risk management.

- **Installing recent software versions and patches**
  Applications should always be up-to-date with regard to version and patch level. This ensures that applications are protected against potential threats in the best possible way. SAP Note 1224599, for example, contains information on the patch level that should be installed to prevent SAP Web Dispatcher being blocked due to a high number of Internet requests (denial of service attack). The current release of SAP Web Dispatcher is Release 7.11. This note also applies to version and patch level updates of the operating system that runs SAP Web Dispatcher. Support is provided for AIX, Sun Solaris, HP UNIX, UNIX (Tru64), Windows, Linux, AS/400, and z/OS, for example.
- **Avoiding system information in error messages**
  System-generated error messages usually contain comprehensive information on the system, the application, and the security configuration (even passwords in some cases); this is intended and useful in the case of troubleshooting. However, this is also a good source of information for potential attackers looking for system and security gaps. So it is a common method for attacks from the Internet and intranet to trigger system errors on purpose and then examine the error messages. Refer to SAP Note 870127 to reduce this risk.
- **Using individual error messages**
  Error messages can also include system information that can be used by potential attackers to plan system attacks. You can significantly reduce the risk of making critical system information accessible in error messages by creating

your own error messages that contain less detailed information or an error code that can only be understood by internal employees, for example. SAP Web Dispatcher can be configured for such a behavior by providing the error message in a separate text file and storing this file under a respective path at the operating system level. The following parameter supports this configuration:

```
icm/HTTP/error_template_path=/usr/sap/B6M/D13/data/icmerror.
```

You can also deactivate the error message function. This can be done using the following parameter setting:

```
is/HTTP/show_detailed_errors=FALSE
```

- **Configuring the URL filter to block system-specific URLs**
  As a middleware solution, SAP Web Dispatcher receives external requests and redirects them to a specific system service or SAP message server that forwards the external requests to the corresponding SAP back-end system in turn. External requests are always made via URL calls that start specific activated services. In this context, SAP Web Dispatcher can filter these external URLs calls. This function should be used to reduce the risk of system-specific information being called from the outside. These kinds of system-specific URLs that can be accessed from the outside can display internal system data and configurations and thus present points of attack. You can avoid this using the following configuration in the *ptabfile* parameter file:

```
D /sap/public/icman/*
D /sap/public/ping
D /sap/public/icf_info/*
D /SAP/wdisp/information
```

- **Securing the administrative access to SAP Web Dispatcher**
  You should secure the operating system interface for the SAP Web Dispatcher administration. The following measures are available for this purpose:
  - You can implement an SSL communication for administrative access by configuring the `icm/HTTP/admin` administrator interface (`PORT` option) for an SSL port.
  - In addition, you can ensure that SAP Web Dispatcher can only be accessed from the intranet by a specific number of authorized systems (`HOST` option and `CLIENTHOST` option).

  These measures reduce the risk of the administrator password being compromised and enabling unauthorized access to the administration option for SAP Web Dispatcher. The configurations are set in the Web Dispatcher profile file (*sapwebdisp.pfl*).

### Monitoring

SAP Web Dispatcher can be monitored with a monitoring program via a web browser or using the command line program `icmon`. The web-based administration interface for administration and monitoring of SAP Web Dispatcher is started with the web browser. The functionality and setup are comparable to those of the ICM in SAP NetWeaver AS, set with Transaction SMICM. The browser-based administration interface is started via *http://<web dispatcher host>:<web dispatcher port>/sap/wdisp/admin/default.htm*.

The following preconditions for administration with the web browser must be met:

- The most recent version of SAP Web Dispatcher is installed in a directory.
- Packet *icmadmin.SAR* is unpacked in its own directory.
- The value `icm/HTTP/admin` is maintained in the profile of SAP Web Dispatcher, for example, `icm/HTTP/admin_0=PREFIX=/sap/wdisp/admin,DOCROOT=./ admin`.
- A file for authentication of the administrators exists (*icmauth.txt*). The file is automatically generated when starting SAP Web Dispatcher with the `-bootstrap` option.
- SAP Web Dispatcher was configured for SSL, because the password is also transmitted to the monitoring console during log-on access with the web browser.

After the administration interface has been installed, the most important functions of SAP Web Dispatcher can be monitored.

## 14.2 SAProuter

SAProuter is a simple but nevertheless powerful supplement to the security concept of an SAP network. This section describes its part in the risk management area regarding the access to SAP systems.

### 14.2.1 Introduction and Functions

Access to a network is usually protected by firewalls and the package filtering options referring to IP address and domain name. Modern firewalls can also actively read the communication and thus perform additional security tasks. You can increase the level of protection for the network if a network router controls the communication that is permitted by the firewall.

Here, SAProuter is specialized in SAP applications and can protect access to SAP systems from the network side providing the following configurable control options:

- **Protocol filtering**
  Blocking non-SAP protocols
- **Data security**
  Blocking non–SNC communication from unknown communication partners
- **Authentication of the communication partners**
  Blocking communication for incorrect password or no password
- **Controlling permitted source and target systems**
  Blocking unauthorized source and target IP addresses of systems and routers

SAProuter is an application-level proxy that has been specifically developed for the SAP protocols, Dynamic Information and Action Gateway (DIAG) and Remote Function Call (RFC). It can be configured in such a way that it only grants access to specific SAP systems, SAProuter, or SAP GUI users, from and to specific network segments. It runs on UNIX, Windows, and OS/400. As already mentioned, encryption using SNC can also be requested.

The configuration of the SAProuter controls, including passwords, is defined in the corresponding configuration file, which must be protected against unauthorized modification — depending on its security-technical significance. The configuration file is located in the current SAProuter directory in the file system of the server operation system that runs SAProuter.

### 14.2.2 Risks and Controls

Because SAProuter is, itself, a security solution, the risks and controls described in Table 14.2 refer to the security functions provided by SAProuter. In this section, we'll use a simplified version of the risk analysis methodology described in Chapter 1, Risk and Control Management, to identify the main security risks and the necessary controls for SAProuter. The controls are then discussed in more detail in the following sections and illustrated using examples.

| No. | Classification | Description |
|---|---|---|
| 1. | Potential risk | Direct access to an SAP system using the DIAG or RFC protocol:<br>The DIAG (SAP GUI) and RFC protocols enable direct access from a nontrustworthy network to the SAP NetWeaver AS. This eliminates the proposed network segmentation from being established and divided into trustworthy and less trustworthy areas. |

**Table 14.2** Risks and Controls for SAProuter

| No. | Classification | Description |
|---|---|---|
| | Impact | The direct access to the SAP NetWeaver AS from a nontrustworthy network segment increases the potential risks that can ultimately compromise the integrity of the SAP system. In that case, unauthorized accesses to the SAP system are possible. Eventually, unauthorized (financial) transactions can be triggered. |
| | Risk without control(s) | High |
| | Control | Use of SAProuter as a level proxy for SAP applications that use the SAP protocols, DIAG and RFC. According to security requirements, you can request source and target IP addresses, SNC encryption, and password authentication. |
| | Risk with control(s) | Normal |
| | Section | 14.2.4 |

**Table 14.2** Risks and Controls for SAProuter (Cont.)

### 14.2.3 Application Security

We don't need to consider any application security aspects for SAProuter, because this SAP component is exclusively responsible for technical security. You configure the SAProuter table manually in the file system of the operating system of the router server. Because the SAProuter table is the core of router controls, it must be protected against unauthorized and incorrect modification at the operating system level using access controls for the operating system.

### 14.2.4 Technical Security

To ensure that the security routing of SAProuter functions properly, you must terminate the direct communication between the SAP GUI clients and the SAP systems with a restrictive network router or a firewall. You must design the firewall rules in such a way that SAP GUI can only access the SAProuter that forwards the requests to the relevant SAP systems using the DIAG and RFC protocols. SAProuter checks the origin of the requests on the basis of the defined routing rules of the SAProuter table. Figure 14.3 illustrates this relationship.

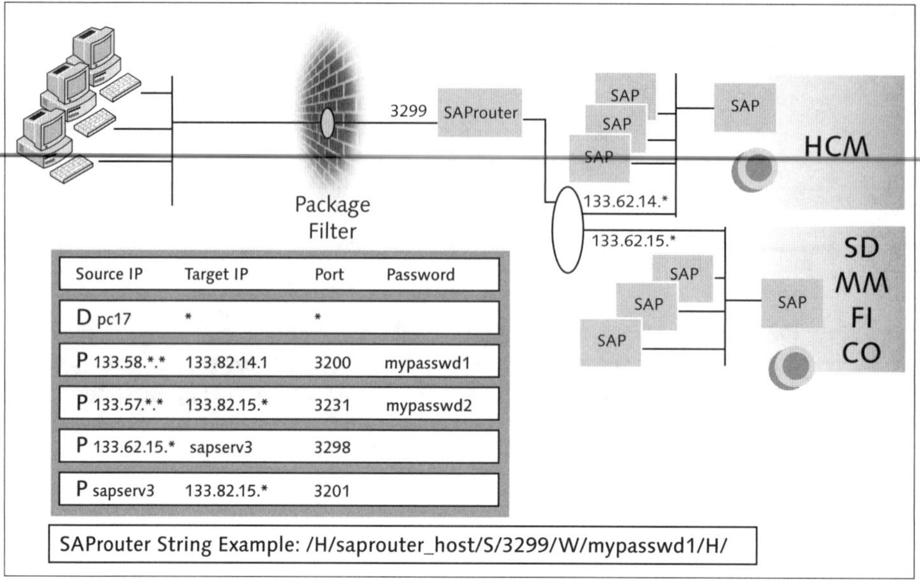


| Source IP | Target IP | Port | Password |
|---|---|---|---|
| D pc17 | * | * | |
| P 133.58.*.* | 133.82.14.1 | 3200 | mypasswd1 |
| P 133.57.*.* | 133.82.15.* | 3231 | mypasswd2 |
| P 133.62.15.* | sapserv3 | 3298 | |
| P sapserv3 | 133.82.15.* | 3201 | |

SAProuter String Example: /H/saprouter_host/S/3299/W/mypasswd1/H/

**Figure 14.3** Example of a Network Architecture with SAProuter and the Corresponding SAProuter Table

The *saprouttab* configuration file contains configuration information for the routing rules of SAProuter. The file is generated as a text file, provided with the respective entries, and stored without file extension at the same location as the SAProuter installation file (Windows: *saprouter.exe*). The configuration file contains a list of entries of the following type:

```
[D|P|S]{#before,#after} <Source IP> <Target IP> <Port> {>Password}
```

- Each line contains the identification code `[D|P|S]` that is used for describing the access right. `D` stands for Deny Connection, `P` stands for Permit Connection (including TCP), while `S` stands for Permit only SAP Protocols.
- The source IP addresses of the SAP GUI clients for which the connections are to be permitted or denied must be entered in the `<Source-IP>`.
- The `<Target-IP>` must be provided with the target addresses of the SAP systems to which access is supposed to be permitted or denied.
- The `<Port>` value must contain the network TCP/IP port used by the message server of the SAP NetWeaver AS for receiving requests.
- Optionally, you can specify a `{Password}` that must also be sent by the SAP GUI client so that the connection is permitted.

As already mentioned, SAProuter can also be configured to only accept or redirect SNC-encrypted communication channels. If the request is a non-SNC request, it is rejected. Entries that start with K define the SNC requests in the configuration file.

The SAProuter string must be entered in SAP GUI so that the SAP GUI client can find and establish the connection to the SAProuter in the network. That string tells SAP GUI through which SAProuter the connection to an SAP system can be established. You can find an example of such a string at the bottom of Figure 14.3. The SAProuter string in SAP GUI contains a password that may be necessary to connect to SAProuter; so adequate measures must be taken to protect the password and restrict access to SAP GUI on local computers. In addition, communication between SAP GUI and SAProuter should be protected through SNC.

## 14.3 SAP Internet Transaction Server (ITS)

SAP ITS was the first application that opened up the SAP system to the Internet. Since then, the "traditional Internet Transaction Server" has gone through significant changes. But information security and risk management still assume critical roles in the ITS's old and new form and are therefore discussed in this section.

**Note**

Originally, SAP ITS was a standalone application that acted as a technological bridge between the HTTP/HTML world of the Internet and the SAP dialog or RFC protocol of the SAP applications. Accordingly, SAP ITS was and still is equipped with the required functional and security-technical options to assume this task. However, this also leads to some restrictions. SAP therefore developed the SAP Web AS (today: SAP NetWeaver AS) to meet the increasing requirements and create a new, more flexible, and more powerful platform for SAP NetWeaver.

So Basis Release 6.20 is the last version that supports SAP ITS as a standalone application. With Basis Release 6.40, SAP ITS was fully integrated with SAP NetWeaver AS. Since Basis Release 7.0, all Internet applications of the standalone ITS must run on the integrated ITS of the SAP NetWeaver AS. The traditional ITS architecture with WGate and AGate and the common administrative user interfaces in SAP NetWeaver 7.0 were removed. So the information security and risk management issues for SAP ITS were shifted toward SAP NetWeaver AS (see Chapter 9).

Nevertheless, Release 6.20 of SAP ITS can still be used in the following cases:

- All systems that run on Basis Release 6.20 or earlier must still use the standalone ITS 6.20 version. The ITS FlowLogic and web reporting (WebRFC) functions are only directly supported by the standalone ITS in combination with Basis Release 6.20. These two functions are no longer available in the integrated ITS version but can be converted to ABAP programming code (see SAP Notes 1057274 and 979467).

- The integrated ITS version only supports the processing of Internet transactions that can be directly executed from a separate SAP NetWeaver AS. That means that Internet transactions cannot be directed to another SAP system as with ITS 6.20.
- Companies still use SAP applications with transactional ABAP applications that can only be addressed as web applications using SAP ITS. SAP ITS transforms the ABAP transactions that have been started this way into HTML format to display them in SAP GUI for HTML.

### 14.3.1 Introduction and Functions

SAP ITS (Release 6.20) is the link between SAP Web AS and SAP GUI for HTML (web browser). It is used to format dynpro-based applications (transactions based on ABAP) in HTML, so they can be displayed and controlled using a web browser.

SAP ITS consists of the following two components: Web Interface Gate (WGate) and Application Interface Gate (AGate). WGate is an extension for a web server that translates the HTTP requests it receives from a web browser into a format that is understood by AGate. The following web browsers are supported:

- Microsoft Internet Information Server (IIS), including the required Information Server Application Programming Interface (ISAPI) by SAP
- Netscape Enterprise Server (NES), including the required Network Server Application Programming Interface (NSAPI) by SAP
- Apache Web Server, including the required Web Server Application Programming Interface (WSAPI) by SAP

AGate then converts the request into a DIAG call (or into an RFC call) and forwards it to the application server. The requested transaction, which must exist as an Internet Application Component (IAC) in the ICF is then called and executed. For this reason, the AGate is the actual gateway in the standalone ITS and in SAP NetWeaver AS for Basis Release 6.40 or earlier releases.

The response is sent from the application server to the AGate, where it is converted into an HTML page. That page is transferred through the WGate to the web browser, where it can be forwarded in HTML format to the requesting web browser. For application server, SAP ITS appears to be a regular SAP GUI, because the request is sent to the SAP system via the DIAG protocol.

Figure 14.4 displays the logical process flow of the web-based user request up to the application server. The following protocols are used between these locations:

- Web browser and web server/WGate: HTTP
- WGate and AGate: SAP-proprietary protocol, similar to the DIAG protocol
- AGate and application server: DIAG and RFC protocol

The configuration illustrated in Figure 14.4 is a dual-host configuration in which WGate and AGate are installed separately on two different servers. However, it is also possible to install WGate and AGate together with the web server to be used on a single machine. This type of configuration is referred to as a single-host configuration. Nevertheless, for security reasons the dual-host configuration is preferable, as described in detail later on.

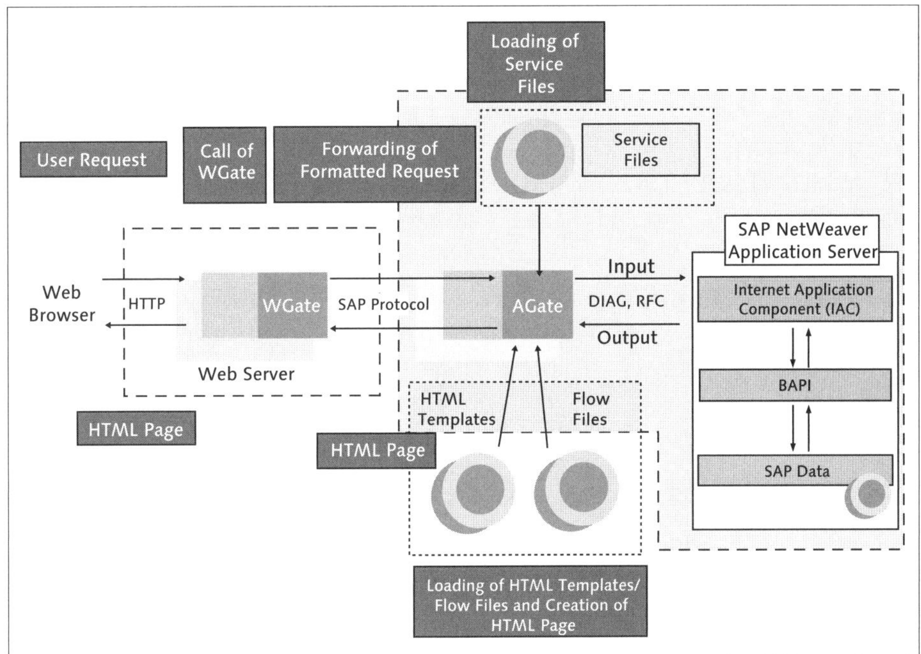


**Figure 14.4** Technical Architecture of the SAP ITS

All services provided by SAP ITS, such as the SAP GUI for HTML access, which is frequently referred to as WebGUI, or the administration console for SAP ITS, and so on, are defined via parameters in service files in the AGate file system. Parameters that are applied to all services are stored in the file *global.srvc*. Specific parameters such as those for the SAP GUI for HTML access are defined in separate files, in this case in *webgui.srvc*; a separate file must be created for each additional service.

The AGate contains other, equally important files, namely the HTML templates and flow files: The HTML template files contain predefined structures that are necessary to complete the individual transactions that are called; the flow files contain information for defining the request flow.

As already mentioned, all of the descriptions only refer to ITS Release 6.20; for Release 6.40, the transaction server has been integrated with the SAP NetWeaver AS. In this context, the WGate functions have been replaced by an integration into the ICM, and the AGate runtime environment has been embedded into the Internet Communication Framework (ICF). The security measures required for the integrated SAP ITS are described in Chapter 9, SAP NetWeaver Application Server. They're identical to the security measures that are required for BSP applications.

### 14.3.2 Risks and Controls

In this section, we'll use a simplified version of the risk analysis methodology described in Chapter 1 to identify the main security risks and the necessary controls for SAP ITS (see Table 14.3). The controls are then discussed in more detail in the following sections and illustrated using examples.

| No. | Classification | Description |
|---|---|---|
| 1. | Potential risk | No access rights for service files have been defined:<br>The rights for accessing the service files (*global.srvc* and so on) at the operating system level of the AGate server have either been incorrectly defined or not defined at all. |
| | Impact | The missing or incorrectly defined access rights for service files enable unauthorized employees or external attackers to modify the configuration of the ITS. This provokes further attempts to compromise the application server. Eventually, unauthorized (financial) transactions may be triggered. |
| | Risk without control(s) | Extremely high |
| | Control | Definition of access rights for the service files for user groups at the operating system level. |
| | Risk with control(s) | Normal |
| | Section | Defining Access Rights for Service Files in Section 14.3.3 |

**Table 14.3** Risks and Controls for SAP ITS

| No. | Classification | Description |
|---|---|---|
| 2. | Potential risk | Lack of an administration concept for SAP ITS:<br>There is no administration concept for SAP ITS. Even operating system (OS) administrators can access the SAP ITS configuration. |
| | Impact | The lack of an administration concept enables third parties to compromise the configuration of the SAP ITS. This can lead to unauthorized accesses to the application server. Eventually, unauthorized (financial) transactions may be triggered. |
| | Risk without control(s) | High |
| | Control | Implementation of an administration concept for SAP ITS. |
| | Risk with control(s) | Normal |
| | Section | Administration Concept in Section 14.3.3 |
| 3. | Potential risk | SAP ITS is configured as a single host:<br>The components of SAP ITS, the web server, WGate, and AGate are installed on one server.<br>The network is not segmented into trustworthy and less trustworthy network zones or DMZs. |
| | Impact | The AGate server that stores the service files can be accessed directly from the Internet. Possible misconfigurations — such as incorrectly defined access rights for the files — enable unauthorized parties to perform further successful attacks even on the back-end application server. |
| | Risk without control(s) | High |
| | Control | Implementation of a network segmentation concept and subdividing the SAP ITS components into corresponding DMZ network areas. |
| | Risk with control(s) | Normal |
| | Section | Installing a DMZ Network Segmentation in Section 14.3.4 |

**Table 14.3** Risks and Controls for SAP ITS (Cont.)

| No. | Classification | Description |
|---|---|---|
| 4. | Potential risk | No encryption of communication channels:<br>The communications connections between the web browser and WGate, WGate and AGate, and between AGate and the application server are not encrypted. |
| | Impact | When accessing the application server through the ITS, authentication data — like user IDs and passwords — is transferred (the access through the SAP ITS involves the same authentication process for a user as the SAP GUI access). Because this data is not encrypted properly, it can be eavesdropped on and then used for an unauthorized logon. The possible effects of this can be extremely negative for the company. |
| | Risk without control(s) | Extremely high |
| | Control | Encryption of all communication paths between the web browser, WGate, and AGate up to the application server. |
| | Risk with control(s) | Normal |
| | Section | Encrypting Communications Connections in Section 14.3.4 |
| 5. | Potential risk | The selected passwords are too simple:<br>The passwords selected for authenticating to the application server through SAP ITS are too simple. This weakens the entire authentication process. |
| | Impact | Passwords that are too obvious make it easier for attackers to get access to the application server. The possible effects of this can be extremely negative for the company. |
| | Risk without control(s) | High |
| | Control | Implementation of a stronger authentication process based on X.509 certificates for application server users. The certificates can be managed by a company-specific public key infrastructure. |
| | Risk with control(s) | Low |
| | Section | Setting Up a Certificate-Based Authentication Process in Section 14.3.4 |

**Table 14.3** Risks and Controls for SAP ITS (Cont.)

| No. | Classification | Description |
|---|---|---|
| 6. | Potential risk | Too many passwords are being used: The users of the application server must memorize a separate password for each individual application. For this reason, they either choose structured passwords, or write down the individual system access data on a piece of paper that they keep somewhere near the local PC. |
| | Impact | Passwords that are too obvious make it easier for attackers to get access to the application server. It will be even easier for them if they can use the passwords that have been written down on the piece of paper. The possible effects of this can be extremely negative for the company. |
| | Risk without control(s) | High |
| | Control | Implementation of an SSO process using the Pluggable Authentication Service (PAS) that's available for SAP ITS. This service enables the integration of the authentication with an external authentication service such as the Windows domain. |
| | Risk with control(s) | Normal |
| | Section | Setting Up an Authentication Service in Section 14.3.4 |

**Table 14.3** Risks and Controls for SAP ITS (Cont.)

### 14.3.3 Application Security

This section describes in more detail the risks and controls that are outlined in Table 14.3 with regard to application security.

#### Defining Access Rights for Service Files

Service files, HTML templates, and flow files are stored on the AGate server in a directory structure of the operating system. Those files must be protected against unauthorized access. For this reason, the access rights for the files must be defined correctly.

The rights are set during the installation process for the SAP ITS. Table 14.4 provides an overview of the available security levels.

| Security Level | OS User Group | Access Rights | Assessment |
|---|---|---|---|
| ITS Administration Group only (high) | ITS administration | Read and write access to all ITS files | This is the highest level of security. Only the SAP ITS administration group can modify all files. All other OS administrators are granted read-only access. This configuration must therefore be used for production systems or for production-related QA systems. |
| | All others | Read access to all ITS files | |
| ITS Administration Group and ITS Users (medium) | ITS administration | Read and write access to all ITS files | This is a medium level of security. In addition to the ITS administration group, which still keeps its full access rights, ITS users are granted partial write access to service files. These users are ITS developers who are defined as a group in the operating system. All other OS administrators are granted read-only access. This configuration should be used for development systems. |
| | ITS Users (developers) | Read access to all ITS files and write access to selected service files and HTML templates that must be edited by a team of developers. | |
| | All others | Read-only access to all ITS files | |
| Everyone (low) | All | Read and write access to all ITS files | This is a low level of security. In this case, all OS administrators are granted write access to all files of the ITS. This level should only be used for internal, non-production-related sandbox systems on the intranet that don't provide access to security-critical applications. |

**Table 14.4** Access Rights for SAP ITS Files

### Administration Concept

The SAP ITS is administrated through a dedicated web application. This administration console must be specified as a service and, as all other services, defined in the file *admin.srvc*. The service can be called via the following sample URL:

*http://www.example.com:1080/scripts/wgate/admin!*

By default, the administration service is called through port 1080. In an Internet usage scenario, this port must be blocked in the external firewall.

The default superadministrator is called `itsadmin`. This name cannot be changed. The superadministrator has full authorization over the SAP ITS administration. It represents the only user account that is authorized to create new administrators for the SAP ITS. For that reason, it is imperative that the default password for the superadministrator be changed immediately after the installation is completed. You should choose a complex password. No more than two administrators, a main administrator and an assistant, should know the details for the `itsadmin` user. If possible, you should ensure that access to the `itsadmin` user is restricted by applying the four-eyes principle. Technically, this is not supported and must therefore be implemented with guidelines at the organizational level.

The administrators created by `itsadmin` are also granted full access to the ITS files and configurations; however, they cannot create any new administrators. But those administrators do have an important authorization — the starting and stopping of the respective SAP ITS instance. Furthermore, because they can restrict the administration right at the SAP ITS instance, the assignment of an administration account should be very restrictive.

In addition, a read-only administration account can be set up for support desk employees who are responsible for performing error searches. Such a read-only administration account enables them to view the SAP ITS files and to check the operational status of the SAP ITS. The read access can also be restricted at the level of SAP ITS instances.

The entire SAP ITS administration assignment occurs at the operating system level, for example, in the Windows registry for a Windows server. The exact definition is described in the SAP ITS manuals.

### 14.3.4 Technical Security

This section describes in more detail the risks and controls that are outlined in Table 14.3 with regard to technical security.

#### Installing a DMZ Network Segmentation

Due to the existing logical separation of WGate and AGate, a DMZ concept can be easily set up (see Figure 14.5). The WGate, which is directly connected to the web server as an Information Server Application Programming Interface (ISAPI, in the case of Microsoft IIS), is located in DMZ 1. Internet access must be configured so that only the web server, including WGate, can be addressed via TCP/IP port 80 or 443 (if HTTPS is configured). All other ports must be blocked in the external firewall.

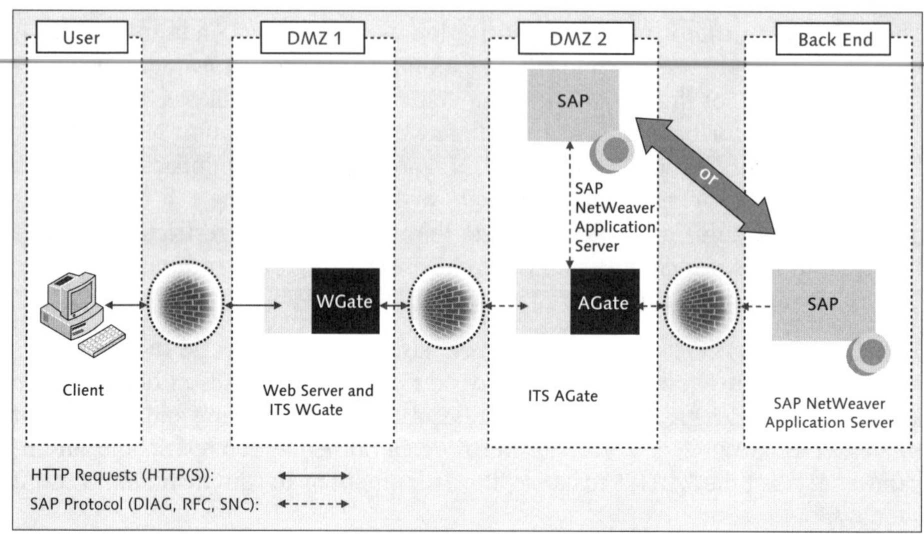


**Figure 14.5** DMZ Network Concept with SAP ITS

The communication between WGate and AGate must also be restricted with the internal firewall to such an extent that communication is only possible between those two servers. Typically, you must configure TCP/IP port 3900 for this (that is, for the first AGate; for AGate clusters, 3901 must be used for the next one, then 3902, and so on).

You can implement an additional security layer by establishing an additional firewall separation between AGate and the application server. In that case, the communication can be restricted even further to a permitted communications connection between AGate and the application server. We recommend this option if the back-end application has a high need for protection.

Another option is to connect the AGate directly with the application server within the same network zone (for example, DMZ 2). That application server can then establish communication with critical back-end applications via RFC connections. That way, you can implement a very detailed structure of permitted communications connections. Moreover, at the network level, you can set up a cascading protection if you so choose.

### Encrypting Communications Connections

As already indicated in Figure 14.5, you can encrypt all communications connections between the client and WGate, WGate and AGate, and between AGate and the application server. This enables you to meet two additional security requirements: You can establish protection against unauthorized access to the data being transferred, and an additional mutual authentication at the technical level between WGate and AGate and between AGate and the application server. The increased stringency of the authentication process is attained by using the digital certificates that are required for encryption according to the X.509 standard.

### HTTPS between Client and WGate

The encryption between the client (web browser) and the WGate can be achieved by using HTTPS. The configuration depends on the web server being used. If you use Microsoft IIS, you must request a digital certificate from a certificate authority, which must then be imported. Once the certificate has been imported, the communications can be switched to HTTPS for the WGate service in a few configuration steps. You can also configure the WGate service to only use HTTPS.

### SNC between WGate and AGate

The SNC connection between WGate and AGate can be established in the same way as the connection between AGate and the application server. In the following text, we'll describe this in more detail. To establish SNC, you must first install the default SAP Cryptographic Library (SAPCRYPTOLIB) in all SAP ITS components, that is, in WGate, AGate, and on the application server. The communications connections can be encrypted according to the Generic Security Services Application Program Interface (GSSAPI) standard only by using the cryptographic programs contained in that library.

Here, you must consider whether you want to use the PSE to assign a certificate to each ITS component (WGate and AGate), or if you want to assign a separate certificate to each component. The advantage of using a PSE, and therefore only one certificate, is that the configuration is less complex and the trust relationship between the ITS components is automatically established. The disadvantage of such a solution is that if the WGate is compromised by an external attack, the trust relationship can be exploited so that the attack can be extended to the back-end application. We therefore recommend that you assign a separate PSE to each component and establish a mutual trust relationship by exchanging the certificates among the ITS components. This is the only way can you establish a technical mutual authentication between the components.

#### SNC between AGate and Application Server

To establish an SNC connection between AGate and application server, you must perform the following steps:

- On the application server:
  - Install the SAPCRYPTOLIB and the license key. Typically, the SAPCRYPTOLIB is copied into the executing directory while the license key is copied into the instance directory. Then, you must set the profile parameters `sec/libsapsecu` and `ssf/ssfapi_lib` to the installation directory of the executing directory.
  - Start the Trust Manager (Transaction STRUST) to set up the PSE for SNC. In the Trust Manager, you must request a digital certificate with a distinguished name for the application server. Once the certificate authority has signed the certificate, you can import it using Transaction STRUST. This step ensures that the application server is assigned a unique digital identity (distinguished name) for the SNC connection.
  - Establish the trust relationship with AGate using the Trust Manager. To do this, the public certificate in the Trust Manager must be imported under the SNC-based PSE to the list for trustworthy certificates using Transaction STRUST.
  - Specify the AGate that is granted access to the application server in table `SNCSYSACL`. You can do this by using Transaction SM30 (Table Maintenance), Transaction SNC0, or Report RSUSR300. The AGate must be defined as an external system with its entire distinguished name.
- Perform the following steps in the AGate using the administration tool for SAP ITS:
  - Install the SAPCRYPTOLIB.
  - Set up an SNC-based PSE using the administration tool. We recommend that you create a separate PSE for the AGate. Access to that PSE is protected by an additional Personal Identification Number (PIN).
  - Save the PSE name of the AGate in the server registry. This is also done using the administration tool.
  - Import the public certificate of the application server (which you must first export there using Transaction STRUST) following the ADVANCED PKI OPERATIONS • IMPORT TRUSTED CERTIFICATE menu path. This way, you can establish a trust relationship with the application server.
  - Then you must maintain the SNC name of the application server in the SAP Connection Maintenance of the administration tool.
  - Restart the AGate at the operating system level.

The SNC connection can be used once the AGate has been restarted. If any problems arise, you can delete the contents of the `sncNameR3` parameter, which results in a deactivation of the SNC connection.

### Setting Up a Certificate-Based Authentication Process

Users who log on to the back-end application of an SAP system via the SAP ITS can do so via their user ID and password, which is similar to the logon procedure via SAP GUI, or by using a digital certificate based on the X.509 standard. In the latter case, however, they will inevitably have to set up an HTTPS connection between the web browser and the web server, including the WGate, which forces a client authentication (mutual authentication). Furthermore, it is advisable that all communications connections — up to and including the application server using SNC — be encrypted.

This mechanism is shown in Figure 14.6. In this context, it is important that the user possesses a digital certificate issued by a trustworthy certificate authority that is either stored as software in the web browser or on a hardware component such as a smart card.

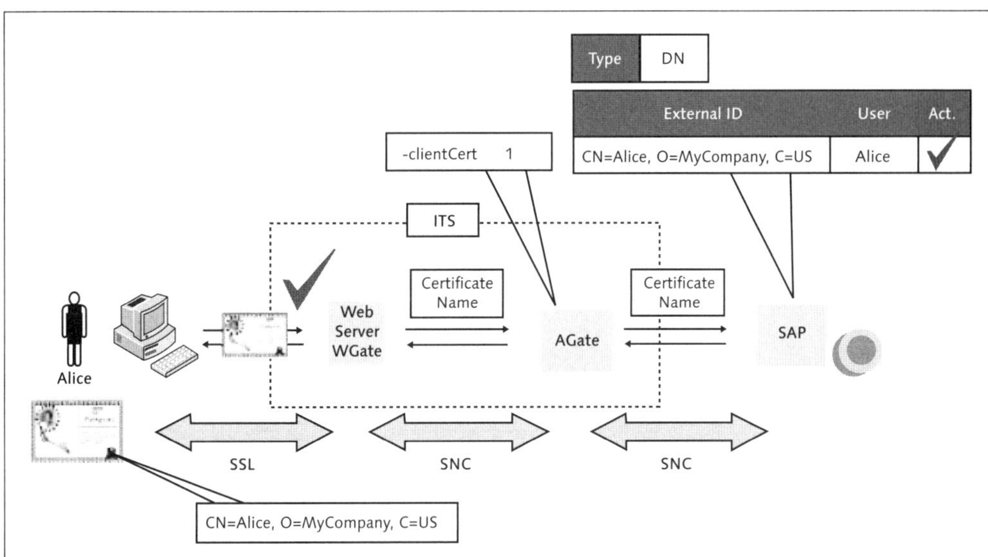


**Figure 14.6** Certificate-Based Logon via SAP Internet Transaction Server

To enable a certificate-based strong authentication via the SAP ITS, you must set the SAP ITS parameter `~clientCert` to the value `1` using the administration tool. Moreover, you must ensure that the distinguished name is synchronized with the user ID that is stored in the application server. For example, the user ID could be ALICE. This synchronization must be done in Table USREXTID, which, for example, can either be managed via Transaction SM30 or by using Report RSUSREXTID, if a lot of users are involved. Once the entries have been activated, the certificate-based user authentication can be used.

To use this option in an enterprise scenario, you should consider using a public key infrastructure, because the digital certificates must be securely managed. A public key infrastructure is most efficient when interacting with an identity and access management solution, because this system is then responsible for distributing the certificates. In that case, all of the identities that are included in the SAP system network are managed centrally.

### Setting Up an Authentication Service

Another option to consider when you want to authenticate users is integrating the SAP ITS authentication mechanism with an external authentication service such as the Windows Kerberos authentication. To do that, you can use the Pluggable Authentication Service (PAS). As shown in Figure 14.7, here, the system trusts an external authentication instance during the authentication process. This way, an additional SSO mechanism is used for distributed SAP applications, because the authentication process is always controlled by the SAP ITS.

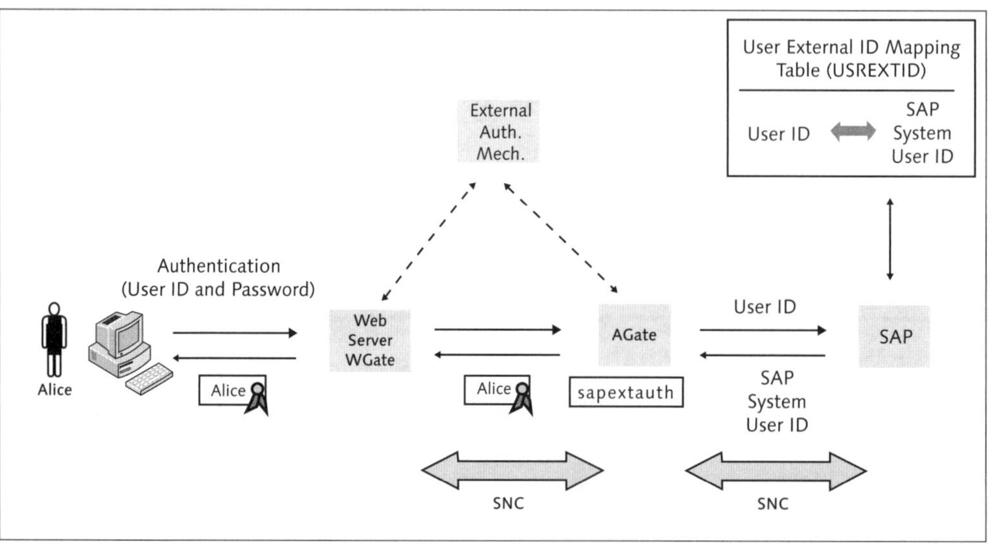


**Figure 14.7** PAS using SAP ITS

The user authentication process functions as follows:

1. The user calls the PAS by entering the corresponding URL.
2. The user enters his credentials for the PAS (for example, a Windows user ID and password).
3. The PAS verifies the user ID and the password. If the details are correct, the user is transferred to the SAP system, which issues an SAP logon ticket (see Chapter 9, SAP NetWeaver Application Server, and Chapter 16, SAP NetWeaver Portal).
4. The SAP system runs a comparison between the external user credentials and the SAP user ID. If the user is also stored as an SAP user, the corresponding SAP system issues an SAP logon ticket, the validity of which is confirmed by a digital signature using the system PSE. The SAP logon ticket is returned as a cookie to the user's web browser.
5. The AGate redirects the user to the SAP system the user had originally requested to access.

The benefit of this process is that the user doesn't need to log on to any other SAP systems. Nevertheless, you should ensure that all communications connections are encrypted; otherwise, potential attackers could be enabled to sniff the SAP logon ticket and hijack the already authenticated logon.

The PAS is available for the standalone ITS 6.20 version for Windows operating systems (Windows NT, 2000 - 2008, and XP). Additional PAS modules are available for a Lightweight Directory Access Protocol (LDAP) bind and X-509 certification services. With SAP NetWeaver 7.0 for the integrated ITS version, the PAS concept was replaced by the enhanced and operating system–independent Java Authentication and Authorization Service (JAAS) (see Chapter 9, SAP NetWeaver Application Server). For ITS 6.20, you can set up the PAS for the WGate or the AGate. You must perform the following steps:

1. Install the PAS module, for example, for Windows (*ntauth.sar*), in the SAP ITS installation directories, *services* and *templates*.
2. Set the following parameters:
   - `~xgateway sapextauth`
     Activates the external authentication.
   - `~extauthtype <NTLM, NTPassword, LDAP, X509, HTTP, DLL>`
     Defines the type of external authentication service.
   - `~extid_type <NT>, <LD>, <UN>, or <user-defined>`
     Defines which user ID is to be returned by the external service, for example, NT ID, or SAP user ID, if `UN` is set.

- `~mysapcomgetsso2cookie 1`
  Defines the acceptance of the SAP logon ticket.
- `~dont_recreate_ticket 1`
  Indicates that the SAP logon ticket is not reissued.
- `~redirectHost <host_name>`
  Name of the SAP system the user is redirected to after a successful authentication.
- `~redirectPath <Path>`
  Defines the path to which the user is redirected.
- `~redirectQS <host_name>`
  Defines the logon parameters for the SAP system the user is redirected to, for example, `client`.
- `~redirectHttps 1`
  Defines that HTTPS is used for the redirection.
- `~login_to_upcase 1`
  Specifies that the entries in table `USREXTID` are maintained using only uppercase letters.

3. Maintain the comparison table for external user IDs and SAP user IDs in table `USREXTID` of the SAP system that issues the SAP logon ticket. To do this, use Transaction SM30 or Report `RSUSREXTID`.

Once you have set these parameters and made all of the necessary settings, you can use SAP ITS to perform an external, delegated authentication. You should note that it is important to ensure that the SAP user IDs are consistently maintained in all accessible SAP systems; otherwise, the mechanism won't work.

*This chapter describes Information Technology (IT) security concepts for SAP NetWeaver Master Data Management (MDM). In this context, it describes sample Best Practices for controlling MDM applications.*

# 15 SAP NetWeaver Master Data Management

Master data, that is, information on employees, customers, suppliers, and materials, is the central type of data that is used and processed in business processes. For this reason, it is subject to specific control requirements. The information that is classified as master data must always be correct, available, and up to date.

Along with transaction data, master data determines the flow of information and actions within an enterprise. A decentralized access to the same master data information is a critical requirement in daily business and administrative processes. It is extremely important to protect master data to ensure the dataset and continuity of business processes that involve the processing of master data, but also because it is critical to the overall success of a company and therefore of internal and external interest.

## 15.1 Introduction and Functions

SAP NetWeaver MDM is used to centrally create, consolidate, and distribute all of the master data that's required in a company's heterogeneous SAP system landscape. SAP NetWeaver MDM, for example, can be used to manage purchasing processes that involve customer, supplier, material, and other types of master data. All of the different departments involved must be able to access the same set of data. The administration of employee and HR data in SAP NetWeaver MDM is another example.

Because customer and supplier data must be protected according to data protection laws, central master data systems are subject to various control measures. SAP NetWeaver MDM can collect and centrally manage data from other systems and also create new data and make it available to other systems (see Figure 15.1).

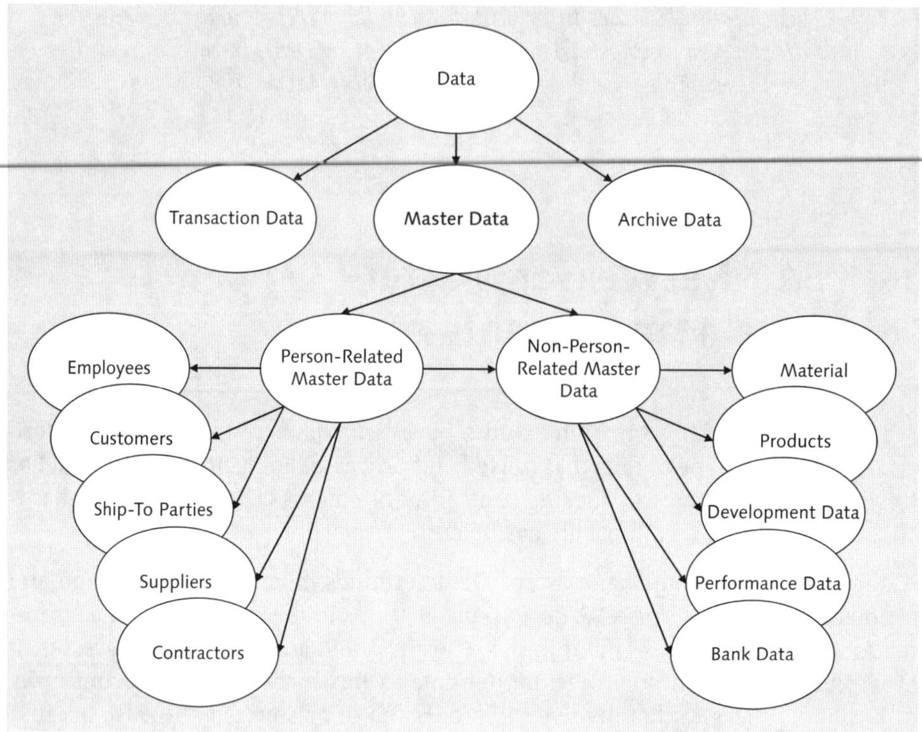


**Figure 15.1** Examples of Master Data

## 15.2 Risks and Controls

Master data such as material data, product development data, or research results involves different risks. The main risks include:

- **Creation of customers as consumers using reference customers in the different SAP systems**
  Mapping and data accesses — the use of master data information in distributed systems can lead to inconsistencies if no central data management system like SAP NetWeaver MDM is used.
- **Distributed master data management**
  Data integrity cannot be attained due to user rights with too many authorizations — master data can be changed by too many users and therefore be processed with errors.

- **Central data storage**
  If authentications and authorizations are violated, many activities enable access to master data, where it can then be manipulated.
- **Numerous systems**
  Typically, central master data systems store the biggest quantity of master data in a company. Therefore, backup and restore systems are particularly important. Neglecting the security of these systems can result in a loss of data integrity and, worst of all, a loss of information.

Personal master data is another central risk. This includes all data that pertains to an individual person. The management of human resources (HR) and partner data also requires adherence to regional data protection laws to ensure a high level of data protection. The following data protection objectives are important in this context:

- Personal master data must be protected using authentication and authorization controls and security measures like encryption and secure communications.
- Personal data can only be managed by a limited number of specifically trained employees. Access to personal data must be limited to auditors so they can retrace the data history. This also includes administrator authorizations.
- Persons on whom data is stored must be allowed to view this data at any time and be informed about any unauthorized attempts to use this data for purposes other than those for which they are intended.
- Adherence to legal regulations is equally important for the company. Control objectives like ensuring integrity, availability, and traceability must be attained by implementing an internal control system. The integration of SAP NetWeaver MDM into this control system is a requirement.
- As soon as personal data has fulfilled its information storage purpose, and as soon as the end of the determined storage period is reached, the data must be permanently deleted. These requirements are met by archiving solutions.

Personal master data contains data that must be protected due to its high degree of sensitivity. Among other information, such data includes details on an employee's origin, political opinion, medical data, and their cooperation with a trade union. For the affected people, this data is very important and must therefore be specifically considered when choosing the appropriate protection measures (see Chapter 21, SAP ERP Human Capital Management and Data Protection). SAP NetWeaver MDM provides a configuration that meets these data protection requirements.

Other risks for SAP NetWeaver MDM, which are described in detail in the following sections, are listed as examples in Table 15.1.

| No. | Classification | Description |
|---|---|---|
| 1. | Risk potential | Inadequate authorization concept:<br>Master data users have full authorization for maintaining specific types of master data, although they should only have partial authorizations. Due to change authorizations, users can change data they have access rights for although they aren't authorized to do so. This can result in data inconsistencies and a violation of the master data integrity. |
| | Impact | The effects comprise disruptions of daily business processes, costly data cleansing measures, and even the complete loss of master data information, including the related process history. |
| | Risk without control(s) | High |
| | Control | Authorizations are restricted, and a well-organized management system only assigns them to those users whose positions require the corresponding activities as well. |
| | Risk with control(s) | Low |
| | Section | 15.3.1 |
| 2. | Risk potential | Inadequate responsibility structure:<br>The technical requirements for solid master data management are met by SAP NetWeaver MDM, however, the task-related and process-related distribution of master data management functions to departments and employees is missing. The risk of noncentral and uncontrollable master data management exists. |
| | Impact | The use of available master data is not protected. Neither the integrity nor completeness of the data, nor its correctness and up-to-dateness is protected. This affects all processes that involve master data. For example, the integrity of pricing information is no longer ensured, which affects follow-up processes. |
| | Risk without control(s) | Extremely high |
| | Control | Implementation and consistent penetration of the information ownership principle to ensure an efficient control of master data using an effective authorization system |
| | Risk with control(s) | Low |

**Table 15.1** Risks and Controls for SAP NetWeaver MDM

| No. | Classification | Description |
|---|---|---|
| | Section | 15.3.1 |
| 3. | Risk potential | Personal data:<br>Master data that is directly or indirectly related to persons (for example, employees, business partners, consultants, and so on) is subject to legal, internal, and ethical requirements. The protection of this data is completely or at least partly jeopardized by insecure authentication, inaccurate user rights, and insufficiently secured interfaces and communication channels. |
| | Impact | The effects involve the theft of information, the manipulation of personal master data, and the circulation of data to unauthorized third parties. |
| | Risk without control(s) | High |
| | Control | The integrity of technical and process-related controls for the protection of data in SAP NetWeaver MDM and master data in the connected systems is an integral part of an internal control system and ensures the protection and compliance of business-relevant master data. |
| | Risk with control(s) | Low |
| | Section | 15.3.1 |
| 4. | Risk potential | Inconsistent master data:<br>The different user management options in an SAP MDM landscape enable the versatile usage of these systems. This involves the potential risk of inconsistent identity management. |
| | Impact | Internal and external users are wrongfully authorized to use systems they shouldn't have access to. The datasets in the different SAP systems don't match. Administration, monitoring, and control become increasingly difficult and are constrained, and therefore, it takes more time and a greater expense to carry out these responsibilities. |
| | Risk without control(s) | High |
| | Control | Implementation and use of a user management system |

**Table 15.1** Risks and Controls for SAP NetWeaver MDM (Cont.)

| No. | Classification | Description |
|---|---|---|
| | Risk with control(s) | Low |
| | Section | 15.3.1 |
| 5. | Risk potential | Anonymous user actions:<br>In SAP NetWeaver MDM, generic users can be defined for the distribution of master data. SAP NetWeaver MDM users who carry out these actions remain anonymous in the change documents. |
| | Impact | Changes to master data can no longer be controlled. This means that using a generic user in SAP NetWeaver MDM enables a person to change or create master data, and the change documents don't indicate any information on the responsible person. |
| | Risk without control(s) | High |
| | Control | The relevant configuration table must contain the ID of the generic user. |
| | Risk with control(s) | Low |
| | Section | 15.3.1 |
| 6. | Risk potential | Inadequately configured communication connections:<br>A large number of RFC and HTTP communication connections to the SAP systems must be configured particularly for SAP NetWeaver MDM. The internal link between SAP NetWeaver MDM and SAP Content Integrator (CI), which runs on Application Server (AS) Java, is based on HTTP and represents an important and very sensitive connection. |
| | Impact | Incorrectly configured RFC connections can easily be compromised by attackers. The internal connection is also used for exchanging highly sensitive master data. If this data is compromised, data inconsistencies in the connected systems can be the result. This endangers the proper operation of the business to a great extent. |
| | Risk without control(s) | High |

**Table 15.1** Risks and Controls for SAP NetWeaver MDM (Cont.)

| No. | Classification | Description |
|---|---|---|
| | Control | Correct configuration of RFC communication destinations and restriction of RFC system user authorizations. In addition, SNC and HTTPS should be used to encrypt the communications connections. |
| | Risk with control(s) | Low |
| | Section | 15.4.1 |

**Table 15.1** Risks and Controls for SAP NetWeaver MDM (Cont.)

## 15.3 Application Security

To ensure the integrity of business transactions and the presentation of information, master data on employees from different departments, subsidiaries of the company, and different geographical regions must always be up to date and complete.

### 15.3.1 Identity Management and Authorizations

Managing authorizations and users involves the use of different components. SAP NetWeaver MDM uses both the authorization concepts in AS ABAP and the J2EE roles in the Java area. Roles and worksets are used in SAP NetWeaver MDM to assign application rights to users.

#### Identity Management

SAP solutions like a central SAP ERP HCM, a Central User Administration (CUA), or external solutions with Lightweight Directory Access Protocol (LDAP) directory services/Active Directory can be used as identity management solutions. In this context, user data is created either in an LDAP directory, in the SAP NetWeaver MDM user administration, or in SAP NetWeaver Portal or the integrated UME.

If an LDAP server and SAP NetWeaver Portal are used, the LDAP synchronization between AS ABAP — for example, CUA — and the LDAP must be configured, which enables the synchronization of data between the back-end system and the LDAP. The administration of the SAP NetWeaver Portal users must be set to LDAP with Read/Write to make sure users can be created and user attributes and passwords can be changed via the UME of the portal. User master data can be managed in SAP NetWeaver Portal, in AS ABAP, or in the LDAP directory service. For consistency, user data should only be modified at one location.

Users can also be administrated with CUA and without an LDAP service. The CUA can, for instance, be set up in SAP NetWeaver MDM — a scenario that represents the logical consequence of the master data concept. Users that have been created in the UME of SAP NetWeaver Portal can also be distributed to the CUA of the connected systems. Therefore, the RFC destinations, technical users with specific standard SAP roles, and CUA subsystems must be defined in the CUA of SAP NetWeaver MDM (Transaction SCUA). This configuration makes it impossible to maintain individual users in the CUA subsystems.

Another option for managing users in SAP NetWeaver MDM is the integration of SAP CI to transfer roles from AS ABAP to the J2EE Engine. The UME administration option of SAP CI also lets you update the roles in the portal. In SAP NetWeaver Portal, users are assigned portal roles that let them generate the portal menu. In the SAP systems (for instance, SAP NetWeaver MDM, SAP Solution Manager), all SAP MDM users are assigned the relevant roles of the back-end. In the SAP CI user administration, UME roles can be assigned in the UME of the relevant J2EE server.

#### Roles

In SAP NetWeaver MDM, authorizations are defined via roles and then assigned to the different users. Three different types of roles are used as:

- ABAP roles
- Portal roles
- CI roles

If synchronized, these roles provide the required user authorizations.

During the installation of SAP CI, the SAP CI roles are synchronized with the AS ABAP roles that are available as groups in the UME of SAP CI. Because the AS ABAP roles are also synchronized with the SAP NetWeaver Portal roles, all roles required for the SAP MDM systems are synchronized and can be used (see Figure 15.2).

The following portal roles can be used in the standard SAP version:

- `com.sap.pct.mdm.master_data_administrator`
  for master data administrators

- `com.sap.pct.mdm.master_data_specialist`
  for master data specialists
- `com.sap.pct.mdm.master_data_manager`
  for master data managers
- `com.sap.pct.mdm.local_data_manager`
  for master data managers (local master data)
- `com.sap.pct.mdm.master_data_user`
  for master data users

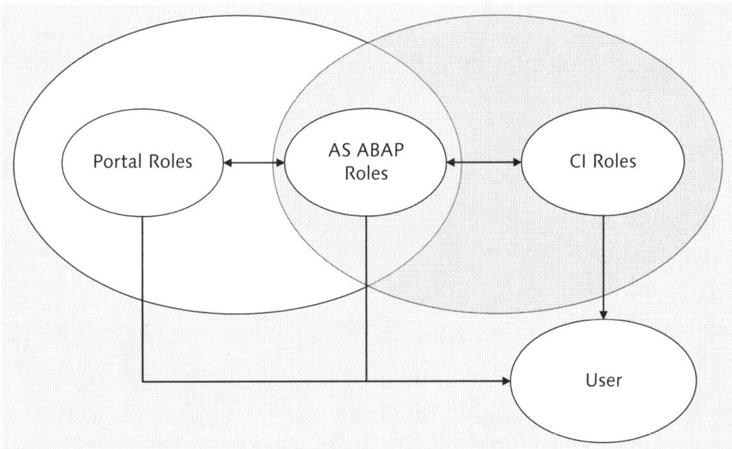


**Figure 15.2** Role Types and Role Synchronization for SAP NetWeaver MDM

When assigning portal roles to users or user groups of SAP NetWeaver Portal, the roles from the data source (for example, SAP NetWeaver MDM) are available as user groups in the UME. The assignment of roles to users in SAP NetWeaver MDM is adopted as an assignment of users to user groups. The link between the portal role and the user group is defined in the UME. This means that in SAP NetWeaver MDM, a user is assigned a role and a corresponding portal role.

SAP NetWeaver MDM users must be assigned the default or equivalent roles `eu_role` and `com.sap.pct.mdm.mdm_default_service` if they are to be granted access to personalization functions in SAP NetWeaver Portal. These roles also control additional functions within SAP NetWeaver MDM. The following composite roles correspond to the portal roles and can be used as templates for customized SAP MDM roles or as usable roles in the standard SAP version:

- `SAP_WP_MDM_MASTER_DATA_ADMIN`
  for master data administrators
- `SAP_WP_MDM_MASTER_DATA_SPEC`
  for master data specialists
- `SAP_WP_MDM_MASTER_DATA_MANAGER`
  for master data managers
- `SAP_WP_MDM_LOCAL_DATA_MANAGER`
  for master data managers (local master data)
- `SAP_WP_MDM_MASTER_DATA_USER`
  for master data users

In addition, the following UME roles in SAP CI can be used in the standard SAP version:

- `CI_MasterDataAdministrator`
  for master data administrators
- `CI_MasterDataSpecialist`
  for master data specialists
- `CI_MasterDataManager`
  for master data managers

The standard SAP version also contains individual roles that are not assigned to any composite roles. Individual and composite roles can be customized according to the requirements of the respective company. In this context, different characteristics and actions can determine and restrict the rights of users. For example, a master data user can be authorized for specific products or business partners.

The Business Server Pages (BSPs) applications (for instance, SAP CRM) use the People-Centric user interface (UI). For this reason, role-dependent links are defined in SAP NetWeaver MDM Customizing. Accordingly, if roles are changed, those changes must also be made in Customizing to ensure that the links continue to function. These settings can be made using Transaction CRMC_BLUEPRINT (URL generation).

In the MDM environment, users are required for creating ID mappings, starting and executing process chains, and sending and receiving messages with SAP NetWeaver PI. These remote users are technical communications users of the user type `C` that execute RFC or Web service calls. For master data management, default SAP roles are available for remote users.

The following default SAP roles are provided as composite roles for remote users of SAP NetWeaver MDM:

- SAP_WP_MDM_REMOTE_ALE_REMOTE (external)
  for outbound and inbound Master Data Server (MDS) and SAP BW data extraction processes
- SAP_WP_MDM_REMOTE_MDM_REMOTE (external)
  for ID mapping (outbound and inbound processes)
- SAP_WP_MDM_REMOTE_CI_REMOTE (external)
  for accessing SAP CI and filling the ID mapping in the master data server (replication)
- SAP_WP_MDM_REMOTE_XI_MDS (external)
  for receiving and processing SAP NetWeaver PI messages in the master data server
- SAP_WP_MDM_MASTER_DATA_ADMIN (external)
  for master data administrators

Table 15.2 lists some examples of user master records to which the composite roles for the remote users listed previously can be assigned in SAP NetWeaver MDM.

| Role in SAP NetWeaver MDM | Technical User |
|---|---|
| SAP_WP_MDM_REMOTE_ALE_REMOTE | ALEREMOTE — As an SAP NetWeaver MDM system user, the ALEREMOTE user is used for communications via Application Link Enabling (ALE). |
| SAP_WP_MDM_REMOTE_MDM | MDM_REMOTE — The MDM_REMOTE user that creates the ID mapping via a web service call from the SAP NetWeaver PI to the MDS is defined in MDS Customizing. |
| SAP_WP_MDM_REMOTE_CI_REMOTE | CIREMOTE — The CIREMOTE user is created during the SAP CI installation process. |
| SAP_WP_MDM_REMOTE_XI_MDS | <MDSsystemname>_XI_LOGON—The user that is required for exchanging messages between SAP NetWeaver PI and the MDS is created during the configuration of PI MDS. This user is defined in a communications channel or in an RFC connection in SAP NetWeaver PI. |

**Table 15.2** SAP NetWeaver MDM Roles for Remote Users

Figure 15.3 illustrates the use of composite roles in SAP NetWeaver MDM for technical remote users in processes that require the same roles.

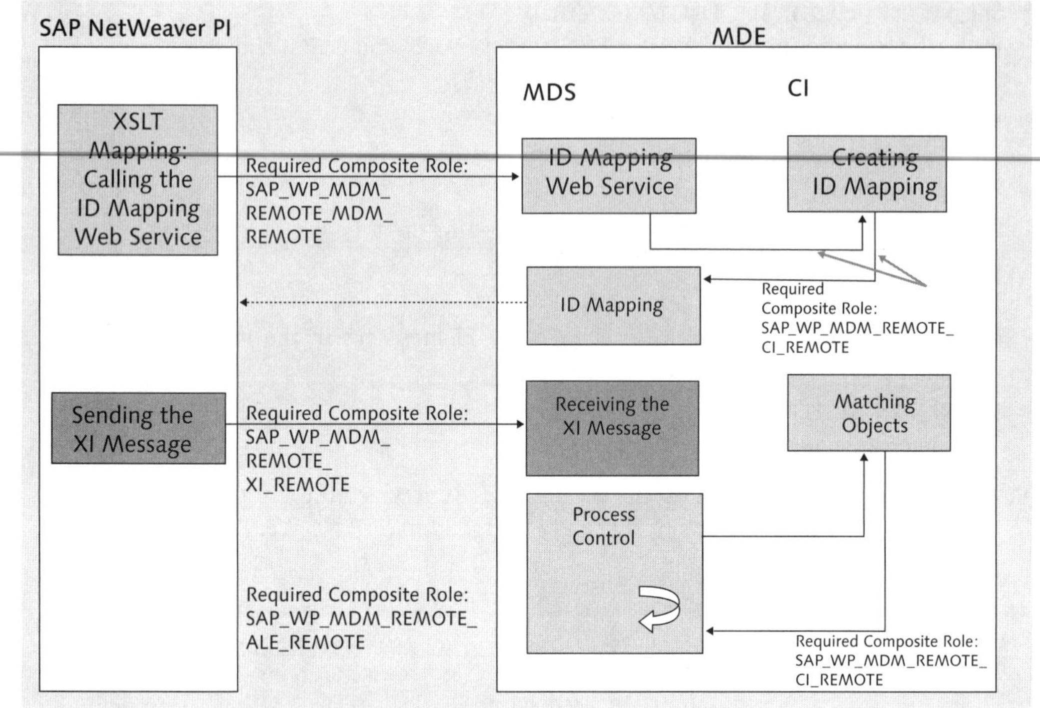


**Figure 15.3** Using Roles for Communications Users in an MDM Landscape

The actions for administrative user rights listed in Table 15.3 are relevant to SAP CI roles.

| Name of CI Role (Technical Name) | Actions in SAP CI |
|---|---|
| Master Data Administrator (`MasterDataAdmin`) | This role enables users to perform the following actions in SAP CI:<br>▸ Performing initial configurations<br>▸ Displaying version information<br>▸ Creating a system in CI<br>▸ Transporting customizing objects<br>▸ Managing jobs<br>▸ Finding ID mappings<br>▸ Displaying category hierarchies<br>▸ Managing identity check settings |

**Table 15.3** CI Roles and Activities

| Name of CI Role (Technical Name) | Actions in SAP CI |
|---|---|
| | ▶ Processing change requests<br>▶ Editing UI customizing<br>▶ Managing default categorization settings |
| Master data manager (`MasterDataManager`) | This role enables users to perform the following actions in SAP CI:<br>▶ Managing jobs<br>▶ Editing category hierarchy mappings<br>▶ Displaying category hierarchies<br>▶ Categorizing products<br>▶ Managing default categorization settings<br>▶ Processing change requests<br>▶ Displaying version information<br>▶ Finding ID mappings<br>▶ Managing identity check settings |
| Master data specialist (`MasterDataSpecialist`) | This role enables users to perform the following actions in SAP CI:<br>▶ Displaying category hierarchies<br>▶ Categorizing products<br>▶ Managing jobs<br>▶ Displaying version information<br>▶ Finding ID mappings |
| `Accessibility` | This role ensures the accessibility of SAP Content Integrator (CI) and must be assigned to the SAP CI UME user groups in addition to the other CI roles, because the accessibility role doesn't enable users to perform any separate actions apart from ensuring the accessibility actions that belong to other SAP CI roles. |

**Table 15.3** CI Roles and Activities (Cont.)

The following SAP CI roles can be assigned to the user groups of the UME during the installation of SAP CI:

- **`MasterDataAdmin`**
  This role is assigned to the UME user group `SAP_WP_MDM_MASTER_DATA_ADMIN`
- **`MasterDataManager`**
  This role is assigned to the UME user group `SAP_WP_MDM_MASTER_DATA_MANAGER`

- `MasterDataSpecialist`
  is assigned to the UME user group SAP_WP_MDM_MASTER_DATA_SPEC

### 15.3.2 Revision Security

In SAP NetWeaver MDM, generic users are also defined for the distribution of master data. It is possible to define more than one generic user for the inbound distribution process, which facilitates the search for business partners according to change document criteria.

Some change documents are not generated with a specific user ID of SAP NetWeaver MDM, but with a generic user of the application. If a business partner change is distributed by the Master Data Client (MDC), the change record is generated with a generic user. The ID of the user who performed the change is not displayed. If the object is changed during staging, the revision entry is also generated with a generic user ID. If you want to include the entries in the search result, the configuration table must contain the ID of this generic user. The user who is responsible for the distribution is defined as a generic user in Customizing.

The integrative examples from the Enterprise Risk Management (ERM) Navigation Control Map emphasize the importance of a holistic view of the SAP NetWeaver components for defining and implementing the necessary security and control measures. In addition to the technical authorizations and finding identity management measures, it is imperative that the management processes and master data owners are known to constantly keep potential risks to a minimum.

## 15.4 Technical Security

This section describes in more detail the risks and controls that are outlined in Table 15.1 with regard to technical security.

### 15.4.1 Communication Security

To ensure that SAP NetWeaver MDM operates correctly, a large number of RFC connections to those SAP systems, which are to be included into the central master data management process, is required. In this context, the technical default settings for the SAP Gateway must be considered, and the authorization restrictions for RFC connections described in Chapter 9, SAP NetWeaver AS. Particularly authorizations for the authorization object S_RFC, whose scope is set too wide, can be used to compromise the system, if the RFC user has the type System or Communication. Moreover, the communication connections should be encrypted using SNC, as described in Chapter 9.

In addition, an HTTP-based communication link is used between SAP NetWeaver MDM and SAP CI. Because SAP CI is based on AS Java, the SSL option for the J2EE Engine must be activated; Chapter 9 describes in detail how this can be done. However, the entry for the HTTP provider in the Visual Administrator must be changed.

Usually, the entry looks like this:

```
(Port:50000,Type:http)
(Port:50001,Type:ssl).
```

This means that TCP/IP port 50000 can be used to address AS Java via HTTP, while port 50001 is used for HTTPS connections. The entry must be complemented as follows:

```
(Port:50000,Type:http,BindAddress:127.0.0.1)
(Port:50001,Type:ssl)
```

This in turn means that an internal server communication is used, as the IP address 127.0.0.1 always designates the local server. This way, it can be ensured that communication between SAP NetWeaver MDM (AS ABAP) and SAP CI (AS Java) always occurs internally.

### 15.4.2 Important Additional Components

The technical security of SAP NetWeaver MDM depends on additional components (see the ERM Navigation Control Map). Particularly for SAP NetWeaver MDM, the technical controls of the following applications and solutions should be considered depending on the scenario used:

- SAP NetWeaver AS (see Chapter 9)
- SAP NetWeaver PI (see Chapter 12, SAP NetWeaver Process Integration)
- SAP ITS (see Chapter 14, Classic SAP Middleware)
- SAP NetWeaver Portal (see Chapter 16, SAP NetWeaver Portal)
- SAP Graphical User Interface (GUI) (see Chapter 28, User Interfaces)
- Web browser (see Chapter 28)

*SAP NetWeaver Portal is a central access point for numerous applications and components. For this reason, the access authorizations stored in the portal and the risk management aspects in the portal context assume a central role with regard to security strategies. These are discussed in this chapter.*

# 16 SAP NetWeaver Portal

Like SAP NetWeaver Application Server (AS), SAP NetWeaver Portal plays a critical role in the SAP NetWeaver system architecture. SAP NetWeaver Portal is a central access portal for internal employees and external customers or business partners. Critical applications and information regarding SAP systems and non-SAP applications can be presented using SAP NetWeaver Portal as an internal portal or as a web portal via the Internet. So portal users only need a web browser to start applications. This also enables user access via mobile devices.

## 16.1 Introduction and Functions

SAP NetWeaver Portal assumes three central tasks:

- The portal function itself includes display options and access to data and applications in a web browser–based front end. This includes management functions, such as user management or monitoring.
- Another central function is the collaboration area, that is, all functions that can be used for synchronous and asynchronous collaboration between colleagues, team members, or business partners. This includes instant messaging, emails, forums, wikis, group calendars, and so on.
- The multichannel access option comprises various functions for providing portal content in mobile infrastructures. This includes Personal Digital Assistants (PDAs) or notebooks, for example, which enable access to SAP NetWeaver Portal.

In addition to web-based access to the portal, secure and role-based control options are supposed to be available for the portal, including access to data and information in SAP and non-SAP systems (see Figure 16.1).

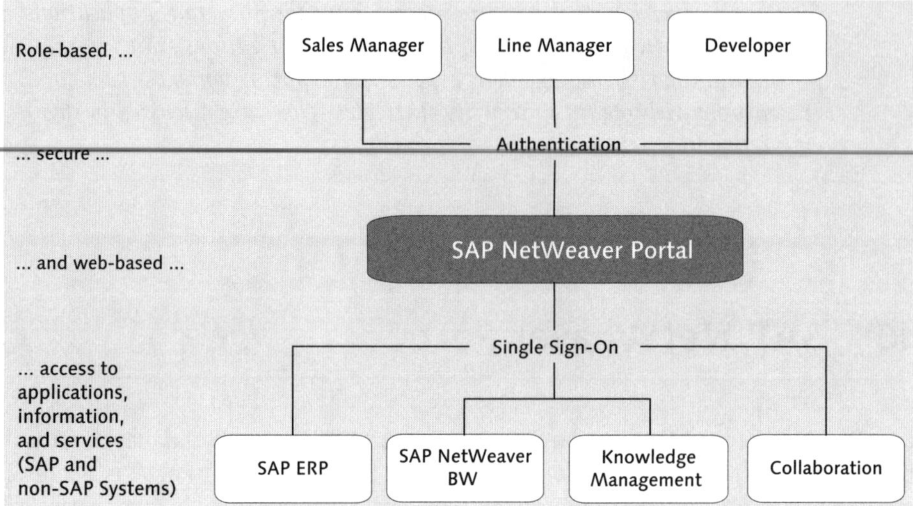


**Figure 16.1** Tasks and Functions in SAP NetWeaver Portal

However, internal and external users of SAP NetWeaver Portal have to undergo identification and authentication processes before they can access the portal. Anonymous access is also possible, but should be sufficiently limited.

A benefit of SAP NetWeaver Portal is the ability to easily implement a Single Sign-On (SSO) mechanism for the associated back-end applications. Users only need to log on once to SAP NetWeaver Portal. SAP NetWeaver Portal then takes over any further authentication to the back-end applications. To do this, the portal can be integrated with the identity management applications that already exist in the company. SSO for SAP applications is based on SAP logon tickets.

In addition to SAP applications, non-SAP applications can also be integrated in SAP NetWeaver Portal. Even links to other external resources can be integrated. In addition, users can customize their content, or they can organize the portal content, like documents, for managing their own information. This makes it possible to integrate a knowledge management functionality in the portal.

The authorization concept for controlling access to portal content and portal functions is based on portal roles and portal user groups to which portal users are assigned. In contrast to the known ABAP authorization concept (Profile Generator, Transaction PFCG), portal roles consist of portal-typical elements. These authorization-determining elements are, for example, iView, Portal Page, Workset, and Access Control Lists (ACL). The elements are considered parts of the portal content and managed in SAP NetWeaver Portal at the organizational level.

### 16.1.1 Technical Architecture

In Release 7.0, two different usage types of SAP NetWeaver Portal are used. They provide the portal users with the respective applications and tools:

- **EP Core usage type**
  The EP Core usage type provides the main functions of SAP NetWeaver Portal, that is, the actual portal, including its standardized interface and basic portal functions.
- **EP usage type**
  The EP usage type is a subarea that contains additional functions and add-on functions, such as collaboration, knowledge management, and so on.

Regarding the security risks and risk management, both usage types are identical; both types are often used in parallel anyway.

Furthermore, all security risks of the SAP NetWeaver AS Java must be considered because SAP NetWeaver Portal is based on AS Java (see Chapter 9, SAP NetWeaver AS). Along with other software components, AS Java forms the entire portal framework. This architecture is illustrated in Figure 16.2. The following text briefly introduces the essential components.

- **Portal server**
  The portal server contains the portal's runtime environment, and the portal runtime, including the application information that is partially returned by the back-end applications (for example, via XML) or other portal content, which is prepared accordingly for the front end (web browser) in the Page Builder. The various content is provided to the users in iViews. An iView is the smallest unit for controlling authorizations and structuring portal pages.

  Portal services comprise the services for managing the iView content. User management (definition of authorizations and roles) via the User Management Engine (UME, see Section 16.1.2, Description of the UME) is significant as well. Another service manages the connections of the individual iViews to the back-end applications via the Connector Framework.

  Other important services include those that provide the navigation service for the entire portal content, the caching service, the portal content handling service, the URL generation service (for example, via SAP Internet Transaction Server (ITS), see Chapter 14, Classic SAP Middleware), and the web service. The latter can be used to access the portal via web services. In turn, it is also possible to call web services. The Portal Content Directory is used to manage the content, that is, all objects (for example, iViews, roles, content, applications, back-end applications). The Portal Content Directory sets the portal roles and their accesses to the individual objects and defines the services that can be called.

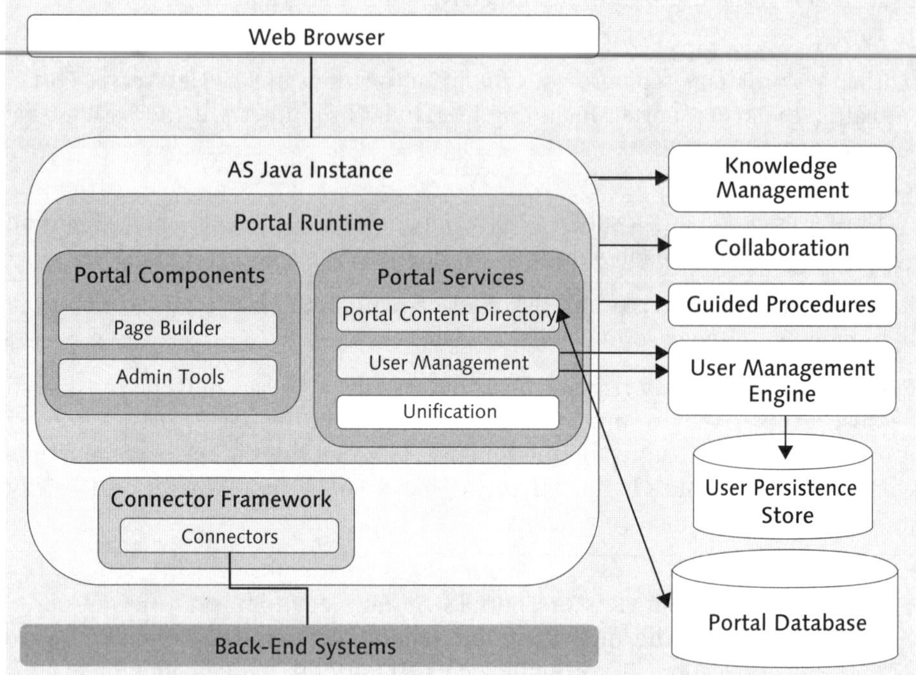


**Figure 16.2** SAP NetWeaver Portal Architecture

- **Knowledge management**
  Knowledge management is an additional component that contains content management, that is, portal content management using administration tools (for creating iViews, layouts, documents, etc.), and the TREX search and classification engine. TREX is the SAP search engine that creates an index across the entire portal content and can be used to search the portal content for keywords or logically related terms. Users can then store the documents and information in the portal for their own information management.
- **Connector Framework**
  The Connector Framework is based on the standardized Java Connection Architecture (JCA). This framework can be used to connect the applications running in the portal to other back-end applications. Connectors for this purpose are already available (for example, for R/3 back-end applications). Connectors can

also be called via Web services and can be used to connect iViews to the back-end applications. The connectors provide an integration form that is independent of the respective back-end application so that the programmer can focus entirely on developing the business logic.

### 16.1.2 Description of the UME

In the portal environment, it is crucial to have a basic understanding of the UME, because this architecture service controls all management of users and their authorizations in SAP NetWeaver Portal. Additional knowledge is also important, because many of the technical controls are implemented using the UME. The UME is usually used with a user-friendly standard user interface for user management within SAP NetWeaver Portal, that is, for assigning portal users, portal groups, and portal roles. This standard user interface enables general manual user management, for example. If they are not managed automatically, Application Programming Interfaces (API) must be controlled via programs.

Figure 16.3 presents an overview of all of the architecture services provided by the UME. The central layer provides the application programming interfaces based on Java that are required by the portal applications (for example, Java-based iViews) to perform, for example, the authentication of a user or to maintain the related master data via automatic programs. These programming interfaces are the following:

- **User API**
  Using the User API, a portal application can call authentication services for existing users and validate their authorization.
- **User Account API**
  The User Account API enables the portal application to create new users, to maintain their master data, and to assign their portal roles, among other things. The User Account API is therefore implemented for management services and — unlike the User API — is not used at runtime.
- **Group API**
  The Group API can be used to create portal user group definitions. Even at runtime, you can query if a user belongs to a specific portal group.
- **Role API**
  The Role API serves for managing the portal roles. It can also be used to assign the portal roles to the users.

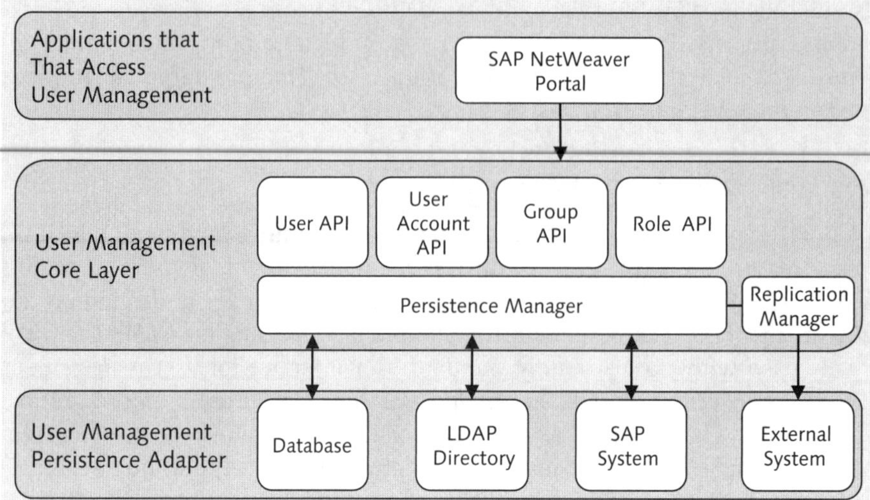


**Figure 16.3** Architecture of the UME

The Persistence Manager controls access to user data via the programming interfaces described. The Persistence Manager performs the task of managing the available storage systems. As persistence storage, the portal database, an external Lightweight Directory Access Protocol (LDAP) directory (for example, identity management systems that already exist in the company), an AS ABAP (for example, of the SAP back-end system), or SAP NetWeaver Identity Management (IdM) can be implemented.

The Persistence Manager can manage several LDAP directories at a time. You therefore have the option of distributing users among the various user storage systems connected to user management, which is particularly important when implementing SAP NetWeaver Portal in Internet scenarios. For example, external users can be made persistent in the portal database, and internal users can be made persistent in an LDAP directory. It is also possible to make this division according to user attributes. For example, the assignment of the portal role to the user can be stored in the portal database, and the corresponding master data can be stored in the LDAP directory.

This distribution is controlled via an XML file, the data source configuration file, which can be set using the config tool at the operating system level (*<AS_Java_host_name>\j2ee\configtool\configtool.bat*), or using the UME configuration functions via *<http or https>://<AS_Java_host_name>:<AS_Java_HTTP_port>/irj*. It is recommended to use one of the UME data source configuration files delivered by SAP. These configuration files are part of the portal installation files and can be obtained via SAP Note 983808, if required. A customized file can only be defined if none of the specified files meets the requirements.

The name of the data source configuration file is defined in the following UME property entry:

```
ume.persistence.data_source_configuration=
  dataSourceConfiguration_new.xml
```

The property is `ume.persistence.data_source_configuration`, which in this case is set to the file *dataSourceConfiguration_new.xml*.

Listing 16.1 shows an example of an XML file where regular users are stored in an LDAP directory (`CORP_LDAP`) and service users are stored in the portal database (`PRIVATE_DATASOURCE`).

```
<dataSource id="PRIVATE_DATASOURCE"
            className="com.sap.security.core.persistence.
              datasource.imp.DataBasePersistence"
            isReadonly="false"
            isPrimary="true">
    <homeFor>
      <principals>
        <principal type="USER">
<!--
KOMMENTAR: If you set the triple attribute values
($serviceUser$,SERVICEUSER_ATTRIBUTE,IS_SERVICEUSER) in a
substructure for the principals (not yet authorized user) of
the type "USER" in your name range, this rule is applied, and
the service users are stored in the PRIVATE_DATASOURCE portal
database.
-->
          <nameSpace name="$serviceUser$">
            <attribute name="SERVICEUSER_ATTRIBUTE">
              <values>
                <value>IS_SERVICEUSER</value>
              </values>
            </attribute>
          </nameSpace>
        </principal>
      </principals>
    </homeFor>
    <notHomeFor>
    </notHomeFor>
    ...
```

```
</dataSource>

<dataSource id="CORP_LDAP"
            className="com.sap.security.core.persistence.
              datasource.imp.LDAPPersistence"
            isReadonly="false"
            isPrimary="true">
    <homeFor>
      <principals>
        <principal type="USER">
<!--
KOMMENTAR: If no substructure for specific principals of the
type "USER" is defined, except for the "notHomeFor" section,
this rule is applied to all other users. This means that all
users except for those with the service user attribute are
stored in the CORP_LDAP LDAP directory.
-->
        </principal>
      </principals>
    </homeFor>
    <notHomeFor>
      <principals>
        <principal type="USER">
<!--
KOMMENTAR: As explained above, this rule applies if a
substructure exists for principals of the type "USER" and the
service user attribute.
-->
          <nameSpace name="$serviceUser$">
            <attribute name="SERVICEUSER_ATTRIBUTE">
              <values>
                <value>IS_SERVICEUSER</value>
              </values>
            </attribute>
          </nameSpace>
        </principal>
      </principals>
    </notHomeFor>
    ...
</dataSource>
```

**Listing 16.1** Example of the dataSourceConfiguration_new.xml File

In addition to the Persistence Manager, the Replication Manager is also responsible for providing a replication service via XML with additional external applications. Therefore, legacy SAP systems (for example, SAP R/3 4.6D up to Release 6.10) can be supported.

## 16.2 Risks and Controls

This section uses a simplified version of the risk analysis methodology described in Chapter 1, Risk and Control Management, to identify the main security risks and the necessary controls for SAP NetWeaver Portal (see Table 16.1). The controls are then discussed in more detail in the following sections and illustrated using examples.

| No. | Classification | Description |
|---|---|---|
| 1. | Potential risk | Authorization concept missing or faulty:<br>Due to an inadequate assignment of rights, users gain access to information and applications in SAP NetWeaver Portal for which they have no authorization. |
| | Impact | Due to their authorizations, users can view or even change confidential business documents. This enables them to perform fraudulent acts or other activities that jeopardize the business. On the other hand, there is the risk that users have insufficient access to the portal so that user authorizations need to be changed frequently. |
| | Risk without control(s) | Extremely high |
| | Control | Portal roles are predefined and assigned authorizations that have been tested and approved by the data or business process owner. Portal roles enable users to only access specific applications and information according to their scope of tasks. |
| | Risk with control(s) | Low |
| | Section | 16.3.1 through 16.3.6 |
| 2. | Potential risk | No information ownership principle:<br>Owners of business processes cannot determine or approve the assignment of portal roles that enable other employees to access their information and applications. |

**Table 16.1** Risks and Controls for SAP NetWeaver Portal

| No. | Classification | Description |
|---|---|---|
| | Impact | Central administrators assign portal roles and the associated authorizations for business process information without the approval of the business process owner. Because of this, authorization accumulations can occur, or the assigned authorizations can no longer be validated due to a lack of transparency. Users therefore gain access to information and functions for which they are not authorized. |
| | Risk without control(s) | Extremely high |
| | Control | A segregation of functions when assigning portal roles is achieved using the delegated administration by involving the information owner (usually the owner of the business process). |
| | Risk with control(s) | Low |
| | Section | 16.3.5 |
| 3. | Potential risk | No holistic authorization concept between SAP NetWeaver Portal and the back-end:<br>Users have incongruent roles in the portal and the corresponding back-end applications, and therefore have either too little or too much authorization. |
| | Impact | Due to excessive authorization, users are able to access information or applications for which they are not authorized. Therefore, they can manipulate information and perform fraudulent activities. On the other hand, it is likely that they cannot perform their tasks due to insufficient authorization and are therefore not productive. |
| | Risk without control(s) | High |
| | Control | Portal roles are synchronized and reconciled with the respective back-end applications. To do this, portal roles can be downloaded into the back-end applications, or the roles can be uploaded to the portal. However, this only applies if the back-end applications are SAP systems. |
| | Risk with control(s) | Low |
| | Section | 16.3.1, 16.3.6 |

**Table 16.1** Risks and Controls for SAP NetWeaver Portal (Cont.)

| No. | Classification | Description |
|---|---|---|
| 4. | Potential risk | No approval process for portal content:<br>There is no approval process when uploading and implementing new portal content if SAP NetWeaver Portal is used in an Internet scenario. |
| | Impact | In an Internet scenario, incorrect portal content is published, which damages the organization's external presentation and reputation. Eventually, this may result in a loss of sales. |
| | Risk without control(s) | High |
| | Control | An appropriate workflow needs to be established that ensures that portal content is checked before it is published. |
| | Risk with control(s) | Low |
| | Section | 16.3.1, 16.3.5, 16.3.7 |
| 5. | Potential risk | No central user persistence store:<br>Master data is stored in several different user persistence storage locations. In addition to this, there is no unified enterprise-wide employee identifier (user name). The master data storage concept thus contains redundancy and the data is inconsistent. |
| | Impact | Inconsistent user master data causes data redundancy, low data integrity, and a lack of transparency. Thus, when changes need to be made (for example, if an employee leaves the enterprise or changes his name), user accounts are not managed in an appropriate manner. The result may be the existence of user accounts with excessive authorizations, which could be exploited by other unauthorized users. There are also the additional administrative costs of maintaining redundant user accounts. This inconsistent master data is often criticized in audits. |
| | Risk without control(s) | Extremely high |
| | Control | Connect SAP NetWeaver Portal to a central LDAP directory that contains the master data of all users in one central location (single source of truth). Alternatively, SAP NetWeaver Portal can also be connected to an existing SAP back-end system that is then used as the main user persistence storage location. |

**Table 16.1** Risks and Controls for SAP NetWeaver Portal (Cont.)

| No. | Classification | Description |
|---|---|---|
| | Risk with control(s) | Low |
| | Section | 16.4.1 |
| 6. | Potential risk | Passwords that are too numerous and too simple (1):<br>Every SAP NetWeaver Portal system or back-end application has its own password. Users need to memorize these different passwords so they often choose simple or even structured passwords, like names of months. In the extreme case, passwords are jotted down somewhere near the desktop. |
| | Impact | An unauthorized user can easily take on another identity and gain more application rights to effect unauthorized and fraudulent transactions. |
| | Risk without control(s) | Extremely high |
| | Control | Using SAP NetWeaver Portal, an SSO mechanism is established between portals or between a portal and the SAP back-end based on SAP logon tickets. The user then only has one user name and one password for all applications connected to SAP NetWeaver Portal. In addition, there needs to be a regulation that passwords are not to be written down on notes close to the desktop and that users must adhere to strict password rules for complex passwords. |
| | Risk with control(s) | Normal |
| | Section | 16.4.2, 16.4.6 |
| 7. | Potential risk | Passwords that are too numerous and too simple (2):<br>Every back-end application has its own password. Users need to memorize these different passwords so they often choose simple or even structured passwords, like names of months. In the extreme case, passwords are jotted down somewhere near the desktop. |
| | Impact | An unauthorized internal user can easily take on another identity and gain more application rights to effect unauthorized and fraudulent transactions. |
| | Risk without control(s) | Extremely high |

**Table 16.1** Risks and Controls for SAP NetWeaver Portal (Cont.)

| No. | Classification | Description |
|---|---|---|
| | Control | Using SAP NetWeaver Portal, an SSO mechanism is established based on an external authentication mechanism (Windows authentication using Microsoft Active Directory) for the Windows system. Users then only need to log on to their Windows accounts on their desktops to access all applications connected to SAP NetWeaver Portal. |
| | Risk with control(s) | Low |
| | Section | 16.4.3 |
| 8. | Potential risk | Passwords that are too numerous and too simple (3):<br>Every back-end application has its own password. Users need to memorize these different passwords so they often choose simple or even structured passwords, like names of months. In the extreme case, passwords are jotted down somewhere near the desktop. |
| | Impact | An unauthorized internal user can easily take on another identity and gain more application rights to effect unauthorized and fraudulent transactions. |
| | Risk without control(s) | Extremely high |
| | Control | Using SAP NetWeaver Portal, an SSO mechanism is established based on person-related digital certificates (X.509 standard) for the individual users. Users are then always authenticated to the portal and its associated applications using their certificates. |
| | Risk with control(s) | Low |
| | Section | 16.4.4 |
| 9. | Potential risk | Misconfigured anonymous access:<br>The portal is misconfigured for anonymous access so that anonymous users can access confidential information. |
| | Impact | Anonymous users can view or manipulate information for which they are not authorized. Therefore, confidential business information is released to the public, which can damage the company's reputation and even result in financial losses. |
| | Risk without control(s) | Extremely high |

**Table 16.1** Risks and Controls for SAP NetWeaver Portal (Cont.)

| No. | Classification | Description |
|---|---|---|
| | Control | Correct configuration of the portal for anonymous users. |
| | Risk with control(s) | Low |
| | Section | 16.4.5 |
| 10. | Potential risk | Misconfigured portal:<br>After initial installation, SAP NetWeaver Portal has not been sufficiently configured regarding information security. |
| | Impact | Due to a misconfiguration of SAP NetWeaver Portal, a directory browsing of SAP NetWeaver Portal might be enabled, for example. Unauthorized content, like exploits, can then be uploaded to the portal. In addition, it might be possible to gain administrative rights. |
| | Risk without control(s) | Extremely high |
| | Control | Adhere to SAP Note 606733, deactivating services that are not required. |
| | Risk with control(s) | Low |
| | Section | 16.4.6 |
| 11. | Potential risk | Circumventing authentication and authorization mechanisms of SAP NetWeaver Portal:<br>SAP NetWeaver Portal services can be accessed directly, circumventing authentication and authorization, by calling the corresponding URL. |
| | Impact | By circumventing the authentication and authorization mechanism of SAP NetWeaver Portal, confidential information can be viewed or manipulated. |
| | Risk without control(s) | Extremely high |
| | Control | Set up security zones for SAP NetWeaver Portal content so that it cannot be called directly by entering the URL. |
| | Risk with control(s) | Low |
| | Section | 16.3.3 |

**Table 16.1** Risks and Controls for SAP NetWeaver Portal (Cont.)

| No. | Classification | Description |
|---|---|---|
| 12. | Potential risk | iViews are not protected sufficiently against unauthorized access:<br>Specific iViews with high security requirements and access to critical or confidential transactions, URLs, or reports are not protected sufficiently against unauthorized access. |
| | Impact | iViews can be started without authorization if they are not secured sufficiently and individually or other security gaps can be exploited by attackers. This can result in considerable damage to the business. |
| | Risk without control(s) | Extremely high for critical iViews |
| | Control | Set up an additional authentication check for the start of individual iViews. This is done by assigning an authentication schema to the property of an iView. |
| | Risk with control(s) | Very low |
| | Section | 16.3.4 |
| 13. | Potential risk | No network strategy:<br>At the network level, there is no sufficient security for the portal due to the fact that the network is not divided into trustworthy and untrustworthy areas using firewalls. |
| | Impact | If a firewall configuration is not used, the security of SAP NetWeaver Portal at the network level is inadequate, and any weak points that there may be in the system can be exploited at the operating system level. This can allow system attackers to obtain administrator authorizations. The portal can therefore be compromised. The final result may be unauthorized manipulation of data or unauthorized execution of financial transactions. |
| | Risk without control(s) | Extremely high |
| | Control | Secure the portal by securing the network. Divide the network segments into less protected, public areas and strictly protected, trustworthy zones. Do this by carefully configuring the network and setting up network-based firewalls and other network components. |

**Table 16.1** Risks and Controls for SAP NetWeaver Portal (Cont.)

| No. | Classification | Description |
|---|---|---|
| | Risk with control(s) | Low |
| | Section | 16.4.7 |
| 14. | Potential risk | External attacks on the application:<br>Applications do not perform adequate checks on the input transferred by the portal user on the application level, such as URL parameters, form field input, and so on. This allows hackers to carry out the following application-level attacks (these are the main methods of attack):<br>Stealth commanding: changing transfer parameters in transactions to obtain a different application status or to modify data, such as product price information of a sales transaction<br>Cookie poisoning and token analysis: enable the hacker to carry out session hijacking<br>Buffer overflow: enables a denial-of-service attack<br>Cross-site scripting: enables the hacker to divert the portal user to the wrong website |
| | Impact | Inadequate checking of input parameters means that the portal application or data can be compromised or portal users can be redirected to unintended websites. Users can obtain advanced access rights without authorization at the application level. This means that back-end applications might be attacked and that data theft or modifications can take place. |
| | Risk without control(s) | Extremely high |
| | Control | Transfer parameters and input fields have to be checked for plausibility and correctness on the server side. It is also recommended that you introduce an application-level firewall. This is particularly relevant for self-developed applications that are to be integrated into the portal. |
| | Risk with control(s) | Low |
| | Section | 16.4.8 |

**Table 16.1** Risks and Controls for SAP NetWeaver Portal (Cont.)

| No. | Classification | Description |
|---|---|---|
| 15. | Potential risk | Unencrypted data transfer:<br>The connection between the front end (browser) and portal server is unencrypted. Further internal downstream communication channels are unencrypted as well. |
| | Impact | If an SSO configuration was implemented in SAP NetWeaver Portal using SAP logon tickets, the session of another user can be copied by "sniffing" and adopting the cookie. Although SAP logon tickets include separate security measures to reduce this risk, a man-in-the-middle attack is possible, where transferred business information can be accessed by unauthorized persons or manipulated by them. Confidential information is publicly available if it is transferred without encryption. Financial losses can be very high for the organization. |
| | Risk without control(s) | Extremely high |
| | Control | The communication between front end (web browser, for example) and SAP NetWeaver Portal and other downstream communication channels is encrypted via Secure Socket Layer (SSL). |
| | Risk with control(s) | Low |
| | Section | 16.4.9 |
| 16. | Potential risk | No virus scan when uploading documents:<br>When uploading documents or other files to SAP NetWeaver Portal (knowledge management, for example), the files are not scanned for potential computer viruses or other exploits. |
| | Impact | An unidentified virus or another exploit can spread through SAP NetWeaver Portal to other systems of the organization and potentially compromise all IT systems of the organization. This can result in substantial damage to the organization due to downtime and recovery of the IT systems. There might also be legal consequences for the organization if the portal turns out to be a "cesspool of viruses." |
| | Risk without control(s) | Extremely high |

**Table 16.1** Risks and Controls for SAP NetWeaver Portal (Cont.)

| No. | Classification | Description |
|---|---|---|
| | Control | Implement an antivirus scan when uploading files to the portal or knowledge management system. This security control is particularly relevant for publicly accessible recruiting portals where attached résumé documents need to be scanned for existing computer viruses or macros. |
| | Risk with control(s) | Low |
| | Section | 16.4.10 |

**Table 16.1** Risks and Controls for SAP NetWeaver Portal (Cont.)

## 16.3 Application Security

This section describes in more detail the risks and controls that are outlined in Table 16.1 with regard to application security.

### 16.3.1 Structure and Design of Portal Roles

The portal authorization concept differs from the traditional ABAP authorization concept, because SAP NetWeaver Portal runs on the AS Java and thus uses the related security technology. This leads to a portal security technology that is specialized in risks and threats from the Internet or intranet.

In combination with the information from risk/threat analyses, you can use the portal security technology to reduce the remaining security risks to an acceptable low level. Figure 16.4 shows how the basic elements are linked: Portal role, UME role, UME action, access control list (ACL), and security zone. All of these elements are further detailed in the following sections.

The design of the authorization concept in the SAP back-end pursues several control objectives with regard to user access to transactions and data. A critical part of the control objectives is the segregation of duties for process steps for which responsibility should not lie with a single user. This segregation of duties is implemented using the four-eyes principle (see Chapter 4, Security Standards).

This can be achieved, for example in the SAP back-end, by separating the process of entering a document (SAP back-end Transaction FB50) from the process of posting the document (SAP back-end Transaction FBV0) so that these process steps are carried out by two different persons. If possible, the same guidelines should also be applied to the portal authorization concept for access to portal functions and content. This approach allows for the benefits of a uniform access concept for the portal and the SAP back-end becoming effective, and supports the control objective that the authorizations of portal users should not exceed the authorizations in the SAP back-end.

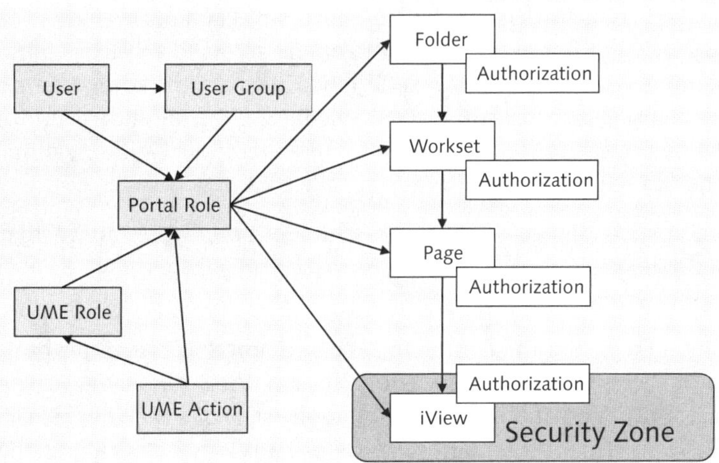


**Figure 16.4** User-Specific Portal Security Elements

To determine potential problems, the portal provides technical information that can be manually obtained in the UME user interface, in the Portal Content Directory, and in the access control list by combining the various display options. However, commercial tools are also available that support this portal authorizations analysis process semi automatically or automatically. These tools reduce the required analysis time and provide options for automatically and periodically running analysis. This enables you to create snapshots of the authorization configuration at defined times and therefore determine and archive the monitoring of compliance with the defined control objectives and changes. It supports the task of management to periodically run analyses and provide data for audits.

### Structure of Portal Roles

The actual difference between the structure of portal roles and ABAP-based roles (Profile Generator, Transaction PFCG), which are traditionally used in most applications in the SAP environment (for example, SAP Enterprise Resource Planning (ERP) Financials, SAP Materials Management (MM), and so on), is that ABAP-based roles specifically define the access to transactions using authorization objects and authorization fields; this is the respective authorization range of a role. For example, a role specifies that a user may start Transaction MM01 (Create Material) and create materials for a specific company code (see Chapter 20, Authorizations in SAP ERP).

Portal roles, in contrast, do not specify access to individual transactions in an SAP back-end system in detail with an authorization range, but do specify access to individual portal content objects that are available in a portal and organized in the Portal Content Directory. The portal can allow for general access to a SAP back-end transaction, for example with the portal object iView. However, the authorization range related to this transaction must still be controlled using the traditional authorizations of ABAP-based roles in the SAP back-end. These traditional authorizations must still be assigned to the user executing the specific iView.

The essential portal objects that can be used to structure portal roles are further described in the following:

- **iViews**
  An iView is an integral part of the complete page of a portal. It can either present information or access to a specific functionality. An iView can also store the call of a back-end application and link it directly to the start of a specific transaction in an SAP system. This is the main purpose of an iView. The iView is the smallest unit for controlling access to the functions in SAP NetWeaver Portal.
- **Worksets**
  A workset groups various iViews in a logical navigation structure according to the respective business aspect. This means that, for example, all iViews concerning Controlling are grouped in one workset. Therefore, a workset is a navigation structure below the portal role.
- **Pages**
  A portal page specifies the visual arrangement of different iViews; it defines the layout. A page can consist of one single iView and can be assigned to a workset.

Portal roles are administrated in the Portal Content Directory (PCD). Using the Role Editor, the roles can be defined in a dedicated directory within the PCD.

**Notes on the Portal Role**

Portal roles are grouped according to the individual job roles of the positions existing in the enterprise. A portal role defines the technical navigation structure and authorizations of a user in SAP NetWeaver Portal. The entire navigation structure of a user is defined by the sum of all portal roles assigned to it. A portal role defines a collective folder for several worksets, pages, and iViews that are to be accessed by the role. Portal roles can be directly assigned to individual users or user groups.

These portal roles and their portal objects can be managed and the hierarchy of the worksets, pages, and so on can be changed using the Role Editor. For example, if more iViews or pages are to be added to the role, you need to navigate to this object in the PCD and right-click to select ADD TO ROLE. You can then insert the new object as a delta link or as a copy. The delta link has the advantage that changes to the original object for example an added iView, are propagated to the related portal role. The portal object that has been inserted using the delta link can accordingly inherit the properties of the original object. If you want to prevent this, you can also break the inheritance relationship. The Role Editor can also be used to edit access control lists and other properties of PCD objects.

#### Authorizations for Portal Roles

An important difference between ABAP roles and portal roles is that in the portal, no authorizations are defined for the back-end application itself. This must still be done in the back-end applications, such as SAP ERP, because the respective authorization system controls all access to its own system. A portal role can only be used to call a transaction in an SAP back-end system.

In the portal, however, access to the individual objects (portal roles, worksets, pages, iViews) is defined via ACLs. There are three authorizations for those objects:

- ADMINISTRATOR
  This authorization controls the administration of the portal objects at administration time.
- END USER
  This authorization controls the call of an object at runtime if the object is executed in the runtime environment of SAP NetWeaver Portal. This does not apply, for example, if the iView starts a transaction on a back-end application, because in this case, only a redirect takes place.
- ROLE ASSIGNER
  This authorization controls the right to assign a portal role to another user. It therefore only exists for objects of the portal role type and for PCD directories that pass the authorizations on to the objects contained therein.

There is one ACL for every object in the PCD. To administer authorizations for these PCD objects (permissions), six access authorization levels are available. These are listed in Table 16.2.

| | Description | | |
|---|---|---|---|
| ACL Definition | Create | Delete | Edit |
| None | The directory of the objects and the objects themselves are not visible in the PCD. This setting only makes sense for pure runtime roles for which the enduser right must be activated. | The directory of the objects and the objects themselves are not visible in the PCD. | The directory of the objects and the objects themselves are not visible in the PCD. |
| Read | The directory of the objects and the objects themselves are visible in the PCD. New objects can be created as an instance of an existing object, as a delta link. | The directory of the objects and the objects themselves are visible in the PCD. Objects cannot be deleted. | The directory of the objects and the objects themselves are visible in the PCD. Objects cannot be edited. |
| Write | This ACL selection only applies to directories in the PCD and not to objects. A role that has write authorization for a directory can create new objects in that directory. | This ACL selection only applies to directories in the PCD and not to objects. Objects cannot be deleted, but directories can. | This ACL selection only applies to directories in the PCD and not to objects. Objects cannot be edited. |
| Read/write | The directory of the objects and the objects themselves are visible in the PCD. New objects can be created as an instance of an existing object, as a delta link. | The directory of the objects and the objects themselves are visible in the PCD. Only the newly created child objects of an existing parent object can be deleted. | The directory of the objects and the objects themselves are visible in the PCD. Only object properties and delta links can be edited. |

**Table 16.2** ACL Definition Administrator for the Design Phase of Portal Objects

| | Description | | |
|---|---|---|---|
| ACL Definition | Create | Delete | Edit |
| Full access | The directory of the objects and the objects themselves are visible in the PCD. New objects can be created as an instance of an existing object, as a delta link. | The directory of the objects and the objects themselves are visible in the PCD. All objects can be deleted. | The directory of the objects and the objects themselves are visible in the PCD. Only object properties and delta links can be edited. |
| Owner | The directory of the objects and the objects themselves are visible in the PCD. New objects can be created without restrictions. | The directory of the objects and the objects themselves are visible in the PCD. All objects can be deleted. | The directory of the objects and the objects themselves are visible in the PCD. All object properties, including authorizations, can be edited. |

**Table 16.2** ACL Definition Administrator for the Design Phase of Portal Objects (Cont.)

At runtime, only the END USER access control list is checked. It can take on two values: possible or not possible. At runtime, when the user is logged on to the portal, the portal object contained in the portal role can be displayed. For customizing the layout, the user can only use those objects for which an authorization has been specified in the END USER access control list.

Direct access to the portal object via the web browser URL is possible only if the END USER access control list has been set for the security zone as well (see Section 16.3.3, Portal Security Zones). However, the iView execution restriction using the ACL only works if the called application is executed in the runtime environment of SAP NetWeaver Portal and if it is a Java application. For iViews that only launch a back-end transaction or application, this access protection does not work. To do this, the authorizations in the back-end application must be set properly.

The ROLE ASSIGNER access control list only exists for the portal role object or can only be defined for PCD directories that pass their authorizations on to the portal roles contained therein via inheritance. The ROLE ASSIGNER access control list can only take on two values: set or not set. A portal role possessing this access control list setting is authorized to assign this role to other users. A delegated user management can be established in this way.

Figure 16.5 summarizes the relationship of portal roles, their assignment to users or user groups, and the (still necessary) specification of authorizations in the back-end applications (ABAP authorizations).

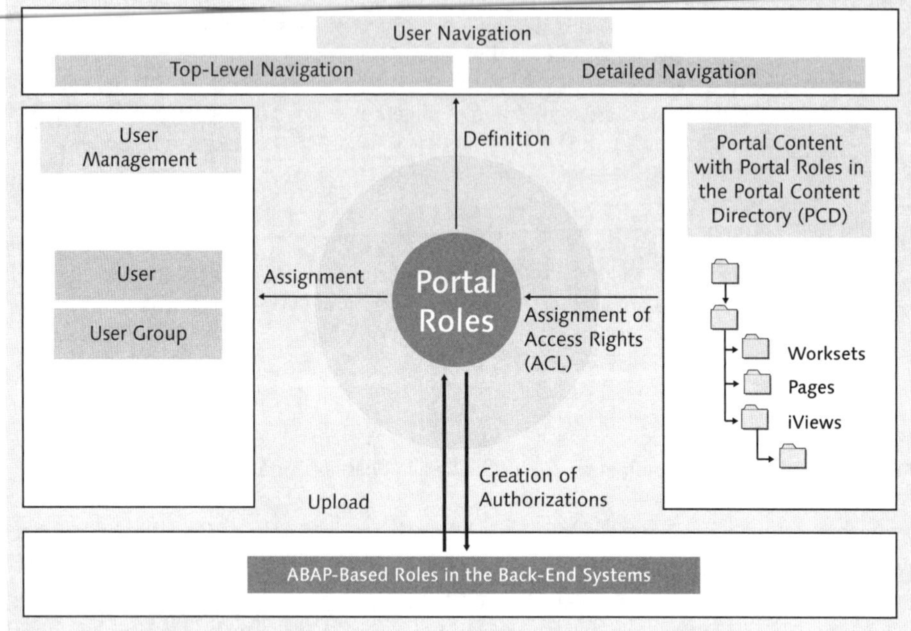


**Figure 16.5** Relationship between Portal Roles and Authorizations in the Back-End Applications

The portal roles are defined with the existing navigation structures via the workset, page, and iView portal objects in the PCD. For access control, there are three access control lists for every object of the design phase and for runtime. Within the back-end applications, the authorizations are still required if an iView calls a back-end application, for example, from SAP ERP. In this context, you have the option to upload roles from the back-end applications and vice versa. The sum of all portal roles assigned to a user defines the user's complete visible navigation structure in the portal.

Table 16.3 provides an overview of the essential tasks and responsibilities for the development and implementation of a portal authorization concept.

| Person Responsible | Task |
|---|---|
| Business process owner | The process owner is responsible for controlling the process. This includes identification and determination of the necessary process controls and criteria for compliance with auditing guidelines. This also applies to portal content and access. The business process owner approves the assignment of internally developed portal content to security zones and the access assignments of users or user groups to portal objects and functions within his area of responsibility. |
| Portal content developer | The developer of the portal content designs the portal content considering the specifications of the overall business security concept. This includes the assignment of portal objects to the PCD and to security zones. |
| Person responsible for portal application security and authorizations | The person responsible for portal security implements the user access to the portal, the defined control objectives, criteria and guidelines for the creation of customer-specific portal roles, and the assignment of the corresponding users or user groups to the portal roles and security zones. |

**Table 16.3** Responsibilities for the Development and Implementation of the Portal Authorization Concept

### 16.3.2 Authorizations for the UME

The UME of SAP NetWeaver Portal is based on AS Java and thus uses the Java security options. Access to the administration functions of the portal user administration is therefore controlled using Java authorizations — so-called UME actions. The standard portal roles for the system and user administration are already provided with the corresponding UME actions (see Table 16.4).

| Portal Role | UME Action |
|---|---|
| Superadministrator | ▸ `UME.AclSuperUser`<br>▸ `UME.Manage_All` |
| User Administrator | ▸ `UME.Manage_All` |
| Delegated User Administrator | ▸ `UME.Manage_Users`<br>▸ `UME.Manage_Role_Assignments` |

**Table 16.4** UME Actions of the Standard Portal Roles

There are additional UME actions, which are not mentioned here, that basically control access to the administrative AS Java functions. Grouped in UME roles, they are assigned to the respective portal roles. In contrast to iViews, which you can also assign to users directly, UME actions or UME roles must be assigned to users via portal roles only. Figure 16.6 illustrates this relationship.

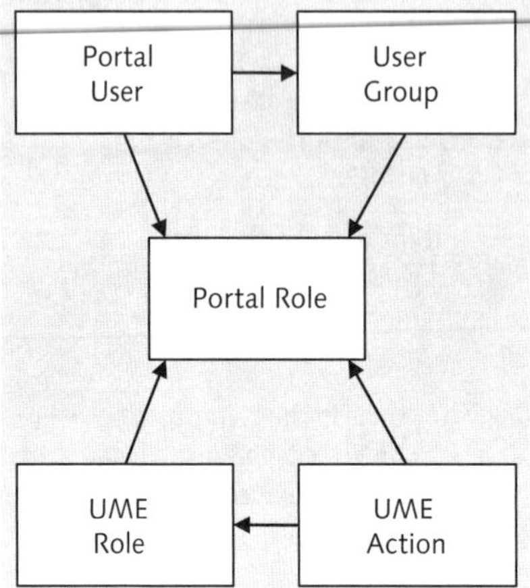


**Figure 16.6** Indirect Assignment of UME Actions and UME Roles

**Note**

You must include UME roles and UME actions in the risk management and overall portal authorization concept, because they control access to AS Java and involve the risk that critical AS Java or portal access authorization security parameters can be changed unauthorized, which results in a security gap.

### 16.3.3 Portal Security Zones

Because the SAP NetWeaver Portal authorization system is based on Java security technology, you can also use another security concept that is implemented as a security zone in the portal. The basic idea is that access to the portal content in the PCD — such as objects and portal services that are arranged in certain Java directories (security zones) at design time — is controlled by assigning authorizations (permissions) for these Java directories. The Java directories that are required for the standard portal installation are created in security zones during the first portal installation.

A user or user group can only start a portal component (an iView, for example) or a portal service, if a permission for the specific security zone exists in which the iView or service reside. So, in addition to the already-introduced portal authorization concept, this permission concept is a second security level. Figure 16.7 describes the assignment of the portal user to the security zone concept.

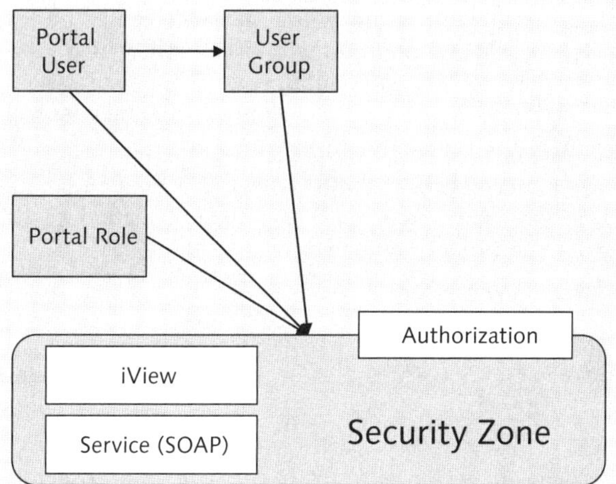


**Figure 16.7** Assignment of Users to the Security Zone

However, this second security level is not activated by default. If risk management requires it, you can activate this additional security option for the portal runtime.

To activate the security zones, the Java Virtual Machine of AS Java (server and instance) must be configured with parameters. To do this, you can work with the Java 2 Enterprise Edition (J2EE) config tool (file: *configtool.bat*), which you can find and launch from the *configtool* directory at the operating system level of AS Java (for example, *<AS_Java_Installation>\j2ee\configtool\configtool.bat*). Use the J2EE config tool to log on to the AS Java, and navigate to the server instance in the server-cluster structure via the menu path: J2EE CLUSTER • INSTANCE NODE • GENERAL • JAVA SETTINGS. For activation, you must enter the following as the Java parameter:

```
-Dcom.sap.nw.sz=true
```

Adding this parameter means that the portal runtime is now constantly in Production Mode status.

After this parameter has been set, all portal users must have the necessary authorizations for the security zone an iView or service has been assigned to. Only then it can be started. How to assign portal objects to security zones and grant user authorizations for security zones is explained later on in this section.

**Note**

When security zones are activated, all portal users, including the users with administrative portal roles (Superadministrator, System Administrator, Content Administrator, and User Administrator), must have the permissions for the appropriate security zones. If certain requirements are not met, it is possible that even users with administrative portal roles will not be able to access the portal due to the activated security zones.

To avoid this risk of a lock-out, you must implement the following configuration before activating the security zones. The EVERYONE portal group must have end user authorizations (permissions) for the following standard portal security zones:

- *ara:/security/sap.com/NetWeaver.Portal/no_safety*
- *ara:/security/sap.com/NetWeaver.UserManagement/no_safety.*

This section provides further information on the configuration of security zones and authorizations.

In general, portal objects and services are assigned to those security zones (permissions) that control access to those portal directories containing the particular portal objects and services in the PCD. This is the case because the objects or services inherit permissions from the directory. If another, for example, higher security zone is required as additional protection for a new customer-specific object or service, the portal developer must assign the object or service to the corresponding overarching security zone during the design phase of the object/service. The portal developer can use one of the following security zones: NO SAFETY, LOW SAFETY, MEDIUM SAFETY, and HIGH SAFETY (see Table 16.5).

For example: An assignment of a test transaction A, `TestTransactionA`, for a vendor with the `abc.com` Vendor ID to the `abc-customer-specific` security zone (SECURITY AREA) with the `high_safety` security level (SAFETY LEVEL) could look as follows:

```
abc.com/abc-customer-specific/high_safety/
  com.sap.portal.prt.cache/components/TestTransactionA.
```

This entry is generated for the example transaction A in the portal file (*portalapp.xml*) when the portal developer uses the UME user interface (Permission Editor) to configure the permissions of the `TestTransactionA` portal object.

You start the Permission Editor via the following menu path in the UME user interface: SYSTEM ADMINISTRATION • PERMISSIONS • PORTAL PERMISSIONS • SECURITY

ZONES. Here, you can select the corresponding object in the directory that opens. By right-clicking on the object and selecting OPEN • PERMISSIONS, you can configure the required setting. Please note that you can define permissions at the directory level and directly at the object or service level. If permissions are configured at the directory level, all objects or services of the respective directory inherit these permissions. This inheritance relationship is no longer valid if the permissions for an object or a service are changed individually.

Security zones offer an additional protection provided by SAP NetWeaver Portal to prevent services that are usually called via an iView from being launched directly via the service URL. Normally, the user can call a specific iView, page, or workset at runtime using his portal role and the associated ACLs or permissions. In case a user wants to bypass this standard security scenario, the user can try to launch the service (or a portal component) — for example, a file upload functionality controlled using an iView — directly by entering the corresponding URL into a Web browser.

**Note**

Using security zones lets you reduce the risk of iViews or services being started via an externally and directly addressed URL bypassing the portal authorization system.

To avoid this security gap, the components and services that have been developed by the customer can be assigned to specific security zones. This task must be carried out by the developer for every Portal Archive Repository (PAR) file containing the services and components using the XML file, *portalapp.xml*. The components and service assignments to the individual security levels can be viewed and modified using the Permission Editor in SAP NetWeaver Portal (see Figure 16.8). These modifications are then reflected in the *portalapp.xml* file.

Like any other objects, security zones can be controlled via the PCD. All security zones can be found under the SECURITY ZONES directory. The next level is the VENDOR ID (the provider of the components and services, like SAP), and the level after that is the SECURITY AREA (like SAP NetWeaver Portal). Within the SECURITY AREA, the SAFETY LEVELS, that is, the security zones, are defined to which the individual components and services are eventually assigned. These safety levels indicate the protection needs of the individual components and services. Services and components that are particularly sensitive must be assigned to the HIGH SAFETY level. There are four safety levels, which are described in Table 16.5.

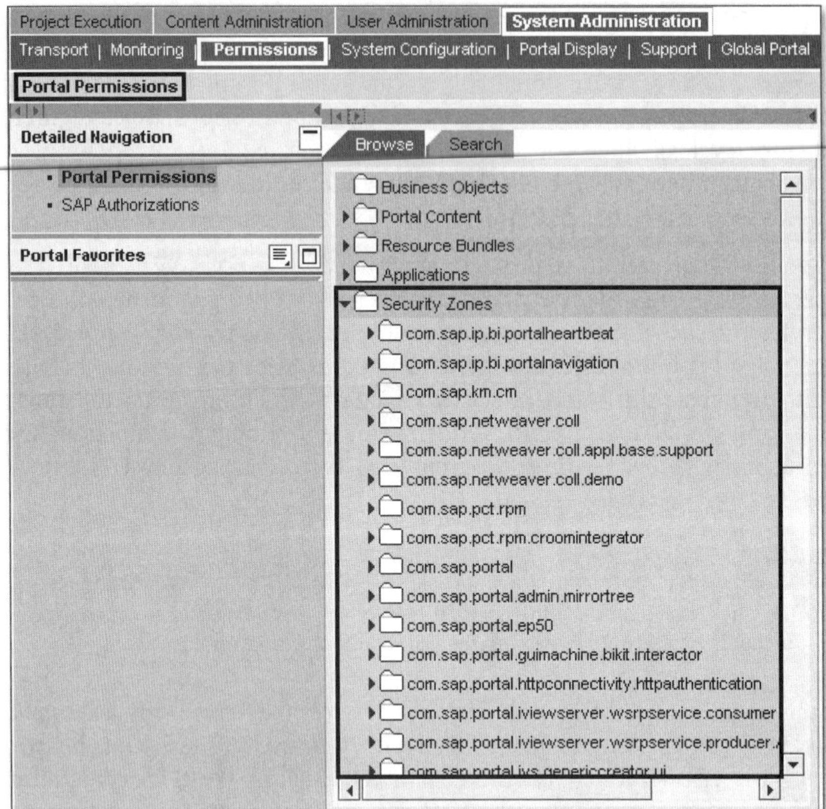


**Figure 16.8** Permission Editor for Security Zones

| Safety Level | Description |
|---|---|
| No Safety | Anonymous users can access components and services assigned to this level. |
| Low Safety | A user must have authenticated to SAP NetWeaver Portal before accessing a service or component assigned to this level. |
| Medium Safety | A user must be assigned to a portal role that is authorized to access components and services assigned to this level. The permissions to this level are assigned to a portal role using an appropriate iView of this zone. |
| High Safety | A user must be assigned to a portal role with advanced permissions for this zone (for example, portal role Content Administrator) to access components and services assigned to this security zone. |

**Table 16.5** Definition of the Security Zones for SAP NetWeaver Portal

Listing 16.2 presents an extract from a *portalapp.xml* file for our example. The `TestTransactionA` component is assigned to the HIGH SAFETY level. For simplification, the sample file does not define a service.

```
Security Zones
  <vendor_ID> = abc.com
    <security_area> = abc-customer-specific
      <safety_level> = high_safety
        <portal_application_name> = com.abc.portal.prt.cache
               components

          <component_name> = TestTransactionA
               services
          <service_name>
```

**Listing 16.2** Example of a portalapp.xml File

For a user to regularly start or call the service or a component using an iView according to his portal role, the user must be assigned to the portal role that has END USER permissions for the security zone which is, in turn, assigned to the service or component. Again, this can be set in the Permission Editor for the SECURITY LEVEL using the inheritance of authorizations via the directory. This means: If you set the END USER permissions for the HIGH SAFETY directory, it also applies to all components and services contained in this directory. However, you can disable inheritance for individual components and services.

In summary, for a user to launch the portal object or service, you must first activate the END USER permissions at the iView level and then the permissions for the respective component or service in the security zone.

**Note**

After the initial installation of SAP NetWeaver Portal, you must implement a basic configuration of the standard authorizations for the PCD and the standard security zones in SAP NetWeaver Portal. This configuration enables administrative standard portal users to execute basic portal functions. For detailed information on the basic configuration after the initial portal installation, refer to "How To... Configure Permissions for Initial Content in SAP NetWeaver Portal SPS 9 and higher" in the SAP Developer Network (SDN) (*http://sdn.sap.com*). The section 16.4.6, Secure Initial Configuration, provides further information on the initial portal configuration and security.

### 16.3.4 Authentication Check for iView Access

Portal iViews are provided with an authentication schema by default. This schema generally consists of the portal user ID and a password. That means that a user who starts an iView for a transaction or portal function must pass this authentication check.

In general, however, this check is performed automatically and is not noticed because the SAP logon ticket that was generated when the portal was accessed for the first time by the user already contains the required authentication. The iView authorization check reads and analyzes this SAP logon ticket. If the check has a positive result, the ticket starts the iView; this process is identical for all iViews.

However, if specific iViews require individual checks, a special authentication process can be requested. This can be an X.509 certificate or any other customer-specific authentication process. You define this individual user authentication in the property configuration of the iView by selecting from the available options. If such a specific authentication is requested by the iView prior to the launch, the check is carried out in the AS Java UME. In this case, a login module that is contained in the UME executes the additional authentication query for the user.

The portal configuration file (*authschemes.xml*) specifies the available authentication options. Table 16.6 lists the options that the portal installation provides by default.

| Name of the Schema | Authentication | Login Module |
|---|---|---|
| `uidpwdlogon` | User ID and password at the portal | `ticket` |
| `certlogon` | X.509 certificate at the portal | `client_cert` |
| `basicauthentication` | HTTP user ID and password at the portal | `ticket` |
| `header` | External products authenticate the user; the user ID is transferred to the portal in the HTTP header. | `header` |
| `anonymous` | No check, no logon ticket | No specific login module |

**Table 16.6** Standard Portal Authentication Options

### 16.3.5 Standard Portal Roles and Delegated User Administration

SAP NetWeaver Portal is developed with predefined standard roles. These portal roles contain authorizations for the standard objects that exist in the portal after its installation. These standard roles enable access to various standalone components of the PCD and UME — they also allow for a segregation of duties for portal administrators.

Task distribution can be observed in the areas of system, content, and user administration. To do this, SAP provides the administrative portal roles, Superadministrator, Content Administrator, System Administrator, and User Administrator (see Table 16.7).

| Portal Role | Description |
|---|---|
| Superadministrator | This portal role is assigned to the initial SAP* portal user and enables the following:<br>▸ Full access, including all rights for all objects in the PCD<br>▸ Full access to all tools of the content, system, and user administrators |
| Content Administrator | This portal role enables access to the following portal tools and content:<br>▸ Content administration (maintenance of portal content), including the option to define portal roles, worksets, pages, and iViews<br>▸ Editors for maintaining portal content, such as the Permission Editor (maintenance of authorizations) and Property Editor (maintenance of object properties)<br>▸ All directories of the PCD if the access control lists have been defined accordingly |
| System Administrator | This portal role enables access to the following portal tools and content:<br>▸ System administration, such as system configurator, transports, authorizations, monitoring, support, and portal display<br>▸ All directories of the PCD if the access control lists have been defined accordingly |
| User Administrator | This portal role enables access to the following portal tools and content:<br>▸ All user management tools for creating new users<br>▸ All tools for assigning roles to the users, administrating the user mapping (mapping of the portal user name to potentially deviating user IDs in back-end applications), user replication with external directories, group administration, etc. |

**Table 16.7** Standard Portal Roles for Administration Tasks

Figure 16.9 shows a list of standard portal roles as they are displayed in the administrative user interface of the UME. The `eu_role` portal role, for example, is a non-administrative role with restricted authorizations (iViews for portal personalization) that is assigned to every portal user.

Roles

| ID | Name | |
|---|---|---|
| content_admin_role | pcd:portal_content/administrator/content_admin | Edit |
| eu_role | pcd:portal_content/every_user/general | Edit |
| super_admin_role | pcd:portal_content/administrator/super_admin | Edit |
| system_admin_role | pcd:portal_content/administrator/system_admin | Edit |
| user_admin_role | pcd:portal_content/administrator/user_admin | Edit |

**Figure 16.9** Selected Standard Portal Roles

The scope of authorizations of these standard administration roles can be fine-tuned using the UME authorization control and therefore adapted to your specific requirements. The significant segregation of functions for defining and assigning portal roles to users can be achieved this way.

To implement the segregation of duties and information ownership principle that has already been introduced to manage ABAP roles and ABAP users, the user administration area provides the option of delegated user administration. It can be set up so that there is still one ultimately responsible user administrator who has the authorization to perform all user management tasks, but who is supported by delegated user administrators. These delegated user administrators can be specified so that they are only authorized to assign users to a portal role if the user administrators and users belong to the same company/subsidiary or department. Portal users can be assigned to an organizational unit (`Org_ID`), such as companies, during the initial configuration of the portal user.

The following technical steps must be carried out to establish delegated user administration for the portal:

1. Define the necessary subsidiaries or departments to which the users can belong. This is done in the config tool for the J2EE Engine of the portal. To do this, the following entry must be added to the `sapum.properties` property (for example, with the sales, marketing, and development departments):

   ```
   ume.tpd.companies=Sales,Marketing,Development
   ```

   Alternatively, you can import a list of subsidiaries and departments from a partner directory on a back-end system into the portal. This option is not discussed here in detail because it depends on the type of directory and on the back-end system.

2. Set the `Check ACL` parameter for the `com.sap.portal.roleAssignment` iView to `true`.
3. Determine one or more delegated user administrators per company, department, and so on by having the responsible user administrator assign the DELEGATED USER ADMIN portal role to these persons. This portal role can be found in the following PCD directory: *pcd:portal_ content/administrator/user_admin/delegated_user_admin_role*.
4. Assign the portal user to a company, department, and so on using the `Org_ID` attribute. This can be done by the user administrator in charge. The following possibilities are available:
   - Use the UME user administration tool in the portal
   - Use the import function in the portal for importing users from an external directory or a file. In this case, the `Org_ID` needs to be defined.
5. As soon as these steps have been completed, the delegated user administrator can create new users for the respective subsidiary or department and assign portal roles for which the ROLE ASSIGNER authorization has been set.

The delegated user administration can be associated with the self-registration of users with the portal. If a user is to be admitted during self-registration as a proper portal user by the user administrator responsible for a specific subsidiary, the following parameter must be defined for the portal in the config tool:

```
ume.logon.selfreg=true
ume.admin.selfreg_company=true
```

In addition, all admissible subsidiaries or departments must be defined. If this is the case, the delegated user administrator receives a notification about the admittance of the user if the user specified his company during the registration process. If this is not the case, the self-registered user retains his guest status.

**Delegation of the Responsibility of Approval**

In this context, the term *company* means that this concept is built according to your own organizational structure so that the responsibility of approval can be delegated to the individual departments. Unfortunately, a full segregation of duties, and thus of the information ownership, is not possible, because the administration of portal roles cannot yet be assigned to the administrators of the individual subsidiaries or departments.

### 16.3.6 Synchronization of Portal Roles with ABAP Roles

Portal roles that are supposed to enable access to data and transactions in the SAP back-end can be synchronized with the respective ABAP roles in the SAP back-end applications. To do this, SAP NetWeaver Portal allows you to upload ABAP roles to the portal, and import portal roles into the SAP back-end applications. However, only the relevant transactions and MiniApps (mobile applications, for example) can be uploaded, not the actual ABAP authorizations that are defined in the authorization objects and profiles. Still, these options are very important, particularly in an SAP application environment, because SAP NetWeaver Portal is becoming increasingly important as a central component and must be synchronized with the back-end applications accordingly. For this reason, both options are discussed in the following sections.

### Uploading ABAP Roles in SAP NetWeaver Portal

First, let's look at how ABAP roles are uploaded from the SAP back-end applications. The following conversion rules are applied:

- Simple ABAP roles are migrated as portal roles (or as worksets) to the portal. Simple ABAP roles are stored in the PCD as portal roles or worksets using the corresponding menu path.
- Composite ABAP roles are created either as portal roles or as worksets in the PCD using the corresponding menu path. The simple ABAP roles contained in the composite role are migrated as well. The menus of the simple ABAP roles are integrated in the main menu of the migrated composite role.
- MiniApps are migrated as iViews.
- In addition to the migration of ABAP roles, all services containing simple roles and composite roles (for example, transactions, MiniApps, URLs) are migrated. This means that all transactions, MiniApps, URLs, and so on that were contained in the "old" ABAP role are available as portal content objects after migration and can be assigned to more portal roles. The transactions contained in the ABAP roles are automatically migrated to iViews that include the transaction call via the default SAP Graphical User Interface (GUI) (SAP GUI for Windows, SAP GUI for Java, or SAP GUI for HTML). These are stored in the PCD under the Migrated Content menu path.
- Even the existing assignment of roles to the users in the back-end applications can be migrated. However, this only works if the users exist under the same user ID in both the portal and the back-end application.
- The authorizations existing in the back-end applications due to authorization objects and profiles are not migrated. Eventually, this means that the authorizations for the back-end applications cannot be specified via SAP NetWeaver Portal. Therefore, this specification of authorizations must remain within the respective SAP back-end applications.

- Derived ABAP roles are not migrated, because they do not differ from the template ABAP roles with regard to their functions, and authorizations are not migrated.

Figure 16.10 summarizes the migration of an ABAP role to a portal role during the upload process.

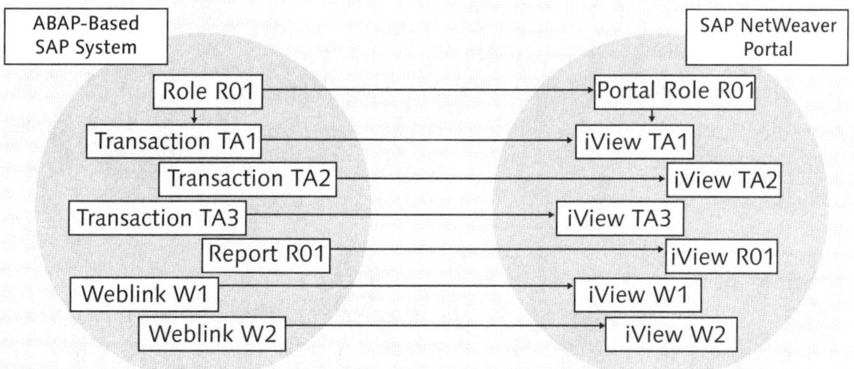


**Figure 16.10** Migration of ABAP Roles to SAP NetWeaver Portal

However, the following restrictions or notes need to be considered for this functionality:

- Simple ABAP roles and composite roles do not have pages that define the layout of the arrangement of the migrated iViews. These pages must be created (for example, using templates) and assigned to the migrated portal roles respectively. However, this is not mandatory but simply improves the layout.
- The role hierarchy and navigation structure must be adapted. The role menus of the migrated ABAP roles correspond to the menus of an ABAP-based SAP backend application that normally has a deep navigation structure with many hierarchical levels. Therefore, removing superfluous navigation levels is recommended.
- The top navigation level needs to be validated as well because it often contains 10 or more entries. A one-to-one migration would mean that in the portal, the first navigation row in the portal menu (in the portal header) would be overloaded.
- Often, you need to consider whether it is more advantageous to migrate ABAP roles to worksets and not directly to portal roles, which, in turn, can be combined more easily to design self-developed portal roles.

- It often makes more sense to only migrate single services, like a transaction, for example, instead of a complete (usually complex) role. Transactions, and thus iViews, can therefore be grouped in a simpler and more structured way to form new portal roles.

Here is a short description of the uploading procedure:

1. The functionality for uploading the ABAP roles from a back-end application can be found in SAP NetWeaver Portal via the following menu path: SYSTEM ADMINISTRATION • TRANSPORT • ROLE UPLOAD.
2. In this menu, you need to select a back-end application.
3. After selection, a list of available ABAP roles that can be uploaded is displayed.
4. After completing this selection, you can choose the following options:
   - UPLOAD USER MAPPING
     If this option is set, the assignment of the ABAP roles to the users is also uploaded apart from the ABAP roles themselves. This option only works if the user IDs in the portal and in the back-end application are identical. This can be achieved by selecting the ABAP back-end application as the user persistence storage location for the portal.
   - UPLOAD INCLUDED SERVICES
     If this option is set, not only is the role structure is uploaded, but also the transactions, URLs, and so on contained therein. These are created as new objects in the PCD.
   - MIGRATE FIRST FOLDER LEVEL AS ENTRY POINT
     If this option is set, all top navigation levels of an ABAP role structure are also specified in the portal role as entry points in the portal main navigation row. However, you need to be careful because the top portal navigation row can quickly be overloaded. Therefore, this option should not be set.
   - CONVERT ROLES TO WORKSETS
     If this option is set, ABAP roles are not directly converted to portal roles, but rather to worksets. These worksets can then be further processed at a later stage and grouped to form a customized portal role.
5. After selecting these options, you can start the process via the Upload button.
6. After uploading, the migrated portal roles can be further processed in the PCD like any other portal role. The roles are stored in the following directory of the PCD: PORTAL CONTENT • MIGRATED CONTENT • SAP COMPONENT SYSTEM • ROLES •

System (system ID plus client of the SAP back-end application). The name of the portal role contains the role description of the SAP back-end application.

- After the upload of the ABAP roles has been completed, the roles can be supplemented with existing predefined SAP business packages. If the uploaded ABAP roles are integrated as delta links into the existing portal roles of the business packages, these are renewed automatically when the ABAP roles are uploaded again at a later stage. This enables consistent portal role maintenance between SAP NetWeaver Portal and back-end applications.

#### Possibility of Distributing Portal Roles to the SAP Back-End Applications

In addition to uploading existing ABAP roles to SAP NetWeaver Portal, you also have the option of distributing portal roles to the associated SAP back-end applications. When distributing portal roles to the back-end applications, the following must be considered:

- During the distribution, only those iViews that contain transactions, MiniApps, and nontransactional services are taken into account. All other objects, such as documents or links, are not distributed. Nontransactional services include iViews that call back-end applications using Business Application Programming Interfaces (BAPIs) and that can display the results of these back-end applications in SAP NetWeaver Portal.
- In addition, the assignments of users to portal roles are optionally distributed to the back-end applications as well. In contrast to the uploading functionality, however, only those users that do not exist in the back-end applications are newly created. Still, you should take care that the user IDs in SAP NetWeaver Portal and in the back-end application are the same. If this is not the case, the SAP NetWeaver Portal user mapping functionality must be used. Also, the user assignment to roles must be adjusted manually using Transaction WP3R.

The role distribution to the back-end applications is illustrated in Figure 16.11. In this example, Transactions T1, T2, and T6, which are called in the System 1 back-end application via the corresponding iViews, are distributed to the back-end application as the ABAP role `A_1`. Using Transaction WP3R, this ABAP role can then be processed, and the authorization objects can be specified accordingly. This ABAP role `A_1` can also be copied to ABAP role `A_2`. This role can then be defined with different authorization values. The assignment of ABAP roles to the users can also be performed using Transaction WP3R. The same applies to Transactions T3, T4, T5, or, respectively, to iViews C, D, and E.

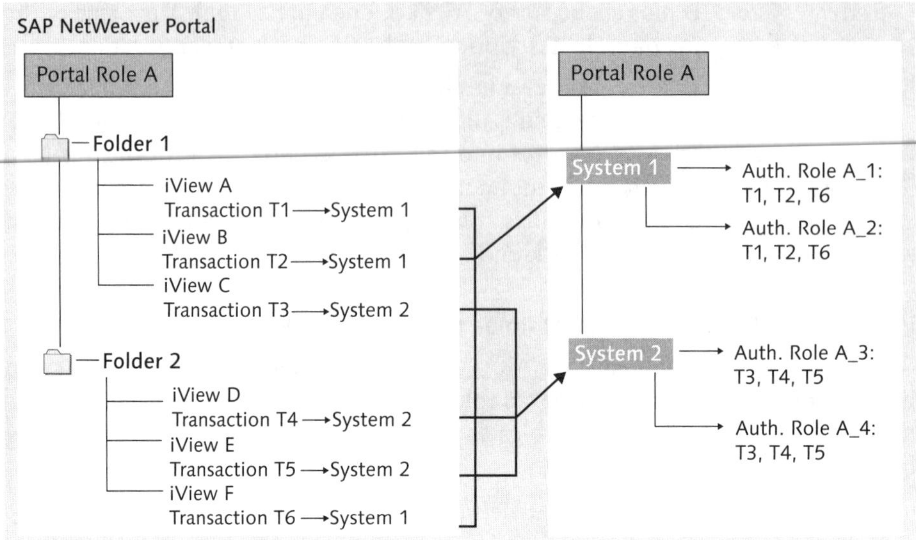


**Figure 16.11** Distribution of iViews to the Corresponding SAP Back-End Applications

The ABAP roles can be implemented in the ABAP authorizations using Transaction WP3R after the portal roles have been distributed to the back-end applications; Transaction PFCG cannot be used for this purpose. These maintenance steps should be regarded in more detail:

1. In the first step, you must distribute the desired portal roles to the corresponding back-end applications. To do this, follow the SYSTEM ADMINISTRATION • PERMISSIONS • SAP AUTHORIZATIONS menu path in SAP NetWeaver Portal. There you will find the portal roles that can be distributed. Select the roles that are supposed to be distributed.
2. In the next step, select the target system to which the roles are supposed to be distributed. As shown in Figure 16.10, only distribute those iViews or transactions from the portal role to the respective back-end application that can be executed there.
3. In the next step, distribute the portal roles with the appropriate name to the back-end application.
4. In the back-end system, you can now maintain the authorizations for the ported portal roles using Transaction WP3R. At first, you must maintain the migrated portal roles. In the initial screen, select the first option, Maintain Authorization Roles, with the respectively ported portal role.

5. In the next step, you can now specify the authorizations.
6. To assign the distributed ABAP roles to the users, you must once again distribute this assignment in the portal. To do this, follow the SYSTEM ADMINISTRATION • PERMISSIONS • SAP AUTHORIZATIONS menu path and go to the TRANSFER USER MAPPING tab. For portal roles that have already been distributed, you can distribute the user assignments to the back-end applications.
7. After distributing the users to the back-end applications, you must select the second option in Transaction WP3R, ASSIGN AUTHORIZATION ROLES TO USERS. With this option, you can assign the distributed portal roles to the selected user.

#### Selection of the Primary System — SAP NetWeaver Portal or Back-End Applications

For synchronizing the roles between SAP NetWeaver Portal and the back-end applications, you must select a primary system. In this regard, you should consider the following aspects:

- If SAP NetWeaver Portal is exclusively used for managing documents or other company-internal content, and if the portal roles for calling the back-end applications are rather simple, you should use SAP NetWeaver Portal as the primary role design system. However, make sure that the ABAP authorization structure does not need to be specified in a very complex manner with numerous company codes, plants, and so on, because in that case, the maintenance effort using Transaction WP3R would be very high.
- If access to back-end applications is managed primarily by using SAP NetWeaver Portal, you should use the back-end applications as primary systems. The roles should be built and managed there and transferred to SAP NetWeaver Portal via the uploading functionality.

Assuming that we have a common business scenario, where SAP NetWeaver Portal is primarily used as a standard entry platform for the back-end applications, you should continue to use the respective back-end applications as primary systems for managing the roles. This solution is much better, because the information ownership principle (segregation of duties) demanded by the Sarbanes-Oxley Act (SOX) can be implemented best by using currently existing external Governance, risk, and Compliance (GRC) tools in SAP BusinessObjects (see Chapter 8, GRC Solutions in SAP BusinessObjects), which can be used to monitor and correct roles and role assignments.

### 16.3.7 Change Management Process for New Portal Content

For SAP NetWeaver Portal, several tools, such as the Portal Development Kit (PDK) or SAP NetWeaver Developer Studio (NWDS), can be used to create new content and store it in the PCD or import it as a PAR file to the portal. This content can also be created directly in the PCD using the iView Wizard. In any case, you need to ensure that an appropriate change management process is implemented, as it also applies as a Best Practice for changes to traditional SAP systems.

To do this, SAP NetWeaver Portal also provides a transport management system that can be used to transport packages from portal objects. Therefore, a three-system landscape with a development (DEV), quality assurance (QAS), and production system (PRD) should exist for the SAP NetWeaver Portal. The development of the new content must take place on the development system and must then be tested on the quality assurance system by key users of strategic business units. On approval, the new content can then be imported into the production environment.

The following principles and Best Practices should be considered during portal content change management:

- Changes to objects on the development system should always be made to the originals and not to copies, because existing changes would otherwise be overwritten again during a succeeding transport.
- A transport is carried out from the development system to a shared transport directory from where the quality assurance and production systems then import their changes.
- Transport packages for the developers must be created at an early stage so that they are able to gradually integrate their modified or newly created objects during the project.
- The developers of new portal content must be responsible for the content they created. They must also confirm when they have placed their content in the provided transport packages.
- The business process owners must be involved in functional tests and approval processes of the new portal content. They must check this content to make sure it functions properly and is textually correct. These checks should also consider required controls or business process controls. In addition, they must give their final approval for import to the production system.
- When finalizing the transport packages, dependencies among objects must be considered. This is important if inheritances are to be transported as well. To do this, a multipackage approach should be used where the object content, portal

structures, and applications are separately exported and imported. The following transport packages should be created:

- **Content transport package**
  This package contains iViews and pages with dependent objects.
- **Structure transport package**
  This package contains pages, worksets, and portal roles without dependent objects.
- **Application transport package**
  This package contains new application elements (PAR files) that include new portal components and services.

When importing multipackages, application packages need to be imported first, then the structure packages, and finally the content transport packages.

Change management should always be well documented. That means that approvals, permissions, test results, and details of changes should be documented sufficiently.

The transport manager is available in SAP NetWeaver Portal via the menu path: SYSTEM ADMINISTRATION • TRANSPORT. Here, you will find the EXPORT AND IMPORT functions. In Export mode, objects can be selected in the PCD that are to be added to a defined transport package. To do this, right-click the appropriate object and select Add to Transport. The transport mechanism is only available to the content administrator to whom the Content Administrator portal role was assigned. This role is a standard role delivered by SAP (see Section 16.3.5, Standard Portal Roles and Delegated User Administration).

## 16.4 Technical Security

This section describes in more detail the risks and controls that are outlined in Table 16.1 with regard to technical security.

### 16.4.1 Connecting SAP NetWeaver Portal to a Central LDAP Directory or SAP System

Because the application landscapes are increasingly complex in most organizations, connecting SAP NetWeaver Portal to a central LDAP directory or identity management system where all user master data is stored and managed is recommended. In simpler scenarios, the SAP NetWeaver Portal user master records can also be stored in an existing SAP system. To do this, SAP NetWeaver AS Release 6.20 or higher is required.

A central LDAP directory has the advantage that the user master records can always be kept consistent across all connected applications (single source of truth). Even when changes occur (for example, due to an employee moving to another department, and so on), this information can immediately be changed in one central place and does not need to be made consistent across several administrative units.

### Description of the LDAP Directory

Technically, LDAP is based on the X.509 standard of the originally defined Directory Access Protocol (DAP), which was relieved of some functionality to increase performance. In the LDAP directory, information can be stored in a flat or deep hierarchy. The following differences between these two hierarchies are illustrated in Figure 16.12.

- In a deep hierarchy, the organizational structure is represented by a directory tree. A distinguished name (DN) is created using the attributes `C` (Country), `O` (Organization), `OU` (Organizational Unit, like subsidiary, department, and so on.), and `UID` (User ID).
- In a flat hierarchy, all organizational elements are mapped at the same level and linked to each other using references (links). In the example, the links are created by entering the members and their user IDs in the appropriate organizational units. The benefit of the flat hierarchy is that employees do not need to be listed several times if they are assigned to an organizational unit more than once. The entire data set that needs to be stored in the LDAP directory can therefore be limited.

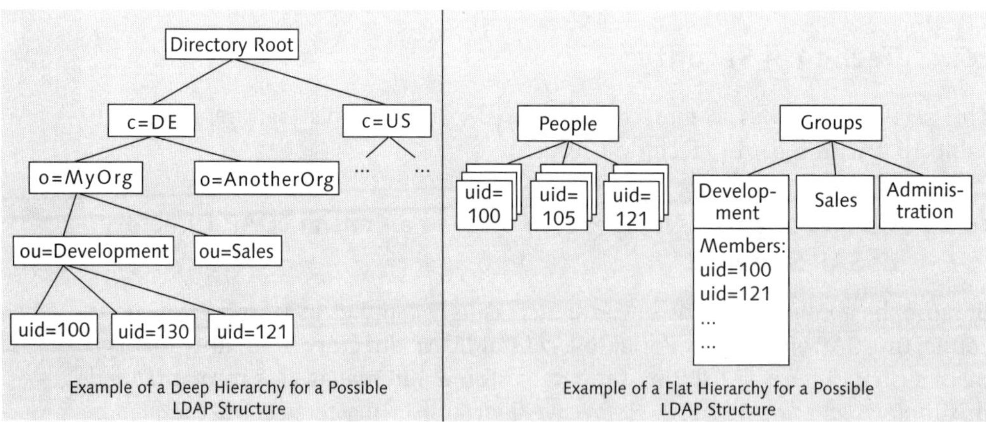


**Figure 16.12** Comparison of Deep and Flat LDAP Hierarchies

### Connecting the LDAP Server to SAP NetWeaver Portal

An LDAP directory is connected to SAP NetWeaver Portal by selecting a data source configuration file (XML file). In SAP NetWeaver Portal, this file can be selected via the following menu path: SYSTEM ADMINISTRATION • SYSTEM CONFIGURATION • UM CONFIGURATION. On the DATA SOURCES tab, the appropriate data source configuration file (for example, READ ONLY NOVELL LDAP SERVER (FLAT HIERARCHY)) can be selected. If no appropriate data source configuration file is available, you can change one accordingly. In addition, the standard data source configuration files delivered with SAP NetWeaver Portal provides numerous configuration options.

If READ ONLY LDAP SERVER (FLAT HIERARCHY) is selected, for example, on the LDAP SERVER tab you need to specify the server name and the technical user for authentication on the LDAP server, and the directory tree for the users (for example, `OU=Users, OU=Development, O=MyOrg, C=DE`). In addition, you need to enter the group path (for example, `OU=Groups, OU=Development, O=MyOrg, C=DE`). You can also create a secure encrypted connection to the LDAP server by setting the SSL option. To do this, however, the external LDAP server must provide an appropriate option as well. After these options have been set, the configuration must be saved and SAP NetWeaver Portal must be restarted. Only then will the settings take effect.

### Connecting SAP NetWeaver Portal to an SAP System

Connecting SAP NetWeaver Portal to an existing AS ABAP (Release 6.20 or higher) is similar to connecting it to an LDAP server. In this case, however, a different data source configuration file needs to be selected. To do this, an XML file can be used to make AS ABAP a user persistence storage location. This option should only be applied in simple enterprise scenarios, though.

### Selecting the Leading User Persistence Storage Location

When connecting SAP NetWeaver Portal to an external user persistence storage location, you should consider which system should act as the leading system. If SAP NetWeaver Portal is supposed to be used as a self-registration platform, you should define SAP NetWeaver Portal as the leading system. If a SAP ERP HCM is already in use and if all employees and their positions in the enterprise are maintained there according to the organizational structure, you should define the SAP ERP HCM system as the leading system. SAP ERP HCM first registers all changes and then affects a transfer to the attached portal LDAP directory. Therefore, you should use the SAP ERP HCM system as the leading user persistence storage location in complex enterprise structures.

In simpler enterprise structures, and if the back-end application is the main application in the enterprise, this back-end application should be used as the leading user persistence storage location. In this case, complete change management, including the SAP roles, can remain within the SAP back-end application.

### 16.4.2 Implementation of an SSO Mechanism Based on a One-Factor Authentication

By default, SAP NetWeaver Portal provides several kinds of user authentication. The simplest option is the standard authentication based on user ID and password. Nevertheless, appropriate rules should be defined for this method as well (see Section 16.4.6). This one-factor authentication can be either *form-based* or *basic*. In an iView, it is form-based, and if it is an HTTP status request of the Type 401, it is basic. The SAP NetWeaver Portal server verifies the entered credentials against the selected user persistence storage.

SAP NetWeaver Portal provides an SSO mechanism based on SAP logon tickets so that the user only has to log on once and doesn't have to reenter his credentials in every single back-end application. This mechanism is summarized in Figure 16.13.

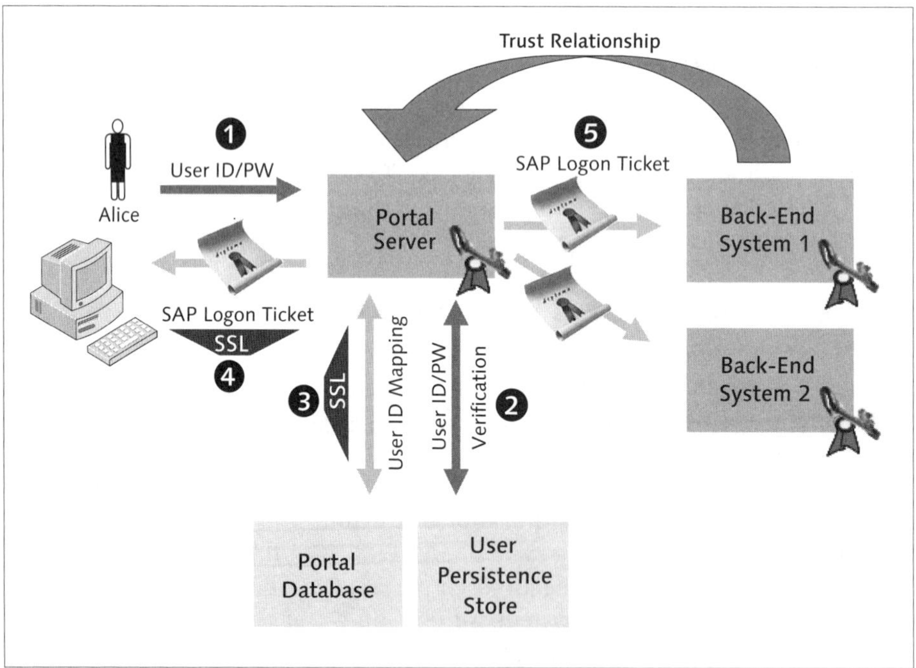


**Figure 16.13** SSO Mechanism in SAP NetWeaver Portal Based on SAP Logon Tickets (Initial Authentication via User ID and Password)

The logon process is as follows:

1. The user enters his credentials (user ID and password) in SAP NetWeaver Portal.
2. The portal server validates the data against the values stored in the user persistence storage of the portal database.
3. If the validation is successful, additional information, such as the mapping of user information, is read from the portal database. This mapping is necessary if the user's user name in the back-end systems is different from the one used in SAP NetWeaver Portal. This assignment is determined in the mapping.
4. The portal server issues an SAP logon ticket (web browser cookie) and digitally signs it with its own certificate. The following information is stored in this SAP logon ticket: the user name used in the back-end application (for example, `AliceM`), the logon name in SAP EP (for example, `Alice.Mueller`), the validity period of the SAP logon ticket, and the SAP system ID of the issuing system (for example, `C11` and `Mandant 000`, AS Java). The ticket does not contain any passwords. Only one different user name can be supported in the back-end applications, which again supports the use of an LDAP directory. In addition, the SAP logon ticket is digitally signed with the private key of the portal certificate and is sent back to the web browser in the form of a cookie.
5. If the user starts a new back-end application using an iView within SAP NetWeaver Portal, the SAP logon ticket is also sent to the back-end application, which then needs to verify it. For the SAP logon ticket to be accepted, the back-end application must be configured so that it accepts SAP logon tickets for authentication. The user name specified in the SAP logon ticket must be known to the application as well, and, most importantly, there must be a trust relationship with the SAP NetWeaver Portal issuing the ticket. The SAP logon ticket will only be accepted for authentication in the back-end application if these requirements are met.

   The back-end application can also be a non-SAP application. For non-SAP applications, there are several possibilities: For example, there are web server filters that can be integrated in a web server as an Information Server Application Programming Interface (ISAPI). There are also Kerberos mapping modules for Internet Information Server (IIS)–based applications (such as Outlook Web Access or SharePoint Portal Server) or Domino filters for Lotus Notes or WebLogic-based web applications.

In the scenario described, however, it is crucial that you define a leading system to issue SAP logon tickets and that you configure all other back-end applications so that these SAP logon tickets are accepted for authentication. Between the back-end applications and the issuing SAP NetWeaver Portal, there must be a trust relationship based on digital server certificates that are stored on the servers.

The following example assumes that an ABAP back-end application is used on an SAP system of a higher release than 6.10. By default, SAP NetWeaver Portal is configured so that it creates SAP logon tickets after a user has been successfully authenticated. The J2EE Engine of SAP NetWeaver Portal is preconfigured for the portal. For a signature to take place, an appropriate server certificate must be stored in the Keystore service of the J2EE Engine that can be accessed via the Visual Administrator.

In the next step, the ABAP back-end system must be configured so that it accepts SAP logon tickets from SAP NetWeaver Portal. This requires the following steps:

1. Add SAP NetWeaver Portal to the component list of the SAP back-end system: To do so, use Transaction SM30 for Table `TWPSSO2ACL`.
2. Insert a new entry in this table using the NEW entry.
3. By default, you must enter the COMMON NAME (CN) of SAP NetWeaver Portal and the ticket-issuing client here. You can refer to the portal server certificate for the common name. The name is usually identical to the SAP system ID (for example, `C11`). For SAP NetWeaver Portal, the default client is `000`. However, these can also be defined in a different way.
4. Enter the following values for SUBJECT NAME, ISSUER NAME, AND SERIAL NUMBER:
   - For SUBJECT NAME, enter the DN of the portal server (for example, `CN=C11, OU=Development,O=SAP,C=DE`).
   - For ISSUER NAME, enter the DN of the issuing certification authority that issued and signed the server certificate for the portal server. For self-signed certificates, this must be the same distinguished name of the portal server that has already been specified under SUBJECT NAME.
   - For SERIAL NUMBER, enter the serial number of the portal certificate.

   After specifying this data, save the entry.
5. The portal server certificate is then imported to the ABAP back-end system using Transaction STRUSTSSO2 or STRUST. To do this, you must select the system PSE.
6. In the Certificate section, select the IMPORT CERTIFICATE function. The system opens a new window providing the IMPORT CERTIFICATE FROM FILE option. Select this option.
7. In the browser, select the portal certificate in DER format that was previously saved from the Keystore of the portal to a file system location.

8. After selecting the appropriate certificate, you can import the portal server certificate.
9. Set the profile parameters `login/accept_sso2_ticket = 1` and `login/create_sso2_ticket = 0` respectively.
10. The ABAP back-end system is now configured to accept SAP logon tickets issued by SAP NetWeaver Portal.

An SSO mechanism can therefore be created based on SAP logon tickets. However, please note that the communication channels among the web browser, the SAP system, and the respective back-end applications should be encrypted via SSL.

**Note**

SAP NetWeaver Portal generates the SAP logon ticket as a web browser cookie for its own network domain. So this logon ticket is not accepted from SAP systems of another network domain. This leads to an SSO restriction for ticket-accepting systems in other network domains. To overcome this bottleneck, you can configure SAP NetWeaver Portal in such a way that it also generates SAP logon tickets for other domains. SAP Note 654982 contains further information on this subject.

### 16.4.3 Implementation of an SSO Mechanism Based on an Integrated Authentication

In a pure intranet scenario, it makes sense to combine the authentication to SAP NetWeaver Portal with the already-performed user authentication to the Windows domain (Windows Active Directory 2000/2003 with Key Distribution Center) based on Kerberos authentication tickets. Because SAP NetWeaver Portal runs on AS Java, authentication methods for this kind of integration are available as of Release 6.40 SP15, particularly the SPNEGO login module.

The SPNEGO login module uses the Generic Security Service Application Programming Interface (GSS-API) to receive the security content of the Kerberos ticket. From this content, the AS Java UME reads the user information (*userPrincipalName*) for the portal, which has already been authenticated by the Windows Active Directory.

If another SSO authentication to back-end applications needs to be carried out, you need to select the SAP logon ticket method again for SAP NetWeaver Portal as presented in Section 16.4.2, Implementation of an SSO Mechanism Based on a One-Factor Authentication. SAP NetWeaver Portal then issues an SAP logon ticket that is used by the back-end applications for further authenticating the user. SAP Note 968191 contains further information on this subject.

Figure 16.14 shows an example architecture for an integrated SSO solution between Microsoft SharePoint 2007, SAP NetWeaver Portal 7.0, and SAP ERP 6.0.

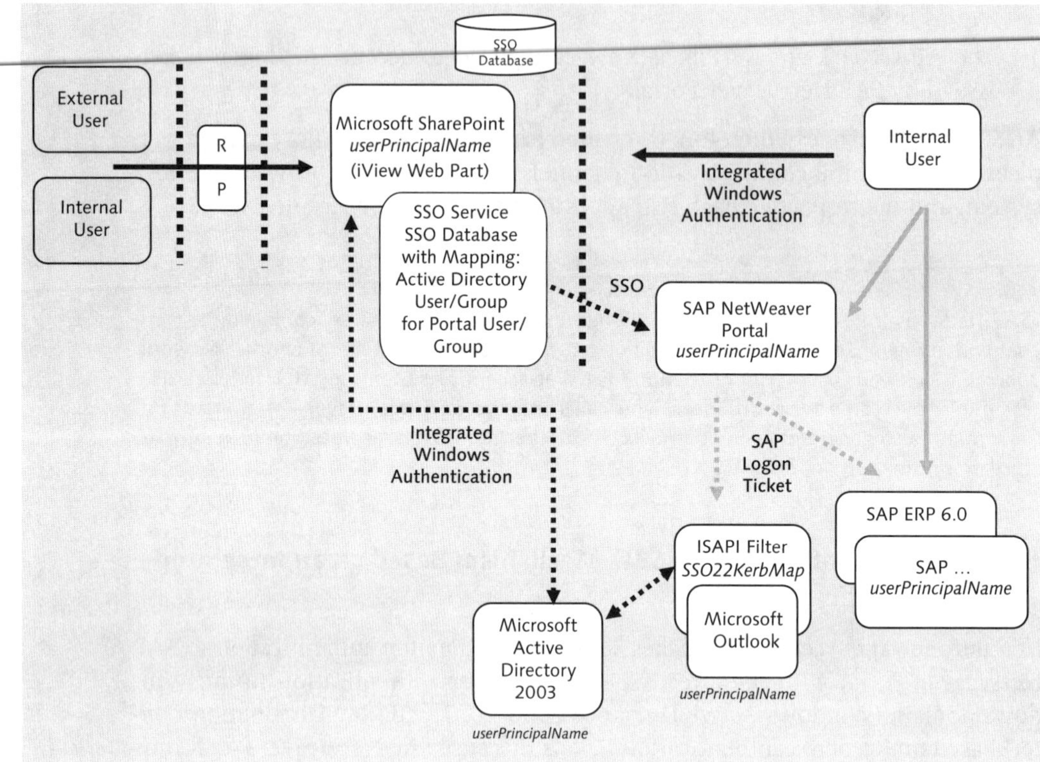


**Figure 16.14** Integrated SSO Solution

**Note**

The Kerberos/SPNEGO-supported Windows authentication also forms the basis for an SSO solution in heterogeneous multidomain architectures if a trust relationship (Windows Trust) has been established between the different domains. If the technical security functions of the technologies are used appropriately, the SSO security risks are on an acceptable level. However, as already mentioned, SSO increases the efficiency of the authentication process, and only the initial authentication involves an authentication risk. Incorrect initial identification or authentication could result in unauthorized access to all applications of the SSO group of applications.

### 16.4.4 Implementation of an SSO Mechanism Based on a Person-Related Certificates

A more sophisticated and secure authentication mechanism is based on the use of person-related X.509 certificates for the users. In this case, the SSL protocol is changed to a mutual authentication. This means that not only must the server provide a certificate to prove its authenticity to the user, but the user also has to prove his identity using a person-related certificate. However, this should be issued by a trustworthy instance like an accredited certificate authority.

For SAP NetWeaver Portal, the SSO process is basically the same as the process using a user ID and password. After the first authentication with person-related certificates, an SAP logon ticket is issued for further authentication to the back-end applications (see Figure 16.15). For verifying person-related certificates, the person-related certificates must be stored in the selected user persistence storage. For the portal database, they must be maintained manually or, when using an LDAP directory, they can be automated by mapping the user certificates stored therein.

The following configuration steps must be carried out to enable a certificate-based authentication for SAP NetWeaver Portal:

1. For the J2EE Engine of SAP NetWeaver Portal, the HTTPS service must be enabled.
2. The person-related certificates exist either in DER or Base64-encoded format.
3. Using the KeyStorage service (accessible via the Visual Administrator), the certificate authority that issued the person-related certificates must be entered in the list of trustworthy instances. In the standard version, all common external certificate authorities are listed there, such as VeriSign, Entrust, and SAP CA.
4. In the Security Provider service, the login module stack must be adjusted by adding the optional `ClientCertLoginModule` for all applications that accept certificates.
5. Finally, either the person-related certificates must be manually added to the user persistence storage, or the certificate attributes need to be mapped to the LDAP entries.

   If the user certificates are stored in an external LDAP directory, the `certificatehash`, `javax.servlet.request.X509Certificate`, and `certificate` attributes need to be set accordingly in the data source configuration file. A data source configuration file can look as shown in Listing 16.3:

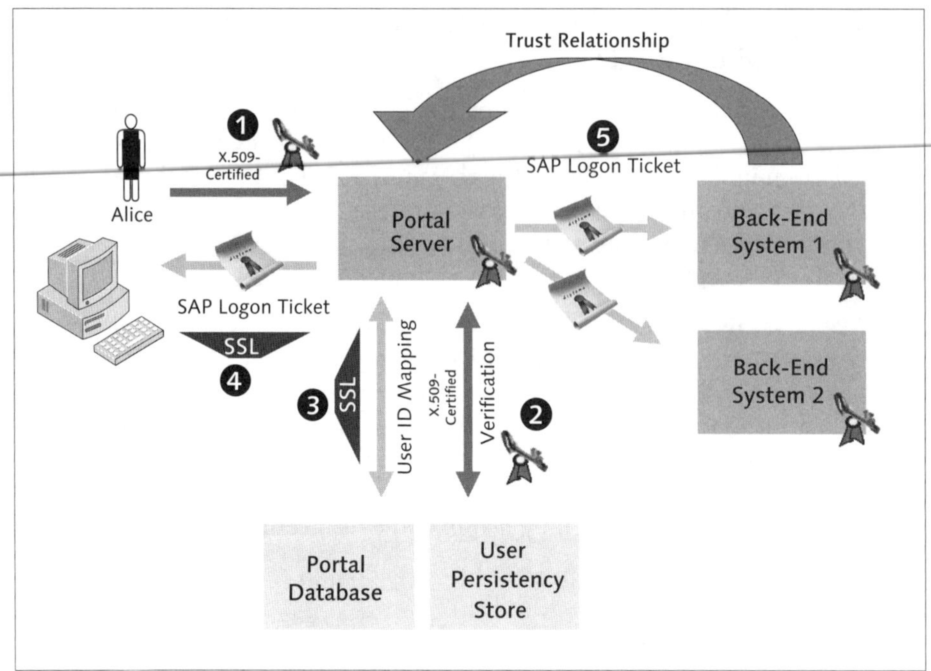


**Figure 16.15** SSO Mechanism in SAP NetWeaver Portal Based on Person-Related Certificates

```
<dataSource id="CORP_LDAP"
            className="com.sap.security.core.persistence.
              datasource.imp.LDAPPersistence"
            isReadonly="false"
            isPrimary="true">
    ...

    <attributeMapping>
      <principals>
        <principal type="account">
          <nameSpaces>
            <nameSpace name="com.sap.security.core.
             usermanagement">
              <attributes>
                ...
                <attribute name="certificatehash">
                  <physicalAttribute name="*null*"/>
                </attribute>
                <attribute name="javax.servlet.request.
                 X509Certificate">
```

```
                  <physicalAttribute name=
                   "usercertificate"/>
                </attribute>
                <attribute name="certificate">
                  <physicalAttribute name=
                   "usercertificate"/>
                </attribute>
              </attributes>
            </nameSpace>
          </nameSpaces>
        </principal>
        ...
      </principals>
    </attributeMapping>
    ...
</dataSource>
```

**Listing 16.3** Example of a Data Source Configuration File

The `certificatehash` attribute must be set to `*null*` because the user certificate cannot be temporarily stored in an LDAP directory. The `javax.servlet.request.X509Certificate` and `certificate` attributes both point to the `usercertificate` LDAP entry. This depends on the LDAP server used, though.

After the configuration has been completed, an SSO mechanism based on person-related certificates can be used. This mechanism can only be effectively implemented, however, if the required certificate management is combined with a public key infrastructure (for example, by Entrust or RSA) and if the certificates are stored in an LDAP directory. This also enables a process for central user management.

### 16.4.5 Configuration for Anonymous Access

SAP NetWeaver Portal can be configured in an Internet scenario so that single pages and iViews can be anonymously started by an Internet user, that is, without previous authentication. If not all of the portal content, but only single iViews, can be viewed anonymously, you need to be particularly careful.

For portal content to be accessed anonymously, named portal users assigned to the group of anonymous users are predefined. These portal users are either defined as normal users or, more favorably, as service users.

To enable an anonymous call, the following UME properties need to be set:

- `ume.login.anonymous_user.mode = 1`
  This value should not be changed.

- `ume.login.guest_user.uniqueids = ...`
  This is a comma-separated list of all anonymous users. By default, this is set to `anonymous`. These users are automatically assigned to the ANONYMOUS USERS GROUP.

For these iViews, pages, and worksets to be accessible anonymously, the authentication scheme in the properties can now be set to `anonymous`. This can be defined in the PCD by right-clicking on the appropriate portal object (IVIEW, PAGE, WORKSET), starting the Object Editor, and entering `anonymous` as the authentication scheme in the advanced mode of the Property Editor.

After performing this step, the Authorization Editor must be used to add the ANONYMOUS USERS GROUP for the END USER authorization. The Authorization Editor can be started by right-clicking on the object and selecting OPEN PERMISSIONS.

After this configuration, all iViews, pages, and worksets configured this way can be launched via anonymous Internet access.

### 16.4.6 Secure Initial Configuration

After the initial installation, you should definitely perform the security measures mentioned in the composite SAP Note 606733 if SAP NetWeaver Portal is used via the Internet. This note includes the following SAP notes:

- 531495 (How to disable directory browsing in the SAP J2EE Engine)
- 602371 (All users for telnet authorized for R/3)
- 603142 (J2EE users after installation without password)
- 604285 (Security vulnerability by unprotected HTTP PUT method)
- 622447 (SAP Biller Direct 2.0 installation note (Java component))
- 646140 (Security check of Internet Sales)
- 705619 (WEB-INF security vulnerabilities in SAP J2EE Engine 6.20)

This composite note is still valid and should always be adhered to.

Using the portal config tool, important UME properties should be defined. These properties are all stored in the *sapum.properties* file. The file is automatically generated during the portal installation and contains configuration parameters that are defined during installation. If required, you can manually adapt the file to your requirements at a later time. You can store this file in various directories at the AS Java operating system level.

Actually, it is located in the PCD portal and can be edited from there in the UME user interface (via the menu path: SYSTEM ADMINISTRATION • SYSTEM CONFIGURA-

TION • UME CONFIGURATION • DIRECT EDITING). Among other options, the maximum length of user IDs can be specified. If you consider synchronization with an SAP back-end system, you should take into account that it currently only supports a maximum length of eight characters. More password policies like complexity and length can be specified here as well. You should use a minimum length of six characters with at least one numeric character. The UME properties can also be used to define the number of failed authentication attempts. Using a minimum number of three attempts is recommended.

In addition, the validity period of SAP logon tickets can be defined in these UME properties. For pure intranet scenarios, the maximum validity should be adjusted to the regular business times. In Internet scenarios, however, you should consider setting much shorter validity periods of, for example, 15 minutes.

### 16.4.7 Secure Network Architecture

To prevent SAP NetWeaver Portal from being directly accessible at the network level from the Internet, you should establish a network zone structure that is commonly used for Internet scenarios and that consists of DMZs. Such network architecture is illustrated in Figure 16.16.

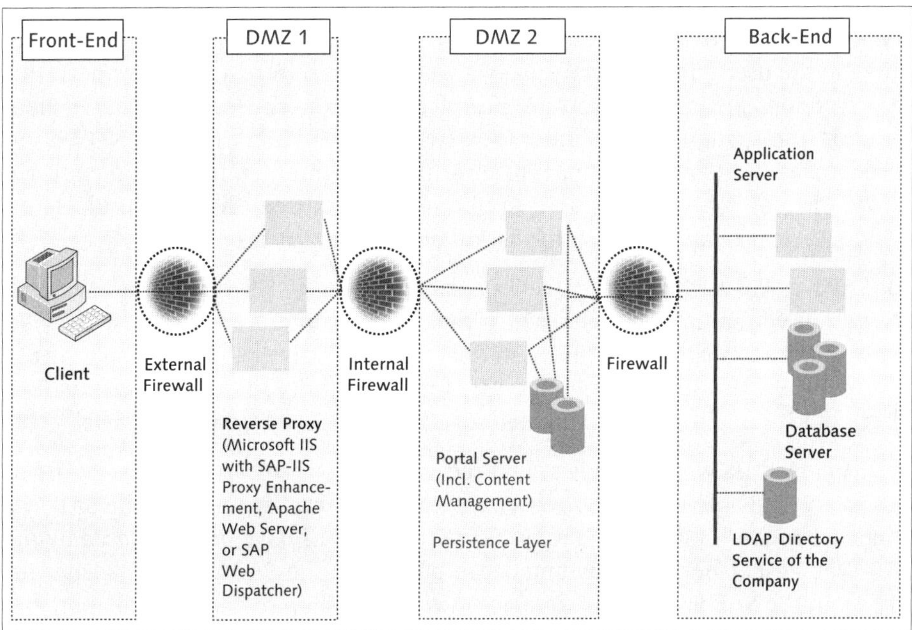


**Figure 16.16** DMZ Network Architecture for Implementing SAP NetWeaver Portal

From the Internet, the client (web browser) can only reach the reverse proxy that is placed in the outer demilitarized zone (DMZ 1). It accepts the HTTP(S) requests and forwards them to the SAP NetWeaver Portal located in the inner demilitarized zone (DMZ 2). The outer firewall only transfers HTTP requests via port 80 or HTTPS requests via port 441. The internal firewall needs to be configured with filter rules that only permit requests from the reverse proxy to SAP NetWeaver Portal. This must be admissible for those ports for which the HTTP or HTTPS services have been defined on the portal. This can easily be checked via the Visual Administrator.

In DMZ 2, the portal database can also be installed, which usually acts as the user persistence storage for external Internet users. For internal users, the company-internal LDAP directory can be used that is located in the back-end. To do this, an appropriate firewall rule must be defined on the back-end firewall. In the back end, the critical back-end applications, such as SAP systems, the database server, and the search and classification engine (TREX) for SAP NetWeaver Portal should be implemented.

Compared to a regular proxy, a reverse proxy functions in the exact opposite way: In company-wide networks, a proxy fulfills the task of bundling and filtering accesses to the Internet. In this case, not every work center can directly access the Internet, but is routed via the proxy, which then acts as the calling instance toward the website selected by the user. The response is then redirected via the proxy to the user's application (usually a web browser). A reverse proxy performs the exact opposite task. It accepts requests coming from the Internet, checks them for correctness, and forwards them to SAP NetWeaver Portal. For SAP NetWeaver Portal, the request does not appear to come from the Internet, but from the reverse proxy. Chapter 9, SAP NetWeaver Application Server, and Chapter 14, Class SAP Middleware, provide further information on reverse proxies.

For SAP NetWeaver Portal, the freely available Apache web server or the Microsoft IIS web server are mainly used, which can also be configured as reverse proxies. The SAP Web Dispatcher discussed in Chapter 14 can also be regarded as a sort of reverse proxy. However, it only provides limited security filter functionality (URL filter), but it can also be implemented together with SAP NetWeaver Portal.

The Microsoft IIS web server is often used as a reverse proxy because it is more or less freely available in a Windows environment. In earlier releases, the SAP system used an ISAPI filter or IISProxy. These two options have been replaced by the SAP Web Dispatcher. SAP customers can download the SAP Web Dispatcher for free from the SAP Service Marketplace (*http://service.sap.com*). Its installation and configuration are very easy if you refer to the available documentation (see Chapter 14). After configuration, the SAP Web Dispatcher functions as a forwarding reverse proxy. This means that original requests with a specific URL arriving at the SAP Web Dispatcher through HTTP port 80, for example, are directed to another SAP NetWeaver Portal port (for example, 4001) with another URL; depending on the configuration, this is done via a mapping table. The URLs provided by SAP NetWeaver Portal are therefore not visible to external users and protected from direct access.

As mentioned earlier, the Apache web server that is available as open software provides specific security checks at the HTTP application protocol level when it is configured as a reverse proxy. These security checks can be activated when the security module `mod_security` is installed. It is recommended to use at least Apache version 2.x. The security filter functionality of the `mod_security` module must be defined using filter rules. The exact configuration of the filter rules can be viewed at *http://www.modsecurity.org*.

The following security checks can be performed using `mod_security`:

- Inbound HTTP requests can be analyzed using predefined filters.
- All paths and parameters of the URLs are first untagged to prevent a normal form from being circumvented with escape sequences, thereby rendering it no longer fit to be analyzed.
- Even `POST` HTTP commands where the control sequences in the HTTP body are forwarded to SAP NetWeaver Portal can be analyzed.
- All HTTP requests can be logged so that you can analyze them in detail at a later stage.
- The HTTP responses can be checked using output rules to ensure that a complete response is sent to the client and does not arrive in separate stages due to a splitting process that would expose it to potential modifications.
- After decryption, HTTPS requests can also be analyzed on the Apache web server.

On the whole, a reverse proxy installation of the Apache web server provides numerous possibilities for ensuring actual Internet security. However, the correct configuration with the appropriate filter rules is rather complex, and its performance is a little weaker compared to the commercial application-level gateways (see Section 16.4.8, Introducing an Application-Level Gateway to Make Portal Applications Secure). Still, this alternative should be considered in a cost/benefit analysis.

### 16.4.8 Introducing an Application-Level Gateway to Make Portal Applications Secure

The network architecture suggested in the previous section in Figure 16.16 only provides sufficient protection against Internet attacks at the network level. It does not ensure sufficient protection against the most common attacks at the application level, though. To counteract these types of attacks, the application itself should be programmed so that every input made by the Internet user is checked for plausibility and correctness in the portal application before it is processed further. On top of this, the use of application-level gateways or application-level firewalls provides additional protection against attacks at the application level. The most common attacks are outlined in Table 16.8.

| Internet Attack | Target | What Happens |
|---|---|---|
| Cookie poisoning | Taking over another identity, session hijacking | With regard to SAP NetWeaver Portal, the authenticity of a user is managed using the SAP logon ticket (a cookie), for example. An attacker can try to take possession of this cookie or to manipulate it and change content so that he can take on the identity of a user who has already been authenticated. |
| Hidden field manipulation | Manipulating data (for example, price information) | In many eShop applications, price information for offered goods is often transferred to a hidden field in the HTTP body. This hidden field can be manipulated to alter the price of goods. Often, hidden fields also contain information about the session state of an application session that was previously authenticated. By means of manipulation, attackers can try to take over the session of another user. |
| Parameter tampering | Fraud | Via the URL, a lot of information is transferred to the server using Common Gateway Interface (CGI) encoding. For example, these parameters provide information about the logged on user or about the user's credit limit. On the server side, the correctness of these parameters is often not verified (for example, when using SAP NetWeaver Portal with the external |

**Table 16.8** Typical Internet Attacks at the Application Level

| Internet Attack | Target | What Happens |
|---|---|---|
| | | Windows authentication service), so these parameters can easily be modified. Therefore, identities can be obtained by fraud or credit limits can be modified, for instance. |
| Buffer overflow | Denial of service | In normal form fields for entering information and for transferring this data to the server, the amount of data transferred is too large. This way, application servers, like the SAP NetWeaver Portal server, might be brought to a crash. |
| Cross-site scripting | Identity theft, fraud | Via normal form fields, JavaScript or ActiveX components are transferred to the server and executed when they are transferred back to other users. They then direct those users to fictitious pages that entice them to enter confidential information. |
| Backdoor and debug options | Taking possession of the server | Often, Internet applications are developed under such high time pressures that developers forget to remove debug options after going live. These debug options can be abused by external attackers. |
| Forceful browsing | Taking possession of the Internet application | The attacker tries to quit the normal logical application flow and take possession of the Internet application by calling modified HTTP responses to achieve more advanced authorization. In SAP NetWeaver Portal, this could be achieved if security zones are not implemented, and services can therefore be called directly via a URL. |
| HTTP response | Phishing, identity theft | The HTTP responses that are intended for the application server and stored in the cache are split, modified, and sent back to the application server. Unprotected services can therefore be called on the application server to promote the attacker to a higher authorization level. |

**Table 16.8** Typical Internet Attacks at the Application Level (Cont.)

| Internet Attack | Target | What Happens |
|---|---|---|
| Stealth commanding | Introducing malware | Attackers often try to introduce their own malware (like Trojans) to application servers using form fields or document upload options. With this malware, further attacks can then be carried out. |
| Script injection (SQL injection) | Fraud, taking over another identity | Using script injection, attackers try to change database entries directly by using the logic of SQL queries. URL header variables are often used to integrate them directly in SQL queries. A modification of these header variables can be used for a script injection. |
| Known vulnerabilities | Taking over the control of the Internet application | Known vulnerabilities in the operating system, for example, that are reported on a regular basis, can be used by attackers for taking over the Internet application. |

**Table 16.8** Typical Internet Attacks at the Application Level (Cont.)

To effectively avert such attacks, adequate server-side checks must be carried out during application development (see also *Sichere ABAP-Programmierung, http://www.sap-press.de/2037*). Along with secure application development, implementation of application-level gateways can provide protection. This kind of application-level gateway must be placed before SAP NetWeaver Portal in DMZ 1. The gateway accepts all requests from the Internet and checks these requests for plausibility and correctness according to rules that were previously defined. Figure 16.17 presents the DMZ network architecture using an application-level gateway.

An application-level gateway considerably improves the options for performing security checks in a normal reverse proxy, as it was described in the previous section. Various commercial products can be used as possible application-level gateways. Most of these commercial products work with a positive security model. This means that Internet requests (HTTP or HTTPS requests) that are not included on the positive access list are blocked.

Basically, this works as follows: A normal and admissible point of entry is defined for the Internet application, such as *http://my.webapplication.com*. Only this URL is permitted as a possible point of entry. If this URL is called, the HTTP response generated in the application server (in this case, SAP NetWeaver Portal) is checked for the new possible links and form fields before it is returned to the client. These potential new branches and input options are stored per user session in the cache of the application-level gateway.

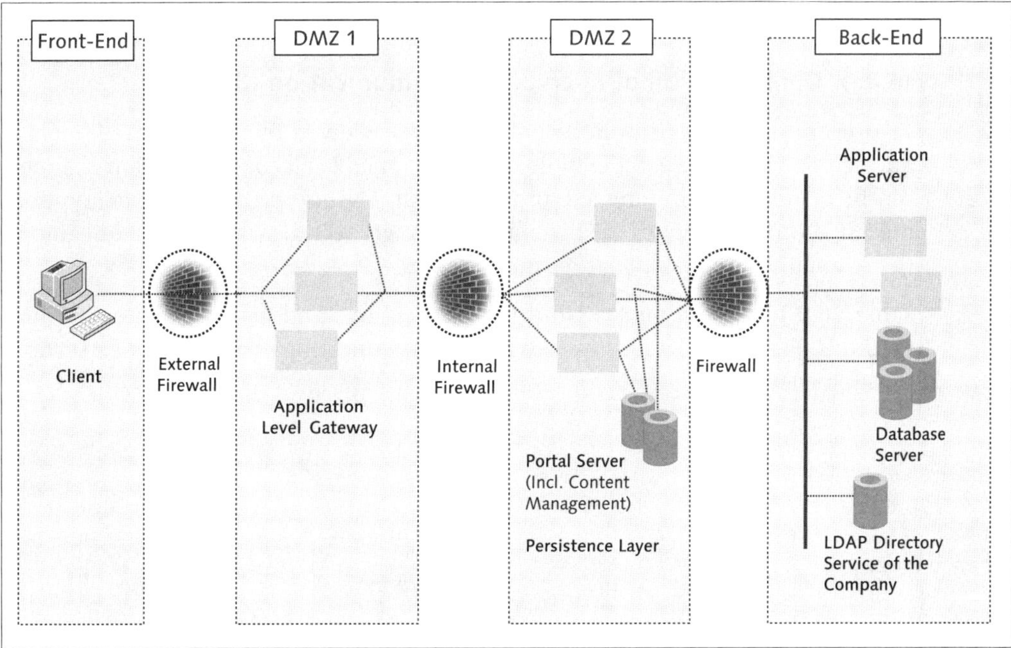


**Figure 16.17** DMZ Network Architecture with Application-Level Gateway

This means that the cache is user-specific, which is achieved via an additional cookie. This cache gradually builds the positive list per user throughout the course of the session. If the user issues a new request, it is checked against the positive list. If it is contained therein, the request is forwarded to SAP NetWeaver Portal. If it is not, the request is blocked. For example, if the user modifies the URL and given parameters, this request would be blocked, as it is identified as not being part of the positive list.

In addition to this positive list, you can also define black lists (for example, special character strings like <, >, /, and so on) that indicate script input in form fields and are therefore blocked. You can also define form field sizes to prevent buffer overflow attacks. Numerous configurations can be specified that will not be discussed in detail. The challenge is often in finding the right balance between security and functional requirements. This is only possible by performing sufficient tests.

Altogether, the security level that can be achieved compared to a traditional reverse proxy is higher because the reverse proxy's configuration and proactive security functions are more complex. This is the case if the web application is built in a very dynamic way, which is common practice today.

### 16.4.9 Configuration of Encrypted Communication Channels

To prevent information from being changed or viewed by unauthorized persons during transport between the individual components, all communication channels can be encrypted using the SSL protocol or an SNC. Apart from just encryption, the SSL protocol provides the benefit of a stronger technical authentication among the communicating architecture components.

Table 16.9 further discusses all of the connections and explains the encryption methods. Figure 16.18 illustrates which communication channels can be secured through encryption.

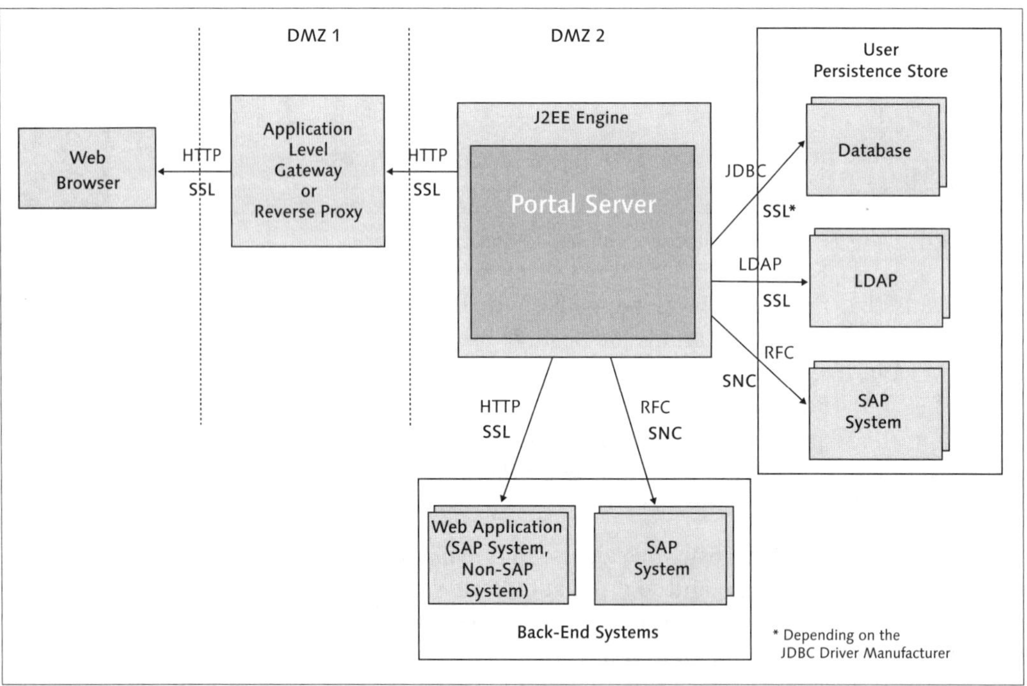


**Figure 16.18** Encryptable Communication Channels for SAP NetWeaver Portal

| Connection | Encryption | Connection Purpose |
|---|---|---|
| Client ↔ reverse proxy | SSL (HTTPS) | Via this connection, the web browser can send an HTTP request to the reverse proxy and receive the HTML responses. |
| Reverse proxy ↔ SAP NetWeaver Portal server | SSL (HTTPS) | After the HTTP(S) request has been validated on the reverse proxy, it is forwarded to SAP NetWeaver Portal. |
| SAP NetWeaver Portal server ↔ portal database | SSL (for JDBC) | Under certain conditions, the portal database is also used as the user persistence storage. In this case, it is recommended to use encryption because the users' credentials are then kept in the database. |
| SAP NetWeaver Portal server ↔ LDAP server | SSL (LDAPS) | If an LDAP server is used as the user persistence storage, it is recommended to use encryption because the users' credentials are stored on the LDAP server and are queried during the authentication process. In this case, the connection is established between the UME and the LDAP server. |
| SAP NetWeaver Portal server ↔ SAP system | SNC | If the SAP system is used as the user persistence storage, the RFC connection that is used between the portal and the SAP system should be appropriately encrypted. To do this, the SNC protocol can be used. The connection is established between the UME and the SAP system. RFC calls can also be used for further function calls on the SAP system that can be secured using SNC. |
| SAP NetWeaver Portal server ↔ web application | SSL | Other web applications that can be addressed using HTTP (for example, on SAP and on non-SAP systems) can be secured again using SSL. |

**Table 16.9** SAP Communication Channels and Encryption Technologies

The exact steps that are necessary to configure the SSL or SNC connections are not further discussed in this chapter because they have already been described in detail in Chapter 9. The required configuration steps are identical. In this context, it should be mentioned that the respective cryptographic libraries have been installed both for the SAP J2EE Engine in SAP NetWeaver Portal and for the SAP back-end systems that are supposed to be connected. In addition, the appropriate certificates for the servers must be implemented because all encryption mechanisms are initially based on asymmetric encryption processes.

### 16.4.10 Implementation of a Virus Scan for Avoiding a Virus Infection

If SAP NetWeaver Portal enables an application to upload a document, there is the risk that this document (attachment) is infected with a virus. To prevent this virus from quickly spreading throughout the organization via the existing office communication platform, SAP provides a certified interface to integrate a virus scanner that scans attachments for potential viruses before they are stored in the database and prevents further storage in case of an infection.

The certified products for the virus scan interface (VSI) can be found in the SAP Service Marketplace under *http://service.sap.com/securitypartners* (also see SAP Note 786179). The VSI is available for both ABAP programs and Java programs running on AS Java.

The essential elements of the VSI are illustrated in Figure 16.19. The interface can be called directly on the relevant server (SAP NetWeaver AS) or via an RFC on a dedicated virus scan server. A dedicated virus scan server is recommended if the virus scan software provided by the individual certified vendor cannot be executed on the same SAP NetWeaver AS or if a high virus scan load is anticipated. The actual virus scan software product of the respective vendor is then connected via the VSI. To do this, an API of the relevant virus software vendor is addressed.

In addition, it is possible to connect several different virus scan products via the virus scan interface if a product does not provide the desired virus definition. To do this, the virus scan products must be assigned to individual virus definition groups. Some groups can be executed locally on the SAP NetWeaver AS and others on a dedicated external virus scan server.

The choice of an external virus scan server mainly depends on the expected load of a potential attachment (document) uploading activity. For classic public Internet job exchanges where a large number of attachments must be managed, it makes sense to implement a dedicated external virus scan server or even a cluster. When selecting a virus scanner, you should pay attention to the functionality of the automated update of the virus definition file. It is crucial that this file is always up to date to ensure good virus protection. In this respect, daily update functionality would be ideal. However, you should always carefully test a virus scanner before using it in the production system. This is necessary to determine or reduce the risk of the scanner manipulating normal functions without reason.

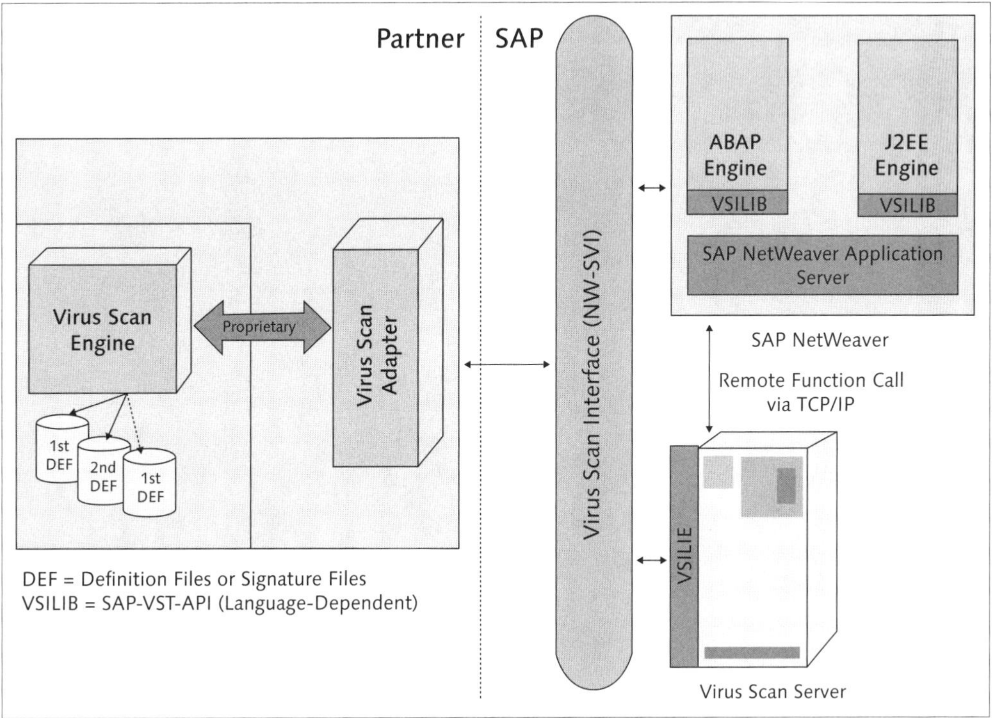


**Figure 16.19** Architecture of the VSI

*Mobile devices provide great options for external and internal access to SAP systems if the security risk to data is recognized and handled appropriately. For this reason, this chapter focuses on the security aspects for use, communication, and data replication within the scope of SAP NetWeaver Mobile.*

# 17 SAP NetWeaver Mobile

International networking and global mobile system access are a requirement for the success of many modern business models. Advanced communication options, and global system accesses and transactions are the way of modern economics; however, this system openness also requires the risk management to establish appropriate restrictions.

In particular, logistics uses mobile scanners to capture goods receipts and goods issued on site and posts them directly to inventory. In addition, customer consultants need a way to close an order directly at a customer's site. The use of mobile devices enables sales staff to improve their relationships with customers. In both examples, the SAP back-end system is accessed via a wireless data network using mobile devices. This scenario results in a major risk potential for data security because the transferred information or the information stored on the mobile device can be confidential and because protecting data in mobile devices or wireless data networks against unauthorized access is not trivial. The goal of this chapter is that you better understand such risks and get to know the security options of SAP NetWeaver Mobile.

## 17.1 Introduction and Functions

Within SAP Business Suite, SAP offers several mobile applications implemented on the basis of SAP NetWeaver Mobile. The applications include mobile asset management within SAP Product Lifecycle Management (PLM), mobile field sales within SAP Customer Relationship Management (CRM), mobile warehouse management within SAP Supply Chain Management (SCM), and many more. SAP NetWeaver Mobile also supports the Radio Frequency Identification (RFID) technology.

Mobile devices include notebooks, netbooks, wireless data input devices, Personal Digital Assistants (PDA), and smartphones. In addition, an application in SAP NetWeaver Mobile enables access to any device on which the client of SAP NetWeaver Mobile (mobile client) can be operated. Controls for security and risk management are included in SAP NetWeaver Mobile and must be set according to your requirements.

SAP NetWeaver Mobile supports two mobile usage scenarios:

- **Online scenario**
  In the online scenario, the mobile device uses a middle layer to connect directly to the back-end application. Data is exchanged directly online.
- **Offline scenario**
  In the offline scenario, the mobile device works independent of the back-end application. Data is exchanged periodically during a synchronization process.

The second scenario occurs more often, because an opportunity to establish a direct connection with the back-end application is not a frequent occurrence. Therefore, the offline scenario is considered to be the more important scenario, and is the model on which the following security considerations are based. The architecture of SAP NetWeaver Mobile is identical in both scenarios, as shown in Figure 17.1. Figure 17.1 also shows the SAP NetWeaver Development Infrastructure (NWDI) and the SAP NetWeaver Developer Studio (NWDS). The two components are not a direct element of SAP NetWeaver Mobile, but they are mentioned here because they form the basis for the design and development environment for mobile applications.

A mobile client is installed on a mobile device as an independent, technical runtime environment. With this component, mobile applications can be developed independent of the operating system on the mobile device. The client assumes responsibility for the following tasks and provides the required interfaces:

- Local data storage
- Data synchronization between the mobile device and the server
- Application management
- Tracing and logging on files that can also be transmitted to the server
- Configuration management for setting application and user parameters
- User Interface (UI) programming models based on Java Server pages (JSPs)/ Abstract Window Toolkit (AWT)
- User management

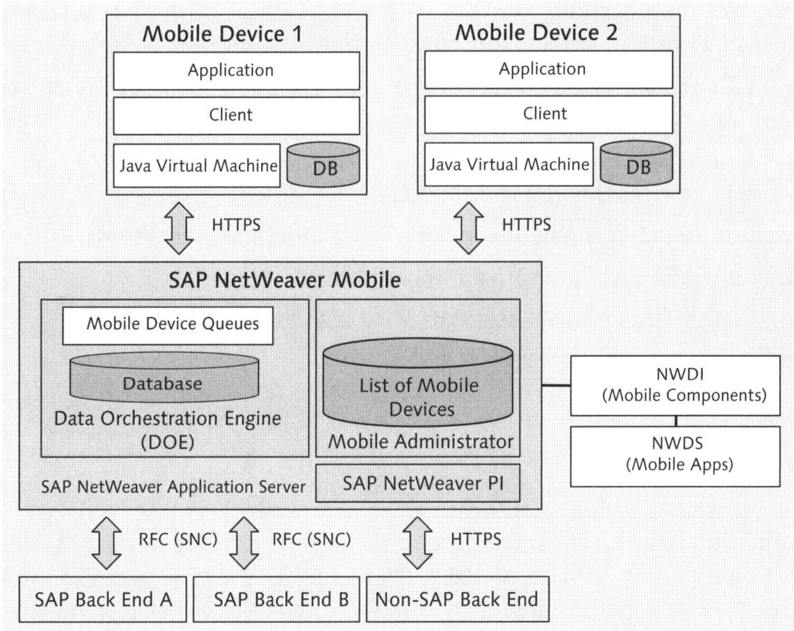


**Figure 17.1** System Architecture of SAP NetWeaver Mobile (Schematic)

SAP NetWeaver Mobile server operates as the middleware and controls the mobile device with its options for data synchronization. It uses SAP NetWeaver AS ABAP and AS Java (J2EE) as the technical runtime environment:

- The Java component is responsible for the following tasks:
  - Synchronization of configuration, application, and user data with the SAP NetWeaver Mobile client
  - Distribution of applications on the individual mobile devices that are connected
  - Encryption of the connection to the client (SSL)
  - Data compression for the transfer of information
  - Control of the relay or communication of application data with the ABAP component
  - SSO
  - Support of the SAP Mobile Development Kit (MDK), tools for developing mobile applications as part of SAP NetWeaver Developer Studio
- The ABAP component is responsible for the following tasks:
  - Control of the processing of asynchronous queuing

- Control of communication with the back-end applications that have been called for synchronous or asynchronous communication
- Management of user rights (authorization concept) and control of the distribution of user rights to the mobile devices that are connected
- Management of applications and control of the distribution of applications to the mobile devices that are connected
- Data replication between client and server and monitoring functions
- User administration and authorization controls
- Synchronization of persistent user data with LDAP directories
- Encryption of RFC connections using SNC.

## 17.2 Risks and Controls

The risks and controls described in this chapter refer exclusively to SAP NetWeaver Mobile. Neither the risks that arise because of the mobile transfer protocol being used (such as GPRS, GSM, UMTS, or WLAN) nor the risks that concern mobile devices themselves (see Chapter 28, User Interfaces) or SAP NetWeaver AS (see Chapter 9, SAP NetWeaver AS) are addressed in more detail here.

This section uses a simplified version of the risk analysis methodology described in Chapter 1, Risk and Control Management, to identify the main security risks and the necessary controls for SAP NetWeaver Mobile (see Table 17.1). The controls are then discussed in more detail in the following sections and illustrated using examples.

| No. | Classification | Description |
|---|---|---|
| 1. | Potential risk | Missing authorization concept for the mobile application:<br>A missing or incomplete authorization concept can give unauthorized users access to functions in the application for which they do not have rights. Other users might have access to a functional scope that is too wide, because no concept for a segregation of duties exists. Legal frameworks can also be disregarded. |
| | Impact | Unauthorized transactions or a missing segregation of duties means that fraudulent actions can be started or that confidential data is compromised. Such actions can include unauthorized financial transactions or violate legal requirements (see Chapter 3, Requirements). |

**Table 17.1** Risks and Controls for SAP NetWeaver Mobile

| No. | Classification | Description |
| --- | --- | --- |
| | Risk without control(s) | Extremely high |
| | Control | Design and implementation of a holistic authorization concept that considers the principle of information ownership and separates functions. This control is an important requirement of the Sarbanes-Oxley Act (SOX), which also applies to mobile applications. The authorization concept should be harmonized with the user-specific authorizations. This means that the scope of authorizations for mobile access should not be wider, but rather smaller than in the SAP back-end. |
| | Risk with control(s) | Normal |
| | Section | 17.3.1 |
| 2. | Potential risk | Missing authorization concept for the administration of SAP NetWeaver Mobile:<br>Unauthorized administrators obtain access to the configuration parameters of SAP NetWeaver Mobile. Administration also lacks the related segregation of duties. |
| | Impact | Unauthorized administrators obtain access to the configuration settings of SAP NetWeaver Mobile, particularly user management and application distribution. Such access endangers the stability of the mobile infrastructure and might allow unauthorized devices to log on to the SAP NetWeaver Mobile server. Ultimately, unauthorized persons can implement changes to the security configuration and enable and execute fraudulent actions, like financial transactions. |
| | Risk without control(s) | Extremely high |
| | Control | Design and implementation of a holistic authorization concept for the administration of SAP NetWeaver Mobile |
| | Risk with control(s) | Normal |
| | Section | 17.3.2 |

**Table 17.1** Risks and Controls for SAP NetWeaver Mobile (Cont.)

| No. | Classification | Description |
|---|---|---|
| 3. | Potential risk | Authorizations of RFC users are too broad:<br>A technical RFC user is required to establish an RFC connection to the back-end applications. This user has more authorizations than required. In some cases, the complete authorization SAP_ALL is granted. |
| | Impact | Although the user types communication and service are typically set, authorizations whose scope is too comprehensive allow for the unauthorized creation of new dialog users in the back-end applications. In this manner, SAP NetWeaver Mobile can become compromised. |
| | Risk without control(s) | High |
| | Control | Restriction of RFC authorizations for the current RFC users to the ABAP function groups that are actually called |
| | Risk with control(s) | Low |
| | Section | 17.3.3 |
| 4. | Potential risk | Unencrypted communication channels:<br>The communications connections between the mobile device and the SAP NetWeaver Mobile server, between AS ABAP and AS Java (via Java Connectors (JCo)), and between the mobile server and back-end applications are unencrypted. |
| | Impact | The information being transmitted can be viewed or manipulated by unauthorized parties. Authentication data between the client and the server can also be spied on. That means that an unauthorized external device can log on to the mobile server and execute application functions or exchange data. Fraudulent activities, such as unauthorized financial transactions, can be performed. |
| | Risk without control(s) | Extremely high |
| | Control | Encryption of the most important communications connections for SAP NetWeaver Mobile |
| | Risk with control(s) | Low |
| | Section | 17.4.1 |

**Table 17.1** Risks and Controls for SAP NetWeaver Mobile (Cont.)

| No. | Classification | Description |
|---|---|---|
| 5. | Potential risk | Passwords that are too simple:<br>The authentication mechanism between the client and the server is based on the user ID and password method. The selected password is too obvious (that is, too easy for hackers to deduce) and authentication on the mobile device itself was deactivated. |
| | Impact | Unauthorized mobile devices can log on to the SAP NetWeaver Mobile server by guessing the password in a brute-force attack. Therefore, data can be exchanged with the back-end applications, unauthorized financial transactions can be executed, or data can be compromised. |
| | Risk without control(s) | Extremely high |
| | Control | Selection of a complex password for authentication of the client to the server for data synchronization. |
| | Risk with control(s) | Normal |
| | Section | 17.4.2 |
| 6. | Potential risk | Superfluous services on the SAP NetWeaver Mobile server:<br>Services on the mobile server have been activated, although they are not required for the synchronization of application data or for online access. |
| | Impact | The superfluous services can be security gaps and therefore be used to compromise the mobile server and assume administration functions without authorization. |
| | Risk without control(s) | Extremely high |
| | Control | Deactivation of superfluous services on the SAP NetWeaver Mobile server. |
| | Risk with control(s) | Normal |
| | Section | 17.4.3 |
| 7. | Potential risk | Missing network segmentation:<br>At the network level, inadequate security of the SAP NetWeaver Mobile server exists, because of not separating the network into trustworthy and nontrustworthy areas with firewalls. |

**Table 17.1** Risks and Controls for SAP NetWeaver Mobile (Cont.)

| No. | Classification | Description |
|---|---|---|
| | Impact | Inadequate security of the mobile server, with appropriate firewall configuration on the network side, leaves any vulnerability at the operating system level open to possible attacks. Hackers might be able to receive administrator rights. Unauthorized access to confidential information can be achieved in this manner; unauthorized financial transactions or manipulations are also possible. Moreover, the mobile server can be the starting point for attacks on other internal networks or systems. |
| | Risk without control(s) | High |
| | Control | Protection of the mobile server with network security is achieved by dividing the network segments into unsecured and trustworthy segments. The control can be implemented by configuring network-based firewalls appropriately. |
| | Risk with control(s) | Normal |
| | Section | 17.4.4 |
| 8. | Potential risk | Missing monitoring concept:<br>No monitoring concept is present for the SAP NetWeaver Mobile system landscape. |
| | Impact | System availability or unavailability cannot be recognized. Users cannot access their applications. The synchronization mechanism is unavailable. This way, the integrity of business data may be violated, and sales revenues can suffer if orders cannot be scheduled in production in a timely manner, for example. |
| | Risk without control(s) | High |
| | Control | Implementation of a system monitoring concept with the required reaction and problem-resolution processes |
| | Risk with control(s) | Normal |
| | Section | 17.4.5 |
| 9. | Potential risk | Negligent use of mobile devices in unsecured networks.<br>The user uses mobile devices in unsecured public networks. |

**Table 17.1** Risks and Controls for SAP NetWeaver Mobile (Cont.)

| No. | Classification | Description |
|---|---|---|
| | Impact | In case of negligent use of mobile devices in unsecured networks, for instance, when logging on to unsecured Internet hot spots, Trojan horses, viruses, and so on can be infiltrated onto the device. This could result in data corruption, data loss, takeover of the device's control by unauthorized persons, or the prerequisite for a subsequent attack on the device. |
| | Risk without control(s) | High |
| | Control | You should avoid the use of unsecured and unknown/suspicious networks. Security applications such as virus scanners should be used for mobile devices, if possible. |
| | Risk with control(s) | Low |
| | Section | 28.3 |
| 10. | Potential risk | Negligent use of mobile devices in public:<br>Users use mobile devices in public places without any protection and foreign; unauthorized persons could view the information displayed on the device. |
| | Impact | Company-internal data and confidential information could be compromised and exploited to the company's disadvantage. Passwords could be spied on during entry. |
| | Risk without control(s) | High |
| | Control | Mobile devices should not be used in public. If this is not possible, you should take appropriate protective measures. |
| | Risk with control(s) | Low |
| | Section | 28.3 |
| 11. | Potential risk | Negligent handling of mobile devices:<br>It is possible that mobile devices can be stolen or lost due to negligence. |
| | Impact | Company-internal information and passwords could become accessible to unauthorized persons. This enables the greatest damage for the information stored in the device or access to the mobile infrastructure and connected networks and systems. |

**Table 17.1** Risks and Controls for SAP NetWeaver Mobile (Cont.)

| No. | Classification | Description |
|---|---|---|
| | Risk without control(s) | High |
| | Control | You should strive for a responsible handling of mobile devices and the security of stored local information through encryption and passwords with high complexity. The technical options and the quality of encryption depend on the device's operating system. Sometimes, only limited encryption options exist. This condition must be considered carefully when you select the technology for the device and the usage scope for functions and data. If possible, you should set a start-up password for the operating system. In case of loss, server access for the respective device must be blocked.<br>SAP NetWeaver Mobile provides the option to destroy client data as soon as a client device that was reported lost tries to access the server. |
| | Risk with control(s) | Normal |
| | Section | 17.4.1, 17.4.2, 28.3 |
| 12. | Potential risk | Security gaps in custom developments of mobile applications.<br>The program code of customer-specific mobile applications developed by the customer was not checked for security and has security gaps. |
| | Impact | Security gaps in the program code offer targets for hackers to compromise data, change or stop the applications' mode of operation, or obtain administrator rights. Unauthorized access to confidential information can be achieved in this manner; unauthorized financial transactions or manipulations are also possible. Moreover, the unsecured program code can be the starting point for attacks to other applications, internal networks, or systems. |
| | Risk without control(s) | High |
| | Control | Custom-developed program code must be checked for security. This means that the coding must comply with approved company programming guidelines and must not contain programming steps that could compromise the security for data, applications, communications, and the authorization concept. To do this, company programming guidelines must be set up and complied with, and programming rules recommended by SAP must be used. |

**Table 17.1** Risks and Controls for SAP NetWeaver Mobile (Cont.)

| No. | Classification | Description |
|---|---|---|
| | Risk with control(s) | Normal |
| | Section | 17.4.6 |

**Table 17.1** Risks and Controls for SAP NetWeaver Mobile (Cont.)

## 17.3 Application Security

This section describes in more detail the risks and controls that are outlined in Table 17.1 with regard to application security.

### 17.3.1 Authorization Concept for Mobile Applications

The basic authorization concept for SAP applications essentially corresponds to the ABAP authorization concept (see Chapter 20, Authorizations in SAP ERP). The same basic principles (information responsibility by business units, risk management, and so on) implemented in stationary SAP applications are applicable to mobile applications integrated in the portfolio of SAP applications. This is an important aspect of compliance with SOX and the generally applicable control objectives and guidelines.

However, special differences must be noted for mobile applications: SAP NetWeaver Mobile is primarily used when it deals with offline applications that synchronize their information with the back-end systems and execute the appropriate transactions remotely. Therefore, authorizations must be controlled on the mobile device and in the back-end applications that are called by the mobile application.

Authorization objects are also used to define the scope of authorizations for mobile applications. But the authorization objects to be used in the mobile application are not created individually and locally in each mobile device. Instead, they're created centrally in the SAP NetWeaver Mobile ABAP server component using the Mobile Component Descriptor (MCD). The MCD defines and describes all parameters of the mobile application: the name of the required mobile software components, version, description, component type (additional required technical runtime components for the mobile device), and so on.

The MCD also defines the authorization objects that should be checked in the mobile application. This setting is made in the dependency definition of the MCD in the Environment tab. The dependency is defined with three parameters:

- DEPENDENCY_TYPE
  This parameter must be set to AUTH_OBJECT and determines the type of dependency to be defined. This example involves a dependency definition for an authorization object.
- DEPENDENCY_NAME
  This parameter specifies the name of the dependency definition.
- DEPENDENCY_VALUE
  This parameter defines an existing ABAP authorization object (for instance, M_MATE_BUK, creation of a material master for a specific company code) that should be checked in the mobile application. The developer must program this authorization object in advance, so that it can be included in the dependency definition. The developer must also provide default values for the dependency definitions. This requires a close cooperation of the business process owner, persons responsible for security and authorizations, and the developers.

The dependency definition determines which authorization objects in the ABAP server component of SAP NetWeaver Mobile must be assigned specific characteristics for the mobile application (for example, using Transaction PFCG) and must later be loaded into the mobile application during synchronization. Accordingly, the authorization objects can be managed just like all other ABAP applications.

In addition to the business authorization objects defined in the dependency definition, the authorization objects must be assigned too, and given characteristics for a role. Roles are listed on the Authorizations tab in the MCD. These authorization objects have a technical orientation and define synchronization authorizations in SAP NetWeaver Mobile and so on. Table 17.2 lists the most important authorization objects and fields. They must be maintained for all users.

In order for a user to work with mobile applications, the ABAP role assigned to that user must include a definition of the mobile application — much like the concept of the S_TCODE for stationary transactions. A MiniApp is created in the ABAP server component of SAP NetWeaver Mobile for the mobile application. The MiniApp has the same name as the mobile application described in the MCD. The MiniApp must then be assigned to a role (for instance with Transaction PFCG, MiniApps tab). The role can then be assigned to the user.

Figure 17.2 illustrates the relationship between mobile application authorizations and authorizations that apply to the server side. The example shows that the MCD and dependency definition can also set the authorization object (Object 3) to NOT CHECKED.

| Authorization Object | Field | Value | Description |
|---|---|---|---|
| S_ME_SYNC | ACTVT (Activity) | 38 (Execute) | This authorization must be assigned to each user. It enables synchronization between the client and server for installation of the mobile application or other components, and for the exchange of business data with back-end applications. |
| S_RFC | ACTVT (Activity) | 16 (Execute) | This authorization must be assigned to each user. It enables execution access to the function group defined in the following description. The function group is required for synchronization between the client and server. |
| | RFC_NAME (Name of the function group) | RFC1<br>SDIRRUNTIME<br>SYST<br>SG00<br>SRFC<br>SYSU | This authorization must be assigned to each user. It enables implementation of the JCo. |
| | | ME_USER | This authorization must be assigned to each user. It enables changes of the synchronization password. |
| | | BWAF_MW | This authorization must be assigned to each user. It enables synchronization of business data with back-end applications. |
| | RFC_TYP | FUGR | Only the value FUGR (function group) can be defined. |

**Table 17.2** Technical Authorization Objects for SAP NetWeaver Mobile

Once an ABAP role for each mobile application has been determined for the ABAP server component of SAP NetWeaver Mobile, the next step assigns the role to the user, after which the mobile application can be distributed to the mobile devices by synchronization. That occurs in two steps. The first step uses the report WAF_DEPLOYMENT_FROM_ROLES to consolidate all roles. It then writes the MiniApps and the corresponding mobile applications (according to the report) to a synchronization directory.

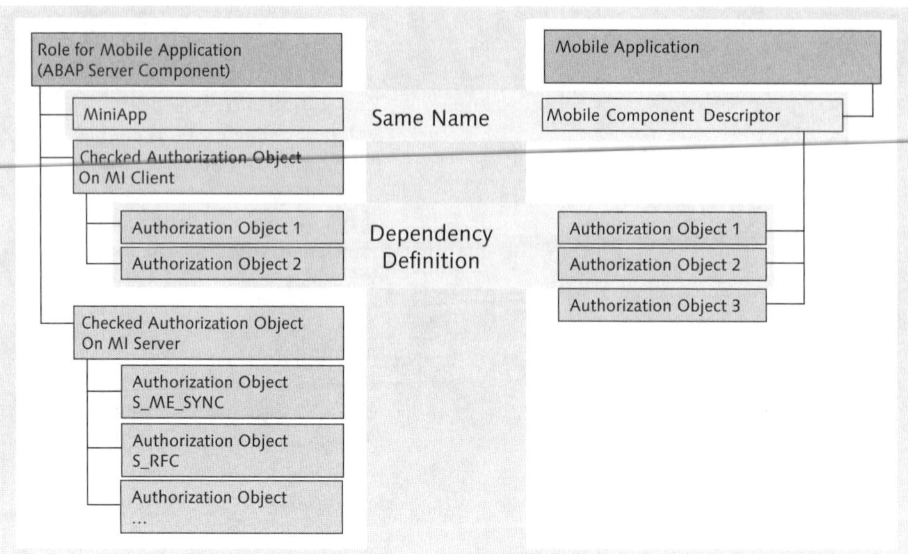


**Figure 17.2** Relationship between Client and Server Authorizations

The synchronization directory can be controlled from the SAP NetWeaver Mobile Web Console, which lets you view and edit the pending distribution of mobile applications for the mobile devices that are available. Theoretically, the Web Console can be used to distribute the mobile application to a user without prior definition of a role. However, this is not advisable because the access controls of the authorization system are bypassed.

The Web Console can also be used to distribute the mobile applications to the mobile devices that are available. This feature can be helpful when a mobile application should not be distributed to all mobile devices. Service `SyncBO MIAUTH` can be started from the SAP Web Console; it handles the distribution of authorizations and mobile applications to the mobile devices.

### 17.3.2 Authorization Concept for Administration

For the administration of SAP NetWeaver Mobile, you need the standard roles for administrative tasks listed in Table 17.3. Following best-practice rules, copies with customer-specific names should be assigned to the users. With this approach, the original remains unchanged; the copy can be customized for specific requirements.

| Role | Description |
|---|---|
| SAP_DOE_ADMINISTRATOR<br>SAP_BC_BASIS_ADMIN | The two standard SAP roles enable administrative access to the Data Orchestration Engine of SAP NetWeaver Mobile, which controls the data exchange between the SAP back-end system and the mobile device. The authorization object MMW_ADM_DS contained in the roles allows for a refined restriction to specific regions and devices. |
| SAP_DOE_TECH_ADMIN<br>SAP_BC_BASIS_ADMIN | The roles control the activation and the generation of data objects and the deletion of data within the Data Orchestration Engine of SAP NetWeaver Mobile. |
| SAP_DOE_DEVRE | This standard role can be assigned to an administrator that is responsible for the administration of the Data Orchestration Engine and the assignment of mobile devices. |
| SAP_DOE_DEVELOPER<br>SAP_BC_DWB_ABAPDEVELOPER | These are typical developer roles that enable access to the design of data objects, to the Data Orchestration Engine, and to design tools in SAP NetWeaver Developer Studio. |
| SAP_DOE_BASIS_DEVELOPER<br>SAP_BC_DWB_ABAPDEVELOPER | These are the administrative roles with access to data (queue), the Data Orchestration Engine, and for authorizations to transport software packages. |
| SAP_DOE_SYNC_ROLE | This administrative role authorizes the user to configure and implement data synchronization between the Data Orchestration Engine and mobile devices. |

**Table 17.3** Standard SAP Roles with Authorizations for the Administration of SAP NetWeaver Mobile

### 17.3.3 Restricting the Authorizations of the RFC User to Back-End Applications

Back-end applications are accessed with an RFC access. Access requires the setup of a technical RFC user in the back-end applications. The ABAP server component of SAP NetWeaver Mobile logs on with the technical user. The type of RFC user is either Communication or Service.

Even if the user type doesn't appear to be critical because no dialog logon is possible, the RFC user may not be assigned a full authorization like SAP_ALL. Instead, the user should contain authorization object S_RFC, which can granularly control the call of the function groups in the back-end applications that are actually needed for the application with authorization field RFC_NAME. Authorized function groups must be at least the same as those of the mobile application itself and of all wrapper and Business Application Programming Interface (BAPI) wrapper function groups.

Chapter 9, SAP NetWeaver Application Server, describes the exact method of limiting the function groups to be assigned properties in authorization object S_RFC. This chapter also describes how an authorization check with trusted RFC calls differs.

## 17.4 Technical Security

This section describes in more detail the risks and controls that are outlined in Table 17.1 with regard to technical security.

### 17.4.1 Setting Up Encrypted Communications Connections

SAP NetWeaver Mobile includes the following three major types of communications connections:

- **Communication between the client and the Java server component**
  This communication is primarily used to distribute the software components, parameter settings, and authorizations, and to synchronize business data and objects. The standard protocol used is HTTP. The underlying carrier protocols are GSM, UMTS, GPRS, or other mobile protocols. SSL (HTTPS) can be used to encrypt the connection.
- **Internal communication between the Java server component and the ABAP server component**
  In this case, communication is implemented via the JCo connection, which corresponds to an RFC connection. The connection can be encrypted with a secure network communication.
- **Communication between the ABAP server component and the respective back-end applications**
  This communication connection is established via RFCs. The connection can also be encrypted with a secure network communication.

Encryption of the first type of communication is imperative, because the client is authenticated to the Java server component of SAP NetWeaver Mobile with a user ID and password. Encryption of the internal JCo and RFC connections with secure network communication is recommended, but not required.

Depending on the potential risks of the mobile application, encryption should be used. The use of SNC should result in a stronger technical authentication among the server components — another reason to recommend implementation. Chapter 9, SAP NetWeaver Application Server, describes how to set up an SNC encryption.

Both sides must be configured to set up the HTTPS connection between the client and the Java server component.

1. The first step configures the server component for the HTTPS service (see Chapter 9).
2. The next step converts the configuration of the client to HTTPS communication. Conversion occurs in the *MobileEngine.config* file, which is located in the *SAP NetWeaver Mobile Client Component Installation Path/Settings* directory. The following parameters must be set:
   - `MobileEngine.Security.SSLSupport = True`
     SSL support is activated in the client.
   - `MobileEngine.Security.HostnameVerifying = True`
     When calling the mobile application with a URL, the server name given in the URL is checked with the server certificate of the SAP NetWeaver Mobile server.
   - `MobileEngine.Sync.ConnectionTimeout = -1`
     This technical parameter optimizes the synchronization performance when SSL is used as the communication protocol.
3. If no trustworthy certificate authority has issued the server certificate of the Java server component (see the list of trustworthy certificate authorities in SAP Note 602993), either the issuing CA certificate or the SAP NetWeaver Mobile server certificate must be defined as trustworthy. Definition occurs in the client with `keytool`. The complete command then appears as follows:

   ```
   keytool -import -alias <Alias-name> -file
   <server-certificate-file> -keystore truststore
   ```

   The alias name is a short form of the digital certificate that is considered trustworthy. This name must be identical to the name of the server certificate.
4. Once configuration is complete, communication between the client and the Java server component occurs with SSL.

### 17.4.2 Securing the Synchronization Communication

As described in the previous section, communication that occurs between the client and the Java server component of SAP NetWeaver Mobile helps to synchronize business transaction data after all components have been installed on the mobile device. Users of the mobile application on the mobile device can have up to three passwords.

- One password is for authentication to the operating system of the mobile device
- The second password is for logging on to the client
- The third password is for authentication to the Java server component for synchronizing the business data

The following minimum criteria apply to all three passwords:

- Password length to be a minimum of eight characters
- At least one special character
- At least one letter
- At least one number

A configuration file on the mobile device stores the password for logging on to the client as a hash value. The user can change it at will. Only the server stores the password for synchronization, however. Various options can force a logon during synchronization with the Java server component. In the file MobileEngine.config, the parameter `MobileEngine.Security.SynchronizationPasswordHandlingOption` can be set as follows:

- `atsync`
  The local password for logging on to the client does not correspond to the synchronization password. The synchronization password must be entered at every synchronization. This is the default setting and is also recommended.
- `local`
  The local password for logging on to the client corresponds to the synchronization password. The synchronization password need not be entered for each synchronization. This setting is not recommended.

  This setting is only a good idea when automatically scheduled synchronizations (controlled with the `Timed Sync` parameter) are to be executed. In this case, it is the only feasible option. However, the risk potential is greater, because synchronization can still occur if the mobile device is stolen, which can lead to erroneous postings.
- `once`
  The local password for logging on to the client does not correspond to the synchronization password. The synchronization password must only be entered once for each logon to the client — at the first synchronization. Follow-up synchronization in the same logon session does not require you to enter the password. This setting is also not recommended.

The logon session must be deactivated after three incorrect logon attempts on the server to avoid successful brute-force attacks. Deactivation is defined with parameter login/fails_to_user_lock. The user account should be locked after three incorrect attempts to log on. Administrators must be informed if a mobile device is stolen so they can lock the user account immediately.

When a JSP-based application (Java application) is installed on the client, a local web server with a configurable log function exists on the client. The Information or Debug parameters must not be set to display mode (verbosity level), because the Jasper log function would also log the synchronization password on the side of the mobile device in this case. The default setting is FATAL, and should be used. You can check the setting in the installation directory of the client on the side of the mobile device in the *server.xml* file in the *conf* subdirectory.

The client also supports the traditional concept of SSO using the SAP logon ticket or the X.509 certificate for user authentication to synchronize data with the server. Chapter 9, SAP NetWeaver Application Server, already presented the associated security risks and measures.

### 17.4.3 Deactivating Unnecessary Services on the SAP NetWeaver Mobile Server

Superfluous services should be deactivated when using SAP NetWeaver Mobile. Deactivation is important for HTTP-based services, because they're made available externally with the Internet Communication Manager (ICM) and called by entering the URL. Demo services can be activated in this manner, for example. But those services have a drawback — they enable attackers to obtain additional system information or nonsecured demo services that can compromise the integrity of the ABAP server. This is why extraneous services must be deactivated in the ABAP server component of SAP NetWeaver Mobile using Transaction SICF.

The services that SAP NetWeaver Mobile doesn't need for administration and runtime should also be deactivated for the Java server component. Chapter 9 describes a possible strategy.

### 17.4.4 Secure Network Architecture

Secure network architecture can also be set up for SAP NetWeaver Mobile via a demilitarized zone (DMZ). The server can be placed behind the first firewall in the external demilitarized zone (DMZ 1). The use of an upstream reverse proxy with SAP NetWeaver Mobile is difficult to configure because of the synchronization mechanism. Figure 17.3 shows the proposed network architecture; however, the figure does not display the intermediate transmission paths, such as a telecommunications provider with a receiving station, conversion of wireless into wired communications, and so on.

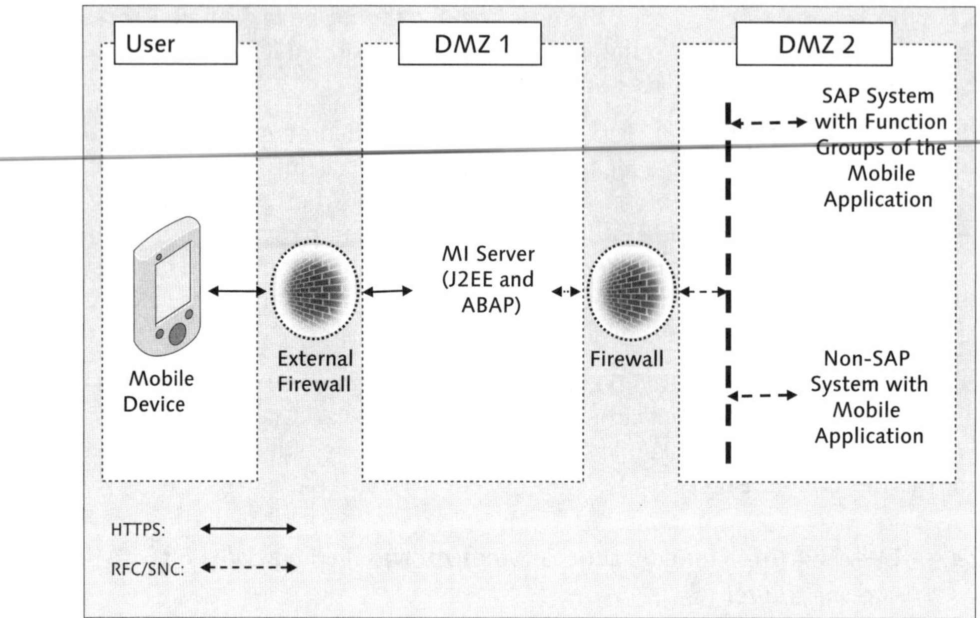


**Figure 17.3** DMZ Network Architecture for SAP NetWeaver Mobile

As mentioned previously, the communication between the individual technical components should be encrypted. If possible, the back-end applications can be placed in the internal demilitarized zone (DMZ 2). Because intelligent synchronization temporarily stores business data on the mobile server, special hardening measures must be used for this server at the operating system level. The hardening measures correspond to those of SAP NetWeaver Application Server. Chapter 9 provides further information on this topic.

### 17.4.5 Monitoring

As holds true for all other SAP systems, SAP NetWeaver Mobile can also be connected to the Computing Center Management System (CCMS) (Transaction RZ20). A monitoring template for SAP NetWeaver Mobile already exists; it can be tailored to meet individual needs. The template supports the following monitoring functions:

- Configuration of SAP NetWeaver Mobile, including all mobile devices, server, and back-end applications
- Heartbeats (all functions of the SAP MI server are active)
- Tracing functions for successful synchronization between the client and the server

- Alarm notifications for memory problems, unavailable services, and so on
- Logging of the intelligent synchronization functions
- Tracing of the client distribution functions and configurations

Activation of CCMS monitoring for SAP NetWeaver Mobile occurs with the SAP_CCMS_MONI_BATCH_DP report, which collects all of the data of the passive data collector MI_*. Transaction RZ21 controls the data collector; it runs every 60 minutes by default. This value can be controlled via Transaction SM36. The connection of the Java server component must be created as a scenario in Transaction GRMG (Generic Request and Message Generator). The scenario must be imported to the Generic Request and Message Generator as an XML configuration file. Then, it can be activated.

It's important that organizational and process support exists for monitoring SAP NetWeaver Mobile. Only the discovery of disruptions and errors within a short period of time can trigger the implementation of the required countermeasures. All tasks and responsibilities of individual administrators involved in the monitoring process must be defined before an actual disruption occurs.

### 17.4.6 Secure Program Code

Program code forms the basis of all applications and is therefore often the main cause for insufficient functions, information quality, or security gaps in IT systems. In general, you should subject all programs created in custom developments to a detailed risk and security analysis. To do this, commercial program code scanners are available, which are a good support for detecting program-related security gaps.

**Note**

The descriptions of this section not only apply to the program code of mobile applications within SAP NetWeaver Mobile, but also to the development of customer-specific program code in general.

However, an initial documentation step should include secure programming rules that represent the guidelines for in-house developers and which form the basis for measuring the security of programs. Because the mobile applications — besides the databases — basically run on two platforms, AS ABAP and AS Java, the same security goals must be implemented in detail for the different platforms.

SAP has provided a checklist of rules for secure program code, which can be used as the starting point and converted in custom business requirements and for the existing risk situation. Table 17.4 presents a summary of the security-relevant risk areas that are considered in this checklist for applications (for instance, Web Dynpro ABAP) which can run on AS ABAP or AS Java.

| Potential Vulnerability | Description |
|---|---|
| Password security | For many applications, passwords still present the traditional method of user authentication. It is the first line of defense against unauthorized access. |
| Secure communication | Data encryption using SSL or SNC increases the data security during transfer. Program code can control the usage of SSL or SNC. |
| Secure Store and Forward (SSF) | The encryption of documents and the use of digital signatures are methods for data backup. |
| Logging of security-relevant data and data changes | Details corresponding to the requirements must be stored in secured log files. |
| Virus scanner interfaces | SAP applications have no internal function to eliminate viruses or Trojans, for example. For this reason, the standard SAP applications include interfaces that can be used to integrate external anti-virus scanners. These interfaces should be considered in custom program code. |
| Cross-site scripting | The risk of cross-site scripting attacks can only be reduced by first checking the data read by HTML pages (forms) and further process permitted commands/data. |
| SQL injection | SQL programming rules and the input evaluation of SQL commands can reduce the risk of this potential vulnerability. |
| Canonicalization | External URLs should be checked prior to accepting them and suspicious URLs should be filtered. |
| Directory traversal | You can reduce the risk that a hacker accesses the file system of SAP NetWeaver AS without authorization by evaluating the externally entered URL data and using an appropriate filtering. The goal of the filtering is to eliminate URL queries that present an unauthorized access to directories and files to be protected. |
| URL Encoding and manipulation | You can reduce the risk that a hacker enters unauthorized HTML commands in URLs by evaluating the externally entered URL data and using an appropriate filtering. The goal of the filtering is to eliminate URL queries that would allow unauthorized access to directories, files, or services to be protected via infiltrated HTML program code. |
| Cookie manipulation | Cookies present a high risk if the program code doesn't contain appropriate compensating security measures. For example, cookies should not contain any identifiable information on persons or systems. |

**Table 17.4** Security-Relevant Risk Areas for SAP Applications

*SAP Auto-ID Infrastructure is the connecting element between SAP systems and Radio Frequency Identification (RFID) applications. For this reason, this chapter focuses on the security aspects for applications, communication, and data security.*

# 18 SAP Auto-ID Infrastructure

Chapter 17, SAP NetWeaver Mobile, already presented an application example for mobile barcode scanners in logistics, which you can use to manually enter the goods receipt and goods issue on site at the warehouse and directly post it in the material stock of the SAP system. The introduction of the barcode scanner in logistics processes results in time and cost savings. It also improves the accuracy and currency of data. However, this solution has some limitations. For example, these limitations exist when you manually scan very large numbers of pieces, very small parts, or if the products that are provided with a barcode are moving. Moreover, for optical scanning, the one-dimensional or two-dimensional barcode IDs in the scanner area must always be visible.

To overcome these and other disadvantages of the manual solution, barcodes are now being replaced with RFID chips, where appropriate. The RFID technology using RFID tags or RFID sensors enable the automatic identification and localization of objects and considerably facilitates the entry and storage of data. Furthermore, you can easily integrate this technology with automated goods movement processes, which almost creates a real-time level for imported data, and process and logistics information.

## 18.1 Introduction and Functions

SAP Auto-ID Infrastructure is the SAP NetWeaver component that utilizes these benefits for the back-end logistics system by providing interfaces and applications, formatting information and data of the automated ID system or sensors, and forwarding it to the applications that process the information. SAP Auto-ID Infrastructure runs on Application Server (AS) ABAP and AS Java, whereas the ABAP stack represents the essential component with regard to user and communication security. Figure 18.1 shows a simplified technical overview of the communication channels of an RFID solution via SAP Auto-ID Infrastructure up to the SAP back-end systems.

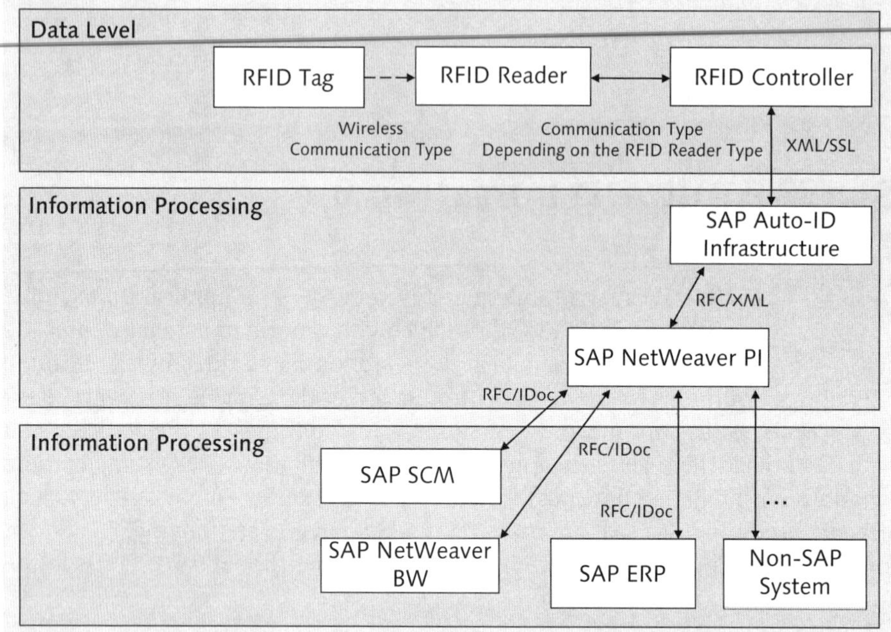


**Figure 18.1** Communication Types between RFID and Back-End Systems

The back-end systems that process the information include the following, for example:

- SAP ERP
- SAP NetWeaver BW
- SAP SCM
- Non-SAP Systems

SAP Auto-ID Infrastructure is flexible and can be adapted to business process conditions. In principle, you can differentiate the following variants:

- As an independent system and without an Enterprise Resource Planning (ERP) connection
- As an independent system, integrated with a logistics system like SAP Supply Chain Management (SCM) and with an ERP connection
- As a local system with direct connection to a central database system

## 18.2 Risks and Controls

SAP Auto-ID Infrastructure as a component of SAP NetWeaver specializes in supporting data processes in heterogeneous system landscapes. This leads to complex questions concerning security and risk management, which must be answered depending on the special integration level with other systems. This chapter therefore discusses risks and controls that exclusively refer to SAP Auto-ID Infrastructure.

The methodology of a possible risk analysis, which was presented in Chapter 1, Risk and Control Management, is now going to be applied to SAP Auto-ID Infrastructure. This section describes the essential security risks and the controls required for this purpose (see Table 18.1). Usually, only system administrators log on to the application for configuration, monitoring, and maintenance tasks of the SAP Auto-ID Infrastructure processes. Therefore, the security risks focus on this area and the communication processes.

| No. | Classification | Description |
|---|---|---|
| 1. | Risk potential | Missing authorization concept for administration functions of SAP Auto-ID Infrastructure:<br>A missing or incomplete authorization concept can give unauthorized users access to functionalities in the application for which they do not have rights. Other users might have access to a functional administration scope that is too wide, because no separation of duties, responsibilities, and functions exists. |
| | Impact | Unauthorized access or missing segregation of duties could lead to an unauthorized access to configuration functions. Users could create misconfigurations, start fraudulent actions, compromise company-internal confidential data, or violate legal regulations. |
| | Risk without control(s) | Extremely high |
| | Control | Design and implementation of an authorization concept that considers the principle of information ownership and segregates duties. For example, the administrator is only granted access that is absolutely necessary for mastering the tasks. |
| | Risk with control(s) | Normal |

**Table 18.1** Risks and Controls for SAP Auto-ID Infrastructure

| No. | Classification | Description |
|---|---|---|
| | Section | 18.3.1 |
| 2. | Risk potential | Missing authorization concept for the administration of SAP Auto-ID Infrastructure:<br>Unauthorized administrators obtain access to the configuration parameters of SAP Auto-ID Infrastructure or the management of RFID devices. Administration also lacks the related segregation of duties. |
| | Impact | Unauthorized administrators obtain access to the configuration settings of SAP Auto-ID Infrastructure, data monitoring and usage of RFID devices, or the general system configuration. This jeopardizes the stability and data protection of SAP Auto-ID Infrastructure, and fraudulent activities could become possible. |
| | Risk without control(s) | Extremely high |
| | Control | Design and implementation of a holistic authorization concept for the administration of SAP Auto-ID Infrastructure with separation of the task areas and responsibilities |
| | Risk with control(s) | Normal |
| | Section | 18.3.2 |
| 3. | Risk potential | Authorizations of RFC users are too broad:<br>A technical RFC user is required to establish an RFC connection to the back-end applications. This user has more authorizations than required. In some cases, the complete authorization SAP_ALL is granted. |
| | Impact | Although the user types communication and service are typically set, authorizations whose scope is too comprehensive allow for the unauthorized creation of new dialog users in the back-end applications. This way, SAP Auto-ID Infrastructure could be further compromised. |
| | Risk without control(s) | High |
| | Control | Restriction of RFC authorizations for the current RFC users to the ABAP function groups that are actually called. |
| | Risk with control(s) | Low |

**Table 18.1** Risks and Controls for SAP Auto-ID Infrastructure (Cont.)

| No. | Classification | Description |
|---|---|---|
| | Section | 18.3.3 |
| 4. | Risk potential | Password that is too simple:<br>The user ID and password method is the SAP Auto-ID Infrastructure authentication mechanism that is typical for administrators. The password selected is too simple, or the password is not kept secret individually, but is used jointly by administrators. |
| | Impact | Unauthorized persons can log on to SAP Auto-ID Infrastructure simply by guessing the password in a brute-force attack. This makes it possible to implement corresponding unauthorized configurations or compromise data. The individual responsibility principle is violated because the identity of an administrator cannot be determined uniquely if the same user IDs and passwords are used. |
| | Risk without control(s) | Extremely high |
| | Control | Selection of an appropriate individual, complex password for the authentication of administrators |
| | Risk with control(s) | Normal |
| | Section | 18.3.4 |
| 5. | Risk potential | Unencrypted communication channels:<br>The communication channels between SAP Auto-ID Infrastructure, AS ABAP, AS Java, communication partners, and SAP back-end applications are unencrypted. |
| | Impact | The information being transmitted can be viewed or manipulated by unauthorized parties.<br>This enables fraudulent actions, such as data theft or data manipulations, which can lead to a compromise of the data integrity. |
| | Risk without control(s) | Extremely high |
| | Control | Encryption of the most critical communication channels from and to SAP Auto-ID Infrastructure |
| | Risk with control(s) | Low |

**Table 18.1** Risks and Controls for SAP Auto-ID Infrastructure (Cont.)

| No. | Classification | Description |
|---|---|---|
| | Section | 18.4.1 |
| 6. | Risk potential | Unnecessary services on the server of SAP Auto-ID Infrastructure:<br>Services, which are available via HTTP(S), on the server have been activated, although they are not required for the synchronization of application data or for online access. |
| | Impact | The unnecessary services can be security gaps and therefore be used to compromise the server of SAP Auto-ID Infrastructure and assume administration functions without authorization. |
| | Risk without control(s) | Extremely high |
| | Control | Deactivation of superfluous services on the server of SAP Auto-ID Infrastructure |
| | Risk with control(s) | Normal |
| | Section | 18.4.2 |
| 7. | Risk potential | Missing network segmentation:<br>Inadequate security of the SAP Auto-ID Infrastructure server against external and internal unauthorized access through a corresponding subdivision into confidential areas through firewall separation |
| | Impact | Inadequate security of the server, with appropriate firewall configuration on the network side, leaves any vulnerability at the operating system level open to possible attacks. Hackers might be able to receive administrator rights. This enables unauthorized access to confidential information or data manipulation.<br>Moreover, the server can be the starting point for attacks on the internal networks/systems. |
| | Risk without control(s) | High |
| | Control | Protection of the SAP Auto-ID Infrastructure server with network security is achieved by dividing the network segments into unsecured and trustworthy segments. The control can be implemented by configuring network-based firewalls appropriately. |

**Table 18.1** Risks and Controls for SAP Auto-ID Infrastructure (Cont.)

| No. | Classification | Description |
| --- | --- | --- |
| | Risk with control(s) | Normal |
| | Section | 18.4.3 |

**Table 18.1** Risks and Controls for SAP Auto-ID Infrastructure (Cont.)

## 18.3 Application Security

This section describes in more detail the risks and controls that are outlined in Table 18.1 with regard to application security.

### 18.3.1 Authorization Concept for SAP Auto-ID Infrastructure

The basic authorization concept for SAP Auto-ID Infrastructure essentially corresponds to the ABAP authorization concept. Although only administration personnel have access, the same basic principles (information responsibility by business units, risk management, and so on) implemented in traditional SAP applications should apply. This observation is an important aspect of compliance with generally applicable business control objectives and guidelines.

The goal is to develop an appropriate authorization concept that weighs the business requirements for functionality, on the one hand, and for security and restrictions, on the other hand. In this context, two important general principles should always be considered:

- The access authorizations should be limited to the necessary minimum.
- The access authorizations should correspond to clearly separated task areas to establish responsibilities.

### 18.3.2 Authorization Concept for Administration

Standard roles are provided for managing and handling RFID devices for SAP Auto-ID Infrastructure. Following the best-practice rule, copies with a customer-specific name should be assigned to the users. With this approach, the original remains unchanged and is not used. The copy can be customized for specific requirements.

The following functional standard roles are offered. They are specialized in the usage and management of mobile RFID devices in conjunction with SAP Auto-ID Infrastructure:

- SAP_AIN_SUPERADMINISTRATOR
- SAP_AIN_SUPERADMINISTRATOR
- SAP_AIN_SUPERVISOR
- SAP_AIN_WORKER
- SAP_XI_MONITOR_ABAP

The standard roles contain authorization objects (/AIN/...), which are specialized in the functions of SAP Auto-ID Infrastructure. Using the individual configuration of these authorization objects, you can also create customer-specific roles that offer a useful separation of task areas and responsibilities.

### 18.3.3 Restricting the Authorizations of the RFC User to Back-End Applications

RFC network connections are predestinated for communication exchange between the system components (see Figure 18.1). To do this, you must set up RFC users for the communication partners.

In general, RFC users are not configured as the user type Dialog and mustn't obtain any full authorization in the form of SAP_ALL. Instead, the users should contain authorization object S_RFC, which can granularly control the call of the function groups in the back-end applications that are actually needed for the application with authorization field RFC_NAME. Authorized function groups must be at least the same as those of the SAP Auto-ID Infrastructure itself.

Chapter 9, SAP NetWeaver AS, describes the exact method of limiting the function groups to be assigned properties in authorization object S_RFC. This chapter also describes how an authorization check with trusted RFC calls differs.

### 18.3.4 Authentication, Password Rules, and Security

Passwords are the simplest method of authentication and are primarily used for the RFC communication in the context of SAP Auto-ID Infrastructure if no trusted RFC communication exists (see Chapter 9). The following minimum criteria should be complied with for strict password rules:

- Password length to be a minimum of eight characters
- At least one special character
- At least one letter
- At least one number

Because SAP Auto-ID Infrastructure runs on SAP NetWeaver Application Server, it is compatible with other authentication methods presented in Chapter 9, SAP Web Application Server. These methods include SSO for SAP GUI, RFC for SNC communication, SAP Logon Tickets, and X.509 certificates. This way, you can integrate the SAP Auto-ID Infrastructure with a holistic authentication principle within the system landscape, which simplifies the risk management with regard to authentication.

## 18.4 Technical Security

This section describes in more detail the risks and controls that are outlined in Table 18.1 with regard to technical security.

### 18.4.1 Setting Up Encrypted Communication Connections

Figure 18.1 at the beginning of this chapter provides an overview of the RFID communication channels that exist up to the SAP back-end. However, the technical data backup within the RFID technology depends on the security requirements and the actual technical preconditions. Modern RFID solutions offer encryption for wireless data transfer.

All other components of SAP NetWeaver are compatible with the data transfer via HTTP(S) and SNC communication and therefore offer a homogeneous and secure encryption technology within heterogeneous systems.

### 18.4.2 Deactivating Unnecessary Services on the Server

Unused services should be deactivated in all components of SAP Auto-ID Infrastructure. This should be a generally applied security measure because services, whether used or not, always represent a vulnerability that hackers can exploit for compromising the system. Chapter 9, SAP NetWeaver Application Server, describes a possible strategy for hardening the server operating systems.

### 18.4.3 Secure Network Architecture

SAP Auto-ID Infrastructure takes center stage in heterogeneous systems and depends on a secure data communication beyond network boundaries and across heterogeneous networks. Because the possible and necessary security measures decisively depend on the participating systems, networks, and their risks, a clear risk analysis must precede a network design phase. The identified risks must be compensated justifiably with technical means, for instance, with elements of network segmentation, network perimeter protection, data encryption, or other security guidelines. When you prepare this concept, you can use the general principles and Best Practices as the basis that were discussed in Chapters 5, Information Technology (IT) Security, 6, Enterprise Risk Management (ERM) Navigation Control Map, and 9, SAP NetWeaver Application Server.

*With its cross-system application options, SAP Solution Manager is ideal for SAP system administration and monitoring. With regard to risks and security, it focuses on the authorization concept and the cross-system management functions.*

# 19 SAP Solution Manager

SAP Solution Manager is the central application for implementing, operating, and optimizing complex SAP NetWeaver system landscapes and its SAP components. SAP Solution Manager facilitates the technical support of the Information Technology (IT) operation and provides tools and functions to improve the reliability of SAP solutions and reduce the total cost of ownership (TCO).

## 19.1 Introduction and Functions

Figure 19.1 shows SAP Solution Manager within a system landscape. The advantage of SAP Solution Manager is that all essential customizing settings can be made in one application. Also, monitoring the operation status with regard to available storage space, workload, logs, and so on, which is very important in terms of security, only occurs in one monitoring console. This enables you to implement any necessary countermeasures to stabilize the complex SAP NetWeaver system landscape. In addition, you can stabilize the operating costs because you don't have to create a new implementation and monitoring solution for each SAP system that is added to the landscape, instead you can simply integrate it with the existing SAP Solution Manager.

In summary, the major benefits of SAP Solution Manager include the following:

- Central point of access
- Central monitoring of all business processes
- Consideration of the dependencies between business processes
- Support of SAP applications in their entire lifecycle

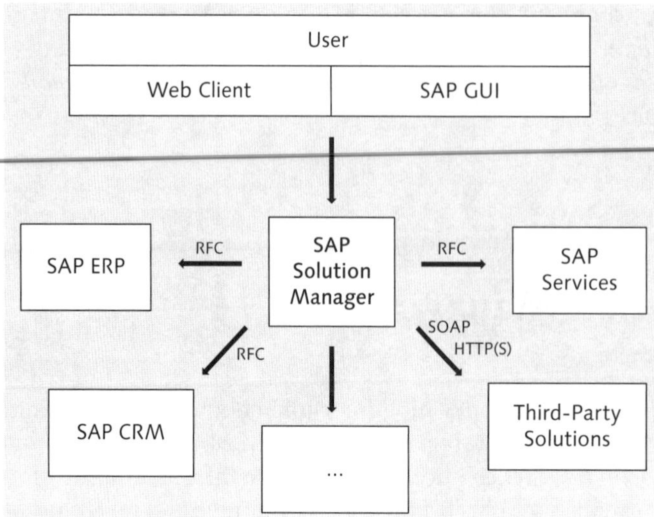


**Figure 19.1** Central Concept of SAP Solution Manager

Moreover, the central functioning provides benefits for risk management if, for example, security-relevant settings can be checked more easily. However, this central access to key information, settings, and monitoring also entails an additional security risk if no appropriate security configurations are made and complied with for SAP Solution Manager. Like all other components of SAP NetWeaver, SAP Solution Manager should be aligned with the general information security guidelines and security concepts of the company.

The following scenarios are supported by SAP Solution Manager on the application side:

- **Implementation and application distribution**
  This scenario is important to the implementation phase of a new implementation project. SAP Solution Manager provides complete project management functionality for this scenario, which contains the documentation of a project in addition to project controlling. The automated test run functionality is important as well. Customer-specific settings of different SAP components can be compared and synchronized.
- **Upgrade**
  Importing necessary application and system upgrades to enter a higher release level can be executed centrally using SAP Solution Manager. This way, it is also possible to monitor and trace the release levels of the connected SAP systems centrally.

- **Change management**
  Change management is one of the most important IT Infrastructure Library (ITIL) processes (see Chapter 4, Security Standards), as new requirements must first be categorized and evaluated. This must be documented accordingly and be released by the persons responsible for change management. Only when a change request has been released can the necessary test be run, which usually happens first in the development system and then in the QA system before the change is transported into the production system. SAP Solution Manager supports this entire IT service process.
- **Help and service desk**
  SAP Solution Manager offers a complete help desk functionality. This functionality mainly captures the problems of users and the solution management using a ticketing system. Solutions to problems are found using integrated knowledge management or by forwarding the problems to a support employee at a higher level. A ticketing solution can be used here. A knowledge base helps support employees find quick and efficient solutions to problems. The knowledge base can be built step by step during the implementation and execution of the test cycles.
- **Service delivery**
  If problems that arrive at the support desk also require an assignment of on-site personnel (second-level support employees) to exchange a hard disk, for example, SAP Solution Manager can be used to coordinate and control that assignment. All units that are connected to SAP Solution Manager and render services can be centrally controlled and support an orientation according to the ITIL. A support function, including a workflow for creating and processing messages, is available to support solution developments.
- **Solution documentation**
  You can centrally edit and store a project and analysis documentation. Modifications and custom development are supported using the Custom Development Management Cockpit.
- **Root cause analysis**
  Different monitoring functions, analysis options, and performance parameters support the examination of problem causes and their solution.
- **Monitoring**
  You can use the monitoring function to control the current status of the used SAP systems in real time; this also includes business process job management. The status is indicated by traffic lights. If the traffic lights are yellow, proactive measures can be used to quickly counteract imminent problems to ensure the availability of the SAP systems and hence the business processes.

Thanks to its extensive functions, SAP Solution Manager plays an important role, particularly in complex SAP system landscapes. Figure 19.2 summarizes the entire functional scope of SAP Solution Manager.

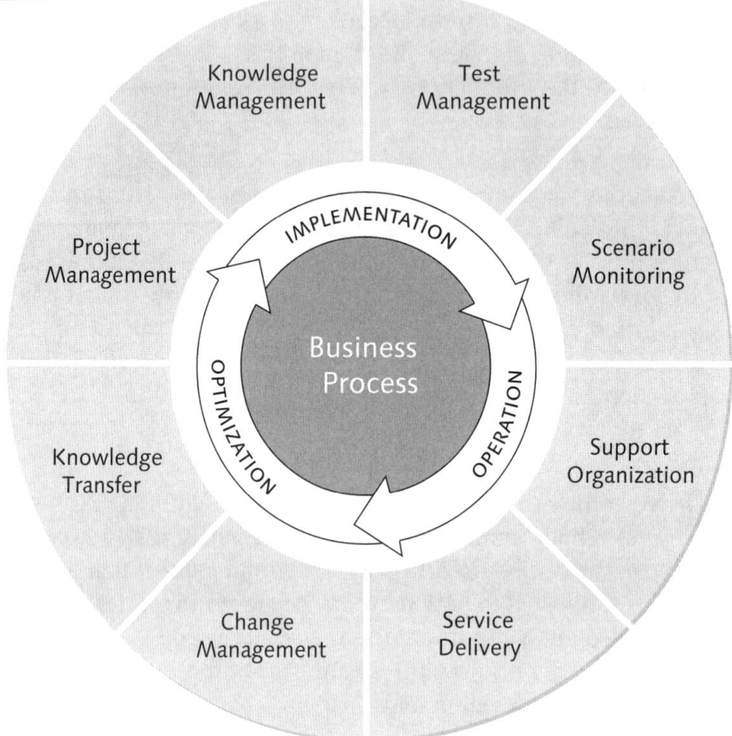


**Figure 19.2** Functional Areas of SAP Solution Manager

## 19.2 Risks and Controls

Because SAP Solution Manager can be used to centrally control and monitor a complex SAP system landscape, and modify critical technical configurations in all integrated SAP systems, a corresponding comprehensive data security and authorization concept is very important. The security methods and solutions that you choose for SAP Solution Manager are determined by an assessment of the requirements and the risk potential of each individual situation. Before you develop the data security and authorization concept, you should first implement a risk analysis like in any other case.

The technical security of SAP Solution Manager is based on the security technologies of SAP NetWeaver Application Server (AS) ABAP and Java (see Chapter 9, SAP NetWeaver AS) and the SAP Graphical User Interface (GUI) (see Chapter 28, User Interfaces). The benefit of this is that already-existing business security concepts and configuration guidelines (baselines) can be used. Therefore, the following only discusses the essential risks presented in Table 19.1.

| No. | Classification | Description |
|---|---|---|
| 1. | Potential risk | Inadequate authorization concept:<br>Users of SAP Solution Manager have authorizations that are too extensive for their actual requirements in terms of information and functions. The reason for this is that the authorization concept is only used as a means of assigning functional authorizations and not as an effective instrument for controlling access and minimizing risks. This application, in particular, enables users to set sensitive technical system configurations from a central point. |
| | Impact | Users have greater authorizations than are necessary for their position and the scope of their work. The unauthorized or unqualified access to high-risk, central technical system configuration settings can result in system instabilities, and may even compromise the entire system. Highly sensitive business processes can be affected and this may result in a loss of revenue for the entire company. |
| | Risk without control(s) | Extremely high |
| | Control | The authorization concept has to take into account both organizational and functional requirements, and make administration simpler and more effective. The relevant risks have to be taken into account in the authorization design process, and methods of continuous management have to be integrated into the change management process. |
| | Risk with control(s) | Normal |
| | Section | 19.3 |
| 2. | Potential risk | No monitoring of the SAP system landscape:<br>The technical operation status of a complex SAP system landscape is not monitored centrally. System breakdowns or critical statuses such as system overloads can't be identified. |

**Table 19.1** Risks and Controls for SAP Solution Manager

| No. | Classification | Description |
|---|---|---|
| | Impact | As critical system statuses can't be identified at an early stage, the availability of the SAP system landscape can't be ensured. Therefore, systems or business processes that must be highly available depending on individual requirements can no longer be ensured. This may lead to an increased loss of revenues.<br>It may also have legal implications, for instance, if a banking application fails and the users affected by this take legal action. |
| | Risk without control(s) | High |
| | Control | A complex SAP system landscape must be monitored using SAP Solution Manager (or a similar partner solution). The monitoring function must be configured in such a way that unstable system statuses can be identified early so that adequate countermeasures can be implemented. |
| | Risk with control(s) | Low |
| | Section | 19.4 |
| 3. | Potential risk | Inadequately configured communication connections.<br>A large number of communication connections to the SAP systems must be configured especially for SAP Solution Manager.<br>In this context, incorrectly configured Remote Function Call (RFC) connections are a potential risk. If authorizations are assigned to RFC system users that go beyond the scope required (for example, when using SAP_ALL), an unnecessarily high potential risk exists. |
| | Impact | Incorrectly configured RFC communication connections can be used to further compromise the system. For example, an RFC system user that has authorizations for all ABAP function groups can be used to create a new dialog user in the target system. That dialog user can be granted a wide range of authorizations and can be misused to carry out unauthorized financial transactions. Moreover, these excessive and unnecessary authorizations are recorded in audits. |
| | Risk without control(s) | Extremely high |

**Table 19.1** Risks and Controls for SAP Solution Manager (Cont.)

| No. | Classification | Description |
|---|---|---|
| | Control | Correct configuration of RFC communication destinations and restriction of RFC system user authorizations to the minimum required. Before you use the trusted RFC connections, you should check to see if the associated risk is justified and whether sufficient compensating security measures are available. |
| | Risk with control(s) | Normal |
| | Section | 19.4 |
| 4. | Potential risk | Insufficient security for user access to SAP Solution Manager: SAP Solution Manager is the central part of the system landscape, is connected with the most essential components of SAP NetWeaver, and provides access to these applications. As a result, SAP Solution Manager is a potential point of attack in case of an unauthorized access to another system. |
| | Impact | An insufficiently secured user access increases the risk of an unauthorized access to important configuration and monitoring functions of SAP Solution Manager. The application runs on AS ABAP and AS Java. You can access the operating system from both platforms. Moreover, SAP Solution Manager is linked with various systems and therefore provides access to these systems. Therefore, the risk exists for SAP Solution Manager to be a predestinated point of attack for unauthorized access to the entire system architecture. |
| | Risk without control(s) | High |
| | Control | Individual user names with individual and complex passwords increase the security in the identification and authentication of the system personnel and also their responsibility for the system access and system activities. |
| | Risk with control(s) | Normal |
| | Section | 19.4 |
| 5. | Potential risk | Insufficient security for stored data and data during transmission. |

**Table 19.1** Risks and Controls for SAP Solution Manager (Cont.)

| No. | Classification | Description |
|---|---|---|
| | | If data communications, for instance, user names and their passwords, are exchanged between the systems without any protection, these could be intercepted during transmission and used for unauthorized access. The same risk applies to the unprotected data transmission. Here, confidential business data could be compromised in the monitoring of business processes or background jobs. As a result, SAP Solution Manager is a potential point of attack in the case of an unauthorized access to data. |
| | Impact | Unprotected data can be accessed by unauthorized users, for example, at the system level, in the data storage, or during the transmission in the network. Financial data or company-strategic information could be viewed without authorization or come into the possession of unauthorized users or competitors. |
| | | This is a violation of customer-specific security requirements, internal company requirements, statutory requirements, and data protection guidelines. |
| | Risk without control(s) | High |
| | Control | Data connections and data storage for potentially confidential data must be secured using data encryption considering a balanced ratio of security costs and justifiable risk. |
| | Risk with control(s) | Normal |
| | Section | 19.4 |

**Table 19.1** Risks and Controls for SAP Solution Manager (Cont.)

## 19.3 Application Security

SAP Solution Manager is supported by SAP NetWeaver AS ABAP and Java. However, it is recommended to configure the User Management Engine (UME) (Java) in such a way that the ABAP stack assumes the user and authorization management so that the user authentication and its authorization checks are based on the traditional ABAP authorization concept (see Chapter 9 and Chapter 20, Authorizations in SAP ERP). The user authorizations should be based on the best-practice method presented in Chapter 20.

SAP Solution Manager already contains preconfigured standard SAP roles with specific authorizations for every Solution Manager function. This is useful because SAP Solution Manager provides a variety of functions that makes it easier for the user to implement an authorization concept. However, you should check to see if the standard roles meet the company's security requirements and the risk tolerance or whether you need new roles with adaptations.

Access to the administrative functions should be distributed across several administrators according to the concept of segregation of duties for task areas. To implement these control objectives, the SAP transactions and authorization objects that are typical for SAP Solution Manager provide the option to issue tailored access authorizations and restrict the use of general, overly broad authorizations. Tables 19.2 and 19.3 list the typical transactions and authorization objects for SAP Solution Manager.

| Transaction | Description |
|---|---|
| DMD | Solution Content Repository: transaction for accessing configuration data that is stored in the general content storage |
| DMDDEF | Solution Metadata Repository: transaction for accessing the maintenance of metadata in the Solution Manager repository |
| DSMOP, DSWP, SOLUTION_MANAGER | SAP Solution Manager: Using these three transactions, you can access the main functions of Maintenance Optimizer. |
| DSWP_WEB, SOLUTION_MANAGER_BSP | SAP Solution Manager (HTML): transactions for supporting access to SAP Solution Manager via a web browser |
| SMAP01 | Maintain Solutions Map Objects: transaction for maintaining the Solution Map objects |
| SMSY | System Landscape: transaction for accessing the system landscape |
| SOLAR01 | Business Blueprint: transaction for accessing the Business Blueprint administration |
| SOLAR01C, SOLAR02 | Configuration: transaction for Business Blueprint configuration |
| SOLAR_CONF | Customizing: transaction for the SAP Solution Manager configuration |
| SOLAR_EVAL | Project Reporting/Analysis: transaction for accessing the analysis and report functions |

**Table 19.2** Important Transactions for SAP Solution Manager

| Transaction | Description |
|---|---|
| SOLAR_MIGRATION | Solution Manager Migration: transaction for data migration within the system landscape |
| SOLAR_PROJECT_CREATE | Solution Manager Project Creation: transaction for creating projects |
| SOLAR_TESTPLAN | Test Plan: transaction for creating a project test plan |
| SOLUTION MANAGER_DIRECTORY | Solution Directory: transaction for maintaining the Solution Manager directory |
| SOLAR_PROJECT_ADMIN | Project Administration: transaction for project maintenance |
| SOLMAP | Maintain Solution Maps: transaction for maintaining the Solution Manager maps |
| /SAPTRX/ASCOSD1 | Define Solution/Scenario: transaction for creating a solution in SAP Solution Manager |
| CRMM_IIA | Interactive Solution Search: transaction for interactive search in solutions |
| ISCB | Define Solution Type: transaction for maintaining the solution type |
| ISCD | Define Solution Categories: transaction for maintaining the solution category |

**Table 19.2** Important Transactions for SAP Solution Manager (Cont.)

| Authorization object | Description | Authorization field | Values |
|---|---|---|---|
| AI_SOL_DIR | Controls access to the Solution Manager directory | ACTVT | 02: Change, modify, delete directory elements |
| S_SMSYEDIT | Controls the authorization for maintaining the Solution Manager system landscape | ACTVT | ▶ 01: Create<br>▶ 02: Change<br>▶ 03: Display<br>▶ 06: Delete<br>▶ 70: Administration (needed to make basic settings; if this authorization is set, the remaining fields are not checked)<br>▶ D1: Copy |

**Table 19.3** Important Authorization Objects for SAP Solution Manager

| Authorization object | Description | Authorization field | Values |
| --- | --- | --- | --- |
| | | SMSYETYPE | Type of system attached to SAP Solution Manager:<br>▶ SYSTEM: SAP system<br>▶ COMPUTER: server<br>▶ DBSYS: database<br>▶ PRODUCT: product<br>▶ LOG_CMP: logical components |
| | | SMSYENAME | Name of system attached to SAP Solution Manager |
| D_SOLUTION | Controls the access to system data of the system landscape defined in SAP Solution Manager. Access to individual customer numbers, installation numbers, and database IDs can be controlled. | DSWPDCUSNO | Existing customer numbers |
| | | DSWPDINSNO | Existing installation numbers |
| | | DSWPDDBID | Existing database ID |
| D_SOLM_ACT | Controls the executable actions that are possible within a monitoring configuration (or solution) | DSWPSOLACT | ▶ 00: Display report<br>▶ 05: Display session<br>▶ 10: Change session<br>▶ 12: Delete session<br>▶ 15: Archive session<br>▶ 20: Change settings (within a monitoring configuration)<br>▶ 25: Start service processing<br>▶ 30: Create service<br>▶ 35: Change global settings |

**Table 19.3** Important Authorization Objects for SAP Solution Manager (Cont.)

| Authorization object | Description | Authorization field | Values |
|---|---|---|---|
| | | | ▸ 40: Create/archive monitoring configuration<br>▸ 50: Delete monitoring configuration |
| D_SOLUTION MANAGERBU | Controls the permitted activities per session type (bundle ID) | DSWPBUNDAC | ▸ 01: Display<br>▸ 02: Change |
| | | DSWPBUNDLE | Session type ID |
| D_SOLUTION MANAGER | Controls the SAP Solution Manager call | ACTVT | 16: Start |
| D_SOL_VIEW | Controls the view that can be displayed in SAP Solution Manager | Solution Manager View | ▸ 10: Display Solution Manager settings<br>▸ 20: Display Solution Manager operations |
| S_RFC | Required for the use of RFC connections. | RFC_TYPE | FUGR |
| | | RFC_NAME | Name of the RFC object that is to be protected (function group). |
| | | ACTVT | 16: Start |
| S_RFC_ADM | Controls the RFC maintenance access using Transaction SM59. | ACTVT | ▸ 01: Create<br>▸ 02: Change<br>▸ 03: Display<br>▸ 06: Delete<br>▸ 36: Advanced management |

**Table 19.3** Important Authorization Objects for SAP Solution Manager (Cont.)

| Authorization object | Description | Authorization field | Values |
|---|---|---|---|
| | | RFCTYPE | ▶ 2: R/2 connection<br>▶ 3: ABAP connection<br>▶ G: HTTP (external)<br>▶ H: HTTP (SAP)<br>▶ M: Logical connection<br>▶ L: CMC connection<br>▶ T: TCP/IP<br>▶ X: ABAP driver |
| | | RFCDEST | Alphanumeric |
| | | ICF_VALUE | Alphanumeric |
| S_RFCAC | Controls the permission for configuring a trusted RFC connection | RFC_SYSID | ID of the calling system |
| | | RFC_CLI | Client the calling system |
| | | RFC_USER | ID of the RFC system user |
| | | RFC_EQUSER | Control flag for users |
| | | RFC_TCODE | Calling transaction code |
| | | RFC_IN | This authorization field is not used currently. |
| | | ACTVT | 16: Start |
| S_RFCACL | Controls the authorizations of RFC system users for an RFC connection to a trusted system. | RFC_SYSID | ID of the calling system |
| | | RFC_CLIENT | ID of the called system |
| | | RFC_USER | ID of the calling system user |

**Table 19.3** Important Authorization Objects for SAP Solution Manager (Cont.)

| Authorization object | Description | Authorization field | Values |
|---|---|---|---|
| | | RFC_EQUSER | Setting whether an RFC system user can be called by another RFC system user with the same ID<br>▶ Y: yes<br>▶ N: no |
| | | RFC_TCODE | Calling transaction code that starts the function in the called system |
| | | RFC_INFO | Additional information for the calling system. However, this field is not currently used. |
| | | ACTVT | 16: Start |

**Table 19.3** Important Authorization Objects for SAP Solution Manager (Cont.)

## 19.4 Technical Security

This section describes in more detail the risks and controls that are outlined in Table 19.1 with regard to technical security.

### 19.4.1 Security Measures for User Access

In principle, you should set up individual user accounts with strict password rules and only assign individual authorizations if a clearly justifiable need exists for the individual tasks of the system or application maintenance. You should avoid generic user names and generally always use individual user names because they also increase the responsibility of application users and system administrators with regard to the uniqueness of log entries.

SAP Solution Manager supports Single Sign-On (SSO) using SAP logon tickets, which is done at the security level of SAP NetWeaver AS. Therefore, SAP Solution Manager is an integral part of SSO within the SAP NetWeaver architecture. Always remember that SSO is not an explicit security measure because the security risk always remains for the initial identification and authentication of a user. The authenticity of a logon ticket in general cannot be better than the initial identification and authentication of a user, which are the basis for creating a logon ticket. Once an SAP logon ticket has been created, several security mechanisms are active that ensure its integrity and authenticity.

### 19.4.2 System Monitoring Function

As mentioned previously, SAP Solution Manager can be used as a central system monitoring and management solution. To do this, the systems to be monitored are connected to the central SAP Solution Manager via the interfaces of the Computing Center Management System (CCMS). Figure 19.3 illustrates this relationship.

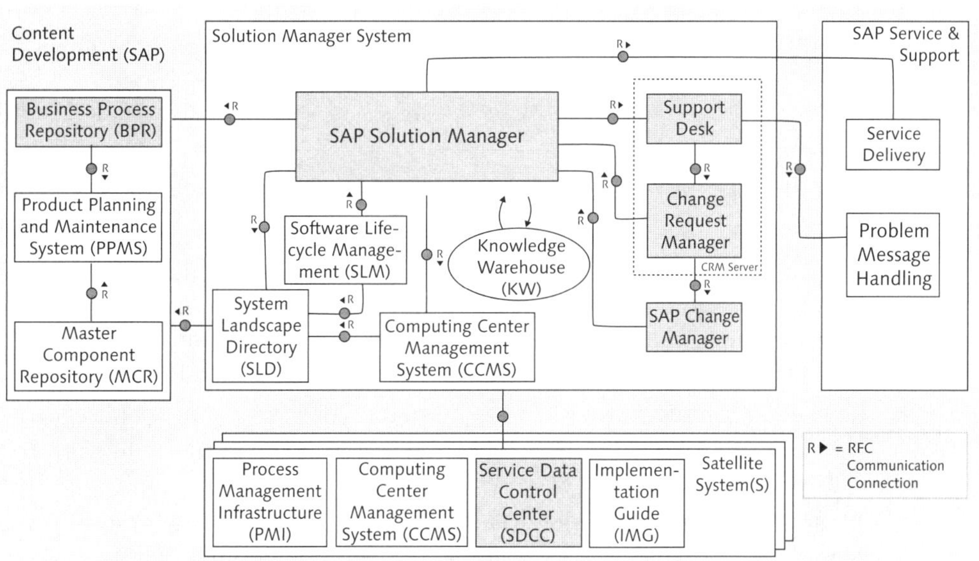


**Figure 19.3** Connecting SAP Systems to Be Monitored to SAP Solution Manager

Within SAP Solution Manager, traffic light functions are available to the operating personnel. These functions can be used to clearly monitor the operation status based on separately configurable system parameters for the defined monitoring configuration. The central monitoring function lets you initiate the necessary countermeasures for system stabilization in real time, if necessary. The overall availability of the SAP system landscape can therefore be kept at a high level.

### 19.4.3 RFC Communication Security

Appropriate RFC communication connections must be implemented when setting up a monitoring configuration. In this context, you must particularly consider the technical default settings for the SAP Gateway, and the authorization restrictions for RFC connections described in Chapter 9 and the information in Table 19.1. Particularly authorizations for the authorization object `S_RFC`, whose scope is set too wide, can be used to compromise the system, if the RFC user has the type System or Communication.

In combination with AS ABAP, SAP Solution Manager also has the function to use a trusted RFC connection to the neighbor system. However, this option entails a very high security risk because this RFC type doesn't require a password for the RFC system user. This means that no authentication of the RFC user is required and the target system provides implicit trust for the identity of the RFC user. This situation is comparable to an SSO concept. But this also has the benefit that no password information needs to be transferred via the network. This RFC connection concept is not mandatory, and the traditional RFC connection using password authentication still applies.

But if trusted RFC is used, the risk management should include the following measures:

- To ensure that no other user other than the RFC system user that was provided with the corresponding limited authorizations in the target system can use the RFC connection, the authorization of this system user should leave the `RFC_USER` field blank in the `S_RFCACL` object (input: ' ') (see Table 19.3).
- The systems connected via RFC must be in the same secured network segment. There is no security if the systems are located in heterogeneous network sections with varying levels of security.
- The systems must meet identical security requirements and be configured according to the same security concept. The same applies to users and RFC system users, that is, both systems have the same level of security, and the users of the source systems would have access to the target system anyway. This emphasizes that the purpose of a trusted connection is to increase the effectiveness of the communication of these two systems.

### 19.4.4 Data Communication Security

Data is exposed to a variety of threats during transfer in the network or in data storage. The resulting risks must be brought to an acceptable level by means of technical countermeasures and continuous maintenance; Chapter 5, Information Technology (IT) Security, provides valuable information on this subject.

With regard to data security during transfer in the company network or the Internet from or to SAP Solution Manager, it is recommended to use Secure Socket Layer (SSL) for HTTP and Secure Network Communication (SNC) connections for RFCs. Because SAP Solution Manager runs on SAP NetWeaver AS, communication via Simple Object Access Protocol (SOAP) (see Chapter 7, Web Services, Enterprise

Services, and Service-Oriented Architectures) is also supported. This variant is used in combination with third-party non-SAP applications.

### 19.4.5 Important Components of SAP NetWeaver

The following SAP NetWeaver components support SAP Solution Manager and its functions. Therefore, the security risks of these components are also security risks for SAP Solution Manager. So their security risks and options for risk management must be considered. The most important components are as follows:

- SAP NetWeaver AS (see Chapter 9)
- SAP NetWeaver Business Warehouse (BW) (see Chapter 10, SAP NetWeaver BW)
- SAP Internet Transaction Server (ITS) (see Chapter 14, Classic SAP Middleware)
- SAP GUI (see Chapter 28)
- Web browser (see Chapter 28)

*This chapter describes Information Technology (IT) security concepts for SAP Enterprise Resource Planning (ERP). The focus is on general authorization concepts and solutions for best-practice controls in ERP.*

# 20 Authorizations in SAP ERP

SAP ERP describes the application portfolio for SAP Enterprise Resource Planning. This includes all of the "modules" of the classic R/3 system, that is, functions that support company activities like financials (SAP ERP Financials), human resources (SAP ERP HCM), or logistics (SAP ERP Operations). SAP ERP is the central back-end system in many companies that operate SAP systems. SAP NetWeaver is the technical basis for SAP ERP applications.

## 20.1 Introduction and Functions

Because the back-end systems process a wide range of business information via transactions and store it in tables or as documents, business, legal, technical, organizational, and other requirements must be considered to sufficiently protect the components or applications of SAP ERP and to ensure security and continuity for achieving the company objectives in the long term. The focus of attention is on core components, such as logistics with sales applications like Sales and Distribution (SD) or Materials Management (MM), financials with Financial Accounting (FI) and Controlling (CO), and HCM as a functional application. The volume of interactive points of contact between users and applications, along with the data quantity in these systems, means that the central back-end systems, in particular, need to be protected from SAP user errors, theft or manipulation of information, and from other attacks damaging the company, its employees, and partners.

In risk management, particular importance is placed on managing internal and external identities to access the SAP ERP system and on the authorization system to define and distribute functions, responsibilities, and access control for business and administrative processes.

## 20.2 Risks and Controls

Risk potential and protection requirements determine the selection of necessary and objective-oriented control measures and security solutions for SAP ERP. Objective requirements and the subjective perception of needs, which may vary due to differences in the company's culture, result in different evaluations of the individual parties involved and persons responsible in the company. This results in an almost chronic lack of attention given to the authorization system.

In the authorization environment, numerous solutions have emerged. In too many cases, these solutions don't address the real problems at all or do so insufficiently, despite their high costs, and they haven't exploited the positive potential of an effective authorization system yet. The evaluation of functions required in SAP ERP and its associated risks, including legal requirements, also determine the use of supported software. The central starting point for evaluating these security solutions is to not only know the risks and their countermeasures, but to also proactively use user rights so that users can work effectively, hackers inside and outside the organization can be fended, and the authorization systems can be managed transparently and effectively. Table 20.1 presents some risks for SAP ERP.

| No. | Classification | Description |
|---|---|---|
| 1. | Potential risk | No authentication:<br>Users of SAP ERP applications receive their user ID and initial password in an unencrypted email, or the initial password is always the same. This allows unauthorized users to access SAP ERP applications and potentially commit criminal offences. |
| | Impact | Unauthorized users use loopholes in authentication mechanisms to access data in back-end systems. Identity theft and unauthorized use of third-party authorizations to access SAP ERP data and transactions are potential effects of this risk. |
| | Risk without control(s) | Extremely high |
| | Control | The authentication mechanism and the associated administrative processes must be strong enough to protect the integrity of authorized users and to only allow access to these users. |
| | Risk with control(s) | Low |

**Table 20.1** Risks and Controls for SAP ERP

| No. | Classification | Description |
|---|---|---|
| | Section | 20.3.1 |
| 2. | Potential risk | Inadequate authorization concept:<br>Users of the various SAP ERP applications have authorizations that are too extensive for their actual requirements in terms of information and functions. The reason for this is that the authorization concept is only used as a means of assigning functional authorizations and not as an effective instrument for minimizing risks and optimizing costs. |
| | Impact | Users have greater authorizations than are necessary for their position and the scope of their work. They thus have read and modify access to high-risk information and data. This is a violation of both internal company requirements and statutory requirements. It creates a situation where process, administrative, and system risks are not controlled. The risk potential is therefore increased rather than minimized. |
| | Risk without control(s) | Extremely high |
| | Control | The authorization concept has to take into account both organizational and functional requirements, and make administration simpler and more effective.<br>The relevant risks have to be taken into account in the authorization design process, and methods of continuous management have to be integrated into the change management process. |
| | Risk with control(s) | Normal |
| | Section | 20.3.2 |
| 3. | Potential risk | Inadequate responsibility structure:<br>The IT department cannot cope in an orderly and organized fashion with the workload of managing users and authorizations. The complexity of the task is increasing, as is the functional workload on the SAP ERP applications. There is also a need for coordination with the user departments, but these leave the task of authorization management up to the IT department. Also, the authorization components are not sufficiently transparent. This results in authorizations that do not accurately reflect the actual requirements of the enterprise. |

**Table 20.1** Risks and Controls for SAP ERP (Cont.)

| No. | Classification | Description |
|---|---|---|
| | Impact | Authorizations are centrally assigned by administrators, even for users in other geographical regions. The actual persons who are responsible for information design — such as process, data, or application owners — are not properly involved in the design of authorization concepts and their daily administration. Thus, not enough attention, or no attention at all, is paid to the basic requirements. The segregation of duties therefore becomes blurred over time. Users are assigned more and more authorizations, and because of time pressures, analyses of the current situation and current requirements never take place. This results in errors and ineffective methods in authorization design, and extra work in terms of technical implementation, distribution, monitoring, and auditing. The security of the SAP ERP applications is thus not guaranteed, and statutory requirements are violated. |
| | Risk without control(s) | Extremely high |
| | Control | Introduce and ensure the consistent implementation of the information ownership principle to effectively control authorizations and users in SAP ERP. |
| | Risk with control(s) | Low |
| | Section | 20.3.4 |
| 4. | Potential risk | The authorization concept is not fully defined:<br>The authorization concepts for SAP ERP and other components partly follow different concepts. This results in individual solutions over the course of the project. Users can have different authorizations in the individual applications. Therefore, either too many or too few authorizations are assigned, which compromises the continuity of the process and the effectiveness of authorization management. |
| | Impact | Authorization errors and inconsistencies compromise operational processes. For example, transactions can no longer be used, which, in turn, results in failures. Systems and employees are not used effectively. |
| | Risk without control(s) | High |

**Table 20.1** Risks and Controls for SAP ERP (Cont.)

| No. | Classification | Description |
|---|---|---|
| | Control | The authorization concepts of the individual applications and systems should usually be part of an overlying comprehensive authorization concept. Authorizations in SAP ERP should be synchronized with the authorizations of SAP NetWeaver Portal and other applications. A shared concept should be the basis for this. Both conceptually and technically, this synchronization process has to ensure that the authorizations exist in all of the various systems, and that the authorizations that have been agreed on are assigned to the users. |
| | Risk with control(s) | Low |
| | Section | 20.3.2 |
| 5. | Potential risk | Identity and change management:<br>There is no central user master data system. Because of the different types of users of SAP systems, there are a number of different solutions, however, the reasons why there are so many are not known. The master data storage system therefore contains redundancies and inconsistencies. The administrative processes do not permit you to make quick organizational changes to employee data or to modify or lock the respective authorizations.<br>Because the HCM organizational structure is not incorporated into the process of assigning authorizations to positions, errors can occur with assigning the correct authorizations to certain user groups. This has an effect on the number of active users in SAP ERP, and it increases the threat from unauthorized employees with corresponding permissions. |
| | Impact | The consistency of user master data is not guaranteed, and modifications are either not implemented or are only implemented after a delay. Employees who have left the enterprise can therefore continue to use their authorizations and access table data and transactional process data in SAP ERP applications while remaining undetected. When an employee changes to a different department or user group, any new authorizations are simply added to their existing ones, which means that their authorizations mount up, along with those that arise as a result of combinations of authorizations. Unwanted authorizations, faulty transactions, unauthorized report running, and serious system errors can all result from excessive authorizations. |

**Table 20.1** Risks and Controls for SAP ERP (Cont.)

| No. | Classification | Description |
|---|---|---|
| | | These risks, in turn, can lead to ineffective administration, a lack of transparency, low levels of control, violations of data protection laws, low levels of security, and potential criminal activity. They can also lead to violations of statutory regulations, such as the Sarbanes-Oxley Act (SOX). |
| | Risk without control(s) | Extremely high |
| | Control | Introduce proper user master data administration by including a central administration system (such as SAP NetWeaver Identity Management (IdM), Central User Administration (CUA), or Lightweight Directory Access Protocol (LDAP)/ Active Directory), and set up a comprehensive, unified identity management system that takes into account all administrative situations that arise in user administration. |
| | Risk with control(s) | Low |
| | Section | 20.3.2 |
| 6. | Potential risk | Password rules:<br>Access to the SAP ERP system is usually controlled by passwords. However, the minimum standards in the system are often not enough to ensure the secure operation of the system. Passwords that are too short can easily be guessed, and old passwords that are not changed regularly lose security as time passes. |
| | Impact | Potential attackers can get hold of passwords that are easily accessible or too simple, and thus gain access to data and transactions. Depending on the authorizations that the user holds, the results of an identity attack can be very serious, and can have financial and internal operational consequences for the enterprise. There may also be violations of statutory regulations. |
| | Risk without control(s) | Extremely high |
| | Control | Passwords must be subject to rules that are defined in accordance with the security requirements of the enterprise. |
| | Risk with control(s) | Normal |
| | Section | 20.3.1 |

**Table 20.1** Risks and Controls for SAP ERP (Cont.)

| No. | Classification | Description |
|---|---|---|
| 7. | Potential risk | Technical problems with authorizations:<br>Authorization components, such as roles, are implemented in the system in such a way that the number of roles increases excessively over time, or the build-up of content causes complexity to increase on an ongoing basis. This affects the degree to which authorizations can be administrated, how roles are assigned to users, the degree to which simple monitoring is possible, and the feasibility of technical checks and audits. This all gives rise to potential risks, both in terms of administration and in the entire area of authorization for SAP ERP authorized users. |
| | Impact | Ineffective authorization management, errors in assigning authorization components to users, and a lack of transparency and clarity leads to higher costs in authorization management and to an increase in risk potential caused by excessive authorizations that have arisen due to the purely technical structure of SAP ERP authorization components.<br>Some functional segregations can no longer be implemented. There may also be violations of internal corporate regulations and statutory regulations. |
| | Risk without control(s) | Extremely high |
| | Control | An agreed authorization strategy must go hand in hand with a clear concept of the technical implementation of authorizations in SAP ERP. To this end, an appropriate authorization and role concept has to be set up. This concept should incorporate all of the components of the theoretical and practical aspects of an authorization system. It should also include best-practice solutions that are based on expert experience. |
| | Risk with control(s) | Low |
| | Section | 20.3.2 |

**Table 20.1** Risks and Controls for SAP ERP (Cont.)

These general risks have to be examined carefully by means of a detailed risk analysis. Table 20.2 shows some of the risks involved with transactions and combinations of transactions.

| Risk | Transaction Codes |
|---|---|
| User can open accounting periods that have already been closed and post documents after the month-end report has been run. | S_ALR_87003642, FBCJ |
| User can create fake General Ledger (G/L) accounts and make unauthorized modifications, and start a posting outside the normal reporting period. | FS00, F-02 |
| User can create a fake stock transport and cause an automatic payment to be made. | ME27, F110 |
| User can make unauthorized changes to a purchasing request and to a purchase order. | MASS, ME52 |
| User can make unauthorized changes to vendor master data and thus cause an unauthorized payment to be made. | FK02, F110 |
| User can create a fake goods receipt, make unauthorized changes, and cause automatic payments to be made. | MB01, F110 |
| User can create purchasing orders and associated credit orders. | ME21, F-41 |
| User can create fake profit accounts and related entries. | KE51, 3KE5 |
| User can make unauthorized changes to vendor master records and create associated invoices. | FK02, F-43 |
| User can make unauthorized changes to material master records and create a related fake purchasing order. | MM02, ME21 |
| User can make unauthorized changes to a vendor master record and cause payments to be made. | FK02, F-44 |
| User can post a credit item and cause an unauthorized payment to be made. | F-02, F-18 |
| User can post a credit item and post and remove fake payments. | F-04, F-18 |
| User can enter a fake goods receipt and post a payment to go with it. | MB01, F-18 |
| User can create a fake vendor master record and make unauthorized changes to a purchasing request. | FK01, MASS |
| User can make unauthorized changes to agreements or contract data and post a corresponding goods receipt. | ME31, MB01 |
| User can make unauthorized changes to main accounts and assign documents. | FS02, FB02 |
| User can make unauthorized changes to asset data and create purchasing orders. | AS02, MASS |
| User can create fake internal orders and post receipts to go with them. | KO01, F-02 |

**Table 20.2** Examples of Risks in Certain Transactions

## 20.3 Application Security

This section describes in more detail the risks and controls that are outlined in Table 20.1 with regard to application security.

### 20.3.1 Authentication

Every user requires a correct user ID and password to log on to a system. This authentication mechanism can be improved, supplemented, or substituted by additional procedures, such as Single Sign-On (SSO), digital certificates, magnetic cards, tokens, biometric identification, and others. SAP supports authentication by user ID and password, single sign-on, and so on, including certificate-based solutions.

If a web browser is used as the front-end client, SAP ERP supports the use of logon tickets for SSO. The users are issued with a logon ticket after they have authenticated themselves in the original SAP system. This ticket then functions as an authentication token for other SAP systems. Thus, to authenticate himself, a user doesn't have to enter a user ID or password; instead, he can directly access systems like SAP ERP once this system has checked his or her logon ticket. As an alternative to user authentication with user IDs and passwords, users who use a web browser as their front end can also use an X.509 client certificate for authentication purposes. The Secure Socket Layer (SSL) protocol is used to authenticate the user on the web server. This protocol does not transfer any passwords.

With authentication methods that use a user ID and password, password rules are particularly important. These rules can be defined in the instance profiles, using Transaction RZ10. They specify, for example, the minimum length of passwords, the validity, rules for automatic locks in the case of incorrect entries of passwords, and so on. Table `USR40` is used to maintain the locking of specific passwords (also referred to as prohibited passwords).

### 20.3.2 Authorizations

The role and authorization concept is the central concept for assigning rights in SAP ERP and all other applications. An enterprise's requirements in terms of application security and the required authorization design are defined as part of an authorization concept for SAP ERP and connected systems.

#### Role Concept

The role concept defines the central starting point when designing and developing the required user authorizations. In SAP ERP, authorizations are required for different applications. Transactions and activities, reports and evaluations, and tables and programs are protected by means of authorization checks.

Transactions are the basic form of access to the SAP system. Transactional Authorizations not only protect transactions and their data, but also restrict organizational and functional elements. Table 20.3 shows an example.

| Transaction | Transaction Code | Restricted to |
|---|---|---|
| Create material | MM01 | Company code |

**Table 20.3** Transaction MM01 with Company Code Check

The necessary authorizations for the transaction are developed in roles and assigned to the individual users. It is also possible to assign roles to a specific organizational unit, such as by position, at the organizational level. The users then receive the relevant authorizations indirectly via the organizational unit in the form of roles.

A transaction usually consists of multiple screens in which data can be created, modified, or displayed. For example, Transaction MM01 is used to create a material master record, Transaction MM02 is used to modify a material master record, and Transaction MM03 is used to display a material master record. The company code is displayed in the company code field, while the material number is displayed in the material number field. Some of these fields contain information that needs to be protected or controlled, and these control points have to be checked accordingly during the running of the transaction.

Usually, there is an ABAP program behind every transaction. The connection to this program is created using Transaction SE93. Authorization checks are built into the program code and have to achieve a positive result when the programs are in use. To this end, the corresponding authorizations are linked to the user master records. In the SAP standard, authorization checks in ABAP programs use authorization objects to assign authorization or restrict access to transaction codes, activities, and data. Developers use various methods to build authorization checks into their programs.

The most common method is an authorization check using the `AUTHORITY-CHECK` ABAP statement, which is used to check a specific authorization object at a specific point in the program (see Figure 20.1). If the check has a positive result, the user of the transaction will have the necessary authorizations in their user master record. If the user does not have sufficient authorization, the program encounters an error, outputs a corresponding error message, and terminates. This intentional termination occurs at the point of control, which is either accepted or rejected. In the case of error messages, a user or administrator can use Transaction SU53 to display more detailed information about the authorization fields.

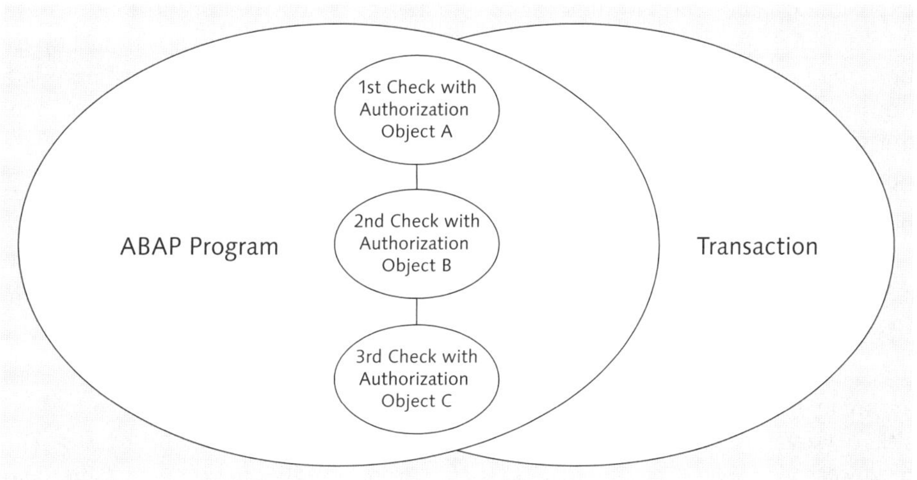


**Figure 20.1** Authorization Check in Program Code

In the SAP standard, every transaction is subject to a check using the S_TCODE authorization object. S_TCODE is checked when the transaction is started. This is the first restriction of users on the transactional level. All other authorizations check access to specific organizational units and activities inside the transactions. Table 20.4 shows an example of authorization objects for Transaction MM01.

| Authorization Object | Authorization Fields | Meaning | Value |
|---|---|---|---|
| S_TCODE | TCD | Transaction code | MM01 |
| M_MATE_BUK | ACTVT | Activity | 01 |
| | BUKRS | Company code | $BUKRS |
| M_MATE_LGN | ACTVT | Activity | 01 |
| | LGNUM | Warehouse number | $LGNUM |
| M_MATE_VKO | ACTVT<br>VKORG<br>VTWEG | Activity<br>Sales organization<br>Sales channel | 01<br>$VKORG<br>$VTWEG |

**Table 20.4** Example of Authorization Objects in Transaction MM01

The authorization objects shown in the example are subject to two checks. First, they are checked with a fixed authorization value, which is "01" in the case of Transaction MM01. Second, there are authorization fields that do not contain any fixed check value. The system dynamically awaits the user's entry in each field to be checked, and then checks the input value against the authorizations. Authorization objects thus control the access to transactions, information groups, and data (for instance, MM01, master data, material), and also to individual organizational units such as a specific company code or material storage location.

The authorization checks in applications make it necessary to implement user permissions in the form of authorizations. The technical implementation of the authorizations is not done via manually created authorization profiles, but in semi-automated processes by means of roles. Roles are developed using the SAP Profile Generator (Transaction PFCG).

Roles are known as design roles in the design phase. As soon as these design roles are mapped in SAP ERP, they become roles. Roles are also referred to in various situations as SAP roles, authorization roles, application roles, or user roles. The predecessor of roles, activity groups, is also used in individual cases in tables and entries in SAP ERP. However, it is roles that are meant in every case, even if the technical names seem to signify activity groups.

A user needs specific permissions and access options within systems so that he can properly use his work center. These access permissions are defined by means of organizationally structured roles. Authorization is therefore the key. An authorization is a set of permitted value assignments that are assigned to users by means of authorization objects. When transactions are called in SAP ERP, authorization objects and authorization values are checked and queried in the user master record. The checked access permissions in the program code of the transaction are assigned in the user master record by means of the relevant authorizations. An authorization is thus a form of permission to access certain transactions under certain conditions. A role contains all of the relevant authorization components and can be assigned to users both individually and in combination with other roles.

### Authorization Components

The main technical components of the SAP authorization system are as follows:

- Authorization object
  - With authorization fields
  - With authorization field values

- Authorization
- Authorization profile
- Authorization role
  - Single roles
  - Composite roles
- Users

The role/authorization role is the unit that contains all of the authorization components mentioned (see Figure 20.2).

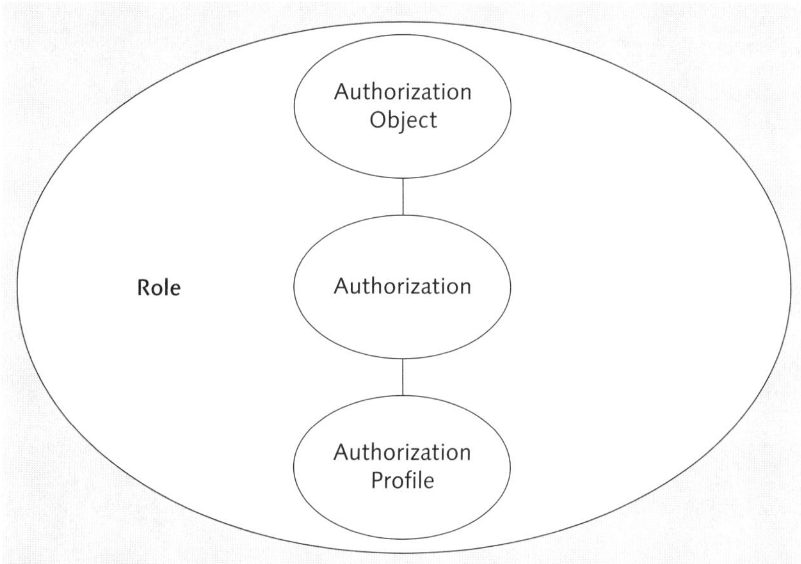


**Figure 20.2** Structure of a Role

From an authorization-checking, point of view, authorization objects are templates that can be used in program code to implement authorization checks in various SAP ERP applications. SAP provides over 800 standard authorization objects. These can be used in standard transactions and programs in ABAP. An authorization object can contain up to ten authorization fields (see Figure 20.3). Authorization objects are divided up according to the individual application, are subject to special naming conventions, and, in conjunction with other authorization objects, can ensure that a program or transaction is protected. Authorization objects are assigned to authorization object classes. This makes it much easier for programmers, administrators, and system auditors to use them and navigate in them.

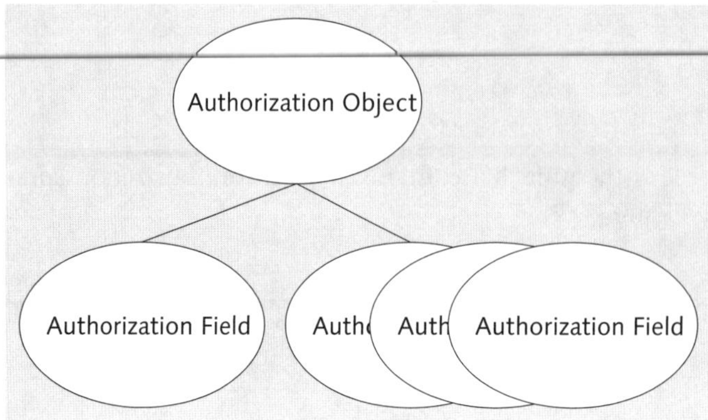


**Figure 20.3** Structure of an Authorization Object

As mentioned previously, authorization objects are templates for (technical) authorizations. An authorization is a specific instance of an authorization object in the SAP system that ensures special functional or organizational accesses within the SAP system. Field content is assigned to an authorization field in the form of authorization field values and is saved as an authorization. Authorizations are assigned to authorization profiles; Table 20.5 shows an example.

| Transaction Code | Check | Check with Authorization Object | Authorization Field | Authorization Field Values |
|---|---|---|---|---|
| MM01 | Company code | M_MATE_BUK | Activity | 01 for Create |
| | | | Company code | – |

**Table 20.5** Example of an Authorization Object and Authorization Object Field Value in Transaction MM01

If an authorization object contains multiple fields, the check always uses an AND operation. The overall check of the authorization object is only considered successful only if the authorization check for each individual authorization field is successful. An authorization itself is a technical component of the overall authorization system. "Authorizations" in this context refers not to user permissions, but to the technical component that is part of the role.

As many authorizations as you like can be created on the basis of an authorization object. Because this is done by using roles, rather than manually, it has no effect on authorization design or authorization management. An authorization contains one authorization object with authorization fields (see Figure 20.4).

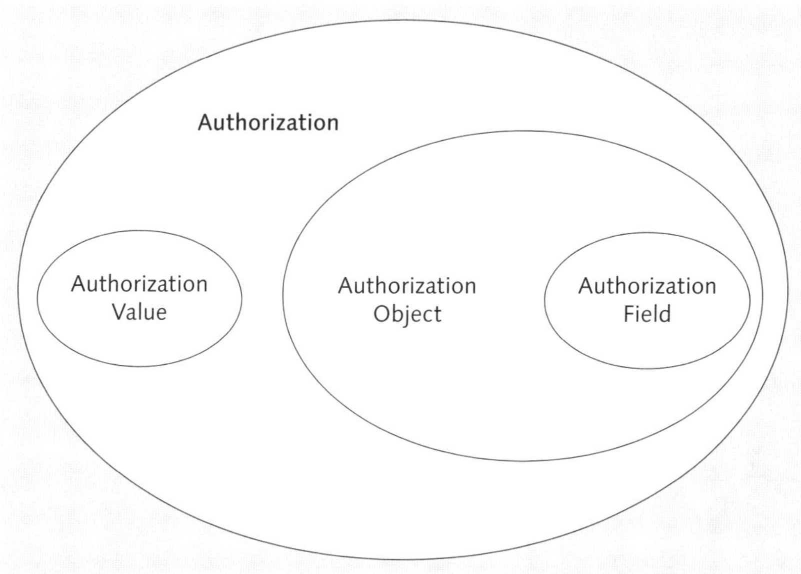


**Figure 20.4** Structure of an Authorization

Authorizations are assigned in an authorization profile, and a profile can contain one or more authorizations (see Figure 20.5).

Authorization profiles, in turn, are a component of the role. Roles themselves are the most important authorization component. The authorizations and authorization profiles with the corresponding content are assigned to users via the role. After roles and the relevant authorization profiles have been assigned to a user, the user then has the permissions to create, display, or change data in SAP ERP. This ensures a controlled form of access to functions, activities, and data. When a user attempts to log on, the central system obtains the relevant authorizations from the user master record in the user storage location. The system then checks the data in this storage location to see whether the required permissions are sufficient. Normally, if the permissions are not sufficient, an error message is output and the selected function terminates.

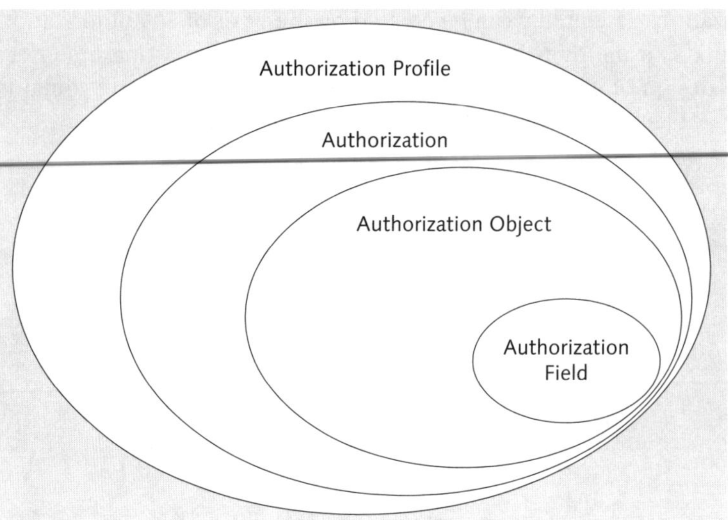


**Figure 20.5** Structure of an Authorization Profile

Figure 20.6 provides a schematic summary of the role concept.

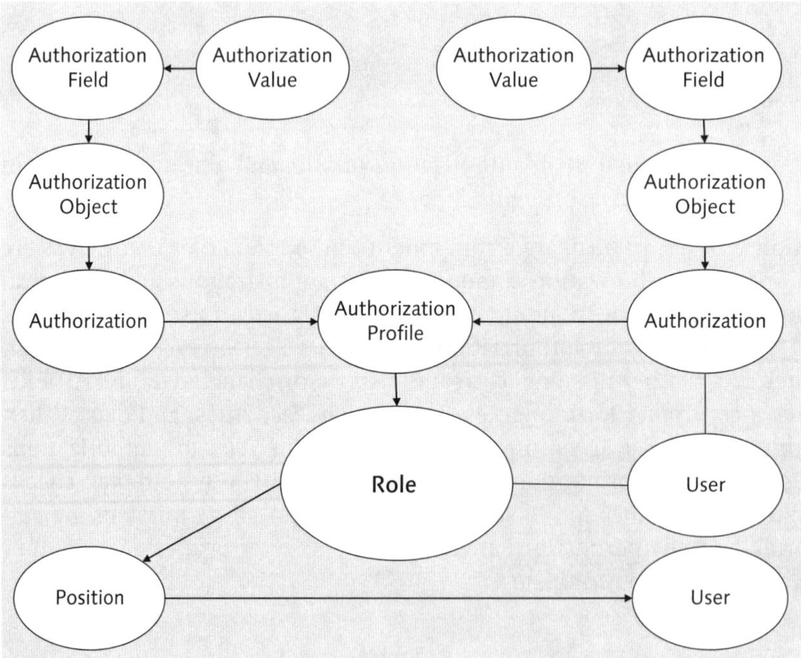


**Figure 20.6** Role Concept

### Role Categories

There are two technical role categories: single roles and composite roles. Single roles are schematically structured in accordance with the role concept described earlier. Composite roles, on the other hand, combine two or more roles to form a combined function role. Role categories can be used to create simple or complex authorization structures. Which role categories are selected as part of the authorization design process should depend on the individual implementation objectives, such as ease of administration, transparency, and security.

### Role types

In terms of content, roles can be grouped into role types (see Figure 20.7). Depending on requirements and various criteria, roles can be subdivided, for example, into roles for users, positions, tasks, individual transactions, or for authorization objects only.

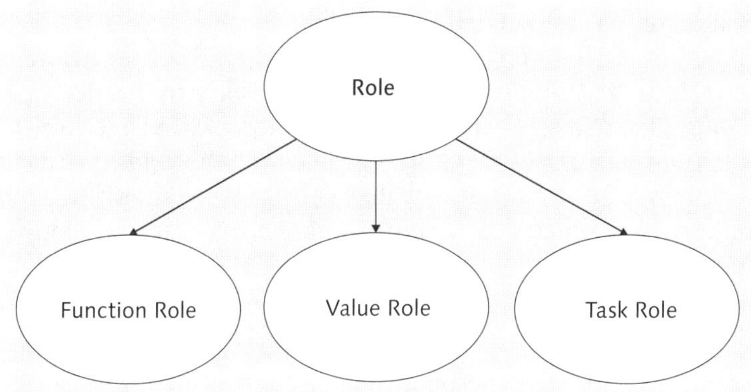


**Figure 20.7** Role Types

- For example, employees who work in the Accounting department most likely require access to Financials transactions for their work. They can then be authorized to access these transactions in a role that suits their function. This kind of role is a function role.
- However, these employees may also require access to transactions in other areas, such as CO. Task roles are used to add on these types of smaller, additional authorizations. The whole set of authorizations is then assigned to the employees by means of a combination of both role types in a composite role.
- Value roles are a special type of role that does not involve transaction assignments. Instead, they only contain specific authorization objects that serve as a

set of authorizations for a position or a user group in terms of the specific form they take and in conjunction with other roles. Value roles are primarily used for authorization concepts where function and value roles are clearly separated and mapped technically.

What role type(s) are selected depends on whether SAP standard solutions or other solutions are used to implement the authorizations. You should critically analyze the requirements in advance and carry out a cost/benefit analysis.

### SAP Profile Generator

SAP ERP contains the Profile Generator, a tool for the technical implementation of authorization components that is used to create, modify, and delete roles and to assign roles to users (Transaction PFCG). The SAP Profile Generator can also be used to group transactions into logical units and to assign authorizations to them. Transactions, reports, and other authorizable elements are selected using the menu or by directly entering the transaction code.

Assigning authorization objects to transactions is defined in tables such as US OBT/ USOBT_C and USOBX/USOBX_C. The Profile Generator collects together the relevant authorization objects, including authorization fields and preset authorization field values, and then, in the next step, creates the authorizations within the role. In doing so, the Profile Generator shows both preset values and the fields that need to be maintained. A traffic light icon indicates the status of the authorizations to be maintained. Authorization objects can also be set to inactive if they no longer need to be maintained.

### Check Indicators

Setting up and maintaining roles has become simpler and clearer thanks to the introduction of the check indicator concept. In the past, authorization objects had to be laboriously identified in the program code, for several years there have been tables that come with this information. Tables USOBT and USOBX in the SAP standard contain the transactions and the relevant authorization objects. Customer tables USOBT_C und USOBX_C are generated first so that every SAP client can individually maintain their transaction values and authorization values without changing the standard. Transaction SU24 is used to maintain these tables.

Check indicators ensure that authorization objects are flagged in accordance with their relevance to the authorization check. Various different check indicators are used to define whether or not an authorization check is used for a specific transaction. This takes place independent of the ABAP program code of the transaction.

The check indicators can deactivate these checks both on the transactional and on the global level.

- "Transactional" in this context means that check indicators can set an authorization object to "inactive" for a specific transaction. In other words, no check will then be carried out.
- "Global" in this context means that an authorization object is deactivated for all transactions in which it was previously checked. These locked authorization objects are then no longer displayed when roles are created.

Another use of check indicators is in relation to the SAP Profile Generator, as shown in Figure 20.8. Check indicators can be set to allow the authorization check to take place, and to display in the Profile Generator the authorization object in question so that the corresponding authorizations can be created there.

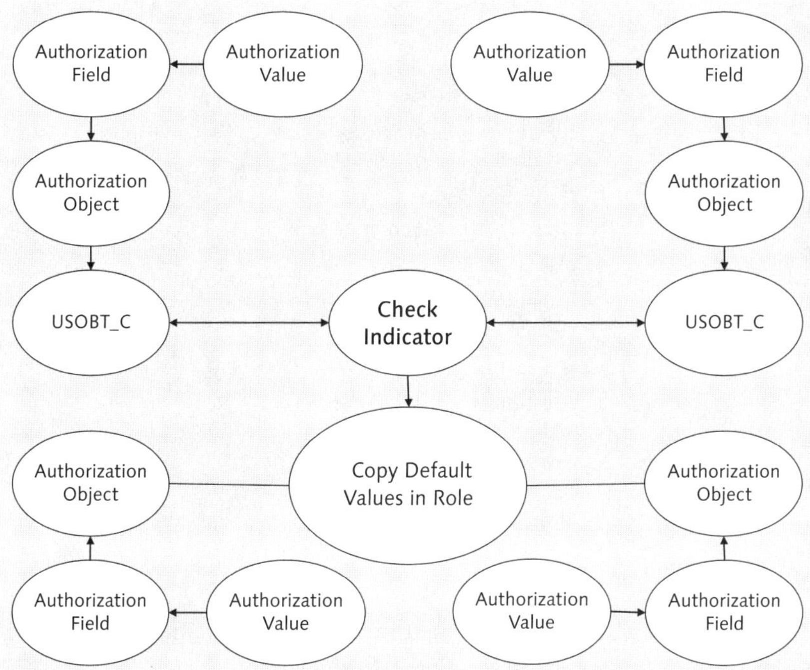


**Figure 20.8** Effect of Check Indicators on Transfer to Transaction PFCG

- Obligatory authorization checks specify that an authorization object must always be checked while the program is running. The authorization object likewise becomes an obligatory authorization object in this case. The check indicator is set to PP or Yes for a specific transaction, which results in the authorization object being proposed for processing in the Profile Generator when a role is created (for example, authorization objects for company code checks).

- Optional authorization checks specify that you can choose whether an authorization object is checked or not. The authorization object in this case becomes a dynamic authorization object. The check indicator is set to P or No for a specific transaction, with the result being that when a role is created, the authorization object is not automatically proposed for processing in the Profile Generator (for example, authorization objects for authorization groups).

Obligatory and optional authorization checks can also be globally defined using the check indicators. Table 20.6 shows the four types of check indicators and their effects on authorization checks.

| Check Indicator | Meaning | Explanation | Authorization objects displayed in Profile Generator? |
|---|---|---|---|
| PP or YES | Check and maintain | The authorization object in question is always checked. | Yes |
| P or NO | Check | The authorization object in question is checked in certain cases. | No |
| N or NO | Do not check | The authorization object in question is never checked. | No |
| U or NO | Unmaintained | The authorization object in question is not entered in tables USOBT (USOBT_C) and USOBX (USOBX_C). This indicator has no effect on the relevance of the check. | No |

**Table 20.6** Check Indicators

After the profile has been created and the authorizations maintained, the authorization profiles can be generated and the role activated.

### Menus

Role menus can also be created in the Profile Generator. Folder and menu structures can also be defined. This is done based on the order of the transactions, reports, and other functions that are to be authorized along with the role. Menus make navigating in and controlling transactions easier for the user. They can also be imported from other menus, such as the SAP menu or area menu, and from other roles or external files, and then processed further. The Menus tab in the SAP Profile Generator is intended for this purpose.

SAP ERP also allows you to create area menus using Transaction SE43. Area menus are used to simplify and standardize navigation aids for organizational and functional units, such as business departments. User groups that need authorization largely to the same functions can control their transactions using an area menu (for example, area menu for sales staff).

### Organizational and Functional Authorizations

Transactional segregation — also referred to as segregation of duties — is not sufficient to guarantee security. In the case of geographical differentiators that require different authorizations, organizational levels with organizational standard fields such as company code or plant can be centrally maintained for the whole role. The authorization values for these fields then no longer have to be individually maintained for every authorization object; instead, they are filled automatically.

The inheritance principle is used for identical roles that are intended to authorize different organizational units. To do this, the SAP Profile Generator allows derivation roles, which consist of a fixed part (transaction and authorization objects outside of the organizational levels) and a variable part (organization levels). Various authorization values can then be assigned to the fields on the organizational levels. All other fields in the function role, which functions as the source of the derivations, are stable. Changes to the function role are passed on via the derived roles. Individual changes to single roles need to be made individually using the SAP Profile Generator. The menu for the derived roles is likewise inherited (see Figure 20.9).

Another way of creating roles with organizational divisions is to use value roles. The value role concept assumes that a risk analysis has confirmed the necessity of organizational and functional divisions. The affected authorization objects are not maintained in the roles; instead, they are set to inactive. However, the authorization checks for these authorization objects still take place. Special authorization object roles, also known as value roles, are created for these authorization checks. These value roles can then be flexibly assigned to different function roles, depending on their own organizational assignment (see Figure 20.10).

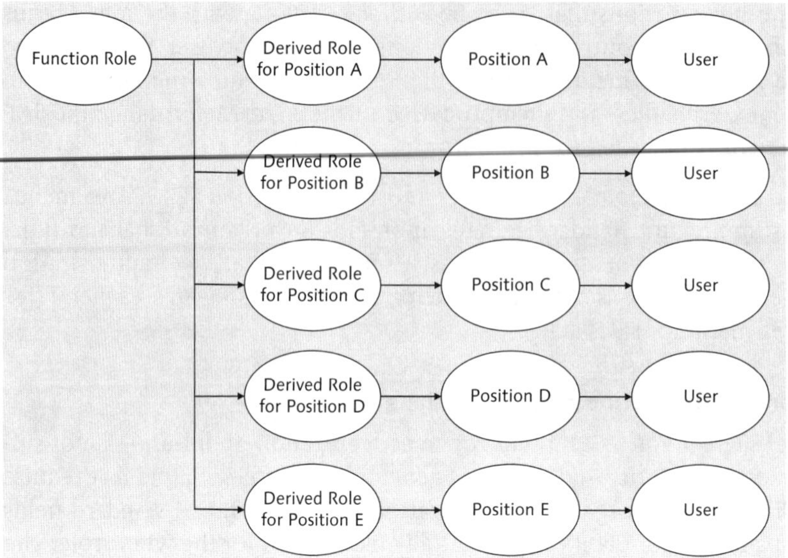


**Figure 20.9** Derived Roles

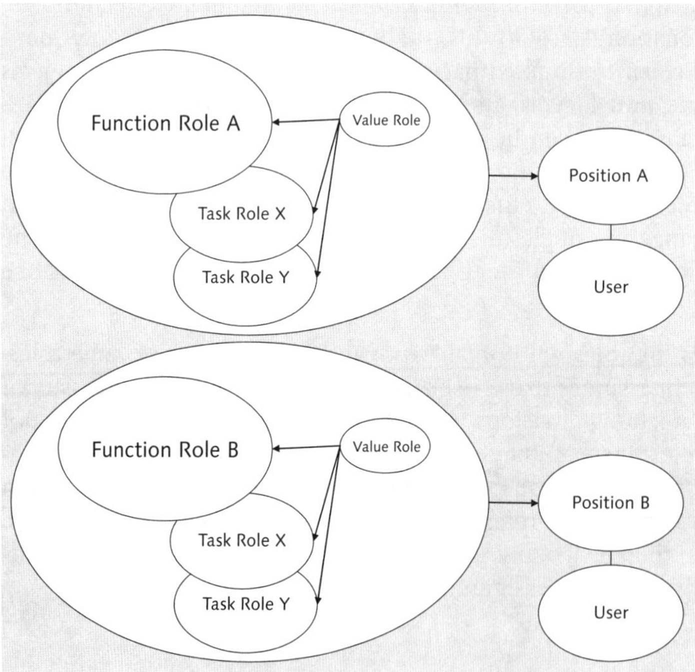


**Figure 20.10** Example of the Value Role Concept in Applications

The benefit of this solution is the flexibility and the transparency that its structure provides. The organizational data and other authorization data are no longer "hidden" in all of the roles; instead, it is always freely accessible in roles specifically intended for this purpose. Not all function and task roles have to be derived — you can also restrict them with a small number of value roles to specific organizational units or other authorization fields.

### Creating and Maintaining User Data

Before you can assign authorizations to users, you have to create user data in SAP ERP. You do this using Transaction SU01 for user master data, or in the CUA function using Transaction SCUG. The CUA allows you to administrate user data, both for SAP ERP systems and for non-SAP systems. Alternatively, you can also implement a complete identity management solution using an identity management system such as SAP NetWeaver IdM for managing all identity data as a whole.

All options can be used with centralized and decentralized user maintenance functions. Transaction SU10 is used for mass changes, that is, if you want to change data such as role assignments, parameters, fixed values, or logon data for a group of users. Users can also be created as reference users and can then function as a template for creating other users. Users can also have an alias. While the standard user ID is 12 characters long, alias can use up to 40 characters.

The CUA is used for maintaining user master data and for assigning roles. The following preparations are required: connect the SAP clients to the logical systems; enter the Application Link Enabling (ALE) distribution model with any partner agreements on the central system and subsystems; and define fields that have to be maintained either locally (client-specific), centrally (system-wide), or by the user. These settings are made in Transactions SCUA and SCUM. Maintaining user data in a consistent manner across multiple systems leads to consistency and transparency in the administrative process. Nonetheless, responsible persons in the business departments should still have a leadership role in assigning authorization data to users.

Either the SAP Profile Generator or Transaction SU01 for user master data is used to assign roles and authorization profiles; the SAP Profile Generator has a tab specifically for this purpose. The user comparison function is an important one here, as it allows all user master tables to be synchronized. You can start this comparison process either from the SAP Profile Generator, using Transaction PFUD, or you can set it to run automatically in a batch process using the program `PFCG_TIME_DEPENDENCY` (call program `RHAUTHUPDATE_NEW`).

The user administration is considerably easier if you use SAP NetWeaver IdM or similar solutions. All user types can be centrally entered and mapped for all systems. The management of the users' lifecycles can now be coupled with authorization mechanisms and implemented across the systems. In the future, this solution will gradually replace the use of the CUA.

The SAP Profile Generator provides a wide range of other functions for implementing and administrating roles in a logical manner. It enables you to copy or delete roles, to choose any profile name you like, and to carry out single or mass changes.

### 20.3.3 Other Authorization Concepts

There are many other ways, besides the role concept, of defining authorizations for specific functions and using them in combination with roles.

#### Authorization Group Concept

Authorization groups are used to indirectly assign SAP values to authorized users (see Figure 20.11). Value assignments are made by means of a group and are then checked as an authorization value. The element to be protected cannot be accessed directly through a special authorization field; instead, it is only accessed through the authorization group for the element. There are authorization groups for different fields; for example, to restrict table authorization groups, document types for Financials via Transaction OVA7, or apply in material master authorization groups.

#### Authorizations for Tables

Like all other data, authorization data is stored in tables in SAP ERP. It is particularly important to protect the content of tables. It is a generally valid rule that in most cases, users do not need direct access to table information. Tables are usually displayed and maintained using transactions and views. To do this, parameter transactions are created and assigned to users via roles. In exceptional cases, direct table maintenance can be used to perform special activities in tables. If you want to control tables directly, this can be done using a number of different transactions, including Transactions SE16 and SM31. The kind of protection that the table has depends on table authorization groups, which are checked by means of the authorization object S_TABU_DIS.

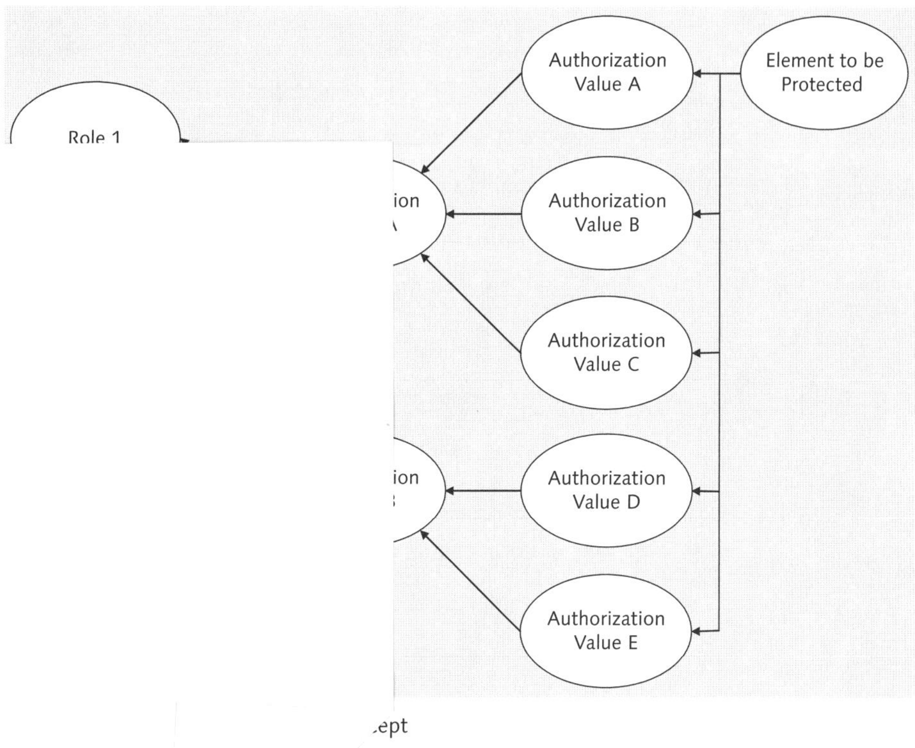


.ept

ɹrdance with the authorization group concept. Several .e authorization group when the system is shipped by SAP. ɩable is assigned to an authorization group; this applies espe- -specific tables. This should be set down in any programmers' .e authorization groups are maintained using Transaction SM31 and the table maintenance view `TDDAT` in table `TBRG`.

Table 20.7 gives an overview of some important tables in the authorization system.

| Technical Name of Table | Meaning of Table |
|---|---|
| `AGR_1016` | Name of role profile |
| `AGR_1250/AGR_1251` | Authorization data for role |
| `AGR_1252` | Organizational levels of authorizations |

**Table 20.7** Authorizations and User Data

| Technical Name of Table | Meaning of Table |
|---|---|
| AGR_PROF | Profile name for role |
| AGR_SELECT | Transaction code for role |
| AGR_TCDTXT | Transaction code for role with text |
| AGR_TCODES | Transaction code for user |
| CRMC_BLUEPRINT | Customer Relationship Management (CRM) Customizing |
| TACT | Standard values for activity codes |
| TACTT | Standard values for activity codes with text |
| TBRG | Authorization groups |
| TDDAT | Table authorization groups |
| TOBJ | Authorization objects |
| TOBJC | Authorization objects and object classes |
| TOBJT | Texts for authorization objects |
| TSTC | Transaction codes |
| TSTCA | Transaction code authorization values |
| TSTCP | Parameters for transactions |
| TSTCT | Transaction texts |
| AUTHA | Application authorization fields |
| AUTHB | Basic application authorization fields |
| USER012 | Authorization information for user maintenance |
| USH04 | History of authorization changes |
| USH10 | History of authorization profile changes |
| USH12 | History of authorization value changes |
| USKRI | Critical authorization combinations (transaction code) |

**Table 20.7** Authorizations and User Data (Cont.)

| Technical Name of Table | Meaning of Table |
|---|---|
| USOBT | Transaction code for the authorization object |
| USOBT_C | Transaction code — authorization object for customers |
| USOBT_CD | History of authorization field changes |
| USOBX | Check table for table USOBT |
| USOBX_C | Check table for table USOBT_C |
| USORG | Organizational level for the SAP Profile Generator |
| USOTT | Transaction code for authorization object |
| USPRO | Authorization profile |
| USR07 | Authorization object and authorization field values of last authorization check that encountered an error |
| USR08 | User menus |
| USR09 | Work areas of user menus |
| USR13 | Authorization short texts |

**Table 20.7** Authorizations and User Data (Cont.)

Authorization object S_TABU_CLI is used to control the maintenance of cross-client tables. Authorization object S_TABU_LIN allows row-based table authorizations.

### Field Group Concept

Some transactions contain specific information that requires protection because of certain risks. The fields in which this information is contained are also protected separately. To do this, the fields in question in the transaction are assigned to a field group. Users obtain access permission to the information in these fields by being assigned to the field group (see Figure 20.12).

The transaction with all other authorizations is assigned to positions or users by means of a role in accordance with the role concept. If users are not assigned to the field group, these users do not have access to the content of the fields that are protected separately. Various applications contain transactions for maintaining field groups, such as AO92, BC65, BUBN, BUCN, and CACS_CSB0103.

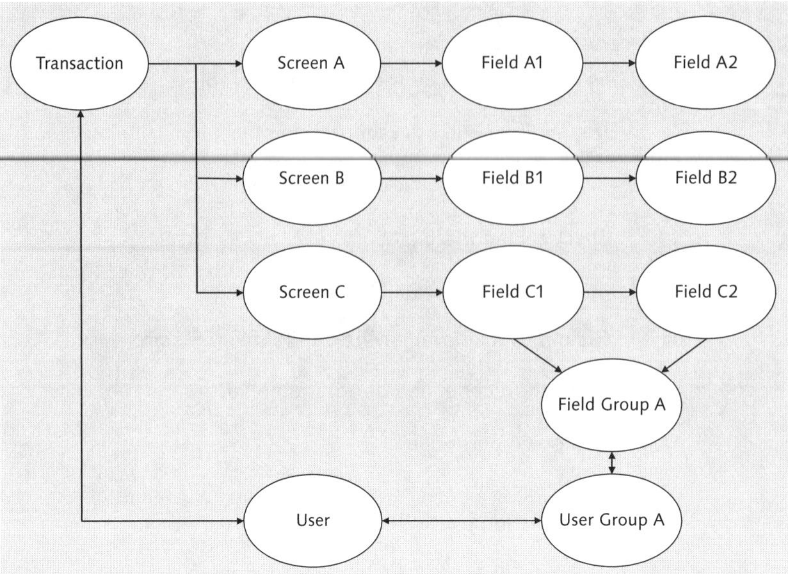


**Figure 20.12** Field Group Authorization Concept

### Authorizations for Reports

Reports and programs are among the most critical information elements, and thus require a high degree of protection. Reports can be controlled by means of transactions and authorization objects, and are therefore authorized in accordance with the role concept. Calls of reports and programs by means of standard transactions such as SA38 or SE38 should be banned, as the risk of errors or serious system complications is very high. In general, programs are not assigned to any authorization group. If the transactions mentioned previously were assigned, this would also mean that authorization to start all programs was assigned as well. You should not allow this kind of access under any circumstances.

Reports can be added to a transaction using either Transaction SE93 or the SAP Profile Generator. In the SAP Profile Generator, you can select reports and assign to them a transaction code that is generated by the SAP system. Because these generated transaction codes do not follow any general naming convention, you should decide in advance whether you want all report transactions to have their own naming convention. If you do want this, the convention will have to be included in the authorization management processes and their documentation.

### Authorizations for Batch Processing

Batch jobs are programs that run in the background of an application. Authorizations for background processing are defined in a batch job authorization concept (see Figure 20.13). The assignment of authorizations in this case is controlled by the background user, the name of the background job, and the activities.

In general, all background jobs have the following criteria:

- Job type (technical, functional, risk)
- Periodic use (daily, weekly, monthly)
- Sporadic use (yes or no)
- Short description of job
- Assignment to role, user, or position

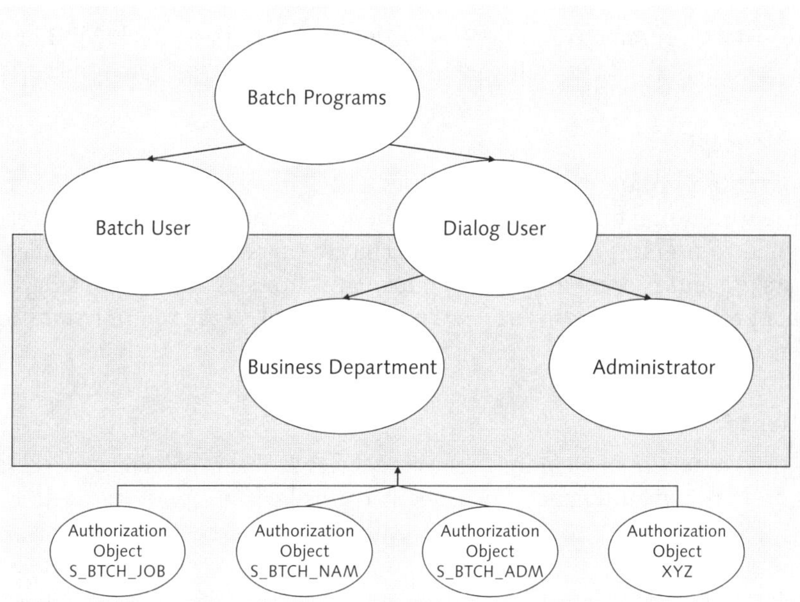


**Figure 20.13** Batch Job Authorizations and Related Authorization Objects

A batch job administrator is responsible for administrating batch jobs. No other user besides the administrator should have administrator permissions. Administrator permissions are controlled by the authorization object `S_BTCH_ADM`.

Batch jobs run under the authorization of either a dialog user or a system user (batch user). It is a common practice to use just one system user that has the

SAP_ALL standard profile as the batch user for all background jobs. This is not a good practice, however, as it contains many risks. There should be several system users for different job categories — for example, one user for all background jobs of logistics applications. The batch users then get exactly the authorizations and permissions that they need to run the relevant batch programs. The authorization object S_BTCH_JOB is used to define these permissions.

Spool requests that are created by background jobs of the logged-on user are handled in the same way as dialog spool requests. Spool requests that are created by background jobs of other users can only be viewed if the user who wants to view them is explicitly named in an authorization with the authorization object S_BTCH_NAM. However, note that in this case, this user can then view all spool requests of the other user. If spool requests are created by a batch user and another user wants to view these requests, the user name of the batch user also has to be explicitly specified.

The various batch programs are subject to further authorization checks, so these authorization objects also have to be defined and assigned for the batch roles.

#### User group concept

Transactional authorization in the form of roles and defined authorization objects is not sufficient for some functions and data. These elements also have to be separately assigned to users in tables that are specifically intended for each application. This assignment process uses user groups. This provides an additional layer of functional protection and also makes it possible to only assign permissions to certain users (see Figure 20.14).

#### Authorizations for Queries

Queries in this context refer to individual user queries to the SAP database. Access to queries and their maintenance functions is controlled by query transactions such as SQ01, SQ02, SQ03, and SQVI. Query authorizations are assigned by means of a combination of views, users, and user groups, and also by using the QuickViews function.

Queries and InfoSets should generally be created in the development system and tested in the test or quality assurance system, as they do involve some risks in terms of security, data protection, and performance. Specific user groups and positions for these queries can then be authorized in the production system. Every authorized user has to be assigned to a query user group; this guarantees that the users can only access queries in their work area.

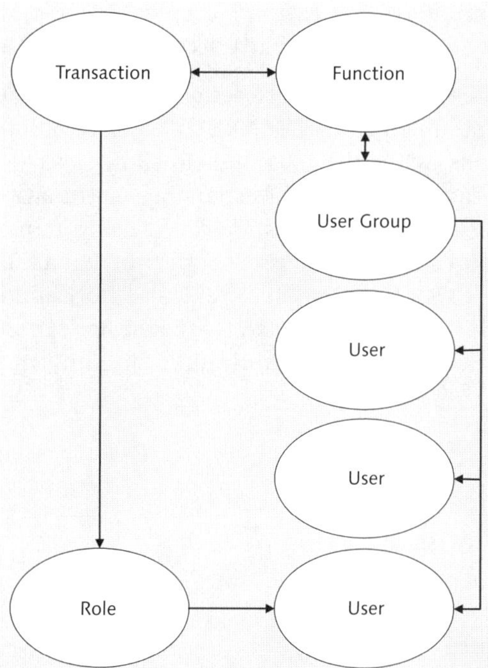


**Figure 20.14** User Groups Authorization Concept

There are special authorization objects for queries, such as S_QUERY, that make access to queries and activities for queries secure. The details of which InfoSets may be accessed have to be specified for each user group. InfoSets themselves are protected by authorization groups. Authorization for queries is then carried out by assigning queries to query user groups.

### Authorizations for Report Writer and Report Painter

The functions of the Report Writer and the Report Painter should only be available to a small number of users, as they can also perform user-specific analyses using specific data and collect this information in reports. The procedure is similar to that of query authorizations. Authorization restrictions are set for reports, the report group, the libraries, and layouts, by means of authorization groups.

### Spool and Printer Authorizations

Security for sensitive spool entries, such as spool entries in Financials, is set up using the Authorization Field in the properties of the relevant spool request. For all sensitive FI reports that are started in the dialog or in background mode, the corresponding value, such as ZFI for the AUTHORIZATION FIELD, for example, is maintained. This protects the spool requests from third-party access.

Spool authorizations (activities and value assignments) are assigned by means of the S_ADMI_FCD and S_SPO_ACT authorization objects. The SPOACTION authorization field is used to set the authorized actions, while the SPOAUTH field allows specific spool entries to be assigned that are protected by the corresponding AUTHORIZATION FIELD (see Figure 20.15). User-specific spool entries are called using Transaction SP02. Transaction SP01 for administration requires special protection. To display and maintain employee-specific spool requests for the ZFI authorization group — for example, for the Accounting department staff — the authorization values shown in Table 20.8 have to be added to the authorization for authorization object S_SPO_ACT.

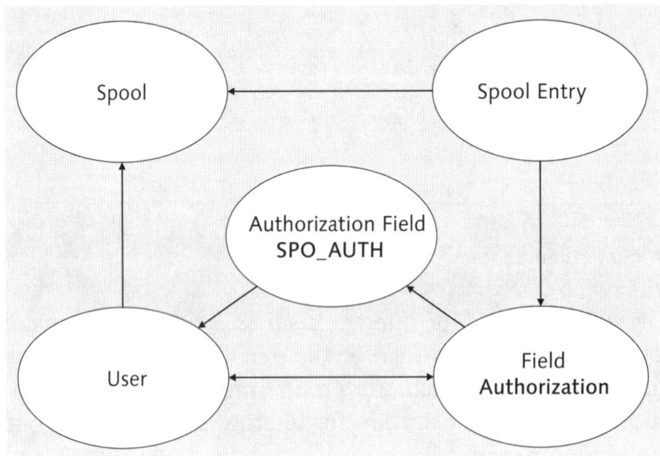


**Figure 20.15** Protecting Spool Requests Using Authorizations

| Spool Authorization Object | Spool Authorization Field | Authorization Value |
|---|---|---|
| S_SPO_ACT | SPOACTION | ATTR |
| S_SPO_ACT | SPOACTION | BASE |
| S_SPO_ACT | SPOACTION | DELE |
| S_SPO_ACT | SPOACTION | DISP |
| S_SPO_ACT | SPOACTION | PRNT |

**Table 20.8** Example of Authorizations of User-Specific Spool Entries

| Spool Authorization Object | Spool Authorization Field | Authorization Value |
|---|---|---|
| S_SPO_ACT | SPOACTION | REDI |
| S_SPO_ACT | SPOACTION | REPR |
| S_SPO_ACT | SPOAUTH | ZFI |

**Table 20.8** Example of Authorizations of User-Specific Spool Entries (Cont.)

For the Accounting department staff to see the spool requests of all other employees in their department, and the contents of these requests, all spool requests created in this department need to be protected by the ZFI authorization value in the Authorizations FIELD. Transaction SP01 has to be assigned for this activity. Then, define authorization object S_SPO_ACT and maintain authorization object S_ADMI_FCD (see Table 20.9).

| Spool Authorization Object | Spool Authorization Field | Authorization Value |
|---|---|---|
| S_ADMI_FCD | S_ADMI_FCD | SP01 |

**Table 20.9** Defining Authorization Object S_ADMI_FCD for Use with Transaction SP01

These settings allow users to view all spool requests that are protected with the ZFI authorization value and to view their own spool requests that were created without an authorization value. Spool requests that are created by background jobs of the logged-on user are handled in the same way as dialog spool requests. Spool requests that are created by background jobs of other users can only be viewed if the authorization is explicitly specified in the S_SPO_ACT authorization object.

Printer authorizations and other output authorizations are protected by the authorization object S_SPO_DEV. A printer concept with its own consistent naming convention will make the administration work a lot easier.

The list of other authorization concepts is a long one: view authorization concept, for example, for master data transactions; authorizations for Human Resources (HR) (SAP ERP HCM), transaction variant concept, transaction group concept, batch input concept, group authorization concept, field group authorization concept, and many others. These concepts provide support for a solid role concept and thus help to safeguard and optimize the security requirements of the enterprise.

### Monitoring and Control

Authorization management has to be controlled and monitored because of the risks involved, and because of how important this area is in terms of assigning and dividing up authorizations, and in restricting functions in SAP ERP and other SAP systems. The aim of controlling and monitoring this area is to reduce the risks associated with authorization management tasks. SAP provides a wide range of methods and solutions for these purposes.

Reports in the Audit Information System (AIS) can be used to analyze financial data for auditors, and for system audits and monitoring. Security information logs, the authorization information system, table logs, and other tools can all be used for controlling purposes for the check functions of the SAP systems. The AIS consists of several evaluation reports that provide information on the authorization system and system settings, and reports for business and balance sheet audits.

With regard to authorization system and system settings, the reports contain analyses for the following:

- System configuration with clients, parameter settings, tables, database and system logs, security audit log analyses, and status displays
- Authorization information, change documents, and access statistics for the Repository Information System
- User authentication information with logon procedures, password rules, and settings for SAP standard users such as `SAP*` and `DDIC`
- Authorization management for users with settings for the SAP Profile Generator, check indicators, system parameters, user overview, information on critical authorizations, and their distribution among users
- Change and transport system
- Batch job processing
- Data protection information
- Information on development and Customizing

These analyses are used for internal monitoring and control within the enterprise, but are also actively used for system checks by external auditors. Access to the AIS is assigned by means of SAP standard roles. The `SAP_AUDITOR` role is defined as a composite role and is made up of all of the individual roles of the AIS and the menu structure required to call reports.

There are two different kinds of standard roles in the AIS: transaction roles, which contain the role menu structure, and pure authorization roles, which contain the authorization objects and definitions. The authorization roles comprise the authorization objects necessary for executing the reports defined in the transaction role, plus definitions. In terms of results, the reports can be either displayed or loaded into the SAP system for further processing. However, this and other AIS functions can only be executed with other authorizations.

Comprehensive control and monitoring solutions are achieved by establishing the Governance, Risk, and Compliance (GRC) solutions in SAP BusinessObjects. Chapter 8, GRC Solutions in SAP BusinessObjects, describes the relevant solution concepts.

### 20.3.4 Best-Practice Solutions

The authorization design concept for SAP ERP must be completely incorporated into an overlying SAP security concept. The objective is to customize the functionality of the application to the requirements of the enterprise. This affects the authorizations, which grant access to functionalities, restrict user permissions, and prevent unauthorized activities.

The authorization system is one of the most important preventive controls in the SAP system. Its functions are intended to prevent potential risks from becoming reality, to minimize risks, and to ensure that the applications can be controlled. These functions reveal the clear necessity for a strategically sound definition of the authorization design concept, its effective technical implementation in the SAP ERP system, and an optimized administration procedure for authorizations and users.

It is therefore very important that the authorization system be incorporated into the internal control and monitoring system in the enterprise. Authorizations should not only be granted not only on the basis of functional and work-related requirements, but also regarded as a wide-reaching control option. The amount of time and attention that designing and implementing authorization structures receives depends on the type of enterprise, individual assessments of the security requirements and statutory regulations, and individual experience, and is in direct proportion to the amount of resources that are assigned to it. It is important in all cases that a requirements analysis is carried out in plenty of time, so that the appropriate controlling and monitoring objectives can be set and incorporated into the authorization design process accordingly.

User and authorization management should be as integrated, controlled, transparent, and effective as possible. When SAP standard tools (such as the SAP Profile Generator and CUA) are used, authorization management and user administration should be kept separate, for technical, organizational, and control reasons. If other integrated solutions are in use, this separation is not necessary, as different, more complex controls are implemented using the information ownership principle.

The amount of work involved in administration (and the associated control functions) can be very high. This leads to the necessity for requirements of authorization design and the administrative processes that keep this administration work at a predictable and manageable level — via clear authorization structures; standardized procedures; a clear definition of tasks and the distribution of responsibilities; a limited number of roles, if possible; and balanced training measures.

Authorization management comprises the creation of roles and all authorization components in use in the system, with the objective of ensuring that the processes in question run smoothly. This means that the responsible persons must be notified immediately of configuration changes, as these changes could affect the assignment of authorizations. Also, an application guide should be created that describes the administrative processes and the application areas of the relevant tools and methods, such as the SAP Profile Generator and authorization concepts. This guide should also describe technical Best Practices for using the tools.

User administration includes activities such as creating, modifying, and deleting users; changing passwords; locking; unlocking, and assigning roles and authorization profiles; and many more. The process that applies in the case of problems or changes should also be documented in a guide, and this guide should be made available to all of the responsible persons.

The overall authorization and user administration process is divided into four main categories:

- Application
- Release
- Implementation
- Information

The information is both a concurrent and a subsequent process to cases in the other three categories. In general, this process can be used to process the cases listed in Table 20.10.

| Category | Case |
|---|---|
| Application | New user requires SAP authorizations. |
| | User switches organizational unit. |
| | User leaves company. |
| | User needs more authorizations. |
| | User cannot log on. |
| | Transaction missing in assigned role. |
| | Transactions have to be removed. |

**Table 20.10** Cases in Authorization and User Administration

| Category | Case |
|---|---|
| | Authorization values are missing. |
| | New authorizations have to be distributed across multiple roles. |
| | Roles are missing. |
| | Authorizations outside of the role concept are missing. |
| Release | New user requires SAP authorizations. |
| | User switches organizational unit. |
| | User leaves company. |
| | User needs advanced authorizations. |
| | User cannot log on. |
| | Transaction missing in assigned role. |
| | Transactions have to be removed. |
| | Authorization values are missing. |
| | New authorizations have to be distributed across multiple roles. |
| | Roles are missing. |
| | Authorizations outside of the role concept are missing. |
| Implementation | New user requires SAP authorizations. |
| | User switches organizational unit. |
| | User leaves company. |
| | User needs advanced authorizations. |
| | User cannot log on. |
| | Transaction missing in assigned role. |
| | Transactions have to be removed. |
| | Authorization values are missing. |
| | New authorizations have to be distributed across multiple roles. |
| | Roles are missing. |
| | Authorizations outside of the role concept are missing. |

**Table 20.10** Cases in Authorization and User Administration (Cont.)

The better integrated the business departments are into the design and authorization management processes, the more successful the implementation of the authorizations and the security of the application processes will be. The following factors are of central importance for a successful authorization system that is defined in the authorization strategy:

- **Functionality**
  Users have to be guaranteed that they will receive the authorizations necessary to complete their work. The minimal principle should be used here.
- **Risk**
  In addition to being taken into account in the authorization design process, risk and control analyses should rank along with functional aspects as a central basis for defining and implementing authorizations. This approach ensures that potential risks are identified, and authorizations can then be used to neutralize, restrict, and control these risks. This also creates the possibility of creating a highly effective authorization system, as minor authorization checks do not have to be included and can thus be deactivated. One of the most important control options in this context is segregation of duties, which can be mapped and enforced by the authorization system.
- **Strategy**
  Make sure that a unified concept is developed. Components and requirements such as risk management, change management, ease of implementation, ease of administration, transparency, ease of control, completeness, ease of auditing, costs, and vision are all part of the strategy. You also have to specify the members of the authorization team, and define how the team is incorporated into the overall strategy and an overlying SAP risk management and IT security team. It is particularly important in this context that you integrate IT staff and staff in the individual business departments in a way that ensures the most efficient form of cooperation possible during the design and implementation phases, and that the business departments take responsibility for authorization management, the applications, and the continuity of the solution. The information ownership principle is a central factor in the long-term success of the investments in this context.
- **Solution**
  The solution(s) should be authoritative and integrated, and have a high degree of automation, so that the implementation team is free to concentrate on quality control and detailed aspects of creating the authorization concept. Because risk potential in general is growing and statutory requirements are increasing all of the time, conventional authorization systems are no longer sufficient. This is why solutions that combine integrated controls with risk management, authorization management, user administration, and compliance management are becoming more widespread.

**Example**

Besides the SAP solutions in GRC, various providers offer a combination of risk and control management, authorization and role management, user administration, change and task management, and integrated workflows (see Figure 20.16). By integrating all of the essential components of a comprehensive authorization and user administration solution, and by allowing for the inclusion of the business areas in a logical way, this solution enables a new standard of quality to be reached, both in the area of technical administration and in the analysis and control of process and application risks.

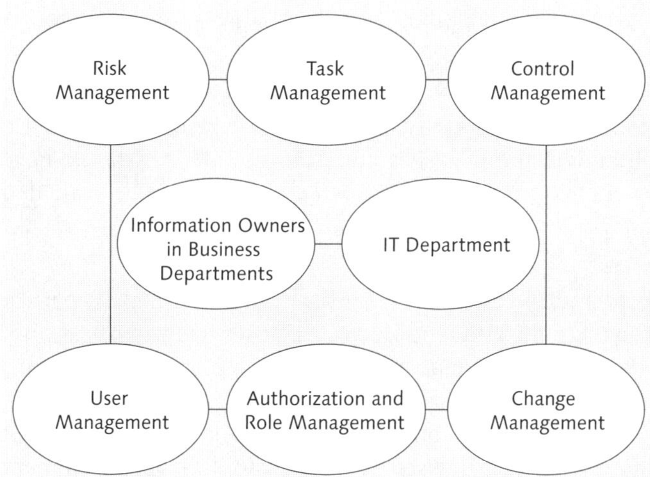


**Figure 20.16** Holistic, Comprehensive, and Effective Risk and Authorization Management

- **Technical implementation**
  Before the technical implementation, you should evaluate the options in the SAP standard tools for identifying risks, creating roles and authorizations, and carrying out the necessary administration and control tasks, and combine them with solutions from other providers, if required.
- **Concepts**
  In the case of role concepts, make sure that the roles follow a clear logical system. Selecting the correct types of roles is just as important for the success of the concept as the role types themselves and their content-related aspects. In most cases, it makes sense to select a combination of role types. Make sure to define in advance the purpose for which a specific role type is intended. It is advisable to use more authorization concepts, if this is required.

- **Transparency**
  It is essential that the authorization concept and the associated processes are simple, easy to understand, and easy to follow for both users and administrators, business departments, and auditors. The responsible persons in the business departments, process owners, data owners, and role owners must clearly understand their role in the internal control process chain and where they fit into the overall process to make effective decisions. Therefore, transparency of the processes and activities is essential for the success of the established internal control systems.
- **User administration**
  User administration is a confidential and highly responsible activity, and should therefore be handled with extreme care. Because it deals with protecting confidential information, authorizations should also be included in the protection area. The processes of creating and modifying user master records and distributing authorizations should be automated as much as possible and should have the highest possible level of control. Solutions such as CUA should be evaluated and used, if required.
- **Naming conventions**
  Assigning a naming convention for every authorization component is part of the design process. Using naming conventions just for user IDs and roles is not enough. Every authorization component, such as table authorization groups, user groups, and material master data authorization groups, should be set in advance in accordance with a naming convention. Make sure when doing this that the names are unique and that they start with a customer-specific element such as Y whenever possible.

Table 20.11 shows some transaction codes that are relevant to authorization and user administration. There are more than 1,000 transactions that can be relevant to good authorization management. The following table provides a selection of these.

| Transaction Code | Transaction |
|---|---|
| AL08 | Display Logged-On Users (All Instances) |
| AUTH_DISPLAY_OBJECTS | Switch Global Authorization Object Check On and Off |
| AUTH_SWITCH_OBJECTS | Display Global Authorization Object Check |
| BALE | Administration Area Menu |
| BALM | ALE Master Data |

**Table 20.11** Selected Transactions for Authorization Management

| Transaction Code | Transaction |
|---|---|
| OOAC | HCM Main Authorization Switch |
| PFCG | SAP Profile Generator |
| ROLE_CMP | Role Comparison for Menus |
| RTTREE_MIGRATION | Report Tree Migration |
| RZ10 | Maintain System Profile Parameters |
| RZ11 | Display System Profile Parameters |
| SALE | ALE Customizing |
| SCC4 | Maintain System Change Option |
| SCUA | CUA Administration (ALE Landscapes) |
| SCUG | CUA Administration (User Maintenance) |
| SCUL | CUA Administration (Distribution Logs) |
| SCUM | CUA Administration (Fields) |
| SE01 | Maintain Special Transport Requests |
| SE03 | Utility Programs for Transport and Correction System |
| SE06 | Set Up Workbench Organizer |
| SE09 | Workbench Organizer |
| SE10 | Customizing Organizer |
| SE11 | Maintain ABAP Dictionary |
| SE16 | Table Display |
| SE43 | Maintain Area Menus |
| SE93 | Transaction Administration |
| SECR | Audit Information System |
| SICF | Protection for Service Level Accesses |
| SLG1 | Application Protocol for Authorization Objects |
| SM01 | Lock and Unlock Transactions |
| SM04 | Display Logged-On Users (Per Instance) |
| SM12 | Delete Locks |
| SM19 | Configure Security Audit |
| SM20 | Analyze Security Audit Log |

**Table 20.11** Selected Transactions for Authorization Management (Cont.)

| Transaction Code | Transaction |
|---|---|
| SM21 | Online Analysis of System Log |
| SM31 | Table Maintenance |
| SM59 | Display and Maintain RFC Destinations |
| SM69 | Define and Maintain Logical Commands |
| SMT1 | Maintain Trusted Relationships between SAP Systems (Target System) |
| SMT2 | Test Trusted Systems (Source System) |
| SO70 | Display Customizing |
| SP01 | Spool Administration |
| SPAD | Set Up Printer |
| SPOR | Implementation Guideline (IMG) |
| SQ01 | Query: Administration of Query User Groups and Functional Areas |
| SQ02 | Query: Administration of InfoSets |
| SQ03 | Query: Start Queries |
| SSO2 | SSO Administration |
| SSO2_ADMIN | Report SS02 Generation |
| ST01 | System and Authorization Trace Functions |
| STAT | Statistical Analysis of User Actions |
| STMS | Administration of Transport System |
| STRUST | Trust Manager |
| STRUSTSSO2 | Trust Manager for SSO |
| SU01 | Maintain Users |
| SU02 | Maintain Authorization Profiles |
| SU03 | Maintain Authorizations |
| SU3 | User Parameters |
| SU10 | Mass Changes to User Master Data |
| SU20 | Maintain Authorization Fields |
| SU21 | Maintain Authorization Objects |
| SU24 | Maintain Check Indicators |

**Table 20.11** Selected Transactions for Authorization Management (Cont.)

| Transaction Code | Transaction |
|---|---|
| SU25 | Upgrade and Migration: Authorizations |
| SU53 | User Information for Authorization Checks |
| SU56 | Display Authorization Checks (if an Error Occurs) |
| SUIM | Authorization Information System |
| SUPO | Maintain Organizational Levels |
| TU02 | Profile Parameters |
| VUSREXTID | User Link (SAP — external) |

**Table 20.11** Selected Transactions for Authorization Management (Cont.)

## 20.4 Technical Security

Solutions for the technical IT security of SAP ERP components have already been described in Chapter 9, SAP NetWeaver AS. Because all applications run on SAP NetWeaver AS, the IT security controls of this platform apply.

*This chapter describes Information Technology (IT) security concepts for SAP Enterprise Resource Management (ERP) HCM taking into account legal data protection requirements. It describes general authorization concepts and solutions for best-practice control methods in applications of SAP Human Capital Management.*

# 21 SAP ERP Human Capital Management and Data Protection

Application security in human resources (HR) is particularly important because personal data protection is required by law. This means that companies are not only morally, but also legally obligated to secure data that is related to persons and employees and stored in SAP systems, and to protect this data from unwanted external access. This chapter first discusses the basic legal requirements of data protection, and then details the specifics of the SAP solution for HR management, SAP ERP HCM.

## 21.1 Introduction and Functions

Data protection is specifically controlled by individual countries through a multitude of laws. For the member states of the European Union, a holistic data protection level exists that is based on the EU data protection guideline (see Official Journal of the European Union No. L 281). The respective member states transfer this EU guideline to applicable national laws. In Germany, for example, the Federal Data Protection Act (BDSG; Bundesdatenschutzgesetz) is applicable, which is used as an example for the following description.

The task of data protection is to protect the identity and the privacy of individuals. This means that the appropriate technical and organizational measures must be taken to protect personal data against misuse and loss.

### 21.1.1 Data Protection in Human Resources

Human Resources is a critical company area in the data protection environment. Regardless of the business sector in which the company operates, employee personal data is processed here. SAP ERP HCM enables you to support many different functional areas (payroll, time management, Human Resources information system, personnel development, organizational structure, and so on). They must be clearly defined and documented in the procedures register (Section 4g Paragraph 2, Section 18 Paragraph 2, BDSG).

In addition to maintaining procedures registers, companies must meet the following requirements from the BDSG:

- Ensuring that the collection, processing, use, and transfer of personal data is permitted
- Training of users (Section 4g Paragraph 1 Sentence 2, BDSG) and duty to maintain confidentiality (Section 5, BDSG)
- Safeguarding the rights of the data subjects for notification (Section 33, Section 19a, BDSG), access to personal data (Section 34, Section 19, BDSG), and rectification, erasure, and blocking of personal data (Section 35, Section 20, BDSG)
- Internal self-control carried out by the data protection official who monitors the proper use of SAP ERP HCM according to Section 4g Paragraph 1 Sentence 1, BDSG; this particularly includes controlling the technical and organizational measures described in the following section.

### 21.1.2 Technical and Organizational Measures

Section 9 of the BDSG and its Annex define that the organization of the company must meet specific data protection and data security criteria. The following describes eight requirements that can be derived from these criteria:

- **Access control**
  Appropriate access control is supposed to prevent unauthorized persons from gaining access to data processing systems. This not only includes data centers but also locations where personal data is processed or stored using information technology. Appropriate access control can be implemented by doing the following:
  - Issuing plant IDs
  - Using ID scanners
  - Implementing visitor regulations
  - Installing video cameras for monitoring plant areas
  - Installing turnstiles
  - Defining security areas

- **Access control**
  Access control and secure authentication measures prevent data processing systems from being used by unauthorized persons. This includes:
  - Protecting company networks using firewalls
  - Providing computers with boot and hard disk passwords
  - Locking computers when leaving work centers
  - Defining and implementing password rules
  - Granting access to SAP ERP HCM and other applications only via user ID and password
- **Access control**
  Access control ensures that users are only assigned the authorization scope that they need for their job. This can be implemented by doing the following, for example:
  - Defining and using the authorization roles that are tailored to the tasks of the respective user
  - Logging activities (table changes, reporting, recording certain activities)
- **Disclosure control**
  When transferring data electronically or using other means of transport, it must be ensured that the data cannot be read, copied, altered, or removed without authorization. Authorized transport must be secured and verifiable. To do this, you can use one of the following methods:
  - Data encryption
  - Logging
- **Input control**
  It must be possible to check and determine by whom data has been entered, altered, and removed. This can be ensured with the following:
  - Appropriate and transparent authorization concepts
  - Access with a unique user identification (no SAP collective users or anonymous users, such as guest users)
  - Logging
  - Double entry, release and control (four-eyes principle)
- **Job control**
  If service providers process data on behalf of others, for example, if payroll processes or hosting processes for the SAP system are outsourced, certain rules must be considered. It must be ensured that the processor only processes personal data according to the instructions of the controller. Commissioned pro-

cessing of data requires contractual stipulations. Section 11, BDSG, defines the minimum requirements for regulation.

- **Availability control**
  It must be ensured that data is protected against accidental destruction or loss. This requires the following:
  - Regular backup copies and outsourced backup archives in separate fire areas (fire protection)
  - Emergency concept for disaster recovery
  - Virus protection
- **Data separation control**
  It must be ensured that data collected for different purposes can be processed separately. This can be ensured with the following:
  - Physical separation of SAP ERP HCM and other SAP systems
  - Logical separation at the client level
  - User roles with the corresponding segregation of duties and gradual authorizations

Prior to implementation (prior to checking according to Section 4d Paragraph 5, BDSG) and at regular intervals afterwards, the data protection official should audit the SAP ERP HCM system. To ensure continuity of these checks, you should use a reusable checklist. You can obtain this checklist from various providers or define it yourself based on the data protection guide of the German-Speaking SAP User Group (Deutschsprachige SAP-Anwendergruppe, DSAG).

## 21.2 Risks and Controls

The following risks exist for HR data and HR systems:

- Unauthorized access to personal data
- Unauthorized execution of master data reports
- Unauthorized downloading of personal data that should be particularly protected
- Unauthorized use of standard SAP tools like Transaction SM30 or SA38 to access HR data
- Unauthorized direct access to personal data with database tables
- Unauthorized use of ad hoc queries to obtain information on employees and other HCM-related information

Appropriate control solutions must ensure, for instance, that only authorized users can delete an employee in the system. In particular, the individual transactions and activities available to perform such tasks must be protected — Transaction PU00 in this example. In other scenarios, the control measures involve a multitude of transactions: For example, only authorized users should have permission to change the wage and salary details for an employee (Transactions PU03 and PA30, Infotype 0003). A detailed risk analysis should therefore provide information on general and detailed risks.

Due to the legal requirements regarding data protection and the required control of personal information, the protection needs in the HR area are especially high. For this reason, SAP ERP HCM contains some advanced authorization solutions in addition to the role concept and all of the authorization concepts described in Chapter 20, Authorizations in SAP ERP. As a rule, authorizations are also defined on the basis of transactions, roles, authorization objects, authorizations, and the other authorization components described earlier in this book. Choosing the right security solution in this context depends on the risk level, the organization, and the internal requirements of a company. In many cases, the role concepts are sufficient to ensure proper protection of personal data.

Table 21.1 provides an overview of the risks related to SAP ERP HCM.

| No. | Classification | Description |
|---|---|---|
| 1. | Potential risk | Inadequate authorization concept:<br>Users of the various SAP ERP applications have authorizations that are too extensive for their actual requirements in terms of information and functions. This also affects employee details, which are to be particularly protected due to their confidential nature (for example, date of birth, income, or qualifications). Because SAP ERP HCM doesn't consist of separate systems, the authorization concept is the most important means available to separate HCM authorizations from other functional authorizations. |
| | Impact | Users have greater authorizations than are necessary for their position and the scope of their work. This includes read and write access to confidential information and data. This situation violates legal requirements such as data protection laws, internal requirements, and the personal rights of employees. Violations of the law on the protection of personal data are evident. The risk of penalization by legal authorities exists. Other risks that result from the knowledge of confidential personal data depend on the type and circumstances of the breach of trust. |

**Table 21.1** Risks and Controls for SAP ERP HCM

| No. | Classification | Description |
|---|---|---|
| | Risk without control(s) | Extremely high |
| | Control | The authorization concept must acknowledge the specific role of HCM-relevant data. The design and implementation of the authorization concept must account for the acknowledgement and application of legal requirements (which data should be protected?), and it must be ensured that the authorizations and administration processes grant access to sensitive personal data only to those employees who have the necessary permission. |
| | Risk with control(s) | Low |
| | Section | 21.3 |
| 2. | Potential risk | Inadequate responsibility structure:<br>The IT department cannot cope in an orderly and organized fashion with the workload of managing users and authorizations. The complexity increases along with the functional workload on the SAP ERP applications; this also affects the applications in SAP ERP HCM. This means that the individual departments must be coordinated; the authorization management is handled by the IT department. Also, the authorization components are not sufficiently transparent. This results in authorizations that do not accurately reflect the actual requirements of the enterprise. This is particularly critical for personal data as the IT administrators are usually not familiar with legal requirements. |
| | Impact | Personal data is not protected or is insufficiently protected. This is a violation of legal requirements, internal company requirements, and the personal rights of the employees. |
| | Risk without control(s) | Extremely high |
| | Control | Introduction and consistent penetration of the principle of information ownership for an efficient control of authorizations and users in SAP ERP HCM, thereby integrating the HCM personnel and the data protection officer. |
| | Risk with control(s) | Low |

**Table 21.1** Risks and Controls for SAP ERP HCM (Cont.)

| No. | Classification | Description |
|---|---|---|
| | Section | 21.3 |
| 3. | Potential risk | Authorization concept is not fully defined:<br>The authorization concepts for SAP ERP HCM have not been defined together and in synch with other SAP applications, but have been set up as individual solutions. Users have different authorizations for HCM data in different systems. This results in either too many or too few authorizations are assigned, which compromises the continuity of the process and the effectiveness of authorization management. Moreover, actual data from the production system can be transferred to the QA or other systems.<br>Information to be protected that has been transferred to a printer outside of the "protection zone" can be accessed by anyone. There is no integration with other authorization concepts like the spool and printer concept. |
| | Impact | Authorization errors and inconsistencies compromise operational processes. Data with a high need for protection can sometimes be accessed by everyone. The effects extend from creating a bad company atmosphere to identity theft, which is a serious violation of legal requirements and a reflection of the company's failure to meet its responsibilities. |
| | Risk without control(s) | High |
| | Control | The authorization concepts of the individual applications and systems should usually be part of an overlying comprehensive authorization concept. Authorizations in SAP ERP should be defined along with the authorizations of SAP ERP HCM. The common concept serves as the basis for the design, implementation, and administrative follow-up processes. |
| | Risk with control(s) | Low |
| | Section | 21.3 |
| 4. | Potential risk | Identity management and change management:<br>There is no central user master data system. The master data storage system therefore contains redundancies and inconsistencies. The administrative processes do not permit you to make quick organizational changes to employee data or to modify or lock the corresponding authorizations. |

**Table 21.1** Risks and Controls for SAP ERP HCM (Cont.)

| No. | Classification | Description |
|---|---|---|
| | | There is no integration of the HCM organizational structure into the process of assigning authorizations. The users in SAP ERP HCM and all other SAP systems are affected by this. |
| | Impact | The transparency of user master data is not guaranteed, and modifications are either not implemented or are implemented only after a delay.<br>Employees who have left the company can thus continue to use their authorizations and access table data and transactional process data in the applications while remaining undetected. When an employee changes to a different department or user group, any new authorizations are simply added to their existing ones, which means that their authorizations mount up, along with those that arise as a result of combinations of authorizations. Unwanted authorizations, faulty transactions, unauthorized starting of reports, and serious system errors can all result from excessive authorizations. These risks, in turn, can lead to ineffective administration, a lack of transparency, low levels of control, violations of data protection laws, low levels of security, and potential criminal activity. |
| | Risk without control(s) | Extremely high |
| | Control | Introduce proper user master data administration by including a central administration system (such as SAP NetWeaver Identity Management (IdM), Lightweight Directory Access Protocol (LDAP), Central User Administration (CUA)), and set up a comprehensive and holistic identity management system that takes into account all administrative situations that arise in user management and organizational structure in SAP ERP HCM. |
| | Risk with control(s) | Low |
| | Section | 21.3 |

**Table 21.1** Risks and Controls for SAP ERP HCM (Cont.)

The general risks listed in Table 21.1 must be supplemented by detailed analyses for SAP ERP HCM to enable a more profound view for specific cases (see Table 21.2). The controls are implemented using transactions or by maintaining and assigning infotypes with regard to authorizations.

| Control Objective | Transaction Code | Infotypes |
|---|---|---|
| The organization plan must be securely maintained and controlled to avoid violations of the functionality of the organizational structure. | ▸ PPOME<br>▸ PPOM_OLD<br>▸ PPOC_OLD<br>▸ PPME<br>▸ PO13<br>▸ PO10<br>▸ PO03 | – |
| An applicant can only be hired if all necessary application documentation and information is available and meets the standard requirements. | ▸ PB30<br>▸ PB40 | 4000 |
| Segregations of duties must be defined between employees who are responsible for recording applicant information, those who hire new employees, and those who initiate wage payments. | ▸ PB30<br>▸ PB40<br>▸ PC00_M99_CALC | ▸ 4000<br>▸ 0001<br>▸ 0002<br>▸ 0008 |
| Only authorized users are allowed to delete an employee's master record. | PA41 | – |
| Only authorized users are allowed to delete employee data. | PU00 | – |
| Only authorized users can change the infotype for status information on wage and salary lists. | ▸ PU03<br>▸ PA30 | 0003 |
| Authorized HR staff and the relevant employees themselves are the only persons who can change the bank data of an employee. | PA30 | 0009 |
| The work plans of employees are kept up to date to ensure they are correct when an employee terminates work. | ▸ PA61<br>▸ PA63 | 0007 |
| Only those employee absences that have been agreed upon and approved are permitted and authorized according to the employee regulations. | PA30 | 2001 |
| The authorization of changes to absence data must be controlled correspondingly. | PA30 | 2013 |

**Table 21.2** Sample Risks for SAP ERP HCM

| Control Objective | Transaction Code | Infotypes |
|---|---|---|
| Authorized HR staff are the only persons who can change bonus payments for employees. | ▶ PA20<br>▶ PA30<br>▶ P16B_ADMIN | ▶ 0002<br>▶ 0006<br>▶ 0008<br>▶ 0009<br>▶ 0011<br>▶ 0014<br>▶ 0015<br>▶ 0149<br>▶ 0150<br>▶ 0151<br>▶ 2010 |
| The employees should be authorized to perform only a selected range of changes to their additional benefits. | ▶ P16B_ADMIN<br>▶ PC00_M99_CALC_SIMU | ▶ 0008<br>▶ 0014<br>▶ 0015<br>▶ 2010 |
| Employees can only view their own wage and salary data. | PC00_M16_CEDT | – |
| The uncontrolled deletion of salary data results for an employee can lead to a change of salary data clusters and a loss of the entire set of salary data. | PU01 | – |
| Only authorized personnel are allowed to view and maintain salary data. | PA30 | ▶ 0008<br>▶ 0014<br>▶ 0015<br>▶ 2010 |
| Salary and wage types must be verified by a second set of eyes prior to being actively used. | PA30 | ▶ 0008<br>▶ 0009<br>▶ 0014<br>▶ 0015<br>▶ 2010 |
| Salary increases have been correctly authorized and controlled in accordance with internal requirements. | ▶ PA30<br>▶ C138 | – |

**Table 21.2** Sample Risks for SAP ERP HCM (Cont.)

| Control Objective | Transaction Code | Infotypes |
|---|---|---|
| Segregations of duties exist between users who maintain master data and those who trigger and start payment runs. | ▸ PC00_M99_PA03_RELEA<br>▸ PC00_M99_PA03_END<br>▸ PC00_M99_PA03_CORR<br>▸ PC00_M99_PA03_CHECK/PA03 | – |
| Only authorized employees are allowed to trigger external payments. | PC00_M99_CIPE | – |
| Employees must not be allowed to approve their own travel requests. | ▸ TRIP<br>▸ TP04<br>▸ TP03<br>▸ TP02<br>▸ TP01 | – |
| Travel expenses can only be approved by authorized persons. | PR05 | – |
| Necessary control measures must be installed to ensure that only authorized employees can access and create bonus data. | PW01 | – |
| The organization plan must be securely maintained and controlled to avoid violations of the functionality of the organizational structure. | ▸ PPOME<br>▸ PPOM_OLD<br>▸ PPOC_OLD<br>▸ PPME<br>▸ PO13<br>▸ PO10<br>▸ PO03 | – |

**Table 21.2** Sample Risks for SAP ERP HCM (Cont.)

## 21.3 Application Security

The ABAP part of SAP ERP HCM consists of a relatively small number of transactions that are protected by a small number of authorization objects. However, the transactions and authorization objects contain many functions and can therefore be used for many different aspects of authorization checks and authorization assignments.

In addition to assigning typical HCM transactions via the general authorization components in SAP ERP HCM (authorization roles, authorization objects like P_TCODE for transaction code checks, or P_PCLX for cluster IDs), specific authorization concepts are also needed to meet data security requirements, particularly for the use of personal data. Additional authorization checks are centrally enabled or disabled by means of a main authorization switch. Along with the authorizations, infotypes determine the level of security in SAP ERP HCM. Infotypes are logical groups of data fields.

The main authorization switch can be used to configure the use of individual authorization objects, the use of inspection procedures, the tolerance period of authorization checks, and the use of structural authorizations in SAP ERP HCM. The main authorization switch can be activated in Customizing using Transaction OOAC. Thus, the transaction itself is also a component of authorization management and must be protected accordingly.

The following inspections can be enabled or disabled using the main authorization switch:

- Tolerance period of the authorization check
- Inspection procedure
- Customized authorization checks
- Master data inspections
- Extended master data inspections
- Structural authorization checks
- Personnel number checks

The main authorization switch (Table T77SO) enables specific inspections in SAP ERP HCM, and it automatically corrects and updates the entries in the USOBT, USOBT_C, USOBX, and USOBX_C authorization tables (see Figure 21.1). SAP ERP HCM supports both types of standard authorization checks: extended and customized.

### 21.3.1 HR Master Data Authorizations

Because the information in SAP ERP HCM usually consists of master data, the protection of master data using specific authorization objects is particularly critical.

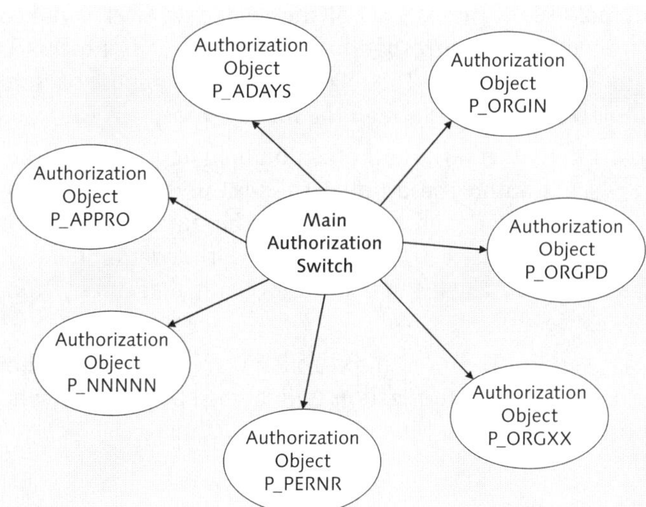


**Figure 21.1** Authorization Control Using the Main Authorization Switch

- The P_ORGIN authorization object restricts authorized access to HCM master data. The authorization object permits authorization checks on transaction data according to criteria like information type and subtype, personnel area, and organizational key. The Authorization Level authorization field is used to assign activities like read and write access. Accesses in the context of asymmetric and symmetric four-eyes principles can also be stored in this field.

  In an asymmetric authorization procedure, different users are assigned different activity rights for manipulating an infotype. This ensures the separation of the creation and release activities in the system by different authorization levels according to the four-eyes principle. In a symmetric authorization procedure, users have the same rights; locked data records can only be released by a second user.
- The P_ORGIN authorization object can be used together with the P_ORGXX authorization object, as a complement of the latter, or P_ORGXX can be used separately and replace P_ORGIN. However, additional or substitutional effects are only possible if the main authorization switch is either enabled or disabled. The P_ORGXX authorization object is used to define responsibilities for personnel administrators. In this context, administrator information from Infotype 0001 is used. It is possible to put restrictions on infotypes and to define different authorization levels.
- The P_PERNR authorization object controls the access to data of individual users and can be activated, for instance, to ensure that users can't change their own

data. The check is only possible if the user ID of the respective user is linked with the personnel number of the corresponding employee. This process is referred to as a personnel number check. The relationship between the personnel number and the user ID is mapped through the link in Infotype 0105.

Just as for P_ORGIN and P_ORGXX, the AUTHC authorization field defines the authorization level, and the P_SIGN authorization object determines the authorizations of the personnel number assigned to the user. The authorizations for activities and personnel numbers interact with the INFTY authorization field for access to HR master data, applicant data, and organizational management. Infotypes are authorized or restricted.

The use of Employee Self-Service (ESS) is also controlled via the P_PERNR authorization object. To do this, the main authorization switch must be activated, and the PSIGN authorization field must be set to authorization value 1.

### 21.3.2 Applicant Authorizations

Information on applicants is controlled via applicant infotypes and checked using the P_APPL authorization object. The time-dependent values of Infotype 0001 enable time-dependent authorizations. The main authorization switch cannot be used for deactivation in this case.

The authorization object uses the VDSK1 authorization field (organizational key). The organizational key enables the definition of more complex roles for the authorization check. In the standard SAP system, the VDSK1 authorization field is a combination of the Personnel Area and Cost Center values. In Customizing you can replace these default values with your own rules that allow combinations of fields from Infotype 0001. This results in new and complex authorization structures (see Figure 21.2).

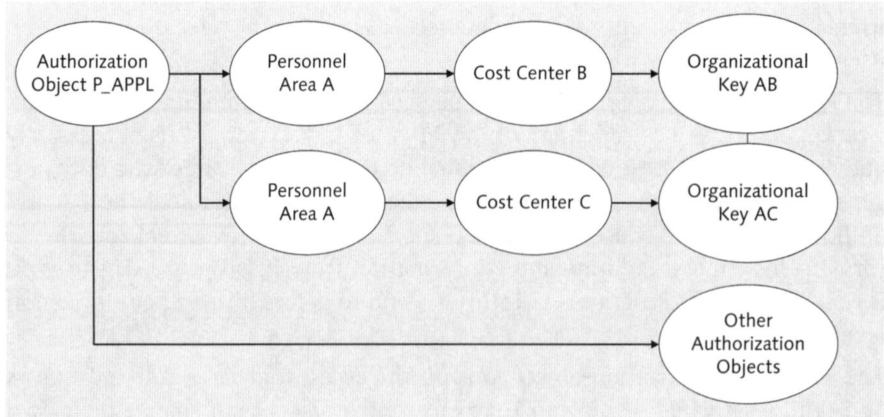


**Figure 21.2** Organizational Key for P_APPL Authorization Object

### 21.3.3 Personnel Planning Authorizations

The personnel planning components can be checked using the PLOG authorization object. The activities are defined using the Function Code authorization field.

### 21.3.4 Reporting Authorizations

The authorization check in HCM reporting is subdivided into a person-related authorization and a data-related authorization. The P_ABAP authorization object enables you to restrict authorization checks. In contrast to the general regular checks, authorization checks are suspended here although they are available. The degree of simplification for the authorization check is defined in the COARS authorization field:

- If the authorization value is set to 2, no authorization check will be performed on the authorization objects of the HCM master data;
- If the value is set to *, no checks will be performed at all.
- If you want to perform an authorization check independent of infotype and organizational assignment, you must use authorization value 1.

### 21.3.5 Structural Authorizations

Structural authorizations define the access rights for organizational units that are defined within the HCM organizational structure. The HR data to be protected are defined via the P object type. Because the individual organizational hierarchies originate from object links (such as Organizational Units • Positions • Persons), different evaluation paths and hence different ways of access are available. Those evaluation paths are defined using structures and can be addressed via structural authorizations. An evaluation or linkage path is defined on the basis of a start object that provides access to personal data. This combination represents the structural profile that enables a user to access organizational units.

For example, the definition of structural profiles determines the object types, the start object, the processing type, the evaluation path, the level of display, and the period. User-specific structural profiles can be created using function modules. Combined with the PLOG authorization object, structural authorizations are also used to protect resource planning data in HR. To use structural authorizations you must set the main authorization switch for the ORGPD authorization field to the value of 1.

Structural authorizations cannot be assigned via roles that were generated in the SAP Profile Generator. The authorizations are defined using Transaction OOSP. The assignment of structural authorizations to users is done via Table T77UA.

### 21.3.6 Authorizations for Personnel Development

Checks that are related to the infotypes for qualification and appraisals (Infotype 0024 and Infotype 0025) can be implemented by activating the main authorization switch. To do this, new entries are necessary in the table of the main authorization switch, T77SO. Those entries correspond to the authorization values in the P_ORGIN authorization object.

### 21.3.7 Tolerance Periods for Authorizations

A user's authorizations are often dependent on validity periods and responsibilities, which can both affect the access rights for specific datasets. Therefore, it is possible to define authorizations that are dependent on a time logic. In this context a distinction is made between the responsibility period of a user and the time logic.

The responsibility period defines infotype rights; the time logic, on the other hand, draws upon the access type and the validity period of the dataset. This combination affects the assignment of authorizations. If the main authorization switch ADAYS is set, you can specify tolerance periods. Those tolerance periods determine the remaining time in which an HR administrator will continue to be responsible for the data of a specific person who has already left the administrator's area of responsibility. The time dependency of infotypes can be set using the Access Authorization switch. The authorization is controlled by the P_ADAYS authorization object.

### 21.3.8 Authorizations for Inspection Procedures

Infotype 0130 controls inspection procedures that can be defined for different purposes by the company. In this context the main authorization switch APPRO must be activated to assign authorizations for inspection procedures. The HCM authorization object P_APPRO is used for assigning the authorizations.

### 21.3.9 Customized Authorization Checks

The P_NNNNN authorization object can be activated using the main authorization switch NNNNN to use it for customized authorization checks. In this context it is important that you maintain the necessary assignments of the checks in Table USOBT_C.

Authorizations in SAP ERP HCM can have a very complex and multifaceted structure. A solid analysis of the requirements and risks is therefore one of the prerequisites for creating an efficient, transparent, and manageable HCM authorization concept.

### 21.3.10 Indirect Role Assignment through the Organizational Structure

Roles can be assigned to users either directly via Transactions SU01, SU10, and PFCG, or indirectly through the organizational structure in SAP ERP HCM. An assignment can, for instance, occur through a job or position. If an employee moves to a different department, the assigned roles are not withdrawn manually from that user, nor are the new roles manually assigned to them — the assignment of the necessary new authorizations instead occurs through the link EMPLOYEE • POSITION. Thus, the employee is automatically assigned the roles indirectly through the position.

The same procedure is applied for new hires or employees who leave the company. This means that the HR administrators are also responsible for some areas related to authorizations. Orderly and constant maintenance of the organizational structure is therefore one of the prerequisites for this method to function properly.

The employees or users are assigned to a job or position that summarizes their activities. They can assign the authorizations in the form of roles to the object types of the organizational structure, which is defined in SAP ERP HCM, for example, to a position. When the assignment of authorizations and user management are made a part of identity management, they can be better controlled and are therefore a more effective component of the internal control system.

### 21.3.11 Additional Transactions Relevant to Internal Controls

In addition to the SAP ERP transactions, the SAP ERP HCM transactions listed in Table 21.3 are also relevant to internal controls.

| Transaction Code | Description |
|---|---|
| P16B_ADMIN | Payroll Administration |
| PA20 | HR Master Data Display |
| PA03 | Maintain Personnel Control Record |
| PA30 | Maintain HR Master Data |
| PA41 | Change Entry/Leaving Date |
| PA61 | Maintain Time Data |
| PA63 | Maintain Time Data |

**Table 21.3** Transactions in SAP ERP HCM Relevant to Controls

| Transaction Code | Description |
|---|---|
| PB30 | Maintain Applicant Master Data |
| PB40 | Applicant Actions |
| PC00_M99_PA03_CHECK | Check |
| PC00_M99_PA03_CORR | Payroll Corrections |
| PC00_M99_PA03_END | Exit Payroll |
| PC00_M99_CALC_SIMU | Simulation |
| PC00_M99_PA03_RELEA | Release Payroll |
| PO03 | Maintain Job |
| PO10 | Maintain Organizational Unit |
| PO13 | Maintain Position |
| PP01 | Maintain Plan Data |
| PPOME | Maintain Organization and Staffing |
| PPOC | Maintain Organizational Structure |
| PPME | Change Matrix Organization |
| PR05 | Travel Expense Manager |
| PU00 | Delete HR Data |
| PU03 | Change Payroll Status |
| PV17 | Billing |
| PW01 | Maintain Incentive Wages Data |
| SBWP | SAP Business Workplace |

**Table 21.3** Transactions in SAP ERP HCM Relevant to Controls (Cont.)

Control tables that allow for a specific view of certain business and employee groups are of particular significance. Examples include:

- Table `T500P` — personnel area
- Table `T501` — employee group
- Table `T503K` and Table `T503T` — employee subgroup
- Table `T549A` — payroll area
- Table `T750F` — applicant subgroup
- Table `T750K` — applicant group

## 21.4 Technical Security

For the evaluation of technical security risks and controls, the following components must be considered:

- SAP NetWeaver Application Server (AS) (see Chapter 9, SAP NetWeaver Application Server)
- SAP Internet Transaction Server (ITS) (see Chapter 14, Classic SAP Middleware)
- SAP graphical user interface (GUI) (see Chapter 28, User Interfaces)
- Web browser (see Chapter 28)

The technical controls described for these components can also be used without limitation for SAP ERP HCM.

*Well-founded company figures and information that allow for an appropriate risk management are important for strategic company decisions. This chapter discusses this process, generally referred to as Strategic Enterprise Management (SEM), with a focus on security risks and controls for user access.*

# 22 SAP Strategic Enterprise Management

Integrated company control is one of the main purposes of any business plan. SAP Strategic Enterprise Management (SAP SEM) is the SAP solution for analyzing important financial data and other freely selectable business performance indicators. The analysis results support the company management in strategic decisions that are supposed to put the company on a secure profitability path with calculable risk, for example. SAP SEM as a subarea of SAP ERP is therefore the functional solution for strategic enterprise management.

## 22.1 Introduction and Functions

The following selected SEM components describe the scope of functions provided by SAP SEM:

- **Business Consolidation**
  Consolidation allows for a performance review of the company or departments for reporting financials, financial status, and profit situation.
- **Business Planning and Simulation**
  Business planning offers applications for supporting the entire business planning process using predefined components ranging from master data entry, to creating planning scenarios, to planning process presentations.
- **Corporate Performance Management**
  This component supports the control of business strategy projects. Here, the focus is on the qualitative or quantitative evaluation and presentation of strategy goals. Applications of this portfolio include the Management Cockpit and the Balanced Scorecard, among others.
- **Risk Management**
  SAP SEM also supports the activities of business risk management, for example,

for identifying, quantifying, or monitoring control risks. It functions supplement the SAP applications portfolio for risk management.

Strategies, planning scenarios, and advanced planning are considered confidential information for competitive reasons and must therefore be protected against unauthorized access. This idea can be emphasized based on some functions and tools that are provided by SAP SEM:

- A freely definable, balanced scorecard can be used to define the most important key figures for measuring company performance. This helps decision-makers tailor their corporate decisions specifically to target weak areas or products in the company.
- The strategic planning functions provide simulation functions that can be used to project the effects certain decisions will have in the future and therefore support the decision-making processes.
- Consolidation and aggregation functions process essential corporate data such as the revenue figures for a specific product by region, or the contribution margin of a particular product.
- The simulation functions, for example, allow for an analysis of the investment capital involved compared to the possible revenue that can be achieved.
  The influence of legal regulations or possible environmental effects can be included in the analysis as well, which, for instance, is a definite requirement for reinsurance transactions.

In view of the examples given for the information options, data security and effective authorization checks for users are of particular importance for security risk management.

## 22.2 Risks and Controls

The security methods and solutions that you choose for SAP SEM are determined by an objective assessment of the requirements and the risk potential of each individual situation. However, different corporate cultures can produce different evaluations of these factors, particularly because SAP SEM processes consolidated enterprise data that is used for making strategic decisions and is therefore exposed to a high risk potential.

Risk evaluation is the central starting point for evaluating security solutions in the SAP environment. The risks that should be evaluated include, for example, situations whereby the enterprise does not comply with the regulations and guidelines of any relevant industry associations, or statutory regulations and guidelines. Table 22.1 contains the main risks in SAP SEM.

| No. | Classification | Description |
|---|---|---|
| 1. | Risk potential | Inadequate authorization concept:<br>Users of SAP SEM are granted authorizations that greatly exceed the actual requirement for information and functionality, because the authorization concept is only used as a means for granting functional authorizations to users, and not as an effective control tool for minimizing risks. With this solution especially, highly sensitive, consolidated enterprise data is processed, the knowledge of which is of high significance, particularly for the competition. |
| | Impact | Users have greater authorizations than are necessary for their position and the scope of their work. Read and write access to high-risk, consolidated financial data and other enterprise key figures is possible. This is a violation of both internal company requirements and statutory requirements. It creates a situation where process, administrative, and system risks are not controlled. The risk potential is therefore increased rather than minimized. In addition, competitors can take possession of important key figures and use this information to improve their own strategic position. Moreover, financial data or company-strategic information on insider trading of stocks or securities could be misused. This is a violation of internal company requirements, statutory requirements, and data protection guidelines. |
| | Risk without control(s) | Extremely high |
| | Control | The authorization concept has to take into account both organizational and functional requirements, and make administration simpler and more effective. The relevant risks have to be taken into account in the authorization design process, and methods of continuous management have to be integrated into the change management process. |
| | Risk with control(s) | Normal |
| | Section | 22.3 |
| 2. | Risk potential | Insufficient security for stored data and data during transmission:<br>Highly sensitive consolidated company data is transferred, processed, and stored in the context of SAP SEM. Knowledge of this data is particularly significant for competitors. |

**Table 22.1** Risks and Controls for SAP SEM

| No. | Classification | Description |
|---|---|---|
| | Impact | Unprotected data can be accessed by unauthorized users, for example, at the system level, in data storage, or during transmission in the network. Financial data or company-strategic information on insider trading of stocks or securities could be misused. In addition, unauthorized users or competitors can take possession of important key figures and use this information to improve their own strategic position. This is a violation of internal company requirements, statutory requirements, and data protection guidelines. |
| | Risk without control(s) | Extremely high |
| | Control | Data must be protected against loss and unauthorized access in the stored state or during transfer. |
| | Risk with control(s) | Normal |
| | Section | 22.4 |

**Table 22.1** Risks and Controls for SAP SEM (Cont.)

## 22.3 Application Security

The security concept for SAP SEM is determined by the execution on Application Server (AS) ABAP. Therefore, the ABAP authorization concept can be used for the user and system access. This concept was already presented in Chapters 9, SAP NetWeaver Application Server, and 20, Authorizations in SAP ERP; the authorization controls discussed there also apply to SAP SEM. In particular, the information ownership method described there should be applied as a best-practice method for the development of user authorizations for SAP SEM.

SAP SEM retrieves data from a connected Business Warehouse (BW) system (see Chapter 10, SAP NetWeaver Business Warehouse). Users who are supposed to have access to such data (for instance, characteristics and key figures) and its analyses must therefore be assigned with the corresponding application authorizations. Here, you should also develop holistic guidelines for user access that are based on the general principles that were developed for Enterprise Resource Planning (ERP) data access. This means that the information access using SAP SEM should not go beyond the scope defined in the ERP or BW system because otherwise the limits defined in the data source system could be exceeded.

## 22.4 Technical Security

Depending on individual configurations, the following components may be important for technical and data security:

- SAP NetWeaver AS (see Chapter 9)
- SAP NetWeaver BW (see Chapter 10)
- SAP Graphical User Interface (GUI) (see Chapter 28, User Interfaces)
- Web browser (see Chapter 28)

Data is exposed to a variety of threats during transfer in the network or in data storage. The resulting risks must be sufficiently minimized to an acceptable level by means of technical countermeasures and continuous maintenance; Chapter 5, Information Technology (IT) Security, provides valuable information on this subject. With regard to the data security during transfer in the company network or the Internet, it is recommended to use Secure Socket Layer (SSL) or Secure Network Communication (SNC) connections.

*This chapter illustrates the complexity of the solution mechanisms and options of the controlling security solutions for SAP Customer Relationship Management (CRM).*

# 23 SAP Customer Relationship Management

With its marketing, sales, and analysis functions and in combination with the logistics functions in SAP Enterprise Resource Planning (ERP), SAP CRM is the central component for customer and client management and for marketing and sales processes in SAP NetWeaver. Customer relationship management focuses on recording and maintaining a company's relationship with its customers. Market and customer analysis functions support the sales department in planning and carrying out targeted actions.

## 23.1 Introduction and Functions

In detail, SAP CRM supports the following business processes:

- **Marketing and sales promotion**
  Here, activities for marketing, business development, and initiation of business contacts are supported.
- **Sales and distribution**
  This process supports all sales and distribution processes, such as planning, implementation, and analysis of sales activities.
- **Service**
  This process supports processes in the service segment to optimize processing.
- **Customer-oriented contact via service centers**
  This process establishes effective communication channels for marketing, sales, and customer service.
- **IP-supported communication management**
  This is an IP-based communication solution that combines all business communication contact channels on a standardized platform.
- **Partner management and indirect sales and distribution**
  Partner management supports the partner management processes in the sales and marketing area via the Internet.

- **Internet as a distribution channel**
  SAP CRM is a web-based platform where e-marketing, e-commerce, e-self-service for customers and many other key processes can be established via Business-to-Business (B2B) and Business-to-Consumer (B2C) scenarios.

## 23.2 Risks and Controls

SAP CRM processes important customer and sales data. While customer data is subject to internal and legal data protection regulations, sales data, such as product and price information or sales figures, often have strategic importance to the company and therefore must be protected. The control measures depend on the classification of the data and the related need for protection (see Table 23.1). Because the technical and business scenarios and the control solutions for application and technical security can be very complex, this chapter only covers a few critical solutions.

Because various user groups and business scenarios are used in SAP CRM, the individual scenarios must be analyzed and secured separately. Integrated systems, such as SAP ERP, SAP ERP HCM, SAP NetWeaver Business Warehouse (BW), SAP NetWeaver Mobile, and so on, also involve different requirements with regard to data synchronization, for example, for user data.

| No. | Classification | Description |
|---|---|---|
| 1. | Potential risk | Business partner and sales data:<br>When SAP CRM converts business partner data to information, it is either subject to a data protection law (see Chapter 21, SAP ERP HCM and Data Protection) or has minimum protection needs.<br>For example, information on the buying behavior, preferences of customers, payment behavior, or bank and credit information, must be protected. Sales information, such as data on sales within a certain period or region, can be anticompetitive if it falls into the possession of unauthorized persons at the wrong time. Furthermore, business partner information, such as customer and client data, can only be transferred to third parties with the explicit permission of the business partner, that is, usually of the customer. This means that (especially) customer and sales data must be protected. |

**Table 23.1** Risks and Controls for SAP CRM

| No. | Classification | Description |
|---|---|---|
| | Impact | Information on business partner and sales data is of particular interest to competitors. Therefore, the data must be protected and the use of the resulting information must be controlled appropriately. |
| | Risk without control(s) | High |
| | Control | The CRM data must be classified according to the required level of protection. Control solutions are defined based on the protection requirements of this data, which are integrated into a comprehensive security strategy. Efficient authorization management helps protect data and activities and ensure that only authorized users have controlled access to it. |
| | Risk with control(s) | Low |
| | Section | 23.3 |
| 2. | Potential risk | Internal and external users:<br>Depending on the scenario, SAP CRM can either be made accessible only to internal users or to external users. This entails an increase in the technical security requirements for the CRM systems. |
| | Impact | External users may inadvertently be authorized to access internal CRM systems. If the technical security measures and the authorization controls are not coordinated exactly, all doors are open for unauthorized access to information. |
| | Risk without control(s) | High |
| | Control | Because different user groups have access to the CRM data, for external<br>authorizations the protection must be ensured not only by the authorization system, but also by technical control measures. |
| | Risk with control(s) | Normal |
| | Section | 23.4 |

**Table 23.1** Risks and Controls for SAP CRM (Cont.)

| No. | Classification | Description |
|---|---|---|
| 3. | Potential risk | Mobile scenarios:<br>Due to the entry of sales information such as purchase orders, confidential data is stored in databases of mobile devices. This means that the security access for mobile clients, the secure synchronization of CRM data with the CRM server, and the protection of CRM back-end systems must be closely monitored. When the relevant data is synchronized and replicated between the mobile client and the CRM server, the validation is usually performed in the CRM back-end system. If the control and protection measures are insufficient, this can result in the falsification or loss of individual data records and even of complete database contents, the loss of synchronicity, or the records can fall into the hands of unauthorized persons. |
| | Impact | The consequences are loss or manipulation of data, which can lead to competitive disadvantages, increased costs, or even legal penalties. |
| | Risk without control(s) | High |
| | Control | Technical and process-related security measures, such as prompt and secure synchronizations and replication of CRM data with the CRM server and the use of consolidated databases, are commonly used standard SAP solutions. In addition, mobile devices must be properly protected by the employees. |
| | Risk with control(s) | Normal |
| | Section | 23.4.1 |

**Table 23.1** Risks and Controls for SAP CRM (Cont.)

## 23.3 Application Security

SAP CRM generally follows the authorization concept rules of the SAP NetWeaver AS (see Chapter 6, Enterprise Risk Management (ERM) Navigation Control Map, Chapter 9, SAP NetWeaver AS, and Chapter 20, Authorizations in SAP ERP). In addition to the role concept, the authorization systems in SAP CRM are complemented by more advanced concepts that protect access to transactions and Business Server Page (BSP) applications. Internal employees must be assigned roles for the internal CRM system, while external business partners or field sales representatives need access to CRM data via portal applications. In addition, internal employees want to access CRM applications from outside the company.

For the different scenarios and the complicated security requirements of CRM systems and applications, different concepts have been established that provide comprehensive data and business activities protection. ABAP authorization roles, portal roles, access control rules, and the business partner principle are some examples of the complex options for controlling authorizations.

### 23.3.1 Authorizations in SAP CRM

The central authorization system is implemented using the SAP NetWeaver AS role concept. Authorizations for business data and transactions in SAP CRM are defined and implemented using the SAP Profile Generator (Transaction PFCG) or other authorization solutions. Additional control options are available for the mobile solutions in SAP CRM. For channel management, SAP CRM provides the Access Control Engine (ACE), which enables a rules-based distribution of authorizations to users (see Figure 23.1).

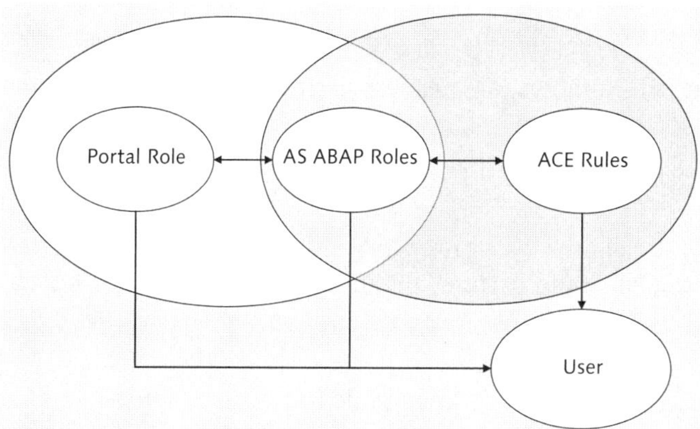


**Figure 23.1** Roles in SAP CRM and Rules-Based Authorizations

The ACE in SAP CRM is an option for controlling user rights within channel management. In contrast to the role authorization concept, the ACE is based on defined rules which are specified in Access Control Lists (ACL). Rules-based access control is the security solution for CRM mass data. The effect of the rules, however, is that they complement the authorizations that have been assigned to a user via the authorization roles.

The function can be maintained in Customizing and can be called via the following menu path: CUSTOMER RELATIONSHIP MANAGEMENT • BASIC FUNCTIONS • ACCESS

Control Engine (Transaction SPRO). SAP CRM references the users that have been created using Transaction SU01. It also references the assigned roles that have been implemented using Transaction PFCG. The ACE uses user IDs to manage the rules-based authorizations, for instance. This means that changes to users also affect the authorizations that are managed by the ACE.

Access control lists can be used to define additional access rights to business data that are based on rules related to users or user groups. Users that have been created using Transaction SU01 are assigned to ACE user groups. The ACE rules are applied in the interaction with portal and CRM back-end roles, for instance, to grant different business partners access to different sets of business information.

Depending on the configured or activated rules, the ACE filters the general and individual rights of users and then releases the relevant information accordingly. Based on the rules, a user of a specific partner company can only access information that is related to this company. In addition, the individual rights of the requesting user are checked. Therefore, the ACE lets you control dynamic authorizations by using hierarchical business partner structures. This means that the ACE is a system for defining user-dependent access rights for information objects. The application can check authorizations for different actions like reading, writing, and deleting information objects in SAP CRM.

For creating the rules, the ACE follows the business partner principle (Transaction BP). The involved partner organizations are mapped as business relationships and information objects using specific elements, some of which are listed here:

- **Actor**
  An actor is an organizational unit that is used as a basis for authorization determinations, such as user, business partner, organizational unit (CRM), region, area, or territory.
- **User context**
  The user context describes the organizational units in relation to the users that are used in the ACE.
- **ACE group**
  The ACE group is a dynamically calculated group of users based on a user's role assignments and the organizational unit to which the user belongs.
- **Activation tool**
  The activation tool is a program that transfers the contents of administrative database tables to runtime information tables. The administrative tables are directly maintained by the administrator, whereas the runtime information tables are used by the ACE for calculating the authorizations.

- **Actions**
  Actions are used to create rules and comprise different individual or composite activities such as writing, deleting, or just reading.
- **Rules**
  A rule is a group of methods that defines how filters can be used to find actors for a user or for an object, or just to find objects. In addition, rules are used to calculate the relationship between users and information objects.
- **Rights**
  Rights define the assignment of rules and actions to user groups.
- **Roles**
  Roles contain authorizations and are assigned to users or organizational levels.

Figure 23.2 shows the hierarchical structure for business partner organizations that are defined as business relationships, and the relationships between information objects and the hierarchical CRM structures. It does not refer to the HCM organizational structure.

Because the organizational structure in SAP CRM serves a different purpose than the organizational structure defined according to Human Resources (HR) aspects in SAP ERP HCM, they can be based on the same technology but shouldn't be synchronized. It definitely makes sense to use different organizational structures even if this increases the maintenance effort.

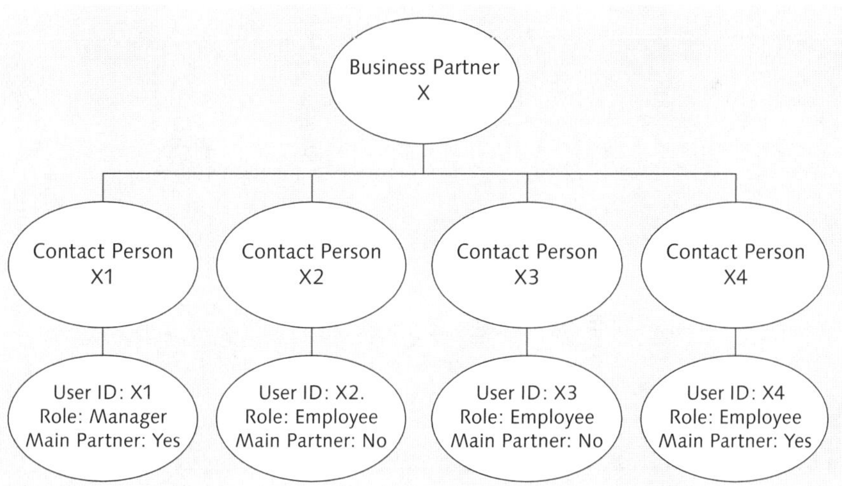


**Figure 23.2** Hierarchical Organizational Structure for Business Partners

The ACE uses this information to define the access to individual objects (for example, a list of customer contacts). Once the access to an individual information object has been defined, the result of the authorization check is temporarily stored in the system cache so that it can be used for further accesses. The actor in this case is the partner company (for example, business partner X).

The example shown in Figure 23.3 illustrates the relationship between information objects and the hierarchical structure for determining rules-based authorizations. Due to the rules-based definition of the access to a list of customer contacts, the authorized list can be built and displayed for a specific user.

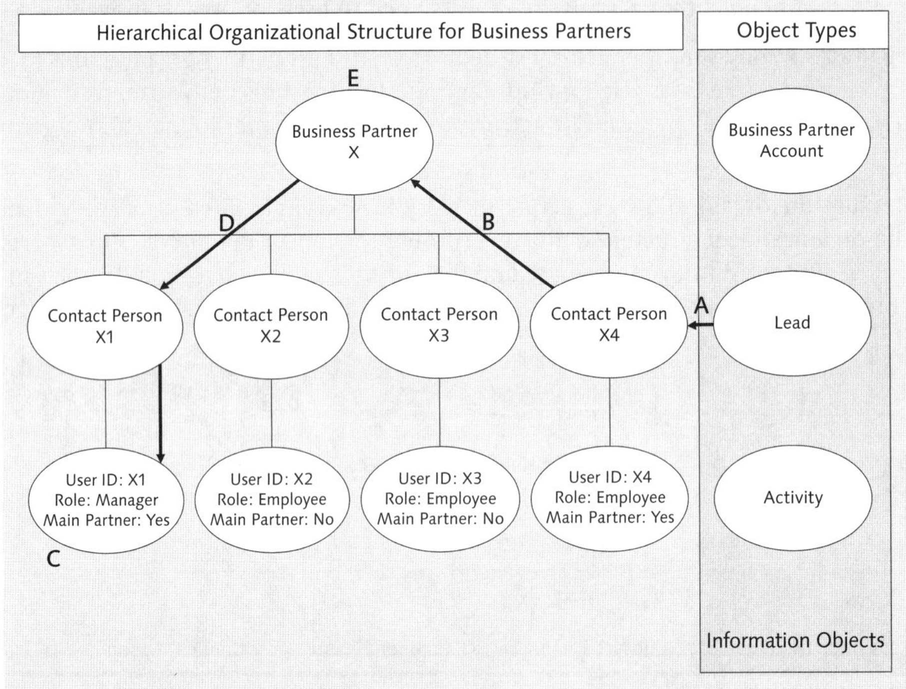


**Figure 23.3** Sample ACE Authorization Check

- **Rule A**: Check the contact person the entry is associated with on the list of customer contacts
- **Rule B**: Check the primary business partner for the contact person
- **Rule C**: Obtain contact data of the contact person
- **Rule D**: Check the primary business partner for the contact person

- **Rule E**: Compare the business partners; if they are identical, the customer contact data can be displayed to the user

Transaction SM30 can be used to manage the elements for the ACE. The individual object types for information objects such as an activity, lead, or user are equipped with rights and rules in this context. If the rights are activated in the ACE administration in Customizing, the results of the activations can be displayed under Statistics. To do this, the views listed in Table 23.2 must be maintained.

| View | Description |
|---|---|
| CRM_ACE_ACTTYP | Definition of the actor type |
| CRM_ACE_AFO_CL | Finding actors of an object |
| CRM_ACE_AFU_CL | Finding actors of a user |
| CRM_ACE_ANGRP | Action group for the ACE |
| CRM_ACE_ANGRPS | Action group for the ACE |
| CRM_ACE_CUSTOM | Customizing for CRM portals |
| CRM_ACE_OBF_CL | Finding objects with filters for the ACE |
| CRM_ACE_OTYPES | Relevant object types for the ACE |
| CRM_ACE_RIGHTS | Rights for the ACE |
| CRM_ACE_RULES | Rules for the ACE |
| CRM_ACE_ST_ACC | Super types for the ACE |
| CRM_ACE_U_GRP | User group for the ACE |
| CRM_ACE_U_GRPS | User group for the ACE |

**Table 23.2** SAP CRM Maintenance Tables (Views) for ACE Administration

Table 23.3 displays an example of rule definitions.

| Relation ID (Rule ID) | Actor Type | Object Type | GetActors FromUser | GetActorFrom Object | GetObjects ByFilter |
|---|---|---|---|---|---|
| MyLeads | Contact | Lead | UserSContacts | LeadSPartner Contacts | * |
| MyCompany Leads | Partner company | Lead | UserSPartner Company | LeadSPartner Company | U.S. leads |

**Table 23.3** Rule Definition for the ACE

The Actor Type is the type of organizational element used with regard to user and information objects. `GetActorsFromUser` determines the actors (for example, the organizational unit) for each user who has been assigned those rights. `GetActorsFromObject` determines the actors in relation to each object that is returned by the rule `GetObjectsByFilter` (see Figure 23.4).

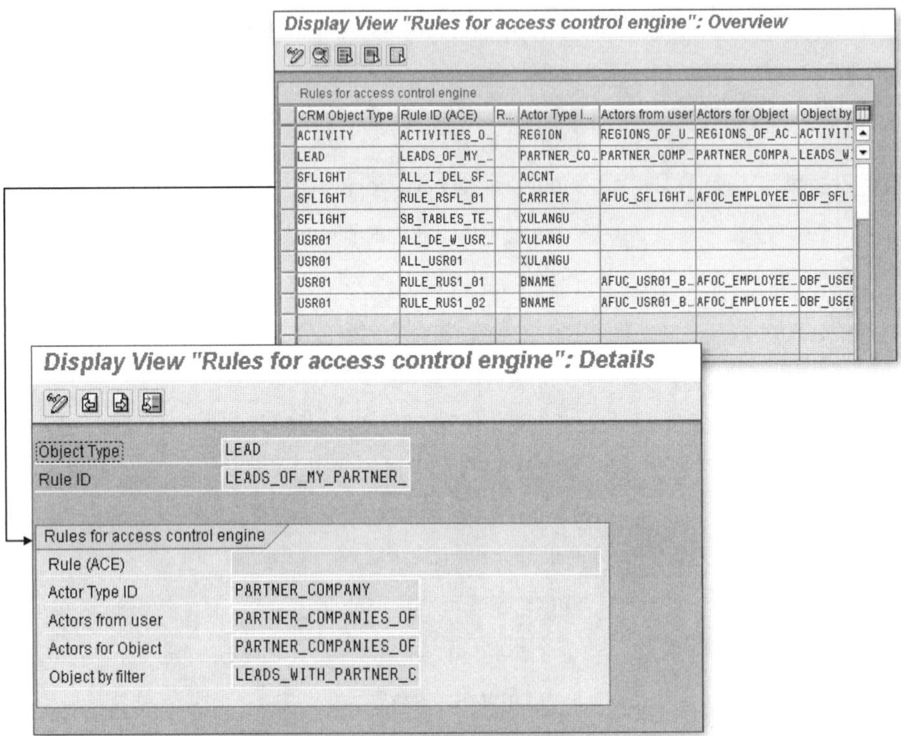


**Figure 23.4** Maintaining Rules and Rights for ACE Object Types

In the administration of rights, permitted actions are defined for the previously defined rules and object types for each user group. User groups are often based on portal roles. Rights describe the relationship between users and objects. Table 23.4 uses the `Lead` CRM object type as an example to describe the maintenance of rights by using rules with predefined actions.

| Right | User Group | Object Type | Rule | Action |
|---|---|---|---|---|
| R318 | All partner roles | Lead | MyCompaniesLeads | Read |
| R315 | Partner manager | Lead | MyCompaniesLeads | Change |
| R316 | All partner roles | Lead | MyLeads | All |

**Table 23.4** Rights Definition for the ACE

### 23.3.2 Authorizations for Portal Roles

The authorizations for portal roles are divided into two categories – rights for administrators and rights for users. In addition to the definition of rights, portal roles are also used to add ACLs to the content in the content management component of SAP NetWeaver Portal. The following tables should be logged for monitoring ACE changes:

- Definition of the actor type with Table CRM_ACE_ACTTYP
- Customizing with Table CRM_ACE_CUSTOM
- Object types with Table CRM_ACE_OTYPES
- Rights with Table CRM_ACE_RIGHTS
- Activated rights with Table CRM_ACE_RIG_RT
- Rules with Table CRM_ACE_RULES
- Assignment of tables to supertypes with Table CRM_ACE_ST_ACC
- Activated user rights with Table CRM_ACE_UGR_RT
- Definition of actors per object with Table CRM_ACE_AFO_CL
- Definition of actors for users with Table CRM_ACE_AFO_CL
- Action groups with Table CRM_ACE_ANGRP
- Assignment of actions to action groups with Table CRM_ACE_ANGRPS
- Definition of objects using a filter with Table CRM_ACE_OBF_CL
- User groups with Table CRM_ACE_U_GRP
- Assignment of users, roles, or groups to user groups with Table CRM_ACE_U_GRPS

Logging these tables can be activated or deactivated in the ABAP Dictionary. Logging can be displayed using Transaction SCU3.

The authorization and control options in SAP CRM provide a lot of different ways to assign and restrict authorizations for necessary functions and actions for internal and external users. The standard SAP tools can be used to create functional and organizational authorizations and to define them using roles. Authorization objects can be assigned the corresponding authorization fields. In addition, dynamic access controls are available that are based on the use of flexible authorization rules and individual information objects.

## 23.4 Technical Security

Depending on operational necessity and security needs, the CRM systems must meet different technical requirements. If CRM applications should be made accessible only for internal employees, it must be ensured that the CRM systems cannot be accessed through the Internet. In that case, the CRM servers should not be outside the demilitarized zone (DMZ).

However, due to organizational and sales-related requirements, internal sales employees may need to be granted access to SAP CRM from outside of the demilitarized zone. This can be the case for employees who work from home or for sales employees who travel to another region. In this case, a Virtual Private Network (VPN) can establish an encrypted data communication.

When granting access rights to external users such as business partners, SAP Web Dispatcher can be used to ensure a higher level of security. SAP Web Dispatcher is only used in CRM and BW back-end systems, whereby the access to the back-end systems is controlled by URL filters. To ensure that all requests from SAP NetWeaver Portal to the CRM system pass through SAP Web Dispatcher, the latter should be set up in DMZ 1 of the ERM Navigation Control Map. Therefore, each URL that needs access to the CRM back-end system must be configured.

### 23.4.1 Technical Protection of the Mobile Application

Specific scenarios that involve mobile applications must be secured according to their protection needs. This applies to the use of special mobile devices, communication and authentication technologies, and to the safeguarding of synchronization and replication scenarios. For the protection of mobile CRM applications, you should consider the technical risks and the corresponding control measures of the SAP NetWeaver Mobile components (see Chapter 17, SAP NetWeaver Mobile) and mobile devices (see Chapter 28, Section 28.3, Mobile Devices).

### 23.4.2 Important Additional Components

The applications contained in SAP CRM are based on SAP NetWeaver components. The technical risks and controls described for those components can also be applied to SAP CRM. Therefore, the technical control measures of the following components should also be considered for SAP CRM:

- SAP NetWeaver AS (see Chapter 9)
- SAP NetWeaver BW (see Chapter 10, SAP NetWeaver Business Warehouse)
- SAP NetWeaver PI (see Chapter 12, SAP NetWeaver PI)
- SAP Web Dispatcher (see Chapter 14, Classic SAP Middleware)
- SAP Internet Transaction Server (ITS) (see Chapter 14)
- SAP NetWeaver Mobile (see Chapter 17)
- Web browser (see Chapter 28)
- Mobile devices (see Chapter 28)

*This chapter describes SAP Supply Chain Management (SCM) as an Enterprise Risk Management (ERM) Navigation Control Map component, based on a sample control solution.*

# 24 SAP Supply Chain Management

In the SAP world, central planning and control processes are mapped using SAP SCM to provide shorter and more effective production cycles. Control measures for protecting planning, purchasing, production, and stockholding data are processed here.

This SAP application contains essential information on the supply chain of a manufacturing company that must be evaluated and protected to ensure the continuity of the production processes and avoid interruptions due to incorrect supplies. Challenges in the production and market supply areas require customized products and services.

## 24.1 Introduction and Functions

To successfully master these challenges, an increasing number of manufacturing companies focus on partnering with service providers, vendors, and customers. This way, they can concentrate on their core business and can also access a multitude of resources to meet their customers' requirements. This approach places new requirements on companies because they have to cooperate in complex collaboration scenarios to remain competitive at a national and global level.

In close collaboration and communication scenarios, applications for demand and requirements planning, for production and detailed scheduling, for global availability checks or transport planning, and for event management, are coupled with solutions for production control, transport management, materials management, and warehousing in SAP ERP. Their processes must be protected in numerous ways. Against this background, an essential economical change takes place for logistics processes. Because the SAP SCM applications map the foundations for the production processes, which involves communication between SAP SCM and other SAP systems that essentially affect the business results, some requirements must be considered when evaluating the data, collaboration scenarios, technical networks, and the need for protection when using SCM solutions.

## 24.2 Risks and Controls

SAP SCM processes important information such as planning and production data. The control measures depend on the classification of the data, the processes, the collaborative scenarios, and the related need for protection (see Table 24.1).

| No. | Classification | Description |
|---|---|---|
| 1. | Potential risk | Inadequate authorization concept:<br>SAP SCM processes information needed to ensure a functioning supply chain. This data is of essential importance for maintaining the production processes and must therefore be protected from unauthorized access, modification, delay, and other risks. |
| | Impact | Unauthorized data access can result in a manipulation of the data, which can severely disturb the production operations and therefore create high extra costs. Securing the undisturbed continuity of those business processes must be a top priority. |
| | Risk without control(s) | High |
| | Control | A solid authorization system, including appropriate controls of access rights to SCM data, SMC functions, and SMC actions are important measures within the internal risk control system. |
| | Risk with control(s) | Low |
| | Section | 24.3 |
| 2. | Potential risk | Inadequate data protection for data communication processes:<br>SAP SCM supports numerous Remote Function Call (RFC) communication connections to connected SAP systems. In this context, incorrectly configured RFC connections are a potential risk. If RFC system users with authorizations that go beyond the necessary scope are used (for instance, when using SAP_ALL), an unnecessarily high potential risk exists. |

**Table 24.1** Risks and Controls for SAP SCM

| No. | Classification | Description |
|---|---|---|
| | Impact | Incorrectly configured RFC communication connections can be used to further compromise the system. For example, an RFC system user that has authorizations for all ABAP function groups or SAP_ALL can be used to create a new dialog user with extensive authorizations in the target system and to initiate unauthorized transactions or data access. Moreover, these excessive and unnecessary authorizations will be criticized in audits. |
| | Risk without control(s) | High |
| | Control | Correct configuration of RFC communication destinations and restriction of RFC system user authorizations to the minimum required. Before you use the trusted-RFC connections, you should check to see if the associated risk is justified and whether sufficient compensating security measures are available. |
| | Risk with control(s) | Normal |
| | Section | 24.4 |

**Table 24.1** Risks and Controls for SAP SCM (Cont.)

## 24.3 Application Security

SAP SCM generally follows the authorization concept rules of the SAP NetWeaver Application Server (AS) (see Chapter 9, SAP NetWeaver AS, and Chapter 6, Enterprise Risk Management (ERM) Navigation Control Map, and Chapter 20, Authorizations in SAP ERP). The authorizations for accessing SAP SCM data and application objects and activities are defined and implemented based on authorization roles. The SAP Profile Generator is one of the main tools used to create roles and authorizations.

SAP provides predefined roles for SAP SCM that you can use as templates for your own customized roles. These predefined roles also include the SAP templates for Advanced Planning and Optimization (APO). The role concept is supported by some additional authorization solutions. The most important concepts are the authorization and filter profiles that are defined as internal controls in SAP SCM Customizing. You can also work with Access Control Lists (ACL), which are used for results forecasting and material replenishment processes.

### 24.3.1 Authorizations for the Integrated Product and Process Engineering (iPPE) Workbench

For applications contained in SAP APO and the iPPE Workbench, iPPE authorization profiles for master data are created in Customizing. These iPPE authorization profiles are defined in the Implementation Guide (IMG) for SAP SCM via the menu path: Advanced Planning and Optimization • Master Data • Integrated Product and Process Engineering (iPPE) • Settings for the iPPE Workbench Professional • Define User Profiles for the iPPE Workbench Professional.

SAP provides standard authorization profiles that can also be used as templates to define your own authorization profiles. These authorization profiles include the following:

- S_PPEALL
  This authorization profile is used for granting user rights for the entire iPPE Workbench.
- S_ASTACT
  This authorization profile is used for granting user rights for process structures within the iPPE Workbench. It involves the Detail Area of the iPPE Workbench.
- S_ASTCMP
  This authorization profile is used for granting user rights for product structures within the Detail Area of the iPPE Workbench.
- SASTFLO
  This authorization profile is used for granting user rights for line structures within the Detail Area of the iPPE Workbench.

The authorizations for the Navigation Area in the iPPE Workbench control the model definitions and objects of SAP Product Lifecycle Management (SAP PLM). Here, the authorizations are maintained via model definitions and SAP PLM.

In contrast to SAP ERP, in the iPPE Workbench reports can be called using the report tree concept. The assignment of reports occurs via iPPE authorization profiles. However, the reports must have been defined for the report trees up front. Integration with SAP NetWeaver Business Warehouse (BW) results in the use of the BW authorization concepts (see Chapter 10, SAP NetWeaver BW).

### 24.3.2 Authorizations for Supply Chain Planning

Authorizations for planners — in other words, for SAP SCP — are also defined in Customizing. Responsibilities are defined via the following menu path: APO • SCP • Specify the Person (Planner) Responsible.

### 24.3.3 Authorizations for SAP Event Management

Information that is used in SAP Event Management is presented in business scenarios to which users are assigned. The assignment controls which parameters and conditions are displayed to a user for a specific scenario. This way, access to information in SAP Event Management is controlled.

The assignment occurs in Customizing as a critical authorization and control measure. To do this, authorization profiles with parameters are defined and then assigned to an event handler type. The users are granted or restricted access to the event handlers. In addition, filter profiles for components of event handlers can be used. The filter profiles are assigned to the corresponding event handler types, which in turn are assigned to authorization roles. Finally, the authorization role is assigned via the User group authorization component to the user who is supposed to be authorized (see Figure 24.1).

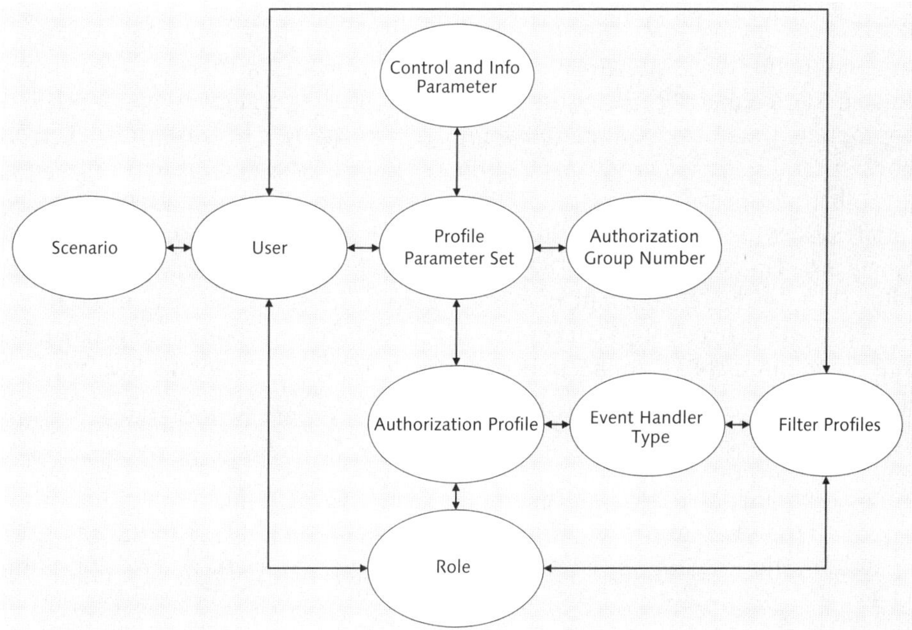


**Figure 24.1** Authorizations for SAP Event Management

The additional authorization solutions, such as access control lists for replenishment applications, help install the necessary controls within SAP SCM. There are, however, some security concerns regarding these solutions, due to the necessity of an RFC connection for a dialog user in the Available-to-Promise (ATP) solution, for instance. These solutions must be complemented by technical security measures to ensure a comprehensive control system.

## 24.4 Technical Security

SAP SCM mainly obtains its information from other SAP systems via internal network connections within the company or via connections to external partner systems. The resulting security risks must be considered in a concept involving the corresponding countermeasures. This section describes in more detail the risk for RFC connections that is outlined in Table 24.1 with regard to technical security. In this context, you must implement the technical default settings, like SNC encryption and authorization restrictions for system users of RFC connections from Chapter 9, SAP NetWeaver AS, and the respective control measures from Table 24.1. RFC user authorizations for the authorization object S_RFC, whose scope is set too unspecific and open, can be used to compromise the system even if the RFC user has the SAP user type System User or Communications User.

In combination with AS ABAP, SAP SCM also provides a function for using a trusted RFC connection to another SAP system. If the connection is not secured appropriately, this option entails a very high security risk because this RFC type doesn't require a password for an authentication of the RFC system user. So if an authentication process for the RFC user is missing, the target system provides implicit trust for the identity of the RFC user. This situation is comparable to the Single Sign-On (SSO) concept. The SSO concept, however, uses initial authentication. This also has the benefit that no password information needs to be transferred via the network. This concept of a trusted RFC connection is not mandatory, and the traditional RFC connection using password authentication still applies.

But if trusted RFC is used, the risk management should include the following measures:

- To ensure that no other user can use the trusted RFC connection, the authorization of this system user should leave the RFC_USER field blank in the S_RFCACL authorization object (input: ' ') (see Chapter 9, SAP NetWeaver Application Server).
- The systems connected via RFC must be located in the same network segment. This architecture avoids additional risks that result from communicating across network boundaries. The security risk increases if the systems are located in heterogeneous network sections with varying levels of security.
- The systems must meet identical security requirements and be configured according to the same well-defined security concept. This also applies to users and RFC system users. This means that both systems have the same level of

security, and users of the source system might have access to the target system anyway. This emphasizes that the purpose of a trusted connection actually is to increase the effectiveness of the communication of these two systems because the RFC system user is not subject to authentication.

In terms of technical security, additional components are important for SAP SCM. In particular, the technical risks and necessary controls of the following components should be considered.

- SAP NetWeaver AS (see Chapter 9) is the business platform for SAP SCM and supports the SCM security functions for data communication in the internal network or via the Internet, using SNC or SSL. SAP NetWeaver AS also supports the categorization of SAP SCM to the SSO environment using SAP logon tickets.
- Within its functionality, SAP SCM supports web services or SAP Enterprise Services (see Chapter 7, Web Services, Enterprise Services, and Service-Oriented Architectures). To start an SCM web service, you require an authorization with the S_SERVICE authorization concept.
- SAP NetWeaver BW (see Chapter 10) is one of the main data sources for SAP SCM.
- SAP Web Dispatcher (see Chapter 14, Classic SAP-Middleware) assumes a critical role as a gateway for external network connections for SCM data communication with external systems.
- SAP Graphical User Interface (GUI) (see Chapter 28, User Interfaces) is the traditional user interface for SAP SCM; the web browser (see also Chapter 28) is the user interface for HTML access to SAP SCM, for example, when calling SCM data from the Internet.

While the application security for SAP SCM can be controlled using the traditional AS ABAP authorization concept, the technical security requires the configuration of a relatively complex framework of measures due to the networking of heterogeneous systems. SAP NetWeaver provides the necessary security technologies for this purpose.

*This chapter introduces you to procurement processes and describes Information Technology (IT) security concepts for SAP Supplier Relationship Management (SRM). It primarily focuses on the authorization concept.*

# 25 SAP Supplier Relationship Management

SAP SRM as an SAP Business Suite component is the SAP solution for purchasing and supplier management. Its goal is to optimize purchasing processes for goods, products, and services and map them securely in all areas of the organization. In this context, the requirements for central procurement management and decentralized organizational requirements are met.

Areas such as continuous procurement management (procure-to-pay), catalog management, strategic purchase and governance in purchasing processes, central contract management, collaboration scenarios, and supplier selection and management are mapped by various components that control the procurement processes separately and in combination with other SAP functions (SAP NetWeaver Business Warehouse (BW), for example) presenting varying commercial scenarios. SRM applications let you map business process scenarios, such as self-service procurement, direct/plan-driven procurement, strategic sourcing, catalog content management, services procurement, and global spend analysis.

## 25.1 Introduction and Functions

Expenditure and procurement process analyses, control measures, and compliance management are essential parts of the security measures in SAP SRM. Here, complex procurement processes and networks with suppliers and manufacturing companies are supported across different value levels to collaborate in continuous procurement processes. These processes include the determination of requirements in decentralized company areas and central awarding and payment processes in the source-to-pay process.

In combination with continuous transparency for supplier selection and contract design, improved supplier management and efficient purchase order handling present critical control instruments for cost control and reduction, for an optimized utilization of resources, and for a targeted improvement of effort and result with regard to external procurement capacities. So SAP SRM itself is a component for implementing corporate governance and effective risk control management in the company.

You can map and implement the following business scenarios using SAP SRM:

- **Self-Service Procurement**
  In this scenario, the employees themselves are responsible for creating and managing the respective ordering processes. The actual processes for purchase orders, incoming goods, and invoicing, however, are carried out in the back-end system.
- **Plan-Driven Procurement**
  This scenario supports the integration of external supplier systems into the procurement process of the SRM systems and the processing of external requirements.
- **Service Procurement**
  In this scenario, external services are procured according to structured service requirements, such as bid invitations.
- **Strategic Sourcing**
  This procurement scenario includes bid invitations, live auctions, and the SAP Bidding Engine component. The result of this process is then used to create the purchase order.
- **Contract Management**
  Contract Management enables you to structure, display, and search for discounts, contact hierarchies, central contacts, or sources of supply in an organized way.
- **Supplier Evaluation**
  Supplier Evaluation lets you manage supplier registrations, their master data, and their categorization, for example, according to quality or business conditions.
- **Catalog Content Management**
  This scenario supports the integration and management of product information with a connection to back-end systems, such as SAP NetWeaver MDM.
- **Analytics**
  Among other things, analytical functions include the monitoring and evaluation of supplier services or the evaluation of internal business tasks.
- **SAP Enterprise Buyer**
  SAP Enterprise Buyer is the central application for controlling the procurement process. SAP Enterprise Buyer enables you to create purchase orders directly in a standardized format using processes that are subject to internal automated controls.

## 25.2 Risks and Controls

Cost controls and continuous supplier management provide potential for improving business performance and results. Depending on the industry, production requirements, and relationships to external suppliers, who significantly affect the quality of your products, the selection of the necessary and appropriate security methods and solutions within SAP SRM depends on your requirements and the respective risk potential. The more procurement processes your production can influence, the more critical are the control and security measures for protecting the internal processes.

Because SAP SRM controls all of the purchasing processes in a company, its security is very important. Fraudulent activity can happen very easily in purchasing processes due to the lack of a segregation of duties. For example, fake supplier master data can be created in the system. They do not exist in real life and are fake companies that allow for fraud if control measures are not sufficient or authorizations are too extensive. From these companies, services (like cleaning services, for example) can be procured which can result in financial losses due to fake invoices.

The components of the Enterprise Risk Management (ERM) Navigation Control Map described in Section 25.4, Technical Security, are especially relevant for technical security. Table 25.1 lists additional risks and controls for SAP SRM as examples.

| No. | Classification | Description |
|---|---|---|
| 1. | Potential risk | Inadequate authorization concept:<br>Users of SAP SRM have authorizations that are too extensive for their actual requirements in terms of information and functions. Reasons for this can be historically grown authorization concepts whose authorization components are used only as a means of assigning functional authorizations and not as an effective instrument for controlling access and minimizing risks. In the case of SAP SRM, it means that the entire purchasing process of the company is involved. |
| | Impact | Users have greater authorizations than are necessary for their position and the scope of their work. This means that specific functional separations and control steps can't be carried out, enabling employees to perform fraudulent actions. |
| | Risk without control(s) | Extremely high |

**Table 25.1** Risks and Controls for SAP SRM

| No. | Classification | Description |
|---|---|---|
| | Control | The authorization concept has to take into account both organizational and functional requirements, and make administration simpler and more effective. The relevant risks have to be taken into account in the authorization design process, and methods of continuous management have to be integrated into the change management process. |
| | Risk with control(s) | Normal |
| | Section | 25.3 |
| 2. | Potential risk | Inadequate data protection for data communication processes:<br>SAP SRM supports numerous communication connections to SAP back-end systems via Remote Function Calls (RFCs) or to other communication partners via HTTP. In this context, incorrectly configured RFC connections or avoiding Secure Socket Layer (SSL) encryption are potential risks.<br>If RFC system users with authorizations that go beyond the necessary scope are used (for instance, when using SAP_ALL), an unnecessarily high potential risk exists. |
| | Impact | Due to inadequate data protection during data transfer, the system can be further compromised and data protection regulations can be violated. In addition, an RFC system user that has authorizations for all ABAP function groups or SAP_ALL can be used to create a new dialog user with extensive authorizations in the target system and to initiate unauthorized transactions or data access. Moreover, these excessive and unnecessary authorizations will be criticized in audits. |
| | Risk without control(s) | High |
| | Control | Correct configuration of RFC communication destinations and restriction of RFC system user authorizations to the minimum required. Before you use the trusted RFC connections, you should check to see if the associated risk is justified and whether sufficient compensating security measures are available. Moreover, SSL encryption should be used for data connections that transfer confidential information. |
| | Risk with control(s) | Normal |
| | Section | 25.4 |

**Table 25.1** Risks and Controls for SAP SRM (Cont.)

## 25.3 Application Security

For the main applications of SAP SRM — SAP Enterprise Buyer, SAP Supplier Management, and Catalog Content Management — the authorization concept for SAP SRM is based on the ABAP authorization concept that is described in great detail in Chapter 20, Authorizations in SAP ERP. For SAP SRM, the concept is mainly enhanced by internal controls, such as specific rules-based queries, that can be used to determine a manager for approving a list of goods ordered by an employee who's assigned to that manager as in the case of SAP Enterprise Buyer, for instance. When the ordering process is completed, the manager must approve the list of goods before it is forwarded to the purchasing group that belongs to the respective department and actually orders the goods from the business partner (supplier, for example). Configurable internal controls enable you to define order and approval limits so that you can monitor and administrate the ordering process. The rules-based queries are controlled by additional attributes that must be assigned to each business partner.

Information on business partners is critical master data for SAP SRM applications. Internal employees are also created as business partners, for example. In addition to normal user master data, they are assigned further attributes that are relevant to the purchasing process; this concept is described in more detail in this chapter later on. First, however, some important authorization objects for SAP SRM are discussed.

### 25.3.1 Important Authorizations

SAP provides SAP SRM with numerous standard roles for positions like employees, managers, purchasing assistants, purchasers, purchasing managers, or catalog managers. These roles can be evaluated for your organization. In contrast to other applications, the purchasing process is typically a rather standardized process, so you should use and customize the SAP standard roles in the SAP SRM environment.

#### Authorization Control for Document Types

To enable better control for access to important document types in the purchasing process, such as requests for quotations, POs, invoices, and so on, even at the organizational level, the Purchasing Organization (PORG), Responsible Purchasing Group (PGR), and Business Transaction authorization fields have been included in the authorization objects of SAP Enterprise Buyer. This not only enables you to define and restrict access to activities, but also to the listed organizational elements.

A purchaser in purchasing group PGR123 has been assigned the authorization object BBP_PD_PO (place purchase orders) via the role SAP_EC_BBP_PURCHASER. In addition to allowing for restrictions to CREATE, CHANGE, DISPLAY, PRINT, and DELETE activities for purchase orders, this also allows for restrictions to purchase orders of the PGR123 purchasing group, the purchasing organization, and the business transaction. A business transaction determines a commissioning process, for example.

The authorization objects described in Table 25.2 demonstrate restriction options using assigned authorization fields.

| Authorization Object | Authorization Field | Description |
|---|---|---|
| BBP_PD_AUC | Internet auction | This authorization object can be used for the Live Auction Cockpit to restrict the purchaser to such an extent that he can only set up and carry out auctions for specific purchasing organizations and groups. |
| BBP_PD_BID | Invitation to bid in an auction | This authorization object can be used for the Live Auction Cockpit and Bidding Engine to restrict the purchaser to such an extent that they can only invite specific business partners (bidders) that are assigned to a specific purchasing organization and group. |
| BBP_PD_CNF | Order confirmation | The purchasing organization and purchasing group are not checked. You can only restrict the permitted action. |
| BBP_PD_CTR | Contracts | The access rights of the purchaser for contracts can be assigned on the basis of controls or restricted using the organizational authorization fields mentioned. |
| BBP_PD_INV | Invoice entry | The purchasing organization and purchasing group are not checked. You can only restrict the permitted action. |
| BBP_PD_PO | Purchase order | With regard to raising purchase orders, the purchaser can be restricted to the purchasing organization and group. |

**Table 25.2** Authorization Objects in SAP SRM

| Authorization Object | Authorization Field | Description |
|---|---|---|
| BBP_PD_QUO | Quotations | This authorization object can be used to restrict the purchaser in such a way that they can only display, accept, and reject quotations for a specific purchasing organization and group. |
| BBP_PD_VL | List of vendors | This authorization object can be used to restrict the purchaser in such a way that they can only enter, display, and change the lists of suppliers of specific purchasing organizations and groups. |
| BBP_PD_SC | Shopping cart | This authorization object is used to control the creation, change, deletion, or printout of an employee's shopping cart. The organizational fields described are not checked in this context. On the other hand, the ownership rule does get checked. This means that an employee can only modify his own shopping cart. The only exception is an employee's substitute, who can be defined using the Requestor attribute. |

**Table 25.2** Authorization Objects in SAP SRM (Cont.)

### Controlling Authorizations for Displaying Purchasing Budgets

In certain cases, the permissions for purchasers to display purchasing budgets that are assigned to specific accounts must be restricted. The purchasing budgets are defined for specific objects (for example, goods) of an account. The BBP_BUDGET authorization object allows for authorization-technical control. This authorization object contains the following authorization fields, which can be complemented with additional values as required:

- **Activity**
  - 03: Display of the complete overview (via RFC connection to Controlling (CO) in SAP Enterprise Resource Planning (ERP)
  - 28: Display of the detailed chart of accounts via a report from SAP NetWeaver BW
- **Assigned account category**
  Selection of the assigned account category
- **Assigned account object**
  Selection of the assigned account object

### Controlling Authorizations for Modifying Purchasing Credit Card Master Data

To make the purchasing process as efficient as possible, certain authorized staff can be given purchasing credit cards for specific organizational groups or for a certain department. The M_BBP_PC authorization object can be used to control the access of the purchaser to the master data of the credit card for maintenance purposes. This authorization object contains the following authorization fields, which can be complemented with additional values for authorization control as required:

- PCINS
  Purchasing credit card organization
- PCNUM
  Purchasing credit card number
- PCBEGRU
  Purchasing credit card group (Purchasing credit cards can be assigned to specific groups. These groups can be used to restrict access to certain cards.)
- PCMAS_ACT
  Possible activities:
  - 01: Create
  - 02: Change
  - 03: Display
  - 04: Display list
  - 05: Delete

### Controlling Authorizations for Maintaining Purchasing Conditions

When considering potential business risks, keep in mind that the maintenance of purchasing conditions is a critical activity. Therefore, the authorizations for maintaining those conditions must be restricted. When restricting authorizations, you can also define which types of contracts can be accessed. In SAP SRM, this is done using the /SAPCND/CM authorization object that belongs to the cross-application authorization objects. This authorization object contains the following authorization fields, which can be complemented with additional values as required:

- **Activity**
  - 01: Create
  - 02: Change
  - 03: Display

- `/SAPCND/AP`
  Because the object is a generic object, the application component for which it is to be applied must be selected here.
- `/SAPCND/US`
  This is the contract conditions method. The maintenance can be restricted to specific methods for determining contract conditions, such as price determination.
- `/SAPCND/CT`
  This is the contract conditions table. The maintenance can be restricted to specific contract conditions tables, such as the control indicator.
- `/SAPCND/TY`
  This is the contract conditions type. The maintenance can be restricted to specific contract conditions types, such as the contract price.

### Controlling Authorizations for the Product Master Data Maintenance

SAP SRM contains several authorization objects for product master data maintenance. The `COM_PRD` authorization object controls if a user who carries out master data management tasks is generally authorized to maintain product master data and, if so, with which activities. Therefore, the relevant authorization field is one of the following:

- **Activity**
  - 01: Create
  - 02: Change
  - 03: Display
  - 06: Delete

The `COM_ASET` authorization object controls whether a user (typically a purchaser) is authorized to maintain product set types or if the user can only display them. Therefore, the only authorization fields available are the following:

- **Activity**
  - 01: Create
  - 02: Change
  - 03: Display
  - 06: Delete

To restrict the product master data maintenance the /SAPCND/CM authorization object must be defined as follows:

- **Activity**
  - 01: Create
  - 02: Change
- /SAPCND/AP
  - BBP
- /SAPCND/US
  - PR
- /SAPCND/CT
  - SAP001, SAP118
- /SAPCND/TY
  - 01PV

### Special Authorization Exceptions

Typically, the S_TCODE authorization object controls the authorization for calling a specific transaction. There are some exceptions in SAP Enterprise Buyer, for example, for transactions that are called using the BBP_FUNCT authorization object. Examples include:

- CR_COMPANY
  Create a new business partner
- MON_ALERTS
  Use monitoring functions
- CR_ASSETS
  Create asset master data
- BE_F4_HELP
  Call a help function
- EVAL_VEND
  Evaluate vendors
- GLOB_ACCSS
  Authorization for confirming purchase orders raised by other users

### Controlling Authorizations for Maintaining Business Partners

The BBP_FUNCT, PLOG, and B_BUPA_RLT authorization objects are relevant to the maintenance of business partners. The BBP_FUNCT authorization object must have the value CR_COMPANY, which means that the user is generally authorized to create business partners. The PLOG personnel planning object from the HR authorization class, which controls checks related to personnel planning and organizational structures, must be assigned the following values:

- PPFCODE
  This field controls the activities a user can execute regarding information types. The possible values are defined in Table T77FC. The value must be set to DISP, which stands for "display."
- PLVAR
  This field specifies which plan version a user is granted access to. The value must be set to 01.
- OTYPE
  This field defines the object type a user has access to. The object type must be set to US and O.
- INFOTYP
  This field specifies which infotypes in SAP ERP HCM a user is granted access to. They can be set to 1000, 1222, 1001, 5500, 5501, 5502, and 5503.
- SUBTYP
  This field determines the subtypes of the defined infotypes a user has access to. A subtype specifically defines the relationships to Infotype 1001. This means that the values 0020, A490, 0200, and A002 must be set.

The B_BUPA_RLT authorization object is used to define which roles can be edited for business partners. For instance, Bidder can be a possible role. This authorization object contains the following authorization fields that can be complemented with additional values, as required:

- **Activity**
  - 01: Create
  - 02: Change
  - 03: Display
- BP_ROLE
  This is the role of the business partner that can be maintained. The following business partners are possible: general business partner, vendor, bidder, component supplier, plant, purchasing organization, service provider, contact person, prospect, employee, organizational unit, Internet user, marketplace supplier, marketplace customer, or financial service provider.

#### Controlling Authorizations for Bidders Regarding Requests for Quotation (RFQs) and Auctions

In SAP Enterprise Buyer, a purchaser can initiate RFQs by using the bidding engine. When doing so, the purchaser can invite selected suppliers to submit a bid, which can be submitted via the web application contained in SAP Enterprise Buyer. Another option for this is to use the Live Auction Cockpit for running an online auction over a certain period of time. In this case, many bidders are simultaneously logged on and submit their pricing offers online. This way, the purchaser can quickly and efficiently determine the best price offer from all bidders.

The authorizations for bidders can also be complemented with specific values. This is important if a supplier wants to have different bidder roles like, for example, the trader who is authorized to negotiate prices and the salesperson who must eventually confirm the bid. The authorization object responsible for this is the BBP_VEND object, which controls the vendor activities. This authorization object can be used to define the following bidder rights:

- Creation of confirmations, such as bid confirmations
- Creation of invoices upon delivery of ordered goods or services
- Submission of bids for an RFQ or the auction

This authorization object contains the following authorization fields that can be complemented with additional values, as required:

- **Activity**
  - 01: Create
  - 02: Change
  - 03: Display
  - 06: Delete
- BBP_OBJTYPE
  This is the document type that can have the following values:
  - BUS2203: Confirmation
  - BUS2205: Invoice
  - BUS2202: Quotation

### Controlling Authorizations for Employees of a Supplier

If SAP Supplier Management is used, which is not necessarily required for SAP SRM, employees of a supplier (business partner) can also process purchase orders, create order confirmations, and carry out other activities through this web-based application. You can also limit the scope of action of the employees of the business partner to certain activities. This is particularly important if the supplier has a large sales organization.

The authorization control is handled by the BBP_SUS_PD authorization object, which contains the following authorization fields that can be assigned the relevant values:

- BBP_OBJTYP
  This is the object type with the possible values:
  - BUS2230: Purchase order
  - BUS2231: Delivery note
  - BUS2232: Order confirmation
  - BUS2233: Confirmation (For confirmations, an additional check is performed against the BBP_FUNCT authorization object with the value GLOB_ACCSS if a user wants to globally confirm all purchase orders that were sent to the business partner.)
  - BUS2234: Invoice
  - BUS2235: Message
- **Activity**
  - 02: Create, change
  - 03: Display
  - 09: Display price (at time of purchase order)

### 25.3.2 Rules-Based Security Checks Using Business Partner Attributes

As noted, in SAP SRM, the underlying ABAP authorization concept is enhanced by specifically programmed, rules-based security queries. The security queries are used on the basis of additional, defined business partner attributes, in particular for release workflows for purchase orders. The business partner attributes are assigned to both internal employees and external suppliers who are both referred to as "business partners" in SAP SRM. A department is also a business partner that must be assigned attributes as well.

The business partner attributes are assigned to the individual business partners by means of an organizational structure that must be specifically defined. Figure 25.1 shows an example of such an organizational structure. There are actually two types of organizational structures: there is the organizational structure of internal business partners with all areas and departments, including the purchasing organization, and there is the external structure that includes all kinds of suppliers. The attributes can be assigned to the departments. If they are, they apply to all employees of a corresponding department, including any additional personal information.

Each department must be assigned a manager. The attributes can also be used to control which purchasing group is responsible for which department. This means, for instance, that purchase orders created in a department must always be processed by the responsible purchasing group. SAP SRM can't function without such an organizational structure. The following transactions are used to create the organizational structure:

- **PPOCA_BBP**
  Initial creation of the organizational plan
- **PPOMA_BBP**
  Changing and maintaining the organizational structure

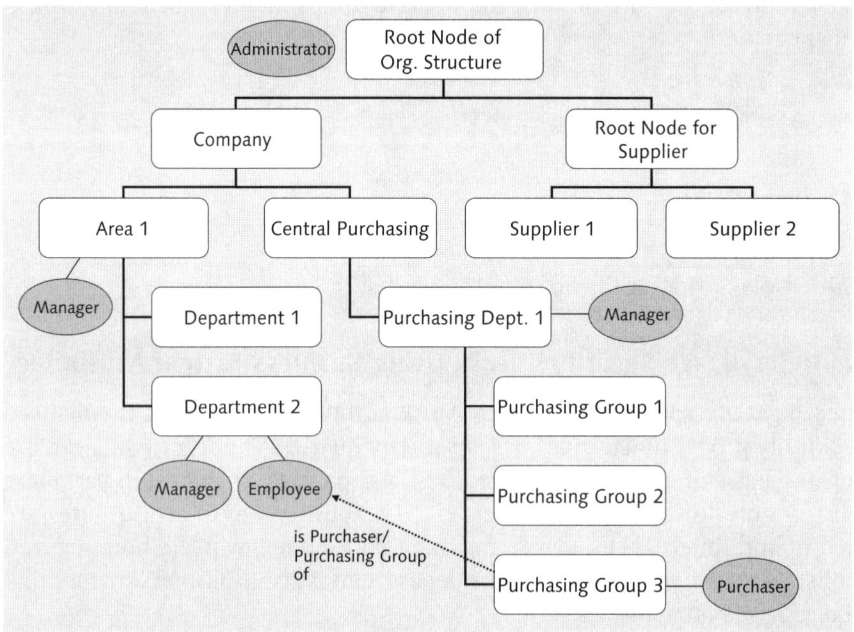


**Figure 25.1** Organizational Structure for SAP SRM

If an internal organizational structure is already available, it can be adopted by an SAP ERP HCM organizational structure; you can also define a new structure that reflects your supplier structure.

Because the business partner attributes are used to run specific security queries, each user must be created as a business partner within SAP SRM, because a regular SU01 user is not sufficient for the use of SAP Enterprise Buyer. Table 25.3 contains important business partner attributes that are used to run rules-based security queries for the release workflow.

| Attribute | Name | Description |
|---|---|---|
| APPRV_LIM | Approval limit | The approval limit presents the total value of a shopping cart ordered by an employee that a responsible user (typically a manager) can approve. |
| BUK | Company code | The company code in the back-end system. Usually, the user inherits the company code from his area or organizational group. The company code in the back-end system determines the company code for which a user can make purchases. The inheritance will be neutralized if a value is specified. |
| CAT | Catalog ID | The catalog ID specifies the goods catalogs from which a user can place purchase orders. |
| CNT | Cost center | This attribute defines the cost center in the back-end system. A user can only place orders for his own cost center. |
| LAG | Storage location | This attribute defines an organizational unit that enables the user to distinguish between different material stocks within the same plant. |
| PM_IPHAS | Phase | Phases divide the lifecycle of an order into several stages (for example, opened and released), and they determine which activities a user is allowed to perform for the order at a certain stage. This attribute is used for selecting orders in the ERP back-end system and is mandatory. |
| PRCAT | Material group | This attribute defines the product categories for which a user has authorizations. It is advisable to define a default value, for instance, if a user only orders office equipment. In that case, the product category should be restricted to Office Equipment. |
| REQUESTER | Requester | This attribute specifies for which organizational units or users the employee is authorized to create shopping carts. A user can select all users of an organizational unit as deviating requesters if the attribute is maintained, for instance, with the entry O 50000019. |

**Table 25.3** Important Business Partner Attributes for Rules-Based Security Queries

| Attribute | Name | Description |
| --- | --- | --- |
| | | If a specific user is to be selected as a requester, the attribute must be maintained as follows: <US><User ID of deviating requester>, for example, USMANAGER22. This attribute must also be maintained for the use of the Purchase as Substitute application. For example, you can specify all employees for whom an assistant is authorized to make purchases. |
| RESP_PRGRP | Responsible purchasing group | This attribute specifies the number of the purchasing group that is responsible for the organizational unit. |
| ROLE | Role (technical ABAP role) | This attribute specifies the role of the user, such as manager, employee, or purchasing assistant. If no approval workflow is used for new users, a default value must be set for the ROLE attribute, for example, SAP_EC_BBP_EMPLOYEE. (If no default value is found, the approval workflow is automatically activated.) |
| SLAPPROVER | Spending limit approver | This attribute specifies the approver used for the approval workflow when the spending limit is exceeded. |
| SPEND_LIM | Spending limit | This attribute defines the value up to which a user can make expenditures. If the value is exceeded, a workflow starts for approving the spending limit. |
| TEND_TYPE | Transaction type: RFQ | This attribute specifies the transaction type for automatically created RFQs, for example, in SAP Product Lifecycle Management (PLM) (collaborative engineering). The attribute must be defined for the purchasing group that is responsible for the organizational unit of the entry channel. The value of this attribute can be inherited. For example, purchasing groups can inherit it from their purchasing organization. |
| TOG | Tolerance group | This attribute defines the tolerance group. This attribute can be used for a user group to define tolerance checks if the quantity or tolerance values for deliveries or invoices have been exceeded. |

**Table 25.3** Important Business Partner Attributes for Rules-Based Security Queries (Cont.)

The approval workflow must be activated as an internal control in Customizing so that the rules-based security queries for the workflow are actually carried out.

### 25.3.3 User Management

Because users are treated as business partners with additional attributes in SAP SRM applications, the user management concepts that are based on Transactions SU01 and PFCG cannot be used without additional enhancements. For example, the web-based application should be used for creating internal SAP Enterprise Buyer users, because it saves the newly created user as a business partner because the user is assigned to a corresponding organizational unit in this case.

That would be the ideal way if an administrator created the users. The administrator would also be able to convert existing SU01 users into business partners by using Transaction USERS_GEN. In that case, the attributes are assigned to the respective organizational unit using Transaction USERS_GEN, and can then be controlled. However, implementing the information ownership principle is not possible here, which means the best-practice method in this case would be to activate the Employee Self-Service (ESS). This self-service must also be activated for external business partners, such as bidders.

In both cases, the user logs on to the SAP Enterprise Buyer application and requests a user ID, including the defined role (for example, employee or bidder). The user can also assign himself to an organizational unit. This action triggers an approval workflow that serves as a control instrument. For an employee, the responsible manager then receives a request to provide the approval via the workflow. For an external business partner, this request is sent to the responsible purchasing group. The roles can be defined upfront for each user so that it is impossible to assign additional roles at a later stage, and an accumulation of functions can be avoided.

Connecting the SRM server to a Central User Administration (CUA) or to SAP NetWeaver Identity Management (IdM) with a corresponding organizational structure according to the SAP ERP HCM concept is not recommended. The reason for this can be found in the SAP SRM business partner principle, the additional attributes of which are not mapped in the HCM organizational structure. In this case, a complex conversion of the HCM infotypes would be necessary. Alternatively, it is possible to connect the SRM server to a Central User Administration, but to permit the user maintenance in the SRM subsystem. The only benefit of this scenario, however, would be that the created SRM business partners would also be available as SU01 users in the CUA system.

## 25.4 Technical Security

SAP SRM is a standalone application within SAP Business Suite. However, it only achieves its business goals if it is linked to SAP back-end systems and to external non-SAP applications (for example, of suppliers) via network connections. The risks and technical security environment for SAP SRM are based on these conditions.

### 25.4.1 Security Environment Based on SAP NetWeaver

The applications contained in SAP SRM are based on the SAP NetWeaver technology platform. SAP SRM contains different predesigned implementation scenarios that can be customized according to specific customer requirements. The technical risks and controls described for the components that are relevant in these scenarios can also be applied to SAP SRM. For the self-service procurement, plan-driven procurement, service procurement, and strategic sourcing scenarios, the following components are relevant:

- SAP NetWeaver AS (see Chapter 9, SAP NetWeaver Application Server) is the technical platform SAP SRM is based on and supports the security functions for data communication in the internal network or via the Internet, using SNC or SSL. The categorization of SAP SRM to a SSO environment using SAP logon tickets is also supported.
- In addition to the SAP ERP back-end system, SAP NetWeaver BW (see Chapter 10, SAP NetWeaver Business Warehouse) is one of the main data sources. Data communication is enabled via RFCs, for example.
- SAP NetWeaver Process Integration (PI) (see Chapter 12, SAP NetWeaver Process Integration) is the middleware component for integrating with SAP or non-SAP systems and also supports the SAP SRM security environment.
- SAP Web Dispatcher (see Chapter 14, Classic SAP Middleware) assumes a critical role as a gateway for external network connections for SRM data communication with external systems and as the first line of defense in the demilitarized zone (DMZ) network segment.
- SAP NetWeaver Portal (see Chapter 16, SAP NetWeaver Portal) is the platform for integration with the Internet and internal HTML access. It also supports integration with an SSO environment using SAP logon tickets and SSL data communication.
- The web browser (see Chapter 28, Section 28.2, Web Browser) is the user interface for HTML access to SAP SRM, for example, when calling data via the Internet. Web browsers support SSL encryption for all types of HTTP communication.

For the Catalog Content Management and Spend Analysis scenarios, you should consider the risks and controls of the following components:

- SAP NetWeaver AS (see Chapter 9)
- SAP NetWeaver BW (see Chapter 10)
- SAP Web Dispatcher (see Chapter 14)
- SAP NetWeaver Portal (see Chapter 16)
- Web browser (see Chapter 28)

For SAP SRM, enterprise services (web services) are also available, for example, for sourcing, service procurement, and contract management. The information security and risk management aspects for enterprise services were already discussed in the context of components that support service-oriented architectures (SOAs) and web service security (see Chapter 7, Web Services, Enterprise Services, and Service-Oriented Architectures). You must also take into account the risks and controls for SAP NetWeaver AS (see Chapter 9) and SAP NetWeaver PI (see Chapter 12).

### 25.4.2 Security Environment for RFC Communication

SAP SRM requires internal and external network connections to partner systems. Connections to other SAP systems (for example, to back-end systems) are usually of the RFC type. The resulting security risks must be considered in a concept involving the corresponding countermeasures. In this context, you must use the technical default settings, like SNC encryption and authorization restrictions, for system users of RFC connections from Chapter 9 and the respective control measures from Table 25.1. In particular, RFC user authorizations for the authorization object `S_RFC`, whose scope is set too wide, can be used to compromise the system even if the RFC user only has the SAP user type System User or Communications User.

In combination with AS ABAP, SAP SRM also provides a function for using a trusted RFC connection to another SAP system. If the connection is not secured appropriately, this option entails a very high risk, because this RFC type doesn't require a password to authenticate the RFC system user. This means that the target system provides implicit trust for the identity of the RFC user. This situation is comparable to SSO. The SSO, however, uses initial authentication. But this also has the benefit that no password information needs to be transferred via the network. This concept of a trusted RFC connection is not mandatory, and the traditional RFC connection using password authentication still applies.

But if trusted RFC is used, the risk management should include the following measures:

- To ensure that no unauthorized user can use the trusted RFC connection, the authorization of the system user should leave the RFC_USER field blank in the S_RFCACL authorization object (input: ' ') (see also Chapter 9, SAP SAP NetWeaver Application Server).
- The systems connected via RFC must be located in the same network segment. This architecture avoids additional risks that result from communications across network boundaries.
- The systems must meet identical security requirements and be configured according to the same well-defined security concept. This also applies to users and RFC system users. This means that both systems have the same level of security, and users of the source system might have access to the target system anyway. This emphasizes that the purpose of a trusted connection is to actually increase the effectiveness of the communication of these two systems, because the RFC system user is not subject to authentication.

While application security for SAP SRM can be mainly controlled using the traditional AS ABAP authorization concept, technical security must consider a multitude of risks due to networking with heterogeneous systems. SAP NetWeaver provides the necessary security technologies for this purpose.

*This chapter discusses the industry-specific solution portfolios of SAP. Different security aspects of the SAP solutions are taken into account as examples of internal and external security.*

# 26 Industry-Specific SAP Solution Portfolios

SAP company software can be used flexibly and universally in many areas. Due to industry-specific requirements, however, some industrial sectors require special solutions that are tailored to the requirements of their respective departments. Over the years, SAP has enhanced its core products with industry-specific solution portfolios, which have found broad market acceptance (see Figure 26.1).

These solutions that are based on SAP NetWeaver, must deal with special threat scenarios.

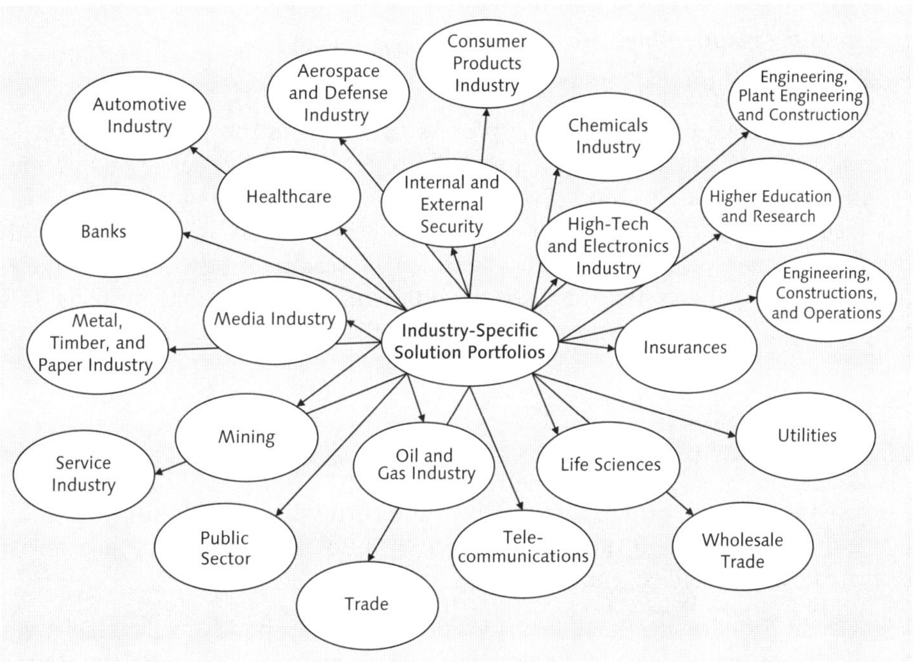


**Figure 26.1** Industry-Specific SAP Solution Portfolios

## 26.1 Introduction and Functions

Apart from general threats and universally valid risk characteristics, there are special instances that occur for every company and organization. In the energy sector, the risks that must be considered are different than those of a financial institution or a trading company. The legal standards also vary greatly in some areas, so risk management must always consider industry-specific needs.

The SAP solutions for the utilities industry, for example, were designed specifically with regard to water and energy applications. With these solutions, the special requirements for gas, water, power, and waste disposal companies of any size can obtain Information Technology (IT) support. A special feature of these solutions is primarily the high integration need of Enterprise Resource Planning (ERP) back-end, web front end, and other SAP systems like SAP NetWeaver Business Warehouse (BW) and SAP ERP HCM up to functionality with mobile scenarios. The following objects can be exchanged during data exchange between SAP Customer Relationship Management (CRM) and the back-end system of an industry solution:

- Business partner contacts (adapter object `SI_BCONTACT`)
- Connection objects/points of consumption (adapter object `SI_CONNOBJ`)
- Contracts (adapter object `SI_CONTRACT`)
- Reporting points (adapter object `SI_POD`)

Integrating mobile devices with the process chains poses the same challenges as for risk management. Apart from physically securing mobile devices and application security with back-end system roles, the SAP Solutions for Mobile Business require synchronization and replication scenarios that are integrated with the security concept. Here, you must consider the security aspects for authentication via trustworthy systems. Due to the different applications and systems, this results in different authorization models that make a holistic SAP security concept indispensable.

## 26.2 Risks and Controls

Because this chapter cannot discuss all of the currently available industry solutions, the following text describes the SAP solutions for internal and external security (SAP for Defense and Security).

With its SAP for Defense and Security solution, SAP responds to the challenges faced by both the police and global relief organizations. Growing threats, terror risks, increased international integration, and global deployment scenarios require an improved synchronization of information and faster decision support. SAP for Defense and Security is the standard SAP solution for deployment planning, maintenance, and materials management and for personnel management, accounting, and the logistic support of mobile units. Despite the requirement of a high degree of standardization, the SAP solution is sufficiently flexible to map the transformations that many armed forces experience today.

Like other solutions, solutions for internal and external security must comply with industry-specific and legal requirements with regard to IT security. However, in contrast to the private sector, the correct implementation of those requirements not only involves material assets, but sometimes even human life or issues of national defense. This results in an enormously high need for protection of the defense-relevant processes and the supporting IT systems.

The high need for protection entails problems that can't be solved by merely using solutions that are freely available on the market. Whereas procurement and approval processes in the private sector are primarily price-oriented, these military processes are also defined by other characteristics, such as branch of service, rank, material category, and (organizational) unit. The procurement processes result in the purchase of hand grenades or life jackets. This means that in terms of both data and strategic considerations, the risk potential is very high.

Another area of concern is asynchronous data storage. As military units can be deployed worldwide, additional risks result from the mobile nature of those deployments. The SAP systems of the mobile systems on a ship or submarine are not continuously connected to a central system. Therefore, specific functions must be carried out in offline mode, which places additional demands on the technical security of the synchronization, the chronological process, and the authorizations to synchronize purchase order lists that have been created offline, for example.

Authentication represents another risk: How, for example, can you ascertain the identity of a commander in offline mode? Because a large quantity of military data and processes is subject to a high degree of confidentiality, the data and processes must be protected — in times of peace and during a war. In a state of defense, mobile devices that contain highly confidential data can fall into the hands of the enemy. For this reason, special requirements exist regarding the storage and transfer of information.

In the following table, the primary focus is on two specific types of risk out of the many additional possible risks (see Table 26.1).

| No. | Classification | Description |
|---|---|---|
| 1. | Risk potential | Support scenarios in the military area:<br>Usually an SAP customer operates a dedicated communications line to transfer error messages to SAP, or to browse through the SAP Notes in the SAP Service Marketplace. SAP employees use this line for issue handling. The customer's SAP Solution Manager also uses this line; for example, to send messages or EarlyWatch data to SAP. |
| | Impact | It is possible that military information is transferred and compromised unintentionally. Moreover, the customer systems can be manipulated. |
| | Risk without control(s) | Extremely high |
| | Control | From a military point of view, the functions mentioned must be separated because the access directions can change, the protocols are not uniform, and logging must be separated according to different activities. Specific qualification criteria must be defined for employees of service organizations. |
| | Risk with control(s) | Normal |
| | Section | 26.3.1 |
| 2. | Risk potential | Deployment scenarios:<br>Employees of armed organizations who are deployed in mobile units are assigned to different organizational structures depending on the type of deployment.<br>Authorizations, technical assignments in SAP systems, and other components must be changed according to the deployment scenarios. Because changes in the systems must be taken care of quickly and be carried out within hours in these situations, the standard SAP tools for role changes do not suffice. |
| | Impact | Employees of unit A move to unit B and must be organizationally assigned there. If the activities, including all those that go along with detailed authorization assignment, can't be carried out immediately, serious consequences during the deployment may result. The system may no longer provide optimal support or any technical support at all. Depending on the type of deployment, national and international interests and those of personal security can be at stake. |

**Table 26.1** Risks and Controls for SAP for Defense and Security

| No. | Classification | Description |
|---|---|---|
| | Risk without control(s) | High |
| | Control | The authorization concepts have been extended by an industry-specific solution to meet the requirements. Authorizations are managed via SAP Role Manager. The immediate and efficient processing of entire organizational units is thus ensured. |
| | Risk with control(s) | Low |
| | Section | 26.3.2 |

**Table 26.1** Risks and Controls for SAP for Defense and Security (Cont.)

## 26.3 Application Security

In addition to the role concept and all of the authorization concepts described in Chapter 20, Authorizations in SAP ERP, there are a few more advanced authorization solutions available. We will describe two of them in this chapter: SAP MaxSecure and SAP Role Manager.

### 26.3.1 SAP MaxSecure Support

Functional separations are required, which are supposed to ensure the integrity and protection of data with highly confidential military or defense-related content with regard to the support accesses listed in Table 26.2. The critical aspects of these types of access are as follows:

- The possibility of an unauthorized, unintentional transfer of data (❶)
- The possibility of an intended data transfer (❷), and in doing so, compromising the data (❸)

| No. | Access | Direction | Dialog |
|---|---|---|---|
| ❶ | SAP Service Marketplace | Customer network → SAP network | No |
| ❷ | Maintenance (SAP Graphical User Interface (GUI) | SAP network → customer network | Yes |
| ❸ | Maintenance (operating system access) | SAP network → customer network | Yes |

**Table 26.2** Types of Access in SAP Support

Control measures for secure authorization (❷) and authentication (❸) provide protection in this respect. However, in national defense organizations, these controls are not always sufficient. Therefore, the accesses are not approved. And company policies prohibit remote access by external employees.

For customers with such an increased need for security, SAP offers SAPMaxSecure Support within the scope of SAP Active Global Support. This support contract is also used in other industries. SAP MaxSecure Support is a specific type of support with additional protective measures. Based on a threat analysis and a customer's need for protection, supplemental technical measures can be added to the standard SAP support link to help considerably reduce existing risks.

For example, in addition to the standard controls used in the relationship between customer and SAP, the tools, protocols, and system levels of the accesses can be defined. A terminal server is responsible for the controls. The SAP employee is granted access via ICA client or pnAgent and can only access the applications published by the customer. The redirection through the terminal server allows for an additional, parallel live observation of the activities, which is also referred to as a shadow session, and a session recording when preserving evidence. The shadow session ensures that legal requirements are adhered to.

The use of encapsulated front-end PCs represents another means of control. This method accounts for the physical separation of the SAP network and the customer's network. However, this control action is rather complex. Although it positively affects security, it also negatively affects support. In high-security environments, these measures represent an important control option that is mandated by internal policies and legal requirements.

When support is needed, an SAP employee takes care of the relevant device, which, if necessary, is located in a specially secured room. The employee opens a terminal session and obtains the tools provided by the customer for a secure logon procedure. Here, the encapsulated system does not allow data to be printed, buffered, or transferred to other media (for instance, a USB flash drive) at the front end. This means that the customer can exert a high degree of control over the support employees who work remotely. If the front-end capsule is considered as a component of the customer network, the support employee de facto belongs to the customer and is thus controlled by them.

### 26.3.2 SAP Role Manager

SAP Role Manager (see Figure 26.2) is another industry solution tool used to assign roles and authorizations to users who are assigned to an organizational structure consisting of structural elements. SAP Role Manager can be used to reassign users, including their authorizations, from one organizational unit to another, in an individual or mass procedure. The call is carried out via Transaction Role Manager (/ISDFPS/ROLE_MANAGER). SAP Role Manager uses reference roles.

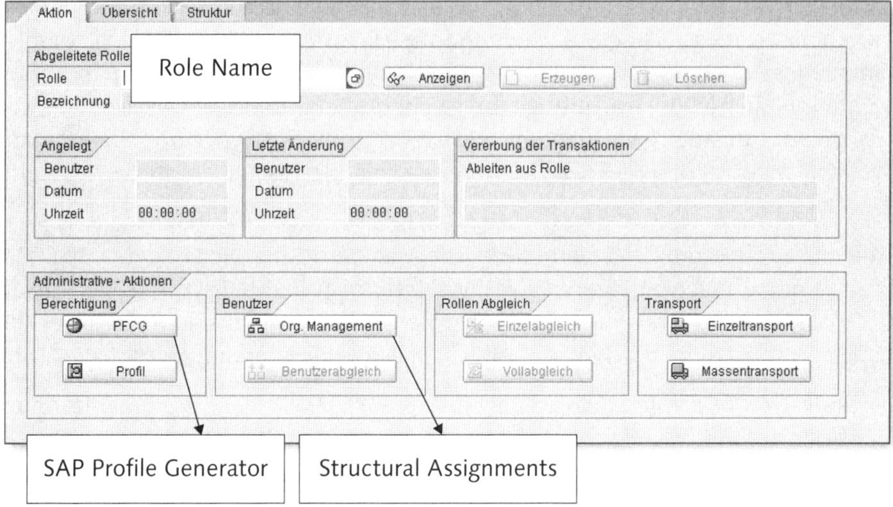


**Figure 26.2** SAP Role Manager

The following tasks can be carried out using SAP Role Manager:

- Defining reference roles
- Deriving roles from reference roles and assigning them to the different users
- Determining authorization values for the relevant organizational-level fields
- Generating authorization profiles
- Addressing the direct navigation to the SAP user administration applications that are relevant to these actions
- Automating the authorization update process using batch jobs

It is necessary to update existing authorizations if the properties or assignments of an organizational structural element are changed.

As described in Chapter 21, SAP ERP Human Capital Management and Data Protection, roles can be assigned indirectly via the HCM organizational structure. These indirect role assignments require the mapping of a corresponding organizational structure in the relevant SAP system. We can distinguish between two different cases:

- A user is assigned the roles that are assigned to the respective person or position, to the superordinate organizational structural element, or to other superordinate organizational objects. The relationship of the role and the assignment object is generated in the SAP Profile Generator.

- A user can be assigned a derived role through the assigned position. SAP Role Manager can be used to assign a role that has been derived from a reference role to a position. Using a Business Add-In (BAdI), the derived role is complemented with values for specific organizational-level fields that are determined via the higher-level structural element. The initial authorization assignment is carried out manually via SAP Role Manager. Updates are performed automatically by the system if SAP Role Manager is scheduled as a job in the corresponding system.

A reference role can be created in SAP Role Manager using the Overview tab. The required name must be entered for the reference role. Then you must click on the Create button to create the reference role. Finally, you must save the role. The Change button can be used to perform changes to the reference roles.

The derivation of a role is stored in Table `/ISDFPS/AGR_DEF`. The organizational level fields are determined for the role and written into Table `AGR_1252`. The creation and assignment of a derived role is carried out via the Action tab in SAP Role Manager. Once you have entered the required name for the derived role, you must click on the Generate button. In the subsequent step, the link between the role and the position is defined through the Create Assignment action. The SAP system then synchronizes the organizational-level fields. The synchronization of the indirect user assignment must be done manually.

The Action and Overview tabs in SAP Role Manager are used to perform further administrative steps. It is possible to navigate to the standard applications of the SAP Profile Generator, for example. Table 26.3 lists the functions and the calls they perform.

| Function | Call |
|---|---|
| PFCG | Roles |
| Profile | Authorizations |
| Org. Management | User assignments |
| User synchronization | User synchronization |
| Individual synchronization | Role synchronization |
| Full synchronization | Role synchronization |
| Individual transport | Transport |
| Mass transport | Transport |

**Table 26.3** Sample Standard Calls in SAP Role Manager

In an individual synchronization, a derived role is synchronized with its reference role. As a result, it adopts all authorization fields from the reference role. The organizational-level fields are not adopted from the reference role. A full synchronization is necessary when the reference role is changed, provided the change should be transferred onto the derived roles. The necessary synchronization of the organizational-level fields is carried out automatically in that case.

To perform necessary role changes in SAP Role Manager, you must select the Overview tab. If the role is a reference role, the system displays all of the roles that have been derived from that role. Changes to a role don't take effect until the respective user logs on to the system again. Changes to an authorization profile are immediately active, but the current transaction must be restarted.

As in the SAP Profile Generator, here traffic lights indicate the status of maintenance actions. Structural assignments of individual derivations to different structural elements (for example, positions) can be controlled via the Org. Management function. If the indirect user assignment (to the authorization roles via the organizational structure) step is performed correctly, the traffic light turns green. To do this, you must use the synchronization functions.

SAP Role Manager assigns the derivation role to an object in the HCM organizational structure to fill the organizational levels of the new derivation that are still empty. The role synchronization then initiates the import of the new auxiliary organizational information for the selected derivation roles. The new structural organizational data originates from different tables that can be addressed using various transactions, such as `/ISDFPS/LS`. The display transactions are `/ISDFPS/TOEACC2`, for organizational elements used to control the cost centers in Accounting, and `/ISDFPS/TOELOG2`, which is used to control the supply relationships in Logistics.

The industry-specific SAP solution portfolios provide a multitude of additional tools that can be used to implement targeted security and control measures, which, in combination with the existing standard solutions, improve the comprehensive internal control structure.

## 26.4 Technical Security

For the evaluation of technical security risks and controls for the industry-specific SAP solution portfolios, the following components must be considered among others:

- SAP NetWeaver Application Server (AS) (see Chapter 9, SAP NetWeaver Application Server)

- SAP NetWeaver Process Integration (PI) (see Chapter 12, SAP NetWeaver Process Integration)
- SAP Internet Transaction Server (ITS) (see Chapter 14, Classic SAP Middleware)
- SAP NetWeaver Portal (see Chapter 16, SAP NetWeaver Portal)
- SAP NetWeaver Mobile (see Chapter 17, SAP NetWeaver Mobile)
- SAP Graphical User Interface (GUI) (see Chapter 28, User Interfaces)
- Web browser (see Chapter 28)

The technical controls described for these components can also be used without limitation for SAP industry solutions applications.

*Database servers are central instances for storing and accessing data. For that reason, database servers are also preferred targets of hacker attacks and must therefore be considered in data security and risk management.*

# 27 Database Server

SAP systems store data in numerous database tables. Their database server is the central storage area for all business data, HR master data, customizing settings, security and authorization configurations, user master data, data dictionary descriptions, and so on. Because databases often contain information that needs to be kept confidential, such as HR data, you usually have to adhere to external legal data protection regulations.

## 27.1 Introduction and Functions

From a technical viewpoint, the database can be implemented in one of two ways. In the first option, it can be implemented on a central database server. Each SAP system would be connected to the central database server and receive its own database instance. In the second option, each SAP system would have its own database on its own database instance.

The advantage of a central database instance is the ability to centralize management of the database more easily. Easier management includes design, backup, and monitoring functions and security management, for example. This approach also allows for a physical separation of the SAP NetWeaver Application Server (AS) and the database, which corresponds to a separation of application logic and data storage. This approach can raise the level of security, because the database server is assigned to a separate, protected network segment.

Most of the manufacturers provide database systems for different operating systems. Basically, this leads to two general aspects that need to be considered for the risk management of database systems: The security concept must include the database itself and the database server, including its operating system. This leads to different complex security configurations, which, however, follow a general rule: As the central data storage locations, database systems must always be available and be able to process data queries or data entries as quickly as possible; in addition, database access must be strictly restricted and controlled so that access is only granted when absolutely necessary. Also, data transfer at the network level to and from the database must be protected against unauthorized access.

Meeting these requirements makes risk analyses and security concepts necessary at all levels of the Open Systems Interconnection (OSI) reference model (see Chapter 5, IT Security). The specific risks and security aspects depend on the database system (manufacturer), operating system, network, applications with database access, external access (Internet), access of database and system administrators, and so on. For this reason, this chapter examines only the basic security principles that apply for the diverse security aspects of database servers.

## 27.2 Risks and Controls

In this section, we'll use a simplified version of the risk analysis methodology described in Chapter 1, Risk and Control Management, to identify the main security-critical risks and the necessary controls for the database server (see Table 27.1). The controls are then discussed in more detail in the following sections and are illustrated using examples.

| No. | Classification | Description |
|---|---|---|
| 1. | Potential risk | Access to database resources has not been restricted:<br>Access rights to important database resources for users of the database server's operating system have not been restricted. |
| | Impact | Security controls within the database management system could be bypassed if access restrictions to database resources are insufficient. Such a situation can compromise the integrity of the database. Unauthorized access that manipulates database tables is also possible. |
| | Risk without control(s) | Extremely high |
| | Control | Access rights for users of the database server's operating system must be limited to the necessary minimum. |
| | Risk with control(s) | Normal |
| | Section | 27.3 |
| 2. | Potential risk | No password change:<br>The passwords for default database users that are used by systems to access the database were not changed or not set. |

**Table 27.1** Risks and Controls for the Database Server

| No. | Classification | Description |
| --- | --- | --- |
| | Impact | If the default passwords are not changed, the database management system and OBDC or JDBC can be used to connect unauthorized to the database. Because standard database users usually have administrator rights and must have them, for example, in SAP systems, users can view and modify tables and objects without authorization. In addition, unauthorized SQL procedures can be installed and executed. They could be used to manipulate data, to generate unauthorized users, or to compromise passwords. |
| | Risk without control(s) | Extremely high |
| | Control | The passwords of default database users must be changed in all cases. The password selected must be sufficiently complex to prevent possible brute-force attacks. If possible, utilize an authentication that is integrated in the operating system using an operating system user (such as `<sapsid>`). |
| | Risk with control(s) | Normal |
| | Section | 27.4.1 |
| 3. | Potential risk | Unnecessary entries of database users:<br>The Database Management System (DBMS) has entries for extraneous database users (such as demo users). |
| | Impact | An attacker can use extraneous database users to compromise the entire database. By exploiting this vulnerability in the system, an attacker can obtain broader rights and thereby view and manipulate tables in the database unauthorized. |
| | Risk without control(s) | High |
| | Control | Remove the unnecessary database user entries in the DBMS. |
| | Risk with control(s) | Normal |
| | Section | 27.4.2 |
| 4. | Potential risk | Unprotected DBMS:<br>Access to the DBMS is inadequately secured. For example, logons to the database are possible from every computer in a less trustworthy network segment. |

**Table 27.1** Risks and Controls for the Database Server (Cont.)

| No. | Classification | Description |
|---|---|---|
| | Impact | Insecure access to the database can compromise tables and the business data they store. |
| | Risk without control(s) | High |
| | Control | Restriction of access to DBMS and use of firewalls to secure access to the database server from a less trustworthy network segment. |
| | Risk with control(s) | Normal |
| | Section | 27.4.3 |
| 5. | Potential risk | Missing data backup concept:<br>No strategy or concept to back up and archive the database. Legal requirements (for example, from the Principles for IT-Supported Accounting Systems) might be disregarded. |
| | Impact | The lack of a database backup concept can lead to a partial or complete loss of all business data. Disregarding legal requirements can lead to fines. |
| | Risk without control(s) | Extremely high |
| | Control | Design and setup of a database backup concept. |
| | Risk with control(s) | Low |
| | Section | 27.4.4 |
| 6. | Potential risk | Unauthorized database queries are not prevented:<br>SQL commands that are sent to the database and data entries made by applications or users are not checked for unauthorized activities. The potential risk is especially high if direct database access is granted (via the Internet, for example). |
| | Impact | Potential attackers can exploit the security gaps of the database or identify passwords. Ultimately, the database can be compromised. SQL injection attacks could compromise the data and database. |
| | Risk without control(s) | High |

**Table 27.1** Risks and Controls for the Database Server (Cont.)

| No. | Classification | Description |
|---|---|---|
| | Control | Filtering of all database queries to eliminate unauthorized SQL commands. |
| | Risk with control(s) | Low |
| | Section | 27.4.5 |
| 7. | Potential risk | Missing upgrade concept:<br>No upgrade concept exists for the database to implement the most recent security patches. |
| | Impact | Security weaknesses are corrected too late with the appropriate patch. A potential attacker can exploit this well known vulnerability. Ultimately, the database can be compromised. |
| | Risk without control(s) | High |
| | Control | Design and implementation of an upgrade concept for the database. |
| | Risk with control(s) | Low |
| | Section | 27.4.6 |

**Table 27.1** Risks and Controls for the Database Server (Cont.)

## 27.3 Application Security

The potential risks listed in Table 27.1 apply to all operating systems of the database servers. Here, a UNIX example is described because the various variants of UNIX are often used as the operating system for SAP database servers. You must be very restrictive when setting access rights to files of database resources, especially where UNIX is concerned. The following sections display the settings for two common database systems, Oracle and DB2.

For DB2 on UNIX, the access rights to database-relevant resources must be set as shown in Table 27.2: `<dbsid>` stands for the database ID. User `db2<dbsid>` is the technical user who installed the database, which runs at the operating system level. This user belongs to UNIX group `SYSADM_GROUP`.

| Directory or File | Access rights in Octal Form | Owner | Group |
|---|---|---|---|
| /db2/db2<dbsid> | 755 | db2<dbsid> | SYSADM_GROUP |
| /db2/<DBSID>/db2dump | 755 | db2<dbsid> | SYSADM_GROUP |
| /db2/<DBSID>/log_dir | 755 | db2<dbsid> | SYSADM_GROUP |
| /db2/<SAPSID>/sapdata* | 755 | db2<dbsid> | SYSADM_GROUP |
| /db2/<SAPSID>/sapdata*/container | 600 | db2<dbsid> | SYSADM_GROUP |
| /db2/<DBSID>/saptempl | 755 | db2<dbsid> | SYSADM_GROUP |

**Table 27.2** Access Rights for DB2 Directories and Files under UNIX

For Oracle on UNIX, the access rights to database-relevant resources must be set as shown in Table 27.3. User `ora<dbsid>` is the technical user who installed the database, which runs at the operating system level. This user belongs to UNIX group `dba` and is also referred to as a database instance user.

| Directory or File | Access rights in Octal Form | Owner | Group |
|---|---|---|---|
| /oracle/<DBSID>/sapdata* | 755 | ora<dbsid> | dba |
| /oracle/<DBSID>/sapdata*/* | 755 | ora<dbsid> | dba |
| /oracle/<DBSID>/sapdata*/*/* | 640 | ora<dbsid> | dba |
| /oracle/<DBSID>/oraarch | 755 | ora<dbsid> | dba |
| /oracle/<DBSID>/oraarch | 640 | ora<dbsid> | dba |
| /oracle/<DBSID>/saparch | 755 | ora<dbsid> | dba |
| /oracle/<DBSID>/sapreorg | 755 | ora<dbsid> | dba |
| /oracle/<DBSID>/sapbackup | 755 | ora<dbsid> | dba |
| /oracle/<DBSID>/dbs | 755 | ora<dbsid> | dba |
| /oracle/<DBSID>/sapcheck | 755 | ora<dbsid> | dba |
| /oracle/<DBSID>/sapstat | 755 | ora<dbsid> | dba |
| /oracle/<DBSID>/saptrace | 755 | ora<dbsid> | dba |
| /oracle/<DBSID>/saptrace/* | 755 | ora<dbsid> | dba |

**Table 27.3** Access Rights for Oracle Directories and Files under UNIX

| Directory or File | Access rights in Octal Form | Owner | Group |
|---|---|---|---|
| /oracle/<DBSID>/saptrace/*/* | 640 | ora<dbsid> | dba |
| /oracle/<DBSID>/origlog* | 755 | ora<dbsid> | dba |
| /oracle/<DBSID>/origlog*/* | 640 | ora<dbsid> | dba |
| /oracle/<DBSID>/mirrlog* | 755 | ora<dbsid> | dba |
| /oracle/<DBSID>/mirrlog*/* | 640 | ora<dbsid> | dba |

**Table 27.3** Access Rights for Oracle Directories and Files under UNIX (Cont.)

## 27.4 Technical Security

This section describes in more detail the risks and controls that are outlined in Table 27.1 with regard to technical security.

### 27.4.1 Changing Default Passwords

Passwords have default settings once the database server has been installed. Every database administrator is generally aware of the passwords, which can also be looked up easily on the Internet. That's why these default passwords must be changed during or after the database installation. The following criteria should be applied when changing the passwords to achieve the necessary level of complexity:

- Password length to be a minimum of eight characters
- At least one special character
- At least one letter
- At least one number

However, the password complexity that can be achieved also depends on the options of the database application. Considering this aspect, the options of older database versions were rather limited. The following tables list the database users for the database systems used primarily with SAP: DB2, Oracle, and SQL Server. The password should be changed for each system. Table 27.4 lists the important technical database users for DB2.

| Name | Type | Method to Change the Password | Description |
|---|---|---|---|
| db2<dbsid> | UNIX and database | UNIX command passwd | Database administrator |
| <sapsid>adm | UNIX and database | DB2 program dscdb6up | The SAP system administrator with authorization to start and stop the database. |
| sapr3 or sap<sapsid> | UNIX and database | DB2 program dscdb6up | This user is the owner of all database objects of an SAP system. AS ABAP uses this user to connect to the database. |
| sap<sapsid>db | UNIX and database | UNIX command passwd | This user is the owner of all database objects of an SAP system. AS Java uses this user to connect to the database. |

**Table 27.4** Important Database Users for DB2

Table 27.5 lists the important technical database users for Oracle databases. Another important feature of the Oracle database is the OPS$ mechanism, which functions as follows:

1. The SAP system authenticates itself to the Oracle database with database user SAPR3 or SAP<SAPSID>: the user's password is stored in table SAPUSER. Authentication does not occur directly. In the first step, the SAP system authenticates itself with user OPS$<UNIX_system_user>. Consider this example: OPS$<SAPSID>adm, where this user represents a UNIX system user and is identified in the database as external.
2. In the second step, the password for user SAPR3 or SAP<SAPSID> is read from table SAPUSER.
3. The third step consists of the login using database user SAPR3 or SAP<SAPSID>.

| Name | Type | Method to Change the Password | Description |
|---|---|---|---|
| <sapsid>adm | UNIX | UNIX command passwd | The SAP system administrator with authorization to start and stop the database. |
| ora<dbsid> | UNIX | UNIX command passwd | Database instance user |

**Table 27.5** Important Database Users for Oracle

| Name | Type | Method to Change the Password | Description |
|---|---|---|---|
| SYS (internal) | Database user | BRCONNECT (as of Release 6.10), SQLPLUS chdpass | Database administrator |
| SYSTEM | Database user | BRCONNECT (as of Release 6.10), SQLPLUS chdpass | Database administrator |
| SAPR3/ SAP<SAPSID> | Database user (SAP system) | BRCONNECT (as of Release 6.10) or the OPS$ mechanism chdpass | This user is the owner of all database objects of an SAP system. The SAP system uses this user to connect to the database. |

**Table 27.5** Important Database Users for Oracle (Cont.)

The advantage of this procedure is that it does not need to exchange a password over an unencrypted communications connection because the external user (OPS$<UNIX_system_user>) has already authenticated itself to the operating system. However, there is the risk that this OPS$ procedure is bypassed by using the *.rhosts* UNIX file. To avoid this, you can deactivate the rlogin UNIX service in the *inetd.conf* configuration file.

Table 27.6 lists the important technical database users for SQL Server. Prior to authenticating on the SQL Server, you should switch to a mixed logon mode with SQL Server and Windows authentication before logging on to the SQL server database.

| Name | Type | Method to Change the Password | Description |
|---|---|---|---|
| sa | Windows and database | Windows operating system command | Database administrator |
| <sapsid> | Windows and database | Windows operating system | This user is the owner of all database objects of an SAP system. The SAP system connects to the database with this user. |
| <sapsid>adm | Windows and database | Windows operating system | The SAP system administrator with authorization to start and stop the database. |
| SAPService <SAPSID> | Windows and database | Windows operating system | Maintenance user in the operating system |

**Table 27.6** Important Database Users for SQL Server

### 27.4.2 Removing Unnecessary Database Users

Extraneous database users, or those users employed for development like demo users, must be deleted. Otherwise, such users can be exploited for unauthorized access. Also, if the database server is to operate for an SAP system, no other application should run at the same time as the database server. For each SAP system, a different database user should also be used for the connection.

### 27.4.3 Limiting Database Access

Access to the database server, for example, with `SQL*NET` commands in the case of Oracle or to other database management systems from the office communications network of the organization must be limited. For Oracle systems, the limitation can occur with file *sqlnet.ora*. This file can specify the IP addresses of the management consoles from which access should be possible.

A firewall is another way of restricting access to the database server in a controlled manner. The firewall rules should be specified so that only SAP systems and the authorized management consoles obtain access to the database server.

The databases use the following default ports:

- SQL Server: TCP/IP port 1433
- Oracle Listener: TCP/IP port 1527
- DB2: TCP/IP port 4402

### 27.4.4 Creation and Implementation of a Database Backup Concept

By now, a database backup concept for databases should be a standard operating procedure. Nonetheless, the following sections briefly describe this necessary risk management measure. Various strategies exist for a data backup concept:

- It's generally simpler to implement a concept for a centrally used database server for all SAP systems, because only one, centrally controlled database has to be managed instead of several, distributed database servers. Accordingly, the database server can also be backed up centrally. The backup can involve a simple design, such as a daily backup run to a backup tape drive. A complete backup occurs at regular intervals; incremental backups of changes occur later. However, this design requires the shutting down of system operations during the backups, which many companies cannot handle.
- A more advanced design synchronizes the database with a parallel database. In this case, all updates of the database are simultaneously executed in a mirrored database. The advantage of this design is that work can continue uninterrupted —

with the mirrored database immediately – should the primary database fail. No time-consuming reconstruction of the database is required and production does not need to grind to a halt.

- Long-term archiving must be regulated by legal requirements. For example, companies must follow the requirements of the Generally Accepted Accounting Principles in the United States (USGAAP). For example, the German Tax Authority requires the following retention periods for data processed and stored in computer based accounting systems (source: Federal Tax Gazette 1995, Part I No. 18, page 738 et seq.):

  *Generally, data performing voucher functions must be retained for six years; data and other necessary records performing journal or account functions for 10 years. The system documentation on the IT-supported accounting system is one of the operating procedures and other organization documents referred to in Section 257 (1) Commercial Code and Section 147 (1) Tax Code, and must generally be maintained for 10 years. Parts of the system documentation performing voucher functions only (such as the documentation on IT-supported voucher generation, from which postings result) generally must be retained for six years. The system documentation can be maintained on microfiche, microfilm, or other data storage media. The retention periods for system documentation begin at the end of the calendar year in which data related to accounting was recorded, generated, or processed using the respective system.*

### 27.4.5 Filtering Database Queries

Applications and users of databases usually use predefined SQL procedures to initiate database queries or data changes. These procedures should normally pass function and security checks before being installed on the production database server. This lets you avoid significant security gaps. You should also regularly check the entire inventory of the SQL procedures that exist on the database server for the existence of unauthorized or unnecessary SQL procedures.

But database queries or data input are also implemented by users making entries in screen fields. This entails the risk that users do not only enter legitimate data, but also forward disallowed SQL commands directly to the database. This leads to a significant security gap with the result that data, passwords, or the entire database can be compromised or advanced permissions at the application level can be obtained. The SQL injection is a commonly known method of attack that exploits this security gap (see Chapter 16, SAP NetWeaver Portal).

You can close this security gap by checking and filtering transfer parameters and input fields for plausibility and correctness. This is especially important for in-house developed applications, which are deployed on the SAP NetWeaver AS for Internet use. Another risk management option is to use commercially available application-level gateways, which can be adapted to the specific existing risk (see Chapter 9, SAP NetWeaver Application Server, and Chapter 16, SAP NetWeaver Portal).

### 27.4.6 Creation and Implementation of an Upgrade Concept

Because they provide central persistence of all business data, database systems require a particularly high level of security protection. They must therefore be upgraded to the latest level of security as soon as possible. The manufacturers of database applications constantly try to make their products more secure. During this process, they discover new vulnerabilities and provide the appropriate patch or upgrade for the next version to improve security.

After having carried out sufficient checks in your test system, you should implement these enhancements; patching must be an essential component of security management, not only for SAP databases and systems. Implementation of new patches must adhere to the requirements of the standard change management processes. Before they can be implemented, patches must undergo a quality assurance process with the required tests.

In certain cases, this process needs to be accelerated because the public release of a security patch also makes the to-be-eliminated security gaps public. Potential hackers can then use this knowledge to identify systems without this patch, exploit the known vulnerability, and compromise these systems.

*The user-friendliness of user interfaces (UIs) determines if the applications are accepted by users. Poor design and complex handling may contribute to the fact that even the best applications are not accepted. Another criterion for the success of a user interface is its ability to integrate information security, which is discussed in this chapter.*

# 28 User Interfaces

UIs are the essential link between user and application. The quality, user-friendliness, and presentation philosophy of user interfaces determine how effectively a person can record and process information from an application. Indirectly, user interfaces also affect the value of an application and its functionality and acceptance. Design and functionality of user interfaces therefore assume a critical role for application manufacturers. Trends and scientific research results may also influence the way users communicate with applications today and in the future.

This section discusses system interfaces from a security and risk management perspective. The following SAP UIs are described as examples:

- SAP Graphical User Interface (GUI) (see Section 28.1, SAP GUI)
- Web browser (see Section 28.2, Web Browser)
- Mobile devices (see Section 28.3, Mobile Devices)

## 28.1 SAP GUI

This section describes Information Technology (IT) security concepts for SAP GUI. It focuses on password security, authentication functions, Single Sign-On (SSO) functions, and Secure, Storage, and Forward (SSF) functions.

### 28.1.1 Introduction and Functions

SAP GUI is the standard SAP front-end for ABAP-based dynpro applications. It is available in three different variants: SAP GUI for Windows, SAP GUI for Java, and SAP GUI for HTML.The latter is actually a web browser that connects to the SAP NetWeaver Application Server (AS) via Internet Transaction Server (ITS) (see

Chapter 14, Classic SAP Middleware). We only mention it here so as to include all variants. The SAP GUI for Java is the version for the UNIX platforms. However, the most popular SAP GUI is SAP GUI for Windows, which is often referred to as WebGUI. Furthermore, because Windows is the most commonly used operating system, the SAP GUI for Windows is the also most widespread SAP client. For that reason, we will use the name SAP GUI for the rest of this chapter.

SAP GUI establishes a connection to the SAP NetWeaver AS using the SAP-specific TCP/IP-supported protocol, Dynamic Information and Action Gateway (DIAG). In doing so, it first connects to the application server's message server, which forwards the request through the dispatcher to an available dialog process of the application server.

The SAP GUI's advantages over other web applications include its faster performance and its ability to map all dynpro functions, some of which are not available in SAP GUI for HTML. Furthermore, as it is standard in most client/server applications, it performs a plausibility check (that is, a verification of the client-side entries according to the specified entry format, for example, for dates) without requiring a roundtrip to the server. The main disadvantage of using the SAP GUI is that it must be distributed across the relevant devices (desktop PCs) and installed by a software distribution mechanism before it can be used. Moreover, the SAP-specific DIAG protocol only enables SAP GUI in Internet scenarios via Virtual Private Network (VPN) dial-up connections.

### 28.1.2 Risks and Controls

In this section, we'll use a simplified version of the risk analysis methodology described in Chapter 1, Risk and Control Management, to identify the main security risks and the necessary controls for SAP GUI (see Table 28.1). The controls are then discussed in more detail in the following sections and illustrated using examples.

| No. | Classification | Description |
|---|---|---|
| 1. | Potential risk | Noncompliance with legal requirements:<br>Due to the noncompliance with legal requirements such as the Electronic Signatures in Global and National Commerce Act (E-Sign), documents are transferred unsigned in a business process. Especially in the pharmaceutical industry, application documents for the approval of a new drug must have a digital signature. |

**Table 28.1** Risks and Controls for SAP GUI

| No. | Classification | Description |
|---|---|---|
| | Impact | The lack of digital signatures and of the frequently necessary encryption enables unauthorized parties, for example, to modify the quantities of ordered goods that have been placed in electronic business processes without the confirmation of the ship-to party. The resulting incorrect deliveries can cause high financial burdens for the company. In the scenario of a drug approval, it would mean that the approval for shipment occurs too late, which would lead to a loss of revenue. |
| | Risk without control(s) | High |
| | Control | The SSF interface, integrated in the SAP GUI can be used to trigger the digital signature function for documents. |
| | Risk with control(s) | Low |
| | Section | 28.1.3 |
| 2. | Potential risk | Passwords that are too numerous and too simple:<br>SAP NetWeaver AS users must memorize a separate password for each SAP and non-SAP application. For this reason, they either choose passwords with a simple structure or write easily accessible notes, which contradicts the idea of the passport. |
| | Impact | Passwords that are too obvious make it easier for attackers to get access to the SAP NetWeaver. It will be even easier for them if they can use the passwords that have been written down. Possible consequences can be extremely negative for the company. |
| | Risk without control(s) | Extremely high |
| | Control | Implementation of an SSO process using the Secure Network Communication (SNC) interface of SAP GUI to integrate the SAP GUI authentication into Windows or UNIX. In that case, the user logs on only once to the operating system and is then granted access to SAP NetWeaver AS due to the integrated SSO authentication mechanism. |
| | Risk with control(s) | Normal |
| | Section | SSO by Integration into the OS Authentication Process in Section 28.1.4 |

**Table 28.1** Risks and Controls for SAP GUI (Cont.)

| No. | Classification | Description |
|---|---|---|
| 3. | Potential risk | Passwords that are too numerous and too simple:<br>SAP NetWeaver AS users must memorize a separate password for each SAP and non-SAP application. For this reason, they either choose passwords with a simple structure, or take notes of the individual system access data. |
| | Impact | Passwords that are too obvious make it easier for attackers to get access to the SAP NetWeaver AS. It will be even easier for them, if they can use the passwords found on an easily accessible note . The possible effects of this can be extremely negative for the company. |
| | Risk without control(s) | Extremely high |
| | Control | Implementation of digital certificates for SSO processes using the SNC interface of SAP GUI. This ensures that each user must use a digital certificate to log on to the relevant SAP NetWeaver AS. The certificate must be issued by a trustworthy certification authority (public key infrastructure) and must be stored or made available in a secure storage location (or on a smart card) on the user's desktop PC. This situation can be attained via a Personal Security Environment (PSE). |
| | Risk with control(s) | Low |
| | Section | SSO Using Digital Certificates in Section 28.1.4 |
| 4. | Potential risk | Missing access control:<br>Unauthorized users, such as external employees, use their SAP GUI installation to obtain access to an SAP NetWeaver AS of the company for which they have no authorization, for example, for the HCM system. |
| | Impact | Because access to the network is unprotected, a potential hacker can address the SAP NetWeaver AS, compromise the password with a brute-force attack, and obtain access to the system. |
| | Risk without control(s) | High |
| | Control | Restriction of SAP NetWeaver AS access using SAProuter for SAP GUI–based access. |

**Table 28.1** Risks and Controls for SAP GUI (Cont.)

| No. | Classification | Description |
|---|---|---|
| | Risk with control(s) | Normal |
| | Section | Restricting Access Using SAProuter in Section 28.1.4 |

**Table 28.1** Risks and Controls for SAP GUI (Cont.)

### 28.1.3 Application Security

Since Release 4.6A, SAP has provided an SSF function that can be used to sign and encrypt electronically stored documents.

#### Types of Signatures

The SSF function can be customized in accordance with the relevant legal requirements. The following scenarios are possible:

- **User signature with person-specific certificate**
  In this case, the user has a person-specific certificate, which is used to generate a signature for a document in the SAP GUI. This is only possible for Windows-based systems. The certificate is issued by a trustworthy Certificate Authority (CA), and the associated private signature key can be stored as software on the hard disk, or on a smart card or another hardware-based storage medium.

  In a regulatory environment, the digital signature must be based on a certificate, which must be issued by an authorized certification service provider. In addition, it must be stored on a secure hardware storage medium such as a smart card. When the certificate is issued, the user must be personally present to provide proof of his identity. Only then can the certificate be called a "qualified certificate." Otherwise, it is referred to as an "advanced digital certificate." If the signature is used among partner companies, the partners can specify the certificate requirements themselves. To use the person-specific signature efficiently, a separate public key infrastructure (PKI) must be used.

  This signature process represents the highest security standard. But it is absolutely necessary that the document to be signed is actually displayed to the signatory in the SAP GUI so that he can sign it digitally with his private signature key.

- **User signature with server certificate**
  This type of signature uses the server certificate or the signature key of the SAP NetWeaver AS instead of the person-specific certificate. The document to be signed is displayed to the user in the SAP GUI and the user must provide proof of his identity by using the SAP user password so that the application server

signs the document on behalf of the user. During the signing process, the signature key of the SAP NetWeaver AS is complemented with the user name of the signatory.

The advantage of this signing process is that no separate Public Key Infrastructure is required because it uses the server certificate; however, the disadvantage is that this type of process cannot be used for interaction with SAP NetWeaver Portal, because the user must provide proof of his identity to the back-end application, which is where the actual signature process occurs.

This process does not comply with the legal requirements in a regulated environment, for example, the German Electronic Signature Act. It is, however, accepted by the American Food and Drug Association (FDA) in the approval process for medication.

- **Server signature**
  As the name implies, this process uses the signature key of the server. There is no interaction with the user. For this reason, this process is applied primarily when the back-end applications are in batch mode, for example, when mass signatures are required. It specifically focuses on protecting documents against unauthorized modification, when the documents are forwarded to business partners. In that case, the business partners can agree on using this type of protection. This process is mainly used in the SAP NetWeaver Process Integration (PI) (Chapter 12) area.
- **Server signature linked to a natural person**
  This type of signature uses the certificate of a natural person (for example, of an authorized signatory) instead of a server certificate. Using a machine-readable system such as a smart card reader, the certificate can also be used in batch-mode operation for mass signatures. In this case, the use of several person-specific certificates is also possible.

  This solution enables you to comply with the requirements set by a regulatory authority, for example, the German Electronic Signature Act, if the smart card reader is located in a secured environment. The use of a public key infrastructure is not mandatory in this scenario; however, the certificates on a smart card must be issued by an accredited certification authority.

### Supported Electronic Document Formats

The following electronically saved document formats are supported by the SSF functions provided by SAP:

- **PKCS#7**
  PKCS#7 stands for Public Key Cryptography Standard (Version 7). This standard was defined by RSA Security and it specifies the secure exchange of documents

through the Internet. PKCS#7 is used to "wrap" the actual document in a new binary format and to assign a signature to it. SAP provides a signature for this format for both the ABAP and the Java stack of the SAP NetWeaver AS.

- **XML**
  XML is the leading standard for information exchange. The document that is supposed to be transferred is converted into an XML format and stored with a signature in an XML structure. The conversion is carried out using an Extensible Stylesheet Language (XSL) definition. The advantage of XML is that this format can be further processed by any web browser. Since Release 6.10, SAP NetWeaver AS supports the XML format; since Release 6.20, you can transfer the structure of XML documents to ABAP formats using XSL Transformation (XSLT). Since Release 6.40, the SAP-specific programming language, Simple Transformations (ST), provides even more powerful XML support.
- **S/MIME**
  S/MIME MIME (Secure Multipurpose Internet Mail Extension) is the standard for signing email. This format has been supported by SAP since Release 6.40.

#### Technical Implementation of the SSF Functions

The SSF library for the ABAP stack of SAP NetWeaver AS is used in ABAP applications. It supports functions for generating and verifying digital signatures (PKCS#7), and those functions that are used for encrypting and decrypting documents. The functions that are used for encrypting and decrypting are provided through the following programming interfaces:

- SSF-Sign generation of digital signatures
- SSF-Verify validity check of digital signatures
- SSF-Envelope encryption of documents
- SSF-Develop decryption of documents

To make these SSF functions available, an external security product is required. The standard product provided with SAP NetWeaver AS is the SAP Security Library (SAPSECULIB). However, this library only supports digital signatures and no cryptographic hardware, such as smart cards, smart tokens, and cryptoboards. Instead of SAPSECULIB, you can also use SAPCRYPTOLIB, which you can download from the SAP Service Marketplace (*http://service.sap.com*).

SAPSECULIB supports the DSA algorithm, whereas SAPCRYPTOLIB supports both the DSA and the RSA algorithms. To decide which algorithm you must use in your signature process depends on the certificate authority that issues the certificate. Most certificate authorities use the RSA algorithm. For SAPCRYPTOLIB, you should note that it is subject to country-specific export regulations. SAP Note 39175 contains further information on this subject.

For document encryption and decryption support at the front end (that is, SAP GUI), and for generating digital signatures using cryptographic hardware, an external security product provided by a certified SAP partner is required. Such security products operate the SSF interface of the SAP system and are certified by SAP for this purpose.

The Java SSF Library supports all Java applications. It is based on the IAIK Toolkit developed by Graz University of Technology in Graz, Austria. This SSF library also supports the generation and verification of digital signatures. For document encryption and decryption, the IAIK Toolkit must be installed, which you can download from the SAP Service Marketplace. For this reason, no external security product provided by an SAP partner is needed, nor does SAP provide a certification program for the Java SSF Library. PKCS#12 and the Java keystore are used for storing the keys, which means that currently digital signatures can only be created without using any cryptographic hardware. In contrast to the library provided for the ABAP stack, the Java library can also generate XML and S/MIME signatures, in addition to the PKCS#7 signature.

A central interface — `IssfData` — is available for the Java version, which contains all of the basic methods such as `sign`, `verify`, `encrypt`, and `decrypt`. This interface is implemented for the different classes (`SsfDataPKCS7`, `SsfDataSMIME`, `SsfDataXML`) that provide specific methods for each document format. An SSF profile containing the private key and the certification path is required for signing and decrypting documents. An SSF Public Address Book (PAB) containing a list of trustworthy root certificates is required for verifying and encrypting documents. The SSF profile is a parameter used by SSF functions that require the private key. For a digital signature, this would correspond with the function `SSF_Sign`, which is used to generate a digital signature. The SSF profile is either the name of a file or a smart card that specifies the public key information, such as the private key and the certification path. The exact form of the profile depends on the security product that is used.

The Private Address Book is a parameter used by SSF functions that require a list of trustworthy certificates. For a digital signature, this would correspond with the `SSF_Verify` function, which is used to verify the digital signature. Depending on the security product that is used, the PAB can be stored in different ways in the system.

As already mentioned, a display component for the document that is supposed to be signed is required specifically for the person-specific and user-specific signature with the server certificate. This signature display component is available specifically for SAP GUI (only for Windows-based versions as of Release 6.40) and for programs that are based on Business Server Pages (BSPs). It is referred to as Signature Control and provides the following functions for programmers:

- `SSFS_Call_Control` launches Signature Control.
- `SSFS_Get_Signature` retrieves the signature value from the Signature Control component.
- `SSFS_Server_Verify` verifies the digital signature via the application server.

The document to be signed is displayed in plain text, HTML, XML, or PDF format in the Signature Control. The signature verification process occurs as follows:

1. A signed document contains the signature value and the digital certificate of the signatory. During verification of the digital signature, cryptographic algorithms are applied to the document and the signature value. If the verification is successful, the document will not have been modified and will have been signed using the private key that belongs to the signatory.
2. Another step must then verify whether the certificate of the signatory is valid and whether it was issued by a trustworthy certificate authority. This is done using the Private Address Book.
3. Then it must be checked if the certificate has been revoked by the Certificate Authority, for example, because the smart card was lost. The certificate authorities provide a list of revoked or invalid certificates (certificate revocation list). You can either download the certificate revocation lists directly from the websites of the Certificate Authorities — within a specified validity period, which needs to be configured accordingly — or, you can use the Online Certificate Status Protocol (OCSP), which is based on HTTP. This new standard is faster, easier to handle, and more reliable than using the certificate revocation lists.
4. The application sends a request to a server application, the OCSP responder, which keeps current status information on the following three responses: "valid," "invalid," or "unknown."

Generally, OCSP services must be purchased; the use of qualified certificates is an exception in this context. Most of the accredited trust centers provide this service free of charge for qualified certificates, because, for example, the German Electronic Signature Act prohibits the use of certificate revocation lists.

#### Saving Digitally Signed Documents

To sign a process step and a document with a digital signature means that the signature must be saved. The application used and the legal framework to be applied determine the way in which the signature is saved. If the signature process must comply with the German Electronic Signature Act, for example, the generic document must be saved to a nonrewritable medium, such as an optical archive.

If the document is modified in subsequent process steps, it must be possible to access the original version of the document at any time. Long-time archiving is another important aspect. If you are legally obligated to archive the signed document for a longer period of time, you must sign the documents with a new qualified digital signature prior to the expiration date of the usage period for the algorithms, or prior to the expiration of a five-year limit. The previous qualified digital signatures must be included in the new signatures, and therefore be preserved so that they cannot be accused of being counterfeit should that occur at a later stage. A qualified timestamp is required for new qualified digital signatures to prevent them from being used and then predated to a time when the security value of the previous digital signature had decreased to such an extent that the creation of counterfeits was possible.

You don't have to generate the new digital signature and the qualified time stamp separately for each electronically signed document. Instead, the documents can be signed with one new digital signature. This process is based on a regulation within the German Electronic Signature Act. Generally, the digital signature regulations can differ depending on the legislations of specific countries, so this needs to be considered.

If the signature process is not subject to any legal requirements, the signature or the signed document could be stored in a database table, an archive, or in a file. SAP NetWeaver provides SAP ArchiveLink, the Archive Development Kit, and Knowledge Management for archiving documents. A revision-proof storage of the data is supported.

#### Installing the SSF Functions

To use the SSF functions, you must first install them. That is done whenever a partner product is used on client computers that run SAP GUI and for the relevant SAP back-end systems, which can also use the SSF functions. The installation procedure itself also depends on the respective partner product.

### 28.1.4 Technical Security

This section describes in more detail the risks and controls that are outlined in Table 28.1 with regard to technical security.

### SSO by Integration into the OS Authentication Process

You can also create an SSO solution based on the traditional SAP GUI. To do that, you must use the SNC interface that is available in the SAP GUI, or the Generic Security Application Programming Interface (GSS-API) that can be used to integrate external partner authentication methods (for example, Windows NTLM or Kerberos SPNEGO).

The partner products must be implemented in the SAP GUI and in the SAP systems for which SSO is supposed to be used. In that case, the authentication occurs outside of the SAP system, for example, in the Windows domain. The successful external authentication is then confirmed to the SAP GUI via the interface and then forwarded to the connected SAP NetWeaver AS. The application server trusts this external authentication through the SNC mechanism and forwards the external user ID (of the operating system), which has been transferred by the SAP GUI, with the SAP user ID stored in the system. If the user IDs are identical or if a unique one-to-one relationship exists, the user can log on to the application server. The assignments of external user IDs to SAP user IDs are stored in Table `USREXTID`, which must be maintained using Transaction SM30. However, this type of authentication is restricted to Windows users.

There are out-of-the-box solutions available for Windows NTLM and Kerberos. To do this, the two libraries gssntlm.dll and gsskrb5.dll are available; the exact installation and integration depend on the respective partner products.

### SSO Using Digital Certificates

It is also possible to integrate the SAP GUI with certificate-based external authentication procedures. Compared to the external authentication in the operating system based on a user ID and password, this method is more secure, because it involves a strong authentication process based on digital certificates (X.509).

But, this method requires the implementation of a process for managing person-specific certificates, which can only be attained by using a PKI. The reason for this is that each employee must be assigned a unique certificate, which must be withdrawn when an employee leaves the company. Moreover, it should be possible to call the certificate from any work center within the company, because usually the work centers aren't related to specific persons. However, if they are, server-based certificate storage locations can be used. In this case, the certificate is imported to the relevant desktop PC when a user logs on to the respective server using a Personal Identification Number (PIN). Another alternative is the use of smart cards (for example, a company badge) for storing the certificates, which is currently one of the most secure and most convenient solutions.

To implement a certificate-based authentication through the SAP GUI to a network of SAP systems that use SSO, you must integrate an external SAP-certified partner product via the SNC interface (GSS-API). You can find a list of the current certified SAP security partners at *http://www.sap.com/solutions/security/technicalresources/index.epx* (link: SECURITY SOFTWARE PARTNERS).

In the following sections, we'll briefly describe the most important steps involved in setting up an SSO solution based on the SAP GUI with digital certificates:

1. First, you must define a naming convention for the SNC name of the user (distinguished name in the X.509 certificate). Make sure the name is unique. You should adhere to the following convention: `CN=Common Name` with a unique use ID, `OU=Organization Unit` (for example, the department), `O=Organization` (name of the company), and `C=Country` (country in which the company is located). For example:

   `CN=SMITH1,OU=SALES,O=SAMPLECOMPANY,C=US`
2. Install the chosen partner product in all SAP systems that use SSO. This step depends on the respective partner product.
3. In the next step, configure the important SNC parameters in the SAP systems. This includes the following parameters:
   - **`snc/enable`**
     Activates SNC on the application server
   - **`snc/user_maint`**
     Transaction SU01, maintenance of the SNC name
   - **`snc/gssapi_lib`**
     Path and file name of the shared GSS-API V2 library (the partner product library)
   - **`snc/identity/as`**
     SNC name of the application server (SAP NetWeaver AS is also assigned an SNC name according to the schema defined).
   - **`snc/data_protection/min`**
     A minimum level of security is required for SNC connections (for example, activation of strong authentication only, or additional activation of data privacy protection)
   - **`snc/accept_insecure_gui`**
     Acceptance of logon attempts by the SAP GUI that are not protected by Secure Network Communication on an SNC-protected application server
   - **`snc/force_login_screen`**
     Displaying the logon screen for each logon that is protected by SNC

4. Maintain the access control list in each SAP system involved. This can be done using Transaction SU01 (entries are case sensitive), or directly in the maintenance of Table USRACL using Transaction SM30. The maintenance of the ACL ensures that each existing user in the SAP system, who is defined with a user ID, is assigned an appropriate SNC name (see Step 1). That way, a unique assignment is guaranteed. Only if this entry exists can an authentication be ultimately performed on the basis of the certificate name.

In general, the use of certificate-based SSO methods is recommended, even though it requires that a PKI be established first, and some additional implementation work. In the long run, it is a worthwhile investment because it eliminates the often-distributed identity management and the related high administration costs, while ensuring a much higher level of security. An authentication solution based on digital certificates is highly recommended, especially in this age of increasing integration of additional business partners and the growing importance placed on securely managing your identities and access rights.

Using SNC is a functional requirement in this scenario. It also supports data protection by means of data encryption methods. Please bear in mind that confidential information or passwords should never be transferred without protection in networks. To do this, SNC provides a well-documented and robust solution (see Chapter 9, SAP NetWeaver Application Server).

The user password, which is transferred by SAP GUI for authentication to the SAP NetWeaver AS, is exposed to an extremely high risk during the transfer. Experience has shown that logon data (user name and password, for example) that was sent via the standard DIAG protocol can be caught in the network and compromised (Sniffing SAP GUI Passwords, Andreas Baus and René Ledosquet, 2009, *http://www.secaron.de/Content/presse/fachartikel/sniffing_diag.pdf*).

### Restricting Access Using SAProuter

Access to an SAP NetWeaver AS can be restricted for the SAP GUI using a SAProuter. The idea is to only grant specific SAP GUI clients access to specific SAP applications on specific SAP systems (see also Chapter 14, Classic SAP Middleware).

## 28.2 Web Browser

For SAP NetWeaver AS Java, SAP NetWeaver Portal, SAP Customer Relationship Management (CRM), and all future web-based applications, the web browser is the universal user interface. Therefore, this section focuses on the general security risks for this front end.

### 28.2.1 Introduction and Functions

The web browser is the universal HTTP platform for interactive access to the various applications within the internal network or Internet. Programming technologies, such as JavaServer Pages (JSPs), BSPs and Web Dynpro, ABAP and Web Dynpro Java, convert content, information, and functions of SAP and non-SAP applications into one presentation format. The advantages are obvious: You don't have to install a proprietary (SAP) front end, and platform-independent web browser and mobile devices can globally support the presentation of SAP application content and functions more easily.

But, the web browser also considerably contributes to information security by enabling data security through SSL encryption at the transport level. However, the standardized and common use of web browsers also involves some security risks. The following sections detail some of the general security risks that do not depend on the specific type of the web browser.

### 28.2.2 Risks and Controls

In this section, the risk analysis methodology described in Chapter 1 is used by the web browser to identify the main security risks and the necessary controls (see Table 28.2). The controls are then discussed in more detail in the following sections and illustrated using examples.

| No. | Classification | Description |
|---|---|---|
| 1. | Potential risk | Missing protection against malware (viruses, spyware, and so on):<br>Inadequate antivirus software is installed on the desktop PC or is not updated. |
| | Impact | The missing protection, especially against Trojans and other malware, enables the unauthorized and unnoticed installation of malware on the desktop PC when downloading content from the Internet and actively using web functions. This allows attackers to lay the foundation for further attacks, for example, for performing unauthorized business transactions or compromising secret business data. This can result in high financial losses. |
| | Risk without control(s) | High |
| | Control | Implementation and, above all, updating of the antivirus software on the desktop PC. |

**Table 28.2** Risks and Controls for Using Web Browsers

| No. | Classification | Description |
|---|---|---|
| | Risk with control(s) | Low |
| | Section | Antivirus Software for the Desktop PC in Section 28.2.4 |
| 2. | Potential risk | Lack of a personal firewall on the desktop PC:<br>No personal firewall is installed on the desktop PC or laptop computer. |
| | Impact | Unauthorized attackers can exploit the open network protocols of the device (especially Netbios) to establish a connection and access business data or log the HTTP communication, especially when using mobile devices that connect to the company network via telecommunications providers. That way, transactions that run in the web browser can be manipulated by unauthorized parties. |
| | Risk without control(s) | High |
| | Control | The implementation of a personal firewall on the desktop PC suppresses access to the PC while being connected to public networks. |
| | Risk with control(s) | Low |
| | Section | Using a Personal Firewall on the Desktop PC in Section 28.2.4 |
| 3. | Potential risk | The security settings in the web browser are too broad and not secure:<br>The security settings (or security levels) in the web browser are too broad and enable the activation of malware on the PC. |
| | Impact | Because the security settings in the web browser are not sufficiently restrictive, malware can be started on the desktop PC. This can ultimately lead to an unauthorized execution of financial transactions or data theft. |
| | Risk without control(s) | High |
| | Control | The security settings of the web browser must be more restrictive. The permission to execute ActiveX controls, in particular, should be regarded as very critical. The execution of Java |

**Table 28.2** Risks and Controls for Using Web Browsers (Cont.)

| No. | Classification | Description |
|---|---|---|
| | | applets and JavaScript should only be permitted to signed versions. When encrypted HTTPS connections are established, the validity of the server certificate must be checked. |
| | Risk with control(s) | Normal |
| | Section | Security Settings for the Web Browser in Section 28.2.4 |

**Table 28.2** Risks and Controls for Using Web Browsers (Cont.)

### 28.2.3 Application Security

There is no specific authorization concept available for using web browsers or SAP GUI for HTML as user interfaces. Access must be restricted via the operating system using Access Control Lists (ACLs).

### 28.2.4 Technical Security

This section describes in more detail the risks and controls that are outlined in Table 28.2 with regard to technical security. In general, you should make sure that you use the latest patch level of your web browser to make your web browser more secure and less vulnerable to potential attacks. The manufacturers of all known web browsers provide corresponding news sites on the web for this very purpose.

#### Antivirus Software for the Desktop PC

It should be a Best Practice that an antivirus solution is set up for desktop PCs. It should be automatically provided with the latest virus definitions. There are a lot of companies that provide various solutions for this purpose. Because the concrete details and installation procedures of these solutions depend on the respective manufacturer, we only mention here that this kind of protection is mandatory. If necessary, due to company requirements, you can also configure the continuous virus protection in such a way that end users cannot control it.

#### Using a Personal Firewall on the Desktop PC

The standard protection for a desktop PC should also include personal firewalls on the user's desktop PC. The firewall should be configured in such a way that individual desktop PC users are not authorized to soften essential security settings of the firewall.

In particular the operation of mobile devices like laptop computers via public or external networks involves a high risk of potential hackers accessing the device via the network. This is facilitated by the fact that the devices, which may also be used in private, are not configured with strict security settings. So it is possible that unnecessary services of the operating system are installed on the laptop computer, which leads to security gaps. If no firewall is used, for example, the Netbios service for mapping drives could be accessed via the public network from the outside. That way, an attacker could try to map the hard drive of the laptop computer and therefore gain access to data or install malware for subsequent attacks.

For this reason, devices that frequently connect to the company network through public networks should be configured in such a way that critical protocols like Netbios cannot be accessed from outside. Access via File Transport Protocol (FTP) and Telnet connections should also be disabled. The best solutions are those that use a central server to configure the firewalls on the devices and notify the central instance of critical incidents. In the case of central monitoring, you can then react to critical events and adjust the firewall configuration accordingly.

#### Security Settings for the Web Browser

Unfortunately, the security settings for the web browser always represent a compromise between the possible level of security and the necessary program functionality. Today many applications use client-side active content/functions (based on JavaScript, Java applets, and ActiveX controls), which is a permanent security risk, because malware can be started on the desktop PC through the web browser. Moreover, many software publishers, including SAP, cannot abandon JavaScript functions entirely, because that would severely restrict the functionality of some applications.

The following introduces some general guidelines for web browser security settings:

- You should only permit JavaScript functions that have been signed by the manufacturer. For all other scripts, you should ensure that the settings are made in such a way that the user is prompted to confirm the execution of the scripts.
- The execution of ActiveX controls should be restricted to signed scripts only as ActiveX controls explicitly permit access to the operating system.
- The same holds true for .NET-relevant components, which should also be permitted only when they have been signed.
- The system should always prompt a user to confirm the downloading of files or programs from the Internet.

- The security setting CHECK FOR REVOCATION, which verifies the validity of a certificate, should also be used to verify server certificates.

## 28.3 Mobile Devices

Information is only useful if it is available – anywhere and anytime. Over the years, mobile devices have undergone such a drastic development and distribution because they increasingly meet this requirement . Nevertheless, the security risk for information that can be accessed via mobile devices must be sufficiently low. This section introduces some basic risks that result from the use of mobile devices. It also discusses the measures for achieving the control objectives and for risk management.

### 28.3.1 Introduction and Functions

If you examine the development of (SAP) business applications from the past to today, one trend is obvious: Information, transaction, business processes, and their flexible integration with specific business areas, customers, and business partners became increasingly important. Local components began to disappear, and for many companies it has become natural that working on a global and mobile scale is possible with no restrictions in terms of location and time. New concepts (Data on Demand for smartphones, for example) and mobile client technologies (for SAP Mobile Sales and SAP NetWeaver Mobile) are additional signs of this trend. So this section – with a focal point on the security and risks of mobile devices – is supposed to provide basic information for your considerations regarding risk management and IT security related to mobile technologies and applications that can be executed regardless of the user's location; the risk potential is too high for IT security being neglected when mobile systems are rolled out.

In general, mobile devices provide the user interface for users who work with mobile applications (see Chapter 17, SAP NetWeaver Mobile). Mobile devices represent a particularly high risk potential for the company, because they are often used to locally store business information, and the loss or theft of these devices can lead to enormous damage if these risks were not considered and the corresponding security measures were not taken in advance. You must also bear in mind that smartphones have been designed for private use, which means that authentication procedures may not always be fully supported as required by the company applications. Therefore, you must run careful risk analyses before developing the security concept and internal usage guidelines for mobile devices.

### 28.3.2 Risks and Controls

This section uses a simplified version of the risk analysis methodology described in Chapter 1, Risk and Control Management to identify the main security risks and the necessary controls for mobile devices (see Table 28.3). The controls are then discussed in more detail in the following sections and illustrated using examples.

| No. | Classification | Description |
| --- | --- | --- |
| 1. | Potential risk | Inadequate multiple-user concept:<br>The multiple-user concept for the mobile device is inadequate. Applications that don't allow for a multiple-user concept, because an authorization control is impossible, are implemented on the mobile device. |
| | Impact | Other users of the mobile device can perform unauthorized back-end transactions. |
| | Risk without control(s) | Extremely high |
| | Control | Only those applications that permit adequate authorization control should be implemented on the mobile device. |
| | Risk with control(s) | Normal |
| | Section | 28.3.3 |
| 2. | Potential risk | Lack of an authentication mechanism:<br>Because simple mobile devices are often designed for private use, such as Personal Digital Assistants (PDAs) or smartphones. They seldom provide secure authentication options for the users of the mobile devices or these options are not used. |
| | Impact | Other unauthorized users can use the mobile device without any prior authentication, and can therefore trigger unauthorized transactions in the connected back-end applications or view confidential information that is stored on the device. |
| | Risk without control(s) | Extremely high |
| | Control | Implementation of an authentication mechanism for the mobile device. The mechanism should be strong, that is, it should use biometrical or certificates-based processes (for example, smart card). |

**Table 28.3** Risks and Controls for Mobile Devices

| No. | Classification | Description |
|---|---|---|
| | Risk with control(s) | Normal |
| | Section | Using Mobile Devices with Authentication Mechanism in Section 28.3.4 |
| 3. | Potential risk | Unencrypted hard disk or storage medium:<br>The hard disk or storage medium of the mobile device is unencrypted. |
| | Impact | In the event of theft or loss of the mobile device, the confidential business data stored on it can be easily viewed. Moreover, the stored passwords can be accessed by unauthorized persons who can use them for an unauthorized logon to the back-end applications. This enables them to carry out unauthorized transactions. |
| | Risk without control(s) | Extremely high |
| | Control | Implementation of an encryption process for the mobile device. |
| | Risk with control(s) | Low |
| | Section | Implementing an Encryption Method for Storage Media in Section 28.3.4 |
| 4. | Potential risk | No antivirus protection:<br>No antivirus protection exists or has been set up on the mobile device. |
| | Impact | When the Internet is used carelessly, viruses or other harmful applets can infect the mobile device and thereby completely disable its functionality. All business data stored on the device can be destroyed or security gaps can be created as the basis for subsequent attacks. Data that hasn't been synchronized with the back-end applications could be lost. |
| | Risk without control(s) | High |
| | Control | Installation of antivirus software on the mobile device. |
| | Risk with control(s) | Low |
| | Section | Implementing Antivirus Protection in Section 28.3.4 |

**Table 28.3** Risks and Controls for Mobile Devices (Cont.)

| No. | Classification | Description |
|---|---|---|
| 5. | Potential risk | Open connection ports:<br>No personal firewall is installed on the mobile device that can be used to restrict access to the web clients of SAP NetWeaver Mobile or SAP Mobile Sales at the protocol and port levels, for example. |
| | Impact | The web server that is available in the SAP NetWeaver Mobile client can be addressed from outside. Directories or passwords that are stored in local directories can also fall into the hands of unauthorized persons. The passwords can be used to launch an attack on the back-end applications from another mobile device. |
| | Risk without control(s) | High |
| | Control | Installation of a personal firewall on the mobile device to restrict access to the device. |
| | Risk with control(s) | Low |
| | Section | Installing a Personal Firewall in Section 28.3.4 |
| 6. | Potential risk | Missing backup concept:<br>The data on the mobile devices is not backed up on a regular basis. |
| | Impact | All business data that is stored on the mobile device and hasn't been synchronized with the back-end applications will be lost. This can lead to inconsistencies in the datasets, for example, if goods receipts are incorrectly posted. |
| | Risk without control(s) | High |
| | Control | Design and implementation of a backup concept for the mobile devices. |
| | Risk with control(s) | Low |
| | Section | Implementing a Backup Concept in Section 28.3.4 |
| 7. | Potential risk | Access rights for important system files are not restricted:<br>The access rights for system files that contain password information are not restricted to authorized users or technical users. |

**Table 28.3** Risks and Controls for Mobile Devices (Cont.)

| No. | Classification | Description |
|---|---|---|
| | Impact | Passwords can be spied on. This enables unauthorized parties to log on to the back-end applications. Unauthorized transactions can be triggered and confidential business information can be viewed. |
| | Risk without control(s) | High |
| | Control | Restriction of access rights for important system files at the operating system level. |
| | Risk with control(s) | Low |
| | Section | Setting Up Access Rights for Important System Files in Section 28.3.4 |
| 8. | Potential risk | Users lack the awareness for security:<br>The user of the mobile device installs, for example, his own software, which has not been verified, or has inadequate theft protection for the device. |
| | Impact | The mobile device and the data that is stored on it can be compromised by unauthorized third parties. |
| | Risk without control(s) | Extremely high |
| | Control | Implementation of a policy and training the user on the correct use of the mobile device. |
| | Risk with control(s) | Normal |
| | Section | Fostering the Users' Security Awareness in Section 28.3.4 |
| 9. | Potential risk | The user uses mobile devices in unsecure public networks.<br>In case of negligent use of mobile devices in unsecure networks or when logging on to unsecured Internet hot spots, for instance, Trojans, viruses, and so on can infiltrate the device. |
| | Impact | This could result in data corruption, data loss, takeover of the device's control by unauthorized persons or lay the foundation for a subsequent attack on the device. |
| | Risk without control(s) | High |

**Table 28.3** Risks and Controls for Mobile Devices (Cont.)

| No. | Classification | Description |
|---|---|---|
| | Control | You should avoid the use of unsecured and unknown/suspicious networks. Security applications such as virus scanners should also be used for mobile devices if possible. |
| | Risk with control(s) | Low |
| | Section | Fostering the Users' Security Awareness in Section 28.3.4 |
| 10. | Potential risk | Violation of the data protection regulations due to careless use:<br>Users use mobile devices in public places without any protection where foreign, unauthorized persons can view the information displayed on the device. |
| | Impact | Company-internal data and confidential information could be compromised and exploited to the company's disadvantage. Passwords could be spied on during entry. |
| | Risk without control(s) | High |
| | Control | The appropriate protective measures should be taken when mobile devices are used in public. Internal regulations must define proper use. |
| | Risk with control(s) | Low |
| | Section | Fostering the Users' Security Awareness in Section 28.3.4 |
| 11. | Potential risk | Loss of the mobile device:<br>Negligence, forgetfulness, or theft is often the cause for the loss of mobile devices and the data stored on them. |
| | Impact | Company-internal information and passwords could become accessible to unauthorized persons. This can allow for significant damage to the information stored in the device and provide access to the mobile infrastructure, to connected networks, and to systems. |
| | Risk without control(s) | High |

**Table 28.3** Risks and Controls for Mobile Devices (Cont.)

| No. | Classification | Description |
|---|---|---|
| | Control | Responsible handling of mobile devices and the security of stored local information through encryption and passwords with high complexity is required. The technical options and the quality of encryption depend on the device's operating system. Sometimes, only limited encryption options exist. This condition must be considered carefully when you select the technology for the device and the usage scope for functions and data. If possible, you should set a password for starting the device's operating system. In case of loss, the access to or from the device to the company network must be blocked as quickly as possible. |
| | Risk with control(s) | Normal |
| | Section | Fostering the Users' Security Awareness in Section 28.3.4 |

**Table 28.3** Risks and Controls for Mobile Devices (Cont.)

## 28.3.3 Application Security

If devices are used for mobile business scenarios based on SAP NetWeaver Mobile, the distribution of mobile applications to the devices must be carried out exclusively via the SAP NetWeaver Mobile synchronization mechanism. Otherwise, the user can install mobile applications that don't allow for a multiuser concept — which includes an adequate authorization concept — or simply disturb the system stability of the mobile device. Applications that haven't been tested can create vulnerabilities, which can, in turn, be exploited by potential attackers. For this reason, the operating system must be configured in such a way that a user cannot install any applications on the mobile device. The manufacturers of mobile devices provide different options to do that.

## 28.3.4 Technical Security

This section describes in more detail the risks and controls that are outlined in Table 28.3 with regard to technical security.

### Using Mobile Devices with Authentication Mechanism

When using mobile devices for business scenarios based on SAP NetWeaver Mobile, it is important that the devices provide authentication mechanisms. You should consider this feature when selecting the devices. It is also essential that you check the reliability of the authentication mechanism prior to selecting a mobile device for a specific business scenario.

There are many different authentication mechanisms available:

- **User name and password**
  This is the standard for mobile notebooks based on Windows operating systems. Most smartphones also provide this option.
- **Biometric fingerprint**
  This initializes the system that the user scans with a fingerprint, ensuring that only he can use the device if the Personal Digital Assistant (PDA) recognizes his fingerprint at the next system startup. However, the scanners that are currently being used are not yet sufficiently reliable, which makes the entire authentication mechanism rather unreliable.
- **Pictograms**
  Instead of using typical passwords that consist of letters, numbers, and so on, the pictogram procedure uses small pictures that the user has to enter for authentication purposes. During the initialization procedure for this method, the user must memorize a small number of pictures (five pictures, for example), which he must later recognize when prompted to choose those five pictures from among a large number of randomly compiled pictures.
- **Signature**
  PDAs that require the use of a stylus allow for an authentication based on signatures. In that case, the user must identify himself with a signature prior to using the device.
- **Smart card**
  In this case, users authenticate themselves via a smart card that stores a corresponding certificate. The device then checks the correctness of the certificate. This method is recommended, because it involves a "two-factor authentication" based on the following questions: "What does the user possess? (smart card)," and "What is the user's secret? (PIN)."

### Implementing an Encryption Method for Storage Media

Because a large quantity of business data must be stored on a hard disk or other storage medium, particularly when using a mobile device based on SAP NetWeaver Mobile or SAP Mobile Sales, you should implement an encryption mechanism for storing data in a persistence storage medium. Depending on the type of device, many third-party vendors provide corresponding options.

### Implementing Antivirus Protection

As you do with stationary personal computers, you should also implement an antivirus protection mechanism for mobile devices. Again, many third-party vendors provide antivirus solutions for small mobile devices.

### Installing a Personal Firewall

If possible, you should also set up a personal firewall on the mobile device because a web server is required, particularly for the SAP NetWeaver Mobile client, which is implemented on the mobile device. The web server is required to display HTML pages on the mobile device and to synchronize with the SAP NetWeaver Mobile server.

The web server is a Tomcat web server, which typically uses TCP/IP port 4444 to connect to the SAP NetWeaver Mobile server. Because the synchronization mechanism is always triggered by the mobile device, we suggest that you close all inbound ports, if the device is used exclusively for mobile purposes. Therefore, the only outbound port is then port 4444, which is to synchronize with the server.

### Implementing a Backup Concept

As mobile devices are often exposed to severe environmental conditions, such as changing temperatures, transport shocks, and so on, the storage media can be damaged. For this reason, the data that is stored on mobile storage media must be backed up daily.

If the mobile device is used exclusively for mobile SAP applications, the backup occurs via the synchronization mechanism (smart synchronization) for business data with the SAP NetWeaver Mobile server. This type of synchronization can be automated using the `timed sync` parameter. During the synchronization process, the required software-related components are also installed on the mobile device so that they don't need to be backed up in a separate procedure. For all other business data that is stored on the mobile device, a separate backup concept provided by third parties must be established.

### Setting Up Access Rights for Important System Files

The SAP NetWeaver Mobile client should be implemented on the mobile device as a service that runs under a specific technical user (typically `SYSADM`). Only this user should be granted access to the installation directory of the client. All other users should be excluded using Access Control Lists (ACLs).

### Fostering the Users' Security Awareness

The last four potential risks in Table 28.3 refer to this section, which focuses on mobile device users. In fact, using a device carelessly or even forgetting it is an enormous risk due to the relatively high level of probability. Because of the human factor involved, the options of eliminating this risk via technical means are limited.

For these cases, internal risk management can establish a code of conduct and policies to mediate this risk. In addition to security-technical equipment and the configuration of the device, a responsible and security-aware use of the mobile device is one of the most important prerequisite for the success of a mobile solution. To achieve this and the information security control objects, every user of a mobile device must be aware of the specifically critical security situation and necessary discipline when using the device.

You should define mandatory regulations regarding the use and behavior in certain situations — as mentioned in Table 28.3 — in a company policy. In addition, information on the proper use, existing risks, Best Practices, and instructions should be provided at regular intervals to counteract decreasing levels of security awareness because the constant use of a device can reduce the already-achieved level of security.

# A Bibliography


- Barta, Alexander; Giller, Barbara; Milla, Aslan: *SAP GRC Access Control*. SAP PRESS 2008.
- Documentations and support documents from the SAP Help Portal of SAP AG: *http://help.sap.com*.
- Esch, Martin; Junold, Anja: *Berechtigungen in SAP ERP HCM*. SAP PRESS 2008.
- IBM Business Consulting Services: *SAP-Berechtigungswesen*. SAP PRESS 2003.
- Karin, Horst; Larson, Bruce M.: "Information Security for the SAP Portal in a Heterogeneous System Landscape, No Security No Sustainable Business", *SAP INFO* 136, 2005.
- Lehnert, Volker; Bonitz, Katharina: *SAP-Berechtigungswesen*. SAP PRESS 2010.
- Linkies, Mario: *Risikomanagement in Zeiten der Finanz- und Wirtschaftskrise*. Thirteenth guest lecture at the Institut für Unternehmensforschung und Unternehmensführung (ifu; institute for operational research and business management) at Martin Luther University Halle-Wittenberg, Germany, 2009.
- Linkies, Mario; Off, Frank: *Sicherheit und Berechtigungen in SAP-Systemen*. SAP PRESS, 1st edition 2006.
- Schöler, Sabine; Zink, Olaf: *Governance, Risk und Compliance mit SAP*. SAP PRESS 2008.
- Wolfgang Lassmann, Gabler: *Wirtschaftsinformatik - Nachschlagewerk für Studium und Praxis. Klinkhardt 2002.*

# B The Authors

**Mario Linkies** studied finance, banking, and foreign trade at Humboldt University in Berlin, Germany. He spent several years in North America, Asia, Scotland, and England. Now he manages LINKIES. Management Consulting (Group) out of Leipzig, Germany and Toronto, Canada.

Mario Linkies has more than 20 years of international experience as a consultant, manager, CEO, author, and guest speaker in the consulting business. He was the Director of Global Enterprise Risk Management Consulting of SAP Group worldwide, and worked at Leipzig Interpelz in Germany, at Shell Chemicals Europe, and at Deloitte in Canada. His work focuses on the consulting topics of SAP security, risk control, solution evaluation, change management and process optimization, and, in particular, strategic consulting, identity, and authorization solutions, data protection, and compliance. His experience is highly appreciated by a wealth of industries and clients — even regarding environmental topics. His customer base includes renowned national and international enterprises and public and governmental organizations.

Mario Linkies is one of the most active global promoters of security topics in the enterprise world, and his numerous initiatives can help you understand the significance of IT security and risk management. He is the co-founder of the SAP Global Security Alliance, and as its speaker he leads the globally organized working group within the framework of the SAP partner organization, International Association for SAP Partners (IA4SP) e. V.

Mario Linkies is married to Oanh; his daughter, Nomiko Taima, is five years old. You can send Mario an email at *mario.linkies@linkies.eu* (*http://linkies.co*) to contact him directly.

**Dr. Horst Karin**, President of DELTA Information Security Consulting Inc., is a specialist in SAP security solutions, consulting in GRC, BusinessObjects, and application integration of SAP with identity management and public key infrastructure solutions. His more than 12 years of SAP, management consulting, and IT auditing enable him to apply his advanced capabilities and experience in helping his customers meet their mission objectives. His consulting service lines also address clients' needs in the area of developing security policies, data privacy, and sustainable compliance. Clients benefit from advice, strategic thinking, improvements in efficiency, resilience, and professional guidance in resolving their challenging security problems.

His international experience derives from consulting projects with more than 50 customers and renowned enterprises, such as The Coca-Cola Company, Procter & Gamble, Eli Lilly and Company, The Royal Bank of Canada, and direct engagements with North American vendors of SAP GRC and IT security products.

Dr. Karin is a graduate of the Technical University in Dresden, Germany and holds a doctorate degree in Physics from the University's Institute for Solid State Physics. He has been certified in SAP, as a CISA, as a CISSP, and in ITIL. After his nine years of research at the Technical University in Dresden, he gained very technical industry experience as a research scientist and engineer in microelectronics R&D. In the following years, he added comprehensive business experience to his portfolio as a security specialist, auditor, and manager at KPMG LLP and Deloitte LLP in Canada. Today, he runs his consulting firm, DELTA Information Security Consulting Inc., in Toronto, Canada.

Dr. Horst Karin is married to Jacqueline Yibin Tan and has two sons, Stefan and Tobias. You can send Horst an email at *hkarin@deltaisc.com* to contact him directly.

# Index

## A

## B



## C

## D

## E

## F



## G

## H



## I

## J



## K

## N



## O



## P

## Q



## R

## S

## V



## W

## X